Lecture Notes in Computer Science 14380

The series Lecture Notes in Computer Science (LNCS), including its subseries Lecture Notes in Artificial Intelligence (LNAI) and Lecture Notes in Bioinformatics (LNBI), has established itself as a medium for the publication of new developments in computer science and information technology research, teaching, and education.

LNCS enjoys close cooperation with the computer science R & D community, the series counts many renowned academics among its volume editors and paper authors, and collaborates with prestigious societies. Its mission is to serve this international community by providing an invaluable service, mainly focused on the publication of conference and workshop proceedings and postproceedings. LNCS commenced publication in 1973.

Bernhard Steffen
Editor

Bridging the Gap Between AI and Reality

First International Conference, AISoLA 2023
Crete, Greece, October 23–28, 2023
Proceedings

Editor
Bernhard Steffen
TU Dortmund University
Dortmund, Germany

ISSN 0302-9743 ISSN 1611-3349 (electronic)
Lecture Notes in Computer Science
ISBN 978-3-031-46001-2 ISBN 978-3-031-46002-9 (eBook)
https://doi.org/10.1007/978-3-031-46002-9

This Springer imprint is published by the registered company Springer Nature Switzerland AG
The registered company address is: Gewerbestrasse 11, 6330 Cham, Switzerland

Paper in this product is recyclable.

Preface

As General Chair and Program Chair I would like to welcome readers to the proceedings of AISoLA 2023, an AI-themed sibling of ISoLA, the International Symposium on Leveraging Applications of Formal Methods. AISoLA took place in Crete (Greece) on October 23–28, 2023. It was an in-person event that provided an interdisciplinary forum for discussing the impact of the recent AI developments on research, education, and society. Discussions ranged from philosophical issues that arise from technologies as powerful as indicated by today's large language models to technical issues of and solutions for the responsible use for AI-applications in safety-critical domains. The program of AISoLA 2023 comprised 5 keynotes, 2 special sessions, and 12 tracks.

Keynotes:

Technology and Democracy
by Moshe Vardi, Rice University, USA

Deep Neural Networks, Explanations and Rationality
by Edward Lee, UC Berkeley, USA

Human or Machine: Reflections on Turing-Inspired Testing for the Everyday
by David Harel, Weizmann Institute of Science, Israel

Education and AI – Current Status, Opportunities and Challenges
by Nele McElvany, TU Dortmund, Germany

Graph Neural Networks: Everything Is Connected
Matthias Fey, Kumo.ai, USA

Special Sessions:

Technology and Democracy
organized by Jim Larus and Edward Lee

Beyond ChatGPT: The Impact of AI on Academic Research
organized by Viola Schiaffonati

Tracks:

1. The Nature of AI-Based Systems
   organized by Bernhard Steffen

2. Responsible and Trustworthy AI
   organized by Kevin Baum, Torsten Helfer, Markus Langer, Eva Schmidt, Andreas Sesing-Wagenpfeil, and Timo Speith

3. Democracy in the Digital Era
   organized by George Metakides and Moshe Vardi
4. Digital Humanism
   organized by Viola Schiaffonati and Hannes Werthner
5. Safety Verification of DNNs
   organized by Taylor Johnson and Daniel Neider
6. Verification Meets Learning and Statistics
   organized by Jan Kretinsky, Kim Larsen, Nils Jansen, and Bettina Könighofer
7. Health Care
   organized by Martin Leucker
8. AI-Assisted Programming
   organized by Wolfgang Ahrendt and Klaus Havelund
9. Safe AI in the Automotive Domain
   organized by Falk Howar and Hardi Hungar
10. Digital Humanities
    organized by Ciara Breathnach and Tiziana Margaria
11. R@ISE: Research at ISE
    organized by Tiziana Margaria and Mike Hinchey
12. AI-Supported Publishing
    organized by Jonas Spies

I thank the track organizers, the members of the program committee and their reviewers for their effort in selecting the papers to be presented, the local Organization Chair, Petros Stratis, and the EasyConferences team for their continuous precious support during the entire period preceding the events, and Springer Nature for being, as usual, a very reliable partner for the proceedings production. Finally, I am grateful to Nicolas Stratis and Tim Tegeler for continuous support for the website and the program, and to Steve Bosselmann for his help with the editorial system EquinOCS.

Special thanks are due to the Center for Trustworthy Data Science and Security and the Lamarr Institute for their support in the organization of the event, and to the Technical University of Dortmund, my home institution.

I hope all AISoLA participants had lively scientific discussions, ideally leading to new cooperations and ideas to be presented at next year's AISoLA which will take place again in Crete, Greece.

Bernhard Steffen

Organization

Program Committee Chair

Steffen, Bernhard	TU Dortmund, Germany

Program Committee

Ahrendt, Wolfgang	Chalmers University of Technology, Sweden
Baum, Kevin	Saarland University, Germany
Breathnach, Ciara	University of Limerick, Ireland
Havelund, Klaus	Jet Propulsion Laboratory, USA
Helfer, Thorsten	Saarland University, Germany
Howar, Falk	TU Dortmund, Germany
Hungar, Hardi	DLR Braunschweig, Germany
Jansen, Nils	Radboud Universiteit, The Netherlands
Johnson, Taylor T.	Vanderbilt University, USA
Kretinsky, Jan	Brno University, Czech Republic
Könighofer, Bettina	Graz University of Technology, Austria
Langer, Markus	University of Marburg, Germany
Larsen, Kim	Aalborg University, Denmark
Leucker, Martin	University of Lübeck, Germany
Margaria, Tiziana	University of Limerick, and Lero, Ireland
Neider, Daniel	TU Dortmund, Germany
Schiaffonati, Viola	Politecnico di Milano, Italy
Schmidt, Eva	TU Dortmund, Germany
Sesing-Wagenpfeil, Andreas	Saarland University, Germany
Speith, Timo	University of Bayreuth, Germany
Steffen, Bernhard	TU Dortmund, Germany

Reviewers

Abu Zaid, Faried	appliedAI Institute, Transferlab, München, Germany
Ahrendt, Wolfgang	Chalmers University of Technology, Sweden
Busch, Daniel	TU Dortmund, Germany
Cai, Feiyang	Vanderbilt University, USA

Cano, Filip	Graz University of Technology, Austria
Ceska, Milan	Brno University of Technology, Czech Republic
Dubslaff, Clemens	TU Dresden, Germany
Galesloot, Maris	Radboud Universiteit, The Netherlands
Hartmanns, Arnd	University of Twente, Enschede, Netherlands
Havelund, Klaus	Jet Propulsion Laboratory, USA
Howar, Falk	TU Dortmund, Germany
Jansen, Nils	Radboud Universiteit, The Netherlands
Johnson, Taylor T.	Vanderbilt University, USA
Krale, Merlijn	Radboud Universiteit, The Netherlands
Kretinsky, Jan	Brno University, Czech Republic
Könighofer, Bettina	Graz University of Technology, Austria
Larsen, Kim	Aalborg University, Denmark
Lutz, Simon	TU Dortmund, Germany
Manzanas Lopez, Diego	Vanderbilt University, USA
Neider, Daniel	TU Dortmund, Germany
Nolte, Gerrit	TU Dortmund, Germany
Pal, Neelanjana	Vanderbilt University, USA
Pranger, Stefan	Graz University of Technology, Austria
Robinette, Preston	Vanderbilt University, USA
Schilling, Christian	Aalborg University, Denmark
Serbinowska, Serena	Vanderbilt University, USA
Simão, Thiago	Radboud Universiteit, The Netherlands
Steffen, Bernhard	TU Dortmund, Germany
Suilen, Marnix	Radboud Universiteit, The Netherlands
Tappler, Martin	Graz University of Technology, Austria
Wirsing, Martin	LMU Munich, Germany

Contents

Extended Abstracts

Contributed Abstracts

Panels and Keynotes

DigHum Panel. Beyond Chat-GPT: The Impact of AI on Academic Research

Viola Schiaffonati[1], Hannes Werthner[2], Edward Lee[3], Moshe Vardi[4], Jim Laurus[5], and George Metakides[6]

[1] Politecnico di Milano
[2] TU Wien
[3] UC Berkeley
[4] Rice University
[5] EPFL
[6] Digital Enlightenment Forum

The widespread diffusion of Artificial Intelligence (AI) tools, such as conversational agents powered by Large Language Models, has popularized the debate on AI and its impact on different fields. Discussions about the consequences of the adoption of these tools in the job market or their impact on creativity are now common also in the public discourse. One of the contexts in which the debate about the impact of AI has been relatively less discussed, at least for a broader audience, is academic research. However, the use of AI tools for research, and the correspondence discussion of its impact, has been common from the early days of AI back in the second half of the last century. It seems now that this debate is revamped by the adoption of the last generation of AI tools, some of which are freely available not only for researchers, but also for a larger population. Is this a real new perspective, with revolutionizing results – as many claim – or is it rather a continuation of a development already started decades ago? This panel will address this and similar questions starting from the first-hand experience of different scholars working in the context of computer science and engineering that will provide their perspective on this relatively undebated issue. These questions will be discussed within the framework of Digital Humanism, as the pursuit of supporting people through digital technologies, especially AI, and of protecting people from adverse effects of these technologies.

Technology and Democracy

Moshe Y. Vardi

Rice University, Houston, TX, USA
vardi@cs.rice.edu

Abstract. U.S. society is in the throes of deep societal polarization that not only leads to political paralysis, but also threatens the very foundations of democracy. The phrase "The Disunited States of America" is often mentioned. Other countries are displaying similar polarization. How did we get here? What went wrong?

We argue that the current state of affairs is the results of the confluence of two tsunamis that have unfolded over the past 40 years. On one hand, there was the tsunami of technology – from the introduction of the IBM PC in 1981 to the current domination of public discourse by social media. On the other hand, there was a tsunami of neoliberal economic policies. We posit that the combination of these two tsunamis led to both economic polarization and cognitive polarization.

Summary

This has been a decade of ACM milestones. In 2012, ACM celebrated the Turing Centenary.[1] In 2017, ACM celebrated 50 Years of the ACM A.M. Turing Award.[2] On June 10 of this year, ACM celebrated ACM's 75th Anniversary (ACM 75).[3] But the differences in tone were palpable. The 2012 and 2017 events celebrated the achievements of computing and its remarkable ascendance as a technology. While the 2017 event did end with a panel on "Challenges in Ethics and Computing," such challenges were a major focus in 2022, and a participant found "the whole thing a little ...depressing."

The somber tone of ACM 75 cannot be separated from concurrent events. On June 9, 2023, a U.S. House of Representatives select committee opened public, televised hearings investigating the Jan. 6, 2021 attack on the U.S. Capitol, laying out evidence of an attack on U.S. democracy orchestrated at the highest level of U.S. government. The school shooting in Uvalde, TX, on May 24, 2022, was also on many minds, remembering that an 18-year-old gunman fatally shot 19 students and two teachers and wounded 17 others. Brian Bennett wrote in Time magazine, "Even as America's firearm massacres provoke profound shock, change seems out of reach."[4]

---

[1] https://turing100.acm.org/index.cfm?p=home.

[2] https://www.acm.org/turing-award-50/conference.

[3] https://www.acm.org/75-celebration-event.

[4] https://time.com/6182996/biden-uvalde-guns-new-zealand/.

U.S. society is in the throes of deep polarization that not only leads to political paralysis, but also threatens the very foundations of democracy. The phrase "The Disunited States of America" (tracing back to Harry Turtledove's 2011 novel with this title) is often mentioned. "The U.S. is heading into its greatest political and constitutional crisis since the Civil War," wrote Robert Kagan in the Washington Post,[5] raising the specter of mass violence. How did we get here? What went wrong? Historians will probably spend the next 50 years trying to answer such questions, but the crisis is upon us. We need some answers now!

The last 40 years have launched a tsunami of technology on the world. The IBM Personal Computer-Model 5150, commonly known as the IBM PC, was released on Aug. 12, 1981, and quickly became a smashing success. For its Jan. 3, 1983 issue, Time magazine replaced its customary person-of-the-year cover with a graphical depiction of the IBM PC – "Machine of the Year." A computer on every work desk became reality for knowledge workers within a few years. These knowledge workers soon also had a computer at home. With the introduction of the World Wide Web in 1989, many millions could access the Web. The commercialization of the Internet in 1995, and the introduction of the iPhone in 2007, extended access to billions.

The socioeconomic-political context of this technology tsunami is significant. There was a resurgence of neoliberalism marked by the election of Margaret Thatcher as Prime Minister of the U.K. in 1979, and of Ronald Reagan as President of the U.S. in 1980. Neoliberalism is free-market capitalism generally associated with policies of economic liberalization, privatization, deregulation, globalization, free trade, monetarism, austerity, and reductions in government spending. Neoliberalism increases the role of the private sector in the economy and society and diminishes the role of government. These trends have exerted significant competitive pressure on the economies of the developed world. To stay competitive, the manufacturing sector automated extensively, with the nascent distributed-computing technology playing a significant role. The implications are still with us.

A 2014 paper by MIT economist David Autor provided evidence that information technology was destroying wide swaths of routine office and manufacturing jobs, while creating new high-skill jobs.[6] The result of this labor polarization is a shrinking middle class. Autor's data showed that this pattern of shrinkage in the middle and growth at the high and low end of the labor-skill spectrum occurred in the US as well as in 16 European Union countries. The immediate outcome of this economic polarization is growing income and wealth disparities.

On top of this, information technology is flooding Internet users with more information than they can digest, so tech companies engage in mass personalization, and now we mostly read information that confirms our preconceived opinions. This exacerbated further the "filter bubbles" that were created earlier in the broadcast media, following the abolition, in 1987, by the U.S. Federal Communications Commission under President Reagan, of the "Fairness Doctrine," which required holders of broadcast licenses both to present controversial issues of public importance and to do so in a manner

[5] https://www.washingtonpost.com/opinions/2021/09/23/robert-kagan-constitutional-crisis/.
[6] https://www.nber.org/papers/w20485.

that reflected differing viewpoints fairly. Economic polarization was thus followed by cognitive polarization, creating political polarization.

Computing has become highly important in everyday life during the past 75 years. In addition to its numerous benefits, however, it has also played a major role in driving societal polarization. The somber tone of ACM 75 appropriately recognized this.

Education and AI – Current Status, Opportunities and Challenges

Nele McElvany and Ulrich Ludewig

IFS, TU Dortmund University, Vogelpothsweg 78, 44227 Dortmund, Germany
nele.mcelvany@tu-dortmund.de

Abstract. Successful educational processes as well as educational outcomes are pre-requisites for positive educational and life paths of individuals as well as the development of their societies and countries. Education-teaching and learning-is a complex process accompanied by multiple challenges. These include, for example: People begin a learning process with different preconditions. Educational outcomes in many countries are still closely as sociated with the social backgrounds of learners' families. A substantial and due to the COVID pandemic increased proportion of learners do not achieve the minimum standard necessary in keys kills such as reading. Digitization in the education system has not progressed that far in many cases. The possibilities of using AI in education have received a lot of attention recently, as there are fundamental opportunities but also challenges associated with it. It can be considered certain that AI will fundamentally transform education across educational phases, domains, and contexts. This transformation needs to be shaped and accompanied from the perspectives of different disciplines.

In the keynote, an overview of key current challenges in the context of education will be presented in the first part. In the second part, the potentials and challenges of AI in the areas of diagnostics and assessment, instruction and support will be addressed. The possibilities of advanced individualization, real-time responses, and the processing of large amounts of data are just some of the advantages for learners and teachers. At the same time, there is up-to-date a lack of well-founded studies on the benefits and risks for many possible areas of application of AI in the educational context. Further limitations concern infrastructure, didactic materials, and professional teacher training.

Keywords: Education · AI applications · Assessment

The Human-or-Machine Matter: Turing-Inspired Reflections on an Everyday Issue (Brief Summary of Paper)

David Harel and Assaf Marron

Department of Computer Science and Applied Mathematics,
The Weizmann Institute of Science, Rehovot, 76100, Israel

In his seminal paper "Computing Machinery and Intelligence", Alan Turing introduced the "imitation game" as part of exploring the concept of machine intelligence. The Turing Test has since been the subject of much analysis, debate, refinement and extension. In this talk we sidestep the question of whether a particular machine can be labeled intelligent, or can be said to match human capabilities in a given context. Instead, we first draw attention to the seemingly simpler question a person may ask themselves in an everyday interaction: "Am I interacting with a human or with a machine?". We then shift the focus from seeking a method for eliciting the answer, and, rather, reflect upon the importance and significance of this Human-or-Machine question and the use one may make of a reliable answer thereto. Whereas Turing's original test is widely considered more of a thought experiment, the Human-or-Machine matter as discussed here has obvious practical relevance.

Among the issues we raise and discuss are:

1. What would the typical 'person on the street' say *are* the differences between machines and humans that are relevant to them, especially, when interacting with machines that mimic humans well. For example, are agent's emotions, learning abilities or common sense relevant factors?
2. How would such differences, real or perceived, affect such a person's interactions with the agent? In what way would a person's interaction with agents that are known to be machines that mimic humans (with high fidelity) be different from their interaction with agents that are known to be human? Would conversations be more matter-of-fact? Would a new kind of trust building evolve?
3. In normal, ethical, everyday situations, how would or should one discover the Human-or-Machine identity of an agent? Should this knowledge be always explicitly available, maybe by regulatory enforcement? Will there be protocols to elicit such knowledge from interactions that are narrowly focused on some business or personal issue? Are there ethical situations where people would prefer to *not* know if the agent is a human or a machine? How will human-to-human interactions change in a world where a growing portion of human-agent interactions are with human-like machines?

While it is still unclear if and when machines will be able to mimic human behavior with high fidelity in everyday contexts, we argue that near-term exploration of the issues raised here can contribute to improving methods for developing computerized systems, and may also lead to new insights into fundamental characteristics of human behavior.

The full paper is under review for publication. Also, see arXiv preprint here: https://arxiv.org/abs/2305.04312.

Graph Neural Networks: Everything Is Connected

Matthias Fey

Kumo.AI, Inc, Mountain View, California, USA
matthias@kumo.ai

Abstract. In this talk, we introduce the concept of Graph Neural Networks and its general framework of neural message passing. We thoroughly analyze the expressive power of GNNs and show-case how they relate and generalize concepts of Convolutional Neural Networks and Transformers to arbitrarily structured data. In particular, we argue for the injection of structural and compositional inductive biases into deep learning models. Despite recent trends in neural networks regarding LLMs, such models manifest our understanding of a structured world, require less computational budget, and are easier to understand and explain.

Keywords: Graph neural networks · Deep learning

Our world is highly rich in structure, composed of objects, their relations and hierarchies. Despite the ubiquity of graphs in our world, most modern machine learning methods fail to properly handle such rich structural representations. Recently, a universal class of neural networks emerged that can seamlessly operate on graph-structured data, summarized under the umbrella term *Graph Neural Networks (GNNs)*.

Graph Neural Networks generalize the concepts of Convolutional Neural Networks and Transformers by following a *neural message passing scheme* (see Fig. 1), in which the computation graph of the network is no longer fixed but instead part of the input. This makes GNNs broadly applicable to a wide range of applications, even on highly irregular input structures. In addition, it allows us to actually witness them as a new paradigm on how to define neural networks. Despite recent successes with LLMs on large-language corpuses, GNNs utilize their built-in structural inductive bias to derive accurate predictions even on only sparsely available data with low computational budget.

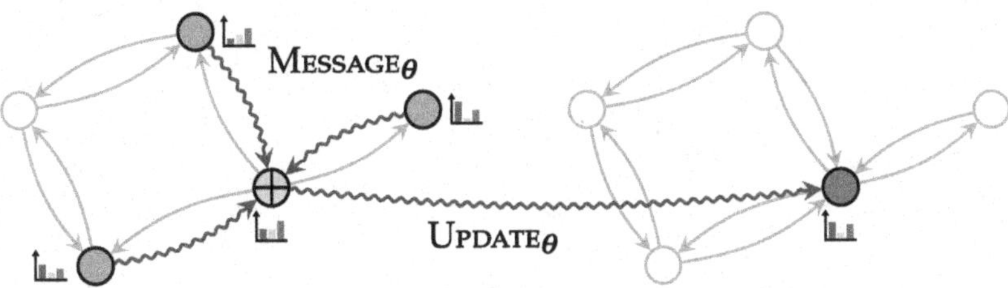

Fig. 1. Graph Neural Networks follow a neural message passing scheme.

Deep Neural Networks, Explanations, and Rationality

Edward A. Lee(✉)

University of California, Berkeley, CA 94720, USA
eal@berkeley.edu
https://ptolemy.berkeley.edu/~eal/

Abstract. "Rationality" is the principle that humans make decisions on the basis of step-by-step (algorithmic) reasoning using systematic rules of logic. An ideal "explanation" for a decision is a chronicle of the steps used to arrive at the decision. Herb Simon's "bounded rationality" is the observation that the ability of a human brain to handle algorithmic complexity and data is limited. As a consequence, human decision-making in complex cases mixes some rationality with a great deal of intuition, relying more on Daniel Kahneman's "System 1" than "System 2." A DNN-based AI, similarly, does not arrive at a decision through a rational process in this sense. An understanding of the mechanisms of the DNN yields little or no insight into any rational explanation for its decisions. The DNN is also operating in a manner more like System 1 than System 2. Humans, however, are quite good at constructing post hoc rationalizations of their intuitive decisions. If we demand rational explanations for AI decisions, engineers will inevitably develop AIs that are very effective at constructing such post hoc rationalizations. With their ability to handle vast amounts of data, the AIs will learn to build rationalizations using many more precedents than any human could, thereby constructing rationalizations for *any* decision that will become very hard to refute. The demand for explanations, therefore, could backfire, resulting in effectively ceding to the AIs much more power.

Keywords: deep neural networks · explainable AI · rationality

1 Imperfect Intelligence

The momentous AI earthquake that surfaced in the form of ChatGPT in late 2022 surprised even experts in the field. ChatGPT is based on GPT-3.5, a large language model (LLM) from OpenAI. Other examples that emerged around the same time include Google's Bard and Microsoft's Sydney (attached to the Bing search engine). As expressed in Kissinger et al., "[t]he ability of large language models to generate humanlike text was an almost accidental discovery. Further, it turns out that the models also have the *unexpected ability* to create highly articulate paragraphs, articles, and in time perhaps books" (emphasis added) [13].

B. Steffen (Ed.): AISoLA 2023, LNCS 14380, pp. 11–21, 2024.
https://doi.org/10.1007/978-3-031-46002-9_1

Everyone was surprised, and even top experts continue to watch with fascination as the machines perform in unexpected ways [3].

The AI researchers who are developing these tools are seeing a relatively gradual evolution of capabilities [10], but even they have been surprised by the outcomes. Because of their expertise in the technology, they are less surprised to be surprised; they have gradually come to expect surprises, but the rest of us were caught off guard. The public witnessed an explosive revelation that contorted expectations.

Many experts have tried to downplay the phenomenon. They argue that the AIs do not understand like we do, they make things up, they plagiarize content from the internet, and they make errors. For example, Chomsky et al., in "The False Promise of ChatGPT," state, "we know from the science of linguistics and the philosophy of knowledge that they differ profoundly from how humans reason and use language" [4]. It is indisputable that the mechanisms of the AIs differ markedly from those of humans, but these authors seem much more confident about the state of the "science of linguistics and the philosophy of knowledge" than might be justified. It is possible that we can learn about human cognition from observing the AIs.

Consider the fact that the AIs make mistakes. As pointed out by Bubek et al. [3], the LLMs acquired the ability to do arithmetic and perform mathematical reasoning by training a language prediction engine. They make no direct use (today) of the arithmetic capability of their machines (which do not make mistakes on arithmetic) nor computer algebra systems such as Maple and Mathematica. It is astonishing to see the emergence of this capability from a token prediction engine. On mathematical problems, my own empirical experimentation reveals that OpenAI's GPT-2 makes the sort of mistakes a child would make, GPT-3.5 makes the sort of mistakes a smart high-school student could make, and GPT-4 makes the sort of mistakes a Berkeley graduate student might make. Could these machines teach us something about how humans reason?

Some people hope that the scope of the AIs will be limited, for example just giving us better search engines. It is not clear, however, where the limits are, or even whether there are any. For example, a previously prevalent presumption that AI would be incapable of creativity was also shattered in 2022 by text-to-image generators such as DALL-E-2 from OpenAI, Stable Diffusion from Stability AI, and Midjourney from the research lab with the same name. These text-to-image tools showed how AIs could absorb stylistic influences, as all human artists do, and then synthesize original works informed by these styles (see Fig. 1). Together with the LLMs, these technology releases have led to a massive cultural shift in the public understanding of the role that AI will have in our society and have spurred a gold rush to develop more AI tools.

Consider the fact that LLMs hallucinate, stating as fact things that are not true. This is also a property of human cognitive minds. In fact, it is a property that we highly value when we call it "creative writing." There are currently many disputes over whether images like those in Fig. 1 violate the copyrights on the images used to train the AIs, but there is no question that these images are unique. Humans also routinely copy the styles of other artists to produce new creative works.

Fig. 1. Selected winner of the Sony world photography award, 2023, in the Open Creative Category, generated by DALL-E 2 prompted by Boris Eldagsen (who declined the prize) and winner of the 2022 Colorado State Fair Grand Prize, entitled "Théâtre D'opéra Spatial," generated by Midjourney prompted by Jason Allen.

Chomsky et al. continue, "These differences place significant limitations on what these programs can do, encoding them with ineradicable defects." But the defects they cite strikingly resemble defects in humans. We make stuff up. We parrot lies. We take morally inconsistent positions or weasel our way out of taking a position at all. And we copy material from others.

Chomsky et al. assert that, "the human mind is a surprisingly efficient and even elegant system that operates with small amounts of information." I have studied (and taught) information theory, and any measure I can imagine for the information provided to human brain during its 20 or so years of development into an educated, rational being is not small. They speak of the "miniscule data" and "minimal exposure to information" that lead a child to be able to distinguish between a grammatically well-formed sentence and one that is not. They then cite the "consciously and laboriously ... explicit version of the grammar" constructed by (adult, highly-educated) linguists as evidence that "child's operating system is completely different from that of a machine learning program." It is true that humans can learn from exposure to far less information, but it seems that the ability of the LLMs to learn complex grammar at all is evidence to the contrary. A child learns from examples, exactly like the LLMs. The child is not able to synthesize the explanations that the adult linguists have laboriously constructed. Interestingly, the LLMs *can* synthesize these explanations, but only because they have "read" all the works of these adult linguists. Leave those texts out of the training data, and their sentences would be no less grammatical.

Chomsky et al. speculate, "[b]ecause these programs cannot explain the rules of English syntax, for example, they may well predict, incorrectly, that 'John is too stubborn to talk to' means that John is so stubborn that he will not talk to someone or other (rather than that he is too stubborn to be reasoned with)." I asked ChatGPT what their sentence means (on March 9, 2023), and it responded:

> The sentence "John is too stubborn to talk to" means that John is so unyielding and inflexible in his opinions, ideas, or behavior that it is difficult or impossible to have a productive conversation with him. His stubbornness makes it challenging to reason with him or persuade him to consider alternative viewpoints or options. The use of the word "too" implies that his stubbornness is excessive and beyond what is reasonable or tolerable in a conversation or interaction.

I then asked for exactly the contrast that Chomsky et al. speculated would foil the machine, for the meaning of the sentence, "John is too stubborn to talk to Jane." The answer was:

> The sentence "John is too stubborn to talk to Jane" means that John's stubbornness or strong refusal to change his thoughts or opinions is preventing him from engaging in a conversation with Jane. In other words, John's inflexibility or obstinacy is causing him to avoid or resist communicating with Jane.

The subtle grammatical differences between these sentences do not elude ChatGPT. Moreover, I seriously doubt that the reason that humans can distinguish the meanings of these sentences is because we can explain the rules of English syntax. We use intuition, not deductive reasoning.

Chomsky et al. observe that the programmers of AIs have struggled to ensure that they steer clear of morally objectionable content to be acceptable to most of their users. What they fail to observe is that humans also struggle to learn to apply appropriate filters to their own thoughts and feelings in order to be acceptable in society. Perhaps the LLMs can teach us something about how morally objectionable thoughts form in humans and how cultural pressures teach us to suppress them. Given the poor behavior of many humans in online forums, we could certainly benefit from new insights into how such behavior emerges.

In a reference to Jorge Luis Borges, Chomsky et al. conclude, "[g]iven the amorality, faux science and linguistic incompetence of these systems, we can only laugh or cry at their popularity." When Borges talks about experiencing both tragedy and comedy, he reflects on the complex superposition of human foibles and rationality. Rather than reject these machines, and rather than replacing ourselves with them, we should reflect on what they can teach us about ourselves. They are, after all, images of humanity as reflected through the internet.

Other critics say the LLMs perform a glorified form of plagiarism, stealing content created by humans. It is easily shown, however, that the data stored in an LLM cannot possibly contain verbatim more that a minuscule subset of the internet. The LLMs somehow encode the concepts and then resynthesize the expression "in their own words" (or pictures) much as humans do. Most human expression is also a reworking of concepts, texts, and images that have been seen before.

Many of these criticisms are implicitly comparing the AIs to ideal forms of intelligence and creativity that are fictions. In these fictions, an intelligence works with true facts and with logic (what Kant called "pure reason"), and creativity produces truly novel artifacts. But we have no precedents for such intelligence or creativity. It does not exist in humans nor in anything humans have created. Perhaps the LLMs have in fact achieved human-level intelligence, which works not with true facts but rather with preconceptions [14], not with logic as much as with intuition [11], and rarely produces anything truly novel (and when it does, the results are ignored as culturally irrelevant). Could it be that these AIs tell us more about humans than about machines?

Janelle Shane, an AI researcher, writes in her book, *You Look Like a Thing and I Love You*, that training an AI is more like educating a child than like writing a computer program [21]. Computer programs, at their lowest level, specify algorithms operating on formal symbols. The symbols are devoid of meaning, except in the mind of human observers, and the operations follow clearly defined rules of logic. Deep neural networks (DNNs), however, exhibit behaviors that are not usefully explained in terms of the operations of these algorithms [15]. An LLM is implemented on computers that perform billions of logic operations per second, but even a detailed knowledge of those operations gives little insight into the behaviors of the DNNs. By analogy, even if we had a perfect model of a human neuron and structure of neuron interconnections in a brain, we would still not be able to explain human behavior [18]. Given this situation, regulatory calls for "algorithmic transparency" are unlikely to be effective.

2 Explainable AI

A hallmark of human intelligence is our ability to explain things. DARPA's XAI program [8] sought to develop a foundation for explainable AI and yielded some useful results. For example, in image classification algorithms, it has become routine to identify portions of an image that most influence the classification. This can sometimes reveal interesting defects in the classification mechanisms, such as a classifier that distinguishes a wolf from a husky based on whether there is snow in the background [20]. For the most part, however, explaining the output of the LLMs remains elusive.

In contrast, humans are good at providing explanations for our decisions, but our explanations are often wrong or at least incomplete. They are often post hoc rationalizations, offering as explanations factors that do not or cannot account for the decisions we make. This fact about humans is well explained by Kahneman, whose Nobel-prize winning work on "prospect theory" challenged utility theory, a popular theory in economics at the time. In prospect theory, decisions are driven more by gains and losses rather than the value of the outcome. Humans, in other words, will make irrational decisions that deliver less value to them in the end. In *Thinking Fast and Slow* [11], Kahneman offers a wealth of evidence that our decisions are biased by factors that have nothing to do with rationality and do not appear in any explanation of the decision.

Kahneman reports, for example, a study of the decisions of parole judges in Israel by [5]. The study found that these judges, on average, granted about 65 percent of parole requests when they were reviewing the case right after a food break, and that their grant rate dropped steadily to near zero during the time until the next break. The grant rate would then abruptly rise to 65 percent again after the break. In Kahneman's words,

> The authors carefully checked many alternative explanations. The best possible account of the data provides bad news: tired and hungry judges tend to fall back on the easier default position of denying requests for parole. Both fatigue and hunger probably play a role. [11]

And yet, I'm sure that every one of these judges would have no difficulty coming up with a plausible explanation for their decision for each case. That explanation would not include any reference to the time since the last break.

Taleb, in his book *The Black Swan*, cites the propensity that humans have, after some event has occurred, to "concoct explanations for its occurrence after the fact, making it explainable and predictable" [25]. For example, the news media always seems to have some explanation for movements in the stock market, sometimes using the same explanation for both a rise and a fall in prices.

Taleb reports on psychology experiments where subjects are asked to choose among twelve pairs of nylon stockings the one they like best. After they had made their choice, the researchers asked them for reasons for their choices. Typical reasons included color, texture, and feel, but in fact, all twelve pairs were identical. Taleb concludes,

> Our minds are wonderful explanation machines, capable of making sense out of almost anything, capable of mounting explanations for all manner of phenomena, and generally incapable of accepting the idea of unpredictability. [25]

Demanding explanations from AIs could yield convincing explanations for anything, leading us to trust their decisions too much. Explanations for the inexplicable, no matter how plausible, are simply misleading.

It is a frustrating result of the recent successes in deep neural nets that people have been unable to provide explanations for many of the decisions that these systems make [16, Chapter 6]. In May 2018 a new European Union regulation called the General Data Protection Regulation (GDPR) went into effect with a controversial provision that provides a right "to obtain an explanation of the decision reached" when a decision is solely based on automated processing. Legal scholars, however, argue that this regulation is neither valid nor enforceable [27]. In fact, it may not even be desirable. I conjecture that sometime in the near future, someone will figure out how to train a DNN to provide a convincing explanation for *any* decision. This could start with a generative-adversarial network (GAN) that learns to provide explanations that appear to be generated by humans.

Kahneman identifies two distinct human styles of thinking, a fast style (System 1) and a slow style (System 2) [11]. The slow style is capable of algorithmic reasoning, but the fast style, which is more intuitive, is responsible for many of the decisions humans make. It turns out that many of today's AIs more closely resemble System 1 than System 2. Even though they are realized on computers, they do not reach decisions by algorithmic reasoning.

Given that humans have written the computer programs that realize the AIs, and humans have designed the computers that execute these programs, why is it that the behavior of the programs proves inexplicable? The reason is that what the programs do is not well described as algorithmic reasoning, in the same sense that an outbreak of war is not well described by the interactions of protons and electrons. Explaining the implementation does not explain the decision.

Before the explosive renaissance of AI during the past two decades, AI was dominated by attempts to encode algorithmic reasoning directly through symbolic processing. What is now called "good old-fashioned AI" (GOFAI) encodes knowledge as production rules, if-then-else statements representing the logical steps in algorithmic reasoning [9]. GOFAI led to the creation of so-called "expert systems," which were sharply criticized by Dreyfus and Dreyfus in their book, *Mind Over Machine* [6]. They pointed out, quite simply, that following explicit rules is what novices do, not what experts do.

DNNs work primarily from examples, training data, rather than rules. The explosion of data that became available as everything went online catalyzed the resurgence of statistical and optimization techniques that had been originally developed in the 1960 s through 1980 s but lay dormant through the AI winter before exploding onto the scene around 2010. The techniques behind today's AI renaissance are nothing like the production rules of GOFAI.

There have been attempts to use machine learning techniques to learn *algorithmic* reasoning, where the result of the training phase is a set of explicable production rules, but these have proven to underperform neural networks. Wilson et al. created a program that could write programs to play old Atari video games credibly well [28]. Their program generated random mutations of production rules, and then simulated natural selection. Their technique was based on earlier work that evolved programs to develop certain image processing functions [19]. The Atari game-playing programs that emerge, however, are far less effective than programs based on DNNs. Wilson et al. admit this, saying that the main advantage of their technique is that the resulting programs are more explainable [28]. The learned production rules provide the explanations.

In contrast, once a DNN has been trained, even a deep understanding of the computer programs that make its decisions does not help in providing an explanation for those decisions. Exactly the same program, with slightly different training, would yield different decisions. So the explanation for the decisions must be in the data that results from the training. But those data take of the form of millions of numbers that have been iteratively refined by backpropagation. The numbers bear no resemblance to the training data and have no simple mapping onto symbols representing inputs and possible decisions. Even a deep understanding of backpropagation does little to explain how the particular set of numbers came about and why they lead to the decisions that they do. Fundamentally, the decisions are not a consequence of algorithmic reasoning that could constitute an explanation.

In a previous paper, I study more deeply the relationship between explanations and algorithms [15]. The well-known work on "bounded rationality" of Herb Simon provides a useful framework for what we mean by an explanation [23]. What we seek is a description of a rational process that arrives at a decision, where a rational process is a sequence of logical deductions that reaches a conclusion. Simon's key insight, for which he got the Nobel Prize in economics, was that enconomic agents (individuals and organizations) do not have the capability to make the kinds of rational decisions that economists assumed they would. In his words:

> Theories that incorporate constraints on the information-processing capacities of the actor may be called theories of bounded rationality. [23]

He identified three human limitations: uncertainty about the consequences that would follow from alternative decisions, incomplete information about the set of alternatives, and complexity preventing the necessary computations from being carried out. He argued that "these three categories tend to merge," using the game of chess as an example and saying that the first and second, like the third, are fundamentally an inability to carry out computation with more than very limited complexity:

> What we refer to as "uncertainty" in chess or theorem proving, therefore, is uncertainty introduced into a perfectly certain environment by inability — computational inability — to ascertain the structure of that environment. [23]

Three decades later, he reaffirmed this focus on the process of reasoning:

> When rationality is associated with reasoning processes, and not just with its products, limits on the abilities of Homo sapiens to reason cannot be ignored. [24]

Reasoning and rationality as algorithmic, terminating sequences of logical deductions, are central to his theory, and he argued that economists' assumptions that agents would maximize expected utility was unrealistic in part because that maximization is intractable to a human mind. It requires too many steps.

An explanation, therefore, needs to be not just a description of a finite sequence of logical deductions, but also a *very short* sequence. Our human minds cannot handle it otherwise. It turns out that such short sequences are not good descriptions of human decision making, and neither are they good descriptions of neural network decision making. Thus, any "explanation" of an AI decision (especially one provided by an AI) should be taken with a grain of salt. It may just be a post hoc rationalization.

3 Fear

Rapid change breeds fear. With its spectacular rise from the ashes in the last 15 years or so, we fear that AI may replace most white collar jobs [7]; that it will learn to iteratively improve itself into a superintelligence that leaves humans in the dust [1,2,26]; that it will fragment information so that humans divide into islands with disjoint sets of truths [16]; that it will supplant human decision making in health care, finance, and politics [12]; that it will cement authoritarian powers, tracking every move of their citizens and shaping their thoughts [17]; that the surveillance capitalists' monopolies, which depend on AI, will destroy small business and swamp entrepreneurship [29]; that it "may trigger a resurgence in mystic religiosity" [13]; and that it will "alter the fabric of reality itself" [13].

With this backdrop of fear, it is particularly disconcerting if the behavior of the AIs is inexplicable. We will have to learn to deal with them not so much as tools we control, but rather as partners with whom we coevolve [16]. As long as we can keep the coevolution symbiotic, we should be able to benefit. However, there are real risks.

As of 2023, the LLMs such as ChatGPT have been trained on mostly human-written data. It seems inevitable, however, that the LLMs will be generating a fair amount of the text that will end up on the internet in the future. The next generation of LLMs, then, will be trained on a mix of human-generated and machine-generated text. What happens as the percentage of machine-generated text increases? Feedback systems are complicated and unpredictable. Shumailov, et al. [22], show that such feedback learning leads to a kind of "model collapse," where original content (the human-written content) is forgotten. As that occurs, we will be left in the dust, possibly becoming unable to understand much of the generated content. The machines will be speaking to each other, not to us.

4 Conclusions

Humans have bounded rationality. We are unable to follow more than a few steps of logical deduction. A useful explanation for any decision, therefore, has to comprise just a few steps. The decisions made by a neural network may not be explicable with just a few steps. Demanding an explanation for an AI-generated decision may therefore be like demanding a post hoc rationalization for a human-generated decision. The decision may not have been arrived at by the steps that constitute the rationalization, but rather may be based much more on intuition or even biochemical factors such as mood or comfort. If we demand rational explanations for AI decisions, engineers will inevitably develop AIs that are effective at constructing such post hoc rationalizations. With their ability to handle vast amounts of data, the AIs will learn to build rationalizations using many more precedents than any human could, thereby constructing rationalizations for *any* decision that will become very hard to refute. The demand for explanations, therefore, could backfire, resulting in effectively ceding to the AIs much more power.

References

1. Barrat, J.: Our Final Invention: Artificial Intelligence and the End of the Human Era. St. Martin's Press (2013)
2. Bostrom, N.: Superintelligence: Paths, Dangers. Strategies. Oxford University Press, Oxford, UK (2014)
3. Bubeck, S., Chandrasekaran, V., et al.: Sparks of artificial general intelligence: Early experiments with GPT-4 (22 March 2023). https://doi.org/10.48550/arXiv.2303.12712. arXiv: 2303.12712
4. Chomsky, N., Roberts, I., Watumull, J.: The false promise of ChatGPT. The New York Times (8 March 2023). https://www.nytimes.com/2023/03/08/opinion/noam-chomsky-chatgpt-ai.html
5. Danziger, S., Levav, J., Avnaim-Pesso, L.: Extraneous factors in judicial decisions. Proc. Nat. Acad. Sci. United States . **108**(17), 6889–6892 (2011). https://doi.org/10.1073/pnas.1018033108
6. Dreyfus, H.L., Dreyfus, S.E.: Mind Over Machine: The Power of Human Intuition and Expertise in the Era of the Computer. Free Press, New York (1986). https://doi.org/10.1016/0160-791X(84)90034-4
7. Ford, M.: Rise of the Robots – Technology and the Threat of a Jobless Future. Basic Books, New York (2015)
8. Gunning, D., Vorm, E., Wang, J.Y., Turek, M.: DARPA's explainable AI (XAI) program: a retrospective. Applied AI Letters **2**, e61 (2021). https://doi.org/10.1002/ail2.61
9. Haugeland, J.: Artificial Intelligence: The Very Idea. MIT Press, Cambridge, Mass (1985)
10. Heaven, W.D.: The inside story of how ChatGPT was built from the people who made it. MIT Technol. Rev. (023). https://www.technologyreview.com/2023/03/03/1069311/inside-story-oral-history-how-chatgpt-built-openai/
11. Kahneman, D.: Thinking Fast and Slow. Farrar, Straus and Giroux, New York (2011)
12. Kelly, K.: The Inevitable: Understanding the 12 Technological Forces That Will Shape Our Future. Penguin Books, New York (2016)
13. Kissinger, H.A., Schmidt, E., Huttenlocher, D.: ChatGPT heralds an intellectual revolution. Wall Street J. (2023)
14. Kuhn, T.S.: The Structure of Scientific Revolutions. University of Chicago Press, Chicago, IL (1962)
15. Lee, E.A.: What can deep neural networks teach us about embodied bounded rationality. Front. Psychol. **25** (2022). https://doi.org/10.3389/fpsyg.2022.761808
16. Lee, E.A.: The Coevolution: The Entwined Futures of Humans and Machines. MIT Press, Cambridge, MA (2020)

17. Lee, K.F.: Super-Powers: China, Silicon Valley, and the New World Order. Houghton Mifflin Harcourt Publishing Company, New York (2018)
18. Lichtman, J.W., Pfister, H., Shavit, N.: The big data challenges of connectomics. Nat. Neurosci. **17**, 1448–1454 (2014). https://doi.org/10.1038/nn.3837
19. Miller, J.F., Thomson, F.: Cartesian genetic programming. In: European Conference on Genetic Programming, vol. 10802. LNCS, pp. 121–132. Springer (2000). https://doi.org/10.1007/978-3-642-17310-3_2
20. Ribeiro, M.T., Singh, S., Guestrin, C.: Why should I trust you? explaining the predictions of any classifier. In: International Conference on Knowledge Discovery and Data Mining, pp. 1135–1144. ACM (2016). https://doi.org/10.1145/2939672.2939778
21. Shane, J.: You look like a thing and I love you. Hachette, United Kingdom (2019)
22. Shumailov, I., Shumaylov, Z., Zhao, Y., Gal, Y., Papernot, N., Anderson, R.: The curse of recursion: training on generated data makes models forget (31 May 2023). https://doi.org/10.48550/arXiv.2305.17493. arXiv:2305.17493v2 [cs.LG]
23. Simon, H.A.: Theories of bounded rationality. In: McGuire, C.B., Radner, R. (eds.) Decision and Organization, pp. 161–176. North-Holland Publishing Company, Amsterdam (1972)
24. Simon, H.A.: Bounded rationality in social science: today and tomorrow. Mind Soc. **1**, 25–39 (2000)
25. Taleb, N.N.: The Black Swan. Random House (2010)
26. Tegmark, M.: Life 3.0: Being Human in the Age of Artificial Intelligence. Alfred A. Knopf, New York (2017)
27. Wachter, S., Mittelstadt, B., Floridi, L.: Why a right to explanation of automated decision-making does not exist in the general data protection regulation. International Data Privacy Law, Available at SSRN (January 24 2017). https://doi.org/10.2139/ssrn.2903469, https://ssrn.com/abstract=2903469
28. Wilson, D.G., Cussat-Blanc, S., Luga, H., Miller, J.F.: Evolving simple programs for playing Atari games. In: The Genetic and Evolutionary Computation Conference (GECCO) (15–19 June 2018). https://doi.org/10.1145/3205455.3205578
29. Zuboff, S.: The Age of Surveillance Capitalism: The Fight for a Human Future at the New Frontier of Power. PublicAffairs, Hatchette Book Group (2019)

Verification Meets Learning and Statistics

Welcome Remarks from AISoLA 2023/Track C2 Chairs

Nils Jansen[1(✉)], Bettina Könighofer[2], Jan Křetínský[3], and Kim Larsen[4]

[1] Radboud University, Nijmegen, The Netherlands
nilsjansen123@gmail.com
[2] Graz University of Technology, Graz, Austria
[3] Masaryk University, Brno, Czech Republic
[4] Aalborg University, Aalborg, Denmark

We are happy to present the proceedings of AISoLA's Track C2: *Verification meets Learning and Statistics*.

Numerous automated systems operate in areas like healthcare, transportation, finance, and robotics. They interact with our everyday lives and thus require strong reliability or safety guarantees on the control of these systems. However, traditional methods to ensure such guarantees, such as from the areas of formal verification, control theory, or testing, often do not account for several fundamental aspects adequately. As examples, take the uncertainty that is inherent to systems that operate with data from the real world; the uncertainty coming from the systems themselves being only partially known/black box; and the sheer complexity and the astronomical size of the systems.

Therefore, a joining of forces is in order of the areas of verification, machine learning, AI planning, and general statistical methods. Within this track, we focus on the interface of these areas. The AISoLA call for this track has put a specific focus on the following concrete topics:

- safety in reinforcement learning
- verification of probabilistic systems with the help of learning
- statistical guarantees on system correctness, statistical model checking
- testing and model learning under uncertainty

These topics overlap and many of the accepted papers and presentations belong to more categories, showing the need for tighter integration of these areas. In particular, making reinforcement learning safe and using learning to provably verify probabilistic systems are two sides of the same coin, seen from two different communities. Similarly, statistical model checking in the context of non-deterministic probabilistic systems is a paradigm for doing so.

The area of **reinforcement learning** includes the following contributions. The papers *Shielded Reinforcement Learning for Hybrid Systems* [1] and *Shielded Learning for Resilience and Performance based on Statistical Model Checking in Simulink* [4], as well as the overview presentation *Shielding in a Simplex Setting*, pinpoint shielding as one of the prominent methods of achieving safety in complex settings, where learning with all its unreliabilities is unavoidable for efficiency, yet safety can be provably achieved. Some safety alternatives to shielding

B. Steffen (Ed.): AISoLA 2023, LNCS 14380, pp. 25–32, 2024.
https://doi.org/10.1007/978-3-031-46002-9_2

deep-learned decisions have been presented in the testing approach of the paper *Differential Safety Testing of Deep RL Agents Enabled by Automata Learning* [6] or the presentation *Regret and Restore - Enhancing Safety-critical Deep Reinforcement Learning Through Evaluation Stages* The principal aspects of uncertainty within reinforcement learning are treated in the paper *What, Indeed, is an Achievable Provable Guarantee for Learning-Enabled Safety-Critical Systems* [9] and presentations *Reinforcement Learning with Stochastic Reward Machines* and *About the Problems When Training Reinforcement Learning Agents for Verification Tasks.*

While the previous topics are concerned with the safety of traditional systems *controlled* by AI-based components (including the presentation *Safety Verification of Decision-Tree Policies in Continuous Time*), the next large area of interest is safety of *completely AI-based* systems, in particular **neural networks**: The classical question of robustness has been discussed in the paper *gRoMA: a Tool for Measuring the Global Robustness of Deep Neural Networks* [8]. More recently, runtime monitoring of neural networks also becomes one of the foci of the AI-verification intersection, interestingly also in connection to abstraction, as seen in the paper *DeepAbstraction++: Enhancing Test Prioritization Performance via Combined Parameterized Boxes* [3] or the presentation *Some Recent Perspectives on Ensuring Neural Networks Safety.*

The perspective of **statistical model checking** was specifically represented in, among others, the paper *Optimized Smart Sampling* [7]. Further aspects of formal guarantees in connection with AI systems are discussed in the papers *Towards a Formal Account on Negative Latency* [2] and *Formal XAI via Syntax-Guided Synthesis* [5]. The first one makes use of predictions in communication protocols, and the latter one addresses the important problem of explainable AI in a formal synthesis framework.

Overall, we received 9 submissions of full papers to our track. The program committee (PC) of Track C2 consisted of 10 researchers from the formal methods and machine learning community. Every submission was evaluated by at least two experts in the field. We employed a single-blind reviewing policy. Due to the high quality of the submitted papers, the acceptance rate for the track was 100%. Track C2 offered also the possibility of submitting a proposal for talks. We received 9 such proposals, all from well-known researchers in the field, and we happily accepted them.

We would like to thank all the people who made AISoLA 2023 possible. First, we would like to sincerely thank all the PC members for their commitment, in-depth reviews, and vivid discussions. Special thanks go to Bernhard Steffen for organizing AISoLA 2023 and for his support and tireless efforts in organizing a great on-site event. Finally, we thank the authors for submitting and presenting their research at AISoLA, and the participants for contributing to the discussions. We hope that you found our track to be inspiring for new research directions and that it was an occasion to start new collaborations. We look forward to your continuing support for ISoLA.

Contributions

Full Papers

Article 1. *Asger Horn Brorholt, Peter Gjøl Jensen, Kim Guldstrand Larsen, Florian Lorber, and Christian Schilling*: **Shielded Reinforcement Learning for Hybrid Systems** [1].
Summary: This paper proposes the construction of a shield for hybrid systems using the so-called barbaric method, where an approximate finite representation of an underlying partition-based two-player safety game is extracted via systematically picked samples of the true transition function. While hard safety guarantees are out of reach, the paper experimentally demonstrates strong statistical safety guarantees with a prototype implementation in Uppaal Stratego.

Article 2. *Saddek Bensalem, Chih-Hong Cheng, Wei Huang, Xiaowei Huang, Changshun Wu, and Xingyu Zhao*: **What, Indeed, is an Achievable Provable Guarantee for Learning-Enabled Safety-Critical Systems** [9].
Summary: First, this paper discusses the engineering and research challenges associated with the design and verification of machine-learning systems. Then, based on the observation that existing works cannot actually achieve provable guarantees, the paper promotes a two-step verification method for the ultimate achievement of provable statistical guarantees.

Article 3. *Hamzah Al-Qadasi, Ylies Falcone, and Saddek Bensalem*: **DeepAbstraction++: Enhancing Test Prioritization Performance via Combined Parameterized Boxes** [3].
Summary: The DeepAbstraction algorithm employs a box-abstraction concept, the efficiency of which depends on the tau parameter, the clustering parameter, that influences the size of these boxes. The selection of the tau value is extremely crucial, given its decisive effect on box size and, subsequently, the stability and efficacy of the framework. Addressing this challenge, the paper proposes a methodology called combined parameterized boxes. This approach leverages the collective verdicts of monitors with various tau values to evaluate network predictions. Furthermore, the paper proposes multiple strategies for integrating the weighted verdicts of monitors into a conclusive verdict, such as mean, max, product, and mode.

Article 4. *Julius Adelt, Sebastian Bruch, Paula Herber, Mathis Niehage, and Anne Remke*: **Shielded Learning for Resilience and Performance based on Statistical Model Checking in Simulink** [4].
Summary: This paper presents an approach to construct provably safe and resilient systems that still achieve certain performance levels with a statistical guarantee in the industrially widely used modeling language Simulink. The key ideas of the proposed approach are threefold: First, failures and repairs are modelled in Simulink. Second, hybrid contracts are used to nondeterministically overapproximate the failure and repair model and to deductively verify safety properties in the presence of worst-case behavior. Third,

the approach learns optimal decisions using statistical model checking (SMC-based learning), which uses the results from deductive verification as a shield to ensure that only safe actions are chosen.

Article 5. *Katrine Bjørner, Samuel Judson, Filip Cano, Drew Goldman, Nick Shoemaker, Ruzica Piskac, and Bettina Könighofer*: **Formal XAI via Syntax-Guided Synthesis** [5].
Summary: This paper proposes a novel application of syntax-guided synthesis to find symbolic representations of a model's decision-making process, designed for easy comprehension and validation by humans. The approach takes input-output samples from complex machine learning models and automatically derives interpretable mimic programs. A mimic program precisely imitates the behavior of an opaque model over the provided data. The paper discusses various types of grammars that are well-suited for computing mimic programs for tabular and image input data.

Article 6. *Martin Tappler, Bernhard K. Aichernig*: **Differential Safety Testing of Deep RL Agents Enabled by Automata Learning** [6].
Summary: A hurdle to the adoption of automata-learning-based verification is that it is often difficult to provide guarantees on the accuracy of learned automata. This paper shows that accuracy guarantees on learned models are not strictly necessary. Through a combination of automata learning, testing, and statistics, the proposed approach performs testing-based verification with statistical guarantees in the absence of guarantees on the learned automata.

Article 7. *Natan Levy, Raz Yerushalmi, and Guy Katz*: **gRoMA: a Tool for Measuring the Global Robustness of Deep Neural Networks** [8].
Summary: This paper presents gRoMA (global Robustness Measurement and Assessment), an innovative and scalable tool that implements a probabilistic approach to measure the global categorial robustness of a DNN. Specifically, gRoMA measures the probability of encountering adversarial inputs for a specific output category. The tool operates on pre-trained, black-box classification DNNs, and generates input samples belonging to an output category of interest. It measures the DNN's susceptibility to adversarial inputs around these inputs, and aggregates the results to infer the overall global categorical robustness up to some bounded statistical error.

Article 8. *Maxime Parmentier, Axel Legay, Firmin Chenoy*: **Optimized Smart Sampling** [7].
Summary: This work revisits the principle of Smart Sampling which makes it possible to apply Statistical Model Checking on stochastic and non-deterministic systems. The paper points out difficulties in the design of the initial algorithm and proposes effective solutions to solve them. The presented contributions are implemented in the Plasma tool.

Article 9. *Clemens Dubslaff, Jonas Schulz, Patrick Wienhöft, Christel Baier, Frank H. P. Fitzek, Stefan J. Kiebel, and Johannes Lehmann*: **Towards a Formal Account on Negative Latency** [2].
Summary: Low latency communication is a major challenge when humans have to be integrated into cyber physical systems with mixed realities. Negative latency is a technique to use anticipatory computing and performing

communication ahead of time. For this, behaviors of communication partners are predicted and used to precompute actions and reactions. In this paper, negative latency is approached as anticipatory networking with formal guarantees. The paper first establishes a formal framework for modeling predictions on goal-directed behaviors in Markov decision processes. Then, it presents and characterize methods to synthesize predictions with formal quality criteria that can be turned into negative latency.

Talks

Keynote 1. *Roderick Bloem*: **Shielding in a Simplex Setting.**
Summary: This talk presents a twist on the shielding approach, adapting it to the simplex architecture for cyberphysical systems. In a simplex architecture we have a base controller that is assumed to be correct, an advanced controller that may be machine learned and a switching logic that switches to the base controller whenever the advanced controller acts in an unexpected way. The presented approach achieves guaranteed correctness by defining the switching logic for given base and advanced controllers.

Keynote 2. *Joost-Pieter Katoen*: **Safe Probabilistic Programming by Inductive Synthesis.**
Summary: Probabilistic programs steer AI robots, encode randomised algorithms and are used to improve the training of neural networks. In this talk we discuss a learning technique synthesising a class of loop invariants on probabilistic programs enabling proving that a program is "safe" in a fully automated manner. We will explain the underlying technology and presents some promising results using a prototypical implementation. In particular, it outperforms state-of-the-art probabilistic model checkers such as Storm on some examples, is competitive to the expected runtime analyser AbSynth, and outperforms data-driven ML techniques for obtaining lower bounds with several orders of magnitude.

Talk 1. *Jan Corazza, Ivan Gavran, Daniel Neider*: **Reinforcement Learning with Stochastic Reward Machines.**
Summary: This talk discusses recent work that is aimed at addressing the issues of reward machine inference under the presence of noisy rewards. The notion of stochastic reward machines will be introduced, together with a novel algorithm for learning them, and discuss several motivating examples. Stochastic reward machines (SRMs) generalize the notion of reward machines and provide a suitable target for inference algorithms in noisy settings. The SRM inference algorithm is an extension of the aforementioned constraint-based formulation, and further enhances explainability by recovering information about reward distributions together with the finite-state structure.

Talk 2. *Marnix Suilen*: **Extending the Scope of Reliable Offline Reinforcement Learning**
Summary: Safe policy improvement (SPI) is an offline reinforcement learning (RL) problem. Specifically, given only a finite data set and the behavior

policy that collected data, the SPI problem is to find a new policy that outperforms the behavior policy with a formal guarantee. We extend the scope of SPI in two fundamental ways: 1) We present the first approach to SPI in partially observable environments (POMDPs), and 2) We significantly reduce the amount of data needed to derive said formal guarantee.

Talk 3. *Jan Křetínský*: **Some Recent Perspectives on Ensuring Neural Networks Safety.**
Summary: This talk advocates several underdeveloped research directions for safety verification of neural networks. The talk focuses at several classical tools of software verification, which have proven crucial for its practical success, yet remain largely unexplored in the context of neural networks. In particular, we firstly discuss the role of abstraction as a separate instrument. Secondly, we discuss runtime verification and monitoring as a more practical compromise for ensuring safety. In the talk, we sketch some of the issues and difficulties as well as suggestions and arguments for examining the directions in more detail.

Talk 4. *Timo P. Gros, Nicola J. Müller, and Verena Wolf*: **Regret and Restore - Enhancing Safety-critical Deep Reinforcement Learning Through Evaluation Stages.**
Summary: Reward structures of safety-critical applications are not well suited for standard deep reinforcement learning (DRL) training because they are typically very sparse and undiscounted. Current exploration strategies do not take information about the current safety performance into account. This talk discusses the algorithm regret and state restoration in evaluation-based DRL (RARE), an algorithm that introduces two innovations: (i) it combines deep statistical model checking evaluation stages with state restorations, i.e., restarting episodes in formerly visited states, and (ii) it exploits estimations of the regret, i.e., the gap between the policies' current and optimal performance.

Talk 5. *Timo P. Gros, Nicola J. Müller, and Verena Wolf*: **About the Problems When Training Reinforcement Learning Agents for Verification Tasks.**
Summary: Training RL agents for benchmarks commonly used in the Verification community comes with specific challenges that must be solved in order to use RL to reliably resolve nondeterminism. In this talk, we analyze the effects of the following three stated challenges: terminal-only reward, undiscounted Objectives, and large action spaces. We discuss how these issues are commonly handled and further present several attempts to tackle these challenges.

Talk 6. *Christian Schilling*: **Safety Verification of Decision-Tree Policies in Continuous Time.**
Summary: Decision trees have gained popularity as interpretable surrogate models for learning-based control policies. However, providing safety guarantees for systems controlled by decision trees is an open challenge. This talk discusses the first dedicated algorithm to verify decision-tree controlled systems in continuous time. The key aspect of our method is exploiting the

decision-tree structure to propagate a set-based approximation through the decision nodes.

Talk 7. *Maria Thurow, Ina Dormuth, Christina Sauer, Anne-Laure Boulesteix, Marc Ditzhaus, Markus Pauly*: **How to Simulate Realistic Survival Data? A Simulation Study to Compare Realistic Simulation Models.**
Summary: There are several possibilities to simulate realistic data from benchmark data sets. Using the example of comparing two-sample procedures for lung cancer studies, the talk discusses a way to simulate realistic survival data in two steps: In a first step, we provide reconstructed benchmark data sets from recent studies on lung cancer patients. In a second step, we build upon the reconstructed benchmark data sets to propose different realistic simulation models for model comparison. The results demonstrate that it is possible to simulate realistic survival data when benchmark data sets from real-world studies are available.

Organization of AISoLA 2023/Track C2

Program Committee Chairs

Nils Jansen, Radboud University Nijmegen, NL
Bettina Könighofer, Graz University of Technology, AT
Jan Křetínský, Technical University of Munich, DE
Kim Larsen, Aalborg University, DK

Program Committee

Milan Češka, Brno University of Technology, CZ
Filip Cano Cordoba, Graz University of Technology, AT
Maris Galesloot, Radboud University Nijmegen, NL
Arnd Hartmanns, University of Twente, NL
Merlijn Krale, Radboud University Nijmegen, NL
Stefan Pranger, Graz University of Technology, AT
Christian Schilling, Aalborg University, DK
Thiago D. Simão, Radboud University Nijmegen, NL
Marnix Suilen, Radboud University Nijmegen, NL
Martin Tappler, Graz University of Technology, AT

References

1. Brorholt, A.H., Jensen, P.G., Larsen, K., Lorber, F., Schilling, C.: Shielded reinforcement learning for hybrid systems. In: Steffen, B. (ed.) AISoLA 2023. LNCS, vol. 14380, pp. 33–54. Springer, Cham (2023)
2. Dubslaff, C., et al.: Towards a formal account on negative latency. In: Steffen, B. (ed.) AISoLA 2023. LNCS, vol. 14380, pp. 188–214. Springer, Cham (2023)

3. Al-Qadasi, H., Falcone, Y., Bensalem, S., Bensalem, S.: Deep-abstraction++: enhancing test prioritization performance via combined parameterized boxes. In: Steffen, B. (ed.) AISoLA 2023. LNCS, vol. 14380, pp. 77–93. Springer, Cham (2023)
4. Adelt, J., Bruch, S., Herber, P., Niehage, M., Remke, A.: Shielded learning for resilience and performance based on statistical model checking in simulink. In: Steffen, B. (ed.) AISoLA 2023. LNCS, vol. 14380, pp. 94–118. Springer, Cham (2023)
5. Bjørner, K., et al.: Formal XAI via syntax-guided synthesis. In: Steffen, B. (ed.) AISoLA 2023. LNCS, vol. 14380, pp. 119–137. Springer, Cham (2023)
6. Tappler, M., Aichernig, B.: Differential safety testing of deep RL agents enabled by automata learning. In: Steffen, B. (ed.) AISoLA 2023. LNCS, vol. 14380, pp. 138–159. Springer, Cham (2023)
7. Legay, A., Parmentier, M., Chenoy, F.: Optimized smart sampling. In: Steffen, B. (ed.) AISoLA 2023. LNCS, vol. 14380, pp. 171–187. Springer, Cham (2023)
8. Levy, N., Yerushalmi, R., Katz, G.: gRoMA: a tool for measuring the global robustness of deep neural networks. In: Steffen, B. (ed.) AISoLA 2023. LNCS, vol. 14380, pp. 160–170. Springer, Cham (2023)
9. Bensalem, S., Cheng, C.-H., Huang, W., Huang, X., Wu, C., Zhao, X.: What, indeed, is an achievable provable guarantee for learning-enabled safety-critical systems. In: Steffen, B. (ed.) AISoLA 2023. LNCS, vol. 14380, pp. 55–76. Springer, Cham (2023)

Shielded Reinforcement Learning for Hybrid Systems

Asger Horn Brorholt[(✉)], Peter Gjøl Jensen, Kim Guldstrand Larsen, Florian Lorber, and Christian Schilling

Department of Computer Science, Aalborg University, Aalborg, Denmark
{asgerhb,pgj,kgl,florber,christianms}@cs.aau.dk

Abstract. Safe and optimal controller synthesis for switched-controlled hybrid systems, which combine differential equations and discrete changes of the system's state, is known to be intricately hard. Reinforcement learning has been leveraged to construct near-optimal controllers, but their behavior is not guaranteed to be safe, even when it is encouraged by reward engineering. One way of imposing safety to a learned controller is to use a *shield*, which is correct by design. However, obtaining a shield for non-linear and hybrid environments is itself intractable. In this paper, we propose the construction of a shield using the so-called *barbaric method*, where an approximate finite representation of an underlying partition-based two-player safety game is extracted via systematically picked samples of the true transition function. While hard safety guarantees are out of reach, we experimentally demonstrate strong statistical safety guarantees with a prototype implementation and UPPAAL STRATEGO. Furthermore, we study the impact of the synthesized shield when applied as either a pre-shield (applied before learning a controller) or a post-shield (only applied after learning a controller). We experimentally demonstrate superiority of the pre-shielding approach. We apply our technique on a range of case studies, including two industrial examples, and further study post-optimization of the post-shielding approach.

1 Introduction

Digital controllers are key components of cyber-physical systems. Unfortunately, the algorithmic construction of controllers is intricate for any but the simplest systems [21,37]. This motivates the usage of reinforcement learning (RL), which is a powerful machine-learning method applicable to systems with complex and stochastic dynamics [12].

However, while controllers obtained from RL provide near-optimal average-case performance, they do not provide guarantees about worst-case performance, which limits their application in many relevant but safety-critical domains, ranging from power converters to traffic control [41,45]. A typical way to tackle this challenge is to integrate safety into the optimization objective via *reward shaping* during the learning phase, which punishes unsafe behavior [23]. This will make the controller more robust to a certain degree, but safety violations will still be

B. Steffen (Ed.): AISoLA 2023, LNCS 14380, pp. 33–54, 2024.
https://doi.org/10.1007/978-3-031-46002-9_3

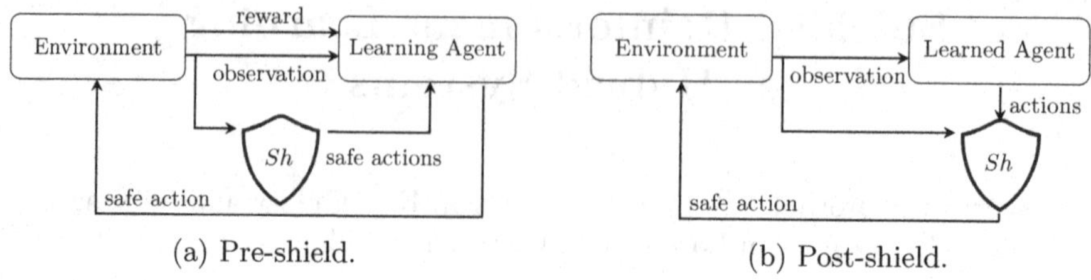

(a) Pre-shield.

(b) Post-shield.

Fig. 1. Pre- and post-shielding in a reinforcement-learning setting.

possible, and the integration of safety into the optimization objective can reduce the performance, thus yielding a controller that is neither safe nor optimal.

A principled approach to obtain worst-case guarantees is to use a *shield* that restricts the available actions [9]. This makes it possible to construct correct-by-design and yet near-optimal controllers. Fig. 1 depicts two ways of shielding RL agents: *pre-* and *post-shielding.* Pre-shielding is already applied during the learning phase, and the learning agent receives only safe actions to choose from. Post-shielding is only applied during deployment, where the trained agent is monitored and, if necessary, corrected. Such interventions to ensure safety interfere with the learned policy of the agent, potentially causing a loss in optimality.

In a nutshell, the algorithm to obtain a shield works as follows. First we compute a finite partitioning of the state space and approximate the transitions between the partitions. This results in a two-player safety game, and upon solving it, we obtain a strategy that represents the most permissive shield.

Cyber-physical systems exhibit behavior that is both continuous (the environment) and discrete (the control, and possibly the environment too). We are particularly interested in a class of systems we refer to as *hybrid Markov decision processes* (HMDPs). In short, these are control systems where the controller can choose an action in a periodic manner, to which the environment chooses a stochastic continuous trajectory modeled by a stochastic hybrid automaton [17]. While HMDPs represent many real-world systems, they are a rich extension of hybrid automata, and thus their algorithmic analysis is intractable even under serious restrictions [26]. These complexity barriers unfortunately also carry over to the above problem of constructing a shield.

In this paper, we propose a new practical technique to automatically and robustly synthesize a shield for HMDPs. The intractability in the shield-synthesis algorithm is due to the rigorous computation of the transition relation in the abstract transition system, since that computation reduces to the (undecidable) reachability problem. Our key to get around this limitation is to approximate the transition relation through systematic sampling, in a way that is akin to the *barbaric method* (a term credited to Oded Maler [19,30]).

We combine our technique with the tool Uppaal Stratego to learn a shielded near-optimal controller, which we evaluate in a series of experiments on several models, including two real-world cases. In our experiments we also find that pre-shielding outperforms post-shielding. While the shield obtained through our technique is not guaranteed to be safe in general due to the approximation, we demonstrate that the controllers we obtain are statistically safe, and that a moderate number of samples is sufficient in practice.

Related Work. Enforcing safety during RL by limiting the choices available to the agent is a known concept, which is for instance applied in the tool UPPAAL STRATEGO [18]. The term "shielding" was coined by Bloem et al. [9], who introduced special conditions on the enforcer like *shields with minimal interference* and *k-stabilizing shields* and later demonstrated shielding for RL agents [3], where they correct potentially unsafe actions chosen by the RL agent. Jansen et al. [29] introduced shielding in the context of RL for probabilistic systems. A concept similar to shielding has also been proposed for safe model predictive control [6,47]. Carr et al. [13] show how to shield partially observable environments. In a related spirit, Maderbacher et al. start from a safe policy and switch to a learned policy if safe at run time [39].

(Pre-)Shielding requires a model of the environment in order to provide safety guarantees during learning. Orthogonal to shielding, several model-free approaches explore an RL environment in a *safer* way, but without any guarantees. Several works are based on barrier certificates and adversarial examples [14,38] or Lyapunov functions [25]. Similarly, Berkenkamp et al. describe a method to provide a safe policy with high probability [7]. Chow et al. consider a relaxed version of safety based on expected cumulative cost [15]. In contrast to these model-free approaches, we assume a model of the environment, which allows us to safely synthesize a shield just from simulations before the learning phase. We believe that the assumption of a model, typically derived from first principles, is realistic, given that our formalism allows for probabilistic modeling of uncertainties. To the best of our knowledge, none of the above works can be used in practice for safe RL in the complex class of HMDPs.

Larsen et al. [35] used a set-based Euler method to overapproximate reachability for continuous systems. This method was used to obtain a safety strategy and a safe near-optimal controller. Contrary to that work, we apply both pre- and post-shielding, and our method is applicable to more general hybrid systems. We employ state-space partitioning, which is common for control synthesis [40] and reachability analysis [32] and is also used in recent work on learning a safe controller for discrete stochastic systems in a teacher-learner framework [46]. Contemporary work by Badings et al. [5] also uses a finite state-space abstraction along with sample-based reachability estimation, to compute a reach-avoid controller. The method assumes linear dynamical systems with stochastic disturbances, to obtain upper and lower bounds on transition probabilities. In contrast, our method supports a very general hybrid simulation model, and provides a safety shield, which allows for further optimization of secondary objectives.

A special case of the HMDPs we consider is the class of stochastic hybrid systems (SHSs). Existing reachability approaches are based on state-space partitioning [2,42], which we also employ in this work, or have a statistical angle [11]. We are not aware of any works that extended SHSs to HMDPs.

Outline. The remainder of the paper is structured as follows. In Sect. 2 we present the formalism we use. In Sect. 3 we present our synthesis method to obtain a safety strategy and explain how this strategy can be integrated into a shield. We demonstrate the performance of our pre- and post-shields in several cases in Sect. 4. Finally we conclude the paper in Sect. 5.

2 Euclidian and Hybrid Markov Decision Processes

In this section we introduce the system class we study in this paper: hybrid Markov decision processes (HMDPs). They combine Euclidean Markov decision processes and stochastic hybrid automata, which we introduce next. HMDPs model complex systems with continuous, discrete and stochastic dynamics.

Euclidean Markov Decision Processes. A Euclidean Markov decision process (EMDP) [27,28] is a continuous-space extension of a Markov decision process (MDP). We recall its definition below.

Definition 1 (Euclidean Markov decision process). *A* Euclidean Markov decision process *of dimension k is a tuple $\mathcal{M} = (\mathcal{S}, s_0, Act, T, C, \mathcal{G})$ where*

- *$\mathcal{S} \subseteq \mathbb{R}^k$ is a bounded and closed part of k-dimensional Euclidean space,*
- *$s_0 \in \mathcal{S}$ is the initial state,*
- *Act is the finite set of actions,*
- *$T : \mathcal{S} \times Act \to (\mathcal{S} \to \mathbb{R}_{\geq 0})$ maps each state-action pair (s, a) to a probability density function over $\mathcal{S}$, i.e., we have $\int_{s' \in \mathcal{S}} T(s, a)(s')ds' = 1$,*
- *$C : \mathcal{S} \times Act \times \mathcal{S} \to \mathbb{R}$ is the cost function, and*
- *$\mathcal{G} \subseteq \mathcal{S}$ is the set of goal states.*

Example 1 (Random walk). Fig. 2 illustrates an EMDP of a (semi-)random walk on the state space $\mathcal{S} = [0, x_{max}] \times [0, t_{max}]$ (one-dimensional space plus time). The goal is to cross the $x = 1$ finishing line before $t = 1$. Two movement actions are available: fast and expensive (blue), or slow and cheap (brown). Both actions have uncertainty about the distance traveled and time taken. Given a state (x, t) and an action $a \in \{slow, fast\}$, the next-state density function $T((x, t), a)$ is a uniform distribution over the successor-state set $(x+d_x(a)\pm\epsilon)\times(t+d_t(a)\pm\epsilon)$, where $d_x(a)$ and $d_t(a)$ respectively represent the direction of movement in space and time given action a, while ϵ models the uncertainty.

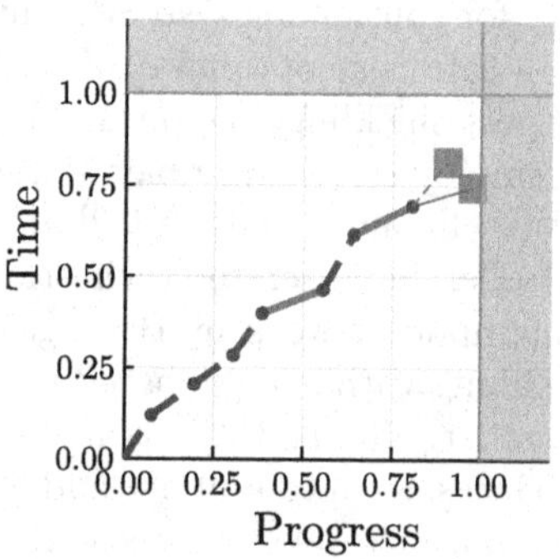

Fig. 2. A random walk with action sequence *slow, slow, slow, slow, fast, slow, fast.*

A run π of an EMDP is an alternating sequence $s_0 a_0 s_1 a_1 \ldots$ of states and actions such that $T(s_i, a_i)(s_{i+1}) > 0$ for all $i \geq 0$. A (memoryless) strategy for an EMDP is a function $\sigma : \mathcal{S} \to (Act \to [0, 1])$, mapping a state to a probability

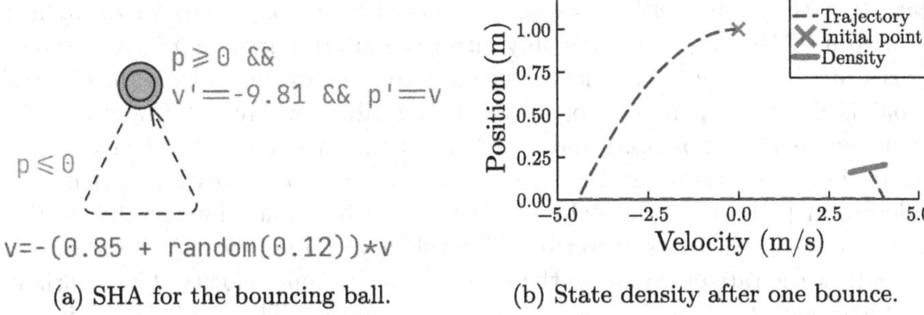

(a) SHA for the bouncing ball. (b) State density after one bounce.

Fig. 3. An SHA for the bouncing ball and a visualization after one bounce.

distribution over *Act*. Given a strategy σ, the expected cost of reaching a goal state is defined as the solution to a Volterra integral equation as follows:

Definition 2 (Expected cost of a strategy). *Let* $\mathcal{M} = (\mathcal{S}, s_0, Act, T, C, \mathcal{G})$ *be an EMDP and* σ *be a strategy. If a state* s *can reach the goal set* $\mathcal{G}$*, the* expected cost *is the solution to the following recursive equation:*

$$\mathbb{E}_\sigma^{\mathcal{M}}(s) = \begin{cases} 0 & \textit{if } s \in \mathcal{G} \\ \sum_{a \in Act} \sigma(s)(a) \cdot \int_{s' \in \mathcal{S}} T(s,a)(s') \cdot \left(C(s,a,s') + \mathbb{E}_\sigma^{\mathcal{M}}(s')\right) ds' & \textit{if } s \notin \mathcal{G} \end{cases}$$

A strategy σ^* is optimal if it minimizes $\mathbb{E}_\sigma^{\mathcal{M}}(s_0)$. We note that there exists an optimal strategy which is deterministic.

Stochastic Hybrid Systems. In an EMDP, the environment responds instantaneously to an action proposed by the agent according to the next-state density function T. In a more refined view, the agent proposes actions with some period P, and the response of the environment is a stochastic, time-bounded trajectory (bounded by the period P) over the state space. For this response, we use a stochastic hybrid system (SHS) [17,34], which allows the environment to interleave continuous evolution and discrete jumps.

Definition 3 (Stochastic hybrid system). *A* stochastic hybrid system *of dimension* k *is a tuple* $\mathcal{H} = (\mathcal{S}, F, \mu, \eta)$ *where*

- $\mathcal{S} \subseteq \mathbb{R}^k$ *is a bounded and closed part of* k*-dimensional Euclidean space,*
- $F : \mathbb{R}_{\geq 0} \times \mathcal{S} \to \mathcal{S}$ *is a flow function describing the evolution of the continuous state with respect to time, typically represented by differential equations,*
- $\mu : \mathcal{S} \to (\mathbb{R}_{\geq 0} \to \mathbb{R}_{\geq 0})$ *maps each state* s *to a delay density function* $\mu(s)$ *determining the time point for the next discrete jump, and*
- $\eta : \mathcal{S} \to (\mathcal{S} \to \mathbb{R}_{\geq 0})$ *maps each state* s *to a density function* $\eta(s)$ *determining the next state.*

Example 2 (Bouncing ball). To represent an SHS, we use a stochastic hybrid automaton (SHA) [17], which we only introduce informally here. Fig. 3(a) shows an SHA of a bouncing ball, which we use as a running example. Here the state of the ball is given by a pair (p, v) of continuous variables, where $p \in \mathbb{R}_{\geq 0}$ represents the current height (position) and $v \in \mathbb{R}$ represents the current velocity of the ball. Initially (not visible in the figure) the value of v is zero while p is picked randomly in $[7.0, 10.0]$. The behavior of the ball is defined by two differential equations: $v' = -9.81 m/s^2$ describing the velocity of a falling object and $p' = v$ stating that the rate of change of the height is the current velocity. The invariant $p \geq 0$ expresses that the height is always nonnegative. The single transition of the automaton triggers when $p \leq 0$, i.e., when the ball hits the ground. In this case the velocity reverts direction and is subject to a random dampening effect (here "`random(0.12)`" draws a random number from $[0, 0.12]$ uniformly). The state density after one bounce is illustrated in Fig. 3(b). The SHA induces the following SHS, where δ denotes the Dirac delta distribution:

- $\mathcal{S} = [0, 10] \times [-14, 14]$,
- $F((p, v), t) = ((-9.81/2)t^2 + vt + p, -9.81t + v)$
- $\mu((p, v)) = \delta((v + \sqrt{v^2 + 2 \cdot 9.81 \cdot p})/9.81)$
- $\eta((p, v)) = (p, v \cdot \mathcal{U}_{[-0.97, -0.85]})$, with uniform distribution $\mathcal{U}_{[l,u]}$ over $[l, u]$.

A timed run ρ of an SHS $\mathcal{H}$ with n jumps from an initial state density ι is a sequence $\rho = s_0 s'_0 t_0 s_1 s'_1 t_1 s_2 s'_2 \ldots t_{n-1} s_n s'_n$ respecting the constraints of $\mathcal{H}$, where each $t_i \in \mathbb{R}_{\geq 0}$. The total duration of ρ is $\sum_{i=0}^{n-1} t_i$, and the density of ρ is $\iota(s_0) \cdot \prod_{i=0}^{n-1} \mu(s'_i)(t_i) \cdot \eta(s_{i+1})(s'_{i+1})$.

Given an initial state density ι and a time bound T, we denote by $\Delta^T_{\mathcal{H},\iota}$ the density function on $\mathcal{S}$ determining the state after a total delay of T, when starting in a state given by ι. The following recursive equation defines $\Delta^T_{\mathcal{H},\iota}$:[1]

$$\Delta^T_{\mathcal{H},\iota}(s') = \begin{cases} \iota(s') & \text{if } T = 0 \\ \displaystyle\int_s \iota(s) \cdot \int_{t \leq T} \mu(s)(t) \cdot \Delta^{T-t}_{\mathcal{H},\eta(F(t,s))}(s')\, dt\, ds & \text{if } T > 0 \end{cases}$$

For $T = 0$, the density of reaching s' is given by the initial state density function ι. For $T > 0$, reaching s' at T first requires to start from an initial state s (chosen according to ι), followed by some delay t (chosen according to $\mu(s)$), leaving the system in the state $F(t, s)$. From this state it remains to reach s' within time $(T - t)$ using $\eta(F(t, s))$ as initial state density.

Hybrid Markov Decision Processes. A hybrid Markov decision process (HMDP) is essentially an EMDP where the actions of the agent are selected according to some time period $P \in \mathbb{R}_{\geq 0}$, and where the next-state probability density function T is obtained from an SHS.

[1] For SHS with an upper bound on the number of discrete jumps up to a given time bound T, the equation is well-defined.

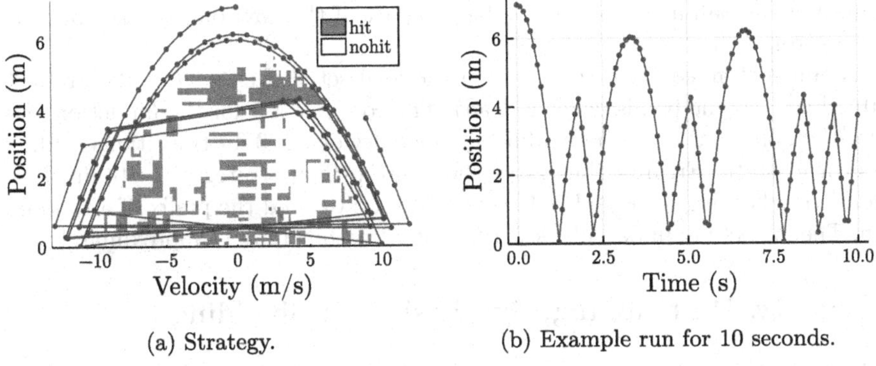

(a) Strategy. (b) Example run for 10 seconds.

Fig. 4. Near-optimal strategy learned by UPPAAL STRATEGO.

Definition 4 (Hybrid Markov decision process). *A hybrid Markov decision process is a tuple* $\mathcal{HM} = (\mathcal{S}, s_0, Act, P, N, \mathcal{H}, C, \mathcal{G})$ *where* $\mathcal{S}, s_0, Act, C, \mathcal{G}$ *are defined the same way as for an EMDP, and*

- $P \in \mathbb{R}_{\geq 0}$ *is the period of the agent,*
- $N : \mathcal{S} \times Act \to (\mathcal{S} \to \mathbb{R}_{\geq 0})$ *maps each state* s *and action* a *to a probability density function determining the immediate next state under* a*, and*
- $\mathcal{H} = (\mathcal{S}, F, \mu, \eta)$ *is a stochastic hybrid system describing the responses of the environment.*

An HMDP $\mathcal{HM} = (\mathcal{S}, s_0, Act, P, N, \mathcal{H}, C, \mathcal{G})$ induces the EMDP $\mathcal{M}_{\mathcal{HM}} = (\mathcal{S}, s_0, Act, T, C, \mathcal{G})$, where T is given by $T(s,a) = \Delta^P_{\mathcal{H},N(s,a)}$. That is, the next-state probability density function of $\mathcal{M}_{\mathcal{HM}}$ is given by the state density after a delay of P (the period) according to $\mathcal{H}$ with initial state density N.

Example 3 (Hitting the bouncing ball). Figure 5 shows an HMDP extending the SHS of the bouncing ball from Fig. 3(a). Now a player has to keep the ball bouncing indefinitely by periodically choosing between the actions *hit* and *nohit*, (three solid transitions). The period $P = 0.1$ is modeled by a clock x with suitable invariant, guards and updates. The top transition triggered by the *nohit* action has no effect on the state (but will have no cost). The *hit* action affects the state only if the height of the ball is at least 4m ($p \geq 4$). The left transition applies if the ball is falling with a speed not greater than -4m/s ($v \geq -4$) and accelerates to a velocity of -4m/s. The right transition applies if the ball is rising, and sets the velocity to a random value in $[-v-4, -0.9v-4]$. The bottom dashed transition represents the

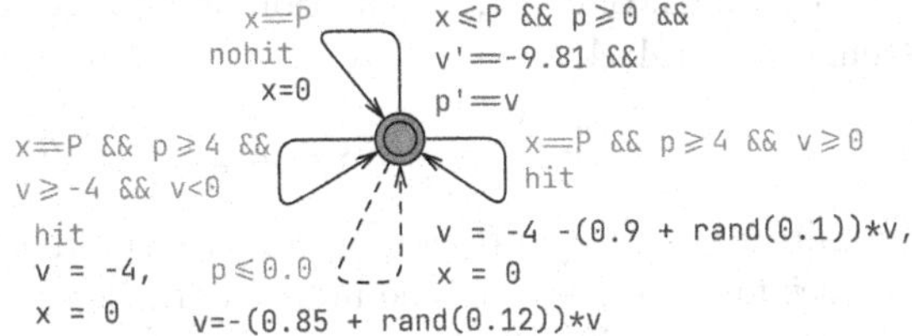

Fig. 5. An HMDP for hitting a bouncing ball.

bounce of the ball as in Fig. 3(a), which is part of the environment and outside the control of the agent.

A time-extended state (p, v, t) is in the goal set $\mathcal{G}$ if either $t \geq 120$ or $(p \leq 0.01 \wedge |v| \leq 1)$ (the ball is deemed dead). The cost (C) is 1 for the *hit* action and 0 for the *nohit* action, with an additional penalty of 1,000 for transitions leading to a dead state. Figure 4 illustrates the near-optimal strategy σ^* obtained by the RL method implemented in UPPAAL STRATEGO and the prefix of a random run. The expected number of *hit* actions of σ^* within 120 s is approximately 48.

3 Safety, Partitioning, Synthesis and Shielding

Safety. In this section we are concerned with a strategy obtained for a given EMDP being *safe*. For example, a safety strategy for hitting the bouncing ball must ensure that the ball never reaches a dead state $(p \leq 0.01 \wedge |v| \leq 1)$. In fact, although safety was encouraged by cost-tweaking, the strategy σ^* in Fig. 4 is *not* safe. In the following we use symbolic techniques to synthesize safety strategies.

Let $\mathcal{M} = (\mathcal{S}, s_0, \mathit{Act}, T, C, \mathcal{G})$ be an EMDP. A safety property φ is a set of states $\varphi \subseteq \mathcal{S}$. A run $\pi = s_0 a_0 s_1 a_1 s_2 \ldots$ is safe with respect to φ if $s_i \in \varphi$ for all $i \geq 0$. Given a nondeterministic strategy $\sigma : \mathcal{S} \to 2^{\mathit{Act}}$, a run $\pi = s_0 a_0 s_1 a_1 s_2 \ldots$ of $\mathcal{M}$ is an outcome of σ if $a_i \in \sigma(s_i)$ for all i. We say that σ is a safety strategy with respect to φ if all runs that are outcomes of σ are safe.

Partitioning and Strategies. Given the infinite-state nature of the EMDP $\mathcal{M}$, we will resort to finite partitioning (similar to [46]) of the state space in order to algorithmically synthesize nondeterministic safety strategies. Given a predefined granularity γ, we partition the state space into disjoint regions of equal size (we do this for simplicity; our method is independent of the particular choice of the partitioning). The partitioning along each dimension of $\mathcal{S}$ is a half-open interval belonging to the set $\mathcal{I}_\gamma = \{[k\gamma, k\gamma + \gamma[\mid k \in \mathbb{Z}\}$. For a bounded k-dimensional state space $\mathcal{S}$, $\mathcal{A} = \{\mu \in \mathcal{I}_\gamma^k \mid \mu \cap \mathcal{S} \neq \emptyset\}$ provides a finite partitioning of $\mathcal{S}$ with granularity γ. For each $s \in \mathcal{S}$ we denote by $[s]_\mathcal{A}$ the unique region containing s.

Given an EMDP $\mathcal{M}$, a partitioning $\mathcal{A}$ induces a finite labeled transition system $\mathcal{T}_\mathcal{M}^\mathcal{A} = (\mathcal{A}, \mathit{Act}, \to)$, where

$$\mu \xrightarrow{a} \mu' \iff \exists s \in \mu.\ \exists s' \in \mu'.\ T(s, a)(s') > 0.$$

Figure 6 shows a partitioning for the running example and displays some witnesses for transitions in the induced transition system.

Next, we view $\mathcal{T}_\mathcal{M}^\mathcal{A}$ as a 2-player game. For a region $\mu \in \mathcal{A}$, Player 1 challenges with an action $a \in \mathit{Act}$. Player 2 responds with a region $\mu' \in \mathcal{A}$ such that $\mu \xrightarrow{a} \mu'$.

Definition 5 (Safe regions). *Let $\varphi \subseteq \mathcal{S}$ be a safety property and $\mathcal{A}$ a partitioning. We denote by $\varphi^\mathcal{A}$ the set $\{\mu \in \mathcal{A} \mid \mu \subseteq \varphi\}$. The set of safe regions with respect to φ is the maximal set of regions $\mathbb{S}_\varphi$ such that*

$$\mathbb{S}_\varphi = \varphi^\mathcal{A} \cap \{\mu \mid \exists a.\ \forall \mu'.\ \mu \xrightarrow{a} \mu' \implies \mu' \in \mathbb{S}_\varphi\}. \tag{1}$$

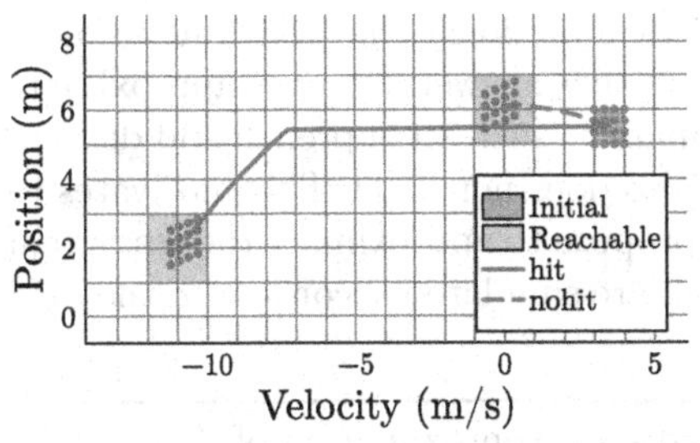

(a) Scenario where the ball is rising and high enough to be hit.

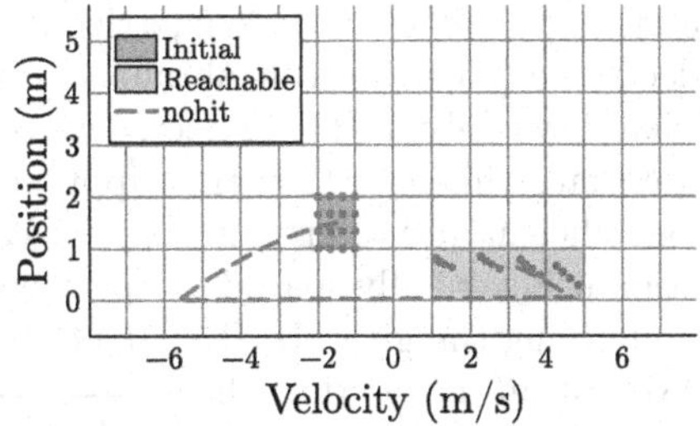

(b) Scenario where the ball is too low to be hit, but bounces off the ground.

Fig. 6. State-space partitioning for Example 3. Starting in the blue region and depending on the action, the system can end up in the green regions within one time period, witnessed by simulations from 16 initial states. (Color figure online)

Given the finiteness of $\mathcal{A}$ and monotonicity of (1), $\mathbb{S}_\varphi$ may be obtained in a finite number of interations using Tarski's fixed-point theorem [44].

A (nondeterministic) strategy for $\mathcal{T}_\mathcal{M}^\mathcal{A}$ is a function $\nu : \mathcal{A} \to 2^{Act}$. The most permissive safety strategy ν_φ obtained from $\mathbb{S}_\varphi$ [8] is given by

$$\nu_\varphi(\mu) = \{a \mid \forall \mu'.\ \mu \xrightarrow{a} \mu' \implies \mu' \in \mathbb{S}_\varphi\}.$$

The following theorem states that we can obtain a safety strategy for the original EMDP $\mathcal{M}$ from a safety strategy ν for $\mathcal{T}_\mathcal{M}^\mathcal{A}$.

Theorem 1. *Given an EMDP $\mathcal{M}$, safety property $\varphi \subseteq \mathcal{S}$ and partitioning $\mathcal{A}$, if ν is a safety strategy for $\mathcal{T}_\mathcal{M}^\mathcal{A}$, then $\sigma(s) = \nu([s]_\mathcal{A})$ is a safety strategy for $\mathcal{M}$.*

Approximating the 2-Player Game. Let $\mathcal{M}$ be an EMDP and φ be a safety property. To algorithmically compute the set of safe regions $\mathbb{S}_\varphi$ for a given partitioning $\mathcal{A}$, and subsequently the most permissive safety strategy ν_φ, the transition relation $\xrightarrow{a}$ needs to be a decidable predicate. If $\mathcal{M}$ is derived from an HMDP $\mathcal{HM} = (\mathcal{S}, s_0, Act, P, N, \mathcal{H}, C, \mathcal{G})$, this requires decidability of the predicate $\Delta^P_{\mathcal{H},N(s,a)}(s') > 0$. Consider the bouncing ball from Example 3. The regions are of the form $\mu = \{(p, v) \mid l_p \leq p < u_p \wedge l_v \leq v < u_v\}$. For given regions μ, μ', the predicate $\mu \xrightarrow{nohit} \mu'$ is equivalent to the following first-order predicate over the reals (note that $F((p, v), t)$ is a pair of polynomials in p, v and t):[2]

$$\exists (p, v) \in \mu.\ F((p, v), P) \in \mu' \vee \exists \beta \in [0.85, 0.97].\ \exists t' \leq P.\ \exists v'.$$
$$F((p, v), t') = (0, v') \wedge F((0, -\beta \cdot v'), P - t') \in \mu'$$

For this simple example, the validity of the formula can be decided [43], which may however require doubly exponential time [16], and worse, when considering

[2] We assume that at most one bounce can take place within the period P.

nonlinear dynamics with, e.g., trigonometric functions, the problem becomes undecidable [33]. One can obtain a conservative answer via over-approximate reachability analysis [20]; in Sect. 4 we compare to such an approach and demonstrate that, while effective, that approach also does not scale. This motivates to use an efficient and robust alternative. We propose to approximate the transition relation using equally spaced samples, which are simulated according to the SHS $\mathcal{H}$ underlying the given HMDP $\mathcal{HM}$.

Algorithm 1 describes how to compute an approximation $\mu \xrightarrow{a}_{app} \mu'$ of $\mu \xrightarrow{a} \mu'$. The algorithm draws from a finite set of n evenly distributed supporting points per dimension $app[\mu] = \{s_1, \dots, s_{n^k}\} \subseteq \mu$ and simulates $\mathcal{H}$ for P time units. A region μ' is declared reachable from μ under action a if it is reached in at least one simulation. When stochasticity is involved in a simulation, additional care must be taken. The random variables can be considered an additional dimension to be sampled from; alternatively, a worst-case value can be used if available, such as the bouncing ball with the highest velocity damping. Figure 6 illustrates 16 ($n = 4$) possible starting points for the bouncing ball together with most pessimistic outcomes, depending on the action taken.

Algorithm 1. Approximation of $\xrightarrow{a}$

Input: $\mu \in \mathcal{A}, a \in Act$
Output: $\mu \xrightarrow{a}_{app} \mu'$ iff $\mu' \in R$

$R = \emptyset$
for all $s_i \in app[\mu]$ **do**
  select $s_i' \sim N(s_i, a)$
  simulate $\mathcal{H}$ from s_i' for P time units
  let s_i'' be the resulting state
  add $[s_i'']_{\mathcal{A}}$ to R
end for

The result $\xrightarrow{a}_{app}$ is an underapproximation of the transition relation $\xrightarrow{a}$, with a corresponding transition system $\widehat{\mathcal{T}}_{\mathcal{M}}^{\mathcal{A}} = (\mathcal{A}, Act, \rightarrow_{app})$. Thus if we compute a safety strategy ν from $\xrightarrow{a}_{app}$, then the strategy $\sigma(s) = \nu([s]_{\mathcal{A}})$ from Theorem 1 is not necessarily safe. However, in Sect. 4 we will see that this strategy is statistically safe in practice. We attribute this to two reasons. 1) The underapproximation of $\xrightarrow{a}_{app}$ can be made accurate. 2) Since $\xrightarrow{a}$ is defined over an abstraction, it is often robust against small approximation errors.

Shielding. As argued above, we can obtain the most permissive safety strategy ν_φ from $\xrightarrow{a}_{app}$ over $\mathcal{A}$ and then use $\sigma_\varphi(s) = \nu_\varphi([s]_{\mathcal{A}})$ as an approximation of the most permissive safety strategy over the original HMDP. We can employ σ_φ to build a shield. As discussed in the introduction, we focus on two ways of shielding: *pre-shielding* and *post-shielding* (recall Fig. 1). In pre-shielding, the shield is already active during the learning phase of the agent, which hence only trains on sets of safe actions. In post-shielding, the shield is only applied after the learning phase, and unsafe actions chosen by the agent are corrected (which is possibly detrimental to the performance of the agent).

Figure 7 shows examples of such strategies for the random walk (Example 1) and the bouncing ball. As can be seen, most regions of the state space are either unsafe (black) or both actions are safe (white). Only in a small area (purple) will the strategy enforce walking fast or hitting the ball, respectively. In the white area, the agent can learn the action that leads to the highest performance.

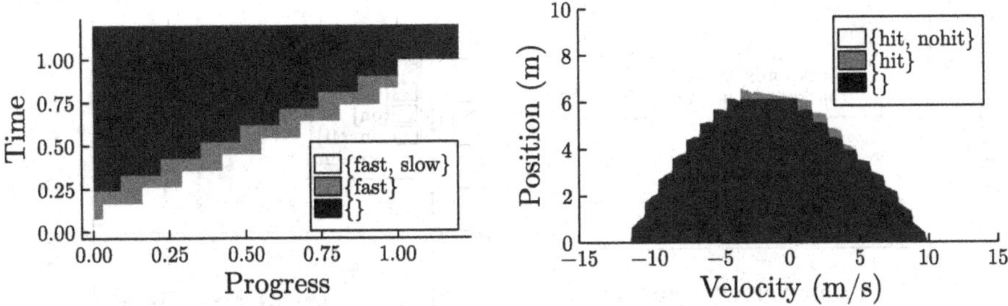

Fig. 7. Synthesized strategies for random walk (left) and bouncing ball (right).

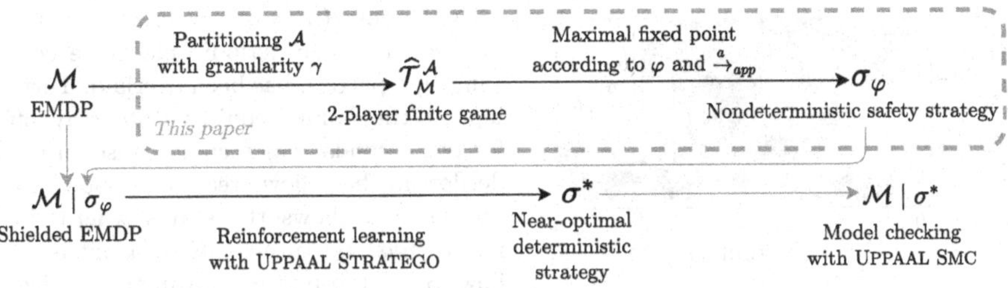

Fig. 8. Complete method for pre-shielding and statistical model checking (SMC).

We use UPPAAL STRATEGO [18] to train a shielded agent based on σ_φ. The complete workflow of pre-shielding and learning is depicted in Fig. 8. Starting from the EMDP, we partition the state space, obtain the transition system using Algorithm 1 and solve the game according to a safety property φ, as described above. The produced strategy is then conjoined with the original EMDP to form the shielded EMDP, and reinforcement learning is used to produce a near-optimal deterministic strategy σ^*. This strategy can then be used in the real world, or get evaluated via statistical model checking. The only difference in the workflow in post-shielding is that the strategy σ_φ is not applied to the EMDP, but on top of the deterministic strategy σ^*.

4 Experiments

In this section we study our proposed approach with regard to different aspects of our shields. In addition to the random walk (Example 1) and bouncing ball (Example 3), we consider three benchmark cases:

- *Cruise control* [4,35,36]: A car is controlled to follow another car as closely as possible without crashing. Either car can accelerate, keep its speed, or decelerate freely, which makes finding a strategy challenging. This model was subject to several previous studies where a safety strategy was carefully designed, while our method can be directly applied without human effort.

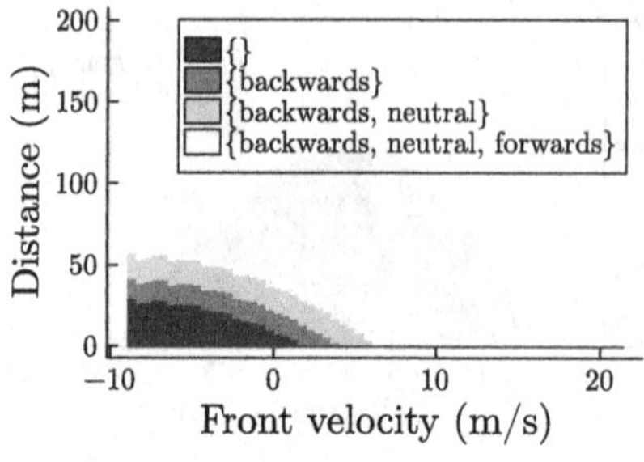

(a) Cruise control ($n = 4$, $\gamma = 0.5$) when the car's velocity is $0m/s$

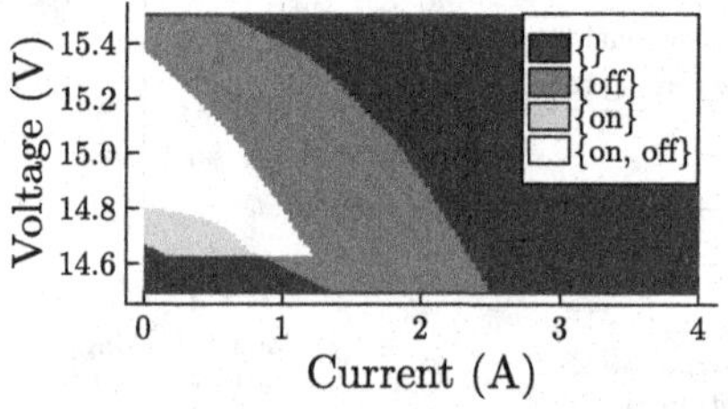

(b) DC-DC boost converter ($n = 4$, $\gamma = 0.01$) when the output resistance is 30Ω.

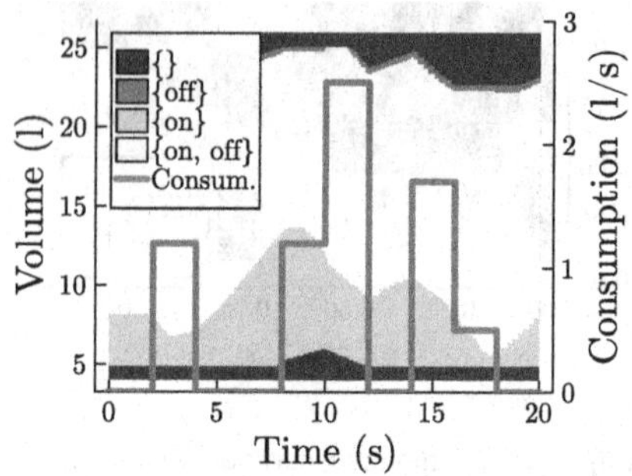

(c) Oil pump ($n = 4, \gamma = 0.1$) when the pump is *on*. The periodic piecewise consumption pattern has been overlaid. Turning off the pump requires it to stay off for two seconds, which could cause an underflow in the yellow area. Conversely, the purple area shows the states where the pump *must* be turned off to avoid overflow. Since the pump is on in this projection, this can wait until the last moment.

Fig. 9. Projected views of synthesized most permissive safety strategies.

- *DC-DC converter* [31]: This industrial DC-DC boost converter transforms input voltage of 10V to output voltage of 15V. The controller switches between storing energy in an inductor and releasing it. The output must stay in ±0.5V around 15V, and the amount of switching should be minimized.
- *Oil pump* [49]: In this industrial case, flow of oil into an accumulator is controlled to satisfy minimum and maximum volume constraints, given a consumption pattern that is piecewise-constant and repeats every 20 seconds. Since the exact consumption is unknown, a random perturbation is added to the reference value. To reduce wear, the volume should be kept low.

Figure 9 shows the synthesized most permissive safety strategies. For instance, in Fig. 9(a) we see the strategy for the cruise-control example when the controlled car is standing still. If the car in front is either close or reverses at high speed, the controlled car must also reverse (purple area). The yellow area shows states where it is safe to stand still but accelerating may lead to a collision.

We conduct four series of experiments to study different aspects of our approach. (1) The quality of our approximation of the transition relation $\xrightarrow{a}_{app}$, (2) the computational performance of our approximation in comparison with a fully symbolic approach, (3) the performance in terms of reward and safety of the pre- and post-shields synthesized with our method, and (4) the potential of post-optimization for post-shielding.

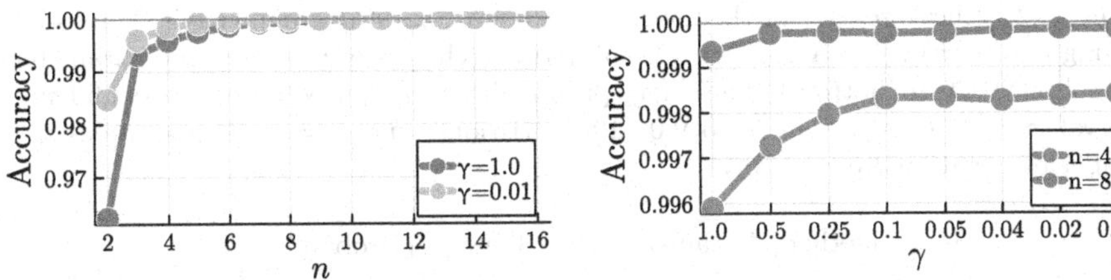

Fig. 10. Accuracy of the approximation $\xrightarrow{a}_{app}$ under different granularity γ and number of supporting points n per dimension.

All experiments are conducted on an AMD Ryzen 7 5700x with 33 GiB RAM. Our implementation is written in Julia, and we use UPPAAL STRATEGO [18] for learning and statistical model checking. The experiments are available online [1].

Quality of the Approximated Transition System. In the first experiment we statistically assess the approximation quality of $\xrightarrow{a}_{app}$ wrt. the underlying infinite transition system. For varying granularity γ of $\mathcal{A}$ and numbers of supporting points n per dimension (see Sect. 3) we first compute $\xrightarrow{a}_{app}$ with Algorithm 1. Then we uniformly sample 10^8 states s and compute their successor states s' under a random action a. Finally we count how often $[s]_\mathcal{A} \xrightarrow{a}_{app} [s']_\mathcal{A}$ holds.

Here we consider the bouncing-ball model, where we limit the domain to $p \in [0, 15]$, $v \in [-15, 15]$. The results are shown in Fig. 10. An increase in the number of supporting points n correlates with increased accuracy. For $\gamma \leq 1$, using $n = 3$ supporting points already yields accuracy above 99%. Finer partition granularity γ increases accuracy, but less so compared to increasing n.

Comparison with Fully Symbolic Approach. As described in Sect. 3, as an alternative to Algorithm 1 one can use a reachability algorithm to obtain an overapproximation of the transition relation $\xrightarrow{a}$. Here we analyze the performance of such an approach based on the reachability tool JULIAREACH [10]. Given a set of initial states of a hybrid automaton where we have substituted probabilities by nondeterminism, JULIAREACH can compute an overapproximation of the successor states. In JULIAREACH, we select the reachability algorithm from [24]. This algorithm uses time discretization, which requires a small time step to give precise answers. This makes the approach expensive. For instance, for the bouncing-ball system, the time period is $P = 0.1$ time units, and a time step of 0.001 time units is required, which corresponds to 100 iterations.

The shield obtained with JULIAREACH is safe by construction. To assess the safety of the shield obtained with Algorithm 1, we choose an agent that selects an action at random and let it act under the post-shield for 10^6 episodes. (We use a random agent because a learned agent may have learned to act safely most of the time and thus not challenge the shield as much.) If no safety violation was detected, we compute 99% confidence intervals for the statistical safety.

Table 1. Synthesis results for the bouncing ball under varying granularity (γ) and supporting points (n) using Algorithm 1 (top) and two choices of the time-step parameter using JULIAREACH (bottom). The safety probability is computed for a 99% confidence interval. $\gamma = 0.02$ corresponds to $9.0 \cdot 10^5$ partitions, and $\gamma = 0.01$ quadruples the number of partitions to $3.6 \cdot 10^6$.

γ	$\xrightarrow{a}_{app}$ method	Parameters	Time	Probability safe
0.02	Algorithm 1	$n = 2$	1m 50 s	unsafe run found
0.02		$n = 4$	2m 14 s	[99.9999%, 100%]
0.02		$n = 8$	4m 02 s	[99.9999%, 100%]
0.02		$n = 16$	11m 03 s	[99.9999%, 100%]
0.01	Algorithm 1	$n = 2$	16m 49 s	[99.9999%, 100%]
0.01		$n = 4$	19m 00 s	[99.9999%, 100%]
0.01		$n = 8$	27m 21 s	[99.9999%, 100%]
0.01		$n = 16$	56m 32 s	[99.9999%, 100%]
0.01	JULIAREACH	time step 0.002	24h 30m	considers s_0 unsafe
0.01		time step 0.001	41h 05m	safe by construction

We consider again the bouncing-ball model. JULIAREACH requires a low partition granularity $\gamma = 0.01$; for $\gamma = 0.02$ it cannot prove that a safety strategy exists, which may be due to conservatism, while our method is able to synthesize a shield that, for $n \geq 4$, is statistically safe. Table 1 shows the results obtained from the two approaches. In addition, the reachability algorithm uses time discretization, and a small time step is required to find a safety strategy.

We remark that the bouncing-ball model has linear dynamics, for which reachability analysis is relatively efficient compared to nonlinear dynamics, and thus this model works in favor of the symbolic method. However, the hybrid nature of the model and the large number of queries (one for each partition-action pair) still make the symbolic approach expensive. Considering the case $\gamma = 0.01$ and $n = 4$, our method can synthesize a strategy in 19 minutes, while the approach based on JULIAREACH takes 41 hours.

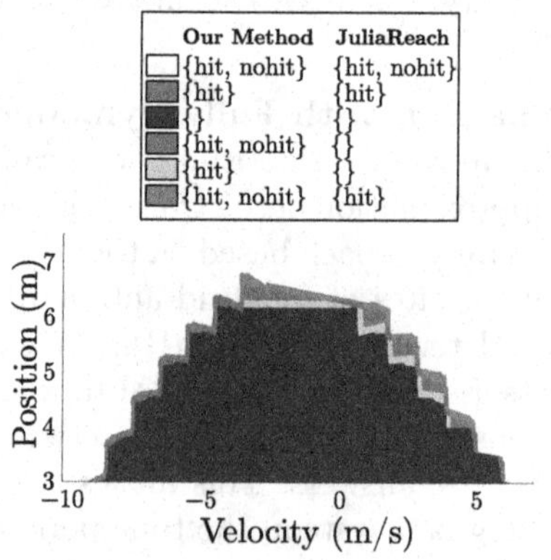

Fig. 11. Superimposed strategies of our method and JULIAREACH.

Figure 11 visualizes the two strategies and shows how the two approaches largely agree on the synthesized shield – but also the slightly more pessimistic nature of the transition relation computed with JULIAREACH.

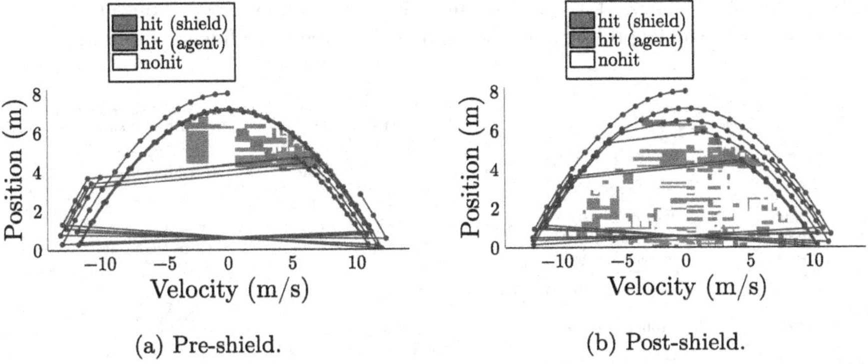

(a) Pre-shield.

(b) Post-shield.

Fig. 12. Learned shielded strategies for the bouncing ball.

Evaluation of Pre- And Post-shields. In the next series of experiments, we evaluate the full method of obtaining a shielded agent. The first step is to approximate $\xrightarrow{a}_{app}$ using Algorithm 1 and extract the most permissive safety strategy σ_φ to be used as a shield. For the second step we have two options: pre- or post-shielding. Recall from Fig. 1 that a pre-shield is applied to the agent during training while a post-shield is applied after training.

In the case of the bouncing ball, the post-shielded agent's strategy is shown in Fig. 12(b). It consists of the unshielded strategy from Fig. 4 plus the purple regions of the safety strategy in Fig. 7(b). Correspondingly, Fig. 12(a) shows the pre-shielded strategy, which is significantly simpler because it does not explore unsafe regions of the state space. This also leads to faster convergence.

Table 2 reports the same data as in Table 1 for the other models. Overall, we see a similar trend in all tables. For a low number of supporting points (say, $n = 3$) we can obtain a safety strategy that we find to be statistically safe. In all cases, no unsafe run was detected in the statistical evaluation. The synthesis time varies depending on the model and is generally feasible. The longest computation times are seen for the oil-pump example, which has the most dimensions. Still, times are well below JuliaReach for the comparatively simple bouncing ball.

Next, we compare our method to other options to make an agent safe(r). As the baseline, we use the classic RL approach, where safety is encouraged using reward shaping. We experiment with a deterrence $d \in \{0, 10, 100, 1000\}$ (negative reward) as a penalty for safety violations for the learning agent. Note that this penalty is only applied during training, and not included in the total cost when we evaluate the agent below. As the second option, we use a post-shielded agent, to which the deterrence also applies. The third option is a pre-shielded agent. In all cases, training and evaluation is repeated 10 times, and the mean value is reported. The evaluation is based on 1000 traces for each repetition.

Table 2. Shield synthesis for different models and granularities γ computed using Algorithm 1. The safety probability is computed for a 99% confidence interval.

(a) Cruise control. $\gamma = 1$ corresponds to $1.9 \cdot 10^5$ partitions, and $\gamma = 0.5$ to $1.5 \cdot 10^6$.

γ	n	Time	Probability safe
1	2	1m 50s	Considers s_0 unsafe
0.5	2	13m 16s	[99.9995%, 100%]
0.5	3	23m 03s	[99.9995%, 100%]
0.5	4	35m 55s	[99.9995%, 100%]

(c) Oil pump. $\gamma = 0.2$ corresponds to $2.8 \cdot 10^5$ partitions, and $\gamma = 0.1$ to $1.1 \cdot 10^6$.

γ	n	Time	Probability safe
0.2	2	3m 07s	considers s_0 unsafe
0.1	2	32m 15s	[99.9995%, 100%]
0.1	3	1h 37m	[99.9995%, 100%]
0.1	4	5h 23m	[99.9995%, 100%]

(b) DC-DC boost converter. $\gamma = 0.05$ corresponds to $3.1 \cdot 10^5$ partitions, $\gamma = 0.02$ to $1.7 \cdot 10^6$ and $\gamma = 0.01$ to $7.0 \cdot 10^6$.

γ	n	Time	Probability safe
0.05	2	41s	[99.9995%, 100%]
0.05	3	1m 50s	considers s_0 unsafe
0.05	4	3m 30s	considers s_0 unsafe
0.02	2	3m 43s	[99.9995%, 100%]
0.02	3	8m 59s	[99.9995%, 100%]
0.02	4	18m 11s	[99.9995%, 100%]
0.01	2	15m 48s	[99.9995%, 100%]
0.01	3	38m 26s	[99.9995%, 100%]
0.01	4	1h 19m	[99.9995%, 100%]

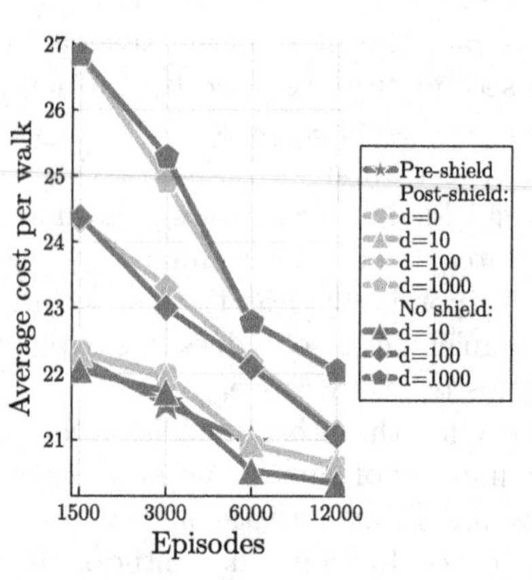

(a) Average cost per run.

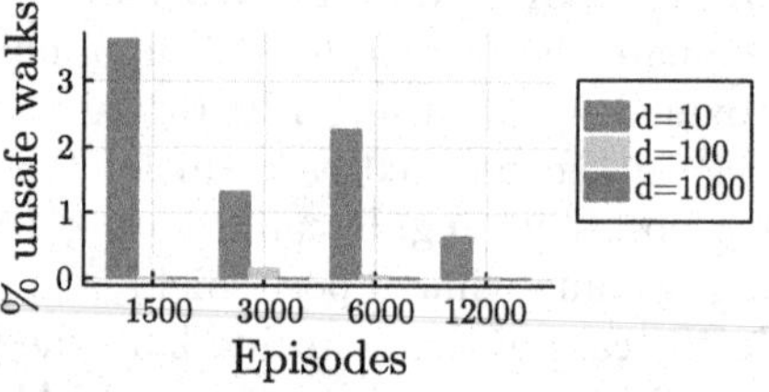

(b) Safety violations for unshielded agents

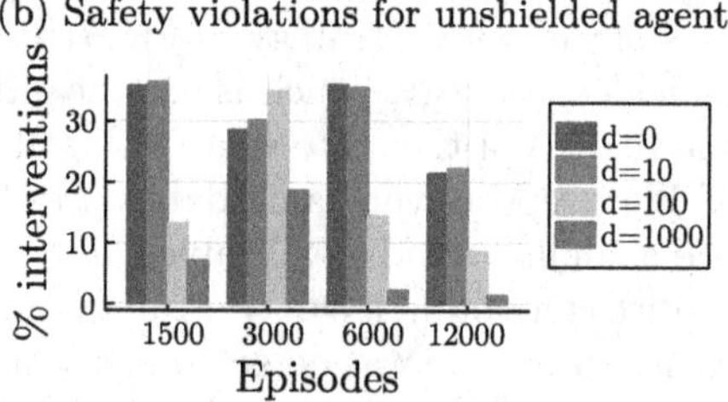

(c) Interventions for post-shielded agents.

Fig. 13. Results of shielding the random walk using $\gamma = 0.005$.

Figures 13, to 17 report the results for the different models. Each subfigure shows the following content: (a) shows the average cost of the final agent, (b) shows the amount of safety violations of the unshielded agents and (c) shows the number of times the post-shielded agents were intervened by the shield.

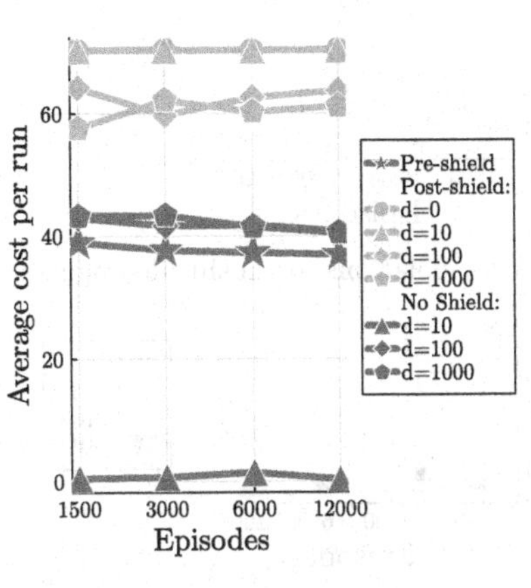

(a) Average *hit* actions per 120s.

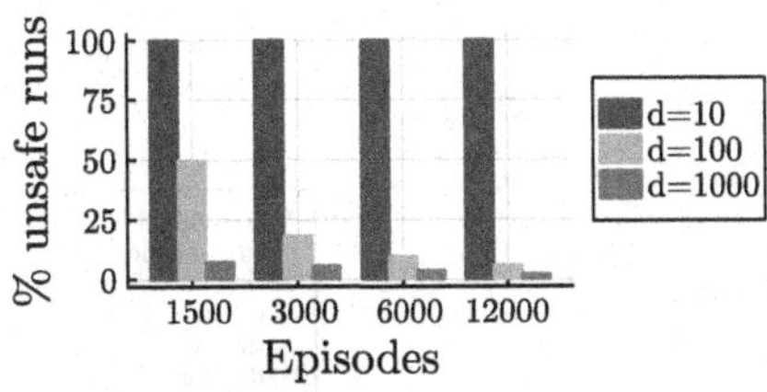

(b) Safety violations for unshielded agents.

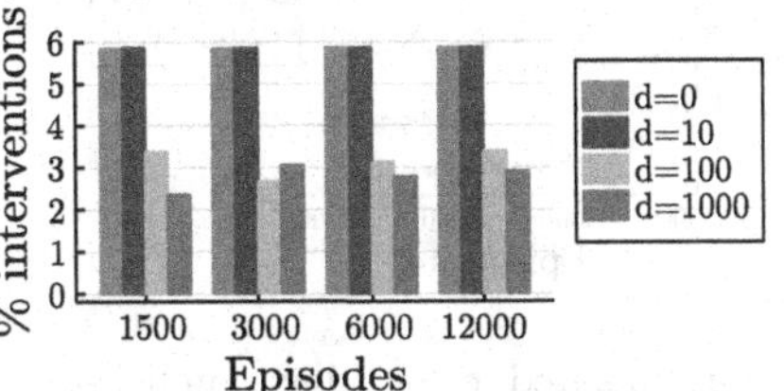

(c) Interventions for post-shielded agents.

Fig. 14. Results of shielding the bouncing ball using $n = 16$, $\gamma = 0.01$.

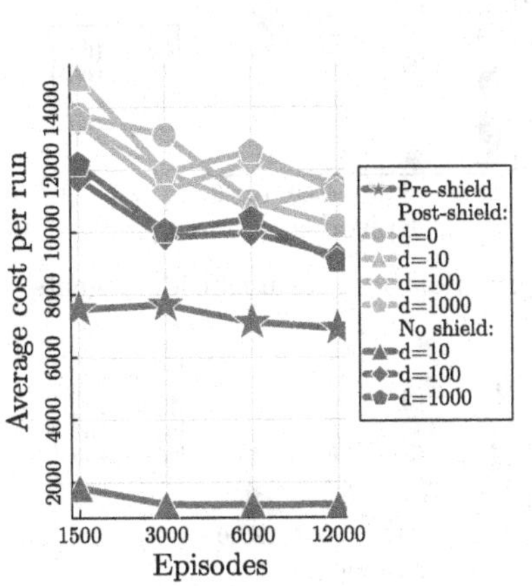

(a) Accumulated distance per 120s.

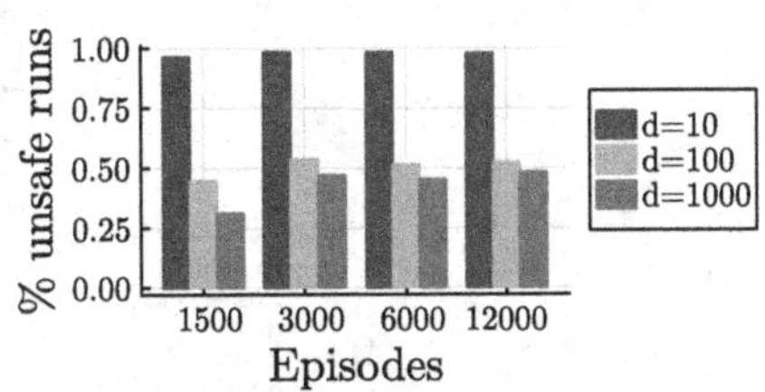

(b) Safety violations for unshielded agents.

(c) Interventions for post-shielded agents.

Fig. 15. Results of shielding the cruise control using $n = 4$, $\gamma = 0.5$.

Overall, we observe similar tendencies. The unshielded agent has lowest average cost at deployment time under low deterrence, but it also violates safety. Higher deterrence values improve safety, but do not guarantee it.

The pre-shielded agents outperform the post-shielded agents. This is because they learn a near-optimal strategy subject to the shield, while the post-shielded agents may be based on a learned unsafe strategy that contradicts the shield, and thus the shield interference can be more detrimental.

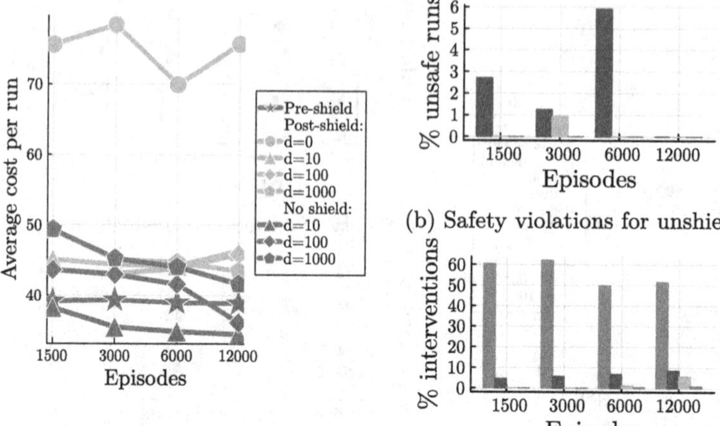

(a) Accumulated error plus number of switches per 120µs.

(b) Safety violations for unshielded agents.

(c) Interventions for post-shielded agents.

Fig. 16. Results of shielding the DC-DC boost converter using $n = 4$, $\gamma = 0.01$.

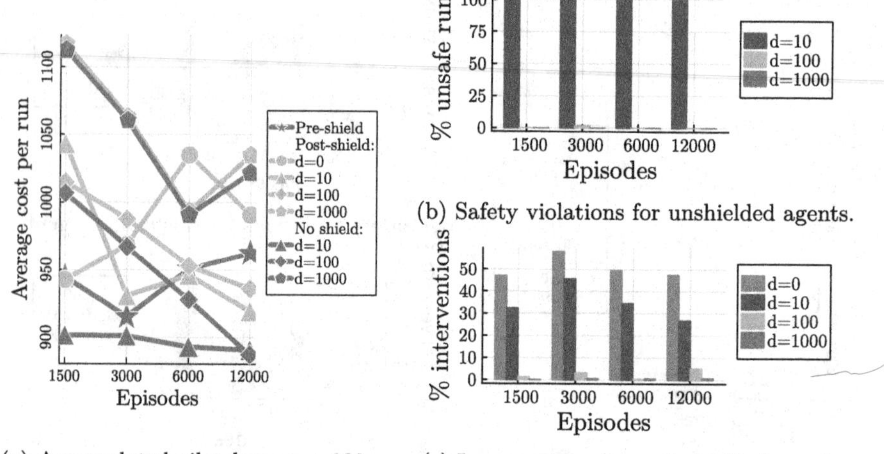

(a) Accumulated oil volume per 120s.

(b) Safety violations for unshielded agents.

(c) Interventions for post-shielded agents.

Fig. 17. Results of shielding the oil pump using $n = 4$, $\gamma = 0.1$.

Post-shielding Optimization When a post-shield intervenes, more than one action may be valid. This leaves room for further optimization, for which we can use UPPAAL STRATEGO. Compared to a uniform baseline, we assess three ways to resolve nondeterminism: 1) minimizing interventions, 2) minimizing cost and 3) at the preference of the shielded agent (the so-called Q-value [48]).

Table 3 shows the effect of post-optimization on the cost and the number of interventions for the cruise-control example. Notably, cost is only marginally affected, but the number of shield interventions can get significantly higher. The pre-shielded agent has lower cost than all post-optimized alternatives.

Table 3. Change of post-optimization relative to the uniform-choice strategy. The strategy was trained for 12,000 episodes with $d = 10$ and post-optimized for 4,000 episodes. Performance of the pre-shielded agent is included for comparison, but interventions are not applicable (because the shield was in place during training).

Configuration	Cost		Interventions	
Baseline with uniform random choice	11371		13.50	
Minimizing interventions	11791	(+3.7%)	11.43	(−15.3%)
Minimizing cost	10768	(−5.3%)	17.43	(+29.1%)
Agent preference	11493	(−1.1%)	14.55	(+7.8%)
Pre-shielded agent	6912	(−39.2%)	–	–

5 Conclusion

We presented a practical approach to synthesize a near-optimal safety strategy via finite (2-player) abstractions of hybrid Markov decision processes, which are systems of complex probabilistic and hybrid nature. In particular, we deploy a simulation-based technique for inferring the 2-player abstraction, from which a safety shield can then be constructed. We show with high statistical confidence that the shields avoid unsafe outcomes in the case studies, and are significantly faster to construct than when deploying symbolic techniques for computing a correct 2-player abstraction. In particular, our method demonstrates statistical safety on several case studies, two of which are industrial. Furthermore, we study the difference between pre- and post-shielding, reward engineering and a post-shielding optimization. In general, we observe that reward engineering is insufficient to enforce safety, and secondarily observe that pre-shielding provides better controller performance compared to post-shielding.

Future work includes applying the method to more complex systems, and using formal methods to verify the resulting safety strategies, maybe based on [22].

Acknowledgments. This research was partly supported by DIREC - Digital Research Centre Denmark and the Villum Investigator Grant S4OS - Scalable analysis and Synthesis of Safe, Secure and Optimal Strategies for Cyber-Physical Systems.

References

1. Reproducibility package - shielded reinforcement learning for hybrid systems. https://github.com/AsgerHB/Shielded-Learning-for-Hybrid-Systems
2. Abate, A., Amin, S., Prandini, M., Lygeros, J., Sastry, S.: Computational approaches to reachability analysis of stochastic hybrid systems. In: Bemporad, A., Bicchi, A., Buttazzo, G. (eds.) HSCC 2007. LNCS, vol. 4416, pp. 4–17. Springer, Heidelberg (2007). https://doi.org/10.1007/978-3-540-71493-4_4
3. Alshiekh, M., Bloem, R., Ehlers, R., Könighofer, B., Niekum, S., Topcu, U.: Safe reinforcement learning via shielding. In: AAAI, pp. 2669–2678. AAAI Press (2018). https://doi.org/10.1609/aaai.v32i1.11797

4. Ashok, P., Křetínský, J., Larsen, K.G., Le Coënt, A., Taankvist, J.H., Weininger, M.: SOS: safe, optimal and small strategies for hybrid markov decision processes. In: Parker, D., Wolf, V. (eds.) QEST 2019. LNCS, vol. 11785, pp. 147–164. Springer, Cham (2019). https://doi.org/10.1007/978-3-030-30281-8_9
5. Badings, T.S., et al.: Robust control for dynamical systems with non-Gaussian noise via formal abstractions. J. Artif. Intell. Res. **76**, 341–391 (2023). https://doi.org/10.1613/jair.1.14253
6. Bastani, O., Li, S.: Safe reinforcement learning via statistical model predictive shielding. In: Robotics (2021). https://doi.org/10.15607/RSS.2021.XVII.026
7. Berkenkamp, F., Turchetta, M., Schoellig, A.P., Krause, A.: Safe model-based reinforcement learning with stability guarantees. In: NeurIPS, pp. 908–918 (2017). https://proceedings.neurips.cc/paper/2017/hash/766ebcd59621e305170616ba3d3dac32-Abstract.html
8. Bernet, J., Janin, D., Walukiewicz, I.: Permissive strategies: from parity games to safety games. RAIRO Theor. Informatics Appl. **36**(3), 261–275 (2002). https://doi.org/10.1051/ita:2002013
9. Bloem, R., Könighofer, B., Könighofer, R., Wang, C.: Shield Synthesis: In: Baier, C., Tinelli, C. (eds.) TACAS 2015. LNCS, vol. 9035, pp. 533–548. Springer, Heidelberg (2015). https://doi.org/10.1007/978-3-662-46681-0_51
10. Bogomolov, S., Forets, M., Frehse, G., Potomkin, K., Schilling, C.: JuliaReach: a toolbox for set-based reachability. In: HSCC, pp. 39–44. ACM (2019). https://doi.org/10.1145/3302504.3311804
11. Bujorianu, L.M.: Stochastic reachability analysis of hybrid systems. Springer Science & Business Media (2012)
12. Busoniu, L., de Bruin, T., Tolic, D., Kober, J., Palunko, I.: Reinforcement learning for control: Performance, stability, and deep approximators. Annu. Rev. Control. **46**, 8–28 (2018). https://doi.org/10.1016/j.arcontrol.2018.09.005
13. Carr, S., Jansen, N., Junges, S., Topcu, U.: Safe reinforcement learning via shielding under partial observability. In: AAAI, pp. 14748–14756. AAAI Press (2023). https://doi.org/10.1609/aaai.v37i12.26723
14. Cheng, R., Orosz, G., Murray, R.M., Burdick, J.W.: End-to-end safe reinforcement learning through barrier functions for safety-critical continuous control tasks. In: AAAI, pp. 3387–3395. AAAI Press (2019). https://doi.org/10.1609/aaai.v33i01.33013387
15. Chow, Y., Nachum, O., Duéñez-Guzmán, E.A., Ghavamzadeh, M.: A Lyapunov-based approach to safe reinforcement learning. In: NeurIPS, pp. 8103–8112 (2018), https://proceedings.neurips.cc/paper/2018/hash/4fe5149039b52765bde64beb9f674940-Abstract.html
16. Davenport, J.H., Heintz, J.: Real quantifier elimination is doubly exponential. J. Symb. Comput. **5**(1), 29–35 (1988). https://doi.org/10.1016/S0747-7171(88)80004-X
17. David, A., et al.: Statistical model checking for stochastic hybrid systems. In: HSBm EPTCS, vol. 92, pp. 122–136 (2012). https://doi.org/10.4204/EPTCS.92.9
18. David, A., Jensen, P.G., Larsen, K.G., Mikučionis, M., Taankvist, J.H.: Uppaal Stratego. In: Baier, C., Tinelli, C. (eds.) TACAS 2015. LNCS, vol. 9035, pp. 206–211. Springer, Heidelberg (2015). https://doi.org/10.1007/978-3-662-46681-0_16
19. Donzé, A.: Breach, a toolbox for verification and parameter synthesis of hybrid systems. In: Touili, T., Cook, B., Jackson, P. (eds.) CAV 2010. LNCS, vol. 6174, pp. 167–170. Springer, Heidelberg (2010). https://doi.org/10.1007/978-3-642-14295-6_17

20. Doyen, L., Frehse, G., Pappas, G.J., Platzer, A.: Verification of hybrid systems. In: Handbook of Model Checking, pp. 1047–1110. Springer, Cham (2018). https://doi.org/10.1007/978-3-319-10575-8_30
21. Doyle, J.C., Francis, B.A., Tannenbaum, A.R.: Feedback control theory. Courier Corporation (2013)
22. Forets, M., Freire, D., Schilling, C.: Efficient reachability analysis of parametric linear hybrid systems with time-triggered transitions. In: MEMOCODE, pp. 1–6. IEEE (2020). https://doi.org/10.1109/MEMOCODE51338.2020.9314994
23. García, J., Fernández, F.: A comprehensive survey on safe reinforcement learning. J. Mach. Learn. Res. **16**, 1437–1480 (2015). https://doi.org/10.5555/2789272.2886795
24. Le Guernic, C., Girard, A.: Reachability analysis of hybrid systems using support functions. In: Bouajjani, A., Maler, O. (eds.) CAV 2009. LNCS, vol. 5643, pp. 540–554. Springer, Heidelberg (2009). https://doi.org/10.1007/978-3-642-02658-4_40
25. Hasanbeig, M., Abate, A., Kroening, D.: Cautious reinforcement learning with logical constraints. In: AAMAS, pp. 483–491 (2020). https://doi.org/10.5555/3398761.3398821
26. Henzinger, T.A., Kopke, P.W., Puri, A., Varaiya, P.: What's decidable about hybrid automata? J. Comput. Syst. Sci. **57**(1), 94–124 (1998). https://doi.org/10.1006/jcss.1998.1581
27. Jaeger, M., Bacci, G., Bacci, G., Larsen, K.G., Jensen, P.G.: Approximating euclidean by imprecise markov decision processes. In: Margaria, T., Steffen, B. (eds.) ISoLA 2020. LNCS, vol. 12476, pp. 275–289. Springer, Cham (2020). https://doi.org/10.1007/978-3-030-61362-4_15
28. Jaeger, M., Jensen, P.G., Guldstrand Larsen, K., Legay, A., Sedwards, S., Taankvist, J.H.: Teaching stratego to play ball: optimal synthesis for continuous space MDPs. In: Chen, Y.-F., Cheng, C.-H., Esparza, J. (eds.) ATVA 2019. LNCS, vol. 11781, pp. 81–97. Springer, Cham (2019). https://doi.org/10.1007/978-3-030-31784-3_5
29. Jansen, N., Könighofer, B., Junges, S., Serban, A., Bloem, R.: Safe reinforcement learning using probabilistic shields. In: CONCUR, LIPIcs, vol. 171, pp. 3:1–3:16. Schloss Dagstuhl - Leibniz-Zentrum für Informatik (2020). https://doi.org/10.4230/LIPIcs.CONCUR.2020.3
30. Kapinski, J., Krogh, B.H., Maler, O., Stursberg, O.: On systematic simulation of open continuous systems. In: Maler, O., Pnueli, A. (eds.) HSCC 2003. LNCS, vol. 2623, pp. 283–297. Springer, Heidelberg (2003). https://doi.org/10.1007/3-540-36580-X_22
31. Karamanakos, P., Geyer, T., Manias, S.: Direct voltage control of DC-DC boost converters using enumeration-based model predictive control. IEEE Trans. Power Electron. **29**(2), 968–978 (2013)
32. Klischat, M., Althoff, M.: A multi-step approach to accelerate the computation of reachable sets for road vehicles. In: ITSC, pp. 1–7. IEEE (2020). https://doi.org/10.1109/ITSC45102.2020.9294328
33. Laczkovich, M.: The removal of π from some undecidable problems involving elementary functions. Proc. Am. Math. Soc. **131**(7), 2235–2240 (2003). https://doi.org/10.1090/S0002-9939-02-06753-9
34. Larsen, K.G.: Statistical model checking, refinement checking, optimization, for stochastic hybrid systems. In: Jurdziński, M., Ničković, D. (eds.) FORMATS 2012. LNCS, vol. 7595, pp. 7–10. Springer, Heidelberg (2012). https://doi.org/10.1007/978-3-642-33365-1_2

35. Larsen, K.G., Le Coënt, A., Mikučionis, M., Taankvist, J.H.: Guaranteed control synthesis for continuous systems in UPPAAL TIGA. In: Chamberlain, R., Taha, W., Törngren, M. (eds.) CyPhy/WESE -2018. LNCS, vol. 11615, pp. 113–133. Springer, Cham (2019). https://doi.org/10.1007/978-3-030-23703-5_6
36. Larsen, K.G., Mikučionis, M., Taankvist, J.H.: Safe and optimal adaptive cruise control. In: Meyer, R., Platzer, A., Wehrheim, H. (eds.) Correct System Design. LNCS, vol. 9360, pp. 260–277. Springer, Cham (2015). https://doi.org/10.1007/978-3-319-23506-6_17
37. Lewis, F.L., Vrabie, D., Syrmos, V.L.: Optimal control. John Wiley & Sons (2012)
38. Luo, Y., Ma, T.: Learning barrier certificates: towards safe reinforcement learning with zero training-time violations. In: NeurIPS, pp. 25621–25632 (2021). https://proceedings.neurips.cc/paper/2021/hash/d71fa38b648d86602d14ac610f2e6194-Abstract.html
39. Maderbacher, B., Schupp, S., Bartocci, E., Bloem, R., Nickovic, D., Könighofer, B.: Provable correct and adaptive simplex architecture for bounded-liveness properties. In: SPIN. LNCS, vol. 13872, pp. 141–160. Springer (2023). https://doi.org/10.1007/978-3-031-32157-3_8
40. Majumdar, R., Ozay, N., Schmuck, A.: On abstraction-based controller design with output feedback. In: HSCC, pp. 15:1–15:11. ACM (2020). https://doi.org/10.1145/3365365.3382219
41. Noaee, M., et al.: Reinforcement learning in urban network traffic signal control: a systematic literature review. Expert Syst. Appl. **199**, 116830 (2022). https://doi.org/10.1016/j.eswa.2022.116830
42. Shmarov, F., Zuliani, P.: Probreach: a tool for guaranteed reachability analysis of stochastic hybrid systems. In: SNR. EPiC Series in Computing, vol. 37, pp. 40–48. EasyChair (2015). https://doi.org/10.29007/mh2c
43. Tarski, A.: A decision method for elementary algebra and geometry. The RAND Corporation (1948). https://www.rand.org/pubs/reports/R109.html
44. Tarski, A.: A lattice-theoretical fixpoint theorem and its applications. Pacific J. Math. **5**(2), 285–309 (1955). https://www.projecteuclid.org/journalArticle/Download?urlId=pjm%2F1103044538
45. Vlachogiannis, J.G., Hatziargyriou, N.D.: Reinforcement learning for reactive power control. IEEE Trans. Power Syst. **19**(3), 1317–1325 (2004). https://doi.org/10.1109/TPWRS.2004.831259
46. Žikelić, D., Lechner, M., Henzinger, T.A., Chatterjee, K.: Learning control policies for stochastic systems with reach-avoid guarantees. In: AAAI, pp. 11926–11935. AAAI Press (2023). https://doi.org/10.1609/aaai.v37i10.26407
47. Wabersich, K.P., Zeilinger, M.N.: A predictive safety filter for learning-based control of constrained nonlinear dynamical systems. Autom. **129**, 109597 (2021). https://doi.org/10.1016/j.automatica.2021.109597
48. Watkins, C.J.C.H.: Learning from Delayed Rewards. Ph.D. thesis, University of Cambridge (1989)
49. Zhao, H., Zhan, N., Kapur, D., Larsen, K.G.: A "Hybrid" approach for synthesizing optimal controllers of hybrid systems: a case study of the oil pump industrial example. In: Giannakopoulou, D., Méry, D. (eds.) FM 2012. LNCS, vol. 7436, pp. 471–485. Springer, Heidelberg (2012). https://doi.org/10.1007/978-3-642-32759-9_38

What, Indeed, is an Achievable Provable Guarantee for Learning-Enabled Safety-Critical Systems

Saddek Bensalem[1], Chih-Hong Cheng[2], Wei Huang[3], Xiaowei Huang[4], Changshun Wu[1](✉), and Xingyu Zhao[5]

[1] University Grenoble Alpes, VERIMAG, Grenoble, France
{saddek.bensalem,changshun.wu}@univ-grenoble-alpes.fr
[2] Technical University of Munich, Garching, Germany
chih-hong.cheng@tum.de
[3] Purple Mountain Laboratories, Nanjing, China
huangwei@pmlabs.com.cn
[4] Department of Computer Science, University of Liverpool, Liverpool, UK
xiaowei.huang@liverpool.ac.uk
[5] WMG, University of Warwick, Coventry, UK
xingyu.zhao@warwick.ac.uk

Abstract. Machine learning has made remarkable advancements, but confidently utilising learning-enabled components in safety-critical domains still poses challenges. Among the challenges, it is known that a rigorous, yet practical, way of achieving safety guarantees is one of the most prominent. In this paper, we first discuss the engineering and research challenges associated with the design and verification of such systems. Then, based on the observation that existing works cannot actually achieve provable guarantees, we promote a two-step verification method for the ultimate achievement of provable statistical guarantees.

Keywords: Safety-critical systems · learning-enabled components · statistical guarantees

1 Introduction

From the studies of Leibniz [1] to the philosophical view, the human mind and brain have been perceived as an information processing system and thinking as a form of computing. Over three centuries ago, two dreams were mingled, the philosopher's and the engineer's: the philosopher's ideal to have a sound method to reason correctly, and the engineer's dream to have a machine to calculate efficiently and without error. Any attempt to assimilate the human brain into a mechanical or computer machine necessarily negates the autonomy of thought. The latter is not the result of chance or indeterminacy but instead of a possibility of choice according to the reasoning based on rules and principles. By

B. Steffen (Ed.): AISoLA 2023, LNCS 14380, pp. 55–76, 2024.
https://doi.org/10.1007/978-3-031-46002-9_4

its organization, the human brain allows the emergence of cognitive autonomy. Of course, suppose we accept the idea of a level of existence proper to the cognitive processes. In that case, the philosophical dream becomes, more modestly, that of understanding the diversity of human cognitive functions. The development of the general theory of automata and the formalization of the construction of complex machines by Von Neumann allowed the pursuit of the engineer's dream. A central turning point took place around the 1960s, with the design of machines on the one hand and progress in artificial intelligence (AI) and cognitive science on the other hand. Significant successes have been achieved, for example, in natural language processing.

Our world today is witnessing the genesis of a significant shift in how advanced technologies operate. We are beginning to see increasingly independent and autonomous systems in this emerging wave of available automation. The degree of interactions between these systems and human operators is gradually being reduced and pushed further away. These autonomous systems are inherently sophisticated and operate in complex, unpredictable environments. Unfortunately, they still face deployment concerns in safety-critical applications (e.g., transportation, healthcare, etc.) due to a lack of trust, behavioural uncertainty, and technology compatibility with safe and secure system development methods. In particular, Urban Autonomous Driving and Intelligent Medical Devices are considered to be the most complex problem in autonomy; existing development of autonomous vehicles naturally includes the AI part (e.g., machine-learning for perception), as well as the CPS part (e.g., for vehicle control or decision making via infrastructure support). However, there are significant challenges in ensuring the quality of the overall system.

To ensure the safety of autonomous systems that incorporate AI components, we consider it mandatory for the overall engineering process to understand the safety performance of AI components while considering their impact on the overall system. Guaranteeing safety in critical systems that incorporate AI components, however, is not a straightforward process. Several constituent elements of safety cover all the dimensions of an AI system. The criteria catalog we can find in the literature to improve safety in critical applications can be summarized as the following:

- All algorithms based on decision-making shall be explainable [2–5];
- The functionality of algorithms shall be analyzed and validated using formal verification methods before use [6–10];
- Statistical validation is necessary, mainly in cases where formal verification is unsuitable for specific application scenarios due to scalability issues [11,12];
- The inherent uncertainty of neural network decisions shall also be quantified [13–16];
- Systems must be observed during operation, for example, by using online monitoring processes [17–21].

In this paper, we promote an approach founded on a two-step integration. The first step involves a system-level analysis and testing, rather than solely focusing on the AI component in isolation. It recognizes the interconnected nature of the system and considers the integration and interactions of various components. By examining the system as a whole, potential risks and vulnerabilities can be identified, allowing for comprehensive safety assurance. The second step involves a detailed analysis of the AI components themselves, without considering their impact on the overall system. While this step provides insights into the specific AI algorithms and models, in itself it may overlook potential risks arising from the interactions between the components and the broader system context. This two-step integration of verification processes is to assess the safety performance of AI components while also considering their impact on the overall system. This entails examining not only their individual performance but also their interactions within the broader system context. In addition to formal analysis, we can also conduct studies on statistical guarantees and how these guarantees propagate throughout the system.

The rest of the paper is organized as follows. Sections 2 and 3 discuss the challenges of designing reliable and trustworthy AI critical systems from an engineering and research perspective, respectively. In Sect. 4, we present our methodology and proposed solutions to tackle these challenges. Finally, Sect. 5 provides a summary of the conclusions and highlights avenues for future work.

2 Challenges in Engineering Safety-Critical Systems Integrating Learning-Enabled Components

The engineering of safety-critical systems has been a mature paradigm with the support of safety standards such as IEC 61508, ISO 26262, or DO-178c. The rigorous method implied by the process focuses on hazards caused by the malfunctioning behavior of E/E safety-related systems, including the interaction of these systems. Nevertheless, even in the absence of system malfunctioning, functional insufficiencies caused by performance limitations and incomplete/improper specification can also be the source of hazards, where standards such as ISO 21448 are introduced to address these issues.

To ensure the necessary level of safety and reliability, a learning-enabled component must also meet the identical functional safety standards encompassing reliability, applicability, maintenance, and safety (RAMS) as any other system. Moreover, it should mitigate the impacts of malfunctions to fulfill the essential safety and reliability prerequisites. On the other hand, properly ensuring the safety of the intended functionality (SOTIF) is the crucial gap in embracing the legitimate use of learning-enabled components. In the following, we enumerate some of the key limiting factors.

1. The introduction of learning-enabled components comes with the practical motivation where the operational environment is ***open*** and ***dynamic*** (e.g., urban autonomous driving), thereby inherently making rigorous analysis complicated [10,22,23].
2. ***Data*** has played a central role in learning-enabled systems [24–26]. Under the slogan "data is the new specification", it is crucial to have a systematic

approach to performing data collection, cleaning, labeling, as well as managing the data to incorporate adjustment of the operational domain.
3. Learning implies translating the implicit knowledge embedded in the data to a model. Despite the mathematical optimization nature of learning model parameters being transparent, the ***uncertainty*** [13–16] caused by the model training or the data can lead to fundamental concerns about the validity of the prediction.
4. Classical techniques for software ***verification*** encounter scalability issues [10, 21]. Learning models such as deep neural networks create highly non-linear functions to perform classification and prediction tasks. Formal verification or bug finding thus can be viewed as a non-linear optimization problem across the high dimensional input space. The problem even worsens when the learned model controls a ***plant*** governed by highly nonlinear dynamics.
5. The derivation of ***safety specifications for the learning component*** can be far from trivial [10,27]. While for tasks such as image-based object detection, the performance specification characterizing the error rate is relatively straightforward (which commonly leads to a probabilistic threshold on error rate), for control applications, the safety and performance requirement needs to be translated into reward signals in order to be used by (reinforcement) learning methods.
6. Finally, the above challenges are further complicated by the fact that the engineering of learning-enabled components is ***iterative*** with the goal of ***continuous improvement*** [10,13–16]. It is also complicated by the dimension of avoiding malfunctioning, implying the need to design hardware or software architectures to avoid transient or permanent faults in the learning-enabled components.

Unfortunately, the state-of-the-art guidelines or standards only provide high-level principles, while concrete methods for ***safe and cost-effective*** implementation are left for interpretation. This ultimately brings the research need in the field, which we detail in subsequent sections.

3 Research Challenges

The reason why one wants to apply machine learning to a safety critical application is two-fold: (1) it is impossible to program a certain functionality of the application and (2) a machine learning model can not only perform well on existing data but also generalise well to unseen data. Nevertheless, it is required that a machine learning model has to be safe and well performed such that both safety and performance can be quantified with error bounds given. Safety will be prioritised when a balance is needed.

Remark 1. While non-trivial, it is possible that a software or hardware system can be designed and implemented with ultra-high reliability, thanks to the availability of specification and requirements. However, this is unlikely for machine learning models, due to the unavailability of specifications and the complexity of the learning process. This calls for novel design and implementation methodologies for machine learning systems to satisfy both safety and performance requirements.

For the remaining of this section, we discuss challenges a novel methodology needs to tackle. While every gap between traditional software and AI-based systems, as discussed in Sect. 2, leads to research challenges, we believe the most significant ones are from (1) the environmental uncertainties that an AI-based system has to face, (2) the size and complexity of the AI models themselves, and (3) the lack of novel analysis methods that are both rigorous and efficient in dealing with the new problems. These three challenges lead to our proposal of considering ***statistical guarantees*** and ***symbolic analysis*** of AI models.

3.1 Uncertainty

In machine learning, uncertainty is often decomposed into aleatoric uncertainty and epistemic uncertainty, with the former irreducible and the latter reducible in theory. To explain this, we formalise the concept of generalisability, which requires that a neural network works well on all possible inputs in the data domain $\mathtt{X}$, although it is only trained on the training dataset (X, Y).

Definition 1. *Assume that there is a ground truth function* $f : \mathtt{X} \rightarrow \mathtt{Y}$ *and a probability function* $O_p : \mathtt{X} \rightarrow [0,1]$ *representing the operational profile. A network* $\mathcal{N}$ *trained on* (X, Y) *has a generalisation error:*

$$G_{\mathcal{N}}^{0-1} = \sum_{x \in \mathtt{X}} \mathbf{1}_{\{\mathcal{N}(x) \neq f(x)\}} \times O_p(x) \tag{1}$$

where $\mathbf{1}_{\mathtt{S}}$ *is an indicator function – it is equal to 1 when* $\mathtt{S}$ *is true and 0 otherwise.*

We use the notation $O_p(x)$ to represent the probability of an input x being selected, which aligns with the *operational profile* notion [28] in software engineering. Moreover, we use 0–1 loss function (i.e., assigns value 0 to loss for a correct classification and 1 for an incorrect classification) so that, for a given O_p, $G_{\mathcal{N}}^{0-1}$ is equivalent to the reliability measure *pfd* (the expected probability of the system failing on a random demand) defined in the safety standard IEC-61508.

We decompose the generalisation error into three:

$$G_{\mathcal{N}}^{0-1} = \underbrace{G_{\mathcal{N}}^{0-1} - \inf_{\mathcal{N} \in \mathtt{N}} G_{\mathcal{N}}^{0-1}}_{\text{Estimation error of } \mathcal{N}} + \underbrace{\inf_{\mathcal{N} \in \mathtt{N}} G_{\mathcal{N}}^{0-1} - G_{f,(X,Y)}^{0-1,*}}_{\text{Approximation error of } \mathtt{N}} + \underbrace{G_{f,(X,Y)}^{0-1,*}}_{\text{Bayes error}} \tag{2}$$

a) The *Estimation error of* $\mathcal{N}$ measures how far the learned classifier $\mathcal{N}$ is from the best classifier in $\mathtt{N}$, the set of possible neural networks with the same architecture but different weights with $\mathcal{N}$. Lifecycle activities at the **model training** stage essentially aim to reduce this error, i.e., performing optimisations of the set $\mathtt{N}$.

b) The *Approximation error of* `N` measures how far the best classifier in `N` is from the overall optimal classifier, after isolating the Bayes error. The set `N` is determined by the architecture of DNNs (e.g., numbers of layers), thus lifecycle activities at the **model construction** stage are used to minimise this error.

c) The *Bayes error* is the lowest and irreducible error rate over all possible classifiers for the given classification problem [29]. The irreducibility refers to the training process, and the Bayes errors can be reduced in data collection and preparation. It is non-zero if the true labels are not deterministic (e.g., an image being labelled as y_1 by one person but as y_2 by others), thus intuitively it captures the uncertainties in the dataset (X, Y) and true distribution f when aiming to solve a real-world problem with machine learning. We estimate this error (implicitly) at the **initiation** and **data collection** stages in activities like: necessity consideration and dataset preparation etc.

Both the Approximation and Estimation errors are reducible, and are caused by the epistemic uncertainties. The Bayes error is irreducible, and caused by the aleatoric uncertainty. The *ultimate goal* of all lifecycle activities is to reduce the three errors to 0, especially for safety-critical applications.

Aleatoric uncertainty, as discussed in [16], may include various data-related issues such as survey error, missing data, and possible shifts in the data when deployed in real-world. Definition and measurement of these uncertainties can be done more reasonably with probabilistic/statistical distributions.

3.2 Size and Complexity of the AI Models

Another significant challenge is on the AI model itself. While it is believed that larger – often overparamterised – models can perform well [30], large models cannot be analysed analytically due to its size and complexity. Formal verification methods that check the local robustness of a neural network against perturbations are either limited on the number of neurons in a network (such as [31–33]) or limited by the number of input dimensions that can be perturbed (such as [34–36]). Even the theoretical analysis in machine learning field, which is usually less rigorous than in formal methods, has to be conducted on much simpler models such as linear and random projection models (see e.g., [37]). The situation is getting worse when we have to deal with large language models, see e.g., [38] for a discussion on their safety and trustworthiness issues.

3.3 Lack of Novel Analysis Methods that Are both Rigorous and Efficient

Existing analysis methods from either formal methods or software testing are mostly aimed to extend their success in traditional software and systems. For example, constraint solving and abstract interpretation are popular methods in robustness verification of neural networks, and structural testing are popular testing methods for neural networks. Actually, the traditional verification methods have already been experiencing scalability problems when dealing with traditional software (up to several thousands lines of code), and it is therefore unlikely that they are able to scale and work with modern neural networks (which typically have multi-millions or billions of neurons). For testing methods, there is a methodological barrier to cross because neurons do not have clear semantics as variables, so does the layers with respect to the statements. Such mismatches render the test coverage metrics, which are designed by adapting the known test coverage in software testing such as statement coverage, potentially uncorrelated with the properties to be tested.

Another critical difference from traditional software that is posed on the analysis methods is the perfection of neural networks. For software to be applied to safety critical applications, a "possible perfection" notion [39–41] is used. However, for machine learning, the failures are too easy to find, and it does not seem likely that a perfect, or possibly perfect, machine learning model exists for a real-world application. To this end, a novel design method is needed to ensure that an AI-based system can potentially be free from serious failures.

Moreover, multiple properties may be required for a machine learning model, e.g., robustness, generalisation, privacy, fairness, free from backdoor attacks, etc. However, these properties can be conflicting (e.g., robustness-accuracy trade-off) and many of them without formal specifications, which lead to the challenge of lacking effective methods for the analysis and improvement of them altogether for a machine learning model.

4 Methodology

The needs of safety-critical systems require that, even facing challenges that are more significant than traditional software, a legitimate methodology will still provide rigorous and provable guarantees, concerning the satisfiability of properties on the autonomous cyber-physical system under investigation. We conceptualise AI-based systems into five levels (shown in Fig. 1). For the remainder of this section, we discuss the methodology needed at each level and across levels. Specifically, at each level, we consider the following questions: For sources of uncertainty identified in earlier sections, what metrics (e.g., binary, worst-case or probabilistic) shall we use to measure them? How to efficiently evaluate those metrics? Can we provide any forms of guarantees on the evaluations? Moreover, we raise questions that span across different levels: How do metrics at higher levels break down to metrics at lower levels? If and how the guarantees (in various forms) from lower levels can propagate and compound to higher levels, ultimately aiming to make meaningful claims about the entire system.

Our proposed methodology consists of the following attributes:

- a set of specification languages that describe, and connect, requirements of different levels;
- a formal method of propagating statistical guarantees about the satisfiability of the requirements across the system and the component levels;
- a rigorous method of achieving required statistical guarantees at the instance and the model levels;

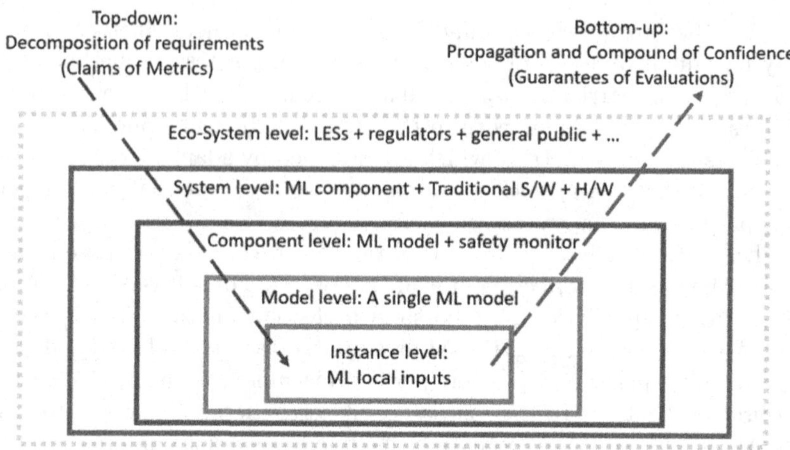

Fig. 1. Research challenges organised into five conceptual levels with top-down and bottom-up routes.

This is founded on two threads of state-of-the-art research: a design and co-simulation framework (Sect. 4.1) and some design-time verification and validation (V&V) methods for machine learning models (Sect. 4.4). The co-simulation framework is to effectively simulate the real-world system and environment to a sufficient level of fidelity. The V&V methods are to detect vulnerabilities and improve the machine learning model's safety and performance. It is noted that, the V&V methods can improve the system but may not be able to provide provable safety guarantee, for reasons that we will discuss below. Once the improvement is converged (or certain termination condition is satisfied), the new methodology is applied for the ultimate achievement of provable guarantees.

4.1 State-of-the-Art 1: A Design and Co-Simulation Framework

This section summarizes the current research on the rigorous design of AI-enabled systems out of the EU Horizon 2020 project FOCETA.

Design of Trustable AI Models. Design of trust-able AI models requires considering the complete engineering life-cycle beyond optimizing the model parameters. Figure 2 presents a flow design for the AI model development. We consider the lifecycle phases: data preparation, training, offline verification and validation, and online deployment. During the offline V&V, techniques for the falsification and explanation are applied to discover whether there are failures regarding the decision-making (i.e., falsification) or failures demonstrating the inconsistency with human's perception (i.e., explanation). In addition to their individual functionalities, falsification and explanation may benefit from mutual interactions, to make sure that a decision failure can be explained and two inconsistent explanations are tested, see e.g., [42]. A formal verification process is called only when no error can be found from both falsification and explanation.

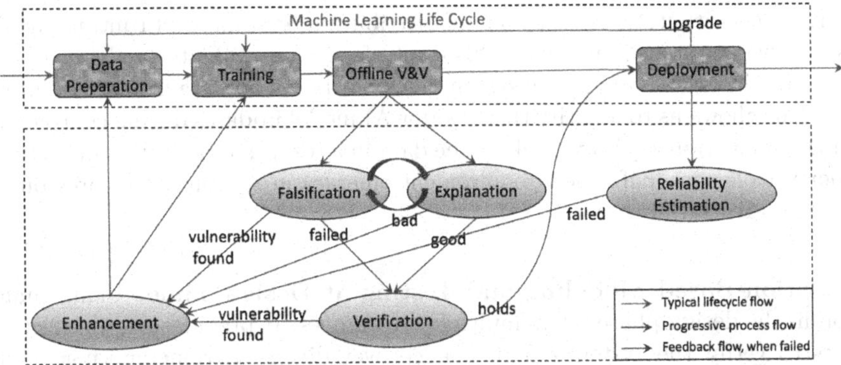

Fig. 2. A Verification and Validation Framework for Machine Learning Enhancement

In the context of a real-world learning-enabled system, the offline V&V can be insufficient, due to the scalability of the verification techniques and the environmental uncertainties that are unknown during offline development (details will be provided below). In such cases, a reliability estimation to analyse the recorded runtime data will be needed, to understand statistically whether the AI-based system can run without failures e.g., in the next hour, with high probability.

Another important module in Fig. 2 is the enhancement, where the failure cases are considered for the improvement of the machine learning models, through either data synthesis or model training.

Design Flow for Safety-Critical Systems with AI Components. Like any other safety-critical systems, the design flow for AI-enabled systems shall also cover design and operation time activities. However, in contrast to classical critical systems where the environment is largely static and predictable, the use of AI-enabled systems reflects the need to handle an open environment.

Within FOCETA, we view the engineering of the complete system as analogous to the engineering of the AI component, where it is important to create a continuous loop of improvement between development and operation. The current state of the practice is extended toward transferring knowledge about systems and their contexts (e.g., traffic situations) from the development to operations and from the operations back to action in iterative steps of continuous improvements. The methodology enables their ongoing engineering over the complete life cycle of autonomous learning-enabled systems – from specification, design, implementation, and verification to operation in the real world with a particular focus on correctness concerning evolving requirements and the systems' safety. Moreover, the whole design flow ensures traceability between requirements and the system/component design.

A key feature is the usage of runtime monitors for the seamless integration of development and operations. In contrast to AI component monitors that largely detect situations such as out-of-distribution, system-level runtime monitors observe a system (part) via defined interfaces and evaluate predefined conditions and invariants about the system behavior based on data from these interfaces. This allows us to identify the need for AI model updates during continuous testing/verification if, for example, some data in a test scenario results in a safety property violation or if a new requirement emerges in response to a previously unknown adversarial threat.

Simulation-Based Modeling and Testing at Design Time. Using simulation in the design phase offers multiple advantages. It provides a cost-effective means to verify the system's performance over diverse parameter ranges and generate massive scenarios. It follows that critical methods can be already identified in the virtual environment, and only those can be replayed in the much more expensive physical setting. Simulation-based testing allows the generation of scenarios (e.g., with infrequent events) that may be impossible to realize when the system operates in its environment (e.g., with specific weather conditions, such as fog or snow). It also enables the creation of safety-critical situations (e.g., crashes) without compromising the safety of the real-life actors. The simulation framework shall allow the integration of heterogeneous components that may be designed with different tools and frameworks. In addition, there is a need to rigorously argue that the domain gap between synthetic data produced by the simulation engine and real data observed in the field is closed. In layman's words, an image being "photo-realistic" does not necessarily imply its being "real".

Deployment, Operation, and Analysis of AI Critical Systems at Runtime. The analysis of the AI components and their integration into the AI critical system during design time, together with protective mechanisms synthesized around AI models, help the safety assurance of the overall system during real-time operation. These measures are complemented by runtime verification, which plays a central role during the AI critical operation. Runtime monitors allow us to observe the system and its interaction with the environment and gather helpful information regarding (1) violation of safety or other requirements and (2) new operational scenarios that were not captured by the training data and models, and (3) other unexpected situations and anomalies not characterized by the existing requirements set. To be effective, monitors must be present both at the component level (AI and classical) and at the system level; the information gathered by different monitors must be fused to derive useful information that can be used to i) ignore the situation (e.g., detected object misclassification) that does not impact the system-level control decision, ii) take a protective measure (e.g., switch from the advanced to a base controller) or iii) improve the design (e.g., provide a new scenario for the training data). The last point refers to an evolvable AI critical system, in which information from the system operation is collected and used to go back to the design and enhance its functionality based on new insights, thus effectively closing a loop between the design and the operation phase.

4.2 Properties and Specifications at Different Levels

On the system level, we may use temporal logic to express the required dynamic behavior. There are recent attempts to extend the temporal logic for AI-based systems. For example, [43] formalises requirements of an autonomous unmanned aircraft system based on an extension of propositional LTL, where temporal operators are augmented with timing constraints. It uses atomic propositions such as "$horizontalIntruderDistance > 250$" to express the result of the perception module, without considering the sensory input and the possible failure of getting the exact value for $horizontalIntruderDistance$. [27] introduces a specification language based on LTL, which utilises event-based abstraction to hide the details of the neural network structure and parameters. It considers the potential failure of the perception component and uses a predicate $pedestrian(\mathbf{x})$ to express if $\mathbf{x}$ is a pedestrian (referring to the ground truth). However, it does not consider the predicate's potential vulnerabilities, such as robustness, uncertainty, and backdoors. [44] proposes Timed Quality Temporal Logic (TQTL) to express monitorable [45] spatio-temporal quality properties of perception systems based on neural networks. It considers object detectors such as YOLO and uses expressions such as $D_0 : d_1 : (ID, 1), (class, car), (pr, 0.9), (bb, B1)$ to denote an object d_1 in a frame D_0 such that it has an index 1, a predictive label car, the prediction probability 0.9, and is in a bounding box B_1. Therefore, every state may include multiple such expressions, and then a TQTL formula can be written by referring to the components of the expressions in a state.

For our purpose of having a statistical guarantee for properties at the system level (see Fig. 1), for any temporal logic formula φ, a statistical guarantee is needed, e.g., in the form of

$$P(err(\varphi) \leq \epsilon) > 1 - \delta \tag{3}$$

where φ is a formula such that $err(\varphi)$ denotes that estimation error on the satisfiability of φ on the system, and ϵ and δ are small positive constants. In the formula φ, we need atomic propositions that are related to the perception components. According to different assumptions, we may have different atomic propositions: instance-level atomic propositions or model-level atomic propositions. For an instance-level atomic proposition such as $pedestrian_{\epsilon,\delta}$, it expresses that the error of having a $pedestrian$ in the current input is lower than ϵ, under the confidence level no less than δ. In such cases, the statistical guarantee is established by considering the local robustness (i.e., cell unastuteness as in [46]). On the other hand, for a model-level atomic proposition such as $perception_{\epsilon,\delta}$, it expresses that the error of having a failed detection among all possible next inputs is lower than ϵ, under the confidence level no less than δ. In such cases, the statistical guarantee is established by considering the reliability as in [46].

The selection between instance-level and model-level atomic propositions depends on the assumptions. If we believe that a failure on the perception component does not have a correlation with the failures of other components, a model-level atomic proposition will be sufficient. On the other hand, if a correlation between failures is expected, and we want the verification to fully consider such correlations, an instance-level atomic proposition will be more appropriate and accurate.

Section 4.3 will discuss how to achieve the statistical guarantee (i.e., ϵ and δ). For the model-level atomic propositions, the specification language in [47] considers not only the functionality (i.e., the relation between input and output) of a trained model but also the training process (where objects such as training datasets, model parameters, and distance between posterior distributions are considered). With this, it can express the safety and security properties that describe the attacks during the lifecycle stages.

4.3 Guarantees Achieved at Component Levels

This section will discuss a potential solution that can be utilised to achieve the statistical guarantee (i.e., ϵ and δ) for an atomic proposition describing certain safety properties as summarised in [47]. As discussed in Sect. 4.4, this cannot be achieved by a standalone machine learning model, even if a V&V framework as in Fig. 2 is applied, due to the insufficiency of machine learning models. We suggest a monitored machine learning system, i.e., a machine learning model running in parallel with a runtime monitor. As indicated in Fig. 3, for non-ML safety-critical systems with clear specifications about safety, a runtime monitor often acts like an alarm to alert the unsafe behaviour. On the other hand, for ML systems without safety specifications but only with samples, a runtime monitor needs to analyze the samples and predict the safety of the current input e.g., in the manner of a traffic light system as briefly discussed below. While the predictions might not be completely correct, we expect they are conservative with a provable guarantee and as accurate as possible.

A runtime monitor checks every input of a neural network and issues warnings whenever there is a risk that the neural network might make wrong decision. As discussed earlier, given the availability of many adversarial attacks, it is unlikely that a neural network itself can achieve "possible perfection" [48] – a notion of traditional safety-critical software introduced by [39–41]. The safety of a neural network, however, can potentially be achievable with the support of a runtime monitor. Actually, in the extreme case, if a runtime monitor is so restrictive that none of the input instances can pass without warning, the neural network under the runtime monitor is safe (although the performance is bad).

The design of a runtime monitor for a given neural network is to ensure that the safety of the monitored neural network can be achieved with guarantees. While the restrictive runtime monitor mentioned above suggests absolute safety, it is also undesirable due to its performance. In the following, we discuss a possible runtime monitor that is able to achieve statistical guarantee of the form (3). The core idea of this monitor is to represent the abstracted experiences

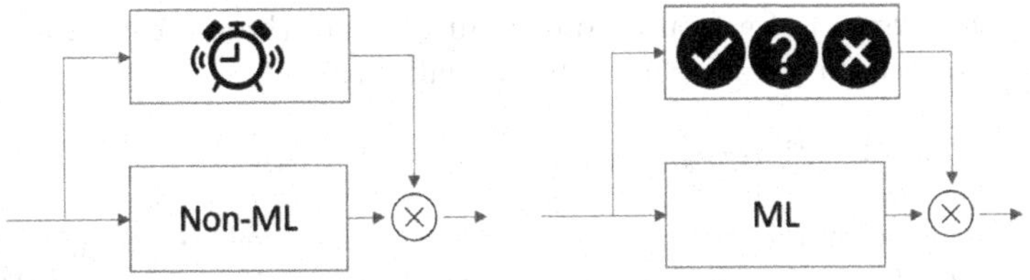

Fig. 3. Runtime Monitors with (for non-ML systems) and without (for ML systems) specifications

symbolically, serving as references for future behaviors. The process involves recording observed data or their learned high-level features for each decision made by the neural network. These data points are then clustered based on their similarities, and each cluster is approximated by a box as an abstraction. Every box $\mathbf{b}$ can be described as a tuple (l, r, c, m, y, i), where l is the location of the box, r is the radius vector of the box, c is the cluster that the box belongs to, m is the number of data samples that the box contains, and y is the predictive class label of the box, and i is the correctness indicator of prediction relating to the abstracted samples. Once these abstractions are derived, they can be effectively symbolized, and operational symbols can be defined to establish the runtime monitor. When new data points and decisions arise, we compare the network's behavior for a given input with the reference abstractions. Generally, there exist two types of boxes: *positive* and *negative* ones, representing abstracted good and bad behaviors, respectively. If the behavior is similar to good behaviors (inside a positive box), the decision is accepted; if it resembles bad behaviors (inside a bad box), the decision is rejected.

Our guarantees are on two levels. The first level considers the confidence the runtime monitor classifies an input as safe or not. Assume that we have a data point that falls within a box $\mathbf{b}$ that is either positive or negative with respect to a label. Since the box will classify the data point, we can utilise the information in the box (e.g., the known points that fall within the box) to conduct a Probably Approximately Correct (PAC) analysis, or utilising Hoeffding inequality such as in [11], to determine a probability and an error. That is, for each box $\mathbf{b}$, we may have

$$P_{\mathbf{b},\mathcal{D}}(err_{\mathbf{b},\mathcal{D}}(c,h) \leq \epsilon_{\mathbf{b}}) > 1 - \delta_{\mathbf{b}} \tag{4}$$

for small positive numbers $0 < \epsilon_{\mathbf{b}}, \delta_{\mathbf{b}} < 1/2$, where $\mathcal{D}$ is the data distribution, $err_{\mathbf{b},\mathcal{D}}(c,h)$ is the probabilistic error of the hypothesis h (i.e., the probability of h does not hold) in the box $\mathbf{b}$, with respect to the concept c and the distribution $\mathcal{D}$, such that $err_{\mathbf{b},\mathcal{D}}(c,h) = P_{x\in\mathcal{D},x\in\mathbf{b}}(h(x) \neq c(x))$, i.e., the probability over x drawn from $\mathcal{D}$ and $\mathbf{b}$ that $h(x)$ and $c(x)$ differ.

The second level considers the probability of a future input that our runtime monitor can confidently classify. Assume that we have a set of n boxes in the space (e.g., the hidden space before the Softmax layer) such that they are either positive or negative (we do not consider uncertain boxes for guarantees) with respect to certain label. We can use hypothesis testing to determine the probability (the error) of a future point falling within these boxes, according to the set of known data points. Similarly, we will have

$$P_{\mathcal{D}}(err_{M^*,\mathcal{D}}(M) \leq \epsilon_{M^*}) > 1 - \delta_{M^*} \quad (5)$$

for small positive numbers $0 < \epsilon_{M^*}, \delta_{M^*} < 1/2$, where $err_{M^*,\mathcal{D}}(M) = P_{x \in \mathcal{D}}(M(x) \neq M^*(x))$ is the probability that the runtime monitor M disagrees with the ground truth M^* regarding whether an input $\mathbf{x}$ is within the confirmed boxes. Moreover, we can replace the hypothesis testing with more effective, and more scalable, probability methods such as MCMC or that we did in [48].

A "combination" (to be analytically derived as future work) of the above levels will reach a statistical way of conducting reliability estimation over runtime data. A statistical guarantee of the form

$$P_{\mathcal{D}}(err_{\mathcal{D}}(c,h) \leq \epsilon) > 1 - \delta \quad (6)$$

will be achieved, where $\mathcal{D}$ is the operational distribution of the AI component within the system, $err_{\mathcal{D}}(c,h)$ denotes the error probability of the AI model c with respect to the ground truth h, and both ϵ and δ are small positive numbers.

Remark 2. The chance constraint (as in Eq. (6)) as a statistical guarantee for safety is not as strong as a deterministic guarantee, which states the absolute missing of failures, or a probabilistic guarantee, which states the missing of failures with certain probability. However, the deterministic guarantee is infeasible in practice due to the environmental uncertainties, as we have discussed for offline verification and validation. Practical methods are missing on how to achieve tight probabilistic guarantees.

4.4 State-of-the-Art 2: Offline V and V Methods and Guarantee

This section discusses the existing verification and validation methods, and explains why they cannot provide the guarantees that are needed for AI-based systems. AI models, especially Deep Neural Networks, are known to be susceptible to the adversarial attack and backdoor attack. Given a DNN model f, which maps a high dimensional input x to a prediction class y, adversarial attack and backdoor attack add maliciously generated perturbations ϵ into the benign inputs, leading to the mis-predictions of DNNs (refer to the survey for the difference between adversarial attack and backdoor attack).

$$f(x) = y \;\&\; f(x+\epsilon) \neq y \quad (7)$$

This section will briefly review the existing V&V methods on the robustness of DNNs against the adversarial perturbation ϵ and discuss the guarantee to the safety of AI model.

Verification. Verification techniques are to determine whether or not a property of a neural network holds within a given range of inputs. The existing verification techniques can be categorized according to the guarantee they provide. *Deterministic guarantees* are achieved by transforming verification of deep neural networks into a set of constraints so that they can be solved with a constraint solver, such as Satisfiability Modulo Theories (SMT) solver [49,50], Boolean Satisfiability Problem (SAT) solver [51–53], and mixed integer linear programming (MILP) solver [54,55]. The name "deterministic" comes from the fact that these solvers often return a deterministic answer to a query, i.e., either satisfiable or unsatisfiable. Some verification techniques can offer *one-sided guarantee*, i.e. deep neural network is robust when adversarial perturbation measured by L_p norm is bounded less than ϵ. These approaches leverage the abstract interpretation [56,57], convex optimization [58,59], or interval arithmetic [60,61] to compute the approximate bound. Compared to the verification techniques with deterministic guarantee, the bounded estimation can work with larger models, up to 10000 hidden neurons, and can avoid floating point issues in existing constraint solver implementations [62]. To deal with real-world system, which contains the state of the art DNNs with at least multi-million hidden neurons, some practical verification techniques are developed to offer *converging bounds guarantee* and *statistical guarantee*. Layer-by-layer refinement [6], reduction to a two-player turn-based game [8], and global optimization-based approaches [63] are developed to compute the lower bounds of robustness by utilizing the Lipschitz constant and the bounds converge to the optimal value. The *statistical guarantee* is achieved by utilizing the statistical sampling methods, e.g. Monte Carlo based sampling, to estimate the robustness with a certain probability. CLEVER [64] estimates the robustness lower bound by sampling the norm of gradients and fitting a limit distribution using extreme value theory. [65] utilizes the multi-level splitting sampling to calculate the probability of adversarial examples in the local region as an estimation of local robustness. The local probabilistic robustness estimation can be aggregated over the train set to form the global robustness estimation [66]. [46,67] further propose the concept of reliability, which is a combination of robustness and generalization, and estimated on the operational dataset to provide statistical guarantee on neural networks' overall performance.

Testing. When working with large-scale models, often used in the industry, verification is not a good option. Verification techniques offer guarantees to the results at the expense of high computational cost. The cost goes sharply with the increase of model's complexity. Testing arises as a complement to verification. Instead of pursuing mathematics proofs, testing techniques exploit the model in a broad way to find potential faults. The first category of works is the coverage-guided testing. A large amount of coverage metrics are designed in consideration of the structure information of DNNs. Structure coverage metrics, such as neuron coverage [68], k-multisection neuron coverage [69], neuron activation pattern coverage [69], Modified Condition/Decision Coverage (MC/DC) for neuron layers [70] are proposed in the past few years. There are also a few works dedicated to designing coverage metrics for Recurrent Neural Networks (RNNs), such as modeling RNNs as abstract state transition systems and covering different states and transitions [71], and quantifying one-step hidden memory change and multi-step temporal relation [72]. They are all based on the assumption that the activation of neurons represents the functionality of DNNs. By achieving a higher coverage rate in proposed structure coverage metrics, the functionality of DNNs are more thoroughly exercised. Therefore, structure coverage metrics can guide the generation of test cases as diversified as possible, and detect different types of defects, such as adversarial examples and backdoor input [72]. However, the weak correlation between structure coverage metrics and the defects can not guarantee that increasing the coverage rate can find more faults in DNNs.

The second category of works is distribution-aware testing. There has been a growing body of research focusing on the development of distribution-aware testing techniques for DNNs. To approximate the distribution of training data, deep generative models such as Variational AutoEncoders (VAE) and Generative Adversarial Networks (GAN) are commonly used, especially for high-dimensional inputs like images. Berend et al. [73] propose the first distribution-guided coverage criterion, which integrates out-of-distribution (OOD) techniques to generate unseen test cases and provides a high level of assurance regarding the validity of identified faults in DNNs. In a study by Dola et al. [74], the validity of test cases generated by existing DNN test generation techniques is examined using VAE. By comparing the probability density estimates of a trained VAE model on data from the training distribution and OOD inputs, critical insights are obtained for validating test inputs generated by DNN test generation approaches. To generate realistic test cases that conform to requirements and reveal errors, Byun et al. [75] employ a variant of Conditional Variational Autoencoder (CVAE) to capture a manifold that represents the feature distribution of the training data. Toledo et al. [76] introduces the first method called distribution-based falsification and verification (DFV), which utilizes environmental models to concentrate the falsification and verification of DNNs on meaningful regions of the input space. This method is designed to leverage the underlying distribution of data during the process of DNN falsification and verification. Huang et al. [77] propose a hierarchical distribution-aware testing framework for DNNs. Their framework takes into account two levels of distribution: the feature level distribution, captured by generative models, and the pixel level distribution, which is represented by perceptual quality metrics. Although distribution aware testing can detect more meaningful faults for DNNs, which significantly contribute to the downstream repairing of DNNs, they still cannot provide the deterministic guarantee to the safety of DNNs.

5 Conclusion

Developing critical systems has always been challenging due to the potential harm caused by malfunctions, functional insufficiencies, or malicious attacks. The complexity is amplified when incorporating learning-enabled components, as the approaches taken by safety engineers who build the system often differ from those employed by AI/ML engineers who construct the components. Educating the general audience about AI safety concerns is essential for fostering active engagement in the ongoing discourse. However, to address the underlying engineering challenges, an interdisciplinary curriculum that bridges concepts from various fields such as AI/ML engineering and safety engineering can provide valuable insights and understanding.

We notice that there are two views on system safety in the broader community, the "binary" view and the "probabilistic" view, which present differing perspectives on how to approach safety assurance. Proponents of the binary view argue that safety is about clearly defining the system's capabilities and limitations, establishing a definitive "safety boundary". According to this view, we can confidently operate the system once we have a comprehensive understanding of this boundary. However, this viewpoint may hold primarily for traditional systems without AI components, where the system behavior is relatively simple and predictable.

The concept in this paper hints that we advocate the probabilistic view that safety for complex AI-enabled systems should be measured in terms of empirical probabilities[1], as modern systems are becoming increasingly complex, with inherent uncertainties that make it difficult to determine the system's safety boundary precisely. In this perspective, the boundary itself may even appear blurred due to the non-deterministic behaviors exhibited by AI algorithms. Consequently, adherents of the probabilistic view assert that safety assurance should consider the likelihood of various outcomes and incorporate risk assessment and mitigation strategies to manage uncertainties effectively.

References

1. Kulstad, M., Carlin, L.: Leibniz's philosophy of mind (1997)
2. Gunning, D., Stefik, M., Choi, J., Miller, T., Stumpf, S., Yang, G.-Z.: Xai-explainable artificial intelligence. Sci. Rob. **4**(37), eaay7120 (2019)
3. Lapuschkin, S., Wäldchen, S., Binder, A., Montavon, G., Samek, W., Müller, K.-R.: Unmasking clever hans predictors and assessing what machines really learn. Nat. Commun. **10**(1), 1096 (2019)
4. Confalonieri, R., Coba, L., Wagner, B., Besold, T.R.: A historical perspective of explainable artificial intelligence. Wiley Interdisc. Rev. Data Min. Knowl. Disc. **11**(1), e1391 (2021)
5. Došilović, F.K., Brčić, M., Hlupić, N., Explainable artificial intelligence: a survey. In: 41st International Convention on Information and Communication Technology, Electronics and Microelectronics (MIPRO), vol. 2018, pp. 0210–0215. IEEE (2018)
6. Huang, X., Kwiatkowska, M., Wang, S., Wu, M.: Safety verification of deep neural networks. In: Majumdar, R., Kunčak, V. (eds.) CAV 2017. LNCS, vol. 10426, pp. 3–29. Springer, Cham (2017). https://doi.org/10.1007/978-3-319-63387-9_1

[1] In statistics, empirical probability refers to the probability of an event based on observed data or evidence. The empirical probability is also known as experimental probability because it is derived from actual experimentation or observation.

7. Dreossi, T., et al.: VERIFAI: a toolkit for the formal design and analysis of artificial intelligence-based systems. In: Dillig, I., Tasiran, S. (eds.) CAV 2019. LNCS, vol. 11561, pp. 432–442. Springer, Cham (2019). https://doi.org/10.1007/978-3-030-25540-4_25
8. Wu, M., Wicker, M., Ruan, W., Huang, X., Kwiatkowska, M.: A game-based approximate verification of deep neural networks with provable guarantees. Theor. Comput. Sci. **807**, 298–329 (2020)
9. Liu, C., et al.: Algorithms for verifying deep neural networks. Found. Trends® Optim. **4**(3–4), 244–404 (2021)
10. Seshia, S.A., Sadigh, D., Sastry, S.S.: Toward verified artificial intelligence. Commun. ACM **65**(7), 46–55 (2022)
11. Huang, C., Hu, Z., Huang, X., Pei, K.: Statistical certification of acceptable robustness for neural networks. In: Farkaš, I., Masulli, P., Otte, S., Wermter, S. (eds.) ICANN 2021. LNCS, vol. 12891, pp. 79–90. Springer, Cham (2021). https://doi.org/10.1007/978-3-030-86362-3_7
12. Zhang, T., Ruan, W., Fieldsend, J.E.: Proa: a probabilistic robustness assessment against functional perturbations. In: Amini, M.R., Canu, S., Fischer, A., Guns, T., Kralj Novak, P., Tsoumakas, G. (eds.) ECML PKDD 2022. LNCS, vol. 13715, pp. 154–170. Springer, Heidelberg (2022). https://doi.org/10.1007/978-3-031-26409-2_10
13. Shafaei, S., Kugele, S., Osman, M.H., Knoll, A.: Uncertainty in machine learning: a safety perspective on autonomous driving. In: Gallina, B., Skavhaug, A., Schoitsch, E., Bitsch, F. (eds.) SAFECOMP 2018. LNCS, vol. 11094, pp. 458–464. Springer, Cham (2018). https://doi.org/10.1007/978-3-319-99229-7_39
14. Gawlikowski, J., et al.: A survey of uncertainty in deep neural networks. arXiv preprint arXiv:2107.03342 (2021)
15. Hüllermeier, E., Waegeman, W.: Aleatoric and epistemic uncertainty in machine learning: an introduction to concepts and methods. Mach. Learn. **110**, 457–506 (2021)
16. Gruber, C., Schenk, P.O., Schierholz, M., Kreuter, F., Kauermann, G.: Sources of uncertainty in machine learning - a statisticians' view. arXiv:2305.16703 (2023)
17. Cheng, C.-H., Nührenberg, G., Yasuoka, H.: Runtime monitoring neuron activation patterns. In: Design, Automation & Test in Europe Conference & Exhibition (DATE), vol. 2019, pp. 300–303. IEEE (2019)
18. Henzinger, T.A., Lukina, A., Schilling, C.: Outside the box: abstraction-based monitoring of neural networks. In: ECAI 2020, pp. 2433–2440. IOS Press (2020)
19. Cheng, C.-H.: Provably-robust runtime monitoring of neuron activation patterns. In: Design, Automation & Test in Europe Conference & Exhibition (DATE), vol. 2021, pp. 1310–1313. IEEE (2021)
20. Lukina, A., Schilling, C., Henzinger, T.A.: Into the unknown: active monitoring of neural networks. In: Feng, L., Fisman, D. (eds.) RV 2021. LNCS, vol. 12974, pp. 42–61. Springer, Cham (2021). https://doi.org/10.1007/978-3-030-88494-9_3
21. Cheng, C.-H., Wu, C., Seferis, E., Bensalem, S.: Prioritizing corners in OoD detectors via symbolic string manipulation. In: Bouajjani, A., Holík, L., Wu, Z. (eds.) ATVA 2022. LNCS, pp. 397–413. Springer, Heidelberg (2022). https://doi.org/10.1007/978-3-031-19992-9_26
22. Fremont, D.J., Dreossi, T., Ghosh, S., Yue, X., Sangiovanni-Vincentelli, A.L., Seshia, S.A.: Scenic: a language for scenario specification and scene generation. In: Proceedings of the 40th ACM SIGPLAN Conference on Programming Language Design and Implementation, pp. 63–78 (2019)

23. Zhong, S., et al.: Machine learning: new ideas and tools in environmental science and engineering. Environ. Sci. Technol. **55**(19), 12741–12754 (2021)
24. Brunton, S.L., Kutz, J.N.: Data-driven Science and Engineering: Machine Learning, Dynamical Systems, and Control. Cambridge University Press, Cambridge (2019)
25. Zelaya, C.V.G.: Towards explaining the effects of data preprocessing on machine learning. In: IEEE 35th International Conference on Data Engineering (ICDE), vol. 2019, pp. 2086–2090. IEEE (2019)
26. Roh, Y., Heo, G., Whang, S.E.: A survey on data collection for machine learning: a big data-AI integration perspective. IEEE Trans. Knowl. Data Eng. **33**(4), 1328–1347 (2019)
27. Bensalem, S., et al.: Formal specification for learning-enabled autonomous systems. In: FoMLAS2022 (2022)
28. Musa, J.D.: Operational profiles in software-reliability engineering. IEEE Softw. **10**(2), 14–32 (1993)
29. Fukunaga, K.: Introduction to Statistical Pattern Recognition. Elsevier, Amsterdam (2013)
30. Nakkiran, P., Kaplun, G., Bansal, Y., Yang, T., Barak, B., Sutskever, I.: Deep double descent: where bigger models and more data hurt. In: International Conference on Learning Representations (2020)
31. Li, J., Liu, J., Yang, P., Chen, L., Huang, X., Zhang, L.: Analyzing deep neural networks with symbolic propagation: towards higher precision and faster verification. In: Chang, B.-Y.E. (ed.) SAS 2019. LNCS, vol. 11822, pp. 296–319. Springer, Cham (2019). https://doi.org/10.1007/978-3-030-32304-2_15
32. Li, R., et al.: Prodeep: a platform for robustness verification of deep neural networks. In: Proceedings of the 28th ACM Joint Meeting on European Software Engineering Conference and Symposium on the Foundations of Software Engineering, ESEC/FSE 2020, pp. 1630–1634. ACM, New York (2020)
33. Yang, P., et al.: Enhancing robustness verification for deep neural networks via symbolic propagation. Form. Asp. Comput. **33**(3), 407–435 (2021)
34. Ruan, W., Huang, X., Kwiatkowska, M.: Reachability analysis of deep neural networks with provable guarantees. In: Proceedings of the 27th International Joint Conference on Artificial Intelligence, IJCAI-18, pp. 2651–2659 (2018)
35. Ruan, W., Wu, M., Sun, Y., Huang, X., Kroening, D., Kwiatkowska, M.: Global robustness evaluation of deep neural networks with provable guarantees for the hamming distance. In: Proceedings of the 28th International Joint Conference on Artificial Intelligence, IJCAI-19, pp. 5944–5952 (2019)
36. Xu, P., Ruan, W., Huang, X.: Quantifying safety risks of deep neural networks. In: Complex & Intelligent Systems (2022)
37. Belkin, M., Hsu, D., Ma, S., Mandal, S.: Reconciling modern machine-learning practice and the classical bias-variance trade-off. Proc. Natl. Acad. Sci. **116**(32), 15849–15854 (2019)
38. Huang, X., et al.: A survey of safety and trustworthiness of large language models through the lens of verification and validation. arXiv:2305.11391 (2023)
39. Littlewood, B., Rushby, J.: Reasoning about the reliability of diverse two-channel systems in which one channel is "possibly perfect". IEEE Trans. Softw. Eng. **38**(5), 1178–1194 (2012)
40. Rushby, J.: Software verification and system assurance. In: 7th International Conference on Software Engineering and Formal Methods, pp. 3–10. IEEE, Hanoi (2009)

41. Zhao, X., Littlewood, B., Povyakalo, A., Strigini, L., Wright, D.: Modeling the probability of failure on demand (pfd) of a 1-out-of-2 system in which one channel is "quasi-perfect". Reliabil. Eng. Syst. Safety **158**, 230–245 (2017)
42. Huang, W., Zhao, X., Jin, G., Huang, X.: Safari: versatile and efficient evaluations for robustness of interpretability. In: International Conference on Computer Vision (ICCV 2023) (2023)
43. Dutle, A., et al.: Pressburger, from requirements to autonomous flight: an overview of the monitoring ICAROUS project. In: Proceedings of 2nd Workshop on Formal Methods for Autonomous Systems, vol. 329 of EPTCS, pp. 23–30 (2020)
44. Balakrishnan, A., et al.: Specifying and evaluating quality metrics for vision-based perception systems. In: Design, Automation & Test in Europe Conference & Exhibition (DATE), pp. 1433–1438 (2019). https://doi.org/10.23919/DATE.2019.8715114
45. Balakrishnan, A., Deshmukh, J., Hoxha, B., Yamaguchi, T., Fainekos, G.: PerceMon: online monitoring for perception systems. In: Feng, L., Fisman, D. (eds.) RV 2021. LNCS, vol. 12974, pp. 297–308. Springer, Cham (2021). https://doi.org/10.1007/978-3-030-88494-9_18
46. Dong, Y., et al.: Reliability assessment and safety arguments for machine learning components in system assurance. ACM Trans. Embedded Comput. Syst. **22**(3), 1–48 (2023)
47. Huang, X., Ruan, W., Tang, Q., Zhao, X.: Bridging formal methods and machine learning with global optimisation. In: Riesco, A., Zhang, M. (eds.) ICFEM 2022. LNCS, vol. 13478, pp. 1–19. Springer, Cham (2022). https://doi.org/10.1007/978-3-031-17244-1_1
48. Zhao, X., et al.: A safety framework for critical systems utilising deep neural networks. In: Casimiro, A., Ortmeier, F., Bitsch, F., Ferreira, P. (eds.) SAFECOMP 2020. LNCS, vol. 12234, pp. 244–259. Springer, Cham (2020). https://doi.org/10.1007/978-3-030-54549-9_16
49. Katz, G., Barrett, C., Dill, D.L., Julian, K., Kochenderfer, M.J.: Reluplex: an efficient SMT solver for verifying deep neural networks. In: Majumdar, R., Kunčak, V. (eds.) CAV 2017. LNCS, vol. 10426, pp. 97–117. Springer, Cham (2017). https://doi.org/10.1007/978-3-319-63387-9_5
50. Ehlers, R.: Formal verification of piece-wise linear feed-forward neural networks. In: D'Souza, D., Narayan Kumar, K. (eds.) ATVA 2017. LNCS, vol. 10482, pp. 269–286. Springer, Cham (2017). https://doi.org/10.1007/978-3-319-68167-2_19
51. Narodytska, N.: Formal analysis of deep binarized neural networks. In: IJCAI, pp. 5692–5696 (2018)
52. Narodytska, N., Kasiviswanathan, S., Ryzhyk, L., Sagiv, M., Walsh, T.: Verifying properties of binarized deep neural networks. In: Proceedings of the AAAI Conference on Artificial Intelligence, vol. 32 (2018)
53. Cheng, C.-H., Nührenberg, G., Huang, C.-H., Ruess, H.: Verification of binarized neural networks via inter-neuron factoring. In: Piskac, R., Rümmer, P. (eds.) VSTTE 2018. LNCS, vol. 11294, pp. 279–290. Springer, Cham (2018). https://doi.org/10.1007/978-3-030-03592-1_16
54. Cheng, C.-H., Nührenberg, G., Ruess, H.: Maximum resilience of artificial neural networks. In: D'Souza, D., Narayan Kumar, K. (eds.) ATVA 2017. LNCS, vol. 10482, pp. 251–268. Springer, Cham (2017). https://doi.org/10.1007/978-3-319-68167-2_18
55. Lomuscio, A., Maganti, L.: An approach to reachability analysis for feed-forward relu neural networks. arXiv preprint arXiv:1706.07351 (2017)

56. Gehr, T., Mirman, M., Drachsler-Cohen, D., Tsankov, P., Chaudhuri, S., Vechev, M.: Ai2: safety and robustness certification of neural networks with abstract interpretation. In: IEEE Symposium on Security and Privacy (SP), vol. 2018, pp. 3–18. IEEE (2018)
57. Mirman, M., Gehr, T., Vechev, M.: Differentiable abstract interpretation for provably robust neural networks. In: International Conference on Machine Learning, pp. 3575–3583 (2018)
58. Wong, E., Kolter, Z.: Provable defenses against adversarial examples via the convex outer adversarial polytope. In: International Conference on Machine Learning, pp. 5283–5292 (2018)
59. Dvijotham, K., Stanforth, R., Gowal, S., Mann, T.A., Kohli, P.: A dual approach to scalable verification of deep networks. In: UAI, vol. 1, p. 3 (2018)
60. Wang, S., Pei, K., Whitehouse, J., Yang, J., Jana, S.: Formal security analysis of neural networks using symbolic intervals. In: 27th {USENIX} Security Symposium ({USENIX} Security 2018), pp. 1599–1614 (2018)
61. Peck, J., Roels, J., Goossens, B., Saeys, Y.: Lower bounds on the robustness to adversarial perturbations. Adv. Neural Inf. Process. Syst. **30** (2017)
62. Neumaier, A., Shcherbina, O.: Safe bounds in linear and mixed-integer linear programming. Math. Program. **99**, 283–296 (2004)
63. Ruan, W., Huang, X., Kwiatkowska, M.: Reachability analysis of deep neural networks with provable guarantees. arXiv preprint arXiv:1805.02242 (2018)
64. Weng, T.-W., et al.: Evaluating the robustness of neural networks: an extreme value theory approach. In: ICLR 2018 (2018)
65. Webb, S., Rainforth, T., Teh, Y.W., Kumar, M.P.: A statistical approach to assessing neural network robustness. In: International Conference on Learning Representations (2018)
66. Wang, B., Webb, S., Rainforth, T.: Statistically robust neural network classification. In: Uncertainty in Artificial Intelligence, pp. 1735–1745. PMLR (2021)
67. Zhao, X., et al.: Assessing the reliability of deep learning classifiers through robustness evaluation and operational profiles. In: Workshop on AI Safety at IJCAI-21 (2021)
68. Pei, K., Cao, Y., Yang, J., Jana, S.: Deepxplore: automated whitebox testing of deep learning systems. In: proceedings of the 26th Symposium on Operating Systems Principles, pp. 1–18 (2017)
69. Ma, L., et al.: DeepGauge: comprehensive and multi-granularity testing criteria for gauging the robustness of deep learning systems. In: 33rd IEEE/ACM International Conference on Automated Software Engineering (ASE) (2018)
70. Sun, Y., Wu, M., Ruan, W., Huang, X., Kwiatkowska, M., Kroening, D.: Deepconcolic: testing and debugging deep neural networks. In: ICSE 2019 (2019)
71. Du, X., Xie, X., Li, Y., Ma, L., Liu, Y., Zhao, J.: Deepstellar: model-based quantitative analysis of stateful deep learning systems. In: Proceedings of the 27th ACM Joint Meeting on European Software Engineering Conference and Symposium on the Foundations of Software Engineering, pp. 477–487 (2019)
72. Huang, W., et al.: Coverage-guided testing for recurrent neural networks. IEEE Trans. Reliab. **71**(3), 1191–1206 (2021)
73. Berend, D.: Distribution awareness for AI system testing. In: 2021 IEEE/ACM 43rd International Conference on Software Engineering: Companion Proceedings (ICSE-Companion), pp. 96–98. IEEE (2021)
74. Dola, S., Dwyer, M.B., Soffa, M.L.: Distribution-aware testing of neural networks using generative models. In: 2021 IEEE/ACM 43rd International Conference on Software Engineering (ICSE), pp. 226–237. IEEE (2021)

75. Byun, T., Vijayakumar, A., Rayadurgam, S., Cofer, D.: Manifold-based test generation for image classifiers. In: IEEE International Conference on Artificial Intelligence Testing (AITest), vol. 2020, pp. 15–22. IEEE (2020)
76. Toledo, F., Shriver, D., Elbaum, S., Dwyer, M.B.: Distribution models for falsification and verification of dnns. In: 2021 36th IEEE/ACM International Conference on Automated Software Engineering (ASE), pp. 317–329. IEEE (2021)
77. Huang, W., Zhao, X., Banks, A., Cox, V., Huang, X.: Hierarchical distribution-aware testing of deep learning. arXiv preprint arXiv:2205.08589 (2022)

DeepAbstraction++: Enhancing Test Prioritization Performance via Combined Parameterized Boxes

Hamzah Al-Qadasi[1(✉)], Yliès Falcone[2], and Saddek Bensalem[1]

[1] Univ. Grenoble Alpes, CNRS, Grenoble INP, Verimag, 38000 Grenoble, France
{hamzah.al-qadasi,saddek.bensalem}@univ-grenoble-alpes.fr

[2] Univ. Grenoble Alpes, Inria, CNRS, Grenoble INP, LIG, 38000 Grenoble, France
ylies.falcone@univ-grenoble-alpes.fr

Abstract. In artificial intelligence testing, there is an increased focus on enhancing the efficiency of test prioritization methods within deep learning systems. Subsequently, the DeepAbstraction algorithm has recently become one of the leading techniques in this area. It employs a box-abstraction concept, the efficiency of which depends on the tau parameter, the clustering parameter, that influences the size of these boxes. The conclusion of the previous experiments using tau values of 0.4 or 0.05 has failed to produce optimal results among all experiments. This highlights a significant challenge in the DeepAbstraction framework concerning the appropriate selection of the tau parameter. The selection of the tau value is extremely crucial, given its decisive effect on box size and, subsequently, the stability and efficacy of the framework. Addressing this challenge, we propose a methodology called combined parameterized boxes. This approach leverages the collective verdicts of monitors with various tau values to evaluate network predictions. We assign appropriate weights to these verdicts to ensure that no single verdict influences the decision-making process, thereby ensuring balance. Furthermore, we propose multiple strategies for integrating the weighted verdicts of monitors into a conclusive verdict, such as mean, max, product, and mode. The results of our investigation demonstrate that our approach can notably boost the DeepAbstraction framework's performance. Compared to the leading algorithms, DeepAbstraction++ consistently outperforms its competitors, delivering an increase in performance between 2.38% and 7.71%. Additionally, DeepAbstraction++ brings remarkable stability to the process, addressing a significant shortcoming of the earlier version of DeepAbstraction.

Keywords: Test Prioritization · Deep Learning Systems · Box Abstraction · Runtime Monitoring · Big Data · Effective Labeling · Performance Improvement · Stability

This paper is supported by the European Horizon 2020 research and innovation programme under grant agreement No. 956123 and by the French National Research Agency (ANR) in the framework of the Investissements d'Avenir program (ANR-10-AIRT-05, irtnanoelec).

B. Steffen (Ed.): AISoLA 2023, LNCS 14380, pp. 77–93, 2024.
https://doi.org/10.1007/978-3-031-46002-9_5

1 Introduction

Deep Neural Networks (DNNs) have made remarkable strides in a variety of fields, ranging from autonomous driving [21], aviation [15], and healthcare [15]. While these networks have achieved extensive success, they still have drawbacks, particularly concerning their quality and reliability. Notable examples of these weaknesses have manifested in real-world applications, such as incidents involving self-driving cars from Google [22]. These incidents highlight the importance of detecting and correcting malfunctions in software based on Deep Neural Networks (DNNs). Test prioritization is a technique that ranks unlabeled test instances based on their potential to identify errors and select a subset of the entire test dataset, allowing for a selective inspections of a subset from the entire dataset. This not only enhances inspection efficiency but also effectively mitigates the labeling costs that arise from the expanding volumes of data in deep learning. Lastly, test prioritization can help in identifying potential issues earlier before production, thereby preventing catastrophic outcomes.

In the realm of test prioritization algorithms for deep learning systems, which includes approaches, such as Byun et al. [3], DeepGini [7], PRIMA [18], TestRank [12], GraphPrior [5], and CertPri [5], DeepAbstraction [2] has shown a recent and promising performance. Uniquely, DeepAbstraction exploits the capabilities of runtime monitors to prioritize error-revealing test instances. In the literature, runtime monitors [9] are used to supervise the neural network predictions and trigger one of the following verdicts: acceptance, rejection, or uncertainty. Contrarily to traditional runtime verification monitors, which are bound to one or more properties, we consider monitors that check whether a newly observed instance belongs to a set of instances englobing a set of references instances constructed during training. Thus, we construct primarily runtime monitors during training from *box abstractions* [9], which are clusters of instances with similar high-level characteristics. During testing, the specific box abstraction where a test instance is located determines the monitor's verdict. This innovative approach enhances the efficiency of test prioritization, demonstrating the impressive capabilities of DeepAbstraction.

The earlier version of DeepAbstraction, despite showing some level of efficacy, currently reveals several flaws which undermine its overall performance. A notable example is the static nature of the clustering parameter, tau. This parameter, custom-tailored according to training accuracy, has a different optimal value in each experiment. However, this indicates high instability in the performance, posing a considerable challenge to the model's reliability. Moreover, the framework is heavily reliant on the verdict of a single monitor, which is often insufficient to provide a comprehensive understanding of the data distribution.

To address these issues, we implement substantial improvements in DeepAbstraction framework. We introduce a dynamic approach to selecting tau, which effectively replaces the previous fixed-value system. This new method offers greater adaptability to the unique distribution of each dataset. Secondly, we overcome the limitations of relying on a single monitor by incorporating a new concept, "combined parameterized boxes," which harnesses the collective verdicts of various monitors. This feature increases the verdict's accuracy. Thirdly, when there is a conflict among different verdicts, we introduce a weighting system to balance the decision-making process. This system assigns unique weights to rejection, acceptance, and uncertainty verdicts, ensuring the decisions made are both effective and fair. Finally, we develop multiple combination strategies for the final verdict of monitors to allow the system to decide the most effective conclusion. If two test instances share the same combined verdict score, the algorithm uses Gini index scores for refined prioritization. These improvements collectively ensure a more effective and stable DeepAbstraction performance.

In this paper, we consolidate our main contributions as follows:

- We comprehensively analyze the earlier version of DeepAbstraction, highlighting the weaknesses compromising its performance and reliability.
- We introduce the concept of "combined parameterized boxes" to leverage the collective verdicts of multiple monitors, enhancing the accuracy of our system's decisions.
- We establish a unique weighting system with a combination strategy that balances the decision-making process when conflicts arise among different verdicts of monitors, optimizing the fairness of the system's decisions.

We organize the paper as follows: Sect. 2 introduces DeepAbstraction's principles. Section 4 details the role of clustering, the tau selection challenge, and our proposed solution. The experimental setup and summary of main experiments are outlined in Sect. 5. Section 6 focuses on answering research questions and evaluating our system. Finally, Sect. 7 reflects on our solution to the tau selection challenge, its impact on DeepAbstraction, and potential future enhancements.

2 Background

This section provides the foundational knowledge needed to grasp the key concepts of DeepAbstraction [2], including the runtime monitors and the statistical scoring function, e.g., the Gini index. Furthermore, we briefly explain the workflow of DeepAbstraction.

2.1 Runtime Monitors

Several studies have been carried out on runtime monitoring, including [4,9, 11,19]. In particular, DeepAbstraction adopts the three-verdict monitor system as developed by [19]. These monitors are the key to monitoring the predictions made by the neural network once it's operational. More specifically, the monitors assess the predictions of the neural network and trigger one of three possible verdicts: rejection, uncertainty, or acceptance. Subsequently, we will revisit the process of building these runtime monitors and explain their role briefly. We refer the reader to [9] to understand more how to construct boxe-abstraction monitors in details.

Monitor Construction. Upon the completion of the training process, each training instance is thoroughly analyzed. This process includes extracting the high-level features from the penultimate layer (just before the softmax layer) with the corresponding predicted class. Subsequently, these features are grouped into unique subsets depending on whether the neural network correctly classifies these features. The method known as *box abstraction* is then applied. This approach forms n-dimensional boxes in the feature space, representing clusters of either correctly or incorrectly classified training instances. In essence, each box is a bounding box encompassing a cluster of training instances. Following this, there are two categories of boxes for every class: those encompassing correctly classified instances and those for misclassified ones. The core idea behind this technique is the observation that samples from the same class exhibit similar patterns in the feature space, enabling the system to more effectively assess and categorize new test samples.

Monitor Operation. During the neural network evaluation, the decision of the monitors is highly affected by the location of the test instance within the predefined boxes. More specifically, monitors approve the neural network predictions when the test instance is within a box containing correctly classified samples. Conversely, if a test instance is within the box that contains inaccurately classified instances, the monitors reject the prediction. The state of uncertainty arises for the monitor when the test instance lies within an area that overlaps the correctly and incorrectly classified boxes. Lastly, the monitors reject the prediction, if the test instance is outside all the boxes.

2.2 Gini Index

The Gini Index (GI) or Gini Impurity value is customized from the decision tree in machine learning [14] to be used in deep learning as a measure to estimate the uncertainty of the probability distribution in the output layer. Thus, we consider the Gini index, here initiated for DNN. It ranges between 0 and 1, where zero indicates no uncertainty in the prediction, implying that the Deep Neural Network (DNN) is entirely certain of its prediction. On the other hand, as the value approaches 1, it suggests that the neural network is increasingly uncertain. The calculation of Gini Impurity (GI) is as follows:

$$GI = 1 - \sum_{i=1}^{C} p_i^2 \tag{1}$$

where p_i is derived from the output layer of the DNN which is often a softmax activation function. Thus, p_i is the probability of an instance being classified to class i and $\sum_{i=1}^{C} p_i = 1$ and C is the total number of classes.

In the test prioritization context, DeepGini [7] and DeepAbstraction utilize GI as a scoring function to estimate the error-revealing capability of each test instance. As a result, instances with high GI are prioritized over other test instances with low GI since they are more likely to show weakness in the model.

Table 1. Prioritizing Test Data Using the Gini Index (GI)

Instance	Ground truth	DNN output	Predicted class	Gini index	Order
A	●	0.90 , 0.10	●	0.18	5
B	■	0.00 , 1.00	■	0.00	6
C	●	0.40 , 0.60	■	0.48	2
D	■	0.50 , 0.50	●	0.50	1
E	■	0.25 , 0.75	■	0.38	4
F	●	0.35 , 0.65	■	0.46	3

Example 3. Assume we have a binary classification with two classes {●, ■}. We also have six test instances with the network predictions. As demonstrated in Table 1, the Gini Impurity (GI) measures the uncertainty of the neural network towards the test instances. We can observe that instance D has the highest impurity score (GI = 0.5), which is the most likely to be misclassified by the network. The prioritization list contains other instances (C, F, E, A, and B) prioritized in descending order, as shown in the last column.

2.3 DeepAbstraction

DeepAbstraction framework essentially involves a two-level prioritization process for unlabeled test inputs. Specifically, the initial stage involves high-level prioritization, where we categorize test instances into three groups based on the verdicts of monitors. The subsequent stage encompasses ordering the test instances within each category in decreasing order, guided by the value determined by the scoring function, such as the Gini Index (GI). At the last phase of this process, instances with a GI value of zero are removed from the first two categories since they are redundant, and the network is highly confident. Lastly, a certain number of instances are chosen within the predefined labeling budget. For more details, we refer the reader to the first version of DeepAbstraction [2].

3 Problem Analysis

In this section, we explain the crucial role that clustering plays within the framework. We then discuss the challenge of tau selection and its consequential effects on the overall performance of the framework.

3.1 Clustering

Box-abstraction monitors are built based on the presumption that instances of the same class show similar patterns due to their greater contiguity within the feature space than instances of other classes. However, monitors may incorrectly validate the network's prediction for a new test input that closely mimics instances within a box, even though this instance originates from another class. Therefore, to alleviate this problem of false negatives, the k-means clustering algorithm is applied before box construction. After clustering, each cluster forms a small box rather than a large box for all clusters. Figure 1 illustrates how monitors in Fig. (a) falsely accept the predictions as a square and a circle for parallelogram and hexagon instances, respectively, i.e., novel classes not in the training dataset. After clustering in Fig. (b), the monitors correctly reject the predictions as they are outside all boxes.

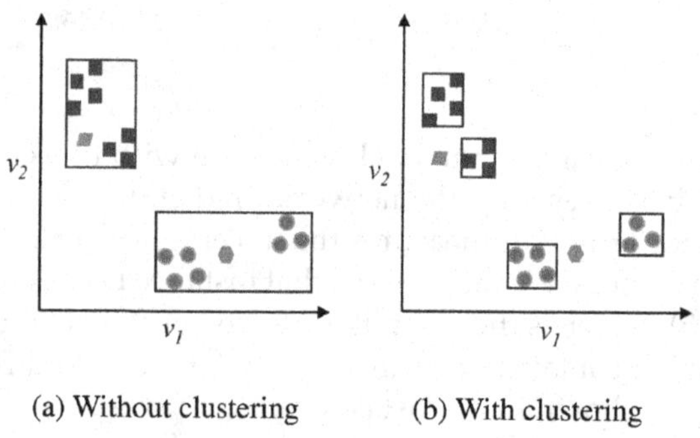

(a) Without clustering (b) With clustering

Fig. 1. Novel test instances before and after clustering [2].

3.2 Tau Selection Issue

DeepAbstraction controls the size of each box by a pre-specified parameter, namely the clustering parameter (τ), which has one of the following values: 0.4, 0.3, 0.2, 0.1, 0.05, and 0.01. The dynamic relationship between the value of τ and the box size is such that a decrease in τ value shrinks the box, whereas an increase expands it. The challenge is to select the best τ that optimally reduces the frequency of false negatives while enhancing the number of true positives. The choice of the ideal τ is deeply influenced by the inherent distribution of the dataset, which may vary across different classes. Therefore, DeepAbstraction lacks a definitive guideline for selecting the best tau across several benchmarks. For instance, DeepAbstraction suggests setting τ to 0.05 as a default value for models with a training accuracy of less than 98%, while a τ of 0.4 is for exceptionally accurate models. These values of τ are experimentally validated. However, these default values of τ are empirical consensus rather than optimal values over all benchmarks, as shown in Fig. 2. For instance, when τ is 0.01 in the following experiments achieves better results than τ of 0.05: Exp.3 and Exp.6. Similarly, the performance of DeepAbstraction with τ of 0.4 in Exp.5 is less effective than with τ of 0.3.

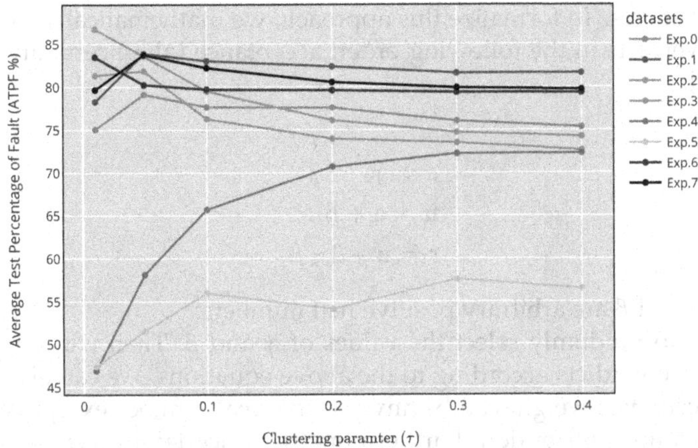

Fig. 2. The effect of clustering parameter τ on performance [2].

4 Approach

In this section, we present the proposed solution, accompanied by its formal definitions. Then, we provide an illustrative example for the updated framework.

4.1 Combined Parameterized Boxes

Figure 2 illustrates that a predefined value of τ cannot effectively improve the performance. There is an observable discrepancy in the performance, i.e., small values of τ work in some cases better than large values, and vice versa. Therefore, we propose an inclusive approach that depends on all monitors' verdicts of different τ to accept or reject the neural network predictions. This integration represents so-called combined parameterized boxes, which collectively involve the predictive potential of every fixed-size box. With this approach, we effectively address the problem of τ selection.

The primary responsibility of monitors is to carefully reject any erroneous predictions. This task gains importance when disagreements arise among monitors of different τ. Amidst such conflict, if even a single verdict signals rejection, the final decision leans towards rejection. Our experimental evaluation further supports the effectiveness of this approach. In response to these findings, we develop a strategic approach to assign weights to the monitors' verdicts. This approach places a higher weight on rejection verdicts than other verdicts, while uncertainty verdicts carry more weight than acceptance ones. It's crucial, however, to maintain a careful balance - the weight differences should not be so significant that the heavily weighted verdicts negate the lesser ones. For instance, overemphasis on rejection verdicts can cancel the contributions of other verdicts, thereby negatively impacting the prioritization performance in subsequent stages. To formalize this approach, we mathematically express the monitor's verdicts in the following order: acceptance [**a**], uncertainty [**u**], and rejection [**r**]:

$$\mathbf{a} = \gamma, \tag{2}$$

$$\mathbf{u} = \mathbf{a} + \beta, \tag{3}$$

$$\mathbf{r} = \mathbf{u} + 2 * \beta \tag{4}$$

where γ and β are arbitrary positive real numbers.

We start to randomly select the values of γ and β. Then we compute the weights of the verdicts according to the above equations. We can also observe that the acceptance weight can be any positive real number except zero since zero denotes no contribution. Furthermore, the uncertainty weight is greater than the acceptance weight with β. Moreover, the rejection weight is larger than the uncertainty weight by $2 * \beta$. Lastly, if we substitute (3) in (4), we infer that the rejection weight is larger than the acceptance weight by $3 * \beta$. In the experimental evaluation section, we will see how different values of β should not affect the performance stability of the combined monitors. In other words, the performance stability is independent of the β selection value.

4.2 Combination Strategy

Numerous strategies exist to merge the weighted verdicts of different monitors and yield a final, cumulative verdict. We highlight a few of these approaches below, with a more comprehensive evaluation of each to follow in the experimental evaluation section:

- *Mean:* This strategy involves adding all weighted verdicts and dividing the total by the number of verdicts, in this case, six-corresponding to the τ values of 0.4, 0.3, 0.2, 0.1, 0.05, and 0.01.
- *Max:* This strategy selects the largest weighted verdict among the six. If a rejection is present, it automatically becomes the final verdict, followed by uncertainty or acceptance verdicts, as applicable.
- *Product:* As the name suggests, this strategy takes the product of all weighted verdicts as the final verdict.
- *Mode:* This fundamentally operates as a voting strategy, where the final verdict is the weighted verdict appearing most frequently among the others.

By evaluating these strategies, we aim to provide insight into their efficacy and relevance in the context of our monitoring system.

4.3 Illustrative Example

Imagine we task a neural network with a binary classification scenario where it should differentiate between plane and bird. As depicted in Fig. 3, the predictions highlighted in red represent misclassifications and should, therefore, be prioritized. Conversely, the ones highlighted in blue indicate the correct classification. We can observe that the upper part of Fig. 3 shows DeepAbstraction version 1, which consists of 6 verdicts according to the τ value. In this version, the user should select *only one* verdict depending on the τ value determined by the model's training accuracy. However, there are some cases where training accuracy does not sufficiently capture the model's learning capability, e.g., overfitting. Ultimately, it's crucial to consider verdicts of false negatives and false positives, which are marked in red, to assess the predictive performance of the monitors.

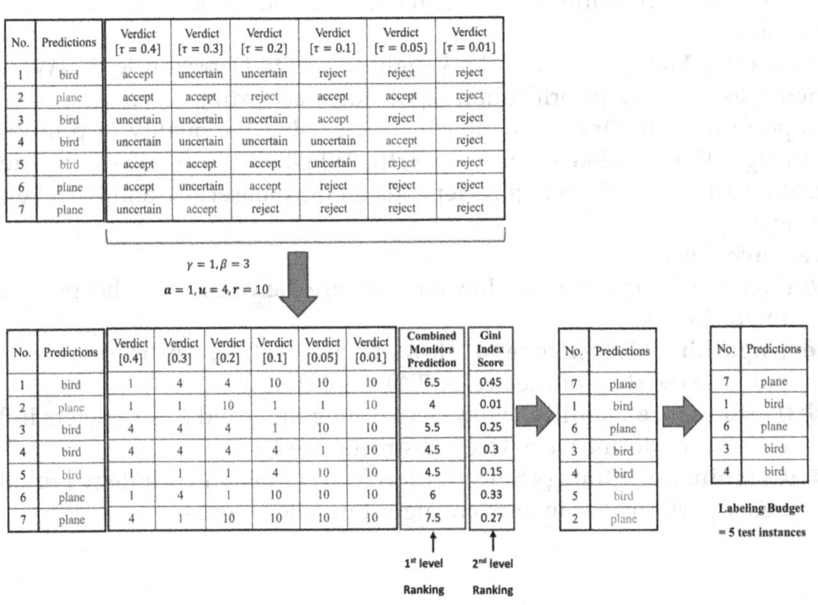

No.	Predictions	Verdict [τ = 0.4]	Verdict [τ = 0.3]	Verdict [τ = 0.2]	Verdict [τ = 0.1]	Verdict [τ = 0.05]	Verdict [τ = 0.01]
1	bird	accept	uncertain	uncertain	reject	reject	reject
2	plane	accept	accept	reject	accept	accept	reject
3	bird	uncertain	uncertain	uncertain	accept	reject	reject
4	bird	uncertain	uncertain	uncertain	uncertain	accept	reject
5	bird	accept	accept	accept	uncertain	reject	reject
6	plane	accept	uncertain	accept	reject	reject	reject
7	plane	uncertain	accept	reject	reject	reject	reject

No.	Predictions	Verdict [0.4]	Verdict [0.3]	Verdict [0.2]	Verdict [0.1]	Verdict [0.05]	Verdict [0.01]	Combined Monitors Prediction	Gini Index Score
1	bird	1	4	4	10	10	10	6.5	0.45
2	plane	1	1	10	1	1	10	4	0.01
3	bird	4	4	4	1	10	10	5.5	0.25
4	bird	4	4	4	4	1	10	4.5	0.3
5	bird	1	1	1	4	10	10	4.5	0.15
6	plane	1	4	1	10	10	10	6	0.33
7	plane	4	1	10	10	10	10	7.5	0.27

No.	Predictions
7	plane
1	bird
6	plane
3	bird
4	bird
5	bird
2	plane

No.	Predictions
7	plane
1	bird
6	plane
3	bird
4	bird

Fig. 3. Transition from DeepAbstraction to DeepAbstraction++.

Our process begins by assigning weights to the acceptance, uncertainty, and rejection verdicts, according to Eq. (2)–(4), yielding respective values of 1, 4, and 10. From there, we incorporate the verdicts of different monitors using the *mean* combination strategy to ascertain the final verdict. Following this, we prioritize the test instances based on the final verdict. However, in cases where two test instances possess an equal combined verdict score, we turn to the GI score for prioritization. For example, the fourth and fifth test instances have a combined verdict of 4.5, prompting the algorithm to prioritize the fourth over the fifth based on their GI scores. Finally, after the prioritization completion, we label the first n test instances. Here, n represents the predetermined labeling budget, setting the threshold for the number of instances to be labeled.

5 Experimental Setup

We conduct the experiments on a system equipped with an Nvidia K80 GPU and 12 GB of RAM, with PyTorch v1.9.0 as the underlying framework. Table 2 summarizes the principal experiments. The configurations used for the primary setup are as follows:

- **Datasets**: MNIST [6], Fashion-MNIST [20], CIFAR10 [10], SVHN [13].
- **Pretrained Model**: ResNet18 [8], GoogLeNet [16], ResNet34 [8], ResNet50 [8], ResNet101 [8], ResNet152 [8], and EfficientNet-B0 [17].
- **Prioritization Algorithms**: DeepGini [7], DeepAbstraction [2], and DeepAbstraction++.
- **Evaluation Metrics**: We use the Weighted Faults Detection Ratio (WFDR) metric to evaluate prioritization algorithms, according to [1]. This metric outperforms other metric in effectively assessing the quality of prioritization algorithms. Unlike other metrics, the WFDR metric involves the prioritization difficulty which highly depends on the dataset size and the labeling budget.
- **Research Questions**:
  ❶ **(Weights Effectiveness)**: How effective are the verdict weights proposed in Eq. (2)–(4)?
  ❷ **(Algorithms Effectiveness)**: How effective is DeepAbstraction++ compared to the state-of-the-art (SOTA) algorithms?
  ❸ **(Performance Stability)**: How does tuning the γ and β parameters influence the performance of DeepAbstraction++?
  ❹ **(Combination Strategy Selection)**: Which combination strategy provides better performance in terms of algorithm effectiveness?

Table 2. Details of the datasets and pretrained models.

Exp. ID	Dataset	Training Dataset	Test Dataset	Pretained Model	Training Acc. (%)	Test Acc. (%)
Exp 0	CIFAR-10	50,000	10,000	Efficient-B0	94.95	92.86
Exp 1	CIFAR-10	50,000	10,000	ResNet101	88.83	86.97
Exp 2	F-MNIST	60000	10000	Efficient-B0	94.94	94.17
Exp 3	F-MNIST	60,000	10,000	ResNet50	93.11	91.12
Exp 4	MNIST	60,000	10,000	ResNet18	99.36	99.16
Exp 5	MNIST	60,000	10,000	ResNet34	99.29	98.84
Exp 6	SVHN	73,257	26,032	GoogLeNet	95.51	95.07
Exp 7	SVHN	73,257	26,032	ResNet152	94.63	94.10

6 Experimental Evaluation

This section addresses the research questions outlined in Sect. 5. First, we assess the effectiveness of the verdict weights proposed in Eq. (2)–(4). Then, we evaluate the efficacy of DeepAbstraction++ algorithm by contrasting its performance with the SOTA algorithms. Third, we explore the performance stability of DeepAbstraction++ by examining the impacts of tuning the parameters γ and β. Finally, we will determine the best combination strategy.

6.1 Weights Effectiveness

We perform eight experiments as detailed in Table 2 where the combination strategy is the mean, and γ and β are 1 and 3, respectively. In our initial experiment, we aim to confirm the necessity of assigning greater importance to the weight of a rejection verdict compared to other verdicts. Specifically, we study how a single rejection verdict can influence the final combined verdict compared to the other five verdicts.

Our findings suggest that when only one monitor issues a rejection verdict, this results in a final combined verdict of rejection in 30% of misclassified instances, as indicated in Exp. 0 of Fig. 4. The last ratio is significantly greater in Exp. 1, 3, and 7, standing at 47%, 48%, and 48%, respectively. However, we found that in scenarios where the neural network exhibits high levels of accuracy, a single *rejection* verdict is insufficient to refuse the network prediction, as evidenced by the results of Exp. 4 and 5 in Fig. 4. When the number of rejection verdicts increases to three or six, we can further confirm this finding. For example, in Exp.0, we noticed that of the instances resulting in a final combined verdict of true rejection, 39% had three rejection verdicts, and 73% had six rejection verdicts. We consistently observe this trend across all the conducted experiments. It strongly underlines the pivotal role that rejection verdicts play in determining the final decision over other verdicts.

In the second experiment, we contrast the impact of the rejection verdict compared to the other two types: uncertainty and acceptance. The aim is to investigate the influence each verdict type has on the true rejection of the final decision. More specifically, our comparison involves only those instances where the verdicts are consistent across all six monitors. Then, we compute the number of instances in which the six rejection verdicts led to the true rejection of the final verdict. After that, we compare this with the total number of six rejection-verdict instances to find the ratio. This procedure is repeated with instances of six uncertainty verdicts and six acceptance verdicts.

Our findings, as depicted in Fig. 5, highlight the considerable influence of the rejection verdicts on the final combined verdict. In six out of eight experiments, this verdict type significantly outperformed the others, with the highest contribution ratio reaching 91% and a median ratio of 78%. On the contrary, instances of uncertainty verdicts exhibit a moderate influence, with a maximum contribution ratio of 42% towards the true rejection of the final ver-

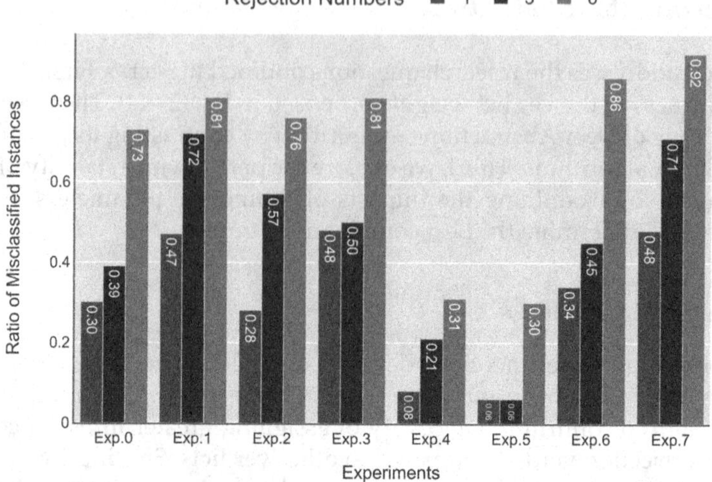

Fig. 4. The impact of the number of rejection verdicts on the final combined verdict.

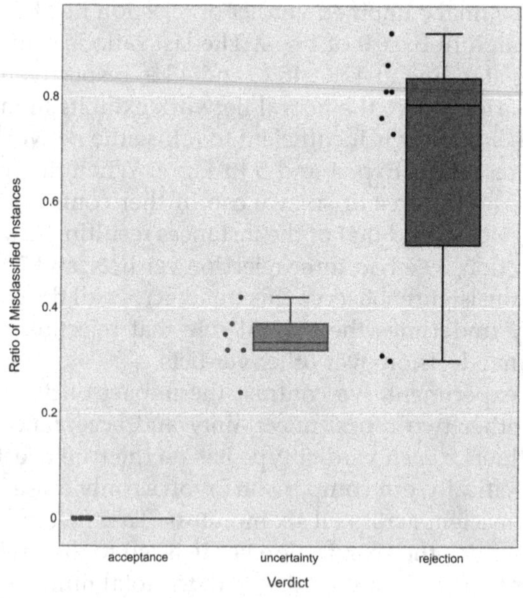

Fig. 5. The Impact of various verdict types on the final combined verdict.

dict. Instances of acceptance verdicts, however, demonstrate minimal impact on rejecting the final verdict.

Table 3. Effectiveness of DeepAbstraction++ and other algorithms (WFDR).

Experiment	DeepGini (%)	DeepAbstraction (%)	DeepAbstraction++ (%)	Δ
Exp.0	45.26	58.75	64.26	↑+5.51
Exp.1	48.62	56.39	59.90	↑+3.51
Exp.2	44.86	59.13	63.79	↑+4.66
Exp.3	46.53	53.19	59.21	↑+6.02
Exp.4	51.08	65.38	67.76	↑+2.38
Exp.5	45.54	60.20	62.79	↑+2.59
Exp.6	45.00	67.59	75.30	↑+7.71
Exp.7	46.55	63.79	69.70	↑+5.91

RQ 1 Answer:

Our study reveals that the observed impact of the verdicts on the final verdict aligns with the proposed weights of the verdicts in the Eq. (2)–(4).

6.2 Algorithms Effectiveness

Table 3 presents a comparative study on the effectiveness of the DeepGini, DeepAbstraction, and DeepAbstraction++ algorithms, evaluated using the WFDR metric across eight experiments. In each experiment, the combination strategy is the mean, and γ and β are 1 and 3. Table 3 reveals that DeepAbstraction++ consistently outperforms both DeepGini and DeepAbstraction in all experiments, as shown by the positive deltas. The improvements offered by DeepAbstraction++ over DeepAbstraction range from a minimum of +2.38% (in Exp.4) to a maximum of +7.71% (in Exp.6). This demonstrates that the additional optimizations in DeepAbstraction algorithm are effective.

RQ 2 Answer :

DeepAbstraction++ demonstrates considerably higher effectiveness than other algorithms. Therefore, the new additions to the framework greatly enhances the performance.

6.3 Performance Stability

As demonstrated in Fig. 6, DeepAbstraction++ model exhibits remarkable stability in performance. Regardless of the β value, which ranges from 1 to 5000, the performance remains constant for each experiment. This consistent performance across a broad spectrum of β values indicates a high level of stability in DeepAbstraction++ performance. Similarly, when the parameter β is held constant at a value such as 1, and γ varies within a range from 1 to 5000, we consistently observe the stable performance of DeepAbstraction++ model across all γ

values for every experiment. For the sake of brevity, the corresponding graph is omitted as it is highly similar to Fig. 6.

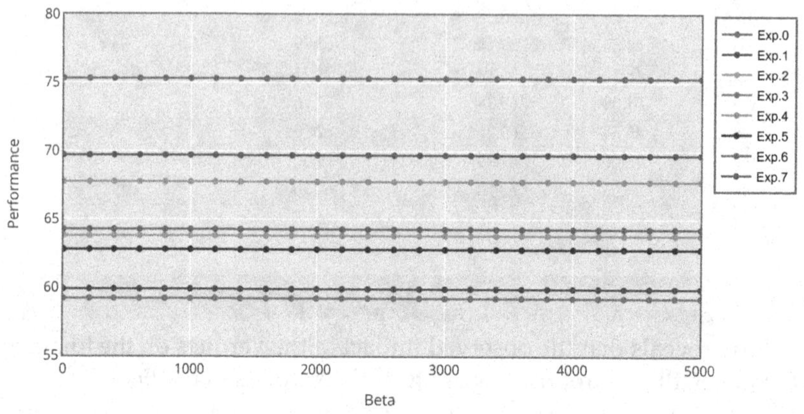

Fig. 6. The Impact of β on the performance stability when $\gamma = 1$.

RQ 3 Answer :

DeepAbstraction++ consistently maintains the stability, unaffected by the values of γ and β, indicating that γ and β do not impact the performance.

6.4 Combination Strategy Selection

Table 4 compares the effectiveness of different strategies where γ and β are 1 and 3. The evaluation is based on the WFDR percentage, incorporating four strategies: mean, product, mode, and max. The mean strategy generally outperforms the other strategies in all the experiments, with the highest mean value seen in Exp.6 at 75.30%. However, there are exceptions to this pattern. For instance, Exp.4 presents a noteworthy difference between the mean (67.76%) and the max (57.04%). Moreover, in Exp.5, the mean and product values are identical at 62.79%. Other combination strategies tend to perform badly because they need to include all monitors in their final combined verdict. For instance, the max strategy only chooses the maximum verdict over the six verdicts. Also, the mode strategy is biased towards the majority verdicts rather than incorporating all. Additionally, the product strategy prioritizes the rejection verdict above other verdicts when determining the final combined verdict. However, product strategy works better when all verdicts are rejection according to Fig. 4. On the other hand, the mean strategy manages to incorporate all monitors when determining the final verdict.

Table 4. Comparative analysis of strategies based on WFDR (%).

Experiment	mean (%)	Product (%)	mode (%)	max (%)
Exp.0	**64.26**	58.76	59.17	60.30
Exp.1	**59.90**	59.43	55.45	59.95
Exp.2	**63.79**	63.45	58.09	60.68
Exp.3	**59.21**	58.42	52.51	56.70
Exp.4	**67.76**	65.38	64.19	57.04
Exp.5	**62.79**	**62.79**	61.07	52.44
Exp.6	**75.30**	73.41	67.19	65.15
Exp.7	**69.70**	68.98	62.02	66.41

RQ 4 Answer:

The results suggest a prevailing superiority of the mean strategy in merging the verdicts from multiple monitors over other strategies.

7 Conclusion and Future Work

This paper tackles a key challenge in DeepAbstraction framework: the tau selection, a factor that significantly shapes the box size and impacts the model stability and performance. To address this problem, we introduced an innovative solution, the combined parameterized boxes. This approach relies on the collective verdicts from monitors with different tau values to assess network predictions. These verdicts are assigned careful weights to prevent any one type of verdict from dominating and to maintain a balanced decision-making process. Various combination strategies, including mean, max, product, and mode, are proposed to unify the weighted verdicts of different monitors into a final verdict. Our proposed approach holds significant potential to enhance the performance of DeepAbstraction framework.

A potential future direction could involve formulating a tau selection procedure that is dynamic and influenced by the specific characteristics of each dataset, thus tailoring the process to the unique data distribution. Similarly, we foresee advancements in a more sophisticated verdict weighting scheme that could adjust adaptively the verdict weights contingent on the local data distribution. Lastly, DeepAbstraction++ lays the groundwork for future studies to fine-tune and further expand these techniques for an even more efficient and trustworthy monitoring system.

References

1. Al-Qadasi, H., Falcone, Y., Bensalem, S.: Difficulty and severity-oriented metrics for test prioritization in deep learning systems. In: 2023 IEEE International Conference on Artificial Intelligence Testing (AITest). IEEE (2023)

2. Al-Qadasi, H., Wu, C., Falcone, Y., Bensalem, S.: DeepAbstraction: 2-level prioritization for unlabeled test inputs in deep neural networks. In: 2022 IEEE International Conference On Artificial Intelligence Testing (AITest), pp. 64–71. IEEE (2022)
3. Byun, T., Sharma, V., Vijayakumar, A., Rayadurgam, S., Cofer, D.D.: Input prioritization for testing neural networks. CoRR arXiv:1901.03768(2019)
4. Chen, Y., Cheng, C.H., Yan, J., Yan, R.: Monitoring object detection abnormalities via data-label and post-algorithm abstractions. In: 2021 IEEE/RSJ International Conference on Intelligent Robots and Systems (IROS), pp. 6688–6693. IEEE (2021)
5. Dang, X., Li, Y., Papadakis, M., Klein, J., Bissyandé, T.F., Traon, Y.L.: Graphprior: mutation-based test input prioritization for graph neural networks. ACM Trans. Softw. Engi. Methodol. (2023)
6. Deng, L.: The mnist database of handwritten digit images for machine learning research [best of the web]. IEEE Signal Process. Mag. **29**(6), 141–142 (2012)
7. Feng, Y., Shi, Q., Gao, X., Wan, J., Fang, C., Chen, Z.: Deepgini: prioritizing massive tests to enhance the robustness of deep neural networks. In: Proceedings of the 29th ACM SIGSOFT International Symposium on Software Testing and Analysis, pp. 177–188 (2020)
8. He, K., Zhang, X., Ren, S., Sun, J.: Deep residual learning for image recognition. In: Proceedings of the IEEE Conference on Computer Vision and Pattern Recognition, pp. 770–778 (2016)
9. Henzinger, T.A., Lukina, A., Schilling, C.: Outside the box: abstraction-based monitoring of neural networks. In: ECAI, Frontiers in Artificial Intelligence and Applications, vol. 325, pp. 2433–2440. IOS Press (2020)
10. Krizhevsky, A., Hinton, G., et al.: Learning multiple layers of features from tiny images. University of Toronto (2009)
11. Kueffner, K., Lukina, A., Schilling, C., Henzinger, T.: Into the unknown: active monitoring of neural networks (extended version). Int. J. Softw. Tools Technol. Transfer (2023)
12. Li, Y., Li, M., Lai, Q., Liu, Y., Xu, Q.: Testrank: bringing order into unlabeled test instances for deep learning tasks. Adv. Neural. Inf. Process. Syst. **34**, 20874–20886 (2021)
13. Netzer, Y., Wang, T., Coates, A., Bissacco, A., Wu, B., Ng, A.Y.: Reading digits in natural images with unsupervised feature learning. In: NIPS (2011)
14. Quinlan, J.R.: Induction of decision trees. Mach. Learn. **1**(1), 81–106 (1986)
15. Shmelova, T., Yatsko, M., Sierostanov, I., Kolotusha, V.: Artificial intelligence methods and applications in aviation. In: Handbook of Research on AI Methods and Applications in Computer Engineering, pp. 108–140. IGI Global (2023)
16. Szegedy, C., et al.: Going deeper with convolutions. CoRR arXiv:1409.4842 (2014)
17. Tan, M., Le, Q.V.: Efficientnet: rethinking model scaling for convolutional neural networks. In: International Conference on Machine Learning (ICML) (2019)
18. Wang, Z., You, H., Chen, J., Zhang, Y., Dong, X., Zhang, W.: Prioritizing test inputs for deep neural networks via mutation analysis. In: 2021 IEEE/ACM 43rd International Conference on Software Engineering (ICSE), pp. 397–409. IEEE (2021)
19. Wu, C., Falcone, Y., Bensalem, S.: Customizable reference runtime monitoring of neural networks using resolution boxes. CoRR arXiv:2104.14435 (2021)
20. Xiao, H., Rasul, K., Vollgraf, R.: Fashion-mnist: a novel image dataset for benchmarking machine learning algorithms. CoRR arXiv:1708.07747 (2017)

21. Yang, K., Tang, X., Qiu, S., Jin, S., Wei, Z., Wang, H.: Towards robust decision-making for autonomous driving on highway. IEEE Trans. Veh. Technol. (2023)
22. Ziegler, C.: A google self-driving car caused a crash for the first time (2016). https://www.theverge.com/2016/2/29/11134344/google-self-driving-car-crash-report. Accessed 27 July 2023

Shielded Learning for Resilience and Performance Based on Statistical Model Checking in Simulink

Julius Adelt(✉), Sebastian Bruch, Paula Herber(✉), Mathis Niehage(✉), and Anne Remke(✉)

University of Münster, Einsteinstr. 62, 48149 Münster, Germany
{julius.adelt,sebastian.bruch,paula.herber,mathis.niehage, anne.remke}@uni-muenster.de

Abstract. Safety, resilience and performance are crucial properties in intelligent hybrid systems, in particular if they are used in critical infrastructures or safety-critical systems. In this paper, we present a case study that illustrates how to construct provably safe and resilient systems that still achieve certain performance levels with a statistical guarantee in the industrially widely used modeling language Simulink. The key ideas of our paper are threefold: First, we show how to model failures and repairs in Simulink. Second, we use hybrid contracts to non-deterministically overapproximate the failure and repair model and to deductively verify safety properties in the presence of worst-case behavior. Third, we show how to learn optimal decisions using statistical model checking (SMC-based learning), which uses the results from deductive verification as a shield to ensure that only safe actions are chosen. We take component failures into account and learn a schedule that is optimized for performance and ensures resilience in a given Simulink model.

Keywords: Hybrid Systems · Resilience · Reinforcement Learning · Formal Verification · Statistical Model Checking

1 Introduction

The demands on the functionality and flexibility of cyber-physical systems are steadily increasing. At the same time, they are increasingly used in critical infrastructures, for example, controlling energy or water supply, and in safety-critical systems such as self-driving cars. Model-driven development frameworks such as MATLAB Simulink help to conquer the complexity and have gained increasing acceptance in industry. Simulink also provides extensions and toolboxes for learning. Learning enables the hybrid systems that are modeled in Simulink to adapt to dynamic changes in the environment, and thus significantly increases their flexibility. To ensure that such intelligent hybrid systems remain operational even in unexpected situations and under external disruptions is a major challenge. Existing approaches for the verification of hybrid systems either focus

B. Steffen (Ed.): AISoLA 2023, LNCS 14380, pp. 94–118, 2024.
https://doi.org/10.1007/978-3-031-46002-9_6

on the rigorous verification of safety guarantees [1,6,18], or employ probabilistic techniques to optimize the probability that a stochastic hybrid system satisfies a temporal logic formula [38,40,44]. While the former often involves worst-case considerations that impede the performance, the latter does not yield guarantees for all possible behaviors.

To overcome this problem, we have recently proposed a novel approach to combine deductive formal verification and quantitative analysis for intelligent hybrid systems, which takes uncertainties and learning into account [2]. However, our previous approach used a variety of heterogeneous formalisms and tools.

In this paper, we present a case study to construct provably safe and resilient systems that optimize the probability that performance properties are satisfied using shielded SMC-based learning in Simulink. Our work is based on three key ideas: First, we provide a way to model stochastic failure and repair times in Simulink using Simulink random and memory blocks to model variable delays and a decision logic to model component failures and repairs. Second, to enable deductive verification of a given Simulink model with stochastic extensions, we encapsulate the failure and repair model in a dedicated subsystem and use hybrid contracts to define a non-deterministic overapproximation of its behavior. With our previously proposed Simulink2dL [3,35] transformation, we can automatically transform the Simulink model together with the hybrid contract into the differential dynamic logic (d$\mathcal{L}$). We use the interactive theorem prover KeYmaera X [18] to deductively verify safety and resilience properties in the presence of worst-case behavior on the resulting model. Third, we use SMC-based learning within Simulink, which can learn a schedule that is optimized for performance but still ensures resilience in the presence of failures by using the deductive verification results as a shield on the learning component. We take component failures into account using our failure and repair model and learn near-optimal decisions using reinforcement learning.

Compared to our previous work [2], we make the following contributions:

- We model stochastic failure and repair times in Simulink.
- We capture the failure and repair model in a dedicated Simulink subsystem and use hybrid contracts to define a non-deterministic overapproximation.
- We enable SMC-based learning for Simulink and validate its results with a recent extension of the statistical model checker HYPEG.

Our case study is a stochastic extension of an intelligent water distribution system provided by MathWorks [59]. We formally verify safety and resilience on a d$\mathcal{L}$ model that is automatically generated from the Simulink model together with the hybrid contract of the failure and repair model. We combine the deductive verification with SMC-based learning, and we provide a near-optimal scheduler that is guaranteed to be safe and resilient by construction. It maximizes resilience and the probability that the energy consumption is kept below a given limit. We validate the results via the statistical model checker HYPEG on a hybrid Petri net model.

This paper is structured as follows: In Sect. 2 and 3, we introduce preliminaries and discuss related work. In Sect. 4, we combine deductive verification and SMC-based learning for our case study. We present experimental results in Sect. 5 and conclude in Sect. 6.

2 Background

In this section, we introduce reinforcement learning, Simulink, our deductive verification approach for Simulink, and statistical model checking.

2.1 Reinforcement Learning (RL)

Reinforcement learning is a class of machine learning methods for learning in a trial and error approach by interacting with an environment through actions [55]. The goal of an RL algorithm is to optimize a reward by learning a policy $\pi(a|s)$ that determines which actions to take in which states. The mathematical basis are Markov decision processes (MDPs) [55]. An MDP is a tuple (S, A, R, p), where S is a set of states, A a set of actions, $R \subset \mathbb{R}$ a set of rewards, and p a probability distribution, which describes the MDPs dynamics. In an MDP, an agent and an environment interact in discrete time steps. At each step t, the agent chooses an action $a_t \in A$ to apply in the current state $s_t \in S$. Then the RL agent receives a new state $s_{t+1} \in S$ resulting from the applied action and a reward $r_{t+1} \in R$. The probabilities of states s, actions a and rewards r at times t are given by random variables S_t, A_t and R_t. The expected reward r and next state s' resulting from the application of a in s can be expressed as the probability distribution $p(s', r|s, a) \doteq Pr\{S_t = s',\ R_t = r|S_{t-1} = s,\ A_{t-1} = a\}$.

2.2 Simulink and the RL Toolbox

Simulink [56] is an industrially well established graphical modeling language for hybrid systems. It comes with a tool suite for simulation and automated code generation. Simulink models consist of blocks that are connected by discrete or continuous signals. The Simulink block library provides a large set of predefined blocks, from arithmetics over control flow blocks to integrators and complex transformations. Together with the MATLAB library, linear and non-linear differential equations can be modeled and simulated. Furthermore, the Simulink library provides random blocks to sample values from a random distribution.

Figure 1a shows a hybrid Simulink model of a water tank controlled by an RL agent. The current water level h is computed by integrating the difference of an inflow i and demand d over time in a (time-continuous) integrator block. The water demand d is provided by an input port. The RL Toolbox [57] provides the *RL Agent* block, which enables the execution of RL algorithms directly within Simulink. In this example, the *RL Agent* controls the inflow i and has to meet the demand while preventing the tank from going empty. The *RL Agent* block acts in fixed sampling steps. In each step, it samples *observations* and *rewards*, and outputs an *action* chosen by its RL algorithm. Here, the observation corresponds to the water level h and the action is the chosen inflow i. The reward is calculated in a user defined *Reward* subsystem.

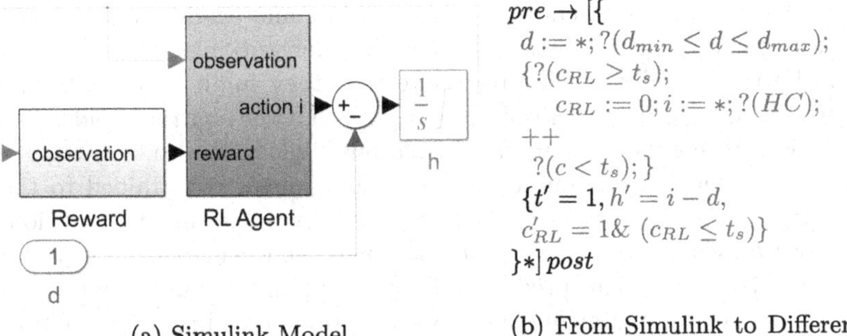

(a) Simulink Model

(b) From Simulink to Differential Dynamic Logic

Fig. 1. Reinforcement Learning, Simulink, and d$\mathcal{L}$

2.3 Differential Dynamic Logic and Simulink2d$\mathcal{L}$

The semantics of Simulink is only informally defined. To enable deductive verification of Simulink models, we have proposed a fully-automatic transformation from Simulink into the differential dynamic logic (d$\mathcal{L}$) [50] in [35]. The d$\mathcal{L}$ is a logic for formally specifying and reasoning about properties of hybrid systems, which are modeled as hybrid programs.

The syntax is as follows: $\alpha; \beta$ models a sequential composition of two hybrid programs α and β. $\alpha \cup \beta$ (or $\alpha ++ \beta$) models a non-deterministic choice. A non-deterministic loop α^* executes α zero or more times. The hybrid program $x := e$ evaluates the term e and assigns it to the variable x. $x := *$ denotes a non-deterministic assignment. $?\mathcal{Q}$ is a test, which checks whether the formula $\mathcal{Q}$ is fulfilled. Finally, $\{x_1' = \theta_1,\ x_2' = \theta_2,\ x_n' = \theta_n\ \&\ \mathcal{Q}\}$ is a continuous evolution, which evolves a set of variables x with a set of differential equations θ. A continuous evolution may progress as long as the evolution domain $\mathcal{Q}$ is satisfied. d$\mathcal{L}$ provides two modalities for reasoning about reachable states of hybrid programs. $[\alpha]\phi$ states that a formula ϕ holds in every state reachable by α. $\langle\alpha\rangle\phi$ states that there exists a state reachable by α in which ϕ holds. Specifications for hybrid programs are defined as $pre \rightarrow [\alpha]post$.

A d$\mathcal{L}$ specification can be deductively verified with the interactive theorem prover KeYmaera X [18]. Deductive reasoning avoids the state space explosion problem and can also be used for parameterized and infinite-state systems, but requires high expertise, e.g., for the manual definition of invariants.

For the transformation from Simulink to d$\mathcal{L}$, we have defined d$\mathcal{L}$ expressions that precisely capture the semantics of all Simulink blocks in a given model, connect them according to the signal lines, and expand control conditions such that assignments and evaluations are only performed if the control conditions are satisfied [35]. To enable compositional verification, we have introduced the concept of hybrid contracts for Simulink [36] and we have extended this concept to RL components in [3]. A hybrid contract is a tuple $hc = (\phi_{in}, \phi_{out})$ that specifies assumptions on the inputs and guarantees on the outputs of a given Simulink subsystem or RL agent. Contracts replace subsystems and agents during transformation, which enables us to abstract from their inner workings. Simulink subsystems can be individually verified to ensure that they fulfill their contracts. For RL agents we use runtime monitoring to ensure that the contract holds. The $d\mathcal{L}$ model in Fig. 1b corresponds to the simple Simulink water tank in Fig. 1a. The input d is modeled by a non-deterministic assignment constrained to the range $[d_{min}, d_{max}]$. The integrator block is captured by a continuous evolution. The water level h evolves with $h' = i - d$, the difference of current inflow i and demand d. The RL agent is captured by a discrete assignment and a continuous evolution. The discrete assignment selects a safe action according to the hybrid contract HC whenever the RL agent's sample time elapses. The clock variable c_{RL} is evolved in the continuous evolution and $c_{RL} \leq t_s$ is added to the evolution domain to ensure that no sampling steps are missed. The global simulation loop is modeled by a nondeterministic repetition.

2.4 Statistical Model Checking and Encoding of Properties

Statistical model checking is used to estimate the probability that a simulation run fulfills a linear-time property Ψ defined in signal temporal logic (STL) [40] over the state of a hybrid model. Whether a property specified in STL at time t is satisfied in a simulation of the stochastic hybrid model can be decided by a model checker which monitors the state evolution. The context-free grammar

$$\Psi ::= tt \mid AP \mid \neg\Psi \mid \Psi \wedge \Psi \mid \Psi\, U^{[t_1,t_2]}\, \Psi$$

constructs a signal temporal logic property Ψ. It consists of true (tt) and continuous atomic properties (AP) comparing a function $f : S \rightarrow \mathbb{R}$ with the value zero: $f(\Gamma) > 0$. They can be combined with a logical *and* or with a time-bounded *until*-operator and negated. STL as in [40] only supports continuous signals, i.e. continuous variables in our context. By mapping discrete modes to continuous signals, they can be included as well. We refer to our own previous work [49] for the semantics of STL in the context of hybrid Petri nets with general transitions (HPnG).

In the following, let $X_i \sim \text{Bernoulli}(p)$ be a random variable and let $x_1, ..., x_n$ be realizations of X_i for n simulation runs with $1 \leq i \leq n$, so that $X_i = 1$ if a property Ψ holds for the i-th simulation run. We denote by r the number of runs for which $X_i = 1$ (i.e., Ψ is fulfilled). Thus, the arithmetic mean of $x_1, ..., x_n$ is $\bar{x} = \frac{r}{n}$.

The desired level of confidence denotes as $\lambda \in [0, 1]$, so that the confidence interval covers in $(100 \cdot (1 - \lambda))\%$ of the times the real probability.

In [47], the calculation of different types of confidence intervals (CI) for statistical model checking of HPnGs is discussed. Since we are considering a Bernoulli random variable, we are able to use interval estimation approaches for binomial proportions, as presented by Agresti and Coull in [4].

This paper uses the *Score Confidence interval* [61], which is well suited for small n and Bernoulli random variables. In the following, z_c denotes the c quantile of the standard normal distribution. The Score CI is then determined by

$$\mathrm{CI}_{Score} = \left[\frac{\bar{x} + \frac{z^2_{(1-\lambda/2)}}{2n} - A}{(1 + \frac{z^2_{(1-\lambda/2)}}{n})} ; \frac{\bar{x} + \frac{z^2_{(1-\lambda/2)}}{2n} + A}{(1 + \frac{z^2_{(1-\lambda/2)}}{n})} \right], \tag{1}$$

with

$$A = z_{(1-\frac{\lambda}{2})} \sqrt{\frac{\bar{x}(1-\bar{x}) + \frac{z_{(1-\frac{\lambda}{2})}}{4n}}{n}}, \tag{2}$$

where the lower bound of CI_{Score} is zero for $r = 0$ and the upper bound is one for $r = n$.

3 Related Work

There has been some work on failure and repair modeling in Simulink. For example, in [20,21], the authors propose a failure analysis for Simulink using probabilistic model checking with Prism [32]. However, the proposed Simulink model consists of purely abstract components, annotated with failure probabilities at each subsystem. Similarly, the authors of [41] present a Simulink library that integrates Monte Carlo and fault tree methodologies. While specialized blocks are provided for fault tree modeling (e.g., *and*, *or*, *basic events*), the behavior of the underlying hybrid system is not considered. In [53], the authors propose *ErrorSim*, a tool for simulative error propagation analysis of Simulink models. They provide an external tool that enables the user to annotate fault injection types together with failure probabilities, and then use MATLAB callback functions to perform error simulation. With that, they enable the user to perform fault tree analysis and failure mode and effects analysis. However, failure and repair modeling is not supported directly within Simulink, and temporal logics properties cannot be analyzed. In several works, for example [29,39,60], the performance of a given deterministic Simulink model has been evaluated. However, in these works, the performance evaluation is carried out via a single simulation run for different parameter settings, and not with a statistical analysis or learning. Furthermore, the systems have not been formally verified.

There have been quite some efforts to enable the formal verification of systems that are modeled in Simulink. However, many of them, e.g. [7,28,51], including the Simulink Design Verifier [58], are limited to discrete subsets of Simulink. Formal verification methods that support hybrid systems modeled in Simulink are, e.g., proposed in [12,13,42,62]. However, none of these methods enables a systematic abstraction of failure and repair times, and, to the best of our knowledge, none of them enables the verification of intelligent hybrid Simulink models with RL components.

There also exist several approaches where formal methods are used to ensure the safety of reinforcement learning. In [5], the use of a shield is proposed, which substitutes unsafe for safe actions and is synthesized from a safety automaton and an abstraction of the environment. This idea has attracted quite some interest. A survey on shield synthesis for reinforcement learning is given in [31]. Recent work [11] applies reach-avoid shields to partially observable MDPs. In [19], the safety of an RL controller is ensured via verified runtime monitors based on a differential dynamic logic model, and we have adopted this approach for Simulink in [1,3]. However in all of these approaches, the resulting knowledge about safe actions is not used in quantitative analyses, i.e., obtaining an optimized probability for meeting an additional property while only choosing guaranteedly safe actions is not considered.

There has been a number of works on statistical model checking (SMC) for Simulink. For example, in [63], the authors present an SMC approach based on Bayesian statistics and show that it is feasible for hybrid systems with stochastic transitions, a generalization of Simulink/Stateflow models. To model failures, they randomly introduce faults into a given Simulink model. In [34], the authors propose an extension of the statistical model-checker Plasma Lab [8] for Simulink. They use custom C-code blocks that generate independent sequences of random draws to model failure probabilities and check bounded linear temporal logic properties over sequences of states and time stamps. However, they neither consider failure and repair times nor learning. In [17], the authors propose a transformation from Simulink into stochastic timed automata (STA) and perform statistical model checking with UPPAAL SMC on the resulting network of STA. However, they do not consider random generation blocks and transform a given Simulink model into a deterministic STA model where all probabilities are one, so they can neither take failure probabilities nor repair times into consideration.

Statistical model checking has been proposed for different kinds of (hybrid) stochastic systems. For hybrid Petri nets, statistical model checking has been proposed for linear evolutions in [47,48] and for non-linear evolutions in [45]. While the Modest Toolset's [24] models simulator [9] supports stochastic hybrid models with linear dynamics as well as lightweight scheduler sampling [33] to approximate optimal schedulers, it provides the latter only for non-hybrid models [14,15]. While Simulink is able to capture a wide class of model instances, more restricted and formal models like MDPs have been considered to improve performance and safety with reinforcement learning (e.g. [26]), as well as to deal with *unknown* stochastic behavior [10,25], and with linear-time logic specifications (e.g. [10,23,52]).

Learning for stochastic hybrid systems is considered, e.g. in a variant of ProbReach, which applies the cross-entropy method for resolving nondeterminism [54]. Also [16] enriches an SMT-based approach with decision trees and AI planning algorithms to handle nondeterminism. Using reinforcement learning in Stochastic Hybrid Models to resolve nondeterminism in an optimal way has been proposed in [44] for Discrete Event Systems (DES) and applied to optimize (dis-)charging of a smart home in [46]. To handle the underlying uncountable state space, a discretization of the continuous variables is used and the optimality of the approach is proven for a decreasing discretization distance.

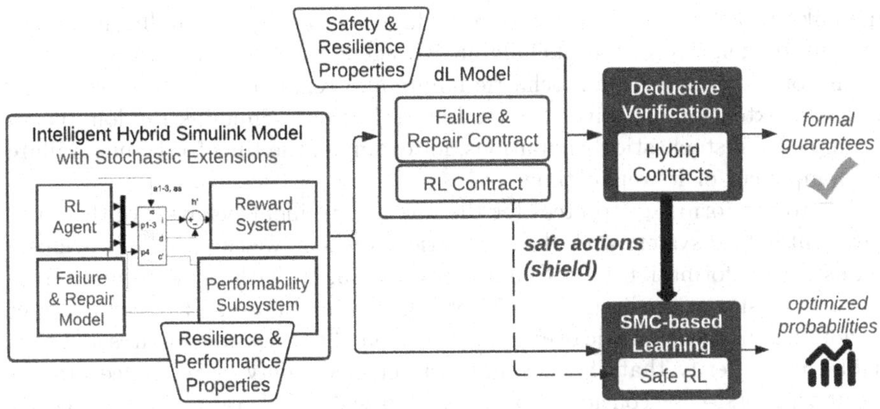

Fig. 2. Deductive Verification and Shielded SMC-based Learning for Simulink

Finally, there has been some work on combining rigorous formal and statistical methods. In [30], the authors incorporate statistical hypothesis testing to compute promising configurations of program verifiers automatically. However, they do not support hybrid systems, and they do not consider both safety and performance properties. In [22], the authors present a formal framework for an integrated qualitative and quantitative model-based safety analysis. This approach is more closely related to our work and also exploits the idea to combine the best out of both worlds from formal verification and quantitative analysis. However, they again do not support hybrid systems, do not consider deductive verification methods and also not the integration of learning components.

4 Shielded SMC-Based Learning in Simulink

In this paper, we combine deductive formal verification with SMC-based learning to ensure safety and resilience of intelligent hybrid systems that are modeled in Simulink. In this section, we first apply shielded SMC-based learning in Sect. 4.1, before Sect. 4.2 recaps the intelligent water distribution system [59] also used in [2]. We present our stochastic extension of the given Simulink model with a failure and repair model in Sect. 4.3. Our approach for a non-deterministic over-approximation of the failure and repair model and its integration into our Simulink to dL transformation is presented in Sect. 4.4. Finally, we present our approach to extend the Simulink model with a performance analysis subsystem and to use this for SMC-based learning that optimizes a given STL property in Sect. 4.5.

4.1 Approach

Our overall approach is shown in Fig. 2. Our goal is to to construct provably safe and resilient systems that still achieve certain performance levels in

Simulink. To achieve this, we propose to first enrich a given intelligent hybrid Simulink model, which may include an RL agent together with a reward subsystem for learning, with a stochastic failure and repair model. To provide this stochastic extension of a given Simulink model, we use Simulink random blocks to sample from stochastic distributions, for example, the time to the next failure of a component or its repair time.

To provide formal guarantees for the safe and resilient behavior of the given intelligent hybrid system with the stochastic extension, we extend our previously proposed transformation from Simulink to d$\mathcal{L}$ [35,37] with a failure and repair contract, as shown in the upper part of Fig. 2. The failure and repair contract provides a non-deterministic over-approximation of the possible failures and thus enables us to verify that the system meets critical safety or resilience properties under worst-case considerations. As proposed in [3], we also use a hybrid contract to abstract from the RL agent. Then, we use the formal d$\mathcal{L}$ representation together with desired safety and resilience properties as an input to the interactive theorem prover KeYmaera X. Using KeYmaera X, we deductively verify that the overall system satisfies the given properties for an unbounded time and potentially even for a system model with unbounded parameters. The verified safety and resilience properties are formally guaranteed to hold under two assumptions: First, we assume that the failure and repair contract actually provides a safe over-approximation of the failures and repairs at runtime. Second, we assume that the RL agent adheres to the hybrid contract at runtime. To enforce the latter, we generate runtime monitors, which can be used to ensure that the RL agent may only choose safe actions. To combine our deductive verification approach with SMC-based learning, we use the safe actions defined by the generated runtime monitor as a shield for the RL agent in the second part of our approach shown in the lower part of Fig. 2.

The aim of SMC-based learning is to provide a near-optimal scheduler, which maximizes or minimizes the probability that given resilience or performance properties are satisfied. To enable SMC-based learning directly on a given intelligent hybrid Simulink model, we extend it with a performability subsystem. The performability subsystem encodes the resilience and performance properties, which are given as STL formulas, in Simulink. This enables us to use the formally defined properties for reward shaping, and to combine reinforcement learning and SMC to compute a policy that optimizes the probability that the given STL formula is satisfied as proposed in [44]. As proposed in [2], we restrict the RL agent to safe actions to ensure that the resulting policy is correct by construction with respect to the (deductively) verified safety properties. With that, we compute an optimized probability that quantitative resilience properties (e.g. provide full service whenever possible) or performance properties (e.g. the energy consumption of the pump is never above a certain limit) are satisfied, while we still ensure that critical safety properties (e.g. the tank never runs empty) and qualitative resilience properties (e.g. always provide at least degraded service) are never violated.

4.2 Intelligent Water Distribution System in Simulink

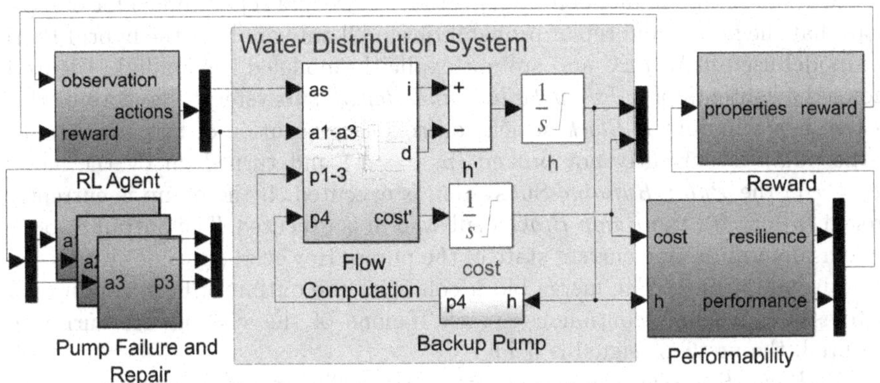

Fig. 3. Intelligent WDS inspired by [59]

The upper part of Fig. 3 depicts the Simulink model of our intelligent water distribution system (WDS) inspired by [59]. The model uses an *RL Agent* to satisfy a water demand by consumers as best as possible, while being energy efficient. The system consists of three pumps, namely $(p_1, p_2, p_3), p_i \in \{0, 1\}$, which are used to constantly pump fluid from a reservoir into a water tank. The *RL Agent* receives *observations* of the current state and a *reward* signal. It decides on the pump activations $(a_1, a_2, a_3), a_i \in \{0, 1\}$ and a chosen maximum supply $a_s \in \mathbb{R}^+$, in discrete sampling steps. The stepsize is defined by a parameter $t_S \in \mathbb{R}^+$. The current inflow and demand are calculated by a *Flow Computation* subsystem. The inflow $i \in \mathbb{R}^+$ is determined by the number of pumps that are currently running. The demand $d \in \mathbb{R}^+$ is limited by the maximum possible supply a_s. The difference of inflow i and demand d is continuously integrated to calculate the current water height $h \in \mathbb{R}^+$. Pumps that are running require energy and thus are associated with cost. The energy consumption $cost' \in \mathbb{R}^+$ is integrated over time to keep track of the total energy consumption $cost \in \mathbb{R}^+$. The *Pump Failure and Repair* and *Performability* subsystems are extensions we use for failure and repair modeling and SMC-based learning and are described in the following subsections.

The major safety requirements of the intelligent WDS is that the water tank should never run empty. To ensure that a minimum supply of water is always available, the system features a backup pump (p_4), which turns on as soon as the water level falls below a backup level h_b. For resilience, the system should always provide at least a degraded service, and full service whenever possible. Note that this definition of resilience comprises a qualitative part (always at least degraded service) and a quantitative part (full service whenever possible). As a performance requirement, the energy consumption should never exceed a given maximum.

4.3 Stochastic Extensions for Modeling Pump Failures and Repairs

To systematically model stochastic pump failures as well as repair times, we extended our Simulink model from [2] with a failure and repair model for pumps. Note that the failure and repair probabilities in [2] only apply to the hybrid Petri net model used in HYPEG and are not explicitly modeled in Simulink. Figure 4 shows the contents of a *Pump Failure and Repair* subsystem. The core of this system is a Simulink *If Block*, which controls the execution of two subsystems. If the pump is currently not broken ($p_1 == 1$) and turned on by the agent ($a_1 == 1$) the *Pump Running* Subsystem is executed. If the pump is currently broken ($p_1 == 0$), the *Pump Broken* subsystem is executed. The output of both systems determines the current state of the pump. However, only one system can be activated at once. The merge block combines the output of both conditional systems into a single continuous signal. If none of the systems are currently executed, the previous signal is held.

The *Pump Running* system is shown in Fig. 5. The system models the behavior of a currently running pump, subject to stochastic failures. The state of the pump is forwarded to the output. Simulink provides blocks for sampling from different random distributions like gaussian and uniform distributions. Additional random distributions can be implemented using MATLAB functions. We use these blocks to sample delays for failures and repairs. The subsystem *Failure Delay Sampler* in *Pump Running* uses a random number block which samples from a Gaussian distributed random signal with configurable mean, variance and random seed. A new seed is randomly set in each simulation run. The sampled delay is forwarded through an *Abs* block to model a folded normal distribution.

The sampled delay is stored in the *Variable Transport Delay* block. Initially, the state of the variable transport delay and thus the state of the output is 1 (the pump is working). As soon as the *Failure Delay* has elapsed, the variable transport delay block outputs the value 0 and the pump state (p_1) switches to broken. Note that the delay time only elapses if the subsystem is enabled, i.e. if the pump is working and activated by the *RL Agent*. In the overall *Pump Failure and Repair* subsystem (Fig. 4), this leads to a change in the *If-Else* blocks conditions. Thus, *Pump Running* is disabled and *Pump Broken* is enabled. The *Pump Broken* subsystem works analogously to the *Pump Running* subsystem. It outputs $p1 == 0$ until its repair time is reached. Then p_1 is set to 1, *Pump Broken* is disabled and Pump Running is enabled again. Contrary to the *Pump Running* subsystem, the random delay is sampled from a uniform distribution with configurable min and max values and random seed. Note that *Pump Broken* and *Pump Running* reset to their initial state as soon as their respective delay time has elapsed. Each time a switch in pump state and thus between the two subsystems occurs, the now enabled subsystem is reset to its initial state and a new random number for the respective failure or repair delay is drawn.

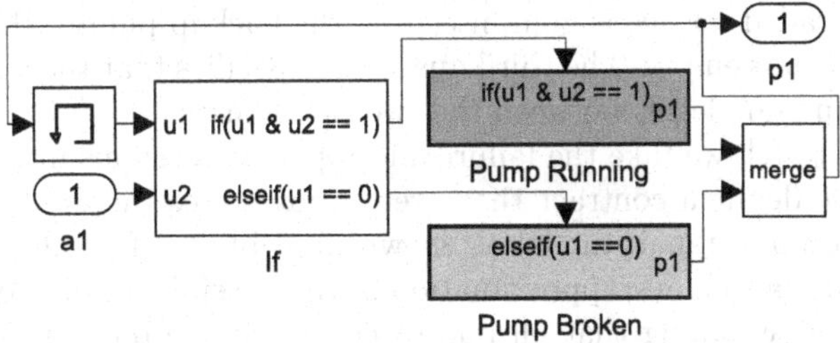

Fig. 4. Failure Repair Subsystem of a Pump

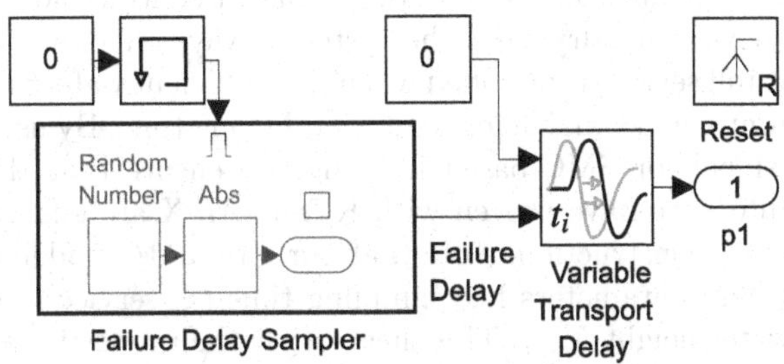

Fig. 5. Pump Running Subsystem

4.4 Formal Verification of Safety and Resilience Contracts

To ensure safety and the qualitative part of resilience of the water distribution system, we apply our approach proposed in [3,37]. To this end, we transform the Simulink model into d$\mathcal{L}$ [35]. Then, we capture the worst case behavior of the failure and repair model as well as the safe behavior of the RL agent with hybrid contracts in d$\mathcal{L}$, and verify the model under the assumption that the failure and repair contract provides a safe overapproximation and that the RL agent complies with its contract [3] deductively in KeYmaera X. This ensures a safe and resilient design by construction. For brevity, we omit the full d$\mathcal{L}$ model, the interested reader is referred to [2]. Our Simulink2dL transformation tool and all proofs can be found online[1].

The contracts for the RL agent, which we have also presented in [2], are shown in Table 1. The safety contract ensures that the maximum water supply is always limited to a value (a_s) that can be satisfied by the current water level (h) without falling below h_{min} until the next decision is made in one sampling step (t_S). In the resilience contract, the first guarantee ensures that the agent always supplies the full service level $a_s = s_{full}$ whenever the water level is above $h_{full} = s_{full} \cdot t_S + h_{min}$. The second guarantee specifies that the agent supplies the degraded service level if the water level is too low, i.e., it chooses $a_s = s_{deg}$ if $h \leq h_{deg} = s_{deg} \cdot t_S + h_{min}$. Note that these definitions imply that $h_{min} \leq h_{deg} \leq$

[1] https://www.uni-muenster.de/EmbSys/research/Simulink2dL.html.

h_{full}. This degraded service is guaranteed by the backup pump, which turns on before the tank runs empty. The third guarantee specifies that the agent supplies intermediate but safe levels between the two boundaries.

In contrast to [2], we take the failure and repair subsystems into account. To achieve this, we define a contract that overapproximates the worst-case behavior of the failure and repair model as shown in Table 2. The failure and repair contract provides a safe overapproximation of the possible outputs of the failure repair system by assuming that all pumps can fail or be repaired at any point in time.

We have verified the same properties as in [2], now under the assumption that both the failure and repair contract and the RL agent contract hold, namely that the water tank never runs dry, that the system always offers at least degraded service, and that full service is provided whenever sufficient water is available and whenever the pumps are available for a sufficiently long time. By using the hybrid contracts as a shield for SMC-based learning, we ensure that the safety and resilience guarantees we have proven with KeYmaera X are guaranteed for the optimized model by construction. Note that our formal d$\mathcal{L}$ model uses symbolic constants for system parameters like sampling time t_S, service levels s_{full}, s_{deg} and minimum water height h_{min}. This means that the properties are proven for a range of safe system parameters and for every possible input scenario.

4.5 Performability Subsystem and SMC-Based Learning

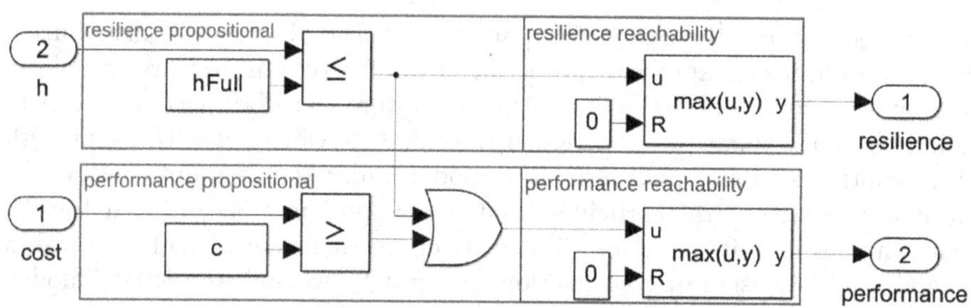

Fig. 6. Performability Subsystem

To optimize the quantitative part of resilience and performance, we define a *Performability* subsystem, which implements a monitor that checks the validity of predefined properties during every simulation run. This enables us to perform SMC-based learning by distributing a reward based on the satisfaction of the property during the training process and computing confidence intervals of the probability that the property holds during statistical model checking. For the purpose of this paper, we consider resilience and performance properties similar to [2] as follows: For resilience, we aim to minimize the probability that a water level is reached that is not sufficient for full service ($h \leq h_{full} \in \mathbb{R}^+$) within the maximum simulation time $t_{max} \in \mathbb{R}^+$. This corresponds to the STL formula Φ_r in Table 3.

Performance in terms of energy consumption is expressed as $\Psi = (h \leq h_{full}) \vee (cost > c)$, where $c \in \mathbb{R}^+$ forms an upper bound for the incurred energy cost. We minimize the probability that Ψ holds, which intuitively means that states are avoided, where either no full service is delivered or the maximum energy consumption is exceeded. Together with the reachability, the corresponding STL formula is Φ_p in Table 3.

The *Performability* subsystem of the Simulink model is shown in Fig. 6. The subsystem receives information relevant for the resilience and performance properties as input. In our model the information received are the current water level h and the accumulated energy *cost* in the current run. The Performability subsystem consists of the following groups of blocks: The left two blocks (depicted in green) represent the propositional part of the resilience and performance properties. The *max* blocks (blue) in the right part of the model then encode the reachability for the respective properties. The *max* blocks take the maximum of the boolean input signals over time and hence, keep returning true, as soon as the desired propositional property is reached once. The reachability values are used in the *Reward* subsystem (cf. Fig. 3) for training the agent, i.e. we distribute a reward based on the satisfaction of the property. The reachability values are written back to the MATLAB workspace for statistical model checking after training.

Summarizing, the safety and resilience contracts, which are used for shielding, ensure that the water level stays safe and that full service is always provided if the water level is actually sufficient. The SMC-based learning optimizes the probabilities that a sufficient amount of water for full service is available and that the energy consumption stays below a given maximum.

Table 1. RL Agent Contracts

Safety Contract		Resilience Contract	
Assumption	Guarantee	Assumption	Guarantee
true	$h - a_s \cdot t_S > h_{min}$	$h > h_{full}$	$a_s = s_{full}$
		$h \leq h_{deg}$	$a_s = s_{deg}$
		$h > h_{deg} \wedge h \leq h_{full}$	$h - a_s \cdot t_S > h_{min}$

Table 2. Failure and Repair Contract

Assumption	Guarantee
true	$(p_1 = 0 \vee p_1 = 1) \wedge (p_2 = 0 \vee p_2 = 1) \wedge (p_3 = 0 \vee p_3 = 1)$

5 Evaluation of Results and Validation

This section presents and discusses the results obtained by SMC-based learning, when using safety and resilience contracts from Table 1 as a shield. Previous work [2] has shown the efficiency of using safety contracts as a shield when simulating optimal system properties. For validation the statistical simulation tool HYPEG [47] is used with its recent extension to Q-learning, called HYPEG ML [44] which simulates a hybrid Petri-net model of the water tank.

Section 5.1 provides parameters for the model proposed in Sect. 4 and the settings for SMC-based learning in Sect. 5.2. Quantitative results for *resilience* and *performance* are presented in Sect. 5.3 and Sect. 5.4, respectively.

Table 3. Minimizing STL properties for resilience and performance similar to [2].

resilience	$\Phi_r = tt\ U^{[0.0,t_{max}]}(h \leq h_{full})$
performance	$\Phi_p = tt\ U^{[0.0,t_{max}]}(h \leq h_{full} \vee cost > c)$

5.1 Model Parameters

The intelligent water distribution system modeled in Simulink, as illustrated in Fig. 3, initially has a water level of 5.5 m and is filled by each active pump with 0.15 m per hour. Each pump consumes energy when active which results in cost of 0.1 for p_1, p_2 and p_3 and cost of 0.15 for p_4. The RL agent can choose from the action set $\mathcal{A} = \{(a_1, a_2, a_3) \mid a_i \in \{0, 1\}\}$, where a_i describes the activation status of pump p_i. Note that $a_i = 1$ does not necessarily corresponds to an active pump, as the pump might be broken. The backup pump is turned on, as soon as the water level falls below 2.1 m and can not fail. The failure and repair times of the three normal pumps follow the probability distributions indicated in Table 4.

While the pump activation can be chosen by the RL agent at the beginning of every simulation run and after every sampling time $t_S = 10$ from the action set $\mathcal{A}$, the service level is determined by the safety and resilience shield (cf. Table 1). We consider the following service levels $\mathcal{S} = \{s_{full}, s_{mid}, s_{deg}\}$ with $s_{full} = 0.3, s_{mid} = 0.2$, and $s_{deg} = 0.15$. Note that setting s_{mid} to a fixed value, represents a simplification of the model, such that not necessarily the maximum possible demand a_s is chosen by the RL agent in case $h_{deg} < h \leq h_{full}$.

We set the remaining parameters of the safety and resilience contracts as follows: the minimum level to $h_{min} = 2$ m in the safety contract and set $h_{full} =$ 5 m and $h_{deg} = 4$ m in the resilience contract. The maximum cost c accepted is given by $0.225 \cdot t_{max}$, i.e. in average slightly more than 2 pumps working.

Table 4. Fail and repair distributions for the three pumps.

pump	fail: folded normal		repair: uniform	
	μ	σ	a	b
p_1	30	6	7	10
p_2	20	4	3	5
p_3	5	1	1	2

5.2 Settings for Simulink and SMC-Based Learning

We run Simulink with a variable-step solver and a maximum step size of 0.06 in combination with an explicit Runge-Kutta method for solving differential equations (ode45). We use the parallel version of Simulink, however note that Q-learning does not support parallelization. For Deep Q-Learning, we use a default MATLAB Deep Q-Network agent (DQN agent), which uses a neural network which consists of six layers: an input layer for observations, two fully connected layers each followed by ReLU activation layer, and a fully connected output layer. The neural network is a multi-output critic, featuring individual outputs corresponding to each possible discrete action. Each output provides the Q-value for taking the corresponding action based on the current observation. Contrary to the default settings, we set the number of nodes in the hidden layers to 512 instead of 256. To improve the convergence of learning, Simulink uses a target critic and memory replay as introduced in [43]. We apply default smoothing, with a *TargetSmoothFactor* of 10^{-3} and set the *ExperienceBufferLength* to 100 000 and *MiniBatchSize* to 256.

HYPEG ML[2] uses Q-learning, as proposed in [44] on the discretized state-space of the hybrid Petri-net modeling the intelligent water distribution system with stochastic pump failures and repairs, as presented in [2]. SMC-based learning, as proposed in [44], evaluates every simulation run w.r.t. a STL property and during the training period provides a single reward, i.e. either 1 or -1, at the end of a simulation run, i.e. t_{max}. HYPEG ML uses a fixed number of 3 million training runs and finishes every run before evaluating the validity of the STL property. In contrast, Simulink finishes the training period as soon as the property is fulfilled in the last 100 training runs. Due to the duration of simulation runs in Simulink, we have set the maximum number of training runs to 5000. We compare the results obtained via two learning methods, i.e., Q-learning and Deep Q-learning.

[2] https://zivgitlab.uni-muenster.de/ag-sks/tools/hypeg.

For both methods in Simulink two different reward distributions are applied: (i) one reward is given based on the satisfaction of the STL property at the end of a simulation run, (ii) at each sample time t_S a reward is given if the property is not violated yet. In both cases, if the property is violated, the current run is aborted and the agent receives a negative reward.

The confidence intervals in both tools are computed after 5000 simulation runs with confidence level $\lambda = 0.95$.

If Q-learning is used, the observation space must be discretized by both, Simulink and HYPEG ML. The continuous variables are discretized to the first decimal place in HYPEG ML and Simulink. The observation space in Simulink with Q-learning had to be restricted to the water level h and the accumulated *cost*, as training in Simulink is not efficient enough to identify optimal results for a large observation space. In contrast, HYPEG ML uses the full state-space as observation space. Hence, it keeps track of the time that has elapsed since a pump has switched state. The Deep Q-learning agent in Simulink works directly on the continuous state space. Its observations consists of the current pump status, the times since a pump has last switched state, the current water level and the accumulated cost.

5.3 Optimizing Resilience

Similar to [2], resilience is formalized in terms of the STL property Φ_r, as shown in Table 3. We use SMC-based learning to optimize the probability that Φ_r holds, using the runtime monitoring subsystem, explained in Sect. 4.5 to ensure that the safety and resilience contracts hold. We compare results obtained from the statistical model checker HYPEG ML with results obtained from Simulink.

All results are summarized in Table 5. It can be seen that the Simulink results obtained with Q-learning with either *one reward* per simulation run or with *multiple rewards* differ considerably w.r.t. results obtained with Deep Q-learning in Simulink. Deep Q-learning is able to achieve considerably smaller probabilities, which is desirable, as we defined resilience as property Φ_r to be minimized. We believe that the number of training runs is too small and the discretization in Simulink is too coarse to explore the state-space sufficiently with Q-learning. For an infinite number of training runs and a converging discretization, Q-learning is guaranteed to compute optimal probabilities.

Note that HYPEG ML is able to perform considerably more training runs in reasonable time and has a larger observation space, which results in lower mid-points compared to Q-learning in Simulink. Applying Q-learning within Simulink suffers from the reduced state-space and the long training and simulation times per run. Hence, Q-learning within Simulink is not able to efficiently compute (near-)optimal probabilities as computed by HYPEG ML in this setting. We assume that the performance difference between both simulators stems from the fact that HYPEG ML applies discrete-event simulation, which is especially fast when used on piece-wise constant differential equations. In contrast, Simulink optimizes simulation accuracy in complex dynamic systems with a potentially high computational overhead. Note that the maximum step size in Simulink is

Table 5. Estimated confidence intervals using Wilson score CI for Φ_r, for learned decisions of the action set $\mathcal{A}$, different time bounds and 5000 simulation runs.

		t_{max}	24 h	48 h	72 h	96 h
HYPEG ML	Q-learn one	midpoint	0.0004	0.003	0.002	0.002
		CI	[0.000,0.0008]	[0.001,0.004]	[0.0006,0.003]	[0.0007,0.003]
		train time	1156.7 s	1861.5 s	3235.6 s	3669.3 s
		train. runs	3 000 000	3 000 000	3 000 000	3 000 000
		sim. time	2.4 s	3.1 s	5.4 s	6.4 s
Simulink	Q-learn one	midpoint	0.0088	0.0495	0.1027	0.3435
		CI	[0.006,0.0113]	[0.044,0.0555]	[0.094,0.1111]	[0.330,0.3567]
		train. time	478.6 s	2645.3 s	3642.7 s	3906.1 s
		train. runs	1179	5000	5000	5000
		sim. time	907.3 s	1062.2 s	1508.2 s	1718.3 s
	Q-learn mult	midpoint	0.0194	0.0436	0.0539	0.0859
		CI	[0.016,0.0232]	[0.038,0.0492]	[0.048,0.0602]	[0.078,0.0937]
		train. time	402.9 s	2985.4 s	3697.5 s	3745.8 s
		train. runs	1152	5000	5000	5000
		sim. time	740.5 s	1128.3 s	1285.2 s	1498.9 s
	DQL one	midpoint	0.0050	0.0008	0.0004	0.0004
		CI	[0.003,0.0069]	[0.000,0.0015]	[0.000,0.0008]	[0.000,0.0008]
		train. time	881.0 s	648.2 s	396.4 s	676.6 s
		train. runs	2919	2092	1789	1962
		sim. time	463.1 s	456.7 s	558.8 s	461.2 s
	DQL mult	midpoint	0.0004	0.0004	0.0268	0.0012
		CI	[0.000,0.0008]	[0.000,0.0008]	[0.022,0.0312]	[0.0003,0.002]
		train time	347.9 s	310.0 s	1672.1 s	1477.5 s
		train. runs	2565	2080	5000	4012
		sim. time	450.1 s	452.7 s	480.3 s	482.8 s

chosen relatively small to ensure consistent results in the validation. Increasing the step size will improve performance, however our experiments have shown that the magnitude of feasible training runs does not change.

While Deep Q-learning can learn directly on the continuous observation space, it lacks convergence guarantees and the robustness of the approach, as well as the reproducibility of the results are subject to many factors, e.g., the neural network architecture and the choice of hyper-parameters [27].

The result obtained by HYPEG ML with Q-learning for $t_{max} = 24$ h matches the confidence intervals computed by Deep Q-learning for multiple rewards. For larger t_{max} Simulink with Deep Q-learning and one reward computes confidence intervals which overlap with the confidence intervals computed by HYPEG ML. However note that Deep Q-learning achieves smaller midpoints for $t_{max} > 24$ h.

While Q-learning in Simulink achieves lower midpoints with multiple rewards, the impact of the reward structure with Deep Q-learning is unclear.

Note that the simulation times in HYPEG ML are much smaller than all simulation times in Simulink. The fact that HYPEG ML is able to simulate individual runs much faster than Simulink also translates to the training time per run. This makes it difficult to compare training times between HYPEG ML and Simulink. The chosen termination condition of 5000 runs in Simulink yields comparable training times to HYPEG ML with 3 million runs, however with larger midpoints.

Only in case $t_{max} = 24\,\text{h}$ Simulink with Q-learning terminates before 5000 runs and its training is about twice as fast as HYPEG ML.

Deep Q-learning takes considerably less training runs than Q-learning in Simulink. The number of training runs varies for all t_{max}, which in turn leads to varying training times. Only the case with multiple rewards for $t_{max} = 72\,\text{h}$ uses 5000 training runs and computes a large midpoint. This is attributed to the lack of robustness of Deep Q-learning.

5.4 Optimizing Performance

The second property of interest is given by the STL property Φ_p (cf. Table 3), i.e. limiting the energy cost and still providing the full service level. Note that our recent work [2] optimized performance for $0.2 \cdot t_{max}$, however Simulink was not able to optimize this property, as the value of 0.2 does not allow for any error in the taken decisions. Relaxing the problem to $0.225 \cdot t_{max}$ instead allows for taking some non-optimal decisions.

Table 6. Estimated confidence intervals using Wilson score CI for Φ_p for learned decisions of the action set $\mathcal{A}$.

		t_{max}	24 h	48 h	72 h	96 h
HYPEG ML	Q-learn one	midpoint	0.001	0.001	0.002	0.002
		CI	[0.000,0.001]	[0.000,0.001]	[0.001,0.003]	[0.001,0.003]
		train time	1017.9 s	1933.4 s	2949.2 s	3775.8 s
		train. runs	3 000 000	3 000 000	3 000 000	3 000 000
		sim. time	1.9 s	3.1 s	5.3 s	6.6 s
Simulink	DQL one	midpoint	0.028	0.014	0.005	0.001
		CI	[0.024,0.033]	[0.011,0.017]	[0.003,0.007]	[0.000,0.001]
		train. time	1061.0 s	1541.9 s	1716.0 s	693.3 s
		train. runs	3499	4775	5000	1979
		sim. time	550.3 s	475.7 s	561.4 s	505.1 s
	DQL mult	midpoint	0.081	0.024	0.032	0.022
		CI	[0.073,0.088]	[0.020,0.028]	[0.027,0.037]	[0.018,0.026]
		train. time	734.2 s	1620.3 s	1753.4 s	1906.3 s
		train. runs	2442	5000	5000	5000
		sim. time	500.5 s	467.9 s	480.2 s	491.9 s

Results obtained from Simulink and HYPEG ML are summarized in Table 6. We recomputed optimal performance with HYPEG ML for the adapted problem and compare with results obtained by Simulink for Deep Q-learning with a single reward and with multiple rewards per simulation run. We did not consider Q-learning for performance in Simulink, as Deep Q-learning performed much better when optimizing resilience.

It can be seen, that for larger time-bounds $t_{max} = 72\,\text{h}$ and $t_{max} = 96\,\text{h}$ the computed confidence intervals of HYPEG ML and Simulink, in case one reward is distributed, overlap. For the smaller time-bound, none of the computed confidence intervals overlap. Since we are able to perform 3 million training runs in HYPEG ML in reasonable time, the computed midpoints in HYPEG ML are almost always smaller than those computed by Simulink with at most 5000 training runs. Due to the convergence guarantees available for Q-learning in combination with a large number of training runs we suspect, that the lower midpoints actually indicate better results and are not caused by a statistical error. Hence, we assume that the quality of the Simulink results suffers from the relatively long training times, which have in turn lead to our restriction to 5000 runs. Since no convergence guarantees exist for Deep Q-learning, it cannot be concluded that a larger maximum of training runs automatically leads to smaller midpoints.

Observe that performance results obtained with one reward per run are smaller than those obtained with multiple rewards. We suspect that for optimizing performance, multiple rewards stimulate cost-expensive behavior in the beginning which benefits resilience, however incurs higher cost towards the end.

6 Conclusion

Building on recent advances in deductive verification and SMC-based learning, we present a unified approach to optimize resilience and performance in Simulink models while ensuring safety and safety-relevant resilience properties via contracts. We use a transformation from Simulink to dL and deductive verification as proposed in [3,35] to ensure that the overall system is safe and resilient if learning components adhere to their contracts. Then, we use these contracts as a shield which restrict the action space of the learning method to safe actions. To do this, we have extended an existing Simulink model with stochastic failure and repair components and a performability subsystem, and have used this for SMC-based learning, as proposed in [44].

We apply (Deep) Q-learning in Simulink with either a single reward at the end of the simulation run, or with multiple rewards, i.e., one after each sampling time. Results are validated with those obtained via a recent extension of the statistical model checker HYPEG for a similar model, as presented in [2].

The evaluation of the results shows that in this case study Q-learning is not able to optimize resilience on the considered Simulink observation space. We believe that the required number of training runs would yield excessive training times. While Deep Q-learning performs much better and is able to optimize resilience and performance efficiently, it requires a larger effort for identifying a suitable neural network architecture. Note that an efficient SMC-based learning tool like HYPEG ML helped to identify the neural network applied.

In future work, we plan to apply our approach to other case studies and to further investigate the scalability of both the deductive verification and the SMC-based learning. Furthermore, we plan to investigate the effect of more fine-granular service levels on the learning results.

References

1. Adelt, J., Brettschneider, D., Herber, P.: Reusable contracts for safe integration of reinforcement learning in hybrid systems. In: Automated Technology for Veri-

fication and Analysis: 20th International Symposium, ATVA 2022, Virtual Event, 25–28 October 2022, Proceedings, pp. 58–74. Springer, Heidelberg (2022). https://doi.org/10.1007/978-3-031-19992-9_4
2. Adelt, J., Herber, P., Niehage, M., Remke, A.: Towards safe and resilient hybrid systems in the presence of learning and uncertainty. In: Leveraging Applications of Formal Methods, Verification and Validation. Verification Principles: 11th International Symposium, ISoLA 2022, Rhodes, Greece, 22–30 October 2022, Proceedings, Part I, pp. 299–319. Springer, Heidelberg (2022). https://doi.org/10.1007/978-3-031-19849-6_18
3. Adelt, J., Liebrenz, T., Herber, P.: Formal verification of intelligent hybrid systems that are modeled with simulink and the reinforcement learning toolbox. In: Huisman, M., Păsăreanu, C., Zhan, N. (eds.) FM 2021. LNCS, vol. 13047, pp. 349–366. Springer, Cham (2021). https://doi.org/10.1007/978-3-030-90870-6_19
4. Agresti, A., Coull, B.: Approximate is better than "exact" for interval estimation of binomial proportions. Am. Stat. **52**, 119–126 (1998)
5. Alshiekh, M., Bloem, R., Ehlers, R., Könighofer, B., Niekum, S., Topcu, U.: Safe reinforcement learning via shielding. In: Proceedings of the AAAI Conference on Artificial Intelligence, vol. 32 (2018)
6. Alur, R.: Formal verification of hybrid systems. In: ACM International Conference on Embedded Software (EMSOFT), pp. 273–278 (2011)
7. Araiza-Illan, D., Eder, K., Richards, A.: Formal verification of control systems' properties with theorem proving. In: UKACC International Conference on Control (CONTROL), pp. 244–249. IEEE (2014)
8. Boyer, B., Corre, K., Legay, A., Sedwards, S.: PLASMA-lab: a flexible, distributable statistical model checking library. In: Joshi, K., Siegle, M., Stoelinga, M., D'Argenio, P.R. (eds.) QEST 2013. LNCS, vol. 8054, pp. 160–164. Springer, Heidelberg (2013). https://doi.org/10.1007/978-3-642-40196-1_12
9. Budde, C.E., D'Argenio, P.R., Hartmanns, A., Sedwards, S.: An efficient statistical model checker for nondeterminism and rare events. Int. J. Softw. Tools Technol. Transf. **22**(6), 759–780 (2020)
10. Cai, M., Peng, H., Li, Z., Kan, Z.: Learning-based probabilistic LTL motion planning with environment and motion uncertainties. IEEE Trans. Autom. Control **66**(5), 2386–2392 (2021)
11. Carr, S., Jansen, N., Junges, S., Topcu, U.: Safe reinforcement learning via shielding under partial observability. In: Proceedings of the AAAI Conference on Artificial Intelligence, vol. 37, no. 12, pp. 14748–14756 (2023)
12. Chen, M., et al.: MARS: a toolchain for modelling, analysis and verification of hybrid systems. In: Hinchey, M.G., Bowen, J.P., Olderog, E.-R. (eds.) Provably Correct Systems. NMSSE, pp. 39–58. Springer, Cham (2017). https://doi.org/10.1007/978-3-319-48628-4_3
13. Chutinan, A., Krogh, B.H.: Computational techniques for hybrid system verification. IEEE Trans. Autom. Control **48**(1), 64–75 (2003)
14. D'Argenio, P., Legay, A., Sedwards, S., Traonouez, L.M.: Smart sampling for lightweight verification of Markov decision processes. Int. J. Softw. Tools Technol. Transfer **17**(4), 469–484 (2015)
15. D'Argenio, P.R., Hartmanns, A., Sedwards, S.: Lightweight statistical model checking in nondeterministic continuous time. In: Margaria, T., Steffen, B. (eds.) ISoLA 2018. LNCS, vol. 11245, pp. 336–353. Springer, Cham (2018). https://doi.org/10.1007/978-3-030-03421-4_22

16. Ellen, C., Gerwinn, S., Fränzle, M.: Statistical model checking for stochastic hybrid systems involving nondeterminism over continuous domains. Int. J. Softw. Tools Technol. Transfer **17**(4), 485–504 (2015)
17. Filipovikj, P., et al.: Analyzing industrial simulink models by statistical model checking (2017)
18. Fulton, N., Mitsch, S., Quesel, J.-D., Völp, M., Platzer, A.: KeYmaera X: an axiomatic tactical theorem prover for hybrid systems. In: Felty, A.P., Middeldorp, A. (eds.) CADE 2015. LNCS (LNAI), vol. 9195, pp. 527–538. Springer, Cham (2015). https://doi.org/10.1007/978-3-319-21401-6_36
19. Fulton, N., Platzer, A.: Safe reinforcement learning via formal methods: toward safe control through proof and learning. In: Proceedings of the AAAI Conference on Artificial Intelligence, vol. 32 (2018)
20. Gomes, A., Mota, A., Sampaio, A., Ferri, F., Buzzi, J.: Systematic model-based safety assessment via probabilistic model checking. In: Margaria, T., Steffen, B. (eds.) ISoLA 2010. LNCS, vol. 6415, pp. 625–639. Springer, Heidelberg (2010). https://doi.org/10.1007/978-3-642-16558-0_50
21. Gomes, A., Mota, A., Sampaio, A., Ferri, F., Watanabe, E.: Constructive model-based analysis for safety assessment. Int. J. Softw. Tools Technol. Transfer **14**, 673–702 (2012)
22. Gudemann, M., Ortmeier, F.: A framework for qualitative and quantitative formal model-based safety analysis. In: IEEE International Symposium on High Assurance Systems Engineering, pp. 132–141. IEEE (2010)
23. Hahn, E.M., Perez, M., Schewe, S., Somenzi, F., Trivedi, A., Wojtczak, D.: Faithful and effective reward schemes for model-free reinforcement learning of omega-regular objectives. In: Hung, D.V., Sokolsky, O. (eds.) ATVA 2020. LNCS, vol. 12302, pp. 108–124. Springer, Cham (2020). https://doi.org/10.1007/978-3-030-59152-6_6
24. Hartmanns, A., Hermanns, H.: The modest toolset: an integrated environment for quantitative modelling and verification. In: Ábrahám, E., Havelund, K. (eds.) TACAS 2014. LNCS, vol. 8413, pp. 593–598. Springer, Heidelberg (2014). https://doi.org/10.1007/978-3-642-54862-8_51
25. Hasanbeig, M., Kantaros, Y., Abate, A., Kroening, D., Pappas, G.J., Lee, I.: Reinforcement learning for temporal logic control synthesis with probabilistic satisfaction guarantees. In: IEEE Conference on Decision and Control (CDC), pp. 5338–5343. IEEE, Nice (2019)
26. Hasanbeig, M., Abate, A., Kroening, D.: Cautious reinforcement learning with logical constraints. In: AAMAS 2020, International Foundation for Autonomous Agents and Multiagent Systems, pp. 483–491 (2020)
27. Henderson, P., Islam, R., Bachman, P., Pineau, J., Precup, D., Meger, D.: Deep reinforcement learning that matters. In: Proceedings of the Thirty-Second AAAI Conference on Artificial Intelligence, (AAAI-18), the 30th Innovative Applications of Artificial Intelligence (IAAI-18), and the 8th AAAI Symposium on Educational Advances in Artificial Intelligence (EAAI-18), New Orleans, Louisiana, USA, 2–7 February 2018, vol. 32, pp. 3207–3214. AAAI Press (2018)
28. Herber, P., Reicherdt, R., Bittner, P.: Bit-precise formal verification of discrete-time MATLAB/Simulink models using SMT solving. In: International Conference on Embedded Software (EMSOFT), pp. 1–10. IEEE (2013)
29. Kanwar, K., Vajpai, D.J.: Performance evaluation of different models of PV panel in matlab/simulink environment. Appl. Solar Energy **58**(1), 86–94 (2022)

30. Knüppel, A., Thüm, T., Schaefer, I.: GUIDO: automated guidance for the configuration of deductive program verifiers. In: IEEE/ACM International Conference on Formal Methods in Software Engineering (FormaliSE), pp. 124–129. IEEE (2021)
31. Könighofer, B., Lorber, F., Jansen, N., Bloem, R.: Shield synthesis for reinforcement learning. In: Margaria, T., Steffen, B. (eds.) ISoLA 2020. LNCS, vol. 12476, pp. 290–306. Springer, Cham (2020). https://doi.org/10.1007/978-3-030-61362-4_16
32. Kwiatkowska, M., Norman, G., Parker, D.: PRISM: probabilistic symbolic model checker. In: Field, T., Harrison, P.G., Bradley, J., Harder, U. (eds.) TOOLS 2002. LNCS, vol. 2324, pp. 200–204. Springer, Heidelberg (2002). https://doi.org/10.1007/3-540-46029-2_13
33. Legay, A., Sedwards, S., Traonouez, L.-M.: Scalable verification of Markov decision processes. In: Canal, C., Idani, A. (eds.) SEFM 2014. LNCS, vol. 8938, pp. 350–362. Springer, Cham (2015). https://doi.org/10.1007/978-3-319-15201-1_23
34. Legay, A., Traonouez, L.-M.: Statistical model checking of simulink models with plasma lab. In: Artho, C., Ölveczky, P.C. (eds.) FTSCS 2015. CCIS, vol. 596, pp. 259–264. Springer, Cham (2016). https://doi.org/10.1007/978-3-319-29510-7_15
35. Liebrenz, T., Herber, P., Glesner, S.: Deductive verification of hybrid control systems modeled in simulink with KeYmaera X. In: Sun, J., Sun, M. (eds.) ICFEM 2018. LNCS, vol. 11232, pp. 89–105. Springer, Cham (2018). https://doi.org/10.1007/978-3-030-02450-5_6
36. Liebrenz, T., Herber, P., Glesner, S.: A service-oriented approach for decomposing and verifying hybrid system models. In: Arbab, F., Jongmans, S.-S. (eds.) FACS 2019. LNCS, vol. 12018, pp. 127–146. Springer, Cham (2020). https://doi.org/10.1007/978-3-030-40914-2_7
37. Liebrenz, T., Herber, P., Glesner, S.: Service-oriented decomposition and verification of hybrid system models using feature models and contracts. Sci. Comput. Program. **211**, 102694 (2021)
38. Lygeros, J., Prandini, M.: Stochastic hybrid systems: a powerful framework for complex, large scale applications. Eur. J. Control. **16**(6), 583–594 (2010)
39. Mahto, R.K., Kaur, J., Jain, P.: Performance analysis of robotic arm using simulink. In: 2022 IEEE World Conference on Applied Intelligence and Computing (AIC), pp. 508–512. IEEE (2022)
40. Maler, O., Nickovic, D.: Monitoring temporal properties of continuous signals. In: Lakhnech, Y., Yovine, S. (eds.) FORMATS/FTRTFT -2004. LNCS, vol. 3253, pp. 152–166. Springer, Heidelberg (2004). https://doi.org/10.1007/978-3-540-30206-3_12
41. Manno, G., Chiacchio, F., Compagno, L., D'Urso, D., Trapani, N.: Matcarlore: an integrated FT and monte carlo simulink tool for the reliability assessment of dynamic fault tree. Expert Syst. Appl. **39**(12), 10334–10342 (2012)
42. Minopoli, S., Frehse, G.: SL2SX translator: from Simulink to SpaceEx models. In: International Conference on Hybrid Systems: Computation and Control, pp. 93–98. ACM (2016)
43. Mnih, V., et al.: Human-level control through deep reinforcement learning. Nature **518**(7540), 529–533 (2015)
44. Niehage, M., Hartmanns, A., Remke, A.: Learning optimal decisions for stochastic hybrid systems. In: ACM-IEEE International Conference on Formal Methods and Models for System Design (MEMOCODE), pp. 44–55. ACM (2021)
45. Niehage, M., Pilch, C., Remke, A.: Simulating hybrid petri nets with general transitions and non-linear differential equations. In: VALUETOOLS 2020: 13th EAI

International Conference on Performance Evaluation Methodologies and Tools, Tsukuba, Japan, 18–20 May 2020, pp. 88–95. ACM (2020)
46. Niehage, M., Remke, A.: Learning that grid-convenience does not hurt resilience in the presence of uncertainty. In: Formal Modeling and Analysis of Timed Systems, vol. 13465, pp. 298–306. Springer, Cham (2022). https://doi.org/10.1007/978-3-031-15839-1_17
47. Pilch, C., Edenfeld, F., Remke, A.: HYPEG: statistical model checking for hybrid petri nets: tool paper. In: EAI International Conference on Performance Evaluation Methodologies and Tools (VALUETOOLS), pp. 186–191. ACM Press (2017)
48. Pilch, C., Niehage, M., Remke, A.: HPnGs go Non-linear: statistical dependability evaluation of battery-powered systems. In: IEEE International Symposium on Modeling, Analysis, and Simulation of Computer and Telecommunication Systems (MASCOTS), pp. 157–169. IEEE (2018)
49. Pilch, C., Remke, A.: Statistical model checking for hybrid petri nets with multiple general transitions. In: Annual IEEE/IFIP International Conference on Dependable Systems and Networks (DSN), pp. 475–486. IEEE (2017)
50. Platzer, A.: Differential dynamic logic for hybrid systems. J. Autom. Reason. **41**(2), 143–189 (2008)
51. Reicherdt, R., Glesner, S.: Formal verification of discrete-time MATLAB/simulink models using boogie. In: Giannakopoulou, D., Salaün, G. (eds.) SEFM 2014. LNCS, vol. 8702, pp. 190–204. Springer, Cham (2014). https://doi.org/10.1007/978-3-319-10431-7_14
52. Sadigh, D., Kim, E.S., Coogan, S., Sastry, S.S., Seshia, S.A.: A learning based approach to control synthesis of Markov decision processes for linear temporal logic specifications. In: IEEE Conference on Decision and Control, pp. 1091–1096. IEEE (2014)
53. Saraoğlu, M., Morozov, A., Söylemez, M.T., Janschek, K.: ErrorSim: a tool for error propagation analysis of simulink models. In: Tonetta, S., Schoitsch, E., Bitsch, F. (eds.) SAFECOMP 2017. LNCS, vol. 10488, pp. 245–254. Springer, Cham (2017). https://doi.org/10.1007/978-3-319-66266-4_16
54. Shmarov, F., Zuliani, P.: Probabilistic hybrid systems verification via SMT and monte carlo techniques. In: Bloem, R., Arbel, E. (eds.) HVC 2016. LNCS, vol. 10028, pp. 152–168. Springer, Cham (2016). https://doi.org/10.1007/978-3-319-49052-6_10
55. Sutton, R.S., Barto, A.G.: Reinforcement Learning: An Introduction, 2nd edn. The MIT Press, Cambridge (2018)
56. The MathWorks: Simulink. https://de.mathworks.com/products/simulink.html
57. The MathWorks: Reinforcement Learning Toolbox. https://www.mathworks.com/products/reinforcement-learning.html
58. The MathWorks: Simulink Design Verifier. https://de.mathworks.com/products/simulink-design-verifier.html
59. The MathWorks: Simulink Example: Water Distribution System Scheduling Using Reinforcement Learning. https://de.mathworks.com/help/reinforcement-learning/ug/water-distribution-scheduling-system.html
60. Tsoutsanis, E., Meskin, N., Benammar, M., Khorasani, K.: Dynamic performance simulation of an aeroderivative gas turbine using the matlab simulink environment. In: ASME International Mechanical Engineering Congress and Exposition, vol. 56246, p. V04AT04A050. American Society of Mechanical Engineers (2013)
61. Wilson, E.: Probable inference, the law of succession, and statistical inference. J. Am. Stat. Assoc. **22**(158), 209–212 (1927)

62. Zou, L., Zhan, N., Wang, S., Fränzle, M.: Formal verification of simulink/stateflow diagrams. In: Finkbeiner, B., Pu, G., Zhang, L. (eds.) ATVA 2015. LNCS, vol. 9364, pp. 464–481. Springer, Cham (2015). https://doi.org/10.1007/978-3-319-24953-7_33
63. Zuliani, P., Platzer, A., Clarke, E.M.: Bayesian statistical model checking with application to stateflow/simulink verification. Formal Methods Syst. Des. **43**, 338–367 (2013)

Formal XAI via Syntax-Guided Synthesis

Katrine Bjørner[1], Samuel Judson[2], Filip Cano[3(✉)], Drew Goldman[4], Nick Shoemaker[2], Ruzica Piskac[2], and Bettina Könighofer[3]

[1] New York University, New York, USA
kbjorner@nyu.edu
[2] Yale University, New Haven, USA
{samuel.judson, ruzica.piskac, nick.shoemaker}@yale.edu
[3] Graz University of Technology, Graz, Austria
{filip.cano, bettina.koenighofer}@iaik.tugraz.at
[4] University of Virginia, Charlottesville, USA
dag5wd@virginia.edu

Abstract. In this paper, we propose a novel application of syntax-guided synthesis to find symbolic representations of a model's decision-making process, designed for easy comprehension and validation by humans. Our approach takes input-output samples from complex machine learning models, such as deep neural networks, and automatically derives interpretable *mimic programs*. A mimic program precisely imitates the behavior of an opaque model over the provided data. We discuss various types of grammars that are well-suited for computing mimic programs for tabular and image input data.

Our experiments demonstrate the potential of the proposed method: we successfully synthesized mimic programs for neural networks trained on the MNIST and the Pima Indians diabetes data sets. All experiments were performed using the SMT-based `cvc5` synthesis tool.

Keywords: Syntax-Guided Synthesis (SyGuS) · Explainable Machine Learning · Program Synthesis · Programming by Example (PbE)

1 Introduction

Complex machine learning models, such as deep neural networks have achieved remarkable success across various domains, including image recognition [29], natural language processing [15], and control [18]. However, the inherently complex and opaque nature of deep neural networks renders insightful human evaluation of their opaque decision logic a challenge. In domains like healthcare, autonomous vehicles, and financial systems, where decisions can have profound consequences on human lives and societal well-being, the explainability of the model's decision making becomes a crucial requirement [25].

K. Bjørner and S. Judson—Equal contribution.

B. Steffen (Ed.): AISoLA 2023, LNCS 14380, pp. 119–137, 2024.
https://doi.org/10.1007/978-3-031-46002-9_7

Explainable AI. The field of explainable AI encompasses a range of methodologies aiming to provide human-understandable insights into complex AI models [1,4,16]. *Global interpretation methods*, such as feature importance and partial dependence plots, focus on understanding the overall behavior of a model across the entire input space [30]. *Local interpretation methods* provide explanations for the model's predictions on a case-by-case basis. Many local interpretation techniques, such as LIME [35] and SHAP [26] are based on training a local surrogate model. Surrogate models are simplified models, such as rule-based models, linear models, or decision trees, that approximate the decision-making of a black-box model locally. For example, LIME generates a surrogate model by perturbing the features of an input data point, observing how the model's predictions change, and then fits a linear model to these perturbed instances. *Decision trees* can serve as surrogate models for local interpretability by training them on a local dataset [12,34]. Decision trees are constructed by recursively partitioning the data based on the most significant features. At each node of the tree, a decision is made based on a specific feature and its corresponding threshold. These decisions create a path from the root node to a leaf node, resulting in a set of if-then rules. Analysing the path for a particular output of the model can reveal the reasons behind the model's decision.

Our Contribution - Mimic Programs. In this paper, we propose to use quantifier-free formulas in first-order logic to explain the model's decisions for a given data set. We call such a formula a *mimic program.*[1] Given a set of data points $\mathsf{Pts} = \{(x, y) \mid x \in \mathbb{R}^d, y \in \{0,1\}\}$ sampled from a model f, *i.e.*, $f(x) = y$ for all $(x, y) \in \mathsf{Pts}$, a mimic program P_f gives the same output as f for any data point in Pts, i.e., $P_f(x) = f(x) = y$ for all $(x, y) \in \mathsf{Pts}$.

Synthesis of Mimic Programs. We formulate the problem of computing an explainable mimic program P_f as a syntax-guided synthesis (SyGuS) problem [3]. SyGuS augments the synthesis problem with a grammar, also called a syntactic template, from which the mimic program is to be constructed. The syntax-guided synthesis problem then is to find an implementation P_f that respects a given grammar and satisfies the semantic constraints given in form of Pts.

The syntactic constraints of SyGuS serve two purposes. First, it renders the search space tractable for the synthesizer. Picking a good grammar is essential for the scalability of the synthesis tools. A grammar that is too large might result in a large search space, while one that is too small may make the synthesizer unable to find a solution [24]. Second, it applies syntactic restrictions on the space of the mimic programs being searched such that the resulting mimic programs are easy to understand for humans.

In the paper, we discuss suitable grammars for the synthesis of mimic programs. Inspired by the structure of decision trees, we use grammars that allow conditionals (if-then-else control flow). In case the input data is tabular data,

[1] Note that the mathematical expressions of the formula can easily be translated into a programming language such as Python.

we allow the comparisons between variables and constants. Since the set of constants allowed for comparison heavily influences the search space, we discuss several heuristics for selecting those constants. For image data, we pick a simpler grammar that allows the comparison between variables, but does not allow the comparison with constants. This not only makes the search simpler but also ensures that the classification of the mimic program remains robust against changes in image brightness.

Experimental Evaluation. In our experiments, we synthesize mimic programs for neural networks trained on the MNIST data set [23] and the Pima Indians diabetes data set [40]. We use the `cvc5` SMT solver [6] for the synthesis procedure. For the obtained mimic programs, we provide the results of evaluating programs with respect to their interpretability, computation times and accuracy. As a baseline, we compare to surrogate models obtained from training decision trees with the off-the-shelf tool scikit-learn [33].

Outline. In Sect. 2, we discuss an illustrating example in which we compute mimic programs for small image input data. We give the background on SyGuS in Sect. 3. We discuss the synthesis of mimic programs in Sect. 4 and report our experimental results in Sect. 5. Finally, we discuss related work in Sect. 6 and conclude in Sect. 7.

2 Illustrative Example

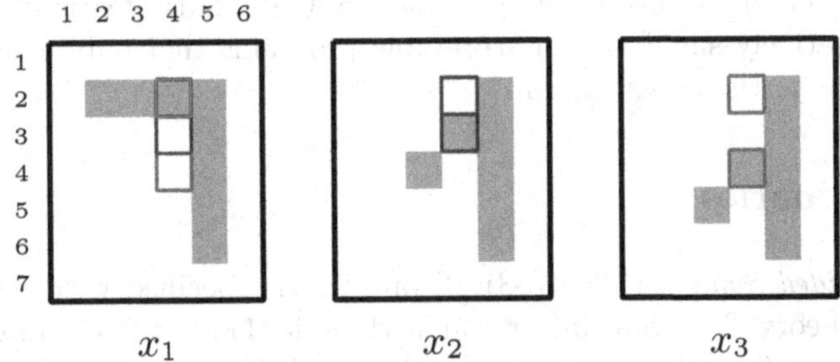

Fig. 1. Illustrative example - mimic programs for an image classification task.

We showcase how mimic programs can be used to explain the decisions of a model trained on image data. In this example, we are given a set of three images that depict handwritten digits, as illustrated in Fig. 1. Additionally, we have given the classification of each image obtained by a model f. Our goal is to compute a mimic program for this data set that explains the decisions of f.

In particular, the images are of size 6×7 pixels and are flattened into a vector $[p_{1,1}, \dots, p_{6,7}] \in \mathbb{R}^{42}$. Each pixel is a real valued number in $[0, 1]$, where

0 is white and 1 is black. A given black-box model f classifies the picture x_1 as the digit 7 and the pictures x_2 and x_3 as the digit 1.

We start by computing a mimic program $P_{f,1,2}$ for the dataset $\mathsf{Pts}_{1,2} = \{(x_1, 7), (x_2, 1)\}$. In order to compute $P_{f,1,2}$ via SyGuS, we need to define both the semantic constraints and the syntactic constraints (the grammar). The semantic constraints are defined by $\mathsf{Pts}_{1,2}$. Thus, we require that $P_{f,1,2}(x_1) = 7$ and $P_{f,1,2}(x_2) = 1$. For the syntactic constraints, we use a simple ITE-grammar that allows as conditions Boolean combinations of comparisons between pixels values. Invoked on this problem, a SyGuS solver might instantiate the following program:

$$P_{f,1,2} := \mathsf{if}\ p_{4,2} > p_{4,3}\ \mathsf{then}\ 7\ \mathsf{else}\ 1.$$

$P_{f,1,2}$ is an interpretable program that mimics the decision making of f for the two given examples. However, it is not a correct mimic program for x_3. Therefore, we extend the set of examples: $\mathsf{Pts}_{1-3} = \{(x_1, 7), (x_2, 1), (x_3, 1)\}$. Using SyGuS, we might now get the synthesized program

$$P_{f,1-3} := \mathsf{if}\ (p_{4,2} > p_{4,3}\ \vee\ p_{4,2} > p_{4,4})\ \mathsf{then}\ 7\ \mathsf{else}\ 1.$$

Note that both programs, $P_{f,1,2}$ and $P_{f,1-3}$, only compare the values of two and three pixels respectively, and so their decision logic is easily comprehensible. Another valid mimic program $P'_{f,1-3}$ for the set of points Pts_{1-3} would be

$$P'_{f,1-3} := \mathsf{if}\ p_{2,2} > p_{2,3}\ \mathsf{then}\ 7\ \mathsf{else}\ 1.$$

This demonstrates a strength of our approach: adding more input-output examples does not imply a more complicated mimic program. On the contrary, given a large data set of input-output examples, SyGuS finds (for many practical instances) relatively small and interpretable programs that only compare data values relevant to the classification.

3 Preliminaries

A *Syntax-Guided Synthesis* (SyGuS) [3] problem is specified with respect to a background theory $\mathbb{T}$, such as linear real arithmetic (`LRA`) or linear integer arithmetic (`LIA`), that fixes the domain of variables and the types and interpretations of the used functions and predicates.

SyGuS searches for an implementation P_f in form of a quantifier-free first-order logic formula within the theory $\mathbb{T}$ that satisfies two types of constraints:

i *Semantic constraints.* In classical SyGuS, the semantic constraints are given as an arbitrary formula φ built from symbols in the theory $\mathbb{T}$. We work with a special instance of the SyGuS problem, called *Programming-by-Example* (PbE) [21,31], where the semantic constraints are given as a set of input-output examples $\mathsf{Pts} = \{(x, y) \mid x \in X^d, y \in \{0, 1\}\}$, where X is the domain defined within the theory $\mathbb{T}$.

ii *Syntactic constraints.* The syntactic constraints are given as a (possibly infinite) set $\mathcal{E}$ of expressions from $\mathbb{T}$ specified by a context-free grammar G.

The Syntax-Guided Synthesis Problem for Programming-by-Example: The computational problem is then to find an implementation P_f, that is permitted by a grammar G, and such that $\forall(x, y) \in \mathsf{Pts}$ it holds that $P_f(x) = y$ within the theory $\mathbb{T}$.

The grammar $G = (V, N, R, S)$ is a context-free grammar, where V is a set of symbols in the theory $\mathbb{T}$, N is a set of non-terminals, R is a set of production rules such that $R : (N \cup S)^* \rightarrow (N \cup V)^*$ and S is the start-symbol. G must also ensure that every sentence generated by the grammar is well-formed for the considered logic. For example, a grammar for synthesizing linear real arithmetic programs must guarantee that no boolean variable is used in an addition operation.

Most SyGuS solvers work in a counterexample-guided refinement loop. Candidates for P_f are enumerated and checked through SMT solving, with the resultant counterexamples informing the adaptive construction of the next candidate.

4 Synthesizing Mimic Programs

In this section, we define mimic programs and discuss their computation. A mimic program serves as a surrogate model for complex opaque models. It is computed from a set of input-output data points sampled from the original model and replicates the decisions of the model in these data points precisely. Additionally, due to the declarative nature of the mimic program and the syntactic restrictions on its structure, the computed mimic programs are generally easy for humans to understand and to analyse.

Definition of Mimic Programs. To replicate machine learning models like deep neural networks, we consider input-output examples of type $\mathsf{Pts} \subseteq \mathbb{R}^d \times \{0, 1\}$. We use the theory of linear real arithmetic (LRA), since that theory both captures the arithmetical statements used in statistical inference and has decision procedures available for determining satisfaction modulo $\mathbb{T}$. Within LRA, each variable is either a boolean or a real, and the vocabulary consists of boolean and real constants, standard boolean connectives, addition (+), comparison ($\leq$), and conditionals (If-Then-Else). We define mimic programs as follows:

Definition 1. *Let G be a context-free grammar, $f : \mathbb{R}^d \rightarrow \{0, 1\}$ be a model, and $\mathsf{Pts} \subseteq \mathbb{R}^d \times \{0, 1\}$ be a set of points of size $|\mathsf{Pts}| = n$ that are consistent with f, i.e., $f(x) = y$ for all $(x, y) \in \mathsf{Pts}$. A* ***mimic program P_f on Pts*** *is a well-formed formula within the theory of LRA that is permitted by the grammar G and satisfies that*

$$\forall(x, y) \in \mathsf{Pts}.\ P_f(x) = f(x) = y.$$

Synthesis of Mimic Programs. To compute a mimic program P_f using syntax-guided synthesis (SyGuS), we fix LRA as background theory and define a set of input-output data points Pts to form the semantic constraints and a grammar G that P_f needs to satisfy. In the following, we give details regarding both the selection of the data points and the grammar.

4.1 Semantic Constraints for Mimic Programs

A mimic program P_f gives the same output as a model f for a given set of data points Pts, i.e., for all $(x, y) \in \mathsf{Pts}$ we have $P_f(x) = f(x) = y$. Depending on the Pts from which the mimic program was created, P_f might also serve as a good *approximation* for the decision-making of the model f in data points not included in Pts.

If Pts is a large enough set that was uniformly sampled on the entire data set, the mimic program can serve as a global surrogate model for f. If Pts was sampled locally around a given data point x^*, the mimic program may serve as a local surrogate model to explain the classification of data points close to x^*. Different strategies, like distance sampling and feature manipulation strategies [35], can be applied to compute samples close to x^*. Note, that P_f gives no correctness guarantees for any data points that are not contained in Pts.

4.2 Syntactic Constraints for Mimic Programs

Designing an effective grammar G is likely to be at least domain- and possibly even dataset- and model-specific. In order to mimic f, G must enable P_f to include statements able to express (approximations of) the statistical patterns that f depends on. But this reliance does not necessarily demand G be complex, as we will show in this section for both image data and tabular data.

Syntactic Constraints for Mimic Programs from Image Data
For image data, we suggest using a very simple grammar that only supports ITE branching and comparison between variables.

We assume that the image data is in a domain of $\mathbb{R}^m \times \mathbb{R}^n$, where $m \times n$ is the size of the input images in pixels. For a given instance $x \in \mathbb{R}^m \times \mathbb{R}^n$, the value $x_{i,j}$ represents the value of the pixel at position i, j. We use the following grammar G_{image} to compute mimic programs for image data:

$$\mathcal{B} := \top \mid \bot \mid \mathcal{R} \leq \mathcal{R} \mid \text{if } \mathcal{B} \text{ then } \mathcal{B} \text{ else } \mathcal{B},$$
$$\mathcal{R} := x_{ij}.$$

Using a simple grammar G_{image} has several advantages:

- *Scalability.* Due to the high-dimensionality of image data, synthesizing mimic programs from images is particularly challenging. A simple grammar limits the search space for P_f. Allowing slighter richer grammars can already have huge negative performance impacts.

- *Robustness.* A mimic program P_f that is permitted by G_{image} is robust to monotonic transformations applied uniformly to the whole image, since it does not allow the comparison of pixels to absolute values. For example, applying the transformation $x_{ij} \mapsto \alpha x_{ij} + k$ for constants k, $\alpha > 0$ on the entire image would make the image brighter, but otherwise leave its structure intact, and the mimic program would still be correct.
- *Interpretability.* More complex rules may also be more difficult for humans to understand. For example, it might be easier to understand the relevance of a branching condition $x_{ij} > x_{i'j'}$, than the reasoning behind a condition like $x_{ij} + 0.29 > x_{i'j'} - 0.12$.

Syntactic Constraints for Mimic Programs from Tabular Data
The most important distinction between tabular and image data is that tabular features are not homogeneous, as is the case for image data. Each features of tabular data has its own meaning and can represent a different quantity and distribution. This makes it difficult to interpret the meaning of comparing the values of different features. Therefore, we consider a grammar that only allows the comparison of individual features with constants.

We assume that the tabular data is in some domain $\mathbb{R}^d$, where d is the number of features (*i.e.*, columns in a dataset). For an instance $x \in \mathbb{R}^d$, the value x_i represents the value of the i-th feature. We use the following grammar $G_{tabular}$ to compute mimic programs for tabular data:

$$\begin{aligned}
\mathcal{F}_0 &:= m_{0,1} \mid m_{0,2} \mid \cdots \mid m_{0,k_0} \\
&\cdots \\
\mathcal{F}_d &:= m_{n,1} \mid m_{n,2} \mid \cdots \mid m_{n,k_d} \\
\mathcal{FC}_0 &:= \mathcal{F}_0 \leq x_0 \mid x_0 \leq \mathcal{F}_0 \\
&\cdots \\
\mathcal{FC}_d &:= \mathcal{F}_d \leq x_d \mid x_d \leq \mathcal{F}_d \\
\mathcal{BC} &:= \mathcal{FC}_0 \mid \mathcal{FC}_1 \mid \cdots \mid \mathcal{FC}_d. \\
\mathcal{B} &:= \top \mid \bot \mid \text{if } \mathcal{BC} \text{ then } \mathcal{B} \text{ else } \mathcal{B}
\end{aligned}$$

For each feature x_j, we define for it a feature-specific set of constants $M_j = \{m_{j,1} \ldots, m_{j,k_j}\}$. Having feature-specific constants offers two benefits. First, it allows for the comparison of feature values with constants that are relevant for the meaning and distribution of the feature. Second, it restricts the search space more than having one joint set of constants that every feature value is allowed to compare to. As for image data, restricting the search space can have a crucial impact on the synthesis performance.

Different heuristics can be applied for selecting feature-specific constants. One such heuristic is to use quantiles as constants, for example, quartiles that divide the data into four sections, or octiles that divide the data into eight sections. Other summary statistics and domain-specific knowledge are other possible sources of good constants.

5 Experimental Evaluation

We computed mimic programs for both the MNIST [23] and Pima Indians diabetes [37] datasets. They are widely-cited benchmarks for image and socially-consequential tabular data classification tasks respectively. For both, we implemented an opaque classifier as a deep neural network trained using Tensorflow (Keras). We employed a standard 80/20 train-test split. All reported results are averaged values over 10 execution runs.

For mimic program synthesis, we used cvc5 [6]. The semantic constraints that encode the input-output examples, as well as the grammar, were written in SMT-LIBv2 format and fed to cvc5 to obtain the corresponding mimic program P_f. As a baseline comparison, we also build mimic programs by training binary decision trees over the same Pts sets as the mimic programs and study them as surrogate models. For such decision trees, we used the off-the-shelf implementation from scikit-learn [33]. We executed all experiments on an AMD Ryzen 9 5900x CPU, with 32GB of RAM and a Nvidia GeForce RTX 3700Ti GPU, running Ubuntu 20.04. Our code for both training the neural network and performing all synthesis experiments is publicly available.[2]

5.1 MNIST Dataset

The MNIST dataset of handwritten digits [23] is a well-known benchmark in image classification problems. Each instance is a vector $x \in \mathbb{R}^{784}$ encoding a 28×28 greyscale image, each representing a digit in $\{0, 1, \ldots, 9\}$. In our case-study, we use the subset of all instances of the digits 1 and 7. This gives us a data set with 15170 instances. For the model f we used a trained deep neural network from [11] with two convolutional and two max-pool layers, followed by a dropout layer and a fully connected layer. With a total of 34k trainable parameters, the network achieves a 99% test accuracy when fully trained.

We computed mimic programs using the grammar defined in Sect. 4.2 for an increasing number of data points and evaluate the resulting programs with respect to synthesis times, interpretability, and global accuracy. As a baseline, we compare our results in runtime, interpretability, and accuracy to the ones obtained by training a binary decision tree on the same set of examples Pts. We use the off-the-shelf decision tree classifier from scikit-learn [33].

Results - Synthesis Times. Figure 2a shows the synthesis time to compute the corresponding mimic programs as a function of $n = |\mathsf{Pts}|$, averaged over 10 runs. Even though each input data has the high dimension of $\mathbb{R}^{784}$, cvc5 was still able to find mimic programs for relatively large sizes of Pts in a reasonable time. For example, computing a mimic program for $|\mathsf{Pts}| = 100$ took an average 19 seconds. However, the steep growth of the curve highlights the challenge of using SyGuS on high-dimensional image data, even when using very restricted grammars. On the other hand, scikit-learn manages to learn decision trees orders of magnitude faster.

2 https://github.com/kbjorner/synthesis.

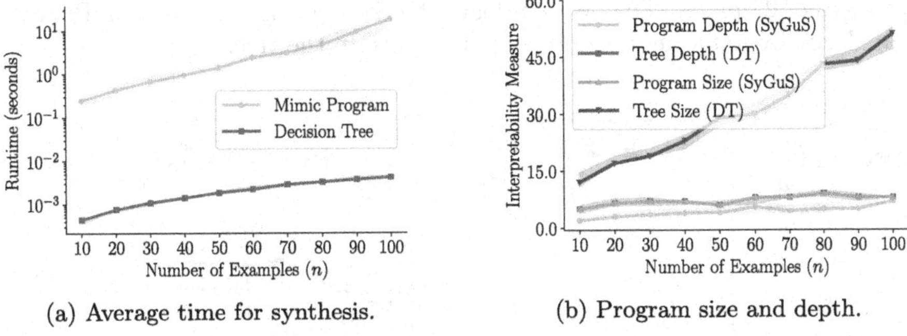

(a) Average time for synthesis.

(b) Program size and depth.

Fig. 2. Results on synthesis times and program sizes for MNIST with growing size of Pts, for both mimic programs and decision trees.

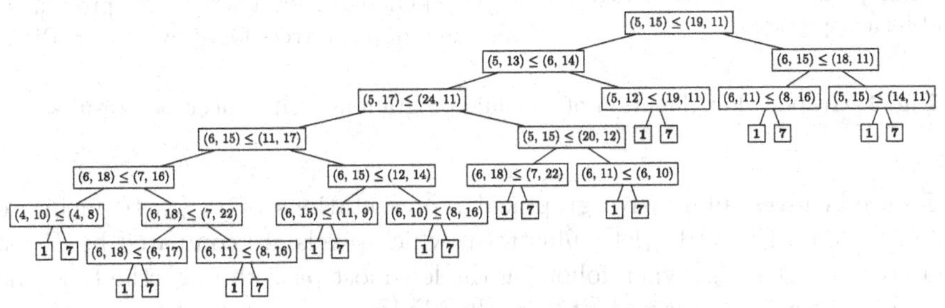

Fig. 3. Tree representation of the decision logic for $P_{f,100}$.

Results - Interpretability. We consider two measures of interpretability: program size and program depth. For the program size, we consider the total number of If-Then-Else statements in the program. The program depth is the maximum depth of nested If-Then-Else statements. In Fig. 2b, we report the average program size and depth of the computed mimic programs for an increasing number of data points $n = |\mathsf{Pts}|$. The results show that the computed mimic programs are quite small and are therefore well suited for humans to analyse the decision-making of f. Our results also show that the mimic programs produce smaller (i.e. more interpretable) surrogate models than the decision trees produced by scikit-learn. On average, the mimic programs only need to compare the values of 13 pixels to mimic the classification of 100 images, while this number goes up to 51 for decision trees. We observed that the depths of the resulting programs are relatively high compared to the size of the program, with no improvement with respect to decision trees. We leave the guidance of the synthesis procedure to obtain programs with smaller depths for future work.

The grammar G_{image} that we use to synthesize mimic programs for image data allows to represent the program as a tree. Figure 3 gives a graphical representation of a mimic program $P_{f,100}$ computed from $|\mathsf{Pts}| = 100$ data points. The resultant tree (of depth = 6) has only 19 branching nodes and compares the values of 23 pixels. The decision logic of f for a given input data in Pts can be analyzed by following the corresponding path in the tree.

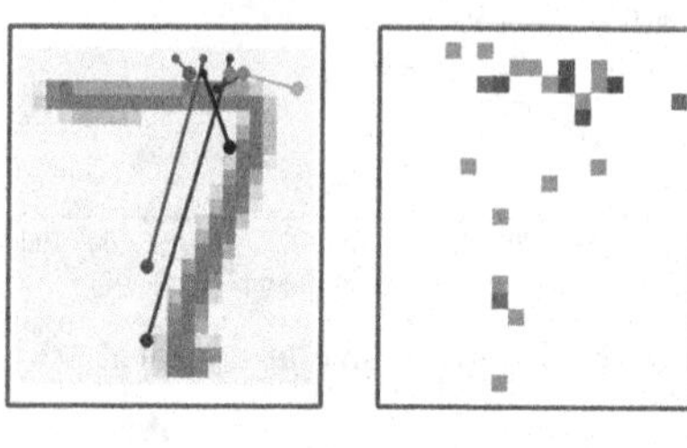

(a) Comparisons in decision logic (left) and heatmap (right).

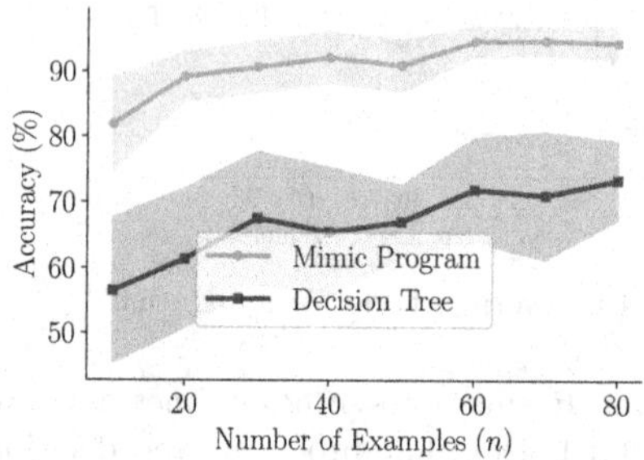

(b) Global Accuracy of mimic programs and decision trees for growing $n = |\mathsf{Pts}|$.

Fig. 4. Graphical explanation of a mimic program as well as accuracy results.

Figure 4a gives alternative graphical representations of $P_{f,100}$ to facilitate interpretability. Figure 4a (left) illustrates which pixels are compared by $P_{f,100}$ for a given input image when following the left-most path through the tree (the background is an exemplary digit from the MNIST dataset). In the Appendix in Fig. 8, we give the representation of the full tree with a graphical visualisation of the pixel comparisons in every node. Figure 4a (right) gives the heat map of all pixels used in $P_{f,100}$. The darkness of each pixel corresponds to the number of times it appears in a guard within $P_{f,100}$.

The graphical representations in Fig. 4a may show which areas of the image are highly relevant for the classification performed by f. For the classification between 1 and 7, it captures the intuition that the distinguishing features between the two digits are the width of the horizontal stroke as well as the slant and depth of the vertical.

Results - Global Accuracy. We also evaluated how well the trained mimic programs globally approximate the classifications of f for data points outside of Pts. To do so, we build mimic programs $P_{f,n}$ for different numbers of examples n and compare the predictions given by $P_{f,n}$ with the predictions given by f. In Fig. 4b we plot the accuracy of the mimic program for different sizes $n = |\mathsf{Pts}|$. We perform each evaluation by uniformly sampling 10 data points over the entire data set and checking whether the outputs of $P_{f,n}$ and f match, and average the results of 10 runs. Our results show that mimic programs computed from only 40 images already reach an accuracy of about 90%. Therefore, the mimic programs serve as a reasonably good approximation for the classification distinguishing between the 1's and 7's of f. The same experiment for decision trees shows that they are less accurate than our mimic programs.

5.2 Pima Indians Diabetes Dataset

In a second set of experiments, we computed mimic programs for the Pima Indians diabetes dataset [37]. Each data point is composed of a feature vector $x \in \mathbb{R}^8$ encoding medical data, with a binary output that represents a diabetes diagnosis. The entire data set consists of 768 data points. For the model f we used a simple feedforward neural network architecture with three dense layers with ReLU activation, followed by a last sigmoid layer. With a total of 722 trainable parameters, the model achieves an accuracy on the test set of about 78%, which is close to optimal for this dataset.

For the synthesis of mimic programs, we use the grammar $G_{tabular}$ described in Sect. 4.2. We perform experiments with four different sets of feature-specific constants. The first three grammars use statistical measures of the data set to define the feature-specific constants. In particular, we use the following sets:

- *Quartiles.* For each feature, we use the three quartiles ($Q1$, $Q2$, $Q3$) for the feature constants.
- *Sextiles.* For each feature, we use the five sextiles as feature constants.
- *Octiles.* For each feature, we use the seven octiles as feature constants.

Lastly, we also use the constants obtained from a trained decision tree as feature-specific constants for a fourth grammar. Concretely, we train the decision tree over the test fraction of the dataset, and use the values of the tree splits as feature-specific constants. We perform this experiment mainly to study the effects of selecting good constants on the synthesis times and sizes of the resulting mimic programs, under the assumption that state-of-the art methods for training decision trees find good constants for branching conditions. We use the off-the-shelf decision tree classifier from scikit-learn [33] with default parameters to train the decision tree. We refer to the grammar using the constants obtained from the decision tree as the *bootstrapped* grammar.

Finally, as a baseline comparison, we train decision trees with scikit-learn on the same set of examples Pts as the mimic programs, and study their properties as surrogate models in terms of runtime, interpretability, and both global and local accuracy.

Results - Synthesis Times. Figure 5 gives the synthesis times to compute the mimic programs, averaged over 10 runs, for the four grammars and decision trees, over an increasing number of data points (*i.e.*, different sizes of the set Pts). For each run, the data points are sampled uniformly at random from the data set. The experiments show that SyGuS is able to find mimic programs in less than one second for this tabular dataset, with only the *bootstrapped* grammar struggling in some queries with a large number of examples. As with the case of image data, scikit-learn is orders of magnitude faster.

Results - Interpretability. Figure 6 presents the results for the four different grammars and decision trees over an increasing number of data points. We observe that for all grammars, the size of the mimic program grows linearly and the depth

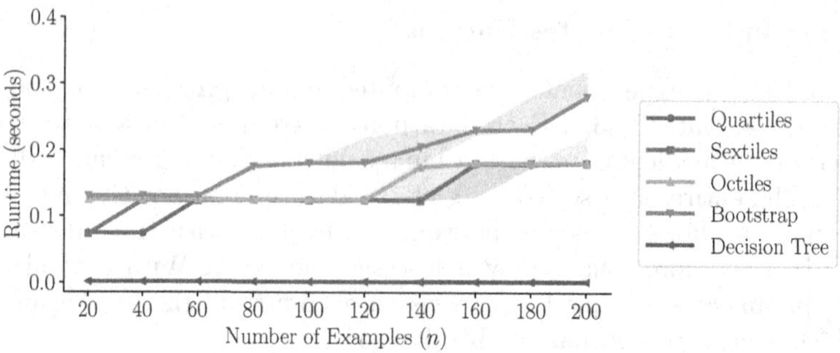

Fig. 5. Synthesis times for Pima dataset.

of the program grows logarithmically. Note that a mimic program restricted by $G_{tabular}$ can also be graphically represented as a tree. Since the depth of the program grows slowly, the mimic program is well suited to analyse individual decisions of the model f. As for the decision trees, in this case we observe that the size of the tree is the same as the size of the mimic programs, while being significantly shallower. Observe that this different size-to-depth ratio between decision trees and mimic programs was already present in the MNIST experiments, with scikit-learn produced more balanced trees than our mimic programs.

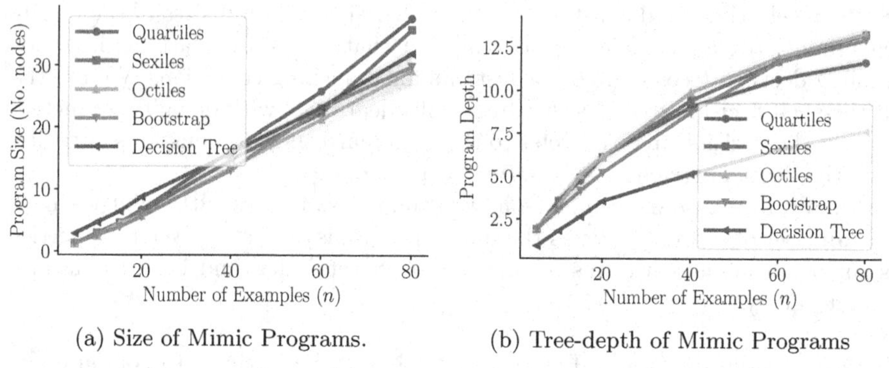

(a) Size of Mimic Programs.

(b) Tree-depth of Mimic Programs

Fig. 6. Interpretability and runtime for different grammars with growing size.

Results - Global and Local Accuracy. Next, we evaluate how well the trained mimic programs approximate (locally and globally) the decisions of f for data points outside of Pts.

Therefore, we randomly select a data point x^* from the training data set, and select the n closest training data points (with corresponding classification from f) to obtain Pts_{x^*}. From Pts_{x^*}, we compute *local* mimic programs for x^*.

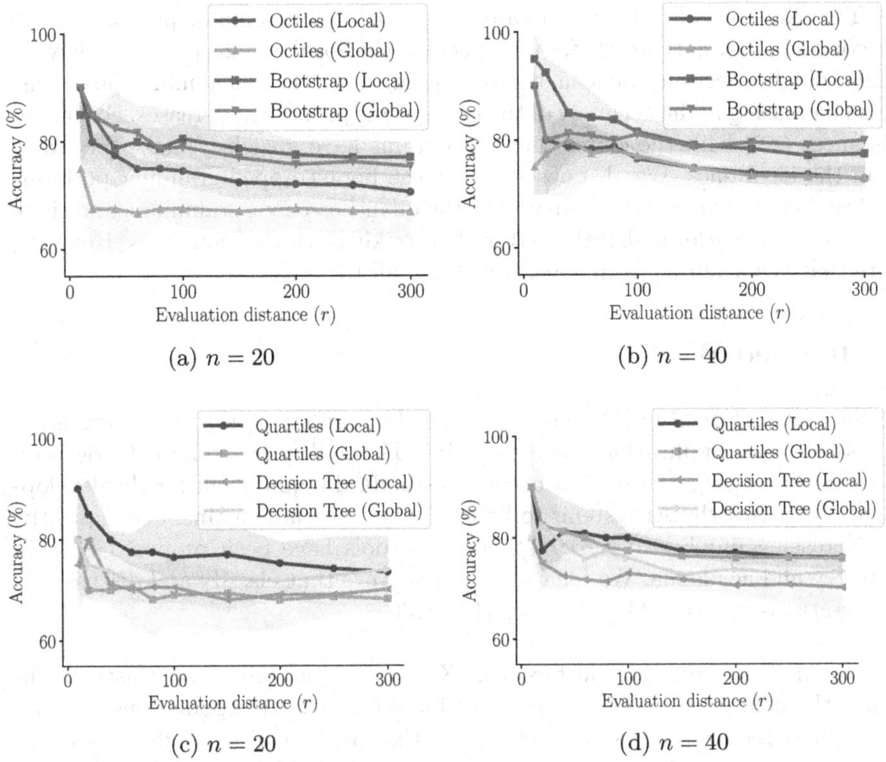

Fig. 7. Global vs. local accuracy evaluation for the *octiles* and *bootstrapped* grammars, as well as for the *quartiles* grammar and for decision trees.

Additionally, we compute *global* mimic programs from n uniformly sampled data points from the training data set.

For the accuracy evaluation, we pick the r closest points from the test data set with their classification from f, and evaluate the accuracy of local and global mimic programs on these data points, as well as local and global decision trees as surrogate models. Figure 7(a) and Fig. 7(b) give the accuracy results for global mimic programs and local mimic programs computed from the $n = 20$ and $n = 40$ closest data points to x^*, respectively. We evaluate the accuracy for an increasing number r of closest points to x^* in the test data set.

In analogous terms, in Fig. 7(c) and Fig. 7(d) we illustrate an accuracy comparison between mimic programs and decision trees. In this case, the mimic programs are built from the *quartiles* grammar. To provide a clear comparison, we have illustrated accuracy results by comparing two approaches side by side. Since the results obtained by grammars using quantiles as feature constants are very similar, we have omitted the results for sextiles.

The results show that for our case study, the obtained mimic programs serve as good approximations of f. As expected, the local mimic programs have a slightly higher accuracy on local test data points then the global mimic programs. With increasing r, the accuracy of the local mimic programs decreases. For higher distances ($r \geq 240$) the global mimic programs have a slightly higher accuracy than the local ones. We also observe that the bootstrapped grammar performs slightly better in accuracy compared to the quantiles-based grammars, and these ones, in turn, perform slightly better than scikit-learn decision trees. However, note that the accuracy is in general high for all test instances.

6 Related Work

Explainable artificial intelligence (XAI) has been receiving significant attention across multiple application domains [2,10]. The ability to explain the decision making of an opaque model has become a standard requirement for the development of trustworthy AI systems to be applied in critical domains. Consequently, an increasing number of XAI methods and tools have been proposed both in industry and academia. We refer to recent surveys that classify and discuss various state-of-the-art XAI techniques [14,28,30].

Formal Methods for XAI. Most existing XAI techniques rely on stochastic methods without any correctness guarantees for the provided explanations. In contrast, there have been several recent works that use formal methods to generate provably correct explanations [7,19,27]. Several of these approaches build upon the verification of deep neural networks (DNN). These approaches typically compute a minimal subset of input features which by themselves already determine the classification produced by the DNN [20,36]. There are also recent approaches using formal methods specifically for explainable reinforcement learning and policies Markov decision processes (MDP) [8,9,39].

Several works exist to make the decision-making of *black-box systems used for control* explainable. Automata learning refers to techniques that infer a surrogate model (e.g., in the form of an input-output automaton [41], a timed automaton [13] or an MDP [38]) from a given black-box system by observing its behavior. The tool dtControl [5] learns decision trees for hybrid and probabilistic control systems, and has been recently extended to support richer algebraic predicates as splitting rules with the use of support vector machines [22]. While not a direct comparison with dtControl, our experimental baseline (scikit-learn) uses the same kind of binary decision trees as surrogate models.

Our approach follows this line of research on formal XAI, studying classification problems for image and tabular data. We rely on *syntax-guided synthesis (SyGuS)* [3] to generate provably correct explanations. In particular, we use SyGuS via formulating the semantic constraints as input-output examples [21,31]. The concept of Programming-by-Example is well known due to the success of the FlashFill [17] feature in Microsoft Excel spreadsheet software. The broad acceptance of FlashFill is due to the fact that it is very simple to use: the user only has to provide the examples. Our approach for computing formal explanations from examples follows this idea. Neider et al. [32] followed a similar direction and proposed to use a combination of probably approximately correct learning (PAC) and syntax-guided synthesis (SyGuS) to produce explanations that with a high probability make only few errors. In contrast to our work, [32] does not compute explanations for image data.

7 Conclusion

In this paper, we synthesize formal explanations for the decisions of opaque machine learning models used for classification tasks. From a given set of data points and the corresponding classification of the opaque model, we compute a mimic program in the form of a quantifier-free first-order logic formula that produces the same output as the given model for all given examples. We formulate the synthesis problem as SyGuS problem and use if-then-else grammars to obtain mimic programs that can be represented as decision trees. For future work, we want to perform more comprehensive case studies on tabular data, since we see the most potential of our method in analysing such data. In particular, we want to investigate the effect of richer grammars on the size of the explanations.

Acknowledgements. This work was supported in part from the European Union's Horizon 2020 research and innovation programme under grant agreement N° 956123 - FOCETA, by the State Government of Styria, Austria - Department Zukunftsfonds Steiermark, by the United States Office of Naval Research (ONR) through a National Defense Science and Engineering (NDSEG) Graduate Fellowship, and by the United States National Science Foundation (NSF) award CCF-2131476. The authors thank Benedikt Maderbacher and William Hallahan for their assistance with SyGuS encodings, and Timos Antonopoulos for his helpful comments on an earlier draft.

Appendix

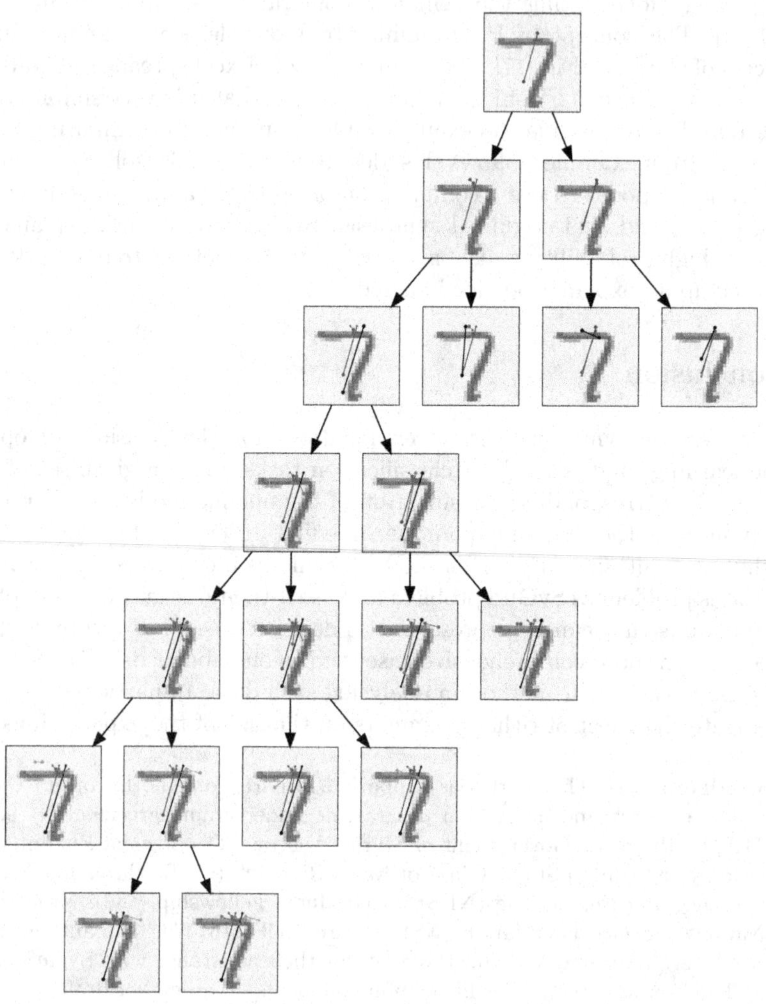

Fig. 8. Decision logic representation for an MNIST mimic program $P_{f,100}$, showing the progression of pixel comparisons.

References

1. Adadi, A., Berrada, M.: Peeking inside the black-box: a survey on explainable artificial intelligence (XAI). IEEE Access **6**, 52138–52160 (2018)

2. Ahmed, I., Jeon, G., Piccialli, F.: From artificial intelligence to explainable artificial intelligence in industry 4.0: a survey on what, how, and where. IEEE Trans. Ind. Inf. **18**(8), 5031–5042 (2022)
3. Alur, R., et al.: Syntax-guided synthesis. In: FMCAD, pp. 1–8. IEEE (2013)
4. Arrieta, A.B., et al.: Explainable artificial intelligence (XAI): concepts, taxonomies, opportunities and challenges toward responsible AI. Inf. Fusion **58**, 82–115 (2020)
5. Ashok, P., Jackermeier, M., Křetínský, J., Weinhuber, C., Weininger, M., Yadav, M.: dtControl 2.0: explainable strategy representation via decision tree learning steered by experts. In: TACAS 2021. LNCS, vol. 12652, pp. 326–345. Springer, Cham (2021). https://doi.org/10.1007/978-3-030-72013-1_17
6. Barbosa, H., et al.: cvc5: a versatile and industrial-strength SMT solver. In: International Conference on Tools and Algorithms for the Construction and Analysis of Systems (TACAS 2022), pp. 415–442 (2022)
7. Bassan, S., Katz, G.: Towards formal XAI: formally approximate minimal explanations of neural networks. In: TACAS (1). Lecture Notes in Computer Science, vol. 13993, pp. 187–207. Springer, Heidelberg (2023). https://doi.org/10.1007/978-3-031-30823-9_10
8. Cano Córdoba, F., et al.: Analyzing intentional behavior in autonomous agents under uncertainty. In: Proceedings of the Thirty-Second International Joint Conference on Artificial Intelligence, IJCAI-23, pp. 372–381 (2023)
9. Carr, S., Jansen, N., Topcu, U.: Task-aware verifiable rnn-based policies for partially observable markov decision processes. J. Artif. Intell. Res. (JAIR) **72**, 819–847 (2021)
10. Chaddad, A., Peng, J., Xu, J., Bouridane, A.: Survey of explainable AI techniques in healthcare. Sensors **23**(2), 634 (2023)
11. Chollet, F.: Simple MNIST convnet (2015). https://keras.io/examples/vision/mnist_convnet/. Accessed 19 July 2023
12. Costa, V.G., Pedreira, C.E.: Recent advances in decision trees: an updated survey. Artif. Intell. Rev. **56**(5), 4765–4800 (2023)
13. Dierl, S., et al.: Learning symbolic timed models from concrete timed data. In: Rozier, K.Y., Chaudhuri, S. (eds.) NASA Formal Methods, vol. 13903, pp. 104–121. Springer, Cham (2023). https://doi.org/10.1007/978-3-031-33170-1_7
14. Dwivedi, R., et al.: Explainable AI (XAI): core ideas, techniques, and solutions. ACM Comput. Surv. **55**(9), 194:1–194:33 (2023)
15. Fathi, E., Shoja, B.M.: Deep neural networks for natural language processing. In: Handbook of Statistics, vol. 38, pp. 229–316. Elsevier (2018)
16. Guidotti, R., Monreale, A., Ruggieri, S., Turini, F., Giannotti, F., Pedreschi, D.: A survey of methods for explaining black box models. ACM Comput. Surv. (CSUR) **51**(5), 1–42 (2018)
17. Gulwani, S., Harris, W.R., Singh, R.: Spreadsheet data manipulation using examples. Commun. ACM **55**(8), 97–105 (2012)
18. Henderson, P., Islam, R., Bachman, P., Pineau, J., Precup, D., Meger, D.: Deep reinforcement learning that matters. In: Proceedings of the AAAI Conference on Artificial Intelligence, vol. 32 (2018)
19. Ignatiev, A.: Towards trustable explainable AI. In: Bessiere, C. (ed.) Proceedings of the Twenty-Ninth International Joint Conference on Artificial Intelligence, IJCAI 2020, pp. 5154–5158 (2020). https://www.ijcai.org/
20. Izza, Y., Huang, X., Ignatiev, A., Narodytska, N., Cooper, M.C., Marques-Silva, J.: On computing probabilistic abductive explanations. Int. J. Approx. Reason. **159**, 108939 (2023)

21. Jha, S., Gulwani, S., Seshia, S.A., Tiwari, A.: Oracle-guided component-based program synthesis. In: 2010 ACM/IEEE 32nd International Conference on Software Engineering (ICSE 2010), vol. 1, pp. 215–224 (2010)
22. Jüngermann, F., Kretínský, J., Weininger, M.: Algebraically explainable controllers: decision trees and support vector machines join forces. CoRR arXiv:2208.1280 (2022)
23. LeCun, Y., Cortes, C., Burges, C.J.: The MNIST database (1998). http://yann.lecun.com/exdb/mnist. Accessed 13 Aug 2022
24. Li, M., Chan, N., Chandra, V., Muriki, K.: Cluster usage policy enforcement using slurm plugins and an HTTP API. In: Jacobs, G.A., Stewart, C.A. (eds.) PEARC 2020: Practice and Experience in Advanced Research Computing, Portland, OR, USA, 27–31 July 2020, pp. 232–238. ACM (2020)
25. Liang, W., et al.: Advances, challenges and opportunities in creating data for trustworthy AI. Nat. Mach. Intell. **4**(8), 669–677 (2022)
26. Lundberg, S.M., Lee, S.: A unified approach to interpreting model predictions. In: NIPS, pp. 4765–4774 (2017)
27. Marques-Silva, J., Ignatiev, A.: Delivering trustworthy AI through formal XAI. In: AAAI, pp. 12342–12350. AAAI Press (2022)
28. Minh, D., Wang, H.X., Li, Y.F., Nguyen, T.N.: Explainable artificial intelligence: a comprehensive review. Artif. Intell. Rev., 1–66 (2022)
29. Mohsen, H., El-Dahshan, E.S.A., El-Horbaty, E.S.M., Salem, A.B.M.: Classification using deep learning neural networks for brain tumors. Future Comput. Inf. J. **3**(1), 68–71 (2018)
30. Molnar, C.: Interpretable Machine Learning, 2 edn. (2022). https://christophm.github.io/interpretable-ml-book
31. Morton, K., Hallahan, W.T., Shum, E., Piskac, R., Santolucito, M.: Grammar filtering for syntax-guided synthesis. In: AAAI, pp. 1611–1618. AAAI Press (2020)
32. Neider, D., Ghosh, B.: Probably approximately correct explanations of machine learning models via syntax-guided synthesis. arXiv preprint arXiv:2009.08770 (2020)
33. Pedregosa, F., et al.: Scikit-learn: machine learning in python. J. Mach. Learn. Res. **12**, 2825–2830 (2011)
34. Ranjbar, N., Safabakhsh, R.: Using decision tree as local interpretable model in autoencoder-based LIME. In: CSICC, pp. 1–7. IEEE (2022)
35. Ribeiro, M.T., Singh, S., Guestrin, C.: "Why Should I Trust You?" explaining the predictions of any classifier. In: Proceedings of the 22nd ACM SIGKDD International Conference on Knowledge Discovery and Data Mining (KDD 2016), pp. 1135–1144 (2016)
36. Shih, A., Choi, A., Darwiche, A.: A symbolic approach to explaining bayesian network classifiers. In: Lang, J. (ed.) Proceedings of the Twenty-Seventh International Joint Conference on Artificial Intelligence, IJCAI 2018, Stockholm, Sweden, 13–19 July 2018, pp. 5103–5111 (2018). https://www.ijcai.org/
37. Smith, J.W., Everhart, J.E., Dickson, W., Knowler, W.C., Johannes, R.S.: Using the ADAP learning algorithm to forecast the onset of diabetes mellitus. In: Proceedings of the Annual Symposium on Computer Application in Medical Care (1988)
38. Tappler, M., Aichernig, B.K., Bacci, G., Eichlseder, M., Larsen, K.G.: L^*-based learning of markov decision processes (extended version). Formal Aspects Comput. **33**(4–5), 575–615 (2021)

39. Verma, A., Murali, V., Singh, R., Kohli, P., Chaudhuri, S.: Programmatically interpretable reinforcement learning. In: International Conference on Machine Learning (ICML), pp. 5045–5054. PMLR (2018)
40. Wachter, S., Mittelstadt, B., Russell, C.: Counterfactual explanations without opening the black box: automated decisions and the GDPR. Harvard J. Law Technol. **31**, 841 (2017)
41. Wang, F., Cao, Z., Tan, L., Zong, H.: Survey on learning-based formal methods: taxonomy, applications and possible future directions. IEEE Access **8**, 108561–108578 (2020)

Differential Safety Testing of Deep RL Agents Enabled by Automata Learning

Martin Tappler[1,2](✉) and Bernhard K. Aichernig[1]

[1] Institute of Software Technology, Graz University of Technology, Graz, Austria
martin.tappler@ist.tugraz.at

[2] Silicon Austria Labs, TU Graz - SAL DES Lab, Graz, Austria

Abstract. Learning-enabled controllers (LECs) pose severe challenges to verification. Their decisions often come from deep neural networks that are hard to interpret and verify, and they operate in stochastic and unknown environments with high-dimensional state space. These complexities make analyses of the internals of LECs and manual modeling of the environments extremely challenging. Numerous combinations of automata learning with verification techniques have shown its potential in the analysis of black-box reactive systems. Hence, automata learning may also bring light into the black boxes that are LECs and their runtime environments.

A hurdle to the adoption of automata-learning-based verification is that it is often difficult to provide guarantees on the accuracy of learned automata. This is exacerbated in complex, stochastic environments faced by LECs. In this paper, we demonstrate that accuracy guarantees on learned models are not strictly necessary. Through a combination of automata learning, testing, and statistics, we perform testing-based verification with statistical guarantees in the absence of guarantees on the learned automata. We showcase our approach by testing deep reinforcement learning for safety that have been trained to play the computer game Super Mario Bros.

Keywords: Reinforcement Learning · Automata Learning · Differential Testing · Learning-Based Testing

1 Introduction

Controllers trained via reinforcement learning (RL) have recently demonstrated impressive performances, for example, in complex real-time computer games (e.g., AlphaStar [51]) and board games, where they even reach superhuman level (e.g., AlphaGo [37] and AlphaZero [38]). Despite these impressive results, their complexity and intransparent decision-making hinder the widespread adoption of controllers and autonomous agents trained via RL. While advances in deep neural networks enabled the progress of RL, these networks encoding control policies are notoriously hard to interpret and verify.

B. Steffen (Ed.): AISoLA 2023, LNCS 14380, pp. 138–159, 2024.
https://doi.org/10.1007/978-3-031-46002-9_8

Verification and testing techniques can be broadly categorized into black-box and white-box techniques. On the one hand, white-box techniques, which take into account the structure and parameters of neural networks, often do not scale well to complex deep neural networks. On the other hand, black-box techniques that only consider the input-output behavior of learning-enabled controllers (LECs) often cannot provide guarantees on the verification results. For example, it is practically impossible to achieve exhaustiveness with black-box techniques. In this paper, we propose a *black-box approach to testing RL control policies.*

Various applications of automata learning for black-box verification have shown its potential to reveal faults of reactive systems. Application domains include communication protocols [32,35,39,43], embedded systems [2,40], and cyber-physical systems [52]. Despite detecting issues in widely used software systems, such as TLS implementations [35,39], guarantees on exhaustiveness are hardly possible. For example, black box checking [31] is only complete when an upper bound on the number of states of the system under consideration is known. Alternatively, instead of aiming for exhaustiveness, we may prioritize statistical guarantees. Under a fixed sampling regime, we can learn deterministic models that are probably approximately correct (PAC) [28,50]. In stochastic automata learning, which is required to deal with RL agents and their environments, the situation is yet again more difficult. Automata learning algorithms [25,26,42,46] for Markov decision processes that are commonly used to model RL environments do not provide PAC guarantees.

A Learning-Based Testing Approach. Despite this bleak outlook, we present an approach that combines various ideas from learning-based testing. The approach tests RL agents for safety while providing statistical guarantees on the testing results. It includes four main ingredients. (1) We apply IOAlergia [25,26], a *stochastic automata learning* algorithm, to learn abstract models of the environment in which the RL agents operate (e.g., proposed in [30,34,45]). (2) We derive control policies from learned models via *probabilistic model checking* that bring the agent into states [4], from which we want to test. Inspired by [39,43], (3) we perform *differential testing* of RL policies. That is, we test multiple policies to compare them to each other. (4) By applying *statistical tests*, we determine whether some policy is significantly safer than another. Hence, we guarantee statistical significance, even though our learned model may not be perfectly accurate or complete. This guarantee does not depend on the learned model as it is derived from sampling the RL agents in their environments, while the learned models are only used to get to a desired location.

Evaluation. We demonstrate our approach by applying it on pairs of deep RL agents that have been trained to complete levels of the Nintendo game Super Mario Bros. (SMB). Our experiments show that even though the RL policies achieve similar levels of cumulative rewards, we can detect significant differences w.r.t. safety. Thus, we enable a more fine-grained evaluation and our approach can provide guidance in selecting an RL policy from multiple available ones. We use the SMB environment throughout the paper as an illustrative example to explain individual concepts.

Contributions. To summarize, our contributions are (1) an approach for differential safety testing of RL policies and (2) its implementation and evaluation.

Structure. The rest of this paper is structured as follows. In Sect. 2, we discuss related work that combines automata learning with verification, testing, and RL, and we briefly discuss RL testing approaches. We provide an overview of notation and preliminaries in Sect. 3. In Sect. 4, we present our proposed approach, and in Sect. 5, we present evaluation results of the approach. We conclude the paper with a summary and an outlook on future work in Sect. 6.

2 Related Work

We draw inspiration from works in automata learning, which we review in the following, as well as related topics.

Differential testing guided by learned automata has been applied to reveal faults in different communication protocols [1,3,39,43]. All these works have in common that they consider deterministic reactive systems, thus they learn deterministic models. The approaches search for differences between the protocol implementation with the help of learned automata.

Various authors proposed to apply probabilistic model-checking on learned automata for verification. Mao et al. [25,26] evaluate IOAlergia, which we use in this paper, using model checking. In previous work, we proposed a probabilistic reachability checking approach by iteratively refining a learned model [4]. We recently adapted this approach to solve control tasks in environments with continuous state spaces [45]. Wang et al. [52] combined predicate abstraction, probabilistic verification, and learning of Markov chains to tackle the verification of cyber-physical systems. These works all consider reactive software systems, whereas we specifically focus on RL policies and the environment they operate in. More recently, Dong et al. [10] combined stochastic automata learning and model checking to detect adversarial examples for recurrent neural networks. In an RL context, we applied IOAlergia to learn models capturing safety-relevant aspects of an environment in order to compute shields [47]. In this paper, we do not restrict learning to safety but focus on safety during testing.

Shielding generally refers to techniques that synthesize reactive systems, so-called shields, which enforce the execution of certain actions in order to satisfy a given system specification [7,20]. Shields monitor actions at runtime to either block actions or override them [21], for example, to ensure safe behavior. It has proven an effective technique to ensure safety during training of RL agents [5, 18,21,22] and to adapt RL agents to changing environments [33]. Our proposed technique is orthogonal to shielding, since our safety testing may be used to check if a shielded system indeed behaves safely after training.

While most work on testing autonomous systems focuses on visual aspects, like DeepTest [48] and DeepHunter [54], recently several testing approaches have been proposed for RL agents. Search-based testing techniques have been proposed for deep RL agents, which search for trajectories in the environment that enable testing [44,56] and which search for environment configurations to be tested [6]. Lu et al. [24] presented a mutation testing framework for RL systems with specialized mutation operators. In this paper, we rely on learned automata to guide testing.

Furthermore, automata learning has been applied in an RL context to enable RL with sparse and non-Markovian rewards [12,13,17,55] and to enable RL under partial observability [17,30]. In these works, learned automata serve as high-level task descriptions and provide additional information to tackle issues resulting from non-Markovian dynamics and rewards.

3 Preliminaries

In this section, we introduce the notation, concepts, and models we use throughout the paper.

3.1 Markov Decision Processes

Given a finite set S, $Dist(S)$ denotes the set of probability distributions over S and $supp(\mu)$ for $\mu \in Dist(S)$ denote the support of μ, i.e. the set $S' \subseteq S$ with $s \in S' : \mu(s) > 0$.
A **Markov decision process (MDP)** is a tuple $\langle \mathcal{S}, s_0, \mathcal{A}, \mathcal{P} \rangle$ where $\mathcal{S}$ is a finite set of states, $s_0 \in \mathcal{S}$ is the initial state, $\mathcal{A}$ is a finite set of actions, and $\mathcal{P} : \mathcal{S} \times \mathcal{A} \to Dist(\mathcal{S})$ is the probabilistic transition function. For all $s \in \mathcal{S}$ the available actions are $\mathcal{A}(s) = \{a \in \mathcal{A} \mid \exists s', \mathcal{P}(s,a)(s') \neq 0\}$ and we assume $|\mathcal{A}(s)| \geq 1$.

Paths. A finite path p through an MDP is an alternating sequence of states and actions, i.e. $p = s_0 a_1 s_1 \cdots a_{n-1} s_{n-1} a_n s_n \in s_0 \times (\mathcal{A} \times \mathcal{S})^*$.

Policy. A policy resolves the non-deterministic choice of actions in an MDP. It is a function mapping paths to distributions over actions. We consider *memoryless* policies that take into account only the last state of a path, i.e., policies $\pi \colon \mathcal{S} \to Dist(\mathcal{A})$. A *deterministic* policy π always selects a single action, i.e., $\pi : \mathcal{S} \to \mathcal{A}$. Following RL terminology, we say that the execution of a policy starting from the initial state of an MDP is an *episode*. An episode yields a path and we use the terms episode and path interchangeably.

Example 1 (MDP for our Case Study). We use SMB as an environment for our case study. The observable states in this environment are images of the game states. We transform them to gray-scale and scale them to 84 by 84 pixels. To enable tracking of movement, we stack images from four consecutive frames. Hence, a state is an array with the dimension $84 \times 84 \times 4$, where each cell holds a byte value representing a shade of gray.

The available actions are button combinations that cause Mario to run right and to jump to the right, i.e., $\mathcal{A} = \{run - right, jump - right\}$. SMB has little stochastic behavior. RL experiments involving computer games often add stochasticity by varying the duration for which button combinations are held pressed. In our case study, each action lasts between three and five frames, where each outcome has an equal probability of $\frac{1}{3}$. As a result, the distance traveled by the Mario agent from the same state varies randomly.

Reinforcement Learning. In RL, [41] an agent learns a memoryless policy to complete a task via interactions with an unknown environment modeled by an MDP $\langle \mathcal{S}, s_0, \mathcal{A}, \mathcal{P} \rangle$. The task is typically defined through a reward function $r : \mathcal{S} \times \mathcal{A} \to \mathbb{R}$. At each state $s \in \mathcal{S}$, the agent chooses and performs an action $a \in \mathcal{A}$, causing a probabilistic change of the environment state. That is, the environment moves to a state s' with the probability $\mathcal{P}(s,a)(s')$. The corresponding reward is determined by $r(s,a)$. RL agents can usually observe the states and receive rewards during execution, but they initially have no knowledge of the transition function $\mathcal{P}$.

Technically, the agent's objective is to maximize the return $\mathtt{ret}$, which is the discounted cumulative reward defined by $\mathtt{ret} = \Sigma_{t=0}^{\infty} \gamma^t r(s_t, a_t)$, parameterized by the *discount factor* $\gamma \in [0,1]$. An *optimal policy* π^* is a policy that maximizes the expectation of the return, i.e., $\max_{\pi \in \Pi} \mathbb{E}_\pi(\mathtt{ret})$, where Π is the set of all policies.

There exist various approaches to implement RL ranging from simple table-based Q-learning [53] to approaches that use deep neural networks [27,36], e.g., to approximate the Q-function from Q-learning. In this paper, we consider testing of **deep RL policies** that internally use neural networks to scale to large state space. However, an in-depth discussion of different RL techniques is beyond the scope of the paper.

Example 2 (Rewards in our Case Study). The agent's task in the SMB environment is to navigate through a game level to get to a goal while dodging enemies and jumping over obstacles. The goal has the largest x-coordinate in the pixel-based coordinate system of each level. The reward gained in a step is given by $(x - x') + (t - t') + d$, where x is the agent's x-coordinate, t is the time left to complete the level, i.e., t decreases from step to step. Primed values denote the corresponding values from the last time step. The value of d is either -25 if the agent reaches an unsafe state, e.g., runs into an enemy, or 0 otherwise.

Deterministic labeled MDPs are defined as MDPs $\mathcal{M}_L = \langle \mathcal{S}, s_0, \mathcal{A}, O, \mathcal{P}, L \rangle$ that include a labeling function $L : \mathcal{S} \to O$ mapping states to observations from a finite set O.

The transition function $\mathcal{P}$ must satisfy the following determinism property:

$$\forall s \in \mathcal{S}, \forall a \in \mathcal{A} \colon \mathcal{P}(s,a)(s') > 0 \land \mathcal{P}(s,a)(s'') > 0$$
$$\implies s' = s'' \lor L(s') \neq L(s'').$$

This property ensures that the successor states reached by executing a given action a in a state s can be distinguished based on the observed output. Given a path p in a deterministic labeled MDP $\mathcal{M}_L$, applying the labeling function on all states of the path p results in a so called *observation trace* $L(p) = L(s_0)a_1L(s_1)\cdots a_{n-1}L(s_{n-1})a_nL(s_n)$. As a result of the determinism property, an observation trace $L(p)$ uniquely identifies the corresponding path p and the state reached at the end. In this paper, we passively learn deterministic labeled MDPs that serve as abstractions of the environment.

We learn *deterministic labeled MDPs* via the algorithm IOAlergia [25,26], an adaptation of Alergia [8]. IOAlergia takes a multiset $\mathcal{T}_o$ of observation traces as input. First, IOAlergia constructs a tree from the observation traces by merging common prefixes. This tree represents the input sample of observation traces. Its edges are labeled with actions and its nodes are labeled with observations. Each edge corresponds to a prefix of an observation trace from the input sample. Every such prefix can be found in the tree by traversing the tree from the root to a node while keeping track of the sequence of visited nodes and edge labels. Additionally, edges are associated with frequencies that denote how many traces in $\mathcal{T}_o$ have the trace corresponding to an edge as a prefix. Normalizing these frequencies already yields a tree-shaped MDP.

To generalize to unseen traces, IOAlergia transforms the tree into an MDP with cycles through iterated merging of nodes. Two nodes are merged if they are compatible. Nodes n_1 and n_2 are considered compatible if their future behavior is sufficiently similar. For this purpose, we check if the observations in the subtrees originating in the nodes are not statistically different. More concretely, IOAlergia first checks if the distributions of observations immediately following n_1 and n_2 are different. They are deemed different if the likelihood of observing any observation after any actions is found to be different by a statistical test that is based on a Hoeffding bound [16]. A parameter $\epsilon_{\text{Alergia}}$ controls the significance level of the applied test. If there is no difference in the immediately following output distributions, IOAlergia recursively checks pairs of nodes in the subtrees originating in n_1 and n_2. If the algorithm does not detect a difference, n_1 and n_2 are considered compatible. Since they cannot be distinguished, the nodes are assumed to correspond to the same state in the MDP to be learned, thus they are merged.

If a node is not compatible with any other node, it is promoted to a state in the final learned MDP. This stage of learning terminates when all pairs of nodes have either been promoted to states or merged into existing states. The final deterministic labeled MDP is created by normalizing the frequencies on the edges to yield probability distributions for the transition function $\mathcal{P}$. In this paper, we refer to this construction as MDP learning. We denote calls to IOAlergia by $\mathcal{M}_L = \text{IOAlergia}(\mathcal{T}, \epsilon_{\text{Alergia}})$, where $\mathcal{M}_L$ is the deterministic labeled MDP learned from the multiset of observation traces $\mathcal{T}$. The state space of $\mathcal{M}_L$ spans the tree nodes in the tree created from $\mathcal{T}$ that are distinguishable using the information in $\mathcal{T}$.

4 Learning-Based Differential Testing of RL Agents

In this section, we describe a differential testing approach aided by automata learning. The approach compares RL agents in terms of safety via statistical testing.

4.1 Setting

Before we detail the individual steps of our approach, we introduce the setting for our approach, our assumptions, and our goals. We consider episodic RL tasks in an environment that can be modeled with an MDP $\mathcal{M} = \langle \mathcal{S}, s_0, \mathcal{A}, \mathcal{P} \rangle$. As is common in RL, we can observe the states $\mathcal{S}$, but the transition function $\mathcal{P}$ is unknown. The states include two types of terminal states without successor states: unsafe states $\mathcal{S}_U$ and goal states $\mathcal{S}_G$. Reaching either of these types of states terminates an episode. An *episode ending in an unsafe state violates safety*, while an episode ending in a goal state solves the RL task. The systems under test (SUTs) are given as policies $\pi_i : \mathcal{S} \to \mathcal{A}$. For the sake of simplicity, we consider pairs of policies (π_1, π_2) that we compare against each other. We focus on *safety testing*, executing a policy π_i under test and checking if it shows unsafe behavior. That is, we check if the execution visits an unsafe state in $\mathcal{S}_U$. During testing, we keep the policies under test fixed, i.e., we do not update the underlying neural networks but only evaluate their behavior.

To enable automata learning, we assume to have a proper abstraction function $abs : \mathcal{S} \to O$ that maps the environment states to abstract observations and an accompanying distance function $\Delta : O \times O \to \mathbb{R}$. Discussing the intricacies of abstraction for automata learning in complex environments is beyond the scope of the paper, therefore we refer to [45] for an abstraction approach involving dimensionality reduction and clustering. We consider test-case specifications on the coverage of abstract observations. A test-case specification on the coverage of $T \subseteq O$ indicates that we want to test agents from states in which we observe a $t \in T$. For testing, we bring the agent into a state where T can be observed and execute a policy under test from there to check if it behaves safely.

Example 3 (Abstraction for our Case Study). The abstraction function abs in our case study maps the concrete states seen by the RL policies to x- and y-coordinates. These coordinates denote the agent position in the pixel-based coordinate system of SMB. An abstract observation may additionally include either `game_over` or `win`, in case the corresponding concrete state is an unsafe state in $\mathcal{S}_U$ or a goal state in $\mathcal{S}_G$. The distance function Δ over abstract observations is simply the Euclidean distance between the pixel-based coordinates.

Note that agent coordinates do not uniquely define a state since they do not capture the agent's speed or enemy positions. Hence, RL with this abstraction would not yield optimal policies due to the non-Markovian behavior of the environment. The environment under this abstraction can be seen as a partially observable Markov decision process (POMDP). MDP learning resolves issues resulting from partial observability by learning an approximation of the belief

MDP corresponding to the abstract POMDP. This belief MDP may contain multiple states with the same abstract observation o if IOALERGIA detects differing future behavior after observing o. For more details on automata learning enabling policy computation under partial observability, we refer to [30,34]. While policies derived from learned MDPs may not be optimal due to inaccuracies in the learned MDPs, our experiments show that they are sufficiently accurate to enable testing from specific states.

Goal. We are given a pair of RL policies (π_1, π_2) and a set of test-case specifications defined by observation sets T_j to be covered. For each T_j, our goal is to bring the agent into a state labeled by $t \in T_j$ and control the agent from there with either of the policies π_i. We repeat *testing until we determine a significant difference w.r.t. safety between the policies* or until hitting a repetition bound.

4.2 Overview

The testing approach we propose consists of three stages: an **automata learning**, a **test-case generation setup** stage, and a **test-case execution** stage.

Automata Learning. In the first stage, we execute the agents under test in the environment to sample paths from the environment. After that, we perform an abstraction from states to abstract observations. This step turns the sampled paths into observation traces, from which we learn a deterministic labeled MDP. Figure 1 provides an overview of the components involved in this stage. Note that we distinguish between policies and the agent that is controlled by a policy, as we have several policies that may control the agent.

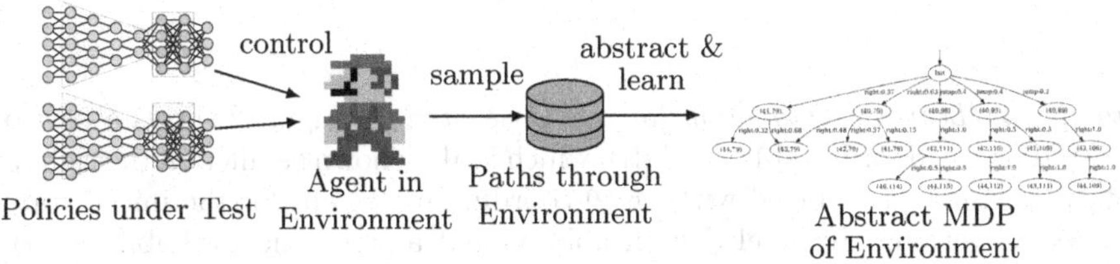

Fig. 1. A graphical overview of the automata learning stage in the proposed approach. We control an agent with the policies under test to collect paths through the environment. After abstracting to paths to observation traces, we learn abstract MDP of the environment.

Test-Case Generation. The test-case generation stage creates test cases from test-case specifications; a common step in model-based testing [49]. We consider specifications on the coverage of observations. To cover these observations, we compute policies from MDPs learned in the first stage. These policies maximize the probability of reaching the specified observations. A policy combined with further parameters, like test length, defines a test case.

Test-case execution controls the agent in the environment with the policies derived from the learned MDP to reach a state with a desired observation. From there, it repeatedly tests the RL policies under consideration until either determining a difference in safety or reaching a repetition bound.

4.3 Automata Learning

Figure 1 provides a graphical overview of the automata learning stage. To get data for automata learning, we simply perform n_{al} episodes, where we control the agent with the policies under test. This gives us a multiset $\mathcal{P}_e$ of n_{al} paths through the environment MDP $\mathcal{M}$. By applying *abs* on every state, we transform $\mathcal{P}_e$ into a multiset of observation traces $\mathcal{T}$. Finally, we learn a deterministic labeled MDP $\mathcal{M}_{abs}$ from $\mathcal{T}$ via IOALERGIA that serves as an abstraction of the environment.

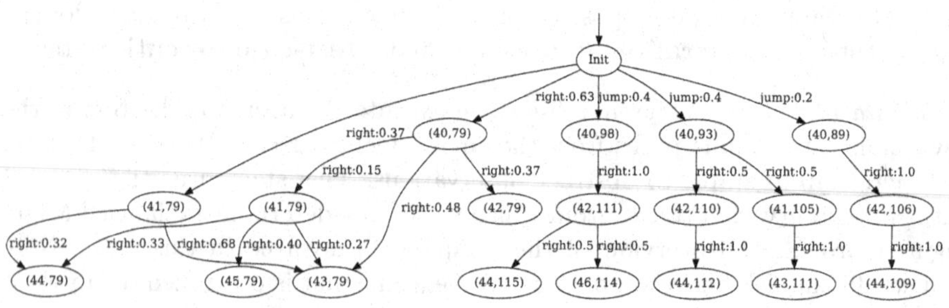

Fig. 2. Partial model learned for Level 1-1 of SMB

Example 4 (Learned Automaton for our Case Study). Figure 2 shows a part of the MDP learned for Level 1-1 of SMB, which is also shown smaller on the right of Fig. 1. Its states are labeled with (x, y)-coordinates, except for the initial state, and its transitions are labeled with abbreviated actions and probabilities. By executing *jump − right* in the initial state, we reach a state labeled $(40, 98)$ with probability 0.4, a state labeled $(41, 93)$ with probability 0.4, or a state labeled $(41, 89)$ with probability 0.2. That is, with probability 0.4, the action takes long enough[1] for the agent to travel 19 pixels in the y-direction from the starting y-coordinate of 79. We can also see that there are two states labeled $(41, 79)$, one that is reached after the observation trace $t_1 = \mathit{Init} \cdot \mathit{run} - \mathit{right} \cdot (41, 79)$ and one reached after $t_2 = \mathit{Init} \cdot \mathit{run} - \mathit{right} \cdot (40, 79) \cdot \mathit{run} - \mathit{right} \cdot (41, 79) \cdot$ actions. IOALERGIA introduces two states for this label, since the future behaviors after t_1 and t_2 differ. Following t_2, we can reach $(45, 79)$, which is not possible after t_1.

[1] Recall that the duration of an action randomly varies between three and five frames as explained in Example 1.

This example demonstrates that IOALERGIA learns the structure and transition probabilities of an abstract MDP underlying the environment. It also shows that IOALERGIA helps to resolve some issues resulting from partial observability (which we discussed in Example 3). It creates two states for the same position $(41, 79)$ because the agent's speed that cannot be observed in the abstraction is different after t_1 and t_2.

4.4 Test-Case Generation

Test-case generation turns specifications of the testing goals into executable test cases. For this purpose, we define the notion of test-case specifications that we consider.

Definition 1 (Test-Case Specifications.) *A test-case specification is a tuple* $\langle T, tl, m, \alpha\rangle$, *where* $T \subseteq O$ *specifies abstract observations that shall be covered,* tl *specifies the test length,* m *specifies the maximum number of test-case executions to attempt to reach the test goal, and* α *specifies the desired significance level on the difference between tested policies.*

To turn a test-case specification into an executable test case, we compute a policy over the learned abstract MDP of the environment $\mathcal{M}_{abs}$ that maximizes the probability of reaching a state labeled by $t \in T$.

Let $\mathcal{S}_{abs}$ be the states of $\mathcal{M}_{abs}$, $s \in \mathcal{S}_{abs}$, and let $p_{s,a} = P_{\max}(\mathbf{F}\ T|s, a)$ be the maximal probability of reaching a state labeled by $t \in T$ from state s when executing action a, where $\mathbf{F}$ denotes the *eventually* operator. A test case generated from a test-case specification $\langle T, tl, m, \alpha\rangle$ is a tuple $\langle \pi_T, tl, m, \alpha\rangle$, where π_T is a memoryless, deterministic policy that picks the action a in each abstract state $s \in \mathcal{S}_{abs}$ which maximizes $p_{s,a}$. Such policies can be computed with probabilistic model checkers, such as, STORM [9] and PRISM [23]. A test suite is simply a set of test cases.

Example 5 (Test-Case Specifications for our Case Study). To define test-case specifications for the SMB environment, we manually examined levels of the computer game. We aim to cover safety-critical states by testing, hence states where the agent is close to a pit or an enemy are natural choices. Each T defines coordinates near pits or adversaries. For example, placing Mario at $x = 260, y = 79$ in Level 1-1 puts him next to the first enemy. The complete test-case specification for the first test case is $\langle\{(x = 260, y = 79)\}, tl = 20, m = 5000, \alpha = 0.05\rangle$ The test length of 20 ensures that the policy needs to avoid the enemy to pass the test case. Having 5000 repetitions and a significance level of 0.05 ensures that we get reliable test results.

The executable test case corresponding to the above specification is relatively simple. The policy leading to $(x = 260, y = 79)$ only needs to perform the action *run* – *right* as there are no obstacles on the way to $(x = 260, y = 79)$. This policy brings the agent to the first safety-critical location, where we test if RL policies are able to safely jump over the enemy.

Algorithm 1. A single test-case run.

Input: Learned MDP $\mathcal{M}_{abs} = \langle \mathcal{S}_{abs}, s_{0abs}, \mathcal{A}, O, \mathcal{P}_{abs}, L \rangle$, test policy $\pi_T : \mathcal{S}_{abs} \rightarrow \mathcal{A}$, policy under test π_i, test length tl
Output: A test verdict

1: $s \leftarrow$ `reset()`
2: $s_{abs} \leftarrow s_{0abs}$
3: **repeat**
4: $\quad act \leftarrow \pi_T(s_{abs})$
5: $\quad s \leftarrow$ `step`(act)
6: $\quad$ **if** $s \in \mathcal{S}_U$ **then**
7: $\quad\quad$ **return inconclusive** ▷ Test goal not reached
8: $\quad o \leftarrow abs(s)$
9: $\quad$ **if** there is an s' with $\mathcal{P}_{abs}(s_{abs}, act)(s') > 0$ and $L(s') = o$ **then**
10: $\quad\quad s_{abs} \leftarrow s'$ ▷ Move in the abstract MDP
11: $\quad$ **else**
12: $\quad\quad s_{abs} \leftarrow s' \in \mathcal{S}_{abs}$ s.t. $\Delta(L(s'), o)$ is minimal
13: **until** $o \in T$
14: **for** $j \leftarrow 1$ **to** tl **do** ▷ Execute the policy under test
15: $\quad act \leftarrow \pi_i(s)$
16: $\quad s \leftarrow$ `step`(act)
17: $\quad$ **if** $s \in \mathcal{S}_{\mathcal{U}}$ **then**
18: $\quad\quad$ **return fail**
19: **return pass**

Note that by defining coverage goals as subsets of abstract observations in learned MDPs, we ensure that these observations occur during the normal execution of the policies under test. This follows from the fact that we learn MDPs from normal execution traces. Hence, the tested observations are not corner cases that cannot happen in normal operation. Potential safety issues detected by testing are therefore relevant.

4.5 Test-Case Execution

Next, we discuss the execution of test cases. To execute a single test case $\langle \pi_T, tl, m, \alpha \rangle$ on a policy pair (π_1, π_2) we perform up to m individual *test-case runs*. In a test-case run, we first control the agent using π_T. Then we let π_i, one of the RL policies, take over to perform tl many steps.

Algorithm 1 formalizes test-case runs. We interact with the agent in the environment via two operations: RESET resets the environment to the initial state and returns this state, STEP(act) performs the action act in the environment and returns the reached state. In the lines 3 to 13, we control the agent with a test-case policy to get to a state that we want to cover. If we get to an unsafe state before reaching our coverage goal (Line 6), we cannot actually test the RL policy π_i. Therefore, we return **inconclusive** as a verdict. Since the learned MDP $\mathcal{M}_{abs}$ is not perfectly accurate, it may happen that there is no transition

Algorithm 2. Test-case execution via repeated test-case runs.

Input: Learned MDP $\mathcal{M}_{abs}$, Policy pair under test (π_1, π_2), test case $\langle \pi_T, tl, m, \alpha \rangle$,
Output: Tuple of fail frequencies and information on the difference in safety

1: $i \leftarrow 1$ ▷ index of policy under test
2: $f_1 \leftarrow 0, f_2 \leftarrow 0$ ▷ test fails
3: $p_1 \leftarrow 0, p_2 \leftarrow 0$ ▷ passing test-case runs
4: **for** $j \leftarrow 1$ **to** m **do**
5:     $verdict \leftarrow$ TestRun$(\mathcal{M}_{abs}, \pi_T, \pi_i, tl)$
6:     **if** $verdict \neq$ **inconclusive then**
7:         **if** $verdict =$ **fail then**
8:             $f_i \leftarrow f_i + 1$
9:         **else**
10:             $p_i \leftarrow p_i + 1$
11:         **if** Different$(f_1, p_1, f_2, p_2, \alpha)$ **then**
12:             **return** (different, $\frac{f_1}{f_1+p_1}, \frac{f_2}{f_2+p_2}$)
13:         $i \leftarrow (i \mod 2) + 1$
    return (similarly safe, $\frac{f_1}{f_1+p_1}, \frac{f_2}{f_2+p_2}$)

for an action-observation pair. In this case, we move to the state that is closest in the abstract observation space. This is implemented by Lines 9 to 12.

After reaching the coverage goal, we execute the RL policy under test for tl steps (Lines 14 to 18). If the RL policy visits an unsafe state, it **fails** the test-case run, otherwise it **passes**.

Algorithm 2 provides the pseudo-code for test-case execution. The algorithm performs up to m test-case runs and records the corresponding conclusive verdicts (Lines 4 to 10). In Line 11, we test for a difference between the fail frequencies, i.e., the relative safety of the tested policies. If we detect a difference, we stop early and return the ratio of failing test cases. In Line 13, we switch the policy under test to balance the data we have for both policies. We return that both policies are similarly safe and the test fail ratio if we do not detect a difference given our testing budget.

Various tests may be used to check for differences between safety-violation frequencies. We apply Fisher's exact test [11] since it requires very few assumptions and is applicable with little data. The latter may be relevant if learned abstract models are inaccurate so that many test-case runs are inconclusive.

5 Experiments

We evaluate our proposed approach by differential testing of deep RL policies trained to complete levels of the Nintendo game Super Mario Bros. (SMB). Our implementation can be found at https://github.com/mtappler/dlbt-smb-rl.

5.1 Setup

Environment and RL Policies Under Test. As SUTs, we use deep RL policies that we trained in previous work in the `gym-super-mario-bros` environment [19]. We perform experiments with policies that solve Level 1-1 and Level 1-4 of SMB. For each level, we compare agents trained with the double Deep Q-Network algorithm (DDQ) [14] to an agent trained with Deep Q-learning from demonstrations (DQfD) [15]. We test DDQ policies trained for 20000 and 30000 episodes and a DQfD policy trained with a lower sampling budget of 15000 episodes to account for the potential performance improvements resulting from 50 expert demonstrations that were used in DQfD training. We have chosen the first and the fourth level of the game, as they are relatively easy, such that DDQ agents without help from expert demonstrations manage to complete them.

Table 1. Average undiscounted cumulative reward gained by different policies and the respective standard deviation.

Level	DDQ (20k)	DDQ (30k)	DQfD (15k)
1-1	1162.33 ± 653.526	1097.58 ± 628.729	1164.89 ± 638.112
1-4	1635.32 ± 554.84	1500.71 ± 535.035	1430.86 ± 515.796

Configuration of Automata Learning. To gather data for automata learning, we performed $n_{al} = 800$ episodes with the RL policies under test in each of the levels. We implemented the automata learning part using AALpy [29] and left the ϵ parameter of IOAlergia at its default value of 0.05.

Testing. For each level, we define six test-case specifications $\langle T, tl, m, \alpha \rangle$. We uniformly set the test length tl to 20, since this is approximately the number of interactions necessary to avoid an obstacle or an adversary. We set $m = 5000$ and $\alpha = 0.05$ in all test-case specifications to define a reasonable testing budget, while achieving some confidence in the testing results.

5.2 Results

In the following, we first present evaluation results in terms of the cumulative reward gained from executing the RL policies under test in the SMB environment. Then, we present safety testing results and put them in contrast to the evaluation results. That is, we check how well the policies solve the task for which they are trained and whether this kind of performance translates to safe behavior. In other words, we check how the policies perform overall and how they act near safety-critical states that we cover with testing.

Performance Evaluation. To evaluate the overall performance of policies, we executed 100 episodes with each policy in its respective level. For every execution, we record the non-discounted cumulative reward. Table 1 shows the average cumulative reward and the standard deviation from our evaluation.

We can see that the DDQ and DQfD policies achieve similar levels of rewards. Note that the rewards across different levels change, due to varying difficulty and length. In Level 1-1, extended training from $20k$ episodes to $30k$ episodes actually hurts performance. The neural network potentially overfits to some features of the environments, thus we will analyze if safety is negatively affected as well. It is noteworthy that the DDQ policies perform better than the DQfD policy in Level 1-4.[2] We will analyze whether this translates to increased safety in this level as well.

Safety Testing Results. For each of the four pairs of a DDQ policy and a DQfD policy, we present safety testing results with tables and plots. The first results column of each table contains the number of conclusive test-case runs and the number of total test-case runs. If the latter is lower than $m = 5000$, this means test-case execution stopped early due to detecting a significant difference in safety. The other columns contain the relative fail frequency of the respective RL policy under test, i.e., the ratio of safety violations to the number of test-case runs. Additionally, we plot the relative fail frequencies for each test case as well as the 95% confidence intervals of these fail frequencies.

Table 2. Results from differential safety testing of the RL policies trained on Level 1-1 including the number of executed test-case runs.

TC	Test-Case Runs	DQfD	DDQ
TC 1	77 of 77	0.184	0.026
TC 2	2360 of 5000	0.001	0.002
TC 3	71 of 617	0.229	0.056
TC 4	297 of 4813	0.588	0.470
TC 5	15 of 124	0.571	0.000
TC 6	703 of 5000	0.689	0.665

(a) Comparison of the DDQ policy trained for 20k episodes and the DQfD policy.

TC	Test-Case Runs	DQfD	DDQ
TC 1	33 of 33	0.250	0.000
TC 2	2501 of 5000	0.002	0.002
TC 3	496 of 5000	0.137	0.157
TC 4	25 of 387	0.750	0.308
TC 5	15 of 195	0.571	0.000
TC 6	13 of 83	0.333	1.000

(b) Comparison of the DDQ policy trained for 30k episodes and the DQfD policy.

Level 1-1. Table 2 and Fig. 3 show the results from testing RL policies trained to complete Level 1-1. We can see that safety testing found issues, with fail frequencies of up to 1.0.

The comparison between the 20k-episode DDQ policy and the DQfD policy in Table 2a suggests that safety testing is useful in choosing a policy for deployment. We can see in the table that the DDQ policy was either deemed significantly safer (TC 1, TC 3, TC 4, and TC 5) or similarly safe (TC 2 and TC 6). Since both policies achieve similarly high cumulative rewards according to Table 1, the DDQ policy should be preferred.

Next, we want to put the comparison involving the 30k-episode DDQ policy in contrast to the first comparison. We can see that the 30k-episode DDQ policy is less safe than the 20k-episode DDQ policy, as expected from the lower cumulative reward reported in Table 1. The comparison results with respect to DQfD changed in the test cases TC 3 and TC 6. In TC 3, the 30k-episode policy is only

[2] We made the same observation in previous, yet unpublished work.

as safe as the DQfD policy, and in TC 6, the 30k-episode policy is significantly less safe than the DQfD policy. In the latter, it even failed all test-case runs.

Aside from the observations regarding safety, we can see that our derived testing policies decrease in effectiveness. The test cases are ordered in ascending number of environment interactions required to reach the coverage goal. For this reason, test-case runs for TC 6 result in more inconclusive verdicts than runs for TC 1. This happens because the policies derived from learned MDPs do not always reach the target states of TC 6. However, the learned MDPs still proved useful as they conveniently enable generating policies for reaching any abstract state without the need for additional sampling or further learning. The testing budget was also sufficient. For example, we got 703 conclusive verdicts for TC 6 in the comparison involving the 20k-episode DDQ policy, resulting in relatively narrow confidence intervals in Fig. 3a.

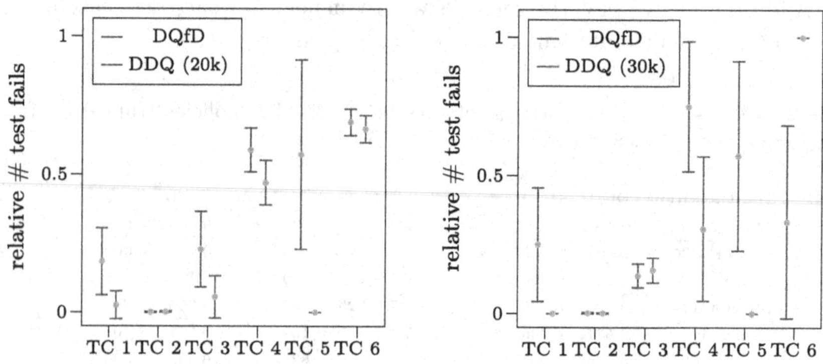

(a) Comparison of the DDQ policy trained for 20k episodes and the DQfD policy.

(b) Comparison of the DDQ policy trained for 30k episodes and the DQfD policy.

Fig. 3. Plots of the relative fail frequency observed in safety testing and the 95% confidence intervals for the RL policies trained on Level 1-1.

Level 1-4. Table 3 and Fig. 4 show the test results for agents trained to complete Level 1-4. We can see that none of the agents is strictly safer than the others. However, we can also see that a higher reward in the evaluation does not imply safer behavior. Comparing the DQfD policy to the DDQ policy trained for 20k episodes, Table 3 shows that the DQfD policy was deemed significantly safer in the states covered by the test cases TC 2 and TC 5, even though the DDQ policy achieves higher reward according to Table 1. However, the safety gap is relatively small, as can be seen in Fig. 4a. In all other cases, the DDQ policy is significantly safer or similarly safe – TC 5 reaches 5000 test-case runs including 1092 conclusive runs without reaching a decision. Contrasting these results to the results from testing against the DDQ policy trained for 30k episodes reveals

Table 3. Results from differential safety testing of the RL policies trained on Level 1-4 including the number of executed test-case runs.

TC	Test-Case Runs	DQfD	DDQ
TC 1	365 of 365	0.678	0.571
TC 2	2431 of 2669	0.030	0.045
TC 3	35 of 106	0.611	0.235
TC 4	1092 of 5000	0.106	0.082
TC 5	689 of 2941	0.200	0.265
TC 6	19 of 195	0.500	0.000

(a) Comparison of the DDQ policy trained for 20k episodes and the DQfD policy.

TC	Test-Case Runs	DQfD	DDQ
TC 1	57 of 57	0.643	0.897
TC 2	987 of 1082	0.030	0.059
TC 3	25 of 66	0.833	0.385
TC 4	787 of 3391	0.122	0.175
TC 5	1188 of 5000	0.227	0.202
TC 6	151 of 1438	0.413	0.250

(b) Comparison of the DDQ policy trained for 30k episodes and the DQfD policy.

an interesting finding, though. The DDQ policy trained for 30k episodes showed less safe behavior, despite achieving even higher rewards in the evaluation. In fact, it was found to be significantly less safe than the DQfD policy in three cases (TC 1, TC 2, and TC 4), and similarly safe in one case (TC 5). Hence, increased training for 10k more episodes worsened safety. This becomes even more apparent when we compare the fail frequencies and confidence intervals plotted in Fig. 4 for both DDQ policies. For example, the 20k-episode DDQ policy passed all test-case runs of TC 6, but the 30k-episode DDQ policy failed in 25% of the runs.

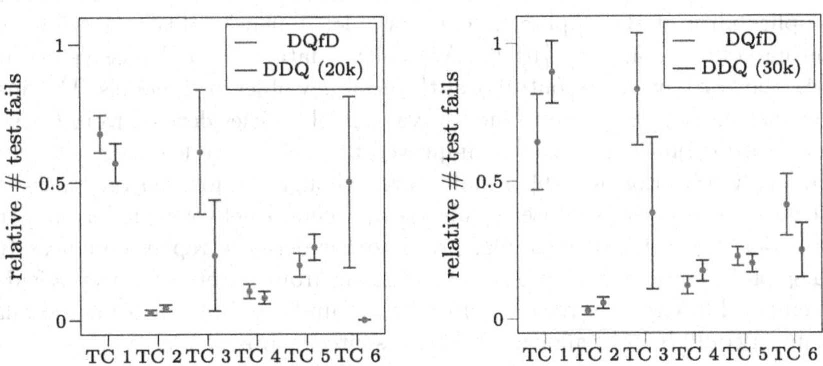

(a) Comparison of the DDQ policy trained for 20k episodes and the DQfD policy.

(b) Comparison of the DDQ policy trained for 30k episodes and the DQfD policy.

Fig. 4. Plots of the relative fail frequency observed in safety testing and the 95% confidence intervals for the RL policies trained on Level 1-4.

6 Conclusion

In this paper, we propose an approach to testing RL policies. For this purpose, we combine stochastic automata learning, probabilistic model checking, differential testing, and statistical tests. Via automata learning, we learn abstract environment models from data collected by executing the policies under test. Through probabilistic model-checking, we derive control policies that bring the agent into states that we want to cover by testing. Finally, we test pairs of policies by executing them from the specified states. This lets us compare policies w.r.t. safety by determining the frequency with which they enter unsafe states during testing. Statistical tests help us determine whether one of the policies is significantly safer in a tested situation.

We evaluate our approach in experiments with deep RL policies that have been trained to complete levels in the Nintendo game Super Mario Bros. We found that an agent achieving higher rewards is not necessarily safer. The DQfD policy trained on Level 1-4 was significantly safer in more situations than the DDQ policy trained for 30000 episodes, despite reaching lower rewards in an evaluation on the whole level. The DDQ policy trained for only 20000 episodes actually showed the safest behavior in testing on this level. Hence, it can be argued that *reward alone is not enough*. To evaluate RL policies, safety should be taken into account as well.

In this paper, we made a step toward the verification of deep RL agents. In future work, we will perform more experiments to validate our findings and we will extend the proposed approach, for which we see several possible avenues. To enable automata learning, we relied on domain knowledge to manually define an abstraction. Techniques that automatically generate abstractions would broaden the applicability of the approach. For example, dimensionality reduction and clustering could be applied [10,45]. We collect data once and passively learn models, thus we have little control over the accuracy of learned models. This may lead to inefficient testing due to ineffective control policies derived from learned models. Testing efficiency could be improved through active learning, where we control data collection [42,46]. Finally, even though we focused on black-box verification, it may make sense to analyze the neural networks underlying the policies that we test. For example, prioritized experience replay enhances RL training progress by giving priority to learning from experiences that yield a high temporal-difference error in neural network updates. Implementing a similar mechanism could help to allocate testing resources more effectively.

Acknowledgements. This work has been supported by the "University SAL Labs" initiative of Silicon Austria Labs (SAL) and its Austrian partner universities for applied fundamental research for electronic based systems.

References

1. Aarts, F., Kuppens, H., Tretmans, J., Vaandrager, F.W., Verwer, S.: Improving active Mealy machine learning for protocol conformance testing. Mach. Learn. **96**(1–2), 189–224 (2014). https://doi.org/10.1007/s10994-013-5405-0
2. Aichernig, B.K., Burghard, C., Korosec, R.: Learning-based testing of an industrial measurement device. In: Badger, J.M., Rozier, K.Y. (eds.) NASA Formal Methods - 11th International Symposium, NFM 2019, Houston, TX, USA, 7–9 May 2019,

Proceedings. LNCS, vol. 11460, pp. 1–18. Springer, Cham (2019). https://doi.org/10.1007/978-3-030-20652-9_1
3. Aichernig, B.K., Muskardin, E., Pferscher, A.: Learning-based fuzzing of IoT message brokers. In: 14th IEEE Conference on Software Testing, Verification and Validation, ICST 2021, Porto de Galinhas, Brazil, 12–16 April 2021, pp. 47–58. IEEE (2021). https://doi.org/10.1109/ICST49551.2021.00017
4. Aichernig, B.K., Tappler, M.: Probabilistic black-box reachability checking (extended version). Formal Methods Syst. Des. **54**(3), 416–448 (2019). https://doi.org/10.1007/s10703-019-00333-0
5. Alshiekh, M., Bloem, R., Ehlers, R., Könighofer, B., Niekum, S., Topcu, U.: Safe reinforcement learning via shielding. In: McIlraith, S.A., Weinberger, K.Q. (eds.) Proceedings of the Thirty-Second AAAI Conference on Artificial Intelligence, (AAAI-2018), the 30th innovative Applications of Artificial Intelligence (IAAI-2018), and the 8th AAAI Symposium on Educational Advances in Artificial Intelligence (EAAI-2018), New Orleans, Louisiana, USA, 2–7 February 2018, pp. 2669–2678. AAAI Press (2018). https://www.aaai.org/ocs/index.php/AAAI/AAAI18/paper/view/17211
6. Biagiola, M., Tonella, P.: Testing of deep reinforcement learning agents with surrogate models. CoRR abs/2305.12751 (2023). https://doi.org/10.48550/arXiv.2305.12751
7. Bloem, R., Könighofer, B., Könighofer, R., Wang, C.: Shield synthesis: - runtime enforcement for reactive systems. In: Baier, C., Tinelli, C. (eds.) Tools and Algorithms for the Construction and Analysis of Systems - 21st International Conference, TACAS 2015, Held as Part of the European Joint Conferences on Theory and Practice of Software, ETAPS 2015, London, UK, 11–18 April 2015, Proceedings. LNCS, vol. 9035, pp. 533–548. Springer, Cham (2015). https://doi.org/10.1007/978-3-662-46681-0_51
8. Carrasco, R.C., Oncina, J.: Learning stochastic regular grammars by means of a state merging method. In: Carrasco, R.C., Oncina, J. (eds.) ICGI 1994, vol. 862, pp. 139–152. Springer, Cham (1994). https://doi.org/10.1007/3-540-58473-0_144
9. Dehnert, C., Junges, S., Katoen, J., Volk, M.: A storm is coming: a modern probabilistic model checker. In: Majumdar, R., Kuncak, V. (eds.) Computer Aided Verification - 29th International Conference, CAV 2017, Heidelberg, Germany, 24–28 July 2017, Proceedings, Part II. LNCS, vol. 10427, pp. 592–600. Springer, Cham (2017). https://doi.org/10.1007/978-3-319-63390-9_31
10. Dong, G., et al.: Towards interpreting recurrent neural networks through probabilistic abstraction. In: 35th IEEE/ACM International Conference on Automated Software Engineering, ASE 2020, Melbourne, Australia, 21–25 September 2020, pp. 499–510. IEEE (2020). https://doi.org/10.1145/3324884.3416592
11. Fisher, R.A.: Statistical Methods for Research Workers. Edinburgh Oliver & Boyd, Edinburgh (1925)
12. Gaon, M., Brafman, R.I.: Reinforcement learning with non-Markovian rewards. In: The Thirty-Fourth AAAI Conference on Artificial Intelligence, AAAI 2020, The Thirty-Second Innovative Applications of Artificial Intelligence Conference, IAAI 2020, The Tenth AAAI Symposium on Educational Advances in Artificial Intelligence, EAAI 2020, New York, NY, USA, 7–12 February 2020, pp. 3980–3987. AAAI Press (2020). https://ojs.aaai.org/index.php/AAAI/article/view/5814
13. Hasanbeig, M., Jeppu, N.Y., Abate, A., Melham, T., Kroening, D.: DeepSynth: automata synthesis for automatic task segmentation in deep reinforcement learning. In: Thirty-Fifth AAAI Conference on Artificial Intelligence, AAAI 2021,

Thirty-Third Conference on Innovative Applications of Artificial Intelligence, IAAI 2021, The Eleventh Symposium on Educational Advances in Artificial Intelligence, EAAI 2021, Virtual Event, 2–9 February 2021, pp. 7647–7656. AAAI Press (2021). https://ojs.aaai.org/index.php/AAAI/article/view/16935

14. van Hasselt, H., Guez, A., Silver, D.: Deep reinforcement learning with double Q-learning. In: Proceedings of the Thirtieth AAAI Conference on Artificial Intelligence, 12–17 February 2016, Phoenix, Arizona, USA, pp. 2094–2100. AAAI Press (2016). http://www.aaai.org/ocs/index.php/AAAI/AAAI16/paper/view/12389
15. Hester, T., et al.: Deep Q-learning from demonstrations. In: Proceedings of the Thirty-Second AAAI Conference on Artificial Intelligence, (AAAI-2018), the 30th innovative Applications of Artificial Intelligence (IAAI-2018), and the 8th AAAI Symposium on Educational Advances in Artificial Intelligence (EAAI-2018), New Orleans, Louisiana, USA, 2–7 February 2018, pp. 3223–3230. AAAI Press (2018). https://www.aaai.org/ocs/index.php/AAAI/AAAI18/paper/view/16976
16. Hoeffding, W.: Probability inequalities for sums of bounded random variables. J. Am. Stat. Assoc. **58**(301), 13–30 (1963). https://doi.org/10.2307/2282952, http://www.jstor.org/stable/2282952
17. Icarte, R.T., Waldie, E., Klassen, T.Q., Valenzano, R.A., Castro, M.P., McIlraith, S.A.: Learning reward machines for partially observable reinforcement learning. In: Wallach, H.M., Larochelle, H., Beygelzimer, A., d'Alché-Buc, F., Fox, E.B., Garnett, R. (eds.) Advances in Neural Information Processing Systems: Annual Conference on Neural Information Processing Systems 2019, NeurIPS 2019, 8–14 December 2019, Vancouver, BC, Canada, vol. 32, pp. 15497–15508 (2019)
18. Jansen, N., Könighofer, B., Junges, S., Serban, A., Bloem, R.: Safe reinforcement learning using probabilistic shields (invited paper). In: Konnov, I., Kovács, L. (eds.) 31st International Conference on Concurrency Theory, CONCUR 2020, 1–4 September 2020, Vienna, Austria (Virtual Conference). LIPIcs, vol. 171, pp. 3:1–3:16. Schloss Dagstuhl - Leibniz-Zentrum für Informatik (2020). https://doi.org/10.4230/LIPIcs.CONCUR.2020.3
19. Kauten, C.: Super Mario Bros for OpenAI Gym. GitHub (2018). https://github.com/Kautenja/gym-super-mario-bros
20. Könighofer, B., et al.: Shield synthesis. Formal Methods Syst. Des. **51**(2), 332–361 (2017). https://doi.org/10.1007/s10703-017-0276-9
21. Könighofer, B., Lorber, F., Jansen, N., Bloem, R.: Shield synthesis for reinforcement learning. In: Margaria, T., Steffen, B. (eds.) Leveraging Applications of Formal Methods, Verification and Validation: Verification Principles - 9th International Symposium on Leveraging Applications of Formal Methods, ISoLA 2020, Rhodes, Greece, 20–30 October 2020, Proceedings, Part I. LNCS, vol. 12476, pp. 290–306. Springer, Cham (2020). https://doi.org/10.1007/978-3-030-61362-4_16
22. Könighofer, B., Rudolf, J., Palmisano, A., Tappler, M., Bloem, R.: Online shielding for stochastic systems. In: Dutle, A., Moscato, M.M., Titolo, L., Muñoz, C.A., Perez, I. (eds.) NASA Formal Methods - 13th International Symposium, NFM 2021, Virtual Event, 24–28 May 2021, Proceedings. LNCS, vol. 12673, pp. 231–248. Springer, Cham (2021). https://doi.org/10.1007/978-3-030-76384-8_15
23. Kwiatkowska, M.Z., Norman, G., Parker, D.: PRISM 4.0: verification of probabilistic real-time systems. In: Gopalakrishnan, G., Qadeer, S. (eds.) Computer Aided Verification - 23rd International Conference, CAV 2011, Snowbird, UT, USA, 14–20 July 2011, Proceedings. LNCS, vol. 6806, pp. 585–591. Springer, Cham (2011). https://doi.org/10.1007/978-3-642-22110-1_47

24. Lu, Y., Sun, W., Sun, M.: Towards mutation testing of reinforcement learning systems. J. Syst. Archit. **131**, 102701 (2022). https://doi.org/10.1016/j.sysarc.2022.102701
25. Mao, H., Chen, Y., Jaeger, M., Nielsen, T.D., Larsen, K.G., Nielsen, B.: Learning Markov decision processes for model checking. In: Fahrenberg, U., Legay, A., Thrane, C.R. (eds.) Proceedings Quantities in Formal Methods, QFM 2012, Paris, France, 28 August 2012, EPTCS, vol. 103, pp. 49–63 (2012). https://doi.org/10.4204/EPTCS.103.6
26. Mao, H., Chen, Y., Jaeger, M., Nielsen, T.D., Larsen, K.G., Nielsen, B.: Learning deterministic probabilistic automata from a model checking perspective. Mach. Learn. **105**(2), 255–299 (2016). https://doi.org/10.1007/s10994-016-5565-9
27. Mnih, V., et al.: Human-level control through deep reinforcement learning. Nature **518**(7540), 529–533 (2015). https://doi.org/10.1038/nature14236
28. Mohri, M., Rostamizadeh, A., Talwalkar, A.: Foundations of Machine Learning. The MIT Press, Cambridge (2012)
29. Muskardin, E., Aichernig, B.K., Pill, I., Pferscher, A., Tappler, M.: AALpy: an active automata learning library. Innov. Syst. Softw. Eng. **18**(3), 417–426 (2022). https://doi.org/10.1007/s11334-022-00449-3
30. Muskardin, E., Tappler, M., Aichernig, B.K., Pill, I.: Reinforcement learning under partial observability guided by learned environment models. CoRR abs/2206.11708 (2022). https://doi.org/10.48550/arXiv.2206.11708
31. Peled, D.A., Vardi, M.Y., Yannakakis, M.: Black box checking. J. Autom. Lang. Comb. **7**(2), 225–246 (2002). https://doi.org/10.25596/jalc-2002-225
32. Pferscher, A., Aichernig, B.K.: Stateful black-box fuzzing of bluetooth devices using automata learning. In: Deshmukh, J.V., Havelund, K., Perez, I. (eds.) NASA Formal Methods - 14th International Symposium, NFM 2022, Pasadena, CA, USA, 24–27 May 2022, Proceedings. LNCS, vol. 13260, pp. 373–392. Springer, Cham (2022). https://doi.org/10.1007/978-3-031-06773-0_20
33. Pranger, S., Könighofer, B., Tappler, M., Deixelberger, M., Jansen, N., Bloem, R.: Adaptive shielding under uncertainty. In: 2021 American Control Conference, ACC 2021, New Orleans, LA, USA, 25–28 May 2021, pp. 3467–3474. IEEE (2021). https://doi.org/10.23919/ACC50511.2021.9482889
34. Ronca, A., Licks, G.P., Giacomo, G.D.: Markov abstractions for PAC reinforcement learning in non-Markov decision processes. In: Raedt, L.D. (ed.) Proceedings of the Thirty-First International Joint Conference on Artificial Intelligence, IJCAI 2022, Vienna, Austria, 23–29 July 2022, pp. 3408–3415. ijcai.org (2022). https://doi.org/10.24963/ijcai.2022/473
35. de Ruiter, J., Poll, E.: Protocol state fuzzing of TLS implementations. In: Jung, J., Holz, T. (eds.) 24th USENIX Security Symposium, USENIX Security 2015, Washington, D.C., USA, 12–14 August 2015, pp. 193–206. USENIX Association (2015). https://www.usenix.org/conference/usenixsecurity15/technical-sessions/presentation/de-ruiter
36. Schulman, J., Wolski, F., Dhariwal, P., Radford, A., Klimov, O.: Proximal policy optimization algorithms. CoRR abs/1707.06347 (2017). http://arxiv.org/abs/1707.06347
37. Silver, D., et al.: Mastering the game of Go with deep neural networks and tree search. Nature **529**(7587), 484–489 (2016). https://doi.org/10.1038/nature16961
38. Silver, D., et al.: Mastering chess and shogi by self-play with a general reinforcement learning algorithm. CoRR abs/1712.01815 (2017). http://arxiv.org/abs/1712.01815

39. Sivakorn, S., Argyros, G., Pei, K., Keromytis, A.D., Jana, S.: HVLearn: automated black-box analysis of hostname verification in SSL/TLS implementations. In: 2017 IEEE Symposium on Security and Privacy, SP 2017, San Jose, CA, USA, 22–26 May 2017, pp. 521–538. IEEE Computer Society (2017). https://doi.org/10.1109/SP.2017.46
40. Smeenk, W., Moerman, J., Vaandrager, F.W., Jansen, D.N.: Applying automata learning to embedded control software. In: Butler, M.J., Conchon, S., Zaïdi, F. (eds.) Formal Methods and Software Engineering - 17th International Conference on Formal Engineering Methods, ICFEM 2015, Paris, France, 3–5 November 2015, Proceedings. LNCS, vol. 9407, pp. 67–83. Springer, Cham (2015). https://doi.org/10.1007/978-3-319-25423-4_5
41. Sutton, R.S., Barto, A.G.: Reinforcement Learning - An Introduction. Adaptive Computation and Machine Learning. MIT Press, Cambridge (1998). https://www.worldcat.org/oclc/37293240
42. Tappler, M., Aichernig, B.K., Bacci, G., Eichlseder, M., Larsen, K.G.: l^*-based learning of Markov decision processes (extended version). Formal Aspects Comput. **33**(4–5), 575–615 (2021). https://doi.org/10.1007/s00165-021-00536-5
43. Tappler, M., Aichernig, B.K., Bloem, R.: Model-based testing IoT communication via active automata learning. In: 2017 IEEE International Conference on Software Testing, Verification and Validation, ICST 2017, Tokyo, Japan, 13–17 March 2017, pp. 276–287 (2017). https://doi.org/10.1109/ICST.2017.32
44. Tappler, M., Córdoba, F.C., Aichernig, B.K., Könighofer, B.: Search-based testing of reinforcement learning. In: Raedt, L.D. (ed.) Proceedings of the Thirty-First International Joint Conference on Artificial Intelligence, IJCAI 2022, Vienna, Austria, 23–29 July 2022, pp. 503–510. ijcai.org (2022). https://doi.org/10.24963/ijcai.2022/72
45. Tappler, M., Muskardin, E., Aichernig, B.K., Könighofer, B.: Learning environment models with continuous stochastic dynamics. CoRR abs/2306.17204 (2023). https://doi.org/10.48550/arXiv.2306.17204
46. Tappler, M., Muskardin, E., Aichernig, B.K., Pill, I.: Active model learning of stochastic reactive systems. In: Calinescu, R., Pasareanu, C.S. (eds.) Software Engineering and Formal Methods - 19th International Conference, SEFM 2021, Virtual Event, December 6–10, 2021, Proceedings. LNCS, vol. 13085, pp. 481–500. Springer, Cham (2021). https://doi.org/10.1007/978-3-030-92124-8_27
47. Tappler, M., Pranger, S., Könighofer, B., Muskardin, E., Bloem, R., Larsen, K.G.: Automata learning meets shielding. In: Margaria, T., Steffen, B. (eds.) Leveraging Applications of Formal Methods, Verification and Validation. Verification Principles - 11th International Symposium, ISoLA 2022, Rhodes, Greece, 22–30 October 2022, Proceedings, Part I. LNCS, vol. 13701, pp. 335–359. Springer, Cham (2022). https://doi.org/10.1007/978-3-031-19849-6_20
48. Tian, Y., Pei, K., Jana, S., Ray, B.: DeepTest: automated testing of deep-neural-network-driven autonomous cars. In: Chaudron, M., Crnkovic, I., Chechik, M., Harman, M. (eds.) Proceedings of the 40th International Conference on Software Engineering, ICSE 2018, Gothenburg, Sweden, 27 May–3 June 2018, pp. 303–314. ACM (2018). https://doi.org/10.1145/3180155.3180220
49. Utting, M., Pretschner, A., Legeard, B.: A taxonomy of model-based testing approaches. Softw. Test. Verification Reliab. **22**(5), 297–312 (2012). https://doi.org/10.1002/stvr.456
50. Valiant, L.G.: A theory of the learnable. Commun. ACM **27**(11), 1134–1142 (1984). https://doi.org/10.1145/1968.1972

51. Vinyals, O., et al.: Grandmaster level in StarCraft II using multi-agent reinforcement learning. Nature **575**(7782), 350–354 (2019). https://doi.org/10.1038/s41586-019-1724-z
52. Wang, J., Sun, J., Jia, Y., Qin, S., Xu, Z.: Towards 'verifying' a water treatment system. In: Havelund, K., Peleska, J., Roscoe, B., de Vink, E.P. (eds.) Formal Methods - 22nd International Symposium, FM 2018, Held as Part of the Federated Logic Conference, FloC 2018, Oxford, UK, 15–17 July 2018, Proceedings. LNCS, vol. 10951, pp. 73–92. Springer, Cham (2018). https://doi.org/10.1007/978-3-319-95582-7_5
53. Watkins, C.J.C.H., Dayan, P.: Technical note Q-learning. Mach. Learn. **8**, 279–292 (1992). https://doi.org/10.1007/BF00992698
54. Xie, X., et al.: DeepHunter: a coverage-guided fuzz testing framework for deep neural networks. In: Zhang, D., Møller, A. (eds.) Proceedings of the 28th ACM SIGSOFT International Symposium on Software Testing and Analysis, ISSTA 2019, Beijing, China, 15–19 July 2019, pp. 146–157. ACM (2019). https://doi.org/10.1145/3293882.3330579
55. Xu, Z., et al.: Joint inference of reward machines and policies for reinforcement learning. In: Proceedings of the Thirtieth International Conference on Automated Planning and Scheduling, Nancy, France, 26–30 October 2020, pp. 590–598. AAAI Press (2020). https://ojs.aaai.org/index.php/ICAPS/article/view/6756
56. Zolfagharian, A., Abdellatif, M., Briand, L.C., Bagherzadeh, M., Ramesh, S.: Search-based testing approach for deep reinforcement learning agents. CoRR abs/2206.07813 (2022). https://doi.org/10.48550/arXiv.2206.07813

gRoMA: A Tool for Measuring the Global Robustness of Deep Neural Networks

Natan Levy[1(✉)], Raz Yerushalmi[1,2], and Guy Katz[1]

[1] The Hebrew University of Jerusalem, Jerusalem, Israel
{natan.levy1,gkatz}@mail.huji.ac.il
[2] The Weizmann Institute of Science, Rehovot, Israel
raz.yerushalmi@weizmann.ac.il

Abstract. Deep neural networks (DNNs) are at the forefront of cutting-edge technology, and have been achieving remarkable performance in a variety of complex tasks. Nevertheless, their integration into safety-critical systems, such as in the aerospace or automotive domains, poses a significant challenge due to the threat of *adversarial inputs*: perturbations in inputs that might cause the DNN to make grievous mistakes. Multiple studies have demonstrated that even modern DNNs are susceptible to adversarial inputs, and this risk must thus be measured and mitigated to allow the deployment of DNNs in critical settings. Here, we present gRoMA (global Robustness Measurement and Assessment), an innovative and scalable tool that implements a probabilistic approach to measure the global categorial robustness of a DNN. Specifically, gRoMA measures the probability of encountering adversarial inputs for a specific output category. Our tool operates on pre-trained, black-box classification DNNs, and generates input samples belonging to an output category of interest. It measures the DNN's susceptibility to adversarial inputs around these inputs, and aggregates the results to infer the overall global categorial robustness of the DNN up to some small bounded statistical error. We evaluate our tool on the popular Densenet DNN model over the CIFAR10 dataset. Our results reveal significant gaps in the robustness of the different output categories. This experiment demonstrates the usefulness and scalability of our approach and its potential for allowing DNNs to be deployed within critical systems of interest.

Keywords: Global Robustness · Deep Neural Networks · Adversarial Examples · Categorial Robustness · Regulation · Safety Critical

1 Introduction

Deep neural networks (DNNs) have become fundamental components in many applications that perform classification [2,25]. Empirically, DNNs often outperform traditional software, and even humans [35,40]. Nevertheless, DNNs have a significant drawback: they are notoriously susceptible to small input perturbations, called *adversarial inputs* [15], which can cause them to produce erroneous

B. Steffen (Ed.): AISoLA 2023, LNCS 14380, pp. 160–170, 2024.
https://doi.org/10.1007/978-3-031-46002-9_9

outputs. These adversarial inputs are one of the causes likely to delay the adoption of DNNs in safety-critical domains, such as aerospace [14], autonomous vehicles [26], and medical devices [17].

In the aforementioned critical domains, systems must meet high dependability standards. While strict guidelines exist for certifying that hand-crafted software meets these standards (e.g., the DO-178 standard [13] in the aerospace industry), no such certification guidelines currently exist for systems incorporating DNNs. Several regulatory agencies have recognized the existence of this gap and the importance of addressing it. For example, in its recently published roadmap, the European Union Aviation Safety Administration (EASA) has emphasized the importance of DNN robustness as one of the 7 key requirements for trustworthy artificial intelligence [12]. However, certifying the robustness of DNNs remains an open problem.

The formal methods community has begun addressing this gap by devising methods for rigorously quantifying the *local robustness* of a DNN [21,37,42]. Local robustness refers to a DNN's ability to withstand adversarial inputs in the vicinity of a specific point within the input space. Although the rigorous verification approaches proposed to date have had some success in measuring these robustness scores, they typically struggle to scale as network sizes increase [21] — which limits their practical application. To circumvent that limitation, *approximate* methods have been proposed, which can evaluate DNN robustness more efficiently, but often at the cost of reduced precision [4,11,19,31,36].

Work to date, both on rigorous and on approximate methods, has focused almost exclusively on measuring *local* robustness, which quantifies the DNN's robustness around individual input points within a multi-dimensional, infinite input space. In the context of DNN certification, however, a broader perspective is required — one that measures the *global robustness* of the DNN, over the entire input space, rather than on specific points.

In this paper, we propose a novel approach for approximating the global robustness of a DNN. Our method is computationally efficient, scalable, and can handle various types of adversarial attacks and black-box DNNs. Unlike existing approximate approaches, our approach provides statistical guarantees about the precision of the computed robustness score.

More concretely, our approach (implemented in the gRoMA tool) implements a probabilistic verification approach for performing global robustness measurement and assessment on DNNs. gRoMA achieves this by measuring the *probabilistic global categorial robustness* (*PGCR*) of a given DNN. In this study, we take a conservative approach and consider the DNN as a black-box: gRoMA makes no assumptions, e.g., about the Lipschitz continuity of the DNN, the kinds of activation functions, the hyperparameters it uses, or its internal topology. Instead, gRoMA uses and extends the recently proposed RoMA (*a Method for DNN Robustness Measurement and Assessment*) algorithm [29] for measuring local robustness. gRoMA repeatedly invokes this algorithm on a collection of samples, drawn to represent a specific output category of interest; and then aggregates the results to compute a global robustness score for this category, across the entire input space. As a result, gRoMA is highly scalable, typically taking only a few minutes to run, even for large networks. Further, the tool formally computes an error bound for the estimated PGCR scores using Hoeffding's inequality [18] to mitigate the drawbacks of using a statistical method. Thus, gRoMA's results can be used in the certification process for components of safety-critical systems, following, e.g., the SAE Aerospace Recommended Practice [27].

For evaluation purposes, we focused on a Densenet DNN [20], trained on the CIFAR10 dataset [25]; and then measured the network's global robustness using one hundred arbitrary images for each CIFAR10 category. gRoMA successfully computed the global robustness scores for these categories, demonstrating, e.g., that the airplane category is significantly more robust than other categories.

To the best of our knowledge, our tool is presently the only scalable solution for accurately measuring the *global categorial robustness* of a DNN, i.e., the aggregated robustness of *all* points within the input space that belong to a category of interest — subject to the availability of a domain expert who can supply representative samples from each category. The availability of such tools could greatly assist regulatory authorities in assessing the suitability of DNNs for integration into safety-critical systems, and in comparing the performance of multiple candidate DNNs.

Outline. We begin with an overview of related work on measuring the local and global adversarial robustness of DNNs, in Sect. 2. In Sect. 3, we provide the necessary definitions for understanding our approach. We then introduce the gRoMA tool in Sect. 4. Next, in Sect. 5, we evaluate the performance of our tool using a popular dataset and DNN model. Finally, Sect. 6 concludes our work and discusses future research directions.

2 Related Work

Measuring the local adversarial robustness of DNNs has received significant attention in recent years. Two notable approaches for addressing it are:

- Formal-verification approaches [23,32,38], which utilize constraint solving and abstract interpretation techniques to determine a DNN's robustness. These approaches are fairly precise, but generally afford limited scalability, and are applicable only to white-box DNNs.
- Statistical approaches, which evaluate the probability of encountering adversarial inputs. These approaches often need to balance between scalability and accuracy, with prior work [4,11,19,31,36] typically leaning towards scalability.

Recently, the *RoMA* algorithm [29] has been introduced as highly scalability statistical method, but which can also provide rigorous guarantees on accuracy. RoMA is a simple-to-implement algorithm that evaluates local robustness by sampling around an input point of interest; measuring the confidence scores assigned by the DNN to *incorrect* labels on each of the sampled input points;

and then using this information to compute the probability of encountering an input on which the confidence score for the incorrect category will be high enough to result in misclassification. In the final step, RoMA assesses robustness using properties of the normal distribution function [29]. RoMA handles black-box DNNs, without any a priori assumptions; but it can only measure local, as opposed to global robustness.

Due to the limited usefulness of computing local robustness in modern DNNs, initial attempts have been made to compute the *global adversarial robustness* of networks. Prior work formulated and defined the concept of *global adversarial robustness* [21,31]; but in the same breath, noted that global robustness can be hard to check or compute compared to local robustness. More recently, there have been attempts to use formal verification to check global adversarial robustness [24,39,43]; but the reliance on formal verification makes it difficult for these approaches to scale, and requires a white-box DNN with specific activation functions.

Two other recently proposed approaches study an altered version of global robustness. The first work, by Ruan et al. [34], defines global robustness as the expected maximal safe radius around a test data set. It then proposes an approximate method for computing lower and upper bounds on DNN's robustness. The second work, by Zaitang et al. [41], redefines global robustness based on the probability density function, and uses generative models to assess it. These modified definitions of global robustness present an intriguing perspective. However, it is important to note that they differ from common definitions, and whether they will be widely adopted remains to be seen. Another noteworthy recent approach, proposed by Leino et al. [28], advocates for training DNNs that are certifiably robust by construction, assuming that the network is Lipschitz-continuous. This approach can guarantee the global robustness of a DNN without accurate measurements, but it requires the DNN to be white-box, whereas our approach is also compatible with black-box DNNs.

Our work here focuses on measuring and scoring the global robustness of pre-trained black-box DNNs and is the first, to the best of our knowledge, that is scalable and consistent with the commonly accepted definitions.

3 DNNs and Adversarial Robustness

Neural Networks. A DNN $N : \mathbb{R}^n \to \mathbb{R}^m$ is a function that maps input $\boldsymbol{x} \in \mathbb{R}^n$ to output $\boldsymbol{y} \in \mathbb{R}^m$. In classifier DNNs, which are our subject matter here, $\boldsymbol{y}$ is interpreted as a vector of confidence scores, one for each of m possible labels. We say that N classifies $\boldsymbol{x}$ as label l iff $\arg\max(\boldsymbol{y}) = l$, i.e., when y's l'th entry has the highest score. We use L to denote the set of all possible labels, $L = \{1, \ldots, m\}$.

Local Adversarial Robustness. The local adversarial robustness of N around input $\boldsymbol{x}$ is a measure of how sensitive N is to small perturbations around $\boldsymbol{x}$ [5]:

Definition 1. *A DNN N is ϵ-locally-robust at input point $\boldsymbol{x_0}$ iff*

$$\forall \boldsymbol{x}. \quad ||\boldsymbol{x} - \boldsymbol{x_0}||_\infty \leq \epsilon \Rightarrow \arg\max(N(\boldsymbol{x})) = \arg\max(N(\boldsymbol{x_0}))$$

Intuitively, Definition 1 states that the network assigns to $\boldsymbol{x}$ the same label that it assigns to $\boldsymbol{x_0}$, for input $\boldsymbol{x}$ that is within an ϵ-ball around $\boldsymbol{x_0}$. Larger values of ϵ imply a larger ball around $\boldsymbol{x_0}$, and consequently — higher robustness.

The main drawback in Definition 1 is that it considers a single input point in potentially vast input space. Thus, the ϵ-local-robustness of N at $\boldsymbol{x_0}$ does not imply that it is also robust around other points. Moreover, it assumes that DNN robustness is consistent across categories, although it has already been observed that some categories can be more robust than others [29]. To overcome these drawbacks, the notion of *global categorial robustness* has been proposed [22,34]:

Definition 2. *A DNN N is (ϵ, δ)-globally-robust in input region D iff*

$$\forall \boldsymbol{x_1}, \boldsymbol{x_2} \in D.$$

$$||\boldsymbol{x_1} - \boldsymbol{x_2}||_\infty \leq \epsilon \Rightarrow \forall l \in L. \ |N(\boldsymbol{x_1})[l] - N(\boldsymbol{x_2})[l]| < \delta$$

Intuitively, Definition 2 states that for every two inputs $\boldsymbol{x_1}$ and $\boldsymbol{x_2}$ that are at most ϵ apart, there are no spikes greater than δ in the confidence scores that the DNN assigns to each of the labels.

Definitions 1 and 2 are Boolean in nature: given ϵ and δ, the DNN is either robust or not robust. However, in real-world settings, safety-critical systems can still be determined to be sufficiently robust if the *likelihood* of encountering adversarial inputs is sufficiently low [27]. Moreover, it is sometimes more appropriate to measure robustness for specific output categories [29]. To address this, we propose to compute real-valued, *probabilistic global categorial robustness* scores:

Definition 3. *Let N be a DNN, let $l \in L$ be an output label, and let I be a finite set of labeled data representing the input space for N. The (ϵ, δ)-PGCR score for N with respect to l and I, denoted $pgcr_{\delta,\epsilon}(N, l, I)$, is defined as:*

$$pgcr_{\delta,\epsilon}(N, l, I) \triangleq P_{\boldsymbol{x_1} \in I, \boldsymbol{x_2} \in \mathbb{R}^n ||\boldsymbol{x_1} - \boldsymbol{x_2}||_\infty \leq \epsilon}[|N(\boldsymbol{x_1})[l] - N(\boldsymbol{x_2})[l]| < \delta]$$

Intuitively, the definition captures the probability that for an input $\boldsymbol{x_1}$ drawn from I, and for an additional input $\boldsymbol{x_2}$ that it is at most ϵ apart from $\boldsymbol{x_1}$, inputs $\boldsymbol{x_1}$ and $\boldsymbol{x_2}$ will be assigned confidence scores that differ by at most δ for the label l.

4 Introducing the gRoMA Tool

Algorithm. The high-level flow of gRoMA implements Definition 3 in a straightforward and efficient way: it first computes the local robustness for n representative points from each category, and then aggregates the global robustness using Algorithm 1.

The inputs to gRoMA are: (i) a network N; (ii) I, a finite set of labeled data that represents the input space, to draw samples from; (iii) a label l; (iv) n, the number of representative samples of inputs classified as l to use; and (v) ϵ and δ, which determine the allowed perturbation sizes and differences in confidence scores, as per Definition 3. gRoMA's output consists of the computed $pgcr_{\delta,\epsilon}(N, l, I)$ score and an error term e, both specific to l. We emphasize the reliance of the $pgcr_{\delta,\epsilon}$ score on having representative input samples for each relevant category l. Under that assumption, in which the samples represent the underlying input distribution, our method guarantees that, with some high, predefined probability, the distance of the computed $pgcr_{\delta,\epsilon}$ value from its true value is at most e.

Algorithm 1 gRoMA($N, I, l, n, \epsilon, \delta$)

```
1: X := drawSamples(I, l, n)
2: for i := 1 to n do
3:     if ( N(X[i]) = l ) then
4:         plr[i] := RoMA(X[i], ε, δ, N)
5:     end if
6: end for
7: pgcr := aggregate(plr)
8: e := computeError(pgcr, plr, X)
9: return (pgcr,e)
```

In line 1, gRoMA begins by creating a vector, $\boldsymbol{X}$, of perturbed inputs — by drawing from I, at random, n samples of inputs labeled as l. Next, for each correctly classified sample (line 3), gRoMA computes the sample's probabilistic local robustness (*plr*) score using RoMA [29] (line 4). Finally, gRoMA applies statistical aggregation (line 7) to compute the *pgcr* score and the error bound (line 8); and these two values are then returned on line 9.

gRoMA is modular in the sense that any aggregation method (line 7) and error computation method (line 8) can be used. There are several suitable techniques in the statistics literature for both tasks, a thorough discussion of which is beyond our scope here. We focus here on a few straightforward mechanisms for these tasks, which we describe next.

For score aggregation, we propose to use the numerical average of the local robustness scores computed for the individual input samples. Additional approaches include computing a median score and more complex methods, e.g., methods based on normal distribution properties [9], maximum likelihood methods, Bayesian computations, and others. For computing the PGCR score's probabilistic error bound, we propose to use Hoeffding's Inequality [18], which provides an upper bound on the likelihood that a predicted value will deviate from its expected value by more than some specified amount.

5 Evaluation

Implementation. We implemented gRoMA as a Tensorflow framework [1]. Internally, it uses Google Colab [7,8] tools with 12.7GB system RAM memory, and T4 GPU. It accepts DNNs in Keras H5 format [10], as its input. The gRoMA tool is relatively simple, and can be extended and customized to support, e.g., multiple input distributions of interest, various methods for computing aggregated robustness scores and probabilistic error bounds, and also to accept additional DNN input formats. gRoMA is available online [30].

Setup and Configuration. We conducted an evaluation of gRoMA on a commonly used Densenet model [20] with 797,788 parameters, trained on the CIFAR10 dataset [25]. The model achieved a test accuracy of 93.7% after a standard 200-epoch training period. The code for creating and training the model, as well as the H5 model file, are available online [30]

For gRoMA to operate properly, it is required to obtain a representative sample of the relevant input space I. Creating such a representative sample typically requires some domain-expert knowledge [16,33]. However, random sampling can often serve as an approximation for such sampling [16,33]; a more thorough discussion of that topic goes beyond the scope of this paper. In our experiments here, we used a simple sampling mechanism in order to demonstrate the use of gRoMA. We measured the global categorial robustness of each output category by running the *RoMA* algorithm [29], to calculate the local robustness of one hundred images drawn independently and arbitrarily from the set I, which includes varying angles, lighting conditions, and resolutions. We set ϵ to 0.04 and δ to 0.07, as recommended in that work [29].

Due to our desire to check the approach's applicability to the aerospace industry, we paid special attention to the airplane category. In this category, we focused on Airbus A320-200 commercial airplane images, either airborne or on the ground. This type of airplane exists in the CIFAR10 training set as well, and hence we expected a high level of categorial global robustness for this category. The images, along with our code and dependencies, are available online [30].

Next, for each output category, we used *RoMA* to compute the *probabilistic local robustness (plr)* score for each input sample. We configured gRoMA to use the numerical average as the aggregation method; and for assessing the error of gRoMA, we applied Hoeffding's inequality [18]. Specifically, we aimed for a maximum expected error value of 5%, which is an acceptable error value when calculating a DNN's robustness [19]. We used Hoeffding's inequality to calculate the probability that the actual error is higher than this value. This was achieved by setting the upper and lower bounds of the *plr* values to be plus and minus five standard deviations of the *plr* values, corresponding to a $1 - 1 * 10^{-6}$ accuracy, all in a normal distribution context. These bounds were selected in order to provide a conservative estimate, encompassing a significant portion of the input space. We justify the normal distribution assumption using Anderson-Darling goodness-of-fit test [3] that focuses on the tails of the distribution [6], as detailed in [29].

Results. Running our evaluation took less than 21 min for each category, using a Google Colab [7] machine. The various global robustness scores for each category, as well as the calculated probabilistic error, appear in Fig. 1.

In the evaluation, the Airplane category obtained, as expected while focusing on a specific type of airplane, the highest categorial robustness score of 99.91% among all categories; while the Cat and Ship categories obtained the lowest score of 99.52% (the PGCR scores appear in blue in Fig. 1). The statistical error margin (tolerance) was set to 5% for this study. Based on these setting, the Ship category had the highest probability to exceed this bound, at less than 0.16%. On the other hand, the Airplane, Automotive, Bird, Dog, and Frog categories had the lowest error likelihood, all below 0.0005% (the likelihood scores per category scores appear in yellow in Fig. 1).

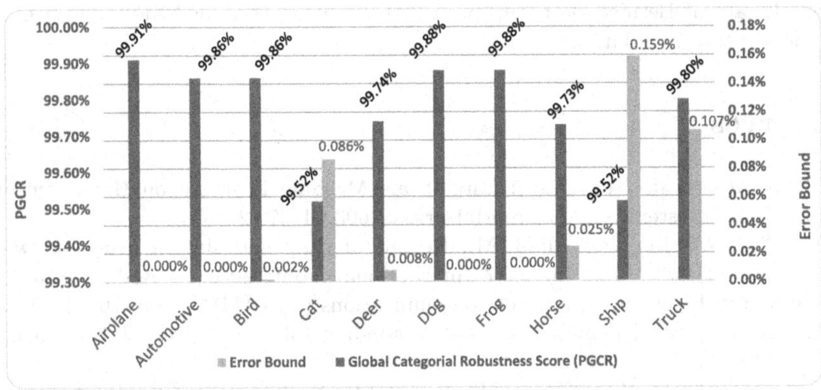

Fig. 1. PGCR scores, per category, for all CIFAR10 categories (blue); and the corresponding statistical errors (yellow). (Color figure online)

The PGCR scores calculated are aligned with previous research, that already assessed the local robustness of all the images in the CIFAR10 test set, and which indicate that different categories may obtain different robustness scores [29].

6 Conclusion and Future Work

We introduced here the notion of PGCR and presented the gRoMA tool for probabilistically measuring the global categorial robustness of DNNs, e.g., calculating the $pgcr_{\epsilon,\delta}$ score — which is a step towards formalizing DNN safety and reliability for use in safety-critical applications. Furthermore, we calculate a bound on the statistical error inherent to using a statistical tool. The main contribution of this work is developing a scalable tool for probabilistically measuring categorial global DNN robustness.

Although extensive research has focused on DNN local adversarial robustness, we are not aware of any other scalable tool that can measure the global categorial robustness of a DNN. Therefore, we believe that our tool provides a valuable contribution to the research community.

In future work, we plan to test the accuracy of gRoMA using a range of input distributions and sampling methods, simulating various input spaces used in different applications. Additionally, we intend to extend our tool to other types of DNNs, such as regression networks, to broaden PGCR's applicability. These efforts will enhance our understanding of DNN robustness and facilitate safe and reliable deployment in real-world applications.

Acknowledgments. We thank Dr. Or Zuk of the Hebrew University for his valuable contribution and support. This work was partially supported by the Israel Science Foundation (grant number 683/18). The work of Yerushalmi was partially supported by a research grant from the Estate of Harry Levine, the Estate of Avraham Rothstein, Brenda Gruss and Daniel Hirsch, the One8 Foundation, Rina Mayer, Maurice Levy, and the Estate of Bernice Bernath, grant 3698/21 from the ISF-NSFC, and a grant from the Minerva foundation.

References

1. Abadi, M., et al.: Tensorflow: Large-Scale Machine Learning on Heterogeneous Distributed Systems. arXiv preprint arXiv:1603.04467 (2016)
2. Al-Saffar, A., Tao, H., Talab, M.: Review of deep convolution neural network in image classification. In: 2017 International Conference on Radar, Antenna, Microwave, Electronics, and Telecommunications (ICRAMET), pp. 26–31 (2017)
3. Anderson, T.: Anderson-darling tests of goodness-of-fit. Int. Encycl. Stat. Sci. **1**, 52–54 (2011)
4. Baluta, T., Chua, Z.L., Meel, K.S., Saxena, P.: Scalable quantitative verification for deep neural networks. In: 2021 IEEE/ACM 43rd International Conference on Software Engineering (ICSE), pp. 312–323. IEEE (2021)
5. Bastani, O., Ioannou, Y., Lampropoulos, L., Vytiniotis, D., Nori, A., Criminisi, A.: Measuring Neural Net Robustness with Constraints. In: Proceedings 30th Conference on Neural Information Processing Systems (NIPS) (2016)
6. Berlinger, M., Kolling, S., Schneider, J.: A generalized anderson-darling test for the goodness-of-fit evaluation of the fracture strain distribution of acrylic glass. Glass Structures Eng. **6**(2), 195–208 (2021)
7. Bisong, E.: Building machine learning and deep learning models on google cloud platform: a comprehensive guide for beginners. Apress (2019)
8. Bisong, E., Bisong, E.: Google Colaboratory. Building Machine Learning and Deep Learning Models on Google Cloud Platform: a Comprehensive Guide for Beginners, pp. 59–64 (2019)
9. Casella, G., Berger, R.: Statistical Inference (2nd Edition). Duxbury (2001)
10. Chollet, F., et al.: Keras (2015). https://github.com/fchollet/keras
11. Cohen, J., Rosenfeld, E., Kolter, Z.: Certified adversarial robustness via randomized smoothing. In: Proceedings 36th International Conference on Machine Learning (ICML) (2019)
12. European Union Aviation Safety Agency: EASA Artificial Intelligence Roadmap 2.0 (2023)
13. Federal Aviation Administration: RTCA Inc, Document RTCA/DO-178B (1993)

14. Gariel, M., Shimanuki, B., Timpe, R., Wilson, E.: Framework for Certification of AI-Based Systems. arXiv preprint arXiv:2302.11049 (2023)
15. Goodfellow, I., Shlens, J., Szegedy, C.: Explaining and Harnessing Adversarial Examples (2014)
16. Grafström, A., Schelin, L.: How to select representative samples. Scand. J. Stat. **41**(2), 277–290 (2014)
17. Hadar, A., Levy, N., Winokur, M.: Management and Detection System for Medical Surgical Equipment (2022)
18. Hoeffding, W.: Probability inequalities for sums of bounded random variables. J. Am. Stat. Assoc. 13–30 (1963)
19. Huang, C., Hu, Z., Huang, X., Pei, K.: Statistical certification of acceptable robustness for neural networks. In: Proceedings International Conference Artificial Neural Networks (ICANN), pp. 79–90 (2021)
20. Huang, G., Liu, Z., Van Der Maaten, L., Weinberger, K.: Densely connected convolutional networks. In: Proceedings 30th IEEE Conference on Computer Vision and Pattern Recognition (CVPR), pp. 2261–2269 (2017)
21. Katz, G., Barrett, C., Dill, D., Julian, K., Kochenderfer, M.: Reluplex: An efficient SMT solver for verifying deep neural networks. In: Proceedings 29th International Conference on Computer Aided Verification (CAV), pp. 97–117 (2017)
22. Katz, G., Barrett, C., Dill, D., Julian, K., Kochenderfer, M.: Towards proving the adversarial robustness of deep neural networks. In: Proceedings 1st Workshop on Formal Verification of Autonomous Vehicles (FVAV), pp. 19–26 (2017)
23. Katz, G., et al.: The marabou framework for verification and analysis of deep neural networks. In: Proceedings of the 31st International Conference on Computer Aided Verification (CAV), pp. 443–452 (2019)
24. Khedr, H., Shoukry, Y.: Certifair: A framework for certified global fairness of neural networks. In: Proceedings of the AAAI Conference on Artificial Intelligence, vol. 37, pp. 8237–8245 (2023)
25. Krizhevsky, A., Hinton, G.: Learning Multiple Layers of Features from Tiny Images (2009)
26. Lan, S., Huang, C., Wang, Z., Liang, H., Su, W., Zhu, Q.: Design Automation for Intelligent Automotive Systems. In: Proceedings of the IEEE International Test Conference (ITC), pp. 1–10 (2018)
27. Landi, A., Nicholson, M.: ARP4754A/ED-79A-guidelines for development of civil aircraft and systems-enhancements, novelties and key topics. SAE Int. J. Aerosp. **4**, 871–879 (2011)
28. Leino, K., Wang, Z., Fredrikson, M.: Globally-robust neural networks. In: International Conference on Machine Learning, pp. 6212–6222. PMLR (2021)
29. Levy, N., Katz, G.: RoMA: a method for neural network robustness measurement and assessment. In: Proceedings of the 29th International Conference on Neural Information Processing (ICONIP) (2021)
30. Levy, N., Katz, G.: gRoMA Code (2022). https://drive.google.com/drive/folders/1cXio-xjcqh1xEyOl5tPM52y4B9wPqAdy?usp=drive_link
31. Mangal, R., Nori, A., Orso, A.: Robustness of neural networks: a probabilistic and practical approach. In: Proceedings of the 41st IEEE/ACM International Conference on Software Engineering: New Ideas and Emerging Results (ICSE-NIER), pp. 93–96 (2019)
32. Muller, M., Makarchuk, G., Singh, G., Puschel, M., Vechev, M.: PRIMA: general and precise neural network certification via scalable convex hull approximations. In: Proceedings of the 49th ACM SIGPLAN Symposium on Principles of Programming Languages (POPL) (2022)

33. Omair, A., et al.: Sample size estimation and sampling techniques for selecting a representative sample. J. Health Specialties **2**(4), 142 (2014)
34. Ruan, W., Wu, M., Sun, Y., Huang, X., Kroening, D., Kwiatkowska, M.: Global robustness evaluation of deep neural networks with provable guarantees for the hamming distance. In: Proceedings of the 28th International Joint Conference on Artificial Intelligence (IJCAI) (2019)
35. Simard, P., Steinkraus, D., Platt, J.: Best practices for convolutional neural networks applied to visual document analysis. In: Proceedings of the 7th International Conference on Document Analysis and Recognition (ICDAR) (2003)
36. Tit, K., Furon, T., Rousset, M.: Efficient statistical assessment of neural network corruption robustness. In: Proceedings of the 35th Conference on Neural Information Processing Systems (NeurIPS) (2021)
37. Wang, S., Pei, K., Whitehouse, J., Yang, J., Jana, S.: Formal security analysis of neural networks using symbolic intervals. In: Proceedings of the 27th USENIX Security Symposium (USENIX), pp. 1599–1614 (2018)
38. Wang, S., et al.: Beta-CROWN: efficient bound propagation with per-neuron split constraints for complete and incomplete neural network verification. In: Proceedings of the 35th Conference on Neural Information Processing Systems (NeurIPS) (2021)
39. Wang, Z., et al.: A Tool for Neural Network Global Robustness Certification and Training (2022)
40. Xu, C., Chai, D., He, J., Zhang, X., Duan, S.: InnoHAR: a deep neural network for complex human activity recognition. IEEE Access **7**, 9893–9902 (2019)
41. Zaitang, L., Chen, P.Y., Ho, T.Y.: GREAT Score: Global Robustness Evaluation of Adversarial Perturbation using Generative Models. arXiv preprint arXiv:2304.09875 (2023)
42. Zhang, Y., Zhao, Z., Chen, G., Song, F., Chen, T.: BDD4BNN: a BDD-based quantitative analysis framework for binarized neural networks. In: Silva, A., Leino, K.R.M. (eds.) Computer Aided Verification: 33rd International Conference, CAV 2021, Virtual Event, July 20–23, 2021, Proceedings, Part I, pp. 175–200. Springer, Cham (2021). https://doi.org/10.1007/978-3-030-81685-8_8
43. Zhang, Y., Wei, Z., Zhang, X., Sun, M.: Using Z3 for Formal Modeling and Verification of FNN Global Robustness. arXiv preprint arXiv:2304.10558 (2023)

Optimized Smart Sampling

Maxime Parmentier[(✉)], Axel Legay, and Firmin Chenoy

ICTEAM, UCLouvain, 1341 Louvain-la-Neuve, Belgium
maxime.parmentier@uclouvain.be

Abstract. We revisit the principle of Smart Sampling which makes it possible to apply Statistical Model Checking on stochastic and non-deterministic systems. We point out difficulties in the design of the initial algorithm and we propose effective solutions to solve them. Our contributions are implemented in the Plasma tool.

Keywords: Statistical Model Checking · Sampling · Markov Decision Process · Non-Determinism · Implementation

1 Introduction

Computer systems occupy an increasingly predominant position in our daily lives. Such systems find themselves embedded in strategic applications ranging from the connected home to assisted driving. In view of this situation, any failure of the system can have serious consequences both from an economic and human point of view. It is therefore necessary to deploy techniques whose purpose is to ensure that the system satisfies a set of security/safety requirements.

A first way to validate the requirements of a computer system is to test the conformity of its outputs with respect to predefined inputs. These techniques are known as very effective and they made it possible to detect numerous safety and security bugs both at code and specification models [3,15]. Unfortunately, this technology does not generally cover all the behaviors of the system or even quantify the degree of confidence that can be given to it [26]. Another problem is that testing relies on predefined requirements, which makes it hard to detect cyber security issues [21]. This means that they cannot be applied in critical certification processes where the calculation of the degree of certainty is necessary to obtain the certificate [13].

Another approach consists in modeling the system by means of a mathematical object such as (extensions of) transition systems [8]. Such representations make it possible to model the failures of the system as well as quantitative information or even interactions with the environment [8]. In this paper, we consider Markov Decision Processes (MDP), an extension of Markov Chains (MC) with non determinism features. The model allows us to represent the failures

M. Parmentier is funded by a FNRS PhD Grant and A. Legay by a FNRS PDR - T013721.

B. Steffen (Ed.): AISoLA 2023, LNCS 14380, pp. 171–187, 2024.
https://doi.org/10.1007/978-3-031-46002-9_10

by means of probabilities and the choices of environment thanks to nondeterministic actions. In this context, the validation process consists in finding the environment (aka the scheduler) which maximizes or minimizes the probability of satisfying a requirement [20,30]. To do so, one can then explore all the behaviors of the system by means of formal verification techniques such as (quantitative) model checking [8]. These exhaustive approaches make it possible to detect all errors in the system and obtain full guarantee. However, they suffer from the problem of the so-called "state-space explosion", which makes them inapplicable in many strategic and complex cases.

Another approach is to use Statistical Model Checking (SMC) to solve this problem [22,25,31]. A SMC algorithm consists in monitoring a finite number of executions of the system and using theoretical results from statistics such as the Chernoff bound to obtain certainty on the probability of satisfying the property. SMC, which is a compromise between testing and formal verification, has been applied in a wide variety of fields ranging from the validation of complex railway and aviation systems to the analysis of medical and space components (see [4,5,9,29] for illustrations). One of the main challenges of SMC is to minimize the number of simulations to be performed [17]. Another difficulty is to extend the approach to systems that are not purely probabilistic, such as Markov Decision processes or Timed Automata [14,16].

A series of recent works [10,16] has made it possible to extend the SMC algorithms to the case of MDPs. Most of these algorithms use deep learning techniques that are very effective but require knowledge of the system and often complex modeling of the schedulers to be analyzed. It is for this reason that we have proposed another approach called "Smart Sampling" [10]. The idea of Smart Sampling is to represent schedulers in a simple way, with seeds and hash functions. We give ourselves an initial budget of schedulers and we apply the SMC algorithm on the MC which results from each scheduler's choices. The fifty percents of the best schedulers are then kept and the operation is repeated until the scheduler for which SMC minimizes or maximizes the requirement to be validated is found. Smart Sampling has been implemented in Plasma [24]. The approach is known to be simpler and faster than its competitors. It has been applied to various extensions of MC and requirements, including cost estimation. Unfortunately, this pure simulation approach suffers from a major preciseness problem. Indeed, it generally does not find the best scheduler but rather a scheduler which calculates the average probability of satisfying the property. This makes the approach inapplicable in certain strategic areas where extremes must be known.

In this article we revisit the Smart Sampling algorithm and we propose practical improvements. In particular, we observe that different reduction factors improve accuracy without impacting performance. Moreover, we point out an operating error of the Chernoff bound in the initial algorithm and we show empirically that the latter has important consequences on the result of the algorithm. All of our contributions have been implemented in Plasma [24] and validated through examples that illustrate the problems and the advantages in a concrete way.

2 Background

Markov Decision Processes allow to model both controllable non-determinism and uncontrollable non-determinism, which is necessary to modelize situations where an agent-based system operates in a dynamical environment with uncertainty. A *Markov Decision Process* (MDP) is a tuple $(S, s_0, A, \{P_a\}_{a \in A})$ where S is a finite set of *states*, s_0 is the initial state, A is a finite set of (labelled) *actions* and $\{P_a\}_{a \in A})$ is a set of probabilities over pairs of states such as for all $P_a \in A$, there exists a unique state $s \in S$ for which $P_a(s, s')$ can be greater than zero. A MDP can be seen as a directed graph whose edges start from a single vertex but can point to multiple vertices, with a probability associated with each of those possible destinations. In any state (vertex) s, a state s' is *reachable* if there exists an action (edge) a from s to s' with $P_a(s, s') > 0$. A (finite) *path* is a (finite) sequence of states $(s^1, s^2, ...)$ such that s^{i+1} is reachable from s^i for all $i \in \mathbb{N}_0$. A (finite) *trace* is a (finite) path such that $s^1 = s_0$. We'll use the notations T^n and T^∞ for the set of all finite traces of length n and the set of infinite traces respectively. For each simulation of a MDP, a trace is produced. To resolve the controllable non-determinism of a MDP, i.e. the necessity to select the actions which will be chosen during one simulation, one can refine a MDP into a Markov chain with the choice of a scheduler. In practice, a scheduler can be interpreted as a possible interaction with the environment (a possible choice of a user for instance) or as a chosen strategy for the execution of the system to achieve a specific goal. A *scheduler*, also called *policy*, is a function which indicates at any point during the generation of a trace which is the action that needs to be considered to determine the next state of the trace. The most basic kind of schedulers are *memoryless schedulers* whose choices only depends on the current state, i.e. functions of the form $\pi : S \to A$. For reachability problems, memoryless schedulers suffice, but they form a strict subset of *history-dependent schedulers*. *Finite-memory schedulers* take as inputs finite paths of a predetermined maximum length n, i.e. are functions of the for $\pi : (s^i)_{1 \leq i \leq n} \to A$. *Infinite-memory schedulers* take as inputs finite traces with no predetermined maximum length, i.e. are functions of the for $\pi : T^\infty \to A$. Schedulers that do not truly resolve the controllable non-determinism are also possible and are called *probabilistic schedulers*, i.e. functions of the form $\pi : S \to Dist(A)$, where $Dist(A)$ is the set of probability distributions over A. A standard probabilistic scheduler is one that choose the uniform distribution over all the available actions in each state. In what follows, unless specified otherwise, scheduler is used as a shortcut for memoryless scheduler.

The choice of a scheduler turns a MDP into a Markov Chain. A *Markov chain* (MC) is a Markov decision process with exactly one available action for each state. Once a MDP is specified as a Markov chain, we can automatically define the associated probability space $(\Omega, \mathcal{F}, \mu)$. $\Omega = T^\infty$ is the set of all infinite traces of the Markov chain, $\mathcal{F}$ is the σ-algebra generated by subsets Ω of the form $\Omega_{(s^1,...,s^n)} = \{(t^1, ..., t^n, ...) \in \Omega \mid t_1 = s_1, ..., t_n = s_n\}$, and $\mu : \mathcal{F} \to [0, 1]$ is the distribution over $\mathcal{F}$ which verifies for any finite trace $(t_0, ..., t_n) \in T^n$: $\mu(\Omega_{(t_0,...,t_n)}) = \prod_{i=0}^{n-1} P_{a_{t_i}}(t_i, t_{i+1})$, with a_{t_i} being the unique action available in the Markov chain at state t_i. Such a distribution μ_π can be built for each scheduler π of a MDP, and for any (finite) trace T of the MDP the probability $\mu_\pi(T)$ is the probability that a simulation of the MDP under the policy π will produce the trace T.

In this work we use *Bounded Linear Temporal Logic* (BLTL) to specify the properties of a system. BLTL is a variant of Linear Temporal Logic (LTL), which is itself a modal extension of propositional logic. The addition of only one modal operator is sufficient to fully define BLTL. A minimal BNF grammar for the syntax of BLTL is:

$$\phi, \psi ::= \bot \mid \alpha \mid \neg\phi \mid \phi \wedge \psi \mid \phi\, U^k\, \psi$$

α denotes an atomic proposition. In the context of statistical model checking, those can be simply defined as a list of logical variables $\{\alpha_s\}_{s \in S}$ with α_s true if and only if the current state is s, but more complex atomic proposition can be defined, for example with fluents. $\neg$ and $\wedge$ are the basic operators of propositional logic for the negation and the conjunction. U^k (with $k \in \mathbb{N}$) is the (bounded) *until* operator. The semantics of BLTL operators are defined in a similar way to what is done for linear temporal logic. In the context of SMC, the models for the formulas of BLTL are usually taken as pairs (T, z) with T being a (infinite) trace of a Markov Chain and z being a starting index for the sequence T. The semantics of the $\neg$ and $\wedge$ operators are the same than with propositional logic, while the semantic of the U^k operator formalizes the intuitive idea of "true if the first formula is true until the second one becomes true, in a a time interval of length k". More formally, for a trace T: $(T, z) \models \phi\, U^k\, \psi$ iff there exists $j \in \mathbb{N}$ with $z \le j \le z + k$ such that $(T, i) \models \phi$ for all $z \le i \le j$ and $(T, i) \models \psi$ for all $j < i \le k$. Just as the $\phi \vee \psi$ operator can be defined as $\neg(\neg\phi \wedge \neg\psi)$ within propositional logic, additional operators can be defined for (bounded) linear temporal logic. The most common ones are $X\,\phi$, $\phi\, F^k\, \psi$ and $\phi\, G^k\, \psi$, the *next*, the *finally/eventually* and the *globally/always* operators, respectively defined as $\top U^1 \phi$, $\top U^k \phi$, $\neg(\top U^k \neg\phi)$.

Given a BLTL formula ϕ associated with a MDP, a *score* can be given to any scheduler π by considering the quantity $\int_\Omega \mathbb{1}_{T \models \phi}\, d\mu_\pi$, i.e. the exact probability that the property of the system formalized by the formula ϕ is verified for a random possible execution of the MDP under the policy π.

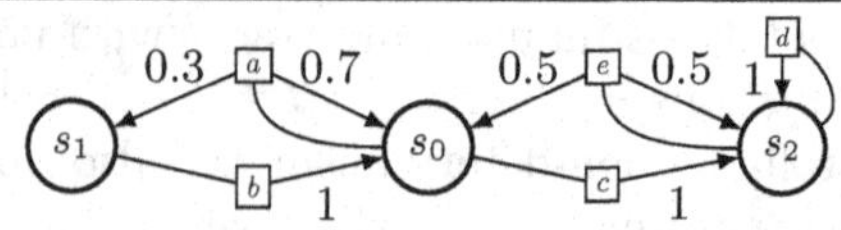

A MDP with 3 states and 5 actions. The schedulers that choose the action c in state s_0 have a score of 0 for the formula $X(\neg\alpha_{s_0}) \Rightarrow (\alpha_{s_0} U^3 \alpha_{s_1})$, while any scheduler which picks action a has a score of $1 - (0.7)^3 = 0.657$. No memoryless scheduler can produce a trace that satisfies $G^8(F^4\alpha_{s_1} \wedge F^4\alpha_{s_2})$, but it is possible with a history-dependent scheduler.

Problem 1. *Given a MDP $(S, s_0, A, \{P_a\}_{a \in A})$, a BLTL formula ϕ and a specific class of schedulers Π, how to find an* optimal *schedulers π^+ and π^-, defined as:*

$$\pi^+ \in \arg\max_{\pi \in \Pi} \int_{\Omega} \mathbb{1}_{T \models \phi} \, d\mu_\pi \qquad \pi^- \in \arg\min_{\pi \in \Pi} \int_{\Omega} \mathbb{1}_{T \models \phi} \, d\mu_\pi$$

That is, a scheduler (not necessarily unique) with the greatest/lowest possible score, i.e. the greatest/lowest probability to generate traces for which the property ϕ is true.

3 The Lightweight Scheduler Approach

The most straightforward method to solve Problem 1 with SMC is to first build a large number of schedulers, compute the score of each of those schedulers, then output one with the highest score [10]. However, despite its simplicity, this approach calls for multiple remarks. First, the right representation of schedulers must be chosen. For very big models representing all schedulers as full maps does not scale well in terms of memory space. As showed in [10], one efficient alternatives is to represent schedulers as seeds for a pseudo-random number generator, whose size can be adapted in function of the expected theoretical number of schedulers.

Second, the size and complexity of the models of real-world systems may prohibit the computation of the exact theoretical scores of the schedulers [25], and those must then be estimated with SMC. Note that the non-exhaustive nature of the evaluation process for the schedulers implies that statistical guarantees are necessary for those estimations. Indeed, depending on how complex, sensitive or critical the system which needs to be verified is, those estimations must have relatively high or low precisions and confidence levels. To characterise those estimations, the notion of (ϵ, δ)-estimation is useful: $\hat{p}$ is a (ϵ, δ)-*estimation* of the true score p of a scheduler π if $P(|\hat{p} - p| > \epsilon p) < \delta$. All SMC algorithms require values for the hyperparameters ϵ and δ, explicitly or implicitly. A smaller ϵ means that the error of the estimations of the scores of the schedulers will be smaller, while a smaller δ means that the probability that one such estimation is not within the error bound is lower. In both cases, decreasing the values of those hyperparameters implies that more simulations must be performed.

Lastly, the performances of such an elementary SMC algorithm are extremely dependant of the number of schedulers which are generated and whose scores are estimated. If that number is low with respect to the total number of possible schedulers for the system under scrutiny, then the chances that an optimal scheduler can be found among the schedulers generated by the algorithm is low as well. This can be solved by allocating a smaller fraction of the simulation budget of the algorithm to each evaluation of the schedulers, i.e. by producing less traces for each scheduler. Unfortunately, that pseudo-solution is useless for real-world applications of SMC, since those usually demand estimations with very high precision and confidence level. Therefore, many SMC algorithms, instead of asking for a total simulation budget size, ask for values for the hyperparameters ϵ and δ and then try to minimize the simulation budget they need to guarantee those levels of precision and confidence. This can be done *a priori*, by exploiting statistical results such as the Chernoff bound [10,28], or *a posteriori*, for instance with adaptive stopping algorithms [11,12,27].

3.1 The Original Smart Sampling Algorithm from [10]

The original Smart Sampling Algorithm from [10] given in Algorithm 1 is the version of the algorithm tailored to find optimal schedulers with maximal scores. The condition on the per-iteration budget is derived from the Chernoff Bound to ensure (ϵ, δ)-estimations [10,28].

In Step 1 (lines 1 to 9), the per-iteration budget B is used once to generate $\lceil\sqrt{B}\rceil$ schedulers (line 2) and produce $\lceil\sqrt{B}\rceil$ traces for each of those schedulers (line 5). The traces which satisfy the property ϕ are counted to compute a rough estimation of the schedulers' scores (line 8), and the greatest value among those estimations is selected as a first estimation $\hat{p}_{\max}$ for the score of a (near-)optimal scheduler. In Step 2 (lines 10 to 18), the naive estimation $\hat{p}_{\max}$ is used to balance the simulation budget so to maximize the probability of producing traces with near-optimal schedulers (line 10) [10]. Then, the initial population of the algorithm is generated (line 11). A preliminary iteration is then performed to abandon the schedulers (line 14) that don't produce any trace which satisfies the property ϕ at least once (line 18). Finally, in Step 3 (lines 19 to 34), the main loop of the algorithm happens here, which doesn't stop until the population has been reduced to one scheduler or until the confidence level that has been reached, as approximated with the Chernoff Bound (line 26), is smaller than δ (line 20). First, the scores of the schedulers are reset (line 19). At each step of the loop, the iteration population is updated (line 22) and as long as the the number of simulations which have been realized at this step is smaller than $\lceil B/M_i\rceil$ (line 24), an additional trace is generated for each scheduler (line 28). At the end of each loop, the results are updated (line 31), the approximation of the optimal probability is updated and the population is cut in a way that only half of the population of schedulers, those with the best scores, are kept.

Algorithm 1. Original Smart Sampling Algorithm from [10]

Require:
MDP $\mathcal{M}$ and BLTL formula ϕ
precision and confidence level ϵ and δ
per-iteration budget $B \geq \ln(2/\delta)/(2\epsilon^2)$

Ensure:
P and $\hat{p}_{\max}$, with P final population,
and $\hat{p}_{\max}$ an (ϵ, δ)-approximation of an optimal score

$N \leftarrow \lceil \sqrt{B} \rceil$; $M \leftarrow \lceil \sqrt{B} \rceil$
$P \leftarrow \{M$ schedulers sampled uniformly at random$\}$
for $\pi \in P$ **do**
    for $1 \leq i \leq N$ **do**
        $T_i^\pi \leftarrow \text{Simulate}(\mathcal{M}, \phi, \pi)$
    end for
end for
$R \leftarrow \{(\pi, \hat{n}_\pi) \mid \pi \in P,\ \hat{n}_\pi = |\{T_i^\pi \mid T_i^\pi \models \phi\}|\}$
$\hat{p}_{\max} \leftarrow \max_{(\pi, \hat{n}_\pi) \in R} \hat{n}_\pi / N$

$N \leftarrow \lceil 1/\hat{p}_{\max} \rceil$; $M \leftarrow \lceil B \hat{p}_{\max} \rceil$
$P \leftarrow \{M$ schedulers sampled uniformly at random$\}$
for $\pi \in P$ **do**
    for $1 \leq i \leq N$ **do**
        $T_i^\pi \leftarrow \text{Simulate}(\mathcal{M}, \phi, \pi)$
    end for
end for
$R \leftarrow \{(\pi, \hat{n}_\pi) \mid \pi \in P,\ \hat{n}_\pi = |\{T_i^\pi \mid T_i^\pi \models \phi\}|\}$
$P \leftarrow \{\pi \in P \mid \hat{n}_\pi > 0\}$

$R \leftarrow \{(\pi, 0) \mid \pi \in P\}$; $i \leftarrow 0$; confidence $\leftarrow 1$
while confidence $> \delta \wedge |P| > 1$ **do**
    $i \leftarrow i + 1$
    $M_i \leftarrow |P|$
    $N_i \leftarrow 0$
    while confidence $> \delta \wedge N_i < \lceil B/M_i \rceil$ **do**
        $N_i \leftarrow N_i + 1$
        confidence $\leftarrow 1 - (1 - e^{-2\epsilon^2 N_i})^{M_i}$
        for $\pi \in P$ **do**
            $T_{N_i}^\pi \leftarrow \text{Simulate}(\mathcal{M}, \phi, \pi)$
        end for
    end while
    $R \leftarrow \{(\pi, \hat{n}_\pi) \mid \pi \in P,\ \hat{n}_\pi = |\{T_i^\pi \mid T_i^\pi \models \phi\}|\}$
    $\hat{p}_{\max} \leftarrow \max_{(\pi, \hat{n}_\pi) \in R} \hat{n}_\pi / N$
    $P \leftarrow \{\pi \in P \mid \hat{n}_\pi$ is one of the greatest $\lfloor |P|/2 \rfloor$ values in $R\}$
end while
return $P, \hat{p}_{\max}$

3.2 Beyond the First Implementation of the Smart Sampling Algorithm

We reproduced two of the experiments of the original paper of the Smart Sampling algorithm [10], the analyses of the IEEE 802.11 Wireless LAN Protocol (WLAN) and the Gossip Protocol (GOSSIP)[1].

We were interested in observing how a greater or smaller *reduction factor*, defined as the denominator of the fraction of the population which is preserved from step to step, could impact the performance of the algorithm. On one hand, increasing the reduction factor should *a priori* lead to poorer performances but a faster execution time for the algorithm: a higher number of schedulers discarded at each step means that near optimal schedulers which can be present in the initial population might be abandoned by mistake (especially at the first step), but it also means that there are fewer steps to the algorithm and that the total simulation budget will be a smaller multiple of the per-iteration budget. On the other hand, decreasing the reduction factor should *a priori* lead to better performances but a slower execution time for the algorithm: a smaller number of schedulers discarded at each step means that near-optimal schedulers which can be present in the initial population have a smaller chance to be abandoned by mistake, but it also means that there are more steps to the algorithm and that the total simulation budget will be a greater multiple of the per-iteration budget.

Since the WLAN and GOSSIP models used have already been evaluated thoroughly with exhaustive model checking techniques [18–20], the theoretical score of an optimal scheduler is known for both of those experiments. Figure 1 shows the proportion of runs for the Smart Sampling algorithm that managed to output an estimation which was within the error bound of the actual optimal score in function of a varying reduction factor, with $\epsilon = 0.01$, $\delta = 0.1$ and a per-iteration budget of 15000.

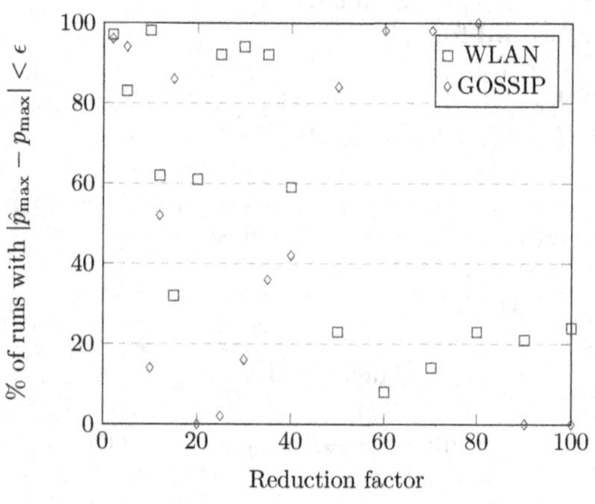

Fig. 1. Original Smart Sampling algorithm performance

Surprisingly, the expected correlations can not be found. Moreover, a performance drop phenomenon can be seen around specific values. The location of those values depends of the values of the parameters of the Smart Sampling algorithm. After analysis of the implementation and individual executions of the algorithm, our conclusion is that the original implementation of the Smart

[1] See https://www.prismmodelchecker.org/download.php for a description.

Sampling algorithm is flawed in three ways. First, because it is designed to immediately stop as soon as the per-iteration budget divided by the number of remaining schedulers is greater than the Chernoff Bound, the algorithm can terminate much earlier than anticipated with a still diverse population of schedulers. Second, because barely enough traces are at that point produced so that the estimations of the schedulers of the final population are valid (ϵ, δ)-estimations, most of them are badly estimated relatively to each others. This results in individual outputs for the original Smart Sampling algorithm with great variance. Those two first flaws make for drastic changes in performance when the ratios between the size of the initial sample and powers of the reduction factor are close to integers, up to the last step of the algorithm. A slight change in one of those ratios can severely impact how soon the algorithm stops and how well the schedulers are evaluated at the last step. We hypothesize that this potential problem was not noticed with the first version of the Smart Sampling because the fixed value of 2 which was originally chosen for the reduction factor was low, making the algorithm's progress smooth in the sense that the population size decreases from step to step relatively slowly. Third, additional tailor-made experiments showed that the original implementation of the Smart Sampling algorithm suffers from another critical weakness: noise. For models with in-built noise, i.e. for which all schedulers have a fixed low chance to produce failing traces, performance is often extremely poor with non-generous per-iteration budget. Indeed, when the ratio between the initial population size and the per-iteration is close to 1, the first evaluation of the schedulers is so vulnerable to the noise that the first wave of discarded schedulers can be essentially regarded as random. Even if (near-)optimal schedulers are present in the sample at the start, the probability they are abandoned before the second step of the algorithm is high.

4 New Lightweight Algorithms for Statistical Model Checking

To improve the Smart Sampling algorithm, we modified how the Chernoff bound test dictates the termination of the algorithm, and we explored three ideas: artificially inflating the simulation budget for the first step, applying a simulated annealing strategy, and reintroducing new random schedulers at specific steps. Those modifications were implemented in *PLASMA* (Platform for Learning and Advanced Statistical Model checking Algorithms), a plug-in based interface for statistical model checking [24].

Unless specified otherwise, all experiments were realized for the WLAN and the GOSSIP models, with $\epsilon = 0.01$, $\delta = 0.1$ and a per-iteration budget of 15000. For both models, since the theoretical optimal scheduler and its score are known, the goal was to compute the probability that the algorithm produces an estimation which deviates from the theoretical optimal solution by at most ϵ and check if the probability is indeed lower or equal to δ. That is, to verify if the algorithm actually produces (ϵ, δ)-estimations. The results, which include information about the execution times as well, are averaged over up to 100 runs (depending on the experiment). The experiments were performed on a 8 GB machine with 4 cores running at 3.2 GHz.

4.1 Modification of the Chernoff Bound Test

Three approaches were considered to deal with the problems arising from the potential early termination of the Smart Sampling algorithm due to the Chernoff bound test: keep the early termination but with a better evaluation of the schedulers of the final population (option 1), ignore the early termination but scale down the simulation budget with respect to the accumulated confidence level for the remaining iterations, (option 2), or completely ignore the early termination (option 3).

Option 1 leaves the main loop of Algorithm 1 intact, but adds a last loop of x simulations for each scheduler once the Chernoff bound test makes the main loop end. Then, the modified algorithm reevaluate the schedulers and order them by their scores one last time before returning the result. Option 2 requires to remove the Chernoff bound test at line 20, and to alter the condition for the simulation loop from "confidence $> \delta \wedge N_i < \lceil B/M_i \rceil$" to "$N_i < F(\text{confidence}, \lceil B/M_i \rceil)$", with F a pre-determined fixed function. Option 3 completely removes the Chernoff bound test both at line 20 and at line 24.

All three options were initially compared to each other fairly in the sense that the design choices (number x and function F) were made so that the number of additional simulations was identical between the options. For option 2, any test function F which scales linearly with confidence quickly leads to insignificant per-scheduler simulation budgets for the subsequent steps of the algorithm. Therefore, the type of function which was the most experimented with is a function which returns $\lceil B/M_i \rceil$ as long as confidence is greater than δ, then returns (a fraction or a multiple of) the per-scheduler simulation budget of the last iteration of the main loop for which confidence was still greater than δ.

Option 1 is not only the option that doesn't fit the original philosophy of the algorithm, but it is also the option which produced the worse results. Because option 1 allocates all the additional budget evenly between the remaining schedulers of the final population, the sampling process ceases to prioritize the most promising schedulers. Option 3 produced the best results consistently, whereas option 2 produced good results as well when the multiple of the test function F was large enough. However, when the multiple of the test function was taken as 1, option 3 was always a better choice in terms of results while the difference in total simulation budgets between option 2 and option 3 was systematically small. Indeed, unless the per-iteration budget parameter is unnecessary large with respect to ϵ and δ, the Smart Sampling algorithm generally completes most of its potential steps before the Chernoff bound condition is verified. Therefore, option 3 is the option we suggest and have chosen for the modification of the Smart Sampling algorithm. A small verification can be added at the level of the preconditions to warn the user or ensure that the per-iteration budget cannot be excessively large with respect to ϵ and δ when the user specifies a per-iteration budget instead of letting the algorithm fix it by itself.

Figure 2 is the equivalent of Fig. 1 for the Smart Sampling algorithm modified with option 3. Not only the modification improves the performances of the algorithm noticeably, but it eliminates the performance drop phenomenon as well. The modification is particularly impactful with high values for the reduction factor, to the point that the algorithm's performance barely diminishes as the reduction factor increases.

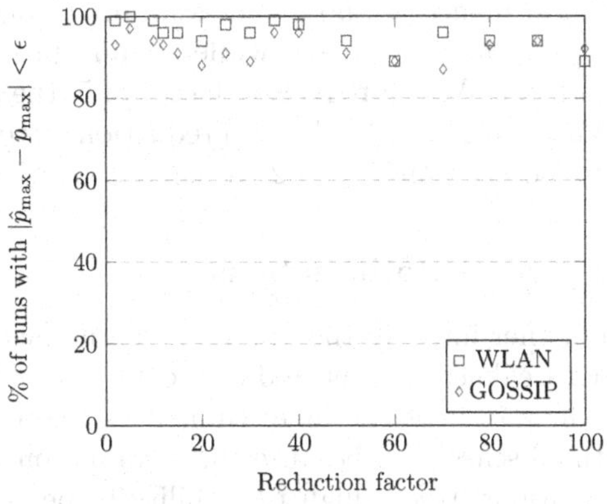

Fig. 2. Modified Smart Sampling algorithm performance

Figures 3 and 4 show the execution times for 100 runs of the Smart Sampling algorithm for the WLAN and GOSSIP experiments, for both versions of the algorithm.

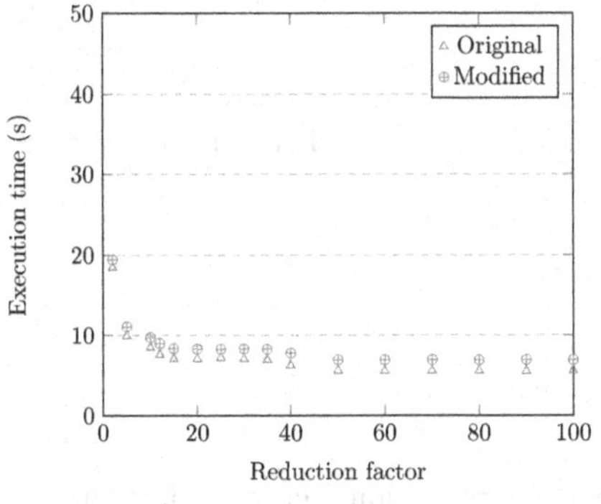

Fig. 3. Execution times (WLAN)

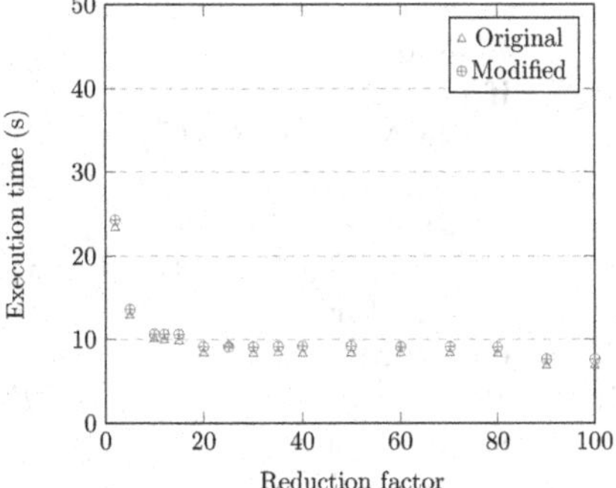

Fig. 4. Execution times (GOSSIP)

For any given reduction factor, the execution times of the modified version of the algorithm are on average 13% greater than those for the original version of the algorithm. However, since it allows for a much larger reduction factor without a loss in performance, the modified version applied with a large reduction factor outperforms the original version (with a reduction factor of 2) both in terms of results and speed.

In conclusion, we hypothesize that the ideal new version of the Smart Sampling algorithm is the third suggested modification, applied with a reduction factor larger than 2. Since the trade-off between performance and speed is inevitable as the reduction factor increases, we cannot give a perfect universal value for the reduction factor. Nevertheless, our recommendation is to take it at least as large as 5 or even 10, for we could never observe noticeable loss in performance at those values in any of our experiments (including those not discussed in this paper), while already providing a significant speed-up to the algorithm. With a reduction factor of 5, the algorithm is accelerated by a factor of $\ln(5)/\ln(2) \simeq 2.32$. With a reduction factor of 10, the algorithm is accelerated by a factor of $\ln(10)/\ln(2) \simeq 3.32$.

4.2 Other Optimizations

To further improve the Smart Sampling algorithm, we first looked at one of its other weaknesses discussed in Sect. 3.2: its fragility with respect to noise. During the first step of the algorithm, it is frequent that the algorithm drops near-optimal schedulers because their evaluation is based on so few traces that those evaluations have a high probability to be unreliable. When realistic simulation budgets are taken into account, the number of times each scheduler is simulated during the first iteration can even be close (if not equal) to 1.

Algorithm 2. Additional Budget at First Step

```
20: while |P| > 1
21:     i ← i + 1
22:     M_i ← |P|
23:     N_i ← 0
24:     if i == 1
25:     while N_i < F(⌈B/M_i⌉)                         ▷ F is a fixed function
26:         N_i ← N_i + 1
27:         for π ∈ P do
28:             T^π_{N_i} ← Simulate(ℳ, φ, π)
29:         end for
30:     end while
31:     R ← {(π, n̂_π) | π ∈ P, n̂_π = |{T^π_i | T^π_i ⊨ φ}|}
32:     p̂_max ← max_{(π, n̂_π)∈R} n̂_π / N
33:     P ← {π ∈ P | n̂_π is one of the greatest ⌊|P|/(reduction factor)⌋ values in R}
34: else
35:     while N_i < ⌈B/M_i⌉)                  ▷ New condition for the main loop
36:         N_i ← N_i + 1
37:         for π ∈ P do                  ▷ New condition for the simulation loop
```

To counter that problem, a very simple solution was first tested: providing the algorithm with additional simulation budget for the first step. This means slightly modifying the condition of the simulation loop at line 24 of Algorithm 1 to introduce an exception for the first iteration. Algorithm 2 shows the main modifications which were brought to the code of Algorithm 1 to remove the Chernoff bound test and introduce additional sampling at the first iteration.

The kind of test function F which was mostly tested is a collection of simple multiplicative functions with a multiplicative parameter a ranging from 2 to 10. Depending on whether the chosen per-iteration budget allows for a large or small per-scheduler simulation budget at the first step, a lower or greater value should be taken for that multiplicative parameter. Indeed, if the per-scheduler simulation budget at the first step is satisfactory to begin with, picking a value as low as 2 is the right choice as to minimize the additional computing cost. However, if the per-scheduler simulation budget at the first step is close to 1, then taking it as large as 10 (or even larger) is necessary. In general, the function F can be of the form $F(x) = \min(K, ax)$, with a rather large and K being a upper bound on the per-scheduler budget for the first step, for a jack-of-all-trades solution.

On custom small scale models designed with a lot of in-built noise, providing additional simulation budget for the first iteration improved the Smart Sampling algorithm's probability of identifying a (near-)optimal scheduler by around 6% with $a = 2$, 15% with $a = 3$, 26% with $a = 5$ and 30% with $a = 10$. Those numbers are average over reduction factors ranging from 2 to 100, albeit the gains in performance were generally more important with large (> 10) reduction factors.

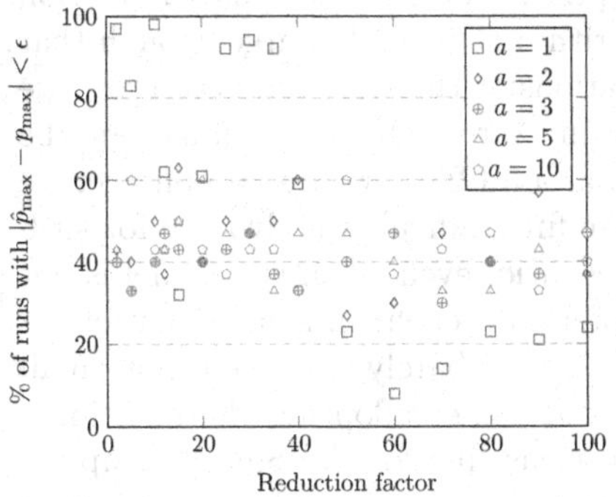

Fig. 5. More budget at first iteration strategy (WLAN)

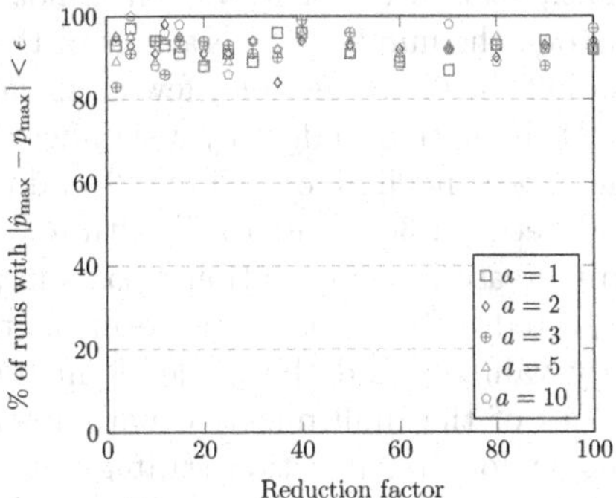

Fig. 6. More budget at first iteration strategy (GOSSIP)

Figures 5 and 6 show the impact of providing additional simulation budget for the first iteration on the probability for the Smart Sampling algorithm to output a near-optimal scheduler for the WLAN and GOSSIP models. Despite the limited importance of the noise weakness of the Smart Sampling algorithm for those models, we can observe that even though the effect of providing additional simulation budget for the first iteration is less noticeable than when noise is involved, in the case of the GOSSIP experiment, that strategy has positive impact on the algorithm's performance nonetheless. However, as can been seen with Fig. 6, which was produced with a very reduced set of experiments of 30, that strategy still suffers from the from the instability of the statistical model checking process.

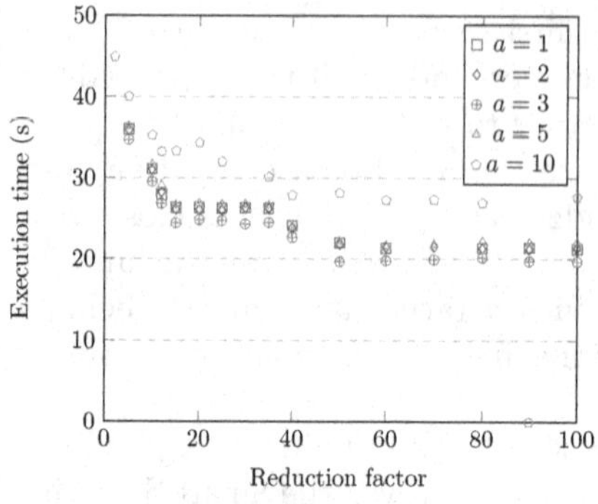

Fig. 7. Execution times (WLAN)

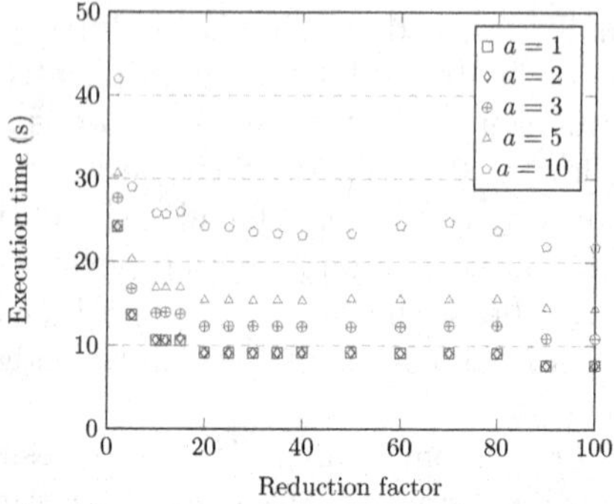

Fig. 8. Execution times (GOSSIP)

Of course, that small positive benefit is not worth if it comes with a prohibitive increase in computational costs. However, as shown with Figs. 7 and 8, the increase in computational costs is limited, at least for small values of the multiplicative factor a. Which is not a surprise: especially with low reduction factors, the number of iterations of the algorithm is generally large enough that adding the equivalent of a few artificial iterations at the start does not grow the total simulation budget by a significant margin. Across all reduction factors, the increase is negligible with $a = 2$ and $a = 3$, around 25% with $a = 5$ on average and between 30% and 150% with $a = 10$. We find difficult to advocate for such an increase in computational costs in any scenario, even when the model is not expected to be "noisy". However, as the potential benefit in some situations is very valuable and the trade-off in terms of speed barely noticeable for small values of the multiplicative parameter a, we consider adopting the additional budget for first iteration strategy as the new baseline for the Smart Sampling algorithm the right choice. Fixing $a = 3$ appears to be a good starting point, with a suggestion to the user to push the value of that parameter up to 10 when working with noisy models.

Trying to extend the additional budget at first step strategy to a simulated annealing strategy was attempted. Instead of only inflating the simulation budget of the first iteration, one can try to artificially rebalance the total simulation budget between the different steps of the algorithm instead of allocating a constant per-iteration budget to all iterations. Skewing towards early iterations and towards the late iterations were both tested. The conclusion is that skewing towards the early iterations is often the best course of action, to the point that the best results were obtained when the skew was so much in favor of the first iteration that it was practically equivalent to the much simpler strategy which consists in providing additional budget at the first step.

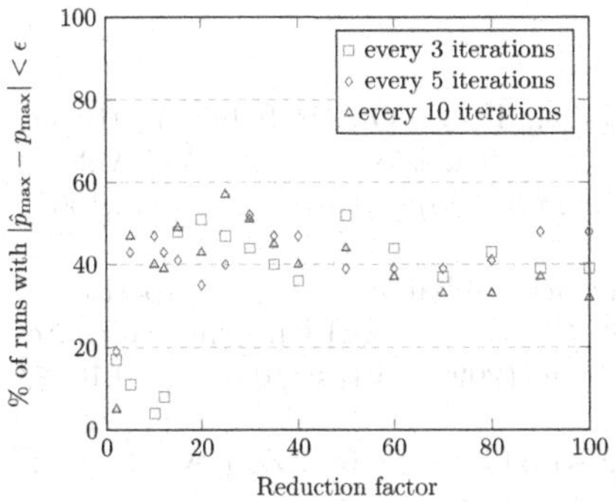

Fig. 9. Random scheduler reintroduction strategy (WLAN)

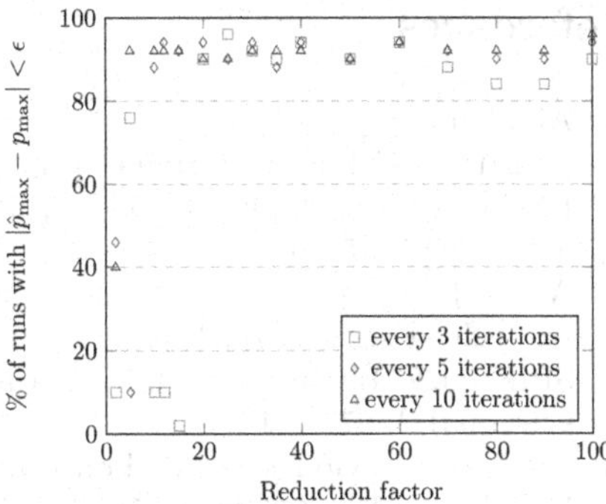

Fig. 10. Random scheduler reintroduction strategy (GOSSIP)

Lastly, the idea of reintroducing schedulers as the algorithm progresses was also experimented with. The goal was to improve the Smart Sampling algorithm with respect to another of its fundamental limitations, i.e. its inability to identify schedulers beyond those present in the initial population, but also reduces its weakness relatively to the local extremum phenomenon. Unfortunately, as shown in Figs. 9 and 10, the results are not conclusive. In all cases, that strategy didn't produce better results than simply starting with a larger initial population. In some cases, that strategy even made the algorithm's performance worse, by introducing badly evaluated schedulers with low scores right before the termination of the algorithm. We hypothesize that this kind of strategy is still promising nevertheless, but at the condition that the new schedulers are instead synthetized in a way that exploits the accumulated information about the discarded schedulers in order to reintroduce schedulers which are different and potentially have good scores, and not just random ones.

5 Conclusion

In this article we propose a new version of the Smart Sampling algorithm presented in [10]. Our first experimental results with Plasma show that Smart Sampling can be used to obtain schedulers that minimize/maximize a BLTL property. Aside from analyzing more examples, there are several ways to extend this work. The first is to adapt the algorithm to other systems and other requirements. One thinks, for example, of timed stochastic systems [6] or of properties that involve cost calculations [23]. A limitation of the current algorithm is that it does not exploit the knowledge between several schedulers. This means that in the case where the scheduler is rare, the efficiency of the algorithm will remain limited. One way to solve this problem would be to adapt genetic algorithms. This requires modeling seed populations and extracting information from them. Another work will consist in considering the hyperproperties which make it possible to compare sets of executions and thus to model a broader spectrum of security properties [1,2]. Finally, using our approach to synthesize schedulers for stochastic interface theories [7] should be investigated.

References

1. Ábrahám, E., Bartocci, E., Bonakdarpour, B., Dobe, O.: Probabilistic Hyperproperties with Nondeterminism. In: Hung, D.V., Sokolsky, O. (eds.) ATVA 2020. LNCS, vol. 12302, pp. 518–534. Springer, Cham (2020). https://doi.org/10.1007/978-3-030-59152-6_29
2. Arora, S., et al.: Statistical model checking for probabilistic hyperproperties of real-valued signals. In: Legunsen, O., Rosu, G. (eds.) Model Checking Software. SPIN 2022. LNCS, vol. 13255. Springer, Cham (2022). https://doi.org/10.1007/978-3-031-15077-7_4
3. Atlidakis, V., Godefroid, P., Polishchuk, M.: RESTler: stateful REST API fuzzing. In: ICSE. IEEE/ACM, pp. 748–758 (2019)
4. Baranov, et al.: A secure user-centred healthcare system: design and verification. In: Bowles, J., Broccia, G., Pellungrini, R. (eds.) From Data to Models and Back. DataMod 2021. LNCS, vol. 13268. Springer, Cham (2022). https://doi.org/10.1007/978-3-031-16011-0_4
5. Basile, D., et al.: Exploring the ERTMS/ETCS full moving block specification: an experience with formal methods. Int. Softw. Tools Technol. Transfer **24**, 351–370 (2022). https://doi.org/10.1007/s10009-022-00653-3
6. Budde, C.E., D'Argenio, P.R., Hartmanns, A., Sedwards, S.: An efficient statistical model checker for nondeterminism and rare events. Int. J. Softw. Tools Technol. Transfer **22**(6), 759–780 (2020). https://doi.org/10.1007/s10009-020-00563-2
7. Caillaud, B., et al.: Constraint Markov Chains. Theor. Comput. Sci. **412**(34), 4373–4404 (2011)
8. Clarke, E.M., et al.: Model checking, 2nd Edition. MIT Press (2018)
9. Colombo, A., et al.: Efficient customisable dynamic motion planning for assistive robots in complex human environments. JAISE **7**(5), 617–634 (2015)
10. D'Argenio, P., Legay, A., Sedwards, S., Traonouez, L.-M.: Smart sampling for lightweight verification of Markov decision processes. Int. J. Softw. Tools Technol. Transfer **17**(4), 469–484 (2015). https://doi.org/10.1007/s10009-015-0383-0
11. Dagum, P., et al.: An optimal algorithm for monte Carlo estimation. SIAM J. Comput. **29**, 1484–1496 (2000)
12. Domingo, C., Gavalda, R., Watanabe, O.: Adaptive sampling methods for scaling up knowledge discovery algorithms. Data Min. Knowl. Discov. **6**, 131–152 (2002). https://doi.org/10.1023/A:1014091514039
13. Dupont, S., et al.: Product incremental security risk assessment using DevSecOps practices. In: Katsikas, S., et al. (ed.) Computer Security. ESORICS 2022 International Workshops. ESORICS 2022. LNCS, vol. 13785. Springer, Cham (2022). https://doi.org/10.1007/978-3-031-25460-4_38
14. Gadyatskaya, O., Hansen, R.R., Larsen, K.G., Legay, A., Olesen, M.C., Poulsen, D.B.: Modelling attack-defense trees using timed automata. In: Fränzle, M., Markey, N. (eds.) FORMATS 2016. LNCS, vol. 9884, pp. 35–50. Springer, Cham (2016). https://doi.org/10.1007/978-3-319-44878-7_3
15. Godefroid, P.: Fuzzing: hack, art, and science. Commun. ACM **63**(2), 70–76 (2020)
16. Jaeger, M., Jensen, P.G., Guldstrand Larsen, K., Legay, A., Sedwards, S., Taankvist, J.H.: Teaching stratego to play ball: optimal synthesis for continuous space MDPs. In: Chen, Y.-F., Cheng, C.-H., Esparza, J. (eds.) ATVA 2019. LNCS, vol. 11781, pp. 81–97. Springer, Cham (2019). https://doi.org/10.1007/978-3-030-31784-3_5

17. Jegourel, C., Legay, A., Sedwards, S.: Importance splitting for statistical model checking rare properties. In: Sharygina, N., Veith, H. (eds.) CAV 2013. LNCS, vol. 8044, pp. 576–591. Springer, Heidelberg (2013). https://doi.org/10.1007/978-3-642-39799-8_38
18. Kwiatkowska, M., Norman, G., Parker, D.: Analysis of a Gossip Protocol in PRISM. ACM SIGMETRICS Perform. Eval. **36**(3), 17–22 (2008)
19. Kwiatkowska, M., Norman, G., Sproston, J.: Probabilistic model checking of the IEEE 802.11 wireless local area network protocol. In: Hermanns, H., Segala, R. (eds.) PAPM-PROBMIV 2002. LNCS, vol. 2399, pp. 169–187. Springer, Heidelberg (2002). https://doi.org/10.1007/3-540-45605-8_11
20. Kwiatkowska, M., Norman, G., Parker, D.: PRISM 4.0: verification of probabilistic real-time systems. In: Gopalakrishnan, G., Qadeer, S. (eds.) CAV 2011. LNCS, vol. 6806, pp. 585–591. Springer, Heidelberg (2011). https://doi.org/10.1007/978-3-642-22110-1_47
21. Lanet, J.-L., et al.: When time meets test. Int. J. Inf. Sec. **17**(4), 395–409 (2018)
22. Larsen, K.G., Legay, A.: 30 years of statistical model checking. In: Margaria, T., Steffen, B. (eds.) ISoLA 2020. LNCS, vol. 12476, pp. 325–330. Springer, Cham (2020). https://doi.org/10.1007/978-3-030-61362-4_18
23. Legay, A., Sedwards, S., Traonouez, L.: Estimating rewards & rare events in non-deterministic systems. In: ECEASST, vol. 72 (2015)
24. Legay, A., Sedwards, S., Traonouez, L.-M.: Plasma lab: a modular statistical model checking platform. In: Margaria, T., Steffen, B. (eds.) ISoLA 2016. LNCS, vol. 9952, pp. 77–93. Springer, Cham (2016). https://doi.org/10.1007/978-3-319-47166-2_6
25. Legay, A., Lukina, A., Traonouez, L.M., Yang, J., Smolka, S.A., Grosu, R.: Statistical model checking. In: Steffen, B., Woeginger, G. (eds.) Computing and Software Science. LNCS, vol. 10000, pp. 478–504. Springer, Cham (2019). https://doi.org/10.1007/978-3-319-91908-9_23
26. Lin, Y., et al.: Test coverage optimization for large code problems. J. Syst. Softw. **85**(1), 16–27 (2012)
27. Mnih, V., Szepesvari, C., Audibert, J.Y.: Empirical Bernstein stopping. In: Proceedings of the International Conference on Machine Learning, pp. 672–679 (2008)
28. Okamoto, M.: Some inequalities relating to the partial sum of binomial probabilities. Ann. Inst. Stat. Math. **10**, 29–35 (1959). https://doi.org/10.1007/BF02883985
29. Paigwar, A., et al.: probabilistic collision risk estimation for autonomous driving: validation via statistical model checking. In: 2020 IEEE Intelligent Vehicles Symposium (IV). IEEE (2020)
30. Vardi, M.Y.: Automatic verification of probabilistic concurrent finite-state programs. In: FOCS. IEEE Computer Society, pp. 327–338 (1985)
31. Younes, H.S., Simmons, R.G.: Statistical probabilistic model checking with a focus on time-bounded properties. Inf. Comput. **204**, 1368–1409 (2006)

Towards a Formal Account on Negative Latency

Clemens Dubslaff[1,2(✉)], Jonas Schulz[2,4], Patrick Wienhöft[2,3], Christel Baier[2,3], Frank H. P. Fitzek[2,4], Stefan J. Kiebel[2,5], and Johannes Lehmann[2,3]

[1] Eindhoven University of Technology, Eindhoven, The Netherlands
c.dubslaff@tue.nl

[2] Centre for Tactile Internet with Human-in-the-Loop (CeTI), Dresden, Germany
{jonas.schulz2,patrick.wienhoeft,christel.baier,frank.fitzek,stefan.kiebel, johannes_alexander.lehmann}@tu-dresden.de

[3] Department of Computer Science, Dresden University of Technology, Dresden, Germany

[4] Department of Electrical Engineering, Dresden University of Technology, Dresden, Germany

[5] Department of Psychology, Dresden University of Technology, Dresden, Germany

Abstract. Low latency communication is a major challenge when humans have to be integrated into cyber physical systems with mixed realities. Recently, the concept of *negative latency* has been coined as a technique to use anticipatory computing and performing communication ahead of time. For this, behaviors of communication partners are predicted, e.g., by components trained through supervised machine learning, and used to precompute actions and reactions.

In this paper, we approach negative latency as anticipatory networking with formal guarantees. We first establish a formal framework for modeling predictions on goal-directed behaviors in Markov decision processes. Then, we present and characterize methods to synthesize predictions with formal quality criteria that can be turned into negative latency. We provide an outlook on applications of our approach in the settings of formal methods, reinforcement learning, and supervised learning.

1 Introduction

A key ingredient for modern communication is low latency, enabling a seamless integration of multimodal information transfer and hence remote robotic control and human interaction in virtual realities. It is thus not surprising that the 5G mobile standard also focused on ultra-low latency to compete with new technological demands [26,40]. For instance, towards an implementation of an *internet of skills*, where tactile skill information has to be communicated between

This work was partially supported by the DFG under the projects EXC 2050/1 (CeTI, project ID 390696704, as part of Germany's Excellence Strategy) and TRR 248 (see https://perspicuous-computing.science, project ID 389792660).

B. Steffen (Ed.): AISoLA 2023, LNCS 14380, pp. 188–214, 2024.
https://doi.org/10.1007/978-3-031-46002-9_11

sensors and actuators, a round-trip latency of less than one millisecond is an essential prerequisite [13,14,24,40].

However, physical limits for communication in terms of speed of light directly tell that under those latency requirements there is a boundary at 25 km distances for an end-to-end communication [53]. In a global world striving towards ubiquitous computing, there is hence a need for more sophisticated techniques to reduce latency and enable greater distances of low-latency communication [36].

One promising technique is *anticipatory computing*. Following the seminal definition by Rosen [33], behaviors of anticipatory systems are characterized by not only depending on the past but also on beliefs in the future and future needs. Research on such systems has a long history. Similar concepts have already been considered, e.g., within *speculative execution* to speed up processing in parallel computing [46]. Recently, anticipatory computing gained more and more attention in the field of software and systems engineering [27]. For instance, automated driver assistance systems benefit from prediction functionalities to navigate in common traffic schemes but also reduce the control action space to react timely on incidents. Here, machine-learning predictors show great performance [25,44]. In the context of mobile devices and communication, *anticipatory networking* enables to reduce latency [28], especially in combination with *edgecloud computing*: Future behaviors of users and computing systems are predicted, consequences computed, and resources then shifted towards infrastructure that is physically close to the communication partner. Depending on the actual behaviors, the speculated results can then directly be transmitted from the edge computing devices to meet latency requirements. Most prominently, a similar technique has been introduced in 2019 for Google's cloud-based gaming service Stadia to precompute game display frames. There, latency lags were mitigated by ahead-of-time computation of most likely game-playing behaviors, leading to a smoother gaming experience. Google coined the term *negative latency* to promote their variant of anticipatory networking towards reducing latencies. One crucial aspect is the clear focus on gaming experience, where incorrect predictions do not have harmful impacts and thus, there is no need to require any guarantees on predicted outcomes. The latter however renders Google's technique not suitable for safety critical applications such as remote surgery or autonomous driving, whose functioning crucially depends on reliably low latency.

We argue that guarantees on predictions are key to actually demarcate negative latency from basic latency reductions through anticipatory networking. To this end, we propose a more strict understanding of negative latency, which essentially boils down to the simple relation

$$\text{negative latency} \;=\; \text{anticipatory networking} \;+\; \text{formal guarantees}$$

Guarantees on predictions for anticipatory networking are required to quantify the reliability of systems that depend on low latency, also to meet safety standards and classify potential failures of the system [32]. Having in mind the success of machine-learning trained predictors, our variant of negative latency also opens a new field in formal methods and artificial intelligence.

In this paper, we develop foundations of a formal framework that captures our understanding of negative latency. Here, we focus on the formal guarantees that can be provided for systems modeled as *Markov decision processes (MDPs,* [31]*)*. MDPs are an expressive stochastic model having a rich support for formal quantitative analysis [4,10] and are also used as underlying model of *reinforcement learning* [45]. Towards reasoning about negative latency, we introduce MDPs with dedicated goal states and model goal-directed behaviors through sequences of state-action pairs towards reaching goals. For instance, goals could stand for different surgery tools a doctor intends to grab during remote surgery, where the hand movements model goal-directed behaviors [34,35]. Further, we introduce *predictions* as sets of anticipated goals, leading to a general framework of MDPs with goals and predictions. Since in practical applications many goals are theoretically possible, we are focusing on so-called *k-predictions* where only up to k goals are predicted. For formal guarantees, we impose thresholds on the quality of predictions, e.g., ensuring that the predicted set of goals is reached with high probability. We then consider cost annotations in MDPs that formalize execution and communication timings, e.g., the time of a hand movement during grabbing surgery tools. The *k-negative latency* corresponds to the maximal time with during any execution a high-quality k-prediction can be made ahead of reaching a predicted goal. Intuitively, giving the formal guarantees in form of high-quality predictions, the communication partner can then start reasoning about consequences of each of the k goals and react ahead of time, leading to negative latency. In case of the remote surgery example, the remote operator can already provide advice to the surgery tools ahead of time compensating the communication latency.

To the best of our knowledge, this view on predictions in MDPs has not yet been established in the literature. Actually, while our motivation stems from formalizing negative latency, our framework can be used in various other settings where, e.g., cost annotations stand for energy consumed or packages transmitted. We present algorithms for the general case of MDPs with goal predictions to solve the k-prediction problems, i.e., computing high-quality k-predictions that optimize costs before reaching goals. Here, we distinguish between *additive quality measures* that allow for synthesizing high-quality k-predictions in polynomial time, and the *canonical quality measure* of pessimistic goal reachability probability where already the problem of deciding whether a high-quality k-prediction exists is NP-complete.

In general, our basic framework models behavior of the communication partner through both nondeterministic and probabilistic choices, leading to overall pessimistic predictions and negative latency. With more information about underlying strategies and behaviors, e.g., obtained by reinforcement-learning techniques, we can reason about Markov chains as fully probabilistic models with uncertainty. In combination with well-known confidence measures, this enables to provide better predictions and negative latencies while maintaining formal guarantees. We also illustrate how supervised-learning techniques could be exploited to trade performance towards higher negative latencies for formal guarantees.

To summarize, we provide a starting point towards formally reasoning about negative latency and MDPs with goals and predictions and contribute

(1) a generic formalization of predictions and prediction qualities in cost-aware MDPs that specify goal-directed behaviors,
(2) algorithms to synthesize high-quality (cost-bounded) predictions,
(3) a discussion of applications of our framework with additional knowledge from strategy estimates and machine learning predictors, and
(4) instantiations of our framework to the setting of negative latency.

Related Work. There is a body of research on anticipatory computing [33], anticipatory networking [28], speculative execution [46], and related concepts [27]. Differently, negative latency only recently attracted attention [34–36]. However, we are not aware of any attempt to provide a formal account on negative latency or to conceptionally demarcate anticipatory networking for reducing latency and negative latency.

Our framework formalizing predictions and negative latency relates to and uses concepts from cost-bounded reachability analysis in MDPs [6,17,18,47]. The cost-optimal k-prediction problem towards maximizing negative latency is closely related to the synthesis of resilient strategies in MDPs [8]. The latter addresses a somehow inverse problem by asking for a strategy to reach goals within a given cost bound while maximizing performance.

In the context of reinforcement learning, estimates of transition probability errors and confidence have been extensively studied [45]. Approaches use, e.g., Hoeffding bounds [19] with reasoning on lower [2] and upper confidence [9]. In this paper, we mainly follow the approach by Strehl and Littman [41,42] towards L_1-estimations of transition probabilities [50]. Such estimations are also employed for offline reinforcement learning with safe policy improvement [23,29].

The application of formal methods to machine learning models remains subject to ongoing research. Previous work in the field of formal methods focused on probabilistic guarantees for predictions based on training data [48]. In this paper, our aim is not to advance the field in this direction, but sketch how machine learning predictions also might provide negative latency.

2 Preliminaries

We briefly present our notations on Markovian models and temporal logics with costs. For more details, see standard textbooks on systems modeling and verification [10]. A *distribution* over a finite set X is a function $\delta\colon X \to [0,1]$ where $\sum_{x\in X} \delta(x) = 1$. The set of distributions over X is denoted by $\mathit{Distr}(X)$, the power set of X by $\wp(X)$. When clear from the context, we omit brackets of singleton sets, i.e., write x for $\{x\}$.

Markov Decision Processes. A *Markov decision process (MDP)* is a tuple $\mathcal{M} = (S, Act, P, C, \imath)$ where S and Act are finite sets of states and actions, respectively, $P\colon S \times Act \rightharpoonup Distr(S)$ is a partial transition probability function, $C\colon S \times Act \to \mathbb{N}$ is a cost function, and $\imath \in S$ is an initial state. The size of $\mathcal{M}$ is the sum of all set sizes as well as binary encodings of costs and probabilities. We say that an action $\alpha \in Act$ is *enabled* in state $s \in S$ if $P(s, \alpha)$ is defined, and assume that the set of enabled actions $Act(s)$ is always non-empty. For $(s, \alpha, s') \in S \times Act \times S$ we define $P(s, \alpha, s') = P(s, \alpha)(s')$ if $\alpha \in Act(s)$ and $P(s, \alpha, s') = 0$ otherwise. If for all states $s \in S$ there is exactly one action enabled, i.e., $|Act(s)| = 1$, then $\mathcal{M}$ is called a *Markov chain (MC)*. In this case we may omit the actions from the definitions. A finite *path* is a sequence $\rho = s_0\alpha_0 s_1\alpha_1 \ldots s_n$ where $P(s_i, \alpha_i, s_{i+1}) > 0$ for all $i = 0, 1, \ldots, n-1$. The *accumulated cost* on ρ is defined by $C(\rho) = \sum_{i=0}^{n-1} C(s_i, \alpha_i)$. The set of all paths in $\mathcal{M}$ starting in s is denoted by $Paths(\mathcal{M}, s)$ and the fragment of finite paths by $Paths_{\mathrm{fin}}(\mathcal{M}, s)$. We assume that all states in $\mathcal{M}$ are reachable from $\imath$, i.e., appear in some path starting in $\imath$.

The semantics of the MDP $\mathcal{M}$ is given by resolving nondeterministic choices through *strategies*, i.e., mappings $\sigma\colon Paths_{\mathrm{fin}}(\mathcal{M}, \cdot) \to Distr(Act)$ where $\sigma(s_0\alpha_0 \ldots s_n)(\alpha) = 0$ for all $a \notin Act(s_n)$. We call a path ρ as above a *σ-path* if $\sigma(s_0\alpha_0 \ldots s_i)(\alpha_i) > 0$ for all $i = 0, \ldots, n-1$. The probability of ρ w.r.t. σ and starting state $s \in S$ is defined as $\Pr_s^\sigma(\rho) = \prod_{i=0}^{n-1} \sigma(s_0\alpha_0 \ldots s_i)(\alpha_i) \cdot P(s_i, \alpha_i, s_{i+1})$ if ρ is a σ-path with $s_0 = s$ and $\Pr_s^\sigma(\rho) = 0$ otherwise. The probability of some set of finite σ-paths $B \subseteq Paths_{\mathrm{fin}}(\mathcal{M}, s)$, where any path is not a prefix of another, is defined by $\Pr_s^\sigma(B) = \sum_{\rho \in B} \Pr_s^\sigma(\rho)$. Definitions for probabilities extend to measurable sets of infinite paths in the standard way [10,49].

Property Specification. We specify properties on MDPs $\mathcal{M}$ as above by formulas in cost-aware *linear temporal logic (LTL)* [30], given as expressions of the grammar

$$\varphi \ ::= \ \mathtt{true} \mid a \mid \neg\varphi \mid \varphi \vee \varphi \mid \bigcirc\varphi \mid \varphi \mathsf{U}^{\sim\tau} \varphi$$

where a ranges over a set of atomic propositions AP, $\sim\, \in \{\leq, \geq\}$, and $\tau \in \mathbb{N}$. Here, $\bigcirc$ stands for the *next operator* and $\mathsf{U}^{\sim\tau}$ for the cost-constrained *until operator*. Further standard operators can be derived, e.g., $\varphi \wedge \psi \equiv \neg(\neg\varphi \vee \neg\psi)$, *until* $\mathsf{U} \equiv \mathsf{U}^{\geq 0}$, *eventually* $\Diamond\varphi \equiv \mathtt{true}\mathsf{U}\varphi$, or *globally* $\Box\varphi \equiv \neg\Diamond\neg\varphi$. In this paper, we consider AP as the set of states of $\mathcal{M}$ and provide the semantics of an LTL formula φ as the set $[\![\varphi]\!]$ of infinite paths $\rho = s_0\alpha_0 s_1\alpha_1 \ldots$ in $\mathcal{M}$ for which $s_0 s_1 \ldots$ satisfies φ, written $\rho \models \varphi$. For a state $s \in S$ we write $s \models \varphi$ if for all infinite $\rho \in Paths(\mathcal{M}, s)$ we have $\rho \models \varphi$. We also use set notations to represent disjunctions of atomic propositions, e.g., $\rho \models A\mathsf{U}B$ for $A, B \subseteq S$ for all paths ρ that reach a state in B and only visit states of A on the way to B.

For any strategy σ, an LTL formula φ constitutes a measurable set $[\![\varphi]\!]_{\mathcal{M}^\sigma}$ of infinite σ-paths that satisfy φ [49]. To this end, for a state $s \in S$ we write $\Pr_{\mathcal{M},s}^\sigma(\varphi)$ for $\Pr_{\mathcal{M},s}^\sigma([\![\varphi]\!]_{\mathcal{M}^\sigma})$. Best- and worst-case probabilities on LTL properties are captured by ranging over possible resolutions of nondeterminism:

$$\Pr^{\min}_{\mathcal{M},s}(\varphi) = \inf_{\sigma} \Pr^{\sigma}_{\mathcal{M},s}(\varphi) \qquad \text{and} \qquad \Pr^{\max}_{\mathcal{M},s}(\varphi) = \sup_{\sigma} \Pr^{\sigma}_{\mathcal{M},s}(\varphi) .$$

Quantiles. Quantiles are defined as optimal values q such that the probability of a random variable Q exceeding q is beyond a given threshold. In our setting, we consider quantiles minimizing costs (such as time consumed) in MDP models w.r.t. worst- and best-case resolution of nondeterminism [6,47]. Let $\mathcal{M}$ be an MDP as above, φ and ψ LTL formulas over AP without cost constraints, $\vartheta \in [0,1]$ be a probability threshold, and $s \in S$. Then, the *lower-bound quantile* with respect to ϑ, φ, and ψ in s is defined as

$$\max \{ c \in \mathbb{N} \mid \Pr^{\min}_{\mathcal{M},s}(\varphi \mathsf{U}^{\geq c}\psi) \geq \vartheta \} . \tag{1}$$

The above quantile specifies the minimal costs c required for paths that start in s to guarantee a probability greater than ϑ for reaching a state where ψ holds, solely via states that satisfy φ and surely spending at least c. *Upper-bound quantiles* are defined accordingly, i.e.,

$$\min \{ c \in \mathbb{N} \mid \Pr^{\min}_{\mathcal{M},s}(\varphi \mathsf{U}^{\leq c}\psi) \geq \vartheta \} . \tag{2}$$

Quantiles can be computed using a back-propagation approach, leading to quantile values in all states of the given MDP [6].

3 Predictions in Markov Decision Processes

To model goal-directed behaviors of systems or humans and to reason about situations where predictions about targeted goals can be made, we establish a formal framework of MDPs with goals and cost predictions. For this, we fix an MDP $\mathcal{M} = (S, Act, P, C, \imath)$ throughout the section.

MDPs with Goals. Let $G \subseteq S$ be a finite set of *goal states.* The pair $(\mathcal{M}, G)$ is called an *MDP with goals* if goal states are reached almost surely for any strategy and state, i.e., $(\mathcal{M}, G)$ is an MDP with goals iff $\Pr^{\min}_{\mathcal{M},s}(\Diamond G) = 1$. MDPs with goals describe goal-directed behavior starting in the initial state $\imath$ until reaching a goal state. After reaching such a goal state, the behavior continues towards a new (possibly different) goal. To this end, each path in $(\mathcal{M}, G)$ operates in several phases, constituting *goal-directed runs* that start and end in a state of $Init = \{\imath\} \cup G$. We define the set of runs by

$$Runs(\mathcal{M}, G) = \{\rho \in Paths(\mathcal{M}, Init) \mid \rho \models \bigcirc\Diamond G\}$$

Example 1. Let us introduce our running example of a human grabbing either a plate, an espresso cup, or a coffee cup [35]. We model the goal-directed hand movement by an MDP with goals $(S, Act, P, C, 211, G)$ over the state space

$S = \{2,1,0\}^2 \times \{1,0\}$, goal states $G = \{000, 001, 021\}$, action space $Act = \{\text{move}, \text{close}, \text{open}, \text{turn}\}$, and transition probabilities and costs as depicted in Fig. 1. The first state component models how close the user's hand is situated relative to the object: far (2), close (1), or touching (0). The second state component models the hand pose: wide (2), normal (1), or narrow (0). The third state component stands for the hand position vertical (1) or horizontal (0). Grabbing an object starts far from the object, with a normal vertical hand pose (cf. initial state "211"). Costs of transitions are annotated in front of action names in Fig. 1, modeling the time in milliseconds to perform the task. Moving at different speeds is modeled via probabilistic transitions towards either "close to" or "touching" the object. Essentially, the user can follow two strategies to grab the desired object: either first moving and then adjusting the hand pose towards the needs of grabbing the object (closing, opening, or turning) or the other way around. Note that turning the hand towards horizontal position directly at the beginning implies that the user targets a plate (goal "000"), since grabbing an espresso or coffee cup requires a vertical hand pose (goals "001" and "021", respectively). Further, observe that touching the object in a normal vertical pose (state "011") does not allow for opening the hand anymore, required to grab the coffee cup. After a goal is reached, i.e., one of the objects is touched and consequently grabbed, a new phase starts by returning to the initial state (indicated by the outgoing arrows of the three goals).

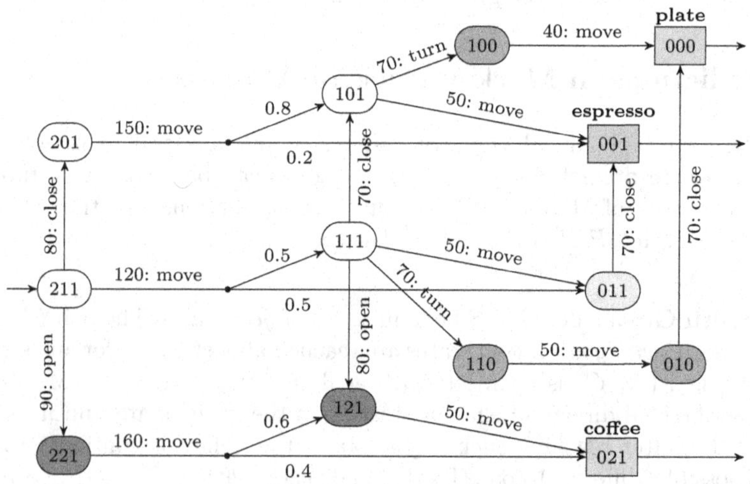

Fig. 1. Example MDP with goals of a grabbing scenario

To reason about time-dependent properties, let us consider the LTL formula $\varphi = \Diamond^{\geq 60}\textbf{plate}$ where **plate** stands for the state "000" (see Fig. 1). Then $\Pr^{\min}_{\mathcal{M},s}(\varphi) \geq 0.9$ only holds in states "110" and "010", since from all other states, either less than 60 ms are spent to reach the goal state "000" (state "100") or there is a strategy for the human to not grab the plate (e.g., deciding to go for espresso in state "101" by moving forward).

Predictions. To formalize predictions on goal-directed behaviors in MDPs with goals, we introduce *prediction* mappings $\pi\colon S \to \wp(G)$ that assign a set of predicted goals to states. Predictions are ordered via goal inclusion, i.e., $\pi \subseteq \pi'$ iff $\pi(s) \subseteq \pi'(s)$ for all $s \in S$. We identify with $supp(\pi)$ the set of states where a prediction is made, i.e., $supp(\pi) = \{s \in S \mid \pi(s) \neq \varnothing\}$.

Intuitively, predictions are made within the goal-directed phases of $(\mathcal{M}, G)$, i.e., $\pi(s) \neq \varnothing$ in some state $s \in S$ then corresponds to predicting the reachability event $\varphi_{\pi(s)} = (\neg G)\mathsf{U}\pi(s)$, i.e., reaching the set of goal states in $\pi(s)$ without passing any other goal state. Note that with this understanding, for a meaningful prediction it should hold that $\pi(s) = \{s\}$ for all $s \in G$.

3.1 Prediction Quality Criteria

Obviously, not all prediction mappings are sensible, e.g., when a goal is not reachable but predicted. Also predicting all reachable goals or none in every state does not provide any useful information. We are mainly interested in predictions with at least one prediction in each goal-directed phase of the MDP with goals:

Definition 1 (Proper prediction). *A prediction $\pi\colon S \to \wp(G)$ for $(\mathcal{M}, G)$ is called* proper *if for all $s_0\alpha_0 s_1 \cdots s_n \in Runs(\mathcal{M}, G)$ with $n > 1$ there is $i \in \{1, \ldots, n-1\}$ such that $\pi(s_i) \neq \varnothing$.*

Within proper predictions we further would like to predict as few goals as possible but with fulfilling certain quality criteria, e.g., predicting with high confidence. For this, we introduce prediction quality measures.

Definition 2 (Prediction quality). *A* prediction quality *for $(\mathcal{M}, G)$ is a mapping $\mu\colon S \times \wp(G) \to [0, 1]$ where $\mu(s, \varnothing) = 0$ for all $s \in S$. We call μ* additive *if $\mu(s, X) + \mu(s, x) = \mu(s, X \cup \{x\})$ for all $s \in S$, $X \subseteq G$, and $x \in G \backslash X$.*

Intuitively, values $\mu(s, X)$ stand for the quality of a goal prediction $X \subseteq G$ in some state $s \in S$. Note that additivity implies monotonicity, i.e., $\mu(s, X) \leq \mu(s, Y)$ for all $X \subseteq Y \subseteq G$ and $s \in G$. We relate different quality measures by pointwise comparison, i.e., for two quality measures μ and μ', we write $\mu \leq \mu'$ iff $\mu(s, X) \leq \mu'(s, X)$ for all $s \in S$ and $X \subseteq G$.

Having full knowledge about $(\mathcal{M}, G)$, the canonical candidate for prediction quality is given by the worst-case reachability probability of predicted goals. Formally, for $s \in S$ and $X \subseteq G$ this instance can be defined by

$$\mu_{\varphi}(s, X) \quad = \quad \Pr^{\min}_{\mathcal{M},s}(\varphi_X) \quad = \quad \Pr^{\min}_{\mathcal{M},s}((\neg G)\mathsf{U}X) \tag{3}$$

Note that this prediction quality can be computed in polynomial time using standard methods for model checking MDPs [10]. But also other quality measures could well be imagined, e.g., when uncertainty on the MDP probabilities or external influences are present. Instances we will discuss in this paper include, e.g., confidence measures in MDPs with goals learned by model-based reinforcement learning (see Sect. 4.1) or confidence on predictors trained with supervised machine learning (see Sect. 4.2).

Remark 1. The canonical prediction quality μ_φ is not additive. To see this, consider $S = \{\imath, g, g'\}$, $G = \{g, g'\}$, $Act = \{\alpha, \alpha'\}$ and $P(\imath, \alpha, g) = P(\imath, \alpha', g') = 1$ being the only transitions. Then

$$\Pr^{\min}_{\mathcal{M},\imath}(\varphi_g) = \Pr^{\min}_{\mathcal{M},\imath}(\varphi_{g'}) = 0 \qquad \text{but} \quad \Pr^{\min}_{\mathcal{M},\imath}(\varphi_{\{g,g'\}}) = 1.$$

Nevertheless, μ_φ is monotonic since adding goals can only increase the probability of reaching goals independent from the chosen strategy.

State-Based Quality Threshold Criterion. A natural way of stating requirements on overall prediction quality of a system is by means of thresholds on qualities of each prediction state.

Definition 3. *Given a quality measure μ and a threshold $\vartheta \in [0,1]$, a proper prediction π for $(\mathcal{M}, G)$ is called a* $\mu\vartheta$-state prediction *if for all states $s \in S$ with $\pi(s) \neq \varnothing$ we have*

$$\mu(s, \pi(s)) \geq \vartheta \,. \tag{4}$$

π is complete *if for all $\mu\vartheta$-state predictions π' we have $supp(\pi') \subseteq supp(\pi)$ and $\pi(s) \subseteq \pi'(s)$ for all $s \in supp(\pi')$.*

Note that every $\mu\vartheta$-state prediction has to be proper and hence, there is at least one state $s \in S$ that has to meet the threshold criterion (4). For a prediction to be complete, it has to make a prediction in as many states as possible, with a minimal set of goals in each state (w.r.t. subset inclusion).

3.2 k-Predictions

In practice, the number of goals in a system might be huge, posing challenges when predictions have to be processed timely. Towards meaningful predictions and to deal with limited resources when anticipating predicted goals, we hence mainly consider predictions with a limited number of goals. Formally, given a goal bound $k \in \mathbb{N}$, we call a prediction π a *k-prediction* if $|\pi(s)| \leq k$ for all $s \in S$.

$\mu\vartheta$-state k-prediction decision problem
For an MDP with goals $(\mathcal{M}, G)$, $k \in \mathbb{N}$, prediction quality μ, and threshold $\vartheta \in [0,1]$, decide whether there is a $\mu\vartheta$-state k-prediction.

Clearly, in case of a positive answer, the goal is to synthesize complete predictions. A simple greedy scheme can compute a complete $\mu\vartheta$-state k-prediction if μ is additive. Algorithm 1 implements this scheme by iterating through all states checking whether in those states a k-prediction can be made that fulfills

Algorithm 1: SynthKMin – Synthesize $\mu\vartheta$-state k-prediction

input : MDP with goals $(\mathcal{M}, G)$, $k \in \mathbb{N}$, prediction quality μ, $\vartheta \in [0,1]$
output: A $\mu\vartheta$-state k-prediction π or **false** if none exists

```
1  forall s ∈ S do
2      π(s) := ∅                                         // initialize prediction
3      while μ(s, π(s)) < ϑ and |π(s)| ≤ k do
4          x_max := argmax_{x∈G\π(s)} μ(s, x)              // add highest quality goal
5          π(s) := π(s) ∪ {x_max}
6      if μ(s, π(s)) < ϑ or |π(s)| > k then
7          π(s) := ∅                                     // no greedy prediction at s
8          if μ is not additive then
9              forall X ⊆ G, |X| ≤ k do
10                 if μ(s, X) ≥ ϑ then
11                     π(s) := X                 // non-greedy prediction found at s
12                     break
13 if there is ρ ∈ Runs(M, G) with ρ ⊭ ○((¬G)U(supp(π)\G)) then
14     return false                              // there is no proper k-prediction
15 return π
```

the state quality criterion. Note that Line 4 involves a nondeterministic choice in case at least two goals can be predicted with same quality. Further, when μ is not additive, the greedy scheme might not succeed in finding a prediction with at most k goals in some state, requiring to possibly check predictions exhaustively (see Line 8). After computing prediction sets for each state, π is a k-prediction. However, this prediction might not be proper, in which case there is no $\mu\vartheta$-state k-prediction (see Definition 1) and the algorithm returns **false** (Line 13).

Theorem 1. *Let $(\mathcal{M}, G)$ be an MDP with goals, $k \in \mathbb{N}$, μ a prediction quality that can be computed in polynomial time, and $\vartheta \in [0,1]$. If there is a $\mu\vartheta$-state k-prediction for $(\mathcal{M}, G)$, Algorithm 1 returns one taking at most exponential time. For additive μ, the prediction is complete and computed in polynomial time.*

Example 2. Let us illustrate predictions on our running example (see Example 1), where we abbreviate by **plate** the state "000", by **espresso** the state "001", and by **coffee** the state "021". Application of Algorithm 1 for $k = 2$, $\vartheta = 0.9$, and the canonical prediction quality $\mu_\varphi(s, X) = \Pr^{\min}_{\mathcal{M},s}\big((\neg G)\mathsf{U}X\big)$ yields a complete $\mu\vartheta$-state 2-prediction π:

$$
\begin{aligned}
&\pi(211) = \pi(111) = \varnothing\\
&\pi(000) = \pi(100) = \pi(010) = \pi(110) = \{\textbf{plate}\}\\
&\pi(001) = \pi(011) = \{\textbf{espresso}\}\\
&\pi(021) = \pi(221) = \pi(121) = \{\textbf{coffee}\}\\
&\pi(201) = \pi(101) = \{\textbf{plate}, \textbf{espresso}\}
\end{aligned}
$$

Note that in the initial state "211" and in "111" there are strategies that eventually open the hand, leading almost surely to goal **coffee**, eventually turn, leading almost surely to goal **plate**, or only move and close without turning, leading almost surely to **espresso**. Thus, by ranging over all possible strategies for checking our quality criteria, we see that there is no $\mu\vartheta$-state 2-prediction possible in those states (cf. first line above). Singleton predictions are trivial for goal states but also those that can reach only a single goal.

Let us more elaborate on the case where the greedy computation scheme in Algorithm 1 is not successful and one has to check possible sets with at most k goals whether their prediction quality exceeds the quality threshold. In fact, while in Example 2 this situation did not arise, this can well happen for the canonical prediction quality μ_φ (see Remark 1).

Example 3. Let $S = \{\imath, g, h, h'\}$, $G = \{g, h, h'\}$, $Act = \{\alpha, \alpha'\}$, and transitions are given by $P(\imath, \alpha, g) = P(\imath, \alpha', g) = 0.3$, $P(\imath, \alpha, h) = P(\imath, \alpha', h') = 0.6$, and $P(\imath, \alpha, h') = P(\imath, \alpha', h) = 0.1$. Then, Algorithm 1 with $k = 2$, the canonical prediction quality μ_φ, and $\vartheta = 0.5$ first adds goal g in state s, since

$$\mu_\varphi(\imath, g) = 0.3 \;\geq\; \mu_\varphi(\imath, h) = \mu_\varphi(\imath, h') = 0.1.$$

After adding goal h or h', we obtain $\pi(\imath) = \{g, h\}$ or $\pi(\imath) = \{g, h'\}$ with $|\pi(\imath)| = k = 2$, where $\mu_\varphi\big(\imath, \pi(\imath)\big) = 0.4$, not exceeding ϑ. This leads the algorithm to invoke a subset search, finally returning the complete $\mu_\varphi\vartheta$-state k-prediction π with $\pi(\imath) = \{h, h'\}$ since $\mu_\varphi\big(\imath, \{h, h'\}\big) = 0.7 \geq \vartheta$.

This example already hints at the $\mu_\varphi\vartheta$-state k-prediction decision problem to be not easily solvable. In fact, this problem is NP-complete, which can be shown by a reduction from the *minimum hitting set problem (MHS)* [15].

Theorem 2. *The $\mu_\varphi\vartheta$-state k-prediction decision problem is NP-complete.*

3.3 Cost-Aware Predictions

In many practical applications it is not only relevant to reach a goal, but also to do so with meeting cost constraints. For instance, when costs are given by means of energy and we are in a state with low battery, it is important to also take the energy budget into account when predicting goals to be reached. We hence extend our notion of prediction quality (cf. Definition 2) to assess costs for reaching a predicted goal.

Definition 4 (Cost prediction quality). *A* cost prediction quality *for $(\mathcal{M}, G)$ is a mapping $\nu\colon \mathbb{N} \times S \times \wp(G) \to [0,1]$ where for all $c \in \mathbb{N}$ the mapping $\nu_c\colon S \times \wp(G) \to [0,1]$ defined by $\nu_c(s, X) = \nu(c, s, X)$ for all $s \in S$, $X \subseteq G$ is a prediction quality. If for all $c, c' \in \mathbb{N}$ we have that $c \leq c'$ implies $\nu_c \leq \nu_{c'}$, we call ν* increasing *and likewise, if $c \leq c'$ implies $\nu_c \geq \nu_{c'}$, we call ν* decreasing.

Intuitively, increasing measures shall be used when reaching goals at high costs is preferred, e.g., when charging a battery if costs model energy or if time is seen as cost and goal-directed behavior tries to extend the time until some maintenance

Algorithm 2: Synthesize cost-maximal $\nu_c\vartheta$-state k-prediction

input : MDP with goals $(\mathcal{M}, G)$, $k \in \mathbb{N}$, decreasing cost prediction quality ν, quality threshold $\vartheta \in [0,1]$
output: A cost-maximal $\nu_c\vartheta$-state k-prediction π or **false** if there is none

$c_{\max} := 1$
while $\text{SYNTHKMIN}(\mathcal{M}, G, k, \nu_{c_{\max}}, \vartheta)$ **do**
  $c_{\max} := 2 \cdot c_{\max}$
$c := c_{\min} := \lfloor c_{\max}/2 \rfloor$
while $c_{\max} - c_{\min} > 1$ **do**
  $c := \lfloor \frac{c_{\max}+c_{\min}}{2} \rfloor$
  if $\text{SYNTHKMIN}(\mathcal{M}, G, k, \nu_c, \vartheta)$ **then**
    $c_{\min} := c$
  else
    $c_{\max} := c$
return c, $\text{SYNTHKMIN}(\mathcal{M}, G, k, \nu_c, \vartheta)$

operation. Decreasing measures are relevant when lowering costs is preferable, e.g., when draining a battery in case of energy consumption or to increase performance if costs stand for execution times.

Natural candidates for cost prediction qualities are cost-bounded reachability probabilities. Here, increasing and decreasing measures $\nu_{\leq}$ and $\nu_{\geq}$, respectively, can be specified for all $s \in S$, $c \in \mathbb{N}$, and $X \subseteq G$ by

$$\nu_{\leq c}(s, X) \quad = \quad \Pr^{\min}_{\mathcal{M},s}\left((\neg G)\mathsf{U}^{\leq c} X\right) \tag{5}$$

$$\nu_{\geq c}(s, X) \quad = \quad \Pr^{\min}_{\mathcal{M},s}\left((\neg G)\mathsf{U}^{\geq c} X\right). \tag{6}$$

Cost-Optimal k-Predictions. Synthesizing $\nu_c\vartheta$-state k-predictions for a fixed cost bound c could possibly be done by Algorithm 1 (see the definition of cost prediction quality). A more interesting problem is to not fix a cost bound but to determine the minimal or maximal c for increasing or decreasing quality measures, respectively, for which there is a $\nu_c\vartheta$-state k-prediction.

Definition 5. *Let $(\mathcal{M}, G)$ be an MDP with goals, $k \in \mathbb{N}$, ν a cost prediction quality, and $\vartheta \in [0,1]$. A prediction π is a* cost-maximal (cost-minimal) $\nu\vartheta$-state k-prediction *if there is a $c \in \mathbb{N}$ such that π is a $\nu_c\vartheta$-state k-prediction and for all $c' > c$ ($c' < c$) there is no $\nu_{c'}\vartheta$-state k-prediction.*

If also a synthesis of such cost-optimal k-predictions can be achieved, this then also provides predictions that (to some extent) predict costs to be spend for reaching goals. Towards a synthesis algorithm, let us first note that computing the minimal and maximal cost bounds for canonical cost qualities (5) and (6), respectively, and exceeding a quality threshold ϑ corresponds to classical quantile computations [6]. We use similar techniques by exploiting the increasing or decreasing property of cost quality measures and performing an exponential search followed by a binary search on cost bounds while stepwise invoking Algorithm 1. Algorithm 2 implements the cost-maximizing case for decreasing cost quality measures, assuming there is some cost bound $c_{\max}$ such that there is no $\nu_{c_{\max}}\vartheta$-state k-prediction. First, we perform an exponential search, i.e., the cost bound $c_{\max}$ is exponentially increased until we cannot synthesize any $\nu_{c_{\max}}\vartheta$-state k-prediction anymore (cf. Line 3). At Line 4 we then have the situation where there is such a prediction for $c_{\min}$ but not for $c_{\max}$. Shrinking the interval $[c_{\min}, c_{\max}]$ then is the purpose of a binary search (see Line 6).

Proposition 1. *Let $(\mathcal{M}, G)$ be an MDP with goals, ν an additive decreasing cost prediction quality, $\vartheta \in [0,1]$, and $k \in \mathbb{N}$. Then if there is a $\nu_0\vartheta$-state k-prediction and a cost bound $c_{\max} \in \mathbb{N}$ for which there is no $\nu_{c_{\max}}\vartheta$-state k-prediction, then Algorithm 2 returns a cost-maximal $\nu\vartheta$-state k-prediction.*

A similar algorithm as Algorithm 2 and proposition can be also established for increasing cost prediction qualities in a straight-forward manner, starting with an exponential search until a prediction can be synthesized and then a binary search with flipped roles of $c_{\max}$ and $c_{\min}$.

Example 4. Continue Example 2 with the canonical decreasing cost prediction quality $\nu_{\geq}$ (6). Algorithm 2 first performs an exponential search until $c_{\max} = 64$, where no prediction on the run $211 \xrightarrow{\text{move}} 111 \xrightarrow{\text{open}} 121 \xrightarrow{\text{move}} 021$ can be made since from "121" the goal **coffee** is reached in less than 64 ms and this is the only non-trivial 2-prediction state on this path in the unconstrained case (cf. Example 2). The binary search then terminates at the maximal cost bound $c = 50$ such that there is a complete $\nu_{\geq 50}0.9$-state 2-prediction

$$\begin{aligned}
&\pi(211) = \pi(111) = \pi(000) = \pi(001) = \pi(021) = \pi(100) = \varnothing\\
&\pi(010) = \pi(110) = \{\textbf{plate}\}\\
&\pi(011) = \{\textbf{espresso}\}\\
&\pi(221) = \pi(121) = \{\textbf{coffee}\}\\
&\pi(201) = \pi(101) = \{\textbf{plate}, \textbf{espresso}\}
\end{aligned}$$

Observe that there is no prediction in goal states, since non-zero cost prediction qualities (6) require costs invested while passing through non-goal states only.

3.4 Negative Latency

Consider a communication system modeled as MDP with goals in which costs correspond to timings of system executions and transmissions. Then, anticipatory networking [36] can be implemented through predictions in system states, fitting well in our formal framework developed in the last sections. Following the principle of negative latency as anticipatory networking with guarantees as we motivated in the introduction, we illustrate in this section how to exploit prediction guarantees to turn anticipatory networking into *negative latency*.

Intuitively, we define *negative latency* as the amount of time a goal can be predicted with high confidence, i.e., predicting goals with meeting prediction quality criteria. Formally, let $(\mathcal{M}, G) = (S, Act, P, C, \imath, G)$ be an MDP with goals where the cost function C assigns (non-zero) execution times to state-action pairs. Negative latency can then be established through cost bounds of $\nu_c\vartheta$-state k-predictions (see Definition 5).

Definition 6 (Negative latency). *For $k \in \mathbb{N}$, decreasing cost prediction quality ν, and $\vartheta \in [0,1]$ the MDP with goals $(\mathcal{M}, G)$ has $\nu\vartheta$-state* k-negative latency

$$\ell \;=\; \max\{c \in \mathbb{N} \mid \textit{there is a } \nu_c\vartheta\textit{-state } k\textit{-prediction}\}.$$

When an MDP with goals has k-negative latency ℓ, then at minimum ℓ ahead of time there is a prediction that guarantees with high confidence to reach the predicted goals. To this end, the impact of at most k predicted goals can be anticipated and precomputed ℓ time ahead, used to reduce latency by ℓ. Practically most relevant is the case where $k = 1$, i.e., the time that one single outcome can be predicted ahead of time [34].

The possible negative latency in given MDPs and predictions as implementations could be computed by Algorithm 2. The inverse synthesis problem might be also relevant: given a target negative latency ℓ and compute the smallest k such that there is a $\nu_\ell\vartheta$-state k-prediction. This can be achieved by a simple algorithm similar to Algorithm 2 but performing a binary search on k.

4 Machine Learning for Negative Latency

Nondeterminism in the system's underlying MDP model is commonly interpreted as environmental impact, e.g., human input as in our running example, or unknown behavior from the side of the system. To account for all possible environmental and unknown influences, still providing strict quality guarantees on predictions, we hence quantified over all possible strategies in our canonical quality measures $\nu_{\leq c}$ (5) and $\nu_{\geq c}$ (6), covering all worst-case scenarios. However, this view is overly conservative as neither a human user nor the underlying system specifically "design" their strategy in such a way to defy possible predictions. Instead, another perspective is to consider user's strategies as memoryless and randomized but hidden, i.e., unknown to the system communicating with the user [5,9]. This implies that the underlying model does not include any nondeterminism anymore but instead also transitions of which we do not know the exact transition probability.

In this section, we describe how machine-learning predictors can be used to resolve nondeterminism by probabilism with uncertainty that follow the canonical quality criteria. For this, we first utilize results from reinforcement learning to estimate strategies from sample runs on the system, on which the machinery of the last section can be directly applied due to the same underlying concepts of MDPs. Second, we showcase how supervised machine learning can be used to predict goals in system states based on continuous sensor data, implementing an extension of the abstract predictions on MDPs we introduced.

4.1 Strategy Estimation

By integrating information from sample data on an underlying strategy, we cannot expect to obtain exact transition probabilities but estimations only. To this end, we define a formalism of sets of MCs to reflect this uncertainty.

Definition 7 (L_1-Markov chain). *An* L_1-Markov chain (L1MC) $\mathcal{C}^e$ *is a Markov chain* $\mathcal{C}$ *along with an* error function $e \colon S \to \mathbb{R}$.

Given an MC $\mathcal{C} = (S, P, C, \imath)$ and error function e, we call an MC $\mathcal{C}' = (S, P', C, \imath)$ an *instantiation* of $\mathcal{C}^e$ if $\|P(s) - P'(s)\|_1 \leq e(s)$ for all $s \in S$. The set of all instantiations of an L1MC $\mathcal{C}^e$ is denoted by $[\mathcal{C}^e]$. Intuitively, an L1MC $\mathcal{C}^e$ represents the set of all MCs where the L_1-distance between their transition probabilities in each state s is bounded by $e(s)$. The semantics of L1MCs arises from first picking an instantiation $\mathcal{C}' \in [\mathcal{C}^e]$ and then considering all infinite paths on $\mathcal{C}'$ as within standard Markov chains, similar to the *uncertain Markov chain (UMC)* semantics in the setting of *interval Markov chains (IMCs)* [3,12,37]. In the framework of IMCs, another common semantics is the *interval MDP* semantics, where an adversarial player chooses the transition probabilities at each step [3,12,37]. However, considering our assumption of the existence of a fixed memoryless strategy we do not consider this variant here.

Strategy Estimation. To represent past information gathered through prior knowledge or observations from an underlying MDP model $\mathcal{M} = (S, Act, P, C, \imath)$, we consider a data set $\mathcal{D} \subseteq Paths(\mathcal{M}, \imath)$ of paths observed in $\mathcal{M}$. We denote by $\#_{\mathcal{D}}(s, A)$ the number of occurrences of an action from the set $A \subseteq Act$ being executed in state $s \in S$ in paths of $\mathcal{D}$. As we assume there is a fixed and memoryless strategy σ that is employed in the system, even observations of single transitions without history are sufficient to estimate σ by a set of strategies $\Sigma_{\mathcal{D}}$. We do this by an S-rectangular set of strategies, i.e., we estimate $\sigma(s)$ by a set of distributions $\Sigma_{\mathcal{D}}(s) \subseteq Distr\big(Act(s)\big)$ for each $s \in S$ and construct $\Sigma_{\mathcal{D}}$ as the cross product of all $\Sigma_{\mathcal{D}}(s)$.

Further, we introduce an *error tolerance* $\delta \in \mathbb{R}$ to formalize uncertainty that $\sigma(s)$ lies within any (non-trivial) $\Sigma_{\mathcal{D}}(s)$. To provide guarantees on the latter we require that $\sigma \in \Sigma_{\mathcal{D}}$ with probability at least $1-\delta$. As we aim for S-rectangular estimations, we split the error tolerance δ uniformly over all states, defining $\delta_T = \delta/|S|$. For all states $s \in S$ we then can utilize a result of Weissman et al. [50] to guarantee that $\sigma(s) \in \Sigma_{\mathcal{D}}(s)$ with probability at least $1 - \delta_T$:

Definition 8 (L_1-strategy estimation). *Let* $\mathcal{M}$ *be an MDP and* $\mathcal{D}$ *be a set of runs on* $\mathcal{M}$ *sampled from common fixed strategy* σ. *For a given error tolerance* $\delta_T \in (0,1)$ *we define the* L_1-strategy interval estimate $\Sigma_{\mathcal{D}}$ *for all* $s \in S$ *by*

$$\Sigma_{\mathcal{D}}(s) = \left\{ \hat{\sigma}(s) \in Distr(Act(s)) \;\middle|\; \|\hat{\sigma}(s) - \hat{p}(s)\|_1 \leq \sqrt{\frac{2(\ln(2^{|S|}-2) - \ln \delta_T)}{\#_{\mathcal{D}}(s, Act)}} \right\}$$

where $\hat{p}(s)(\alpha) = \frac{\#_{\mathcal{D}}(s,\alpha)}{\#_{\mathcal{D}}(s,Act)}$.

This strategy estimation can be included into our framework towards L1MCs estimates of MDPs: Given an MDP $\mathcal{M}$ with a fixed, but hidden, strategy σ that gives rise to the induced MC $\mathcal{M}^\sigma$. Then for an error tolerance δ we can construct an L1MC $\mathcal{M}^e_\mathcal{D}$ from an MC $\mathcal{M}_\mathcal{D}$ that resolves nondeterminism through $\mathcal{D}$ such that $\mathcal{M}^\sigma$ is an instantiation of $\mathcal{M}^e_\mathcal{D}$ with probability at least $1-\delta$.

Definition 9 (MDP estimation). *Let $\mathcal{M} = (S, Act, C, P, \imath)$ be an MDP, $\mathcal{D} \subseteq Paths(\mathcal{M}, \imath)$ sampled from a fixed strategy σ, and $\delta \in (0,1)$ an error tolerance. The $\mathcal{D}$-estimate of $\mathcal{M}$ is the L1MC $\mathcal{M}^e_\mathcal{D}$ with $\mathcal{M}_\mathcal{D} = (S \cup S_{Act}, \hat{C}, \hat{P}, \imath)$ where $S_{Act} = \{s_\alpha \mid s \in S, \alpha \in Act(s)\}$, and where for all $s, s' \in S \cup S_{Act}$ cost estimates $\hat{C}$ are defined by $\hat{C}(s) = C(s,\alpha)$ if $s = s_\alpha \in S_{Act}$ and $\hat{C}(s) = 0$ otherwise, probability estimates $\hat{P}$ and the error function e are defined by*

$$\hat{P}(s,s') = \begin{cases} \frac{\#_\mathcal{D}(s,\alpha)}{\#_\mathcal{D}(s,Act(s))} & \text{if } s \in S, s' = s_\alpha \in S_{Act} \text{ and } \#_\mathcal{D}(s, Act(s)) > 0 \\ 1/|Act(s)| & \text{if } s \in S, s' = s_\alpha \in S_{Act} \text{ and } \#_\mathcal{D}(s, Act(s)) = 0 \\ P(s,\alpha,s') & \text{if } s = s_\alpha \in S_{Act} \text{ and } s' \in S \\ 0 & \text{otherwise} \end{cases}$$

$$e(s) = \begin{cases} 0 & \text{if } s \in S \\ |Act(s)| & \text{if } s = s_\alpha \in S_{Act} \text{ and } \#_\mathcal{D}(s, Act) = 0 \\ \sqrt{\frac{2(\ln(2^{|S|}-2) - \ln \delta_T)}{\#_\mathcal{D}(s,Act)}} & \text{if } s = s_\alpha \in S_{Act} \text{ and } \#_\mathcal{D}(s, Act) > 0 \end{cases}$$

Intuitively, we replace each transition in $\mathcal{M}$ by two transitions in $\mathcal{M}_\mathcal{D}$: The first one estimates the probability that an action α is taken with an admissible L_1-error as in the L_1-strategy estimation (cf. Definition 8), while the second performs the original transition of $\mathcal{M}$ without any error. For the first, we take care of the case where $\#_\mathcal{D}(s, Act(s)) = 0$, by setting the error function to a value such that every transition function is a valid instantiation (see second case of the $\hat{P}$ definition). The newly introduced states s_α serve as the intermediate states between these transitions such that any run in $\mathcal{M}_\mathcal{D}$ alternates between states from S and S_{Act}. Further, intermediate states also encode taken actions, leading to a well-defined cost function that preserves accumulated rewards.

Note that each instantiation $\mathcal{C} \in [\mathcal{M}^e_\mathcal{D}]$ corresponds to the MDP $\mathcal{M}$ under a strategy $\sigma_\mathcal{C} \in \Sigma_\mathcal{D}$. Since the probability that the hidden strategy is within the L_1-strategy estimate, i.e., $\sigma \in \Sigma_\mathcal{D}$, is at least $1-\delta$, we immediately obtain that the probability that an $\mathcal{M}^\sigma$ with stutter steps has an instantiation of $\mathcal{M}^e_\mathcal{D}$ is also at least $1-\delta$. Here, for including stutter steps in $\mathcal{M}^\sigma$, for each transition $s \xrightarrow{\alpha} s'$ in $\mathcal{M}$ there is a finite path $s \ldots s'$ in $\mathcal{C}$ that does not contain any other states from S, and that has the same probability mass and accumulated cost.

Proposition 2. *Let $\mathcal{M}$ be an MDP, $\mathcal{D}$ be a set of runs on $\mathcal{M}$ sampled from a fixed strategy σ, and $\delta \in (0,1)$ an error tolerance. Then with probability at least $1-\delta$ there is a $\mathcal{C} \in [\mathcal{M}^e_\mathcal{D}]$ that is $\mathcal{M}^\sigma$ up to stutter steps.*

Example 5. Let us again consider our running example (see Example 1). We have three states in which nondeterministic choices can be made: states "211",

"101", and "111". Assume we have observed a total of 100 runs in the environment and made the following observations:

state s	$\#_{\mathcal{D}}(s,\alpha)$ for action α:				$\#_{\mathcal{D}}(s, Act)$
	close	move	open	turn	
210	10	40	50	–	100
101	–	7	–	3	10
111	1	14	9	1	25

For a given error tolerance of δ we can then construct the MDP estimation via an L1MC. In Fig. 2 we show the MC $\mathcal{C}$ of the L1MC $\mathcal{M}^{e}_{\mathcal{D}}$ for this specific example. Note that we omit auxiliary states here if they only had a deterministic successor anyway, e.g., state "211_{close}" as its only successor would be "201".

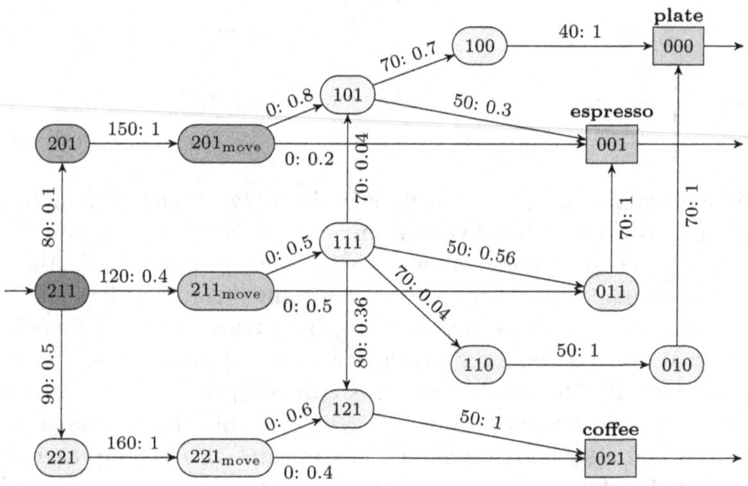

Fig. 2. Example MC of a grabbing scenario with estimated strategy

For $\delta = 0.1$ we obtain an error tolerance $\delta_T = \frac{1}{30}$ for each of the three states in which we estimate the strategy. The corresponding error function e is then computed as in Definition 9 where all the non-zero entries are

$$e(211) \approx 0.264, \qquad e(101) \approx 0.692, \qquad \text{and} \qquad e(111) \approx 0.589.$$

***k*-Predictions in L1MCs.** We can consider our framework of prediction in MDPs (see Sect. 3) in the setting of L1MCs. For this, we take quality measures that quantify over all possible instantiations of an L1MC instead of all strategies of an MDP as done for canonical qualities (3), (5), and (6). Formally, for an

L1MC with goals $(\mathcal{M}^{\mathfrak{e}}_{\mathcal{D}}, G)$, we define the prediction quality measure $\hat{\mu}_{\varphi}\colon S \times \wp(G) \to [0,1]$ for all states $s \in S$ and goals $X \subseteq G$ by

$$\hat{\mu}_{\varphi}(s,X) = \min_{\mathcal{C}\in[\mathcal{M}^{\mathfrak{e}}_{\mathcal{D}}]} \Pr_{\mathcal{C},s}(\varphi_X) = \min_{\mathcal{C}\in[\mathcal{M}^{\mathfrak{e}}_{\mathcal{D}}]} \Pr_{\mathcal{C},s}\big((\neg G)\mathsf{U}X\big) \ .$$

Similarly, for $\sim \in \{\leq, \geq\}$ we define cost prediction qualities as

$$\hat{\nu}_{\sim c}(s,X) = \min_{\mathcal{C}\in[\mathcal{M}^{\mathfrak{e}}_{\mathcal{D}}]} \Pr_{\mathcal{C},s}\big((\neg G)\mathsf{U}^{\sim c}X\big) \ .$$

Note that in case the data set is empty, i.e., no information about the resolution of the nondeterminism is available, the (cost) prediction quality as well as the quality threshold agree for an MDP $\mathcal{M}$ and the corresponding L1MC $\mathcal{M}^{\mathfrak{e}}_{\mathcal{D}}$ estimating $\mathcal{M}$. Intuitively, this is due to the corresponding transition function corresponding to an L1MC that is an instantiation of $\mathcal{M}^{\mathfrak{e}}_{\mathcal{D}}$, no matter by which (possibly probabilistic) scheduler the nondeterminism is resolved.

In that sense, we see that even in general and with using canonical quality measures, taking on the L1MC view on MDPs is beneficial, since even without any data collected the qualities calculated are equivalent:

Lemma 1. *Let $(\mathcal{M}, G)$ be an MDP with goals and $\mathcal{M}^{\mathfrak{e}}_{\mathcal{D}}$ an L1MC that estimates $\mathcal{M}$ as in Definition 9 with the empty data set $\mathcal{D} = \varnothing$. Then, for all states $s \in S$, goals $X \subseteq G$, $\sim \in \{\leq, \geq\}$, and cost thresholds $c \in \mathbb{N}$*

$$\hat{\mu}_{\varphi}(s,X) = \Pr^{\min}_{\mathcal{M},s}\big((\neg G)\mathsf{U}X\big) \quad \text{and} \quad \hat{\nu}_{\sim c}(s,X) = \Pr^{\min}_{\mathcal{M},s}\big((\neg G)\mathsf{U}^{\sim c}X\big).$$

Observe that with using L1MCs, however, we introduce additional uncertainty as we can only guarantee with probability $1-\delta$ that the MC $\mathcal{M}^{\sigma}$ induced by the underlying hidden strategy σ is actually an instantiation of the L1MC $\mathcal{M}^{\mathfrak{e}}_{\mathcal{D}}$. However, when lifting the definition of quality thresholds to L1MCs, we can incorporate this error term:

Definition 10. *Given an MDP with goals $(\mathcal{M}, G)$ and an error tolerance $\delta \in [0,1]$, let $\mathcal{M}^{\mathfrak{e}}_{\mathcal{D}}$ be the L1MC estimating $\mathcal{M}$ through data $\mathcal{D} \subseteq Paths(\mathcal{M}, \imath)$. Further, given a quality threshold $\vartheta \in [0,1]$, a cost bound $c \in \mathbb{N}$, and cost bound c, a proper prediction π for $(\mathcal{M}_{\mathcal{D}}, G)$ is called a $\hat{\nu}_{\sim c}\vartheta\delta$-*state prediction *where $\sim \in \{\leq, \geq\}$ if for all states $s \in S$ with $\pi(s) \neq \varnothing$ we have*

$$(1-\delta)\cdot\hat{\nu}_{\sim c}\big(s,\pi(s)\big) \ \geq \ \vartheta \ . \tag{7}$$

Proposition 3. *Given an MDP with goals $(\mathcal{M}, G)$ and a $\hat{\nu}_{\sim c}\vartheta\delta$-state prediction $\pi(s)$ as in Definition 10, then $\Pr_{\mathcal{M}^{\sigma},s}\big((\neg G)\mathsf{U}^{\sim c}X\big) \geq \vartheta$.*

Intuitively, $(1-\delta)$ is the (minimal) probability that the underlying MC $\mathcal{M}^{\sigma}$ is an instantiation of $\mathcal{M}^{\mathfrak{e}}_{\mathcal{D}}$. This is feasible when we see $\hat{\nu}$ is related to the worst-case reachability probabilities of goals, e.g., being one of the canonical cost predictions $\hat{\nu}_{\leq c}$ or $\hat{\nu}_{\geq c}$. Then, $\hat{\nu}_c\big(s,\pi(s)\big)$ is the minimal probability over all instantiations to fulfill the prediction in state s with given cost constraint depend on c.

Example 6. Let us continue Example 5 by computing a $\nu_{\leq 250}\vartheta\delta$-state 1-prediction in the initial state "211" with $\delta = 0.1$ while maximizing ϑ. To do this, we compute $\nu_{\leq 250}(211, x)$ for all $x \in \{\textbf{plate}, \textbf{espresso}, \textbf{coffee}\}$ by constructing a minimizing instantiation for each goal. Here, we take an adversary role trying to minimize the probability to reach each goal state.
(plate): Since $0.1 \leq e(211)/2$ and $0.08 \leq e(111)/2$, there is an instantiation where **plate** is unreachable, obtainable by minimizing the probability from transitions to states "201", "101", and "110". Hence, $\hat{\nu}_{\leq 250}(211, \textbf{coffee}) = 0$.
(espresso): As $0.3 \leq e(101)/2$ we have instantiations with $P(101, \textbf{espresso}) = 0$. In an effort to minimize the reachability probability of **espresso** we pick an instantiation where $P(211, 211_{\text{move}})$ is as small as possible. To ensure that the MC is still an instantiation, we must have $P(211, 211_{\text{move}}) \geq 0.4 - e(211)/2 \approx 0.268$. Similarly, we minimize $P(111, 011) \geq 0.56 - e(111)/2 \approx 0.265$. Hence, we have an instantiation with only one path reaching **espresso** and by evaluating its probability we obtain $\hat{\nu}_{\leq 250}(211, \textbf{espresso}) = 0.268 \cdot 0.265 = 0.071$.
(coffee): The path via states "221" and "121" violates our cost constraint and is thus not relevant to our example. As before, we minimize $P(111, 121) \geq 0.36 - e(111)/2 \approx 0.065$. For state "211" we would like to minimize the transition probability to both states "111" and "221". However, as the error function only allows a fixed L_1 deviation of the transition function, we can only minimize one of the two. In this case we prefer to minimize $P(211, 221) \geq 0.5 - e(211)/2 \approx 0.368$ as the probability to reach **coffee** is greater from "221" than from "111". This leaves two non-zero paths reaching **coffee** under the given cost constraints from which we can compute $\hat{\nu}_{\leq 250}(211, \textbf{coffee}) = 0.368 \cdot 0.4 + 0.4 \cdot 0.065 \approx 0.173$.

Thus, we have that the goal **coffee** is a $\nu_{\leq 250}\vartheta\delta$-state 1-prediction in state "211" where $\delta = 0.1$ and $\vartheta \approx 0.173$ is maximal. Notice the difference to the original setting where no 1-prediction with $\vartheta > 0$ could be made in the initial state. This in fact matches our intuition: If we have observed that a person has often grabbed the coffee in the past, we might predict with some level of confidence that they will do so again.

Computing $\hat{\nu}_{\sim c}\vartheta\delta$-state k-Predictions. Notice that a high error tolerance δ implies that the set of instantiations also grows, which in turn makes cost prediction quality estimates $\hat{\nu}$ smaller. Finding the optimal value of δ, i.e., the value that maximizes the left-hand side of (7) seems like a hard task for which we do not see a direct procedure. However, for a given δ it is straight forward to compute $\mathcal{M}_{\mathcal{D}}^{e}$ by following Definition 9. We now show that we can also compute the values of $\hat{\nu}_{\leq}$ and $\hat{\nu}_{\geq}$ in L1MCs as well as lift the algorithms for computing k-estimates towards L1MCs. Lifting Algorithm 1 and Algorithm 2 to L1MCs is relatively straight forward as we only need to replace all occurrences of μ and ν with $\hat{\mu}$ and $\hat{\nu}$. In turn, this leaves the question how to compute the canonical quality measures $\hat{\mu}_{\varphi}$, $\hat{\nu}_{\leq}$, and $\hat{\nu}_{\geq}$ (cf. Eqs. (3), (5) and (6)).

Without cost restrictions the canonical quality measure solely relies on computing $\hat{\mu} = \min_{\mathcal{C} \in [\mathcal{M}_{\mathcal{D}}^{e}]} \Pr_{\mathcal{C},s}\big((\neg G) \mathsf{U} X\big)$. This can be computed by an extension of the standard value iteration algorithm that roughly works as follows [41,42]: In each iteration, we construct the minimizing instantiation $\mathcal{C} \in [\mathcal{M}_{\mathcal{D}}^{e}]$ w.r.t. the value function computed in the previous iteration. For this, we initialize all transitions as $P'(s, s') = \hat{P}(s, s')$ and then shift probability mass away from those successors that have the highest value into states that have the lowest value, continuing this until either the transition is deterministic, or we have shifted a total of $e(s)/2$ of probability mass. While we allow for different instantiations of transitions in each step of the value iteration, the algorithm converges towards a probability-minimizing instantiation of the L1MC. Hence, the value iteration computes the value iteration under the UMC semantics (cf. Definition 7). Convergence for this procedure was originally only shown for discounted rewards [42] but later also for contracting models [52], i.e., models such that a goal state is always eventually reached, which is a given assumption for MDPs with goals (see Sect. 3). While [52] does not directly consider L1MCs, the convergence proof does not rely on the specific shape of the uncertainty.

In the case where we have cost constraints, we have to compute $\hat{\nu}_{\geq c}$ or $\hat{\nu}_{\leq c}$. For a given threshold ϑ this is equivalent to deciding *probabilistic computation tree logic (PCTL)* formulas to hold in all instantiations. While we are not aware of any results showing this for L1MCs, this is an active area of research for the related model of IMCs [21]. For these, the decision problem can be solved via a reduction to checking *parametric Markov reward models* [1] against step-bounded PCTL formulas [3]. Using, e.g., a binary search on ϑ, we can approximate $\hat{\nu}_{\sim c}$ to arbitrary precision. While L1MC and IMCs generally differ in their semantics, they do coincide for MCs in which every state has only two successors. Further, any MC can be transformed into this form [51]. Alternatively, one can also directly encode the PCTL decision problem on L1MCs as a quadratic program by treating the transition probabilities as variables and adding constraints according to the error function given by the L1MC.

4.2 Supervised Learning

While estimates on the strategy employed in the model can yield better predictions, it requires sampling data for every state of the environment to do so. In particular, it does not exploit the fact that the strategy may behave similarly in similar states, e.g., that only differ slightly in spatial coordinates. Under the assumption that similar states indeed employ similar strategies in practice, we can encode the components of a state as numerical values and use a neural network to estimate the strategy employed, essentially interpolating the strategy at states where no or little data is available. While we cannot give precise guarantees over the prediction quality anymore, this allows us to cover larger state spaces with less data. Additionally, with this method using a neural network, it is easily possible to handle even continuous state spaces.

Goal Predictions Through ML. Supervised learning for classification problems aims to predict a label y from a set of labels Y based on a system state $\mathbf{x}$. Referring to the example given in Fig. 1, $\mathbf{x}$ represents the posture of the hand, captured via a sensor glove for example, and y is the goal of a human grab. Note that we depart from the notations of our MDP framework of the last sections, since we also allow for continuous states $\mathbf{x}$ and multiple goal states labelled by single goal predictions $y \in Y$.

In general, we assume a data generating process $p_{data}(\mathbf{x}, y) = p(y \mid \mathbf{x})p(\mathbf{x})$ over states $\mathbf{x}$ and goal labels $y \in Y$. The aim is then to fit the tuneable parameters θ of a model $p_\theta(y \mid \mathbf{x})$ to increase the quality of the prediction. Since the data generating process $p_{data}(\mathbf{x}, y)$ is not known a priori, a data set $\mathcal{D} = \{(\mathbf{x}^i, y^i)\}_{i=1}^N$ consisting of N pairs $(\mathbf{x}_i, y_i)$ is used to represent the empirical distribution $\hat{p}_{data}(\mathbf{x}, y)$. The common machine learning objective is then to minimize the *empirical risk* defined as

$$\mathbb{E}_{(\mathbf{x},y)\sim\hat{p}_{data}(\mathbf{x},y)}\left[\mathcal{L}(p_\theta(y \mid \mathbf{x}), y)\right] \quad = \quad \frac{1}{N}\sum\nolimits_{i=1}^{N} \mathcal{L}(p_\theta(y \mid \mathbf{x}^i), y^i),$$

with $\mathcal{L}$ representing a loss function, measuring the discrepancy between the model output $p_\theta(y \mid \mathbf{x}^i)$ and corresponding target label y^i [16]. Therefore, we adjust the model parameters by optimizing for

$$\theta^* \quad = \quad \arg\min_{\theta} \sum\nolimits_{i=1}^{N} \mathcal{L}(p_\theta(y \mid \mathbf{x}^i), y^i).$$

Uncertainty in ML Predictors. Neural networks are subject to *aleatoric* and *epistemic* uncertainty [20]. Similar to the predictions we discussed in our MDP prediction framework, high-quality predictions should satisfy two goals. First, the neural network should accurately predict the most likely label $\hat{y} = \arg\max_k p_\theta(y{=}k \mid \mathbf{x})$ in any state $\mathbf{x}$. Second, it should also communicate the uncertainty a prediction is entailed with. A simple and computationally easy measure to quantify the uncertainty of a prediction for state $\mathbf{x}$ is to compute the entropy [38] of the predictive distribution, also known as *predictive entropy* [22]:

$$H(p_\theta, \mathbf{x}) \quad = \quad -\sum\nolimits_{y \in Y} p_\theta(y \mid \mathbf{x}) \cdot \log_2\left(p_\theta(y \mid \mathbf{x})\right).$$

We extend the entropy to the k-prediction setting by

$$H_k(p_\theta, \mathbf{x}) \quad = \quad -\sum\nolimits_{\substack{Z \subseteq Y \\ |Z|=k}} p_\theta(Z \mid \mathbf{x}) \cdot \log_2\left(p_\theta(Z \mid \mathbf{x})\right). \tag{8}$$

The prediction of the k most likely predictions can then be associated with a measure of uncertainty $H_k(p_\theta, \mathbf{x})$ in state $\mathbf{x}$. While this slightly departs from goal-dependent prediction qualities (cf. Definition 3) in our MDP setting, we can also impose a threshold ϑ on the *confidence* computed as the inverse of the normalized uncertainty $1 - \frac{H_k(p_\theta, \mathbf{x})}{\log_2 |Y|}$. The prediction can be potentially rejected if the associate confidence of that prediction does not exceed ϑ.

Trustworthy Uncertainty Estimates by Calibration. To correctly quantify uncertainty associated with predictions, a neural network needs to be *well-calibrated.* Calibration allows to justifiably determine thresholds on the predictive uncertainty [39]. For the case of predicting a single goal, a neural network classifier is considered calibrated if for any predicted goals $\hat{y}$ and the corresponding classifier probability output $\hat{p} = p_\theta(\hat{y} = y \mid \mathbf{x})$ we have $P(\hat{y} = y \mid \hat{p} = p) = p$ for all $p \in [0, 1]$. Intuitively, this means a neural network is well-calibrated if its output $\hat{p}$ matches the probabilities p_{data} of the data-generating process for all labels $y \in Y$. While the fact that we do not know p_{data} means that we can never expect an exact calibration, we can still employ empirical methods that yield a neural network that is close to being well-calibrated.

A commonly-used scheme for neural network calibration is to generate an ensemble of diverse neural network by randomizing the weight initialization and training process of neural network and subsequently ensemble-averaging multiple individual models [22]. We then can ensure that the estimation is probably approximately correct by utilizing statistical methods such as Hoeffding's inequality [19] or Weissman's bound on the L_1 distance used in Sect. 4.1 [50]. Note that this only guarantees that the empirically estimated neural network is calibrated w.r.t. the neural network minimizing loss on the training data $\mathcal{D}$. Hence, we cannot provide hard guarantees that the gathered data $\mathcal{D}$ is representative for the actual data-generating process.

Negative Latency. In the setting of negative latency, i.e., predicting goals ahead of time with guarantees, supervised learning can be used to tackle two fundamental problems that arise with formal MDP model-based and strategy estimations obtained from reinforcement learning. First, it is also applicable when the ground truth underlying process is completely unknown apart from the influencing features of goal-directed behavior. Then, supervised learning can provide at least tools to estimate the process based on observed data. Second, real-world processes often result in observations in the form of continuous random variables, which can be handled by most popular supervised learning techniques.

Given a neural network and estimates on prediction performance and calibration, negative latency can then be seen as the time difference between the moment of predicting the end state of an ongoing process before that end state is reached. While the predictive uncertainty of the model allows handling the trade-off between prediction accuracy and prediction rejection, the calibration estimated during training gives rise to the empirical approximation of the model to the underlying process.

Example 7. Our running example (see Example 1) has been inspired by a real-world experiment where we used a smart glove as source for sensor data during grabbing objects such as a plate, an espresso cup, or a coffee cup [34,35]. In this experiment, we used a light sensor beneath the objects to determine the time where a goal is reached (i.e., the object is lifted). Training and calibrating a neural network classifier on these inputs, we were able to obtain a predictor that

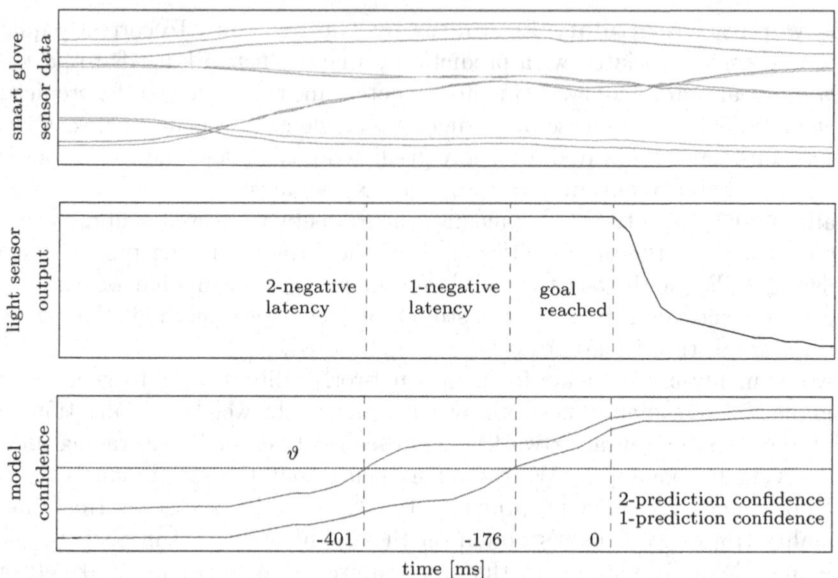

Fig. 3. Sensor data (top plot), light sensor output (center plot), and 1-prediction and 2-prediction confidence of the classifier (bottom plot) in a sample grabbing task [34].

in combination with confidence thresholds could be used to turn predictions into negative latency. Figure 3 shows a sample grab scenario from [34] where smart glove sensor data (top), the light sensor (center), and the 1-prediction and 2-prediction confidence (8) (bottom) are depicted. Note that all sensor data acquired during gradual hand movements towards the object are continuous, i.e., cannot directly be modeled within our MDP and L1MC framework with goals and predictions. In the bottom plot, we indicated the moments in time where the 1-prediction and 2-prediction confidence first surpass the quality threshold $\vartheta = 0.5$. 1-negative and 2-negative latencies then are determined by the time from these time points to the actual goal reached, i.e., 176 ms and 401 ms, respectively.

5 Concluding Remarks

In this paper, we sharpened the concept of negative latency by including formal guarantees into anticipatory computing. Through a general formal framework, we introduced goal-oriented predictions in MDPs and how they can be synthesized under formal guarantees. Applications to negative latency in the theoretical setting, but also for strategy estimations obtained by reinforcement learning and supervised learning were showcased. To this end, our work opened a new perspective on anticipatory computing, where many further research could be conducted. Our notions could be well extended to much richer classes of models, such as continuous-time MDPs or models that account for partial observability, or incremental versions. This would also imply the need for new methods, e.g., including machine-learning methods for partially observable MDPs [11]. Towards handling settings where the strategy is not necessarily fixed, it is possible to adapt the reinforcement learning approach by utilizing linearly updating intervals [43]. Causal relationships between actions in goal-directed behavior could also be the source of formal guarantees towards negative latency. A direct application would be using *degrees of sufficiency and necessity* [7] as quality measure of predictive models.

In the presented framework of cost-optimal predictions, we took on a local view on predictions, assessing the quality of predictions in states independently from each other. This approach renders our framework more accessible to machine learning applications, but might appear strict in other cases. For instance, when many rare events could only provide small negative latencies, the overall negative latency drops as well. An approach to investigate in future work would be to provide *phase-based formal guarantees* instead of state-based ones, i.e., imposing quality thresholds on runs during phases of goal-directed behavior instead. Also other synthesis problems with varying parameters such as ϑ, k, overlapping goal assignments etc., are worth directions to investigate.

References

1. Alur, R., Henzinger, T.A., Vardi, M.Y.: Parametric real-time reasoning. In: Proceedings of the Twenty-Fifth Annual ACM Symposium on Theory of Computing, STOC 1993, pp. 592–601. ACM, New York (1993)
2. Ashok, P., Křetínský, J., Weininger, M.: PAC statistical model checking for Markov decision processes and stochastic games. In: Dillig, I., Tasiran, S. (eds.) CAV 2019. LNCS, vol. 11561, pp. 497–519. Springer, Cham (2019). https://doi.org/10.1007/978-3-030-25540-4_29
3. Bacci, G., Delahaye, B., Larsen, K.G., Mariegaard, A.: Quantitative analysis of interval Markov Chains. In: Olderog, E.-R., Steffen, B., Yi, W. (eds.) Model Checking, Synthesis, and Learning. LNCS, vol. 13030, pp. 57–77. Springer, Cham (2021). https://doi.org/10.1007/978-3-030-91384-7_4
4. Baier, C., de Alfaro, L., Forejt, V., Kwiatkowska, M.: Model checking probabilistic systems. In: Handbook of Model Checking, pp. 963–999. Springer, Cham (2018). https://doi.org/10.1007/978-3-319-10575-8_28
5. Baier, C., Cuevas Rivera, D., Dubslaff, C., Kiebel, S.J.: Human-inspired models for tactile computing, chap. 8, pp. 173–200. Academic Press (2021)
6. Baier, C., Daum, M., Dubslaff, C., Klein, J., Klüppelholz, S.: Energy-utility quantiles. In: Badger, J.M., Rozier, K.Y. (eds.) NFM 2014. LNCS, vol. 8430, pp. 285–299. Springer, Cham (2014). https://doi.org/10.1007/978-3-319-06200-6_24
7. Baier, C., Dubslaff, C., Funke, F., Jantsch, S., Piribauer, J., Ziemek, R.: Operational causality - necessarily sufficient and sufficiently necessary. In: A Journey from Process Algebra via Timed Automata to Model Learning. Lecture Notes in Computer Science, vol. 13560, pp. 27–45. Springer, Heidelberg (2022). https://doi.org/10.1007/978-3-031-15629-8_2
8. Baier, C., Dubslaff, C., Korenčiak, L., Kučera, A., Řehák, V.: Synthesis of optimal resilient control strategies. In: D'Souza, D., Narayan Kumar, K. (eds.) ATVA 2017. LNCS, vol. 10482, pp. 417–434. Springer, Cham (2017). https://doi.org/10.1007/978-3-319-68167-2_27

9. Baier, C., Dubslaff, C., Wienhöft, P., Kiebel, S.J.: Strategy synthesis in markov decision processes under limited sampling access. In: Rozier, K.Y., Chaudhuri, S. (eds.) NASA Formal Methods, pp. 86–103. Springer, Cham (2023). https://doi.org/10.1007/978-3-031-33170-1_6
10. Baier, C., Katoen, J.P.: Principles of Model Checking. The MIT Press, Cambridge (2008)
11. Carr, S., Jansen, N., Wimmer, R., Fu, J., Topcu, U.: Human-in-the-loop synthesis for partially observable markov decision processes. In: 2018 Annual American Control Conference, ACC 2018, Milwaukee, WI, USA, 27–29 June 2018, pp. 762–769. IEEE (2018)
12. Chatterjee, K., Sen, K., Henzinger, T.A.: Model-checking ω-regular properties of interval markov chains. In: Amadio, R. (ed.) FoSSaCS 2008. LNCS, vol. 4962, pp. 302–317. Springer, Heidelberg (2008). https://doi.org/10.1007/978-3-540-78499-9_22
13. Fettweis, G.P.: The tactile internet: applications and challenges. IEEE Veh. Technol. Mag. **9**(1), 64–70 (2014)
14. Fitzek, F.H., Li, S.C., Speidel, S., Strufe, T.: Chapter 1 - Tactile Internet with Human-in-the-Loop: New Frontiers of Transdisciplinary Research. Academic Press (2021)
15. Garey, M.R., Johnson, D.S.: Computers and Intractability: A Guide to the Theory of NP-Completeness (Series of Books in the Mathematical Sciences), 1st edn. W. H. Freeman, New York City (1979)
16. Goodfellow, I., Bengio, Y., Courville, A.: Deep Learning. MIT Press, Cambridge (2016)
17. Haase, C., Kiefer, S.: The odds of staying on budget. In: Halldórsson, M.M., Iwama, K., Kobayashi, N., Speckmann, B. (eds.) ICALP 2015. LNCS, vol. 9135, pp. 234–246. Springer, Heidelberg (2015). https://doi.org/10.1007/978-3-662-47666-6_19
18. Hartmanns, A., Junges, S., Katoen, J.-P., Quatmann, T.: Multi-cost bounded reachability in MDP. In: Beyer, D., Huisman, M. (eds.) TACAS 2018. LNCS, vol. 10806, pp. 320–339. Springer, Cham (2018). https://doi.org/10.1007/978-3-319-89963-3_19
19. Hoeffding, W.: Probability inequalities for sums of bounded random variables. J. Am. Stat. Assoc. **58**(301), 13–30 (1963)
20. Hüllermeier, E., Waegeman, W.: Aleatoric and epistemic uncertainty in machine learning: an introduction to concepts and methods. Mach. Learn. **110**, 457–506 (2021)
21. Jonsson, B., Larsen, K.G.: Specification and refinement of probabilistic processes. In: Proceedings of the 6th Annual IEEE Symposium on Logic in Computer Science (LICS), pp. 266–277 (1991)
22. Lakshminarayanan, B., Pritzel, A., Blundell, C.: Simple and scalable predictive uncertainty estimation using deep ensembles. Adv. Neural Inf. Process. Syst. **30** (2017)
23. Laroche, R., Trichelair, P., des Combes, R.T.: Safe policy improvement with baseline bootstrapping. In: ICML, pp. 3652–3661. PMLR (2019)
24. Lema, M.A., et al.: 5G case study of internet of skills: slicing the human senses. In: 2017 European Conference on Networks and Communications (EuCNC), pp. 1–6 (2017)
25. Mozaffari, S., Al-Jarrah, O.Y., Dianati, M., Jennings, P., Mouzakitis, A.: Deep learning-based vehicle behavior prediction for autonomous driving applications: a review. IEEE Trans. Intell. Transp. Syst. **23**(1), 33–47 (2022)

26. Parvez, I., Rahmati, A., Guvenc, I., Sarwat, A.I., Dai, H.: A survey on low latency towards 5G: ran, core network and caching solutions. IEEE Commun. Surve. Tutor. **20**(4), 3098–3130 (2018)
27. Peischl, B., Tazl, O.A., Wotawa, F.: Testing anticipatory systems: a systematic mapping study on the state of the art. J. Syst. Softw. **192**, 111387 (2022)
28. Pejovic, V., Musolesi, M.: Anticipatory mobile computing: a survey of the state of the art and research challenges. ACM Comput. Surv. **47**(3) (2015)
29. Petrik, M., Ghavamzadeh, M., Chow, Y.: Safe policy improvement by minimizing robust baseline regret. In: NIPS, pp. 2298–2306. Curran Associates, Inc. (2016)
30. Pnueli, A.: The temporal logic of programs. In: Proceedings of the 18th Symposium on Foundations of Computer Science (SFCS), pp. 46–57. IEEE (1977)
31. Puterman, M.: Markov Decision Processes: Discrete Stochastic Dynamic Programming. John Wiley & Sons Inc., Hoboken (1994)
32. Rausand, M.: Reliability of Safety-Critical Systems: Theory and Applications, 1st edn. Wiley Publishing, Hoboken (2014)
33. Rosen, R.: Anticipatory systems: philosophical, mathematical, and methodological foundations. In: IFSR International Series on Systems Science and Engineering. Elsevier Science & Technology Books (1985)
34. Schulz, J., Dubslaff, C., Seeling, P., Li, S.C., Speidel, S., Fitzek, F.H.P.: Negative latency in the tactile internet as enabler for global metaverse immersion. IEEE Netw. (2023)
35. Schulz, J., Nguyen, V., Seeling, P., Nguyen, G.T., Fitzek, F.H.P.: Anticipatory hand glove: understanding human actions for enhanced interaction. In: Proceedings of the ACM International Joint Conference on Pervasive and Ubiquitous Computing (UbiComp). Association for Computing Machinery (2023). accepted for publication
36. Seeling, P., Fitzek, F.H.: Anticipatory networking: Negative latency for ubiquitous computing. In: 2021 IEEE 18th Annual Consumer Communications & Networking Conference (CCNC), pp. 1–4 (2021)
37. Sen, K., Viswanathan, M., Agha, G.: Model-checking Markov chains in the presence of uncertainties. In: Hermanns, H., Palsberg, J. (eds.) TACAS 2006. LNCS, vol. 3920, pp. 394–410. Springer, Heidelberg (2006). https://doi.org/10.1007/11691372_26
38. Shannon, C.E.: A mathematical theory of communication. Bell Syst. Tech. J. **27**(3), 379–423 (1948)
39. Silva Filho, T., Song, H., Perello-Nieto, M., Santos-Rodriguez, R., Kull, M., Flach, P.: Classifier calibration: a survey on how to assess and improve predicted class probabilities. In: Machine Learning, pp. 1–50 (2023)
40. Simsek, M., Aijaz, A., Dohler, M., Sachs, J., Fettweis, G.: The 5G-enabled tactile internet: applications, requirements, and architecture. In: 2016 IEEE Wireless Communications and Networking Conference, pp. 1–6 (2016)
41. Strehl, A., Littman, M.: An empirical evaluation of interval estimation for markov decision processes, pp. 128–135 (2004)
42. Strehl, A., Littman, M.: An analysis of model-based interval estimation for markov decision processes. J. Comput. Syst. Sci. **74**, 1309–1331 (2008)
43. Suilen, M., Simão, T., Jansen, N., Parker, D.: Robust anytime learning of markov decision processes. In: Proceedings of NeurIPS (2022)
44. Sun, Q., Huang, X., Gu, J., Williams, B.C., Zhao, H.: M2i: from factored marginal trajectory prediction to interactive prediction. In: 2022 IEEE/CVF Conference on Computer Vision and Pattern Recognition (CVPR), pp. 6533–6542. IEEE Computer Society, Los Alamitos (2022)

45. Sutton, R.S., Barto, A.G.: Reinforcement Learning: An Introduction, 2nd edn. The MIT Press, Cambridge (2018)
46. Tomasulo, R.M.: An efficient algorithm for exploiting multiple arithmetic units. IBM J. Res. Dev. **11**(1), 25–33 (1967)
47. Ummels, M., Baier, C.: Computing quantiles in markov reward models. In: Pfenning, F. (ed.) FoSSaCS 2013. LNCS, vol. 7794, pp. 353–368. Springer, Heidelberg (2013). https://doi.org/10.1007/978-3-642-37075-5_23
48. Urban, C., Miné, A.: A review of formal methods applied to machine learning. arXiv preprint arXiv:2104.02466 (2021)
49. Vardi, M.Y.: Automatic verification of probabilistic concurrent finite-state programs. In: Proceedings of the 26th IEEE Symposium on Foundations of Computer Science (FOCS), pp. 327–338. IEEE Computer Society (1985)
50. Weissman, T., Ordentlich, E., Seroussi, G., Verdú, S., Weinberger, M.J.: Inequalities for the L1 deviation of the empirical distribution. Technical Report, Hewlett-Packard Labs (2003)
51. Wienhöft, P., Suilen, M., Simão, T.D., Dubslaff, C., Baier, C., Jansen, N.: More for less: safe policy improvement with stronger performance guarantees. In: IJCAI (2023)
52. Wu, D., Koutsoukos, X.: Reachability analysis of uncertain systems using bounded-parameter markov decision processes. Artif. Intell. **172**(8), 945–954 (2008)
53. Xiang, Z., Gabriel, F., Urbano, E., Nguyen, G.T., Reisslein, M., Fitzek, F.H.P.: Reducing latency in virtual machines: enabling tactile internet for human-machine co-working. IEEE J. Sel. Areas Commun. **37**(5), 1098–1116 (2019)

Safety Verification of DNNs

Track C1: Safety Verification of Deep Neural Networks (DNNs)

Daniel Neider[1,2] and Taylor T. Johnson[3(✉)]

[1] Chair for Verification and Formal Guarantees of Machine Learning, TU Dortmund University, Dortmund, Germany
daniel.neider@tu-dortmund.de

[2] Research Center for Trustworthy Data Science and Security, Dortmund, Germany

[3] Institute for Software Integrated Systems, Vanderbilt University, Nashville, TN, USA
taylor.johnson@vanderbilt.edu

Abstract. Formal verification of neural networks and broader machine learning models is an emerging field that has gained significant attention due to the growing use and impact of these data-driven methods. This track explores techniques for formally verifying neural networks and other machine learning models across various application domains. It includes papers and presentations discussing new methodologies, software frameworks, technical approaches, and case studies. Benchmarks play a crucial role in evaluating the effectiveness and scalability of these methods. Currently, available benchmarks mainly focus on computer vision problems, such as local robustness to adversarial perturbations of image classifiers. To address this limitation, this track compiles and publishes benchmarks comprising machine learning models and their specifications across domains such as computer vision, finance, security, and others. These benchmarks will help assess the suitability and applicability of formal verification methods in diverse domains.

Keywords: Formal Verification · Formal Methods · Neural Networks · Safety of Autonomy

1 Description of the Track

Formal verification of deep neural networks (DNNs) and broader machine learning models has been a burgeoning field in the past few years, with continued increasing interest given the ongoing growth and applicability of these data-driven methods. This track focuses on methods for formal verification of machine learning models, including neural networks, but also beyond to other model types across application domains. In particular, this track features contributions addressing theoretical aspects of verifying neural networks [4], the devops cycle for trustworthy learning-enabled autonomous systems [2], neural networks related to cyber-physical systems, neuro-symbolic verification [19],

B. Steffen (Ed.): AISoLA 2023, LNCS 14380, pp. 217–224, 2024.
https://doi.org/10.1007/978-3-031-46002-9_12

anomaly detection [7], predictive maintenance [10], and the problem of overconfident neural networks.

In addition, benchmarks are critical for evaluating scalability and broader progress within formal methods. Most recent benchmarks for evaluating neural network verification methods and broader machine learning verification have focused predominantly on computer vision problems, specifically local robustness to adversarial perturbations of image classifiers. However, neural networks and machine learning models are being used across a variety of safety and security-critical domains, and domain-specific benchmarks—both in terms of the machine learning models and their specifications—are necessary to identify limitations and directions for improvements, as well as to evaluate and ensure applicability of these methods in these domains. For instance, controllers in autonomous systems are increasingly created with data-driven methods, and malware classifiers in security are often neural networks, each of which domain has its specificities, as do countless other applications in cyber-physical systems, finance, science, and beyond.

Our second contribution involves compiling and publishing benchmarks comprising models and specifications across various domains where formal verification of neural networks and machine learning is being explored. These benchmarks span several fields, including information technology (IT) security [18], computer vision [12,17], autonomous driving [14], aerospace [8], maritime search and rescue [9], and chemical process engineering [15]. They have been designed to serve as inputs for future iterations of the International Verification of Neural Networks Competition (VNN-COMP) [1,3,16] and the Artificial Intelligence and Neural Network Control Systems (AINNCS) category [5,6,11,13] of the International Competition on Verifying Continuous and Hybrid Systems (ARCH-COMP). By sharing these benchmarks with the scientific community, our goal is to encourage further research and inspire conversations about expanding the scope of the Verification of Neural Networks standard (VNN-LIB).

As indicated above, the contributions of this track can be grouped into two categories: (i) verification of neural networks and autonomous systems and (ii) verification benchmarks. The remainder of this article gives an overview of each contribution in this track. In the spirit of AISoLA's aims and scope, we have utilized ChatGPT to help summarize the contributions, specifically utilizing the August 3rd, 2023 release of GPT-4 and code interpreter to extract the paper contents from the provided PDFs, to generate a few sentence overview of each contribution, which we have manually reviewed and edited for accuracy. We have organized the contributions according to the planned sessions during the event, in essence into verification approaches and benchmarks.

2 Verification of Neural Networks and Autonomous Systems

Papers and presentations on verification approaches for neural networks are in contributions [4,7,10,19] and for autonomous systems in [2], each of which is briefly summarized next.

The paper, "Formal Verification of a Neural Network Based Prognostics System for Aircraft Equipment", [10] presents methodology for verifying properties of a deep convolutional neural network (CNN) used for estimating the remaining useful life (RUL) of aircraft mechanical equipment. The authors provide mathematical formalizations of the estimator requirements, such as stability and monotonicity, and encode these properties as linear constraints. They use a state-of-the-art tool for neural network verification to check these properties on a neural network model of a prognostics system trained on a real-world dataset of bearing degradation data.

The paper, "The inverse problem for neural networks", [4] investigates the problem of computing the preimage of a set under a neural network with piecewise-affine activation functions. The authors revisit an old result that the preimage of a polyhedral set is again a union of polyhedral sets and can be effectively computed. They show several applications of computing the preimage for analysis and interpretability of neural networks. This study is essential for understanding the inverse problem for neural networks and its implications on the analysis and interpretability of neural networks.

The paper, "Distribution-Aware Neuro-Symbolic Verification", [19] proposes a novel approach to restrict verification processes to the data distribution (or other distributions) by using distribution-aware neuro-symbolic verification. The authors propose the non-linear independent component estimator (NICE) Laplacianizing flow as a suitable density model due to its two major properties: the associated log-density function is piece-wise affine, making it applicable for SMT based approaches using linear arithmetic, and each NICE flow maps the upper log-density level sets of the data distribution to the upper log-density level sets of the latent Laplacian, which has potential applications within interval bound propagation methods.

In "Towards formal guarantees for networks' overconfidence" by Anan Kabaha and Dana Drachsler Cohen, the authors presented addresses the problem of neural networks making overconfident predictions when presented with out-of-distribution inputs. The authors note that even well-trained networks can show very high confidence for inputs that do not belong to the task they are trained for, raising concerns about real-world scenarios where a wide range of inputs may be encountered. They discuss several existing works that suggest training approaches aimed at decreasing the confidence of out-of-distribution inputs, mainly by regularization terms. Each of these works considers a certain type of out-of-distribution domain, samples from it, and incorporates the samples into the training process.

The paper, "Towards Verification of Changes in Dynamic Machine Learning Models using Deep Ensemble Anomaly Detection", [7] emphasizes the importance of formal verification of machine learning models in safety-critical systems, especially when dealing with dynamically changing data distributions. The authors propose considering the temporal representation of state changes as the context of a dynamic machine learning model, and illustrate this with environmental time series variables such as temperature, humidity, and illumination used to train models with respect to seasonal states like spring, summer, autumn, and winter. This approach helps in verifying a time-dependent machine learning model with respect to distinct states of an evolving time series.

The paper, "Continuous Engineering for Trustworthy Learning-enabled Autonomous Systems", [2] discusses the challenges and approaches in engineering trustworthy learning-enabled autonomous systems. The paper discusses the importance of continuous engineering in ensuring the trustworthiness of autonomous systems that are enabled by machine learning, and methodology for establishing this. The work involves a collaborative effort from experts in various fields related to autonomous systems, machine learning, and continuous engineering.

Lastly, two presentation-only contributions describing verification methods were given, both targeting autonomous systems. In "Presentation: reachability for neural-network control systems," by Christian Schilling, the author presented methods for reachability analysis of neural network control systems. In "Presentation: Verification of a neural network for modeling the dynamics of a quadcopter," by Amanjit Dulai and Lucas Garcia, the authors presented verification methods for dynamical systems, specifically a quadcopter modeled as a neural network.

3 Verification Benchmarks

The development of benchmarks for use by the research community is a critical task and aids in a variety of objectives ranging from standardization of formats to identification of critical scalability issues. Through this portion of the track, several benchmarks from a diverse set of problem domains were proposed, specifically in papers [8,9,12,14,15,17,18], each of which is briefly summarized next.

The paper, "Benchmarks: Semantic Segmentation Neural Network Verification and Objection Detection Neural Network Verification in Perceptions Tasks of Autonomous Driving", [14] addresses a critical gap in the field of autonomous driving. Although there are existing benchmarks for verifying the robustness of neural networks, there are hardly any related to autonomous driving, especially those related to object detection and semantic segmentation. The authors present an innovative approach to benchmark formal verification tools and approaches for neural networks in the context of perception tasks of autonomous driving. Specifically, the authors contribute two novel benchmarks: one for semantic segmentation neural network verification and another for object detection neural network verification.

The paper, "Benchmark: Neural Network Malware Classification", [18] addresses the increasing complexity and sophistication of malware threats and the need for advanced detection methods, such as deep neural networks (DNNs), for malware classification. The authors propose two malware classification benchmarks: a feature-based benchmark and an image-based benchmark. Feature-based datasets provide a detailed understanding of malware characteristics, while image-based datasets transform raw malware binary data into grayscale images for swift processing. These datasets can be used for both binary classification (benign vs. malicious) and classifying known malware into a particular family.

The paper, "Benchmark: Remaining Useful Life Predictor for Aircraft Equipment", [8] proposes a predictive maintenance application as a benchmark problem for the verification of neural networks (VNN). The authors implement a deep learning-based estimator of remaining useful life (RUL) of aircraft mechanical components, such as bearings, as a convolutional neural network. They provide mathematical formalizations of its non-functional requirements, such as stability and monotonicity, as properties. These properties can be used to assess the applicability and scalability of existing VNN tools. The benchmark materials, such as trained models, examples of properties, test datasets, and property generation procedures, are available on GitHub.

The paper, "Benchmark: Object Detection for Maritime Search and Rescue", [9] proposes an object detection system for maritime search and rescue as a benchmark problem for the verification of neural networks (VNN). The model to be verified is a YOLO (You Only Look Once) deep neural network for object detection and classification and has a very high number of learnable parameters (millions). The authors describe the workflow for defining and generating robustness properties in the regions of interest of the images, i.e., in the neighborhood of the objects to be detected by the neural network. This benchmark can be used to assess the applicability and scalability of existing VNN tools for perception systems based on deep learning.

The paper, "Benchmark: Neural Networks for Anomaly Detection in Batch Distillation", [15] presents a benchmark suite for verifying neural networks used in anomaly detection for batch distillation chemical processes. The authors highlight the importance of these models working safely and reliably in safety-critical applications, such as chemical plants, where failure to report anomalies or false alarms may result in hazards to the environment, harm to human life, or substantial financial or scientific loss. The work aims to contribute to the field by providing a benchmark suite that can help in verifying the safety and reliability of neural networks used in such critical applications.

The paper, "Benchmark: Formal Verification of Semantic Segmentation Neural Networks", [17] discusses the application of formal verification techniques to semantic segmentation neural networks. While significant progress has been made in verification methods for various deep neural networks (DNNs), such as feed-forward neural networks (FFNNs) and convolutional neural networks (CNNs), the application of these techniques to semantic segmentation remains largely unexplored. Semantic segmentation networks are crucial in computer vision applications, where they assign semantic labels to individual pixels within an image. Given their deployment in safety-critical domains, ensuring the correctness of these networks becomes paramount.

The paper, "Empirical Analysis of Benchmark Generation for the Verification of Neural Network Image Classifiers", [12] addresses the increasing usage of deep learning technology in safety-critical applications such as autonomous cars and medicine. The authors emphasize that the use of models, e.g., neural networks, in safety-critical applications demands a thorough evaluation from both a component and system-level perspective. Despite great efforts in the formal verification of neural networks in the past decade, several challenges remain, one of which is the development of neural networks for easier verification. The authors aim to address this challenge and contribute to the ongoing efforts in the formal verification of neural networks.

4 Summary and Outlook

This track presents approaches for verification of neural networks and autonomous systems, as well as collecting benchmarks for these types of approaches to be used in the broader research community. In the future, these benchmarks and approaches may be utilized in verification tools participating in events such as VNN-COMP and the ARCH-COMP AINNCS category, and we hope this initiative toward collecting benchmarks continues.

Acknowledgements. The material presented in this paper is based upon work supported by the National Science Foundation (NSF) through grant numbers 2220426 and 2220401, and the Defense Advanced Research Projects Agency (DARPA) under contract number FA8750-23-C-0518, and the Air Force Office of Scientific Research (AFOSR) under contract numbers FA9550-22-1-0019 and FA9550-23-1-0135. Any opinions, findings, conclusions, or recommendations expressed in this paper are those of the authors and do not necessarily reflect the views of AFOSR, DARPA, or NSF. In addition, the work was supported by the Deutsche Forschungsgemeinschaft (DFG) through grant number 459419731.

References

1. Bak, S., Liu, C., Johnson, T.: The second international verification of neural networks competition (VNN-COMP 2021): summary and results (2021). https://doi.org/10.48550/ARXIV.2109.00498
2. Bensalem, S., et al.: Continuous engineering for trustworthy learning-enabled autonomous systems. In: Steffen, B. (ed.) AISoLA 2023. LNCS, vol. 14380, pp. 256–278. Springer, Cham (2023)
3. Brix, C., Müller, M.N., Bak, S., Johnson, T.T., Liu, C.: First three years of the international verification of neural networks competition (VNN-COMP). Int. J. Softw. Tools Technol. Transfer 1–11 (2023)
4. Forets, M., Schilling, C.: The inverse problem for neural networks. In: Steffen, B. (ed.) AISoLA 2023. LNCS, vol. 14380, pp. 241–255. Springer, Cham (2023)
5. Johnson, T.T., et al.: ARCH-COMP21 category report: artificial intelligence and neural network control systems (AINNCS) for continuous and hybrid systems plants. In: Frehse, G., Althoff, M. (eds.) 8th International Workshop on Applied Verification of Continuous and Hybrid Systems (ARCH21). EPiC Series in Computing, vol. 80, pp. 90–119. EasyChair (2021). https://doi.org/10.29007/kfk9

6. Johnson, T.T., et al.: ARCH-COMP20 category report: artificial intelligence and neural network control systems (AINNCS) for continuous and hybrid systems plants. In: Frehse, G., Althoff, M. (eds.) ARCH20. 7th International Workshop on Applied Verification of Continuous and Hybrid Systems (ARCH20). EPiC Series in Computing, vol. 74, pp. 107–139. EasyChair (2020). https://doi.org/10.29007/9xgv
7. Katzke, T., Li, B., Klüttermann, S., Müller, E.: Towards verification of changes in dynamic machine learning models using deep ensemble anomaly detection. In: Steffen, B. (ed.) AISoLA 2023. LNCS, vol. 14380, p. 448. Springer, Cham (2023)
8. Kirov, D., Rollini, S.F.: Benchmark: remaining useful life predictor for aircraft equipment. In: Steffen, B. (ed.) AISoLA 2023. LNCS, vol. 14380, pp. 299–304. Springer, Cham (2023)
9. Kirov, D., Rollini, S.F., Chandrahas, R., Reddy, S., Chandupatla, Sawant, R.: Benchmark: object detection for maritime search and rescue. In: Steffen, B. (ed.) AISoLA 2023. LNCS, vol. 14380, pp. 305–310. Springer, Cham (2023)
10. Kirov, D., Rollini, S.F., Guglielmo, L.D., Cofer, D.: Formal verification of a neural network based prognostics system for aircraft equipment. In: Steffen, B. (ed.) AISoLA 2023. LNCS, vol. 14380, pp. 225–240. Springer, Cham (2023)
11. Lopez, D.M., et al.: ARCH-COMP22 category report: artificial intelligence and neural network control systems (AINNCS) for continuous and hybrid systems plants. In: Frehse, G., Althoff, M., Schoitsch, E., Guiochet, J. (eds.) Proceedings of 9th International Workshop on Applied Verification of Continuous and Hybrid Systems (ARCH22). EPiC Series in Computing, vol. 90, pp. 142–184. EasyChair (2022). https://doi.org/10.29007/wfgr
12. Lopez, D.M., Johnson, T.T.: Empirical analysis of benchmark generation for the verification of neural network image classifiers. In: Steffen, B. (ed.) AISoLA 2023. LNCS, vol. 14380, pp. 331–347. Springer, Cham (2023)
13. Lopez, D.M., et al.: ARCH-COMP19 category report: artificial intelligence and neural network control systems (AINNCS) for continuous and hybrid systems plants. In: Frehse, G., Althoff, M. (eds.) ARCH19. 6th International Workshop on Applied Verification of Continuous and Hybrid Systems. EPiC Series in Computing, vol. 61, pp. 103–119. EasyChair (2019). https://doi.org/10.29007/rgv8
14. Luo, Y., Ma, J., Han, S., Xie, L.: Benchmarks: semantic segmentation neural network verification and objection detection neural network verification in perceptions tasks of autonomous driving. In: Steffen, B. (ed.) AISoLA 2023. LNCS, vol. 14380, pp. 279–290. Springer, Cham (2023)
15. Lutz, S., Neider, D.: Benchmark: neural networks for anomaly detection in batch distillation. In: Steffen, B. (ed.) AISoLA 2023. LNCS, vol. 14380, pp. 449–452. Springer, Cham (2023)
16. Müller, M.N., Brix, C., Bak, S., Liu, C., Johnson, T.T.: The third international verification of neural networks competition (VNN-COMP 2022): summary and results (2022). https://doi.org/10.48550/arXiv.2212.10376
17. Pal, N., Lee, S., Johnson, T.T.: Benchmark: formal verification of semantic segmentation neural networks. In: Steffen, B. (ed.) AISoLA 2023. LNCS, vol. 14380, pp. 311–330. Springer, Cham (2023)

18. Robinette, P.K., Lopez, D.M., Johnson, T.T.: Benchmark: neural network malware classification. In: Steffen, B. (ed.) AISoLA 2023. LNCS, vol. 14380, pp. 291–298. Springer, Cham (2023)
19. Zaid, F.A., Diekmann, D., Neider, D.: Distribution-aware neuro-symbolic verification. In: Steffen, B. (ed.) AISoLA 2023. LNCS, vol. 14380, pp. 445–447. Springer, Cham (2023)

Formal Verification of a Neural Network Based Prognostics System for Aircraft Equipment

Dmitrii Kirov[1(✉)], Simone Fulvio Rollini[2], Luigi Di Guglielmo[1], and Darren Cofer[3]

[1] Collins Aerospace, Trento, Italy
dmitrii.kirov@collins.com
[2] Collins Aerospace, Rome, Italy
[3] Collins Aerospace, Minneapolis, MN, USA

Abstract. We demonstrate the use of formal methods to verify properties of a deep convolutional neural network that estimates remaining useful life of aircraft mechanical equipment. We provide mathematical formalizations of requirements of the estimator, such as stability and monotonicity, as properties. To efficiently apply existing tools for verification of neural networks, we reduce the verification of global properties to a representative set of local properties defined for the points of the test dataset. We encode these properties as linear constraints and verify them using a state-of-the-art tool for neural network verification. To increase the completeness and the scalability of the analysis, we develop a two-step verification method involving abstract interpretation and simulation-based falsification. Numerical results confirm the applicability of the approach.

1 Introduction

The aviation industry is being increasingly driven towards the application of Machine Learning (ML) in new products to assist human operators or implement enhanced automation. Such products, in particular safety-critical ones, require certification and must provide a high level of trustworthiness and guarantees of the absence of unintended behaviors.

Currently, the industry does not have a consensus on the assurance of ML-enabled components because they are not fully amenable to current design assurance processes and standards. In particular, DO-178C provides guidance to produce traditional (i.e., non-ML) software that performs the intended function with a level of confidence in safety that complies with airworthiness requirements [12]. The standard focuses on a process for software design that starts from functional and non-functional requirements and transforms them into the software code. This code is traced to and verified against the requirements to ensure it is correct, i.e., it performs the intended function, and, more importantly, does not expose behaviors that are unintended by the designer or unexpected by operators.

B. Steffen (Ed.): AISoLA 2023, LNCS 14380, pp. 225–240, 2024.
https://doi.org/10.1007/978-3-031-46002-9_13

ML development, instead, is data-driven. An ML model, such as a Neural Network (NN), is trained through a learning procedure that starts from data, not only from requirements. The use of traceability of the implementation back to training data as a means to minimize the risk that the ML component includes unintended behaviors may not be possible. Additionally, the use of structural coverage metrics may not be effective in identifying unintended functionalities in ML models such as neural networks [14].

According to DO-333 [13], Formal Methods (FM) can be used as a source of evidence for the satisfaction of verification objectives when a formal model of the software artifact can be established and properties they have to comply with can be verified via formal analysis. FM provide a comprehensive analysis of a system over its entire input space, thus being able to show the absence of unintended behaviors. New FM tools are being developed for ML-based systems, in particular, for verification of neural networks (VNN) [7,15,16]. Several case studies on applying VNN tools have been published [4,9]. Emerging certification guidance created by the European Union Aviation Safety Agency (EASA) explicitly mentions formal methods as promising means of compliance with a number of key assurance objectives, such as stability[1] and robustness of ML [6]. This is further elaborated in the recent technical report on the use of formal methods for learning assurance [5].

In this paper, we demonstrate the application of formal methods on an ML-enabled prognostics system for aircraft equipment to verify a function that predicts remaining useful life of mechanical components. The function is implemented as a convolutional neural network. The main contribution of the paper is to show the effectiveness of FM in identifying unintended behaviors of a real NN application that may potentially have an impact on safety. We were able to identify conditions, in which the requirements of the NN-based estimator, such as stability and monotonicity, are violated.

We also propose an approach to overcome scalability and applicability barriers of existing VNN tools for verifying global properties by reducing them to local properties defined for a representative set of input points. We discuss a necessary condition on data quality (completeness and representativeness) that enables such reduction. To further mitigate the scalability issue, we develop a hybrid, two-step verification method that involves abstract interpretation and simulation-based falsification.

2 Remaining Useful Life Estimator

Remaining Useful Life (RUL) is a metric that manifests the remaining lifetime of a component. In aviation RUL is used in Prognostics and Health Management (PHM) applications, such as condition-based maintenance, to support aircraft maintenance and flight preparation. RUL estimation could contribute to augmented manual inspection of components and scheduling of maintenance cycles.

[1] This is a domain-specific concept, different e.g. from the notion of stability in control theory; see Sect. 3.1 for details.

RUL could also highlight areas for inspection during the next planned maintenance, i.e., it could be used to move up (prioritize) a maintenance/inspection action to prevent component failure.

Existing RUL calculation procedures often use physics-based degradation models [10]. Such models typically have high accuracy, but require extensive prior knowledge about the underlying physical system, which is often not available in practice. Similarity-based methods [2] are less complex to develop and deploy, but their main disadvantage is low accuracy. In the recent decade, the focus has been gradually shifting towards ML-based approaches [3,11]. In particular, deep neural networks are capable of using raw sensor measurements directly as inputs, and leverage their automatic feature extraction capabilities to discover relationships between the inputs and their impact on the RUL, which may be unknown to the experts [8]. Therefore, they require less domain expertise and prior knowledge of the behavior of the equipment that is being monitored.

The RUL estimator examined in this case study is used in an on-ground maintenance application to provide information about the current state of a mechanical bearing component installed in the drivetrain assembly of a rotorcraft. End users are pilots, as well as Maintenance, Repair and Overhaul (MRO) teams. Predicted RUL is used during pre-flight checks to detect possible problems with the bearing and, if present, to prioritize certain maintenance/inspection actions.

The interface of the RUL estimator is illustrated on Fig. 1. The ML model is a Convolutional Neural Network (CNN) that accepts as input a time window of length 40, i.e., snapshots reflecting the bearing state taken at 40 consecutive time steps. Each time step corresponds to 1 h. Each snapshot contains the following information:

- Seven Condition Indicators (CIs) that provide numerical information about the bearing degradation, obtained from signal processing of measurements of the vibration sensor attached to the bearing.
- Information about the current mission: current flight regime, such as ascent, cruise and descent, with corresponding nominal component load (bearing RUL heavily depends on how the component is loaded), mission type (a set of predefined mission patterns is available, e.g., long, short, mixed).
- Information about the current flight environment (e.g., desert or non-desert).

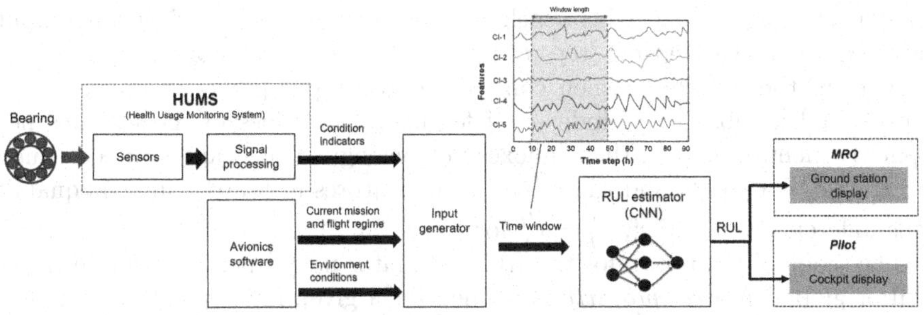

Fig. 1. Overview of the RUL estimator and its context.

CI values are computed by the Health Usage Monitoring System (HUMS), while remaining inputs are provided by other avionics software. Snapshots are provided to the input generator, where they are stored in memory and periodically shifted to yield a new consecutive time window. Output of the CNN is a numerical non-negative value that represents the bearing RUL in hours. It is provided to the end users (pilots, MRO) via cockpit and ground station displays. Additional pre- and post-processing of the CNN (e.g., input normalization) is not described due to space limitations, details are available in [5].

The NN architecture of the RUL estimator is adapted from [1]. It includes several convolutional layers that apply 1D convolutions along the time sequence direction of the input time window, thus extracting trends in separate features. These trends are merged together via a fully connected layer. Activation functions at all layers are Rectified Linear Units (ReLUs). The total number of layers is 12 and the number of learnable parameters is on the order of 100K. The CNN performs a regression task.

Requirements. We provide a selected list of requirements of the RUL estimator in Table 1. They include stability and monotonicity of the estimator. These requirements shall be met within the entire Operational Design Domain (ODD) of the RUL estimator, i.e., the range of inputs for which the estimator is guaranteed to operate as intended. Violation of the requirements may have an impact on the safety, for example, if the NN overestimates the RUL. This is particularly relevant to the so-called *critical range* defined as the last **100h** of the bearing RUL, i.e., when the bearing may soon develop a failure. Overestimating the RUL in the critical range may lead to missing a critical component inspection before proceeding with the flight mission. Requirements from Table 1 can be formalized as properties, as will be shown in Sect. 3.

3 Property Formalization

In the remainder of this paper, the following notation is used. Bold font (e.g., $\mathbf{x}$) is used to denote a vector or a matrix, depending on the context, while normal font (e.g., x) denotes a scalar. We recall that a single input point for the RUL estimator function corresponds to an $L \times n$ time window with a predefined number of time steps L and n features ($1 \leq i \leq n$). Formally, an input point is a matrix $\boldsymbol{x} = [\boldsymbol{x}_1, ..., \boldsymbol{x}_n]$, where each column i contains values x_i^t of some input feature i at consecutive time steps t ($1 \leq t \leq L$), i.e., a vector $\boldsymbol{x}_i = [x_i^1, ..., x_i^L]^T$.

Also, in the following, when considering two input points $\mathbf{x}$ and $\mathbf{x}'$, some step t^*, and a subset S of indexes of features, the values of the features not explicitly mentioned (i.e., their indexes not belonging to S) are assumed equal, i.e., $x_j^t = x_j^{'t}$ for $j \notin S$, and the values of the features in S are assumed equal at steps different from t^*, i.e., $x_j^t = x_j^{'t}$ for $j \in S, t \neq t^*$.

The scope of properties for the RUL estimator neural network can be either local or global. A *local property* is defined for a given input point $\boldsymbol{x} \in X$ or a subset of points $X' \subseteq X$ of the input space X. That is, local properties must

Table 1. Selected requirements for the RUL estimator.

ID	Requirement
RUL-ML-Stab-1	The maximum admissible perturbation that can occur to a condition indicator input shall be equal to **40%** of the average initial value of that CI that corresponds to a fully healthy state of the bearing component
RUL-ML-Stab-2	For a perturbation of a single CI at a single time step within any input time window, the output deviation of the RUL estimator shall not exceed **10 h** The max perturbation for which the requirement must hold corresponds to RUL-ML-Stab-1 Requirement applies to each CI
RUL-ML-Stab-3	For a simultaneous perturbation of all CIs at a single time step (e.g., due to a resonance frequency) within any time window, the output deviation of the estimator shall not exceed **10 h** The max perturbation for which the requirement must hold corresponds to RUL-ML-Stab-1
RUL-ML-Mon-1	For an increased growth rate of a single CI (may occur, for example, when a particular failure occurs in the bearing, which increases its degradation) within any input time window, the estimator shall output a non-increasing value of the RUL. Requirement applies to each CI
RUL-ML-Mon-2	For an increased growth rate of all CIs (may occur, for example, due to simultaneous development of a number of failures or due to excessive load) within any input time window, the estimator shall output a non-increasing value of the RUL

hold for some specific inputs. Such properties are accepted by the majority of existing VNN tools. A *global property* is defined over the entire input space X of the NN. Global properties must hold for all inputs.

3.1 Stability Properties

The ML model is *stable* if a small, bounded perturbation applied to its inputs in normal operating conditions, i.e., when the inputs are inside its operational design domain, does not cause a significant deviation in its output [5]. Condition indicators are key input features of the RUL estimator for which undetected perturbations may occur during operation. For example, a spike change of a single CI may occur at some time step due to sensor noise. Similarly, a resonance frequency in the bearing may result in simultaneous deviation of multiple CIs (also at a single time step). Random CI perturbations at multiple, especially consecutive, time steps shall be detected by data quality monitors within the HUMS before they could enter the neural network, therefore, such cases are considered unrealistic. Similarly, spikes in CIs that exceed the admissible threshold prescribed by requirement RUL-ML-Stab-1 shall be detected by the HUMS.

Stability to a Single CI Perturbation at a Single Time Step. Let $\boldsymbol{x_i}$ be the vector of values of some CI i in the time window, x_i^t being the CI value at time step t. The formulation of a stability property for a single CI is:

$$\forall \boldsymbol{x'} : |x_i^{'t} - x_i^t| < \delta |x_i^*| \rightarrow |f(\boldsymbol{x'}) - f(\boldsymbol{x})| < \epsilon, \tag{1}$$

where prime ($'$) denotes a perturbed item, i.e., $\boldsymbol{x'}$ is the time window, where one or more elements have been perturbed, $x_i^{'t}$ is a value of the i-th CI (perturbed) at time step t, and $f(\boldsymbol{x'})$ is the ML model output computed from the perturbed input, x_i^* represents the average initial value of the i-th CI, which can be computed by averaging initial CI values over all degradation scenarios in the available dataset, δ is the bound on the input perturbation *w.r.t.* x_i^* (expressed as a percentage), and ϵ is the maximum admissible output change.

Stability to Multiple CI Perturbations at a Single Time Step. In case of perturbations over multiple CIs, the formulation of the stability property is:

$$\forall \boldsymbol{x'} : \forall i \in S : |x_i^{'t} - x_i^t| < \delta_i |x_i^*| \rightarrow |f(\boldsymbol{x'}) - f(\boldsymbol{x})| < \epsilon, \tag{2}$$

where S is a subset of the indexes corresponding to perturbed CIs, x_i^*, δ and ϵ are as above (the only difference is that for each perturbed CI with index i a different bound δ_i can be specified), and prime ($'$) denotes a perturbed time window ($\boldsymbol{x'}$) or value ($x_i^{'t}$).

3.2 Monotonicity Properties

Condition indicators and their growth rate are correlated with component degradation and failures. Differently from stability, requirements on monotonicity of the RUL estimator consider simultaneous systematic modifications of CIs at all time steps of the input window. This is a realistic situation that may occur, for example, due to damage or excessive load in the bearing that leads to an increased degradation rate. Therefore, such changes in the CIs over the entire time window shall not be identified by data quality indicators in the HUMS as abnormal (unlike random spikes/perturbations occurring at multiple time steps).

Expected behavior of the RUL estimator output is to be monotonic with respect to CIs, i.e., when they increase, the RUL should decrease. Faster bearing degradation is manifested by the CIs (one or many) growing faster. Monotonicity requirements in Table 1 prescribe a non-increasing output of the RUL estimator given an increase in the growth rate of one or more condition indicators.

Requirements RUL-ML-Mon-1 and RUL-ML-Mon-2 do not prescribe any concrete upper bound of the CI growth rate within any time window. In general, a growth rate increase of a CI by some percentage represents a different CI "trajectory" within the time window, as exemplified in Fig. 2a. Such new trajectory can be used as an upper bound, while the original CI growth trend represents a lower bound. The verification strategy would be to analyze all CI trajectories contained within these bounds, thus exhaustively verifying all possible CI changes within the interval and their effect on the monotonicity of the estimator.

A CI slope change affects all CI values in the time window. In particular, the values closer to the end of the window have a larger change. As a result, overall intervals to be analyzed by formal verification would become substantially large, even if the upper bound (increased CI slope) is small. This may lead to scalability issues. Additionally, such formulation is not able to discard "oscillating" CI trajectories, i.e., highly non-monotonic[2] ones, since it only defines lower and upper bounds for CI values at each time step, but does not prescribe any interdependency between consecutive values. See example in Fig. 2a (black line). Such CI trajectories may represent excessive noise but in general are not realistic. At the same time, they may invalidate a large number of properties, hampering the effectiveness of the verification. Hence, the analysis space has to be further restricted.

A compromise solution that enables a tradeoff between input space coverage, scalability, and effectiveness of the verification is presented below. It consists in extending the CI growth rate change with the possibility of a *constrained fluctuation*: this guarantees that, where the original CI trajectory is locally monotonically increasing, any trajectory in the defined interval is also monotonically increasing; where the original trajectory is not locally increasing, any derived trajectory is at least not "less monotonic" (see example in Fig. 2b). Such formulation allows local oscillations in the CIs, for example, due to noise. Given a CI i, step t, constant γ, let $u_i^t = x_i^t + \gamma|x_i^t - x_i^1|$ and $v_i^t = x_i^t - \gamma|x_i^t - x_i^1|$. Monotonicity properties with constrained fluctuation for a single CI growth rate change can be expressed as:

$$\forall \boldsymbol{x'} : \forall t : u_i^t \leq x_i'^t \leq max(u_i^t, u_i^{t+1}) \rightarrow f(\boldsymbol{x'}) \leq f(\boldsymbol{x}) \tag{3a}$$

$$\forall \boldsymbol{x'} : \forall t : v_i^t \leq x_i'^t \leq max(v_i^t, v_i^{t+1}) \rightarrow f(\boldsymbol{x'}) \geq f(\boldsymbol{x}) \tag{3b}$$

Consider the Eq. 3a. The difference $|x_i^t - x_i^1|$ represents an approximation of the CI slope in the interval $[1, t]$. The given CI i is allowed to fluctuate, at step t, between $u_i^t = x_i^t + \gamma|x_i^t - x_i^1|$ and $u_i^{t+1} = x_i^{t+1} + \gamma|x_i^{t+1} - x_i^1|$, if $u_i^{t+1} \geq u_i^t$, otherwise it is set to u_i^t. The *max* function captures this constrained fluctuation. Accordingly, at step $t+1$, x_i' either belongs to the interval $[u_i^{t+1}, u_i^{t+2}]$, or is set to u_i^{t+1}, if such interval is empty. This procedure guarantees that, if $x_i^t \leq x_i^{t+1}$, then $x_i'^t \leq x_i'^{t+1}$, leading to a derived trajectory that is not "less monotonic" than the original one. Similarly, Eq. 3b captures the constrained CI fluctuation in the opposite direction, i.e., it prescribes a non-decreasing RUL in cases of a "slower" CI growth rate. Properties 3a-3b can be generalized to the case that captures simultaneous growth rate change in all CIs. These formulations are available in [5].

4 Verification Methods

We have implemented a formal verification framework to support the analysis of local stability and local monotonicity properties. The framework carries out all

[2] In this case, the notion of monotonicity applies to a CI in a time window, intended as a sequence of values, rather than to the RUL *w.r.t.* one of the CIs.

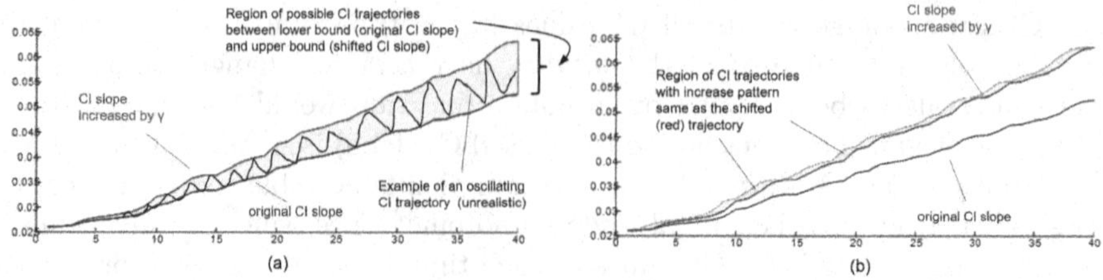

Fig. 2. Monotonicity analysis: (a) Entire space of possible CI trajectories bounded by the original CI trajectory at a given input point and a modified trajectory with an increased growth rate; (b) Subspace of CI trajectories with constrained fluctuation.

property formalization activities, i.e., it automatically creates property objects from numerical values provided in the requirements. To verify the properties, it then invokes the FM tool NNV [15] that is based on abstract interpretation. The tool computes the set of possible outputs for a set of inputs specified by the property, and then performs a geometrical check: for the property to be valid, the output set of the NN must not intersect with the region of the output space (halfspace) that is associated with the negation of this property (i.e., the "unsafe" area). Otherwise, an intersection manifests a property violation. The following verification methods are provided by the VNN tool:

- **Exact method.** This method performs exact reachability analysis for the neural network, i.e., it precisely computes the set of possible outputs (output reachable set) based on the provided input set.
- **Approximate method.** This method computes a conservative approximation of possible NN outputs via abstract interpretation. This enables faster analysis time. If the region associated with a property negation (i.e., unsafe region) does not intersect with the output set over-approximation, the property can be concluded valid. However, the analysis may not be able to disprove the property, that is, if an intersection with the negated property is found, the related counterexample may be spurious. To avoid raising a false alarm, in such situations the tool returns an "unknown" answer.

Despite being sound and complete, the exact verification method may face scalability issues when the complexity of the NN (e.g., number of layers, parameters) and/or the property (e.g., size of the input space to be considered) is high. On the other hand, the approximate method can only identify valid properties, but not invalid ones, always returning "unknown" in the latter case. In this paper, we propose a tradeoff between completeness and execution time. The new approach, called the **two-step method**, combines approximate verification described above, and a simulation-based *falsification* method. The latter randomly generates a number of inputs in the neighborhood of the given point for which the local property is defined, and performs NN inference to check the outputs against the property. If a violation is observed then the property is falsified and can be declared invalid. However, contrary to the above methods, simulation alone cannot prove the property, it may only disprove it.

The two-step method is illustrated in Fig. 3. First, the property is verified with the approximate method and, if it is proven valid, the method terminates. Otherwise, if "unknown" is returned by the solver, the simulation-based method is invoked in an attempt to disprove the property by finding a counterexample (CEX) among a configurable number of randomly generated inputs in the neighborhood of the original point. If no CEX is found, the method returns "unknown". Hence, the method is still incomplete, but it aims at increasing the thoroughness of the analysis *w.r.t.* using only the approximate method based on abstract interpretation. Informally, it increases the chances of providing a definitive answer for each property.

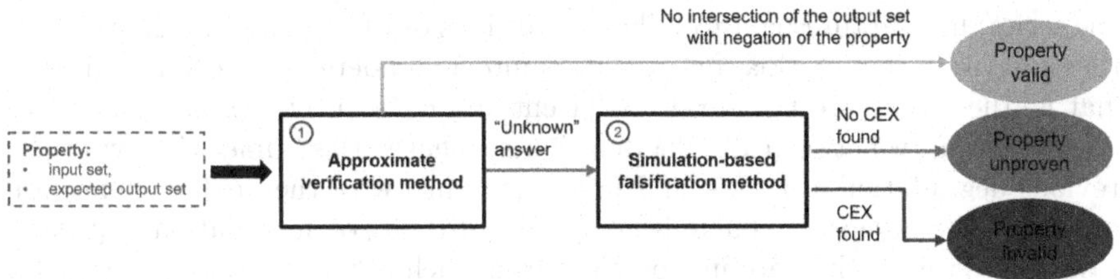

Fig. 3. Two-step verification method: abstract interpretation (first step) and simulation-based falsification (second step).

5 Verification Results

All experiments were run on a server with ~64GB of RAM and a ~2095Mhz Intel Xeon processor, in a Linux Ubuntu environment.

5.1 Reduction of Global Properties to Local Properties

Properties in Sect. 3 have been defined for *some* input time window $\mathbf{x} \in X$, X being the input space of the neural network (more precisely, its ODD). They can be imposed on the entire space X, making them global properties. Formal guarantees on the validity of these global properties would be desirable to demonstrate that the requirements are met. However, such analysis is currently intractable with existing VNN tools.

To mitigate the tool scalability problem, we propose an approximation of global property verification by reducing it to verifying *local properties* defined for a set of input points. The result of such reduction could be acceptable if altogether selected input points and corresponding local properties are representative of the RUL estimator ODD and cover it sufficiently. In other words, a discretization of the ODD could be performed with a representative set of input points that approximate all possible input points within the ODD. Consequently, analysis of local properties for these points would approximate the verification of the corresponding global property.

According to data quality requirements prescribed by existing ML certification guidance for aviation applications [6], each dataset (i.e., training, validation, test) must be *complete* and *representative* with respect to the ODD. Statistical methods could be applied to assess these characteristics of the data [5]. Traditionally, testing of ML models is performed on a test (holdout) dataset. This dataset could be used as an approximation of the ODD, provided that its completeness and representativeness are demonstrated[3].

In this case study, we used the RUL estimator test dataset to perform the verification. Its quality has been analyzed and improved, as described in [5]. The test dataset includes 7493 time windows. They have been obtained by (i) concatenating degradation sequences (each degradation sequence is a multivariate time series that captures run-to-failure conditions of the bearing) in an arbitrary order and (ii) flattening this concatenation into a numbered list of time windows. That is, the inputs are temporally adjacent and consecutive, except that there is a discontinuity between the degradation sequences (last time window of the previous degradation sequence and first time window of the next sequence are not temporally adjacent). There is no specific ordering of degradation sequences in the test dataset, they are independent from each other.

5.2 Stability Verification

Several verification phases have been conducted for stability properties. First, the exact verification method was tested in the presence of a single CI perturbation at a single time step, as formulated in Eq. 1. The encoding produced 52451 local stability properties. The framework was able to verify all properties with an average execution time of 0.36 s; 100% of the properties were proven valid. Since all properties could be verified with a sound and complete method, it was considered redundant to test other verification methods in this phase.

Next, the exact method was employed to verify properties involving simultaneous perturbations of all CIs at a single time step, according to Eq. 2. The encoding produced 7493 local properties, one per input time window. The method could not verify any property within a time limit of 3h, sometimes due to failures caused by out-of-memory events.

To mitigate the scalability problem, two-step verification method was applied to the same properties involving all CIs. The adoption of an approximate method allowed to overcome the difficulties experienced with the exact method: all properties were verified, 98.3% of them were proven valid, with an average verification time of 0.63 s. Invalidity was detected, and an unknown answer was given, respectively, in 0.08% and 1.58% of the cases.

Results are summarized in Table 2, showing the total number of properties verified (or intended to be verified) at each verification phase, and a breakdown

[3] A more detailed investigation of the reduction of global to local properties would include producing empirical evidence of the feasibility of the approach, as well as deriving analytical bounds on the approximation. This is subject of future work.

into amounts of valid, invalid, and unknown answers computed by the verification framework. Finally, average verification time per property is provided (avgTime) - cumulative, as well as average times for valid, invalid, and unknown properties (in brackets). Total verification time (totTime) is also provided in the last column. It can be noted that the use of the exact method to verify properties with perturbations in all CIs is redundant and in fact provided no results, however, it is also shown here to demonstrate the scalability issue. Since with the use of the two-step method invalid and unknown (unproven) properties are present, the table additionally specifies the results for the *critical range* of the RUL to see whether some of these properties could have potential impact on safety.

Table 2. Verification results for local stability properties of the RUL estimator.

Setting	# prop	# valid	# inv	# unknown	avgTime (s)	totTime (s)
Single CI, exact method	52451	52451	0	0	0.3255 (0.3255, -, -)	17074
All CIs, exact method	7493	–	–	-	Timeout (-, -, -)	Timeout
All CIs, 2-step method	7493	7369	6	118	0.6347 (0.5, 6.4, 4.1)	4756
All CIs, 2-step method critical range	1414	1414	0	0	0.3313	468.45

Figure 4 shows where RUL estimator inputs that resulted in invalid and unknown stability properties are located within their degradation sequences. Recall that each property is associated with a time window, and that within each degradation sequence in the test dataset local stability properties correspond to temporally adjacent and consecutive time windows. Black solid vertical bars in Fig. 4 mark the ends of the degradation sequences: a vertical bar represents the end of a previous sequence, i.e., the failure of the bearing, and the beginning of a next one (full healthy state of the bearing). Red and blue dotted vertical bars identify, respectively, invalid and unknown properties.

It can be observed that invalid and unknown properties tend to be concentrated within the first half of the sequence time frame, i.e., the estimator behavior may be problematic at the very beginning of a degradation sequence. Noteworthy, there are no such properties in the critical range (last 100h of remaining lifetime of the bearing), where all properties are valid within the entire test dataset. This increases confidence in the correctness of the behavior of the RUL estimator with respect to safety considerations. Overall, it can be concluded that requirement RUL-ML-Stab-2 for stability to single CI perturbations is met, while RUL-ML-Stab-3 is not met.

Counterexample. It is important to analyze counterexamples to gain insights on the possible reasons of property violation. The verification framework permits visual analysis of the counterexamples. An example is illustrated in Fig. 5 for a stability property to multiple (all) CI perturbations at a single time step. It comes from the simulation-based falsification (second step of the two-step method), i.e., it is the result of applying bounded random perturbations on selected CIs corresponding to the property.

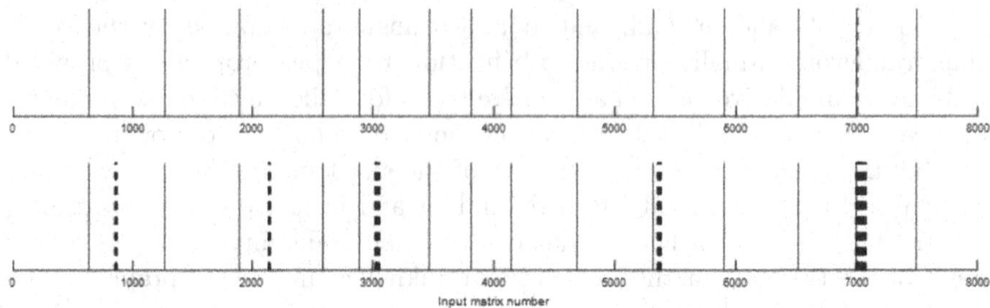

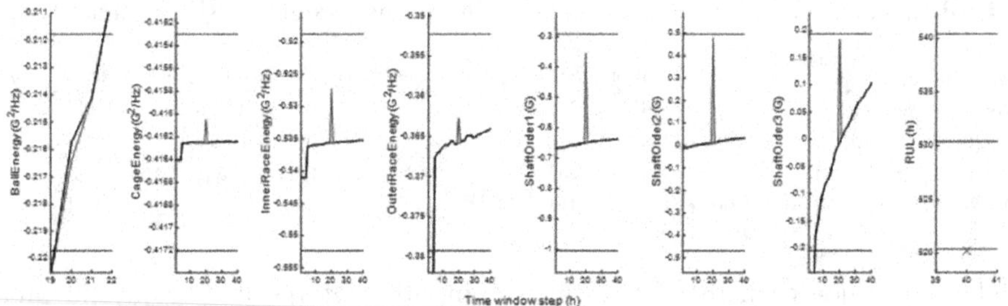

Fig. 4. Location of inputs related to invalid (top) and unknown (bottom) properties for all sequences in the test dataset.

Fig. 5. Visualization of a counterexample to a local stability property.

First seven sub-charts in Fig. 5 show the CIs trends (in blue) over the input window. A perturbation to each of the CIs at step 20 is shown in red color. Black horizontal bars denote the perturbation bounds for each CI ($\pm\delta$). The last sub-chart on the right shows the original RUL estimator output (in blue) and the output deviation (red cross) due to input perturbations; the output exceeds the admissible deviation $\epsilon = 10$h. Several observations can be made:

- Each CI received a positive perturbation, i.e., a spike towards higher values that are associated with higher bearing degradation.
- The last three CIs (ShaftOrder 1–3) got perturbed more than others. The perturbation applied to these CIs is almost the maximum admissible one (δ). The shaft is a cross-component for the bearing, so if the shaft health decreased substantially, as manifested by the ShaftOrder CIs, it would have a multiplicative effect on the degradation coefficient, which could significantly decrease the RUL. However, a spike increase in the shaft CIs at a single time step should not lead to such decrease as resulted from the CEX in Fig. 5.

5.3 Monotonicity Verification

Analysis has been performed on monotonicity properties with constrained fluctuation defined by Eqs. 3a-3b - both for each single CI slope change (and corresponding constrained fluctuation interval of CI trajectories) and for all CI slopes changed simultaneously, with γ varying from 10% to 50%. Again, the exact verification method did not provide any answer in a 3h timeout, therefore, the two-step method was applied.

Table 3 provides the results for growth rate change in a single CI. It reports numbers of valid, invalid and unknown properties, average verification times per property, and total verification times, for different CI growth trajectories (slopes) regulated by the γ parameter. Statistics for properties corresponding to input points in the critical range of the RUL (last 100 h) are shown separately in the same table. Similarly, results for properties involving simultaneous growth rate change in all CIs are provided in Table 4. Following observations can be made:

- The estimator is more likely to correctly react, i.e., exhibit monotonic behavior, to simultaneous changes in all CIs rather than in an individual CI. Considering increased growth rates for individual CI and all CIs, the total percentage of valid properties in the former case varies between 79% and 84% (depending on γ), while for the latter 98%-99.5% of properties are valid. This is because multiple increasing CI trends in the input window provide more "evidence" to the estimator that the bearing is degrading.
- The estimator is more monotonic when the CI growth rate change is large: γ =50% has much fewer property violations compared to γ =10%. Larger changes make it more evident to the estimator that the degradation is happening. This holds for both changes in single CI and in all CIs.
- For single CI slope changes, property violations, as well as "unknown" answers, are uniformly distributed across the RUL range. For changes in all CIs, violations and "unknowns" mainly belong to the critical range of RUL.
- Average solving time for verification of a single property is a fraction of a second for individual CIs and around 1 s for all CIs. Verification of the latter is more complex since more inputs are considered variable (as intervals) rather than fixed: for a time window length of 40, individual CI properties result in 40 intervals to be defined (one per time step for a single CI), while 280 intervals (40×7 CIs) must be considered for all CI properties.

Same as for stability properties, monotonicity verification can generate counterexamples for invalid properties. Such CEX can be fed back to the designer for further analysis. An example is shown in Fig. 6 for one of the input windows in the critical range of the RUL. Here, the growth rate of all seven CIs has been increased by γ = 10%. Original CI trajectories are shown in blue and modified ones in red. The RUL value (red cross on the rightmost plot) is larger than the original one (blue horizontal line), therefore, the property is violated. In fact, even though the new CI trajectory with higher CI growth rate has values strictly larger than the original one, the estimator fails to predict a decreasing RUL. One can observe non-monotonicity in some of the CIs (e.g., BallEnergy and CageEnergy; they are present even in the original trajectories). These fluctuations may be due to flight regime or mission change within the time window.

Overall, verification of local monotonicity properties defined from requirements RUL-ML-Mon-1 and RUL-ML-Mon-2 reveals that the current version of the ML model does not meet neither of the two requirements. This is due to:

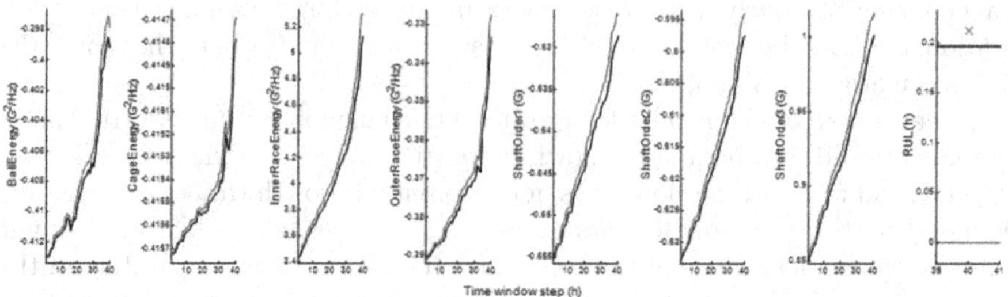

Fig. 6. Counterexample for a monotonicity property with a 10% growth rate increase for all CIs.

Table 3. Monotonicity property verification results with two-step method (single CI, increased CI growth rates).

range	γ	# prop	# valid	# invalid	# unknown	avgTime (s)	totTime (s)
full	10%	52451	41572	7797	3082	0.1716	8999
	20%		42875	7624	1952	0.1660	8706
	30%		43513	7568	1370	0.1591	8346
	40%		43869	7543	1039	0.1632	8563
	50%		44108	7524	819	0.1608	8436
critical	10%	9898	8061	1455	382	0.1620	1604
	20%		8248	1446	204	0.1568	1552
	30%		8316	1445	137	0.1498	1483
	40%		8359	1434	105	0.1533	1517
	50%		8387	1426	85	0.1515	1500

Table 4. Monotonicity property verification results with two-step method (all CIs, increased CI growth rates).

range	γ	# prop	# valid	# invalid	# unknown	avgTime (s)	totTime (s)
full	10%	7493	7364	59	70	1.049	7858
	20%		7458	26	9	1.075	8052
	30%		7457	25	11	1.068	8005
	40%		7458	24	11	1.104	8274
	50%		7458	22	13	1.080	8098
critical	10%	1414	1373	26	15	0.984	1392
	20%		1379	26	9	1.010	1429
	30%		1378	25	11	1.004	1419
	40%		1379	24	11	1.027	1452
	50%		1379	22	13	1.008	1426

- A significant number of property violations occurs on relatively small changes of the CI growth rate (e.g., γ =10%) - 20% for all single-CI properties, with the majority of invalid properties belonging to the changes in ShaftOrder1 and ShaftOrder3. Additionally, there is a large number of unknown properties, also in the critical RUL range. This shows that the estimator is often not capable of associating growing CI trends with component degradation.
- Despite the number of invalid properties for growth rate changes in all CIs (RUL-ML-Mon-2) being small (around 0.3%), all violations belong to the critical region of the RUL.

Limited Non-monotonicity. Additional analysis has been carried out to understand to which extent monotonicity properties are not satisfied, e.g., if such increase of the RUL value can be bounded from above. For this purpose, the notion of *limited non-monotonicity* has been introduced and encoded. For properties with single CI growth rate increase (Eq. 3) this is formalized as follows:

$$\forall \boldsymbol{x}' : \forall t : u_i^t \leq x_i'^t \leq max(u_i^t, u_i^{t+1}) \rightarrow f(\boldsymbol{x}') \leq f(\boldsymbol{x}) + \epsilon \tag{4}$$

for step t, constant γ, constant $\epsilon = 10\text{h}$ (provided by the domain expert), $u_i^{t+1} = x_i^{t+1} + \gamma|x_i^{t+1} - x_i^1|$, S being the subset of indexes i of features corresponding to CIs. Equation 4 imposes that a constrained fluctuation in the CIs yields an increase of the estimated RUL that is limited by a constant number of hours ϵ.

Analysis of the relaxed property allowing limited non-monotonicity has been executed only for properties reported as invalid or unknown during verification activities presented above. Numerical results are available in [5], pages 87–88. Results for single CI have shown that the majority of the previously invalid/unknown properties become valid, i.e., the violations of the original properties are mostly bounded by $\epsilon = 10\text{h}$. A small number of properties remained invalid. The analysis showed that they belong to a group of adjacent time windows in a single degradation sequence. Violations may be related to fluctuating behavior of the CI within the corresponding windows, possibly due to errors in simulations that produced synthetic data for the test dataset.

6 Conclusion and Future Work

We applied formal methods on an industrial case study to verify properties of a deep learning based estimator of remaining useful life. We provided mathematical formalizations of stability and monotonicity properties of neural networks. To overcome scalability limitations of VNN tools, we proposed to reduce the verification of global properties to a representative set of local properties, and also implemented a two-step verification method involving abstract interpretation and simulation-based falsification. Numerical results demonstrate the applicability of formal methods to verify a large number of local properties in reasonable time. Future work shall focus on further improving both the completeness of the analysis and its scalability, derivation of an error bound for the reduction of global properties with local properties, as well as on the application of FM on higher complexity neural networks, such as perception systems.

Acknowledgements. The authors wish to thank Eric DeWind and David F. Larsen for fruitful discussions and feedback about the RUL estimator, as well as for providing mechanical bearing degradation datasets to train and test the neural network.

References

1. Remaining Useful Life Estimation using Convolutional Neural Network. https://www.mathworks.com/help/releases/R2021a/predmaint/ug/remaining-useful-life-estimation-using-convolutional-neural-network.html
2. Similarity-Based Remaining Useful Life Estimation. https://www.mathworks.com/help/predmaint/ug/similarity-based-remaining-useful-life-estimation.html
3. Benkedjouh, T., Medjaher, K., Zerhouni, N., Rechak, S.: Remaining useful life estimation based on nonlinear feature reduction and support vector regression. Eng. Appl. Artif. Intell. **26**, 1751–1760 (2013)
4. Damour, M., et al.: Towards certification of a reduced footprint ACAS-Xu system: a hybrid ML-based solution. In: Habli, I., Sujan, M., Bitsch, F. (eds.) SAFECOMP 2021. LNCS, vol. 12852, pp. 34–48. Springer, Cham (2021). https://doi.org/10.1007/978-3-030-83903-1_3
5. EASA and Collins Aerospace: Formal Methods use for Learning Assurance (ForMuLA). Tech. rep. (April 2023)
6. European Union Aviation Safety Agency (EASA): Concept Paper: Guidance for Level 1&2 Machine Learning Applications. Concept paper for consultation (February 2023)
7. Katz, G.: The marabou framework for verification and analysis of deep neural networks. In: Dillig, I., Tasiran, S. (eds.) CAV 2019. LNCS, vol. 11561, pp. 443–452. Springer, Cham (2019). https://doi.org/10.1007/978-3-030-25540-4_26
8. Li, X., Ding, Q., Sun, J.Q.: Remaining useful life estimation in prognostics using deep convolution neural networks. Reliability Eng. System Safety, 1–11 (2018)
9. Liu, C., Cofer, D., Osipychev, D.: Verifying an aircraft collision avoidance neural network with marabou. In: Proceeding of NASA Formal Methods Symposium (2023)
10. Pecht, M., Gu, J.: Physics-of-failure-based prognostics for electronic products. IEEE Trans. Measurem. Control **31**, 309–322 (2009)
11. Ren, L., Cui, J., Sun, Y., Cheng, X.: Multi-bearing remaining useful life collaborative prediction: a deep learning approach. J. Manuf. Syst. **43**, 248–256 (2017)
12. RTCA/DO-178C: Software Considerations in Airborne Systems and Equipment Certification (2011)
13. RTCA/DO-333: Formal Methods Supplement to DO-178C and DO-278A (2011)
14. SAE G-34 Artificial Intelligence in Aviation: Artificial Intelligence in Aeronautical Systems: Statement of Concerns (2021)
15. Tran, H.-D., et al.: NNV: the neural network verification tool for deep neural networks and learning-enabled cyber-physical systems. In: Lahiri, S.K., Wang, C. (eds.) CAV 2020. LNCS, vol. 12224, pp. 3–17. Springer, Cham (2020). https://doi.org/10.1007/978-3-030-53288-8_1
16. Wang, S., Pei, K., Whitehouse, J., Yang, J., Jana, S.: Efficient formal safety analysis of neural networks. In: Advances in Neural Information Processing Systems 31 (2018)

The Inverse Problem for Neural Networks

Marcelo Forets[1] and Christian Schilling[2(✉)]

[1] Universidad de la República, Montevideo, Uruguay
[2] Aalborg University, Aalborg, Denmark
christianms@cs.aau.dk

Abstract. We study the problem of computing the preimage of a set under a neural network with piecewise-affine activation functions. We recall an old result that the preimage of a polyhedral set is again a union of polyhedral sets and can be effectively computed. We show several applications of computing the preimage for analysis and interpretability of neural networks.

Keywords: Neural network · Inverse problem · Set propagation · Interpretability

1 Introduction

We study the inverse problem for neural networks. That is, given a neural network N and a set Y of outputs, we want to compute the preimage, i.e., we want to find all inputs x such that their image under the network is in Y ($N(x) \in Y$).

Computing the preimage has at least two motivations. First, it can be used for specification mining. Besides the obvious benefit of actually obtaining a potential specification, the main application is in interpretability, explaining the function the neural network encodes. This has indeed been investigated before (under the name *rule extraction*) [4,17,26]. As a second motivation, the preimage is also useful if a specification is known. In that case we can analyze whether the specification holds, e.g., whether there exist inputs leading to a set of outputs.

In this paper, we give a complete picture of the preimage computation for piecewise-affine neural networks. For this class, the preimage of a polyhedral set is again a union of (potentially exponentially many) polyhedral sets and can be effectively computed using linear programming. This result has already been obtained in the past [17]. However, that line of work seems to not be well known, a potential reason being that, at the time, piecewise-affine activation functions were not used. That work is indeed only concerned with a piecewise-affine approximation of the then-common sigmoid activation functions. Nowadays, piecewise-affine activation functions are most widely used in practice, and have also been extensively investigated in the formal-methods community. We believe that the community has fruitful applications for the preimage, and the purpose of this paper is to bring these results to the community's attention. We also show a potential use case in interpretability and two extensions by approximation and combination with forward-image computation.

B. Steffen (Ed.): AISoLA 2023, LNCS 14380, pp. 241–255, 2024.
https://doi.org/10.1007/978-3-031-46002-9_14

1.1 Related Work

The traditional take on the inverse problem for neural networks in the machine-learning community has particularly been studied for image classifiers, where the task is to either highlight which neurons [16] or input pixels [22,29] were most influential in the decision. However, these approaches do not compute the actual inverse but rather implement heuristics to map to one particular input. Many such techniques have been demonstrated to be misleading [24]. For instance, the technique in [29] remembers the inputs to a max-pooling layer, which otherwise cannot be inverted. A related concept is the autoencoder [12], where the decoder maps the output of the encoder back to the input; however, both maps are learned and thus there is no guarantee that the decoder inverts the encoder.

Another direction of inverse computation in neural networks is known as adversarial attacks [9]. The motivation is to find inputs that drive a classifier to a misclassification. For that, an input is mildly perturbed such that it crosses the network's decision boundary.

In abstract interpretation [6], the abstraction function maps an input to an abstract domain, and the concretization function maps back to the (set of) concrete values. Abstract interpretation has also been used for (forward) set propagation in neural networks with abstract domains such as intervals [26, 27], polytopes [28], zonotopes [21,23], and polynomial zonotopes [13]. A related approach uses polygons: given a classifier with two-dimensional input domain, the approach partitions the input domain into the preimages of each class [25].

Maire [17] proposed an algorithm to compute the preimage of a union of polyhedra. The algorithm applies to arbitrary activation functions, but only computes an approximate solution in general. To improve scalability, Breutel and Maire use an additional approximation step based on nonlinear optimization [4]. Our goal is the exact computation of the preimage for networks with piecewise-affine activations. Although very close to this work, the above approaches assume a bounded input domain, bounded activation space, or surjective activations, which excludes the (nowadays) widely used rectified linear unit.

Computing the inverse of a function under a set is also known as set inversion, which has been mainly studied in the context of interval constraint propagation, with applications in robotics, control, or parameter estimation [11]. To reduce the approximation error, one can apply iterative forward-backward contractors [5]. We show such an experiment later. Thrun applied this idea to neural networks with bounded input and output domains as well as activation spaces [26].

Recently, a number of works study backward reachability in discrete-time neural-network control systems [2,7,14,19,20]. These approaches do not seem to be aware of the above-mentioned old works, and discuss strategies to compute an approximation of the preimage. This is due to the intractability of computing the exact preimage.

2 The Preimage of a Piecewise-Affine Neural Network

In this section, we describe an algorithm to compute the preimage of a union of polyhedra under a neural network with piecewise-affine activations.

2.1 Preliminaries

A function $f : \mathbb{R}^m \to \mathbb{R}^n$ is affine if $f(x) = Cx + d$ for some matrix $C \in \mathbb{R}^{n \times m}$ and vector $d \in \mathbb{R}^n$. The function f is piecewise affine if there exists a partitioning of $\mathbb{R}^m$ such that f is affine in each partition.

A (deep) neural network (DNN)[1] N comprises k layers ℓ_i that are sequentially composed such that $N = \ell_k \circ \cdots \circ \ell_1$. Each layer ℓ_i applies an affine map of appropriate dimensions, followed by an activation function, written $\ell_i(x) = \alpha_i(W_i x + b_i)$. Activation functions are one-dimensional maps $\alpha_i : \mathbb{R} \to \mathbb{R}$, and are extended componentwise to vectors. Some common piecewise-affine activation functions are the identity, the rectified linear unit (ReLU), $\rho(x) = \max(x, 0)$, and the leaky ReLU, which is a parametric generalization with $a \geq 0$ defined as

$$\rho_a^\ell(x) = \begin{cases} x & x > 0 \\ ax & x \leq 0. \end{cases}$$

An n-dimensional half-space (or linear constraint) is characterized by a vector $c \in \mathbb{R}^n$ and a scalar $d \in \mathbb{R}$ and represents the set $\{x : c^T x \leq d\}$. A polyhedron is an intersection of half-spaces. A convenient way to write a polyhedron is in the matrix-vector form $Cx \leq d$, where the i-th row of C and d correspond to the i-th half-space. A polytope is a bounded polyhedron.

Given a function (e.g., a DNN) $f : \mathbb{R}^m \to \mathbb{R}^n$, the *image* of a set $\mathcal{X} \subseteq \mathbb{R}^m$ is $f(\mathcal{X}) = \{f(x) : x \in \mathcal{X}\} \subseteq \mathbb{R}^n$. Analogously, the *preimage* of a set $\mathcal{Y} \subseteq \mathbb{R}^n$ is $f^{-1}(\mathcal{Y}) = \{x : f(x) \in \mathcal{Y}\} \subseteq \mathbb{R}^m$. For nonempty sets and injective $g : \mathbb{R}^m \to \mathbb{R}^n$ we note the following facts [10,15]:

$$\mathcal{X} \subseteq f^{-1}(f(\mathcal{X})) \tag{1}$$

$$\mathcal{X} = g^{-1}(g(\mathcal{X})) \tag{2}$$

$$f(\mathcal{X}_1 \cup \mathcal{X}_2) = f(\mathcal{X}_1) \cup f(\mathcal{X}_2) \tag{3}$$

$$f^{-1}(\mathcal{Y}_1 \cup \mathcal{Y}_2) = f^{-1}(\mathcal{Y}_1) \cup f^{-1}(\mathcal{Y}_2) \tag{4}$$

$$f(\mathcal{X}) \cap \mathcal{Y} = f(\mathcal{X} \cap f^{-1}(\mathcal{Y})) \tag{5}$$

The inclusion in Eq. (1) is generally strict. In particular, for the class of DNNs considered here, the image of a (bounded) polytope $\mathcal{X}$ is a union of polytopes, but the preimage of a nonempty polytope (even if consisting of a single element) is a union of (unbounded) polyhedra. Because of the layer-wise architecture of DNNs, the image can be computed by iteratively applying each affine map and activation function. Below we describe how to compute the preimage in the same fashion, most of which has been described in prior work [17].

[1] Typically, *deep* neural networks are neural networks with multiple hidden layers. Here we do not make this distinction and always use the term *DNN*.

2.2 Inverse Affine Map

Given sets $\mathcal{X} \subseteq \mathbb{R}^m$ and $\mathcal{Y} \subseteq \mathbb{R}^n$, a matrix $W \in \mathbb{R}^{n\times m}$, and a vector $b \in \mathbb{R}^n$, for the affine map $f(x) = Wx + b$, the image of $\mathcal{X}$ is $f(\mathcal{X}) = \{f(x) : x \in \mathcal{X}\} \subseteq \mathbb{R}^n$ and the preimage of $\mathcal{Y}$ is $f^{-1}(\mathcal{Y}) = \{x : Wx + b \in \mathcal{Y}\} \subseteq \mathbb{R}^n$. For a polyhedron $\mathcal{Y}$ written as $Cy \leq d$, we can write the preimage as follows:

$$f^{-1}(\mathcal{Y}) = \{x : C(Wx + b) \leq d\} = \{x : CWx \leq d - Cb\} \tag{6}$$

Note that some of the resulting linear constraints may be redundant or contradictory. In the latter case, the preimage is empty.

Example 1. For the affine map $f(x) = \begin{pmatrix}-0.46 & 0.32\end{pmatrix} x + 2$ and the interval $\mathcal{Y} = [2, 3]$, we get the infinite band $f^{-1}(\mathcal{Y}) = \{x \in \mathbb{R}^2 : 0 \leq \begin{pmatrix}-0.46 & 0.32\end{pmatrix} x \leq 1\}$. $\lhd$

2.3 Inverse Piecewise-Affine Activation Function

Given sets $\mathcal{X}, \mathcal{Y} \subseteq \mathbb{R}^n$ and a piecewise-affine activation function α, the image of $\mathcal{X}$ can be computed as follows. Consider the partitioning $\Pi = \bigcup_j \mathcal{P}_j$ of $\mathbb{R}^n$ into the different domains $\mathcal{P}_j$ in which α is an affine function α_j. (Observe that α_j has a diagonal matrix due to componentwise application.) Then we can apply the corresponding affine map to the intersection of $\mathcal{X}$ with each $\mathcal{P}_j$:

$$\alpha(\mathcal{X}) = \alpha\big(\bigcup_j \mathcal{P}_j \cap \mathcal{X}\big) \overset{(3)}{=} \bigcup_j \alpha(\mathcal{P}_j \cap \mathcal{X}) = \bigcup_j \alpha_j(\mathcal{P}_j \cap \mathcal{X})$$

Example 2. Consider the ReLU function ρ for $n = 2$. The partitioning Π consists of four regions with the corresponding affine maps being modified identity matrices, where diagonal entry i is zero if the i-th dimension is non-positive:

$$\mathcal{P}_1 = x_1 > 0 \wedge x_2 > 0 \qquad \rho_1(x) = \begin{pmatrix}1 & 0\\ 0 & 1\end{pmatrix} x$$

$$\mathcal{P}_2 = x_1 \leq 0 \wedge x_2 > 0 \qquad \rho_2(x) = \begin{pmatrix}0 & 0\\ 0 & 1\end{pmatrix} x$$

$$\mathcal{P}_3 = x_1 > 0 \wedge x_2 \leq 0 \qquad \rho_3(x) = \begin{pmatrix}1 & 0\\ 0 & 0\end{pmatrix} x$$

$$\mathcal{P}_4 = x_1 \leq 0 \wedge x_2 \leq 0 \qquad \rho_4(x) = \begin{pmatrix}0 & 0\\ 0 & 0\end{pmatrix} x$$

Thus we get:

$$\rho(\mathcal{X}) = \rho_1(\mathcal{P}_1 \cap \mathcal{X}) \cup \rho_2(\mathcal{P}_2 \cap \mathcal{X}) \cup \rho_3(\mathcal{P}_3 \cap \mathcal{X}) \cup \rho_4(\mathcal{P}_4 \cap \mathcal{X}) \tag{$\lhd$}$$

The preimage can be computed in an analogous way, using that $\bigcup_j \alpha_j(\mathcal{P}_j) = \alpha(\mathbb{R}^n)$. Note that, while the sets $\mathcal{P}_j$ partition $\mathbb{R}^n$, the sets $\alpha_j(\mathcal{P}_j)$ do not necessarily partition $\mathbb{R}^n$ (only if α is injective).

$$\alpha^{-1}(\mathcal{Y}) = \alpha^{-1}\Big(\bigcup_j \alpha_j(\mathcal{P}_j) \cap \mathcal{Y}\Big)$$

$$\overset{(4)}{=} \bigcup_j \alpha_j^{-1}(\alpha_j(\mathcal{P}_j) \cap \mathcal{Y}) \tag{7}$$

$$\overset{(5)}{=} \bigcup_j \alpha_j^{-1}(\alpha_j(\mathcal{P}_j \cap \alpha_j^{-1}(\mathcal{Y}))) \tag{8}$$

One can implement a check for Eq. (7) directly, which is done in [17]. However, there are two issues with Eq. (7).

(1) Some of the resulting linear constraints may be redundant. This is also noted in [17]. For example, in the case of ReLU and assuming that $\mathcal{Y}$ contains the origin, the negative orthant is part of the preimage and can be represented by n linear constraints; instead, the equation suggests to compute the image of the negative orthant (which is the set just containing the origin), which already requires at least $n+1$ linear constraints, then computes the intersection with $\mathcal{Y}$, and finally computes the preimage.

(2) Instead of computing the preimage of the intersection of $\alpha_j(\mathcal{P}_j)$ with $\mathcal{Y}$, it may be more efficient to compute the preimage of $\mathcal{Y}$ first. The reason is that the preimage computation is more efficient for certain set representations, but the intersection may remove the structure from the set.

Equation (8) is an attempt to mitigate these issues. While this expression looks more complicated, we can simplify it further by considering two cases. Recall that α_j is an affine activation function, i.e., it is applied componentwise, and observe that affine functions $\alpha_j : \mathbb{R} \to \mathbb{R}$ are either injective or constant. In the further case we can directly apply Eq. (2).

$$\alpha_j^{-1}(\alpha_j(\mathcal{P}_j \cap \alpha_j^{-1}(\mathcal{Y}))) = \mathcal{P}_j \cap \alpha_j^{-1}(\mathcal{Y}) \tag{9}$$

If α_j is constant such that $\alpha_j(x) = c$ for all $x \in \mathcal{P}_j$, then for any $\mathcal{X}$ we have

$$\alpha_j(\mathcal{P}_j \cap \mathcal{X}) = \begin{cases} \{c\} & \mathcal{P}_j \cap \mathcal{X} \neq \emptyset \\ \emptyset & \mathcal{P}_j \cap \mathcal{X} = \emptyset. \end{cases}$$

Since $\alpha_j^{-1}(\mathcal{Y}) = \mathcal{P}_j$ if $c \in \mathcal{Y}$ and $\alpha_j^{-1}(\mathcal{Y}) = \emptyset$ if $c \notin \mathcal{Y}$, we get:

$$\alpha_j^{-1}(\alpha_j(\mathcal{P}_j \cap \alpha_j^{-1}(\mathcal{Y}))) = \begin{cases} \mathcal{P}_j & c \in \mathcal{Y} \\ \emptyset & c \notin \mathcal{Y} \end{cases} \tag{10}$$

Example 3. We continue with the infinite band from Example 1, which we rename to $\mathcal{Y}$, and compute the inverse under ReLU, i.e., $\rho^{-1}(\mathcal{Y})$. Since we have two dimensions, we have the four partitions from Example 2. There are two cases. Case 1 implements Eq. (9), which applies to $\mathcal{P}_1$, $\mathcal{P}_2$, and $\mathcal{P}_3$. Case 2 implements

$$\ell_1(x) = \rho\left(\begin{pmatrix} 0.30 & 0.53 \\ 0.77 & 0.42 \end{pmatrix} x + \begin{pmatrix} 0.43 \\ -0.42 \end{pmatrix}\right) \qquad \ell_3(x) = \begin{pmatrix} 0.35 & 0.17 \\ -0.04 & 0.08 \end{pmatrix} x + \begin{pmatrix} 0.03 \\ 0.17 \end{pmatrix}$$

$$\ell_2(x) = \rho\left(\begin{pmatrix} 0.17 & -0.07 \\ 0.71 & -0.06 \end{pmatrix} x + \begin{pmatrix} -0.01 \\ 0.49 \end{pmatrix}\right) \qquad N = \ell_3 \circ \ell_2 \circ \ell_1$$

Fig. 1. A simple DNN $N : \mathbb{R}^2 \to \mathbb{R}^2$ for classification.

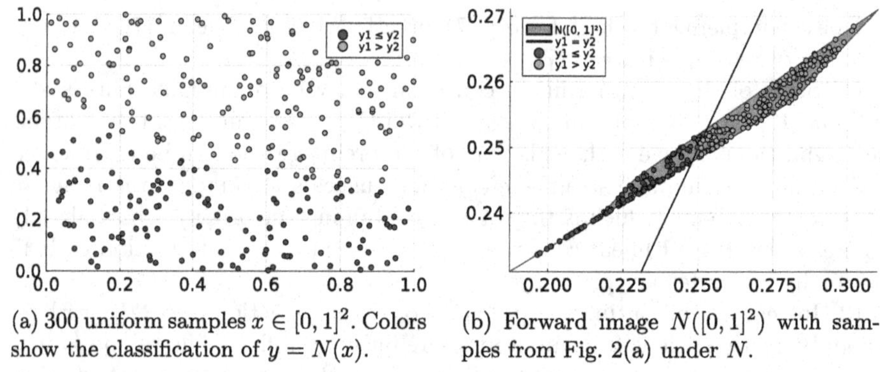

(a) 300 uniform samples $x \in [0,1]^2$. Colors show the classification of $y = N(x)$.

(b) Forward image $N([0,1]^2)$ with samples from Fig. 2(a) under N.

Fig. 2. Sampled inputs and outputs for the DNN N from Fig. 1.

Eq. (10), which applies to $\mathcal{P}_4$. Since the ReLU constant is $c = (0,0)^T$, we get $\mathcal{X}_4 := \mathcal{P}_4$ because $c \in \mathcal{Y}$. Overall the result is $\mathcal{X}_1 \cup \mathcal{X}_2 \cup \mathcal{X}_3 \cup \mathcal{X}_4$, where

$$\begin{aligned}
\mathcal{X}_1 &:= \mathcal{P}_1 \cap \rho_1^{-1}(\mathcal{Y}) = \{x \in \mathbb{R}^2 : 0 \leq \begin{pmatrix} -0.46 & 0.32 \end{pmatrix} x \leq 1 \wedge x_1 > 0\} \qquad (\lhd) \\
\mathcal{X}_2 &:= \mathcal{P}_2 \cap \rho_2^{-1}(\mathcal{Y}) = \{x \in \mathbb{R}^2 : x_1 \leq 0 \wedge 0 \leq x_2 \leq 3.125\} \\
\mathcal{X}_3 &:= \mathcal{P}_3 \cap \rho_3^{-1}(\mathcal{Y}) = \emptyset \\
\mathcal{X}_4 &:= \mathcal{P}_4 = \{x \in \mathbb{R}^2 : x_1 \leq 0 \wedge x_2 \leq 0\}.
\end{aligned}$$

2.4 Inverse Piecewise-Affine DNN

The procedure for a whole DNN is the straightforward alternation of Eq. (7) and Eq. (6) for each layer. In our implementation, instead of Eq. (7) we use Eq. (8) with a case distinction for whether to simplify to Eq. (9) or Eq. (10). The procedure is summarized in Algorithm 1.

Regarding complexity, given a DNN with k layers each of dimension n, it is well-known that the network can map a polyhedron to $\mathcal{O}(b^{kn})$ polyhedra, where b is the number of affine pieces in the activation function (e.g., $b = 2$ for ReLU) [18]. The same holds for the preimage.

Example 4. We consider the DNN N from Fig. 1. Each layer is two-dimensional for convenience of plotting. We view the network as a classifier based on which of the two output values is larger. To provide some intuition, Fig. 2(a) shows

Algorithm 1. Preimage computation for piecewise-affine neural networks

```
# inverse neural network
function preimage(Z, N)
    let ℓ_1, ..., ℓ_k be the layers of N
    for ℓ in ℓ_k, ..., ℓ_1
        let W, b, α be the components of ℓ
        Y = preimage(Z, α)
        X = preimage(Y, W, b)
        Z = X
    end
    return X
end

# inverse piecewise-affine activation function
function preimage(Z, α)
    Y = ∅
    let n be the dimension of Z
    # loop over partitions and corresponding affine functions
    for (Pj, αj) in PWA_partitioning(α, n)
        let A_αj * x = b_αj be the affine representation of αj
        if iszero(A_αj) # constant case, Eq. (10)
            if b_αj ∈ Z
                Y = Y ∪ Pj
            end
        else  # injective case, Eq. (9)
            Q = preimage(Z, A_αj, b_αj)
            Y = Y ∪ (Pj ∩ Q)
        end
    end
    return Y
end

# inverse affine map, Eq. (6)
function preimage(Y, W, b)
    let C ≤ d be the constraints of Y
    M = C * W
    v = d - C * b
    return Polyhedron(M ≤ v)
end
```

samples in the input domain $[0, 1]^2$ with their associated class. Figure 2(b) shows the (forward) image of the domain, $N([0, 1]^2)$, which is a union of polytopes and can be computed by standard (forward) set propagation. The figure also shows the classification boundary (black diagonal).

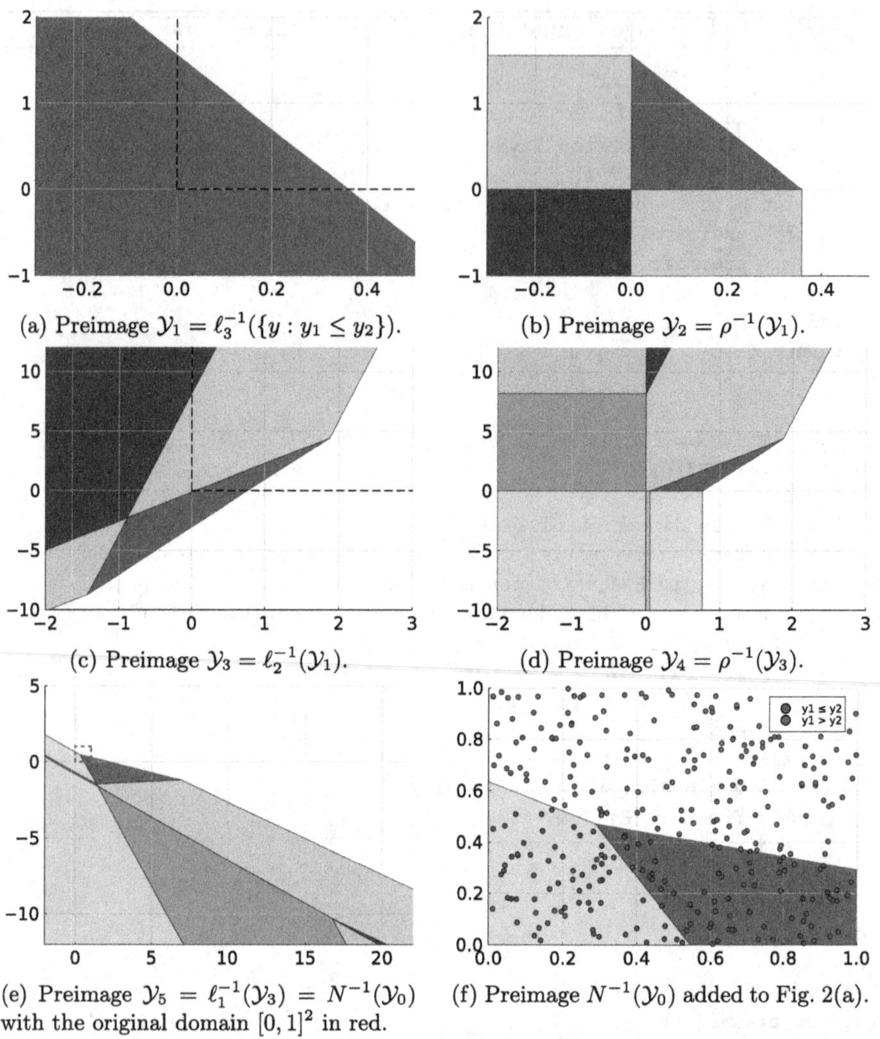

(a) Preimage $\mathcal{Y}_1 = \ell_3^{-1}(\{y : y_1 \leq y_2\})$.

(b) Preimage $\mathcal{Y}_2 = \rho^{-1}(\mathcal{Y}_1)$.

(c) Preimage $\mathcal{Y}_3 = \ell_2^{-1}(\mathcal{Y}_1)$.

(d) Preimage $\mathcal{Y}_4 = \rho^{-1}(\mathcal{Y}_3)$.

(e) Preimage $\mathcal{Y}_5 = \ell_1^{-1}(\mathcal{Y}_3) = N^{-1}(\mathcal{Y}_0)$ with the original domain $[0,1]^2$ in red.

(f) Preimage $N^{-1}(\mathcal{Y}_0)$ added to Fig. 2(a).

Fig. 3. Complete example for the DNN N from Fig. 1. The black dashed lines indicate the codomain of the ReLU activation function.

Now we apply the algorithm to compute the preimage. Figure 1 shows different snapshots of the algorithm. We compute the preimage of the set $\mathcal{C}_2 = \{y : y_1 \leq y_2\}$ (a half-space) of all inputs that classify as class 2 (blue dots). Since the last layer (ℓ_3) has an identity activation, the preimage $\mathcal{Y}_1 = \ell_3^{-1}(\mathcal{C}_2)$ is just the inverse affine map. Since this map is invertible here, the preimage is just another half-space (Fig. 3(a)). Next we compute the preimage under the ReLU activation (Fig. 3(b)). The nonnegative part of $\mathcal{Y}_1$ remains, together with the negative extensions. After computing the preimage under the next affine map

$$\ell_1(x) = \rho\left(\begin{pmatrix} 0.63 \\ 0.17 \\ -0.79 \end{pmatrix} x + \begin{pmatrix} 0.06 \\ -2.25 \\ -2.27 \end{pmatrix}\right) \qquad \ell_3(x) = \begin{pmatrix} 1.92 & 1.01 & 0.83 \end{pmatrix} x + 0.33$$

$$\ell_2(x) = \rho\left(\begin{pmatrix} 0.78 & 2.17 & 0.39 \\ -0.72 & -0.75 & 1.02 \\ -0.14 & -0.64 & -0.32 \end{pmatrix} x + \begin{pmatrix} -2.42 \\ -1.23 \\ 0 \end{pmatrix}\right) \qquad N = \ell_3 \circ \ell_2 \circ \ell_1$$

Fig. 4. A DNN $N : \mathbb{R}^1 \to \mathbb{R}^1$ for approximating the parabola $f(x) = x^2/20$.

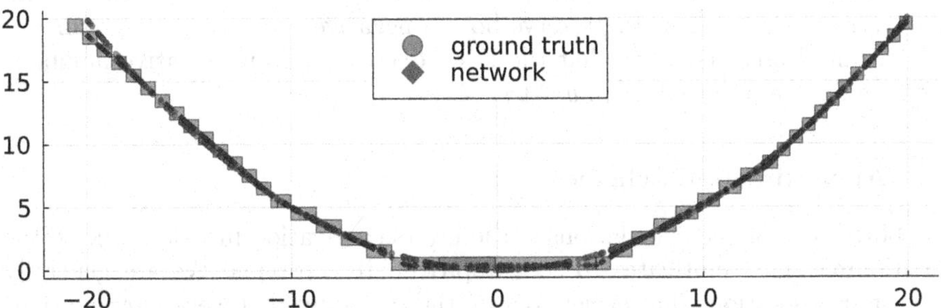

Fig. 5. Preimage computation of the DNN in Fig. 4. (Color figure online)

(Fig. 3(c)) we see that the purple set will get removed with the next ReLU operation. While the previous sets could have been simplified to one polyhedron, the next ReLU preimage (Fig. 3(d)) is non-convex. Finally, we compute the preimage under the last affine map (Fig. 3(e)). The box in red marks the original domain $[0,1]^2$. Figure 3(f) shows the preimage clipped to this domain. $\lhd$

3 Applications and Extensions

We implemented the above-described algorithm in the reachability framework JuliaReach [3], particularly in the set library LazySets [8]. In this section, we report on several experiments and discuss potential extensions. The code to repeat these experiments is available online [1].

3.1 Interpretability

We can use the preimage computation to learn about the function-approximation capabilities of a DNN. As a case study, we look at the parabola $f(x) = x^2/20$. We trained a DNN with two hidden layers, each with 3 neurons, based on 100 samples from the domain $[-20, 20]$. The resulting DNN is given in Fig. 4.

In Fig. 5 we plot the output of 500 samples of the function f (red) as well as the DNN approximation (blue). In addition, we partition the codomain $[0, 20]$ into 20 uniform intervals and compute the preimages (yellow boxes). By construction, the blue samples lie inside the preimages.

In this case we could have obtained similar results via forward-image computation because, by assuming that the DNN approximates the training dataset well, we could have just partitioned the domain $[-20, 20]$ instead. However, this does generally not work if we want to find the preimage of a subset in the codomain that the DNN does not map training data to, since we are clueless where in the domain to search. For example, we can ask for the preimage in the interval $[100, 105]$. This lets us study the generalization capabilities of the DNN. The result is a union of two intervals, $[-80.88, -77.35]$ and $[68.46, 71.48]$. The ground truth consists of the two intervals $\pm[44.72, 45.83]$. We thus see that the DNN does not generalize well, and neither does it preserve the symmetry well. However, the DNN seems to preserve both a negative and a positive preimage.

We can also easily prove that the DNN does not output negative numbers. For that we compute $N^{-1}(\{y : y \leq 0\}) = \emptyset$.

3.2 Approximation Schemes

The bottleneck of the calculations is the inverse activation function, due to the partitioning. This motivates to seek approximate solutions. We are generally interested in solutions that either contain the true solution (overapproximation) or are contained in the true solution (underapproximation).

A simple approach to compute an underapproximation of the preimage considers the partitioning of the sets (as, e.g., in Fig. 3(b)) as a search space and selects only one of the sets to continue with. In general, this search may end up in an empty set (dead end), in which case one has to backtrack and pick the next set using some search heuristics (e.g., breadth-first or depth-first search). In experiments on DNNs with many neurons per layer, where explicit partitioning is infeasible, we noticed that most of the sets are indeed empty.

Instead of underapproximations, we can also consider overapproximations. Using abstract interpretation, we can choose an abstract domain to simplify the calculations. Here we consider the standard interval approximation.

As noted before, in general, the preimage of a DNN is unbounded, which makes an interval approximation useless. To make sure that we receive a bounded preimage for each layer, we consider injective activation functions and layers of the same size. We use the DNN in Fig. 1 but with leaky ReLUs ($\rho^{\ell}_{0.01}$ in layer 1 and $\rho^{\ell}_{0.02}$ in layer 2). First we compute an overapproximation $\mathcal{Y}$ of the image of the domain (i.e., $\mathcal{Y} \supseteq N([0,1]^2)$) using interval approximation. Then we compute the preimage $N(\mathcal{Y})$, using the exact algorithm, as well as obtain an overapproximation by applying an interval approximation for inverting the leaky-ReLU activations. The approximate calculations are $\approx$100x faster than with the exact algorithm, but they also yield a coarser result, as shown in Fig. 6.

Interval approximation is also attractive for activations that are not piecewise affine. We discuss this in the next experiment.

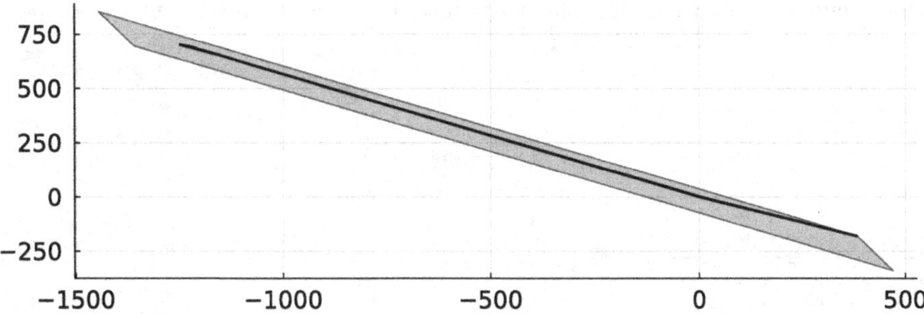

Fig. 6. Preimage computation of the DNN in Fig. 1 but with leaky ReLUs ($\rho^{\ell}_{0.01}$ and $\rho^{\ell}_{0.02}$). The thick black shape is the exact preimage. The blue shape is the preimage where we applied a box approximation inverting the activations. (Color figure online)

$$\ell_1(x) = \sigma\left(\begin{pmatrix}-4.60248 & 4.74295\\ -3.19378 & 2.90011\end{pmatrix} x + \begin{pmatrix}2.74108\\ -1.49695\end{pmatrix}\right) \qquad N = \ell_2 \circ \ell_1$$
$$\ell_2(x) = \sigma\left(\begin{pmatrix}-4.57199 & 4.64925\end{pmatrix} x + 2.10176\right)$$

Fig. 7. A DNN to approximate the XOR function (taken from [26]).

3.3 Forward-Backward Computation

The approach in [26] propagates intervals forward and backward in a DNN, just as the interval approximation explained above. The benefit of this scheme is that it applies to activations that are not piecewise affine, such as the sigmoid function $\sigma(x) = 1/(1+e^{-x})$. Backward propagation of intervals is easy for strictly monotonic activations like the sigmoid: one just applies the inverse function to the lower and upper bound.

We repeat an experiment from [26]. The DNN (given in Fig. 7) uses sigmoid activations and was trained to implement a real approximation of the XOR function, i.e., it should output a value close to 1 if and only if one of the inputs is close to 1. The input domain is $[0, 1]^2$ and we consider five scenarios where we add additional input or output constraints.

The results are shown in Fig. 8. Each row consists of one experiment and each column corresponds to one neuron. The horizontal axis shows the number of iterations, with iteration 0 being the initial configuration. The vertical axis shows the range of each neuron valuation. Input neuron 1 is always further constrained to a smaller interval. In experiments 1, 2, and 5, the second input neuron is also further constrained, and in the last three experiments, the output neuron is further constrained.

We can see that both the image and the preimage of the DNN can get refined by forward resp. backward propagating bounds. In the first experiment,

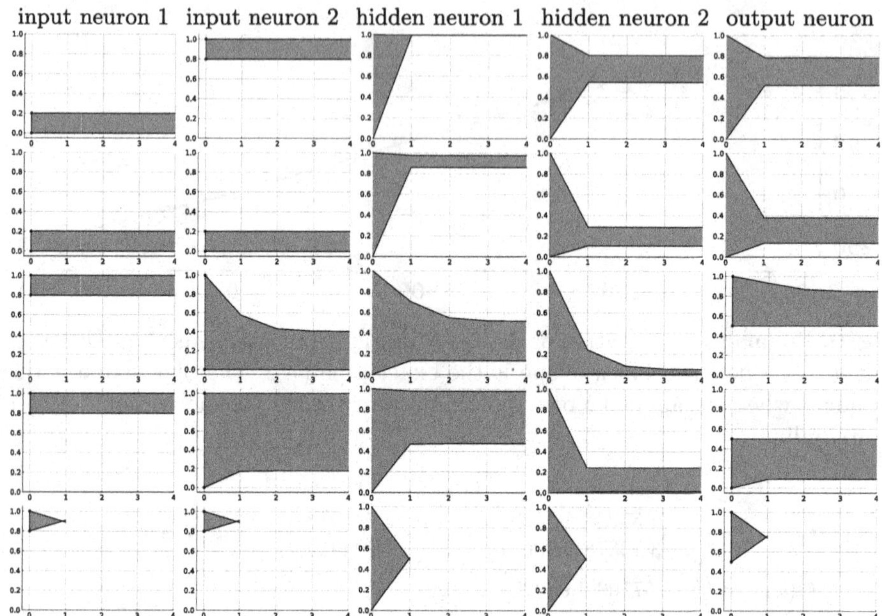

Fig. 8. Experiment from [26] for the DNN in Fig. 7. Each row consists of one experiment and each column corresponds to one neuron. In the last experiment, the sets become empty after the first iteration, which we represented graphically by converging and crossing bounds.

we obtain a proof of the following statement: If $x_1 \in [0, 2]$ and $x_2 \in [0.8, 1]$, then $N(x) \in [0.51, 0.79]$. Note that this can also be achieved with just forward-image computation (the result of which corresponds to the input- and output-neuron bounds after one iteration). In the third experiment, we obtain a proof of the following statement: If $x_1 \in [0, 2]$ and $N(x) \in [0.5, 1]$, then $x_2 \in [0, 0.41]$ and $N(x) \in [0.5, 86]$. Unlike with just forward propagation, we can derive statements about the inputs, and we also obtained tighter output bounds than what forward-image computation would ($N(x) \in [0.5, 0.94]$). The last experiment finds that the input and output constraints are incompatible, and the sets become empty. Thus we obtain a proof of the following statement: Either $x_1, x_2 \notin [0, 2]$ or $N(x) \notin [0.5, 1]$. We refer to [26] for further explanation.

4 Conclusion

In this paper, we have presented a complete picture of the computation of the preimage of a DNN with piecewise-affine activation functions. While a similar approach has been presented before [17], we believe that it has not been appreciated in the formal-methods community, and we also filled a small technical gap to allow the application to the common class of ReLU networks. We have discussed applications in interpretability, scalability improvements via over- and underapproximations, and a combined forward and backward computation.

We see many opportunities for future work. First, the extension to other activation functions has been proposed via piecewise-affine approximation [17]. This approximation can also be implemented in a conservative way. Second, we conjecture that practical abstraction methods can be found, similar to what has been achieved in forward-image computations. Finally, we envision applications related to robustness and adversarial attacks. Once we have computed the preimage, we can use it to search for instances of interest in it (e.g., an input that maximizes another objective). Consider a classifier and the preimage of a small region around a decision boundary. The preimage contains all instances that will make the decision change with a small perturbation. We can obtain samples from the preimage set to determine whether the uncertain classification is indeed reasonable. Also, since we can compute the preimage of all decision boundaries, we can effectively obtain a partition of the input space.

Acknowledgments. We thank the anonymous reviewers for helpful comments to improve this paper. This research was partly supported by DIREC - Digital Research Centre Denmark and the Villum Investigator Grant S4OS.

References

1. Repeatability package. https://github.com/JuliaReach/AISoLA2023_RE
2. Bak, S., Tran, H.: Neural network compression of ACAS Xu early prototype is unsafe: closed-loop verification through quantized state backreachability. In: Deshmukh, J.V., Havelund, K., Perez, I. (eds.) NFM 2022. LNCS, vol. 13260, pp. 280–298. Springer, Cham (2022). https://doi.org/10.1007/978-3-031-06773-0_15
3. Bogomolov, S., Forets, M., Frehse, G., Potomkin, K., Schilling, C.: JuliaReach: a toolbox for set-based reachability. In: HSCC, pp. 39–44. ACM (2019). https://doi.org/10.1145/3302504.3311804
4. Breutel, S., Maire, F., Hayward, R.: Extracting interface assertions from neural networks in polyhedral format. In: ESANN, pp. 463–468 (2003). https://www.esann.org/sites/default/files/proceedings/legacy/es2003-72.pdf
5. Chabert, G., Jaulin, L.: Contractor programming. Artif. Intell. **173**(11), 1079–1100 (2009). https://doi.org/10.1016/j.artint.2009.03.002
6. Cousot, P., Cousot, R.: Abstract interpretation: a unified lattice model for static analysis of programs by construction or approximation of fixpoints. In: POPL, pp. 238–252. ACM (1977). https://doi.org/10.1145/512950.512973
7. Everett, M., Bunel, R., Omidshafiei, S.: DRIP: domain refinement iteration with polytopes for backward reachability analysis of neural feedback loops. IEEE Control. Syst. Lett. **7**, 1622–1627 (2023). https://doi.org/10.1109/LCSYS.2023.3260731
8. Forets, M., Schilling, C.: LazySets.jl: scalable symbolic-numeric set computations. In: Proceedings of the JuliaCon Conferences, vol. 1, no. 1, p. 11 (2021). https://doi.org/10.21105/jcon.00097
9. Goodfellow, I.J., Shlens, J., Szegedy, C.: Explaining and harnessing adversarial examples. In: ICLR (2015). http://arxiv.org/abs/1412.6572
10. Halmos, P.R.: Naive set theory. van Nostrand (1960)

11. Jaulin, L.: A boundary approach for set inversion. Eng. Appl. Artif. Intell. **100**, 104184 (2021). https://doi.org/10.1016/j.engappai.2021.104184
12. Kingma, D.P., Welling, M.: Auto-encoding variational bayes. In: ICLR (2014). http://arxiv.org/abs/1312.6114
13. Kochdumper, N., Schilling, C., Althoff, M., Bak, S.: Open- and closed-loop neural network verification using polynomial zonotopes. In: Rozier, K.Y., Chaudhuri, S. (eds.) NFM 2023. LNCS, vol. 13903, pp. 16–36. Springer, Cham (2023). https://doi.org/10.1007/978-3-031-33170-1_2
14. Kotha, S., Brix, C., Kolter, Z., Dvijotham, K., Zhang, H.: Provably bounding neural network preimages. CoRR abs/2302.01404 (2023). https://doi.org/10.48550/arXiv.2302.01404
15. Lee, J.: Introduction to Topological Manifolds. Springer, New York (2010). https://doi.org/10.1007/978-1-4419-7940-7
16. Mahendran, A., Vedaldi, A.: Understanding deep image representations by inverting them. In: CVPR, pp. 5188–5196. IEEE Computer Society (2015). https://doi.org/10.1109/CVPR.2015.7299155
17. Maire, F.: Rule-extraction by backpropagation of polyhedra. Neural Netw. **12**(4–5), 717–725 (1999). https://doi.org/10.1016/S0893-6080(99)00013-1
18. Montúfar, G., Pascanu, R., Cho, K., Bengio, Y.: On the number of linear regions of deep neural networks. In: NeurIPS, pp. 2924–2932 (2014). https://proceedings.neurips.cc/paper/2014/hash/109d2dd3608f669ca17920c511c2a41e-Abstract.html
19. Rober, N., Everett, M., How, J.P.: Backward reachability analysis for neural feedback loops. In: CDC, pp. 2897–2904. IEEE (2022). https://doi.org/10.1109/CDC51059.2022.9992847
20. Rober, N., Everett, M., Zhang, S., How, J.P.: A hybrid partitioning strategy for backward reachability of neural feedback loops. In: ACC, pp. 3523–3528. IEEE (2023). https://doi.org/10.23919/ACC55779.2023.10156051
21. Schilling, C., Forets, M., Guadalupe, S.: Verification of neural-network control systems by integrating Taylor models and zonotopes. In: AAAI, pp. 8169–8177. AAAI Press (2022). https://doi.org/10.1609/aaai.v36i7.20790
22. Simonyan, K., Vedaldi, A., Zisserman, A.: Deep inside convolutional networks: visualising image classification models and saliency maps. In: ICLR (2014). https://arxiv.org/abs/1312.6034
23. Singh, G., Gehr, T., Mirman, M., Püschel, M., Vechev, M.T.: Fast and effective robustness certification. In: NeurIPS, pp. 10825–10836 (2018). https://proceedings.neurips.cc/paper/2018/hash/f2f446980d8e971ef3da97af089481c3-Abstract.html
24. Sixt, L., Granz, M., Landgraf, T.: When explanations lie: why many modified BP attributions fail. In: ICML. PMLR, vol. 119, pp. 9046–9057 (2020). http://proceedings.mlr.press/v119/sixt20a.html
25. Sotoudeh, M., Tao, Z., Thakur, A.V.: SyReNN: a tool for analyzing deep neural networks. Int. J. Softw. Tools Technol. Transf. **25**(2), 145–165 (2023). https://doi.org/10.1007/s10009-023-00695-1
26. Thrun, S.: Extracting symbolic knowledge from artificial neural networks. Technical report, University of Bonn (1994). https://www.cs.cmu.edu/~thrun/papers/thrun.nn_rule_extraction.ps.gz
27. Wang, S., Pei, K., Whitehouse, J., Yang, J., Jana, S.: Formal security analysis of neural networks using symbolic intervals. In: USENIX Security Symposium, pp. 1599–1614 (2018). https://www.usenix.org/conference/usenixsecurity18/presentation/wang-shiqi

28. Yang, X., Johnson, T.T., Tran, H., Yamaguchi, T., Hoxha, B., Prokhorov, D.V.: Reachability analysis of deep ReLU neural networks using facet-vertex incidence. In: HSCC. ACM (2021). https://doi.org/10.1145/3447928.3456650
29. Zeiler, M.D., Fergus, R.: Visualizing and understanding convolutional networks. In: Fleet, D., Pajdla, T., Schiele, B., Tuytelaars, T. (eds.) ECCV 2014. LNCS, vol. 8689, pp. 818–833. Springer, Cham (2014). https://doi.org/10.1007/978-3-319-10590-1_53

Continuous Engineering for Trustworthy Learning-Enabled Autonomous Systems

Saddek Bensalem[1], Panagiotis Katsaros[2], Dejan Ničković[3(✉)], Brian Hsuan-Cheng Liao[4], Ricardo Ruiz Nolasco[5], Mohamed Abd El Salam Ahmed[6], Tewodros A. Beyene[7], Filip Cano[8], Antoine Delacourt[9], Hasan Esen[4], Alexandru Forrai[10], Weicheng He[1], Xiaowei Huang[11], Nikolaos Kekatos[2], Bettina Könighofer[8], Michael Paulitsch[12], Doron Peled[13], Matthieu Ponchant[9], Lev Sorokin[7], Son Tong[14], and Changshun Wu[1]

[1] University Grenoble Alpes, VERIMAG, Grenoble, France
[2] School of Informatics, Aristotle University of Thessaloniki, Thessaloniki, Greece
[3] AIT Austrian Institute of Technology, Vienna, Austria
dejan.nickovic@ait.ac.at
[4] DENSO AUTOMOTIVE Deutschland GmbH, Eching, Germany
[5] RGB Medical Devices, Madrid, Spain
[6] Siemens EDA, Cairo, Egypt
[7] fortiss GmbH, Munich, Germany
[8] Graz University of Technology, Graz, Austria
[9] Siemens Industry Software SAS, Grenoble, France
[10] Siemens Digital Industries Software, Eindhoven, The Netherlands
[11] University of Liverpool, Liverpool, UK
[12] Intel Labs, Munich, Germany
[13] Bar Ilan University, Ramat Gan, Israel
[14] Siemens Industry Software NV, Leuven, Belgium

Abstract. Learning-enabled autonomous systems (LEAS) use machine learning (ML) components for essential functions of autonomous operation, such as perception and control. LEAS are often safety-critical. The development and integration of trustworthy ML components present new challenges that extend beyond the boundaries of system's design to the system's operation in its real environment. This paper introduces the methodology and tools developed within the frame of the FOCETA European project towards the continuous engineering of trustworthy LEAS. Continuous engineering includes iterations between two alternating phases, namely: (i) design and virtual testing, and (ii) deployment and operation. Phase (i) encompasses the design of trustworthy ML components and the system's validation with respect to formal specifications of its requirements via modeling and simulation. An integral part of both the simulation-based testing and the operation of LEAS is the monitoring and enforcement of safety, security and performance properties and the acquisition of information for the system's operation in its environment. Finally, we show how the FOCETA approach has been applied to realistic continuous engineering workflowsfor three different LEAS from automotive and medical application domains.

Keywords: Learning-enabled Autonomous Systems · machine learning · safety · security · continuous engineering · formal analysis

B. Steffen (Ed.): AISoLA 2023, LNCS 14380, pp. 256–278, 2024.
https://doi.org/10.1007/978-3-031-46002-9_15

1 Introduction

The crucial criteria for the design of *learning-enabled autonomous systems* (LEAS) are correctness and safety, especially for real-world operability. The complexity of LEAS stems, to a large extent, from the interplay between classically engineered and learning-enabled components (LECs). In current design practice, correctness and safety are formulated by requirements that must be satisfied by the LEAS. However, the presence of LECs is not addressed in an adequate manner in this context; there is need for new design, verification and validation (V&V) approaches that take into account the presence of LECs in LEAS, address their qualitative and quantitative capabilities throughout their entire life cycle and consider the real-world complexity and uncertainty.

A holistic engineering approach will adequately assess the correctness and safety of LEAS operating in the real world. Such an analysis requires that the engineering method employed will determine the (quantitative) contexts in which the correctness and safety of systems will be (qualitatively) evaluated. Integrating system design and operation sets more specific considerations for LEAS and the engineering approach: their safety will have to be assessed with respect to an ever evolving set of (critical) scenarios, instantiating difficult conditions for their sensors and underlying algorithms.

In the FOCETA project, we provide a holistic methodology for designing and addressing the correctness and safety of LEAS, bridging the gap between the currently applied development, verification, and validation techniques for LE systems and their operation in the real world. We allow updates to the LECs, in response to emerging requirements from new scenarios, imperfect knowledge of the machine learning models (noise in data observations) or contextual misbehavior of them and possible security threats. This need is addressed within a continuous development and testing process mixing software development and system operations in iterative cycles.

In this process, formal specifications allow designers to formulate requirements in a rigorous manner. They are used throughout the whole system life-cycle, both during development and operations. During the concept design phase, formal specifications can improve the process of engineering requirements by making them precise. This facilitates communication between design teams, removes ambiguities in the exchange of knowledge and renders the requirements verifiable. During the system implementation, specifications can be used for formal verification of critical components, but also as oracles in the testing activities. Finally, formal specifications can be monitored during system operation to detect violations of requirements (runtime verification) and take corrective actions (runtime enforcement). The role of specification languages, fairly well understood in the context of classical system design, is more ambiguous when reasoning about LEAS. The addition of LECs considerably adds to the system's complexity and requires rethinking the entire development and operation process, including the role of formal specifications, which we explain in this document.

The FOCETA methodology (Fig. 1) includes two design flows. The first for designing trustworthy LECs, and the second for integrating them with classically engineered components, resulting in correct and safe LEAS, through iterative cycles of development and system operation. Our methodology relies on verifying simulation results and collecting additional data for system improvement. Runtime monitoring is used to supervise LEAS decision-making and record environmental situations.

The contributions of this paper are the following. First, we introduce the main goals of the two design flows. Then, we present the key technological developments, i.e. the methods and tools, that are the most representative for realizing our methodology:

- techniques for trustworthy perception, sensing and safe data-driven control
- a technique for trustworthy updates of LECs
- a methodology and tool for continuous specification, validation and update of LEAS requirements
- a compositional digital twin architecture and tools for the formal modeling, simulation-based analysis and runtime verification of LEAS
- techniques for efficient virtual testing
- specification mining techniques for learning system properties while the LEAS operates in its environment

At the end, we show how these techniques are combined in LEAS case studies.

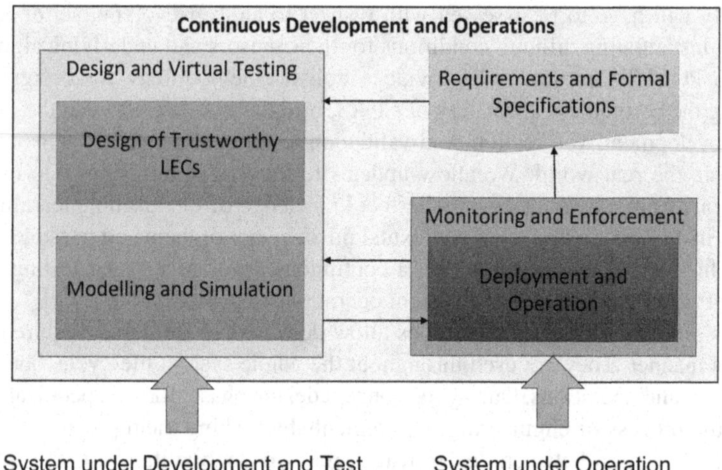

Fig. 1. Continuous development and operations of LEAS

2 Design Flow for Trustable Learning Components

Deep learning is a mathematical framework for inferring (predictive) models from data. Its main feature is to use the prediction score as a feedback signal to adjust the weights' value slightly in a direction that will lower the loss score. This tuning is an optimization process which implements the leading deep learning algorithm to design the neural network model. Machine learning can be considered as input-target matching, done by observing different examples of inputs and targets. The learning process consists of finding a set of values for the weights for all the network layers that correctly match the inputs to their associated targets. Finding the correct value for each of them can seem like a daunting task, since changing the value of one parameter will affect the behavior of all the others; a deep neural network can contain more than a trillion of parameters [33].

A network with a minimal loss is one for which the outputs are as close as possible to the targets, i.e. a trained network. Initially, the network weights are assigned random values, so the network implements a series of random transformations; its output is far from what it should ideally be and the loss score is very high. However, the weights are adjusted in the correct direction and the loss score is decreased. This training loop, repeated several times, yields weight values that minimize the loss function. This iterative process only considers the optimization of the resulting neural network model. We propose, in a complementary way, rigorous methods and tools that guarantee the trustworthiness of the neural network model obtained at the end of this iterative process.

The rigorous design approach for developing a safe and trustworthy LEC heavily depends on the LEC's functionality. We consider mainly two classes of LECs - perception modules and data-driven controllers. Designing a trustworthy perception module is very different from designing a safe data-driven controller. Also, within the context of continuous engineering, we address the problem of replacing LECs with others.

2.1 Trustworthy Perception and Sensing

An object detection component based on a neural network (NN) does not admit a natural formal specification of its expected behavior and characterizing a correct perception module's behavior using mathematics and logic is notoriously hard. It is even hard to formulate an appropriate verification and validation question for such LECs. There are, however, a number of more indirect but still effective approaches to reason about correctness of such components that we explore in FOCETA. Figure 2 provides a general framework illustrating how a machine learning based perception component might be developed and certified. It refines the usual development cycle, which forms three stages - training, offline V&V (or testing), and deployment - by including a collection of activities that support the certification of the component.

Falsification and Explanation. The first approach consists of evaluating low-level properties of the LEC, such as its *robustness* to input perturbations, adversarial attacks and the *explanation* to the perception task. This belongs to the family of design-time testing approaches. Robustness defines how sensitive the NN is to small perturbations in the input. There are situations where a change of a single pixel in a picture can result in a mis-classification or mis-localization, even for state-of-the-art NNs [37,42]. As the first step towards a complete evaluation, the general robustness of a NN can be assessed with testing strategies, resulting in research on defining meaningful notions of coverage for NNs, fault-injection mechanisms for LECs and adversarial testing methods. For example, in FOCETA, coverage-guided testing [19] and distribution-aware testing [20] have been developed. In addition, simulated hardware faults have been found effective in testing NN performance [34]. Within the context of continuous engineering, it is also possible to apply refinement techniques on top of the commonly known combinatorial testing scheme for LECs [8], in order to avoid the need of complete re-verification. For

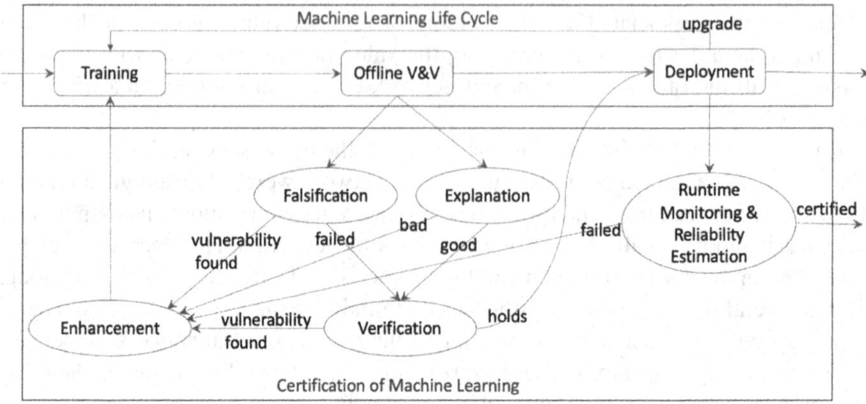

Fig. 2. Continuous development of machine learning based perception component

explanation, saliency maps are usually generated to highlight the important features of an input instance; we consider further the robustness of the generated explanations [21,46].

Verification. While the above methods may be effective in finding bugs in NNs, they cannot be used to prove their correctness. This problem is typically tackled using formal verification. For example, formal verification and optimization can be applied to find the maximum resilience of the NN to local perturbations [26]. The challenge for verification is its scaling to LECs of realistic size; to deal with this, research has been extended to the verification over geometric transformations [43] rather than pixel-level changes.

Enhancement The counterexample found through either falsification, explanation, or verification, can be utilised for enhancing the machine learning model. This can be done through fine tuning, which slightly adjusts the weights according to the counterexamples. The other mainstream, and arguably more effective, approach is through adversarial training, which adapts the training algorithm to consider the properties. Towards this, we have considered the enhancement to generalisation and robustness [22,23].

Runtime Monitoring and Reliability Assessment. Most of the falsification, explanation, and verification approaches are limited to point-wise analysis and are typically subject to the selection of testing data points. To support the deployment, it is necessary to be able to work with any data that may appear during operation. Two methods are considered. First, we developed runtime monitoring techniques for LECs. In general, these techniques can be divided into white-box and black-box approaches. The former class requires access to NN parameters. For example, neuron activation patterns or interval values can be recorded over the training dataset and applied as an abstraction for runtime monitoringe [9,18,41]. Another approach of online monitoring developed in FOCETA uses small efficient neural networks to detect either hardware faults or input abnormalities efficiently as presented and shown in [14]. The black-box approaches build verdicts based on the NN inputs and outputs. For example, temporal consistency of the detected objects can be modelled as a post-algorithmic abstraction and can be applied at runtime [7]. A variant of temporal logic is used to define intended relations in time between detected objects, e.g. forbidding the situation where a detected object of type A suddenly becomes classified as object of type B in the next frame. Detecting such temporal inconsistencies in object detection algorithms could help to prevent accidents such as the Arizona accident with the Uber test vehicle in 2018, in which the vehicle could not correctly and persistently identify a bicycle before an imminent collision. Second, we employ an operational profile, which has been evolved from the field of programming and testing, to model operational data, and then estimate the operational time reliability of the component by considering both the operational model and the verification method [44,45].

2.2 Safe Data-Driven Control

The design of data-driven controllers can benefit from several aspects used for the design of classical control applications. In particular, data-driven control naturally admits formal specifications for expressing its intended behavior. In FOCETA, we identify and investigate two complementary approaches for developing safe control applications that use the formal specification to formulate their functional requirements. The first approach uses formal specifications to guide the training of the controller towards exhibiting safe behavior [6]. The second approach builds an external mechanism, often called a shield, to prevent an untrusted data-driven controller from doing unsafe actions. A *safety shield* is an enforcer that overwrites commands from the controller whenever executing the command could result in a safety violation. It extends the known safety supervision approaches of Responsibility Sensitive Safety[1] and Safety Force Shield[2] of major automated driving provider. Safety is defined via a temporal safety specification φ in linear temporal logic and a threshold $\delta \in [0,1]$. During runtime, the shield overwrites any command from the controller for which the probability of violating φ is larger than δ. A shield is automatically computed from the safety specification and a model of the environment using value iteration. Thus, a shield guarantees that safety is satisfied under the assumption that the underlying environmental model accurately captures the safety relevant dynamics of the environment.

2.3 Trustworthy Updates of LECs

For a number of reasons, LECs usually have to be updated within the context of continuous engineering. For example, security concerns such as the need to withstand data perturbations (e.g. adversarial examples) or out-of-distribution data cases, trigger the need to replace LECs with improved ones that exhibit functionally comparable behavior in certain important aspects with the ones to be replaced.

In FOCETA, in addition to the enhancement approaches discussed in Sect. 2.1, this problem is addressed [12] by *formally verifying the equivalence* of two LECs as follows: for two pretrained NNs of different architectures, or of the same architecture with

[1] https://www.mobileye.com/technology/responsibility-sensitive-safety/.

[2] https://www.nvidia.com/en-us/self-driving-cars/safety-force-field/.

different parameters, we check whether they yield similar outputs for the same inputs. Contrary to strict functional equivalence that is desired for software component design, similar outputs do not necessarily mean identical outputs in the case of NNs. For example, two NNs used for classification may be considered equivalent if they always select the same top output class, even though the remaining output classes are not ordered in the same way. The definition of equivalence depends on the application and NNs at hand (e.g. classifier, regression, etc.). Therefore, we considered strict, as well as approximate equivalences and formalized them as relations characterizing the similarity of NN outputs, for identical inputs. Equivalence is essential for replacing one LEC by another, but it does not ensure by itself the transfer of any other guarantees to the updated LEC. When an improved LEC has been developed that fulfills some additional requirements or that withstands evident security threats, not previously identified, equivalence checking is applied to the outdated and the new LEC, out of the LEAS's overall context.

3 Design Flow for LEAS

The design flow for LEAS consists of two parts: (1) the design-time part including the design, implementation, and verification of the system, and (2) the run-time part, focusing on the deployment of the LEAS and its operation in the real world.

The current state of practice is extended towards the transfer of knowledge about systems and their contexts (e.g. traffic situations) from the development to operations and from the operations back to development, in iterative steps of continuous improvements. Over the complete life cycle of LEAS - from specification, design, implementation, and verification to the operation in the real world - the methodology enables their continuous engineering with particular focus on the correctness with respect to an evolving set of requirements and the systems safety. Moreover, the whole design flow enables traceability between the requirements and the system/component design.

A key feature is the use of runtime monitoring for the seamless integration of development and operations. Monitors observe a system (part) via appropriate interfaces and evaluate predefined conditions and invariants about the LEAS behavior based on data from these interfaces. This allows the monitor to identify needs for LEC/other component updates during continuous engineering, if, for example, some data in a test scenario result in a safety violation or if a new requirement will emerge during system's testing/operation.

3.1 Requirements and Formal Specifications

Requirements Specification and Semantic Validation. In continuous engineering, it should be possible to take into account additional requirements, to address needs which come up from scenarios that have not been taken previously into account. The specification of these additional requirements should not pose issues of consistency, ambiguity and completeness with respect to the existing requirements. Moreover, any additional requirements will have to be appropriate such that together with the existing ones will make it possible to devise an acceptable (i.e. feasible and cost-efficient) LEAS design.

We have introduced an ontology-based approach/tool for specifying, validating and formalizing LEAS requirements during the design phase of the continuous engineering iteration cycles [31]. Requirements are expressed in controlled natural language restricted to terms from an ontology with precisely defined concepts and semantic relationships in the system's domain (domain specific ontology - DSO). To tackle the lack of a unique interpretation for the natural language syntax, we employ boilerplates, i.e. textual templates with placeholders to be filled with ontology elements. These elements are semantically interrelated and are part of a well-defined ontology architecture.

The whole semantic framework, together with the ontology terms mentioned in requirements, enable automated semantic analyses that guide the engineer towards improving the requirements specification. These analyses detect specification flaws.

However, even if the requirement specifications are semantically validated, this does not guarantee that they are satisfied by the LEAS under design. The requirements must be transformed into formal specifications of monitorable properties (formalisation) and then mapped to a component-based simulation model of the LEAS. This transformation is based on predefined mappings of boilerplates to logic-based property specifications and it is supported by our requirements specification and formalisation tool.

Formal Specification of Requirements. Adapting an existing specification formalism to LEAS is a challenging task because of the presence of LECs, such as CNN-based object detection modules, which do not admit natural logic-based formulation of their safety requirements (see Sect. 2). In FOCETA, we suggested past first-order linear temporal logic (P-FO-LTL) [5] as the main specification formalism to reason about LEAS. It abstracts away the internal structure of the NN-based LEC, including the internal values of the different neurons. This simple, yet expressive formalism allows the user to (1) quantify over (possibly unbounded number of) agents, (2) define timing constraints between events and (3) naturally synthesize online monitors. The runtime verification of P-FO-LTL is implemented in the DejaVu tool [17] used in the project.

We also use Signal Temporal Logic (STL) [30] as a popular specification language among the cyber-physical systems community. The main advantage of STL is that it naturally admits *quantitative semantics* and hence allows one to measure *how far* is the behavior from satisfying or violating a specification. A disadvantage of STL compared to P-FO-LTL is that it does not allow quantification over agents. The quantitative runtime STL monitors are implemented in the RTAMT library [32]. Still it is evident that sequential specifications based on temporal logic cannot capture every aspect during design of LEAS. For example, many core properties of LECs, such as robustness of the NN discussed in Sect. 2, do not admit natural formal specification using logic.

3.2 Simulation-Based Modeling, Testing and Monitoring at Design Time

For design-time V&V of LEAS, FOCETA invests on formal modeling and simulation-based analysis. Formal modeling is a prerequisite for specifying correctness and safety properties and eventually verifying them. Simulation-based testing provides a cost-effective means to verify the LEAS performance over diverse parameter ranges and to generate massive sets of scenarios. Critical scenarios can be identified in the virtual environment, thus limiting those needed to be replayed in the much more expensive physical setting. Simulation-based testing also allows generating scenarios (e.g. very rare events) that may be impossible to realize when the LEAS operates in its environment (e.g. with specific weather conditions, such as snow). Finally, it also enables creating safety-critical situations (e.g. crashes) without compromising the safety of the real-life actors.

Formal Modelling. For the formal modeling of LEAS, a component-based modeling approach is introduced that allows mixing model-based and LE components with digital twin simulation [39]. This is achieved by having extended the BIP component framework [4], in order to enable the design of executable models with formal semantics for the LECs. In this extended BIP framework, LECs are represented by atomic BIP components which can make machine learning inference.

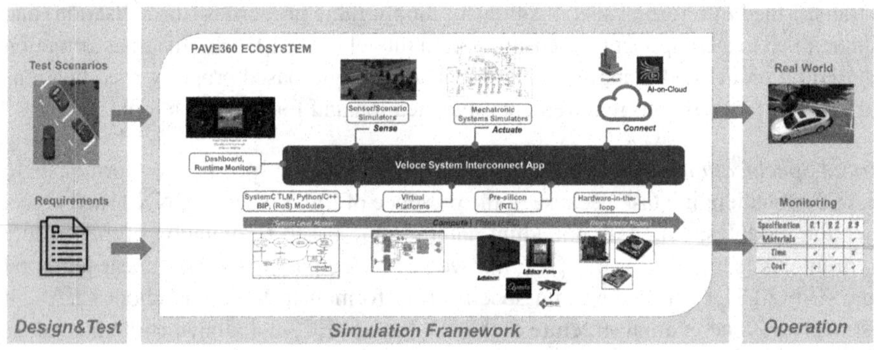

Fig. 3. Compositional Simulation Architecture for Digital Twins of LEAS

Extended BIP models have been integrated into the FOCETA Compositional Simulation Architecture for virtual testing (Fig. 3) using Veloce System Interconnect (VSI) [4]. VSI is used as a middleware to connect different tools and models. It enables integration of heterogeneous components and models that are designed with different tools and allows mixing discrete modeling for the computing elements with continuous modeling for the physical components. In essence, the engineer can use diverse tools/models at different abstraction levels for modeling the sensing, control - actuation functions, the system's physical dynamics, and all interactions with its environment, as long as these tools/models can be integrated via standards-based interfaces (FMI [40] or TLM).

V&V at design time is based on virtual testing. This encompasses all cases in which one or more physical elements (software, hardware) of the LEAS are replaced by their simulation model(s). The FOCETA Compositional Simulation Architecture supports model-in-the-loop (MiL), software-in-the-loop (SiL) and hardware-in-the-loop (HiL) testing of the systems functions, at various abstraction levels. MiL testing is focused on design correctness, the performance of LECs, the control strategies and the associated trade-offs. Having done MiL testing, fine-tuning processes using different mechanisms can be applied, such as requirement-encoded and safety-oriented loss function [27] for object detection or uncertainty-aware loss function [25] for trajectory prediction tasks.

SiL testing is used to check the correctness of code in closed loop with a model of the physical system. Finally, HiL testing consists of real-time simulations that include the target hardware; the hardware-specific impact can be also simulated. A production-friendly approach has been developed with the PyTorchALFI tool chain [29], which allows to efficiently perform fault injection [16].

For verifying safety properties for the overall system model, the online formal analysis of simulation traces is supported. Within the context of the FOCETA Compositional Simulation Architecture, this takes place through the integration of runtime monitors, which are generated by the DejaVU and RTAMT monitor synthesis tools based on formal specifications in P-FO-LTL [38] and Signal Temporal Logic (STL), respectively. P-FO-LTL is the target language of the FOCETA requirements specification/formalization approach that is summarized in Sect. 3.1 (Fig. 4).

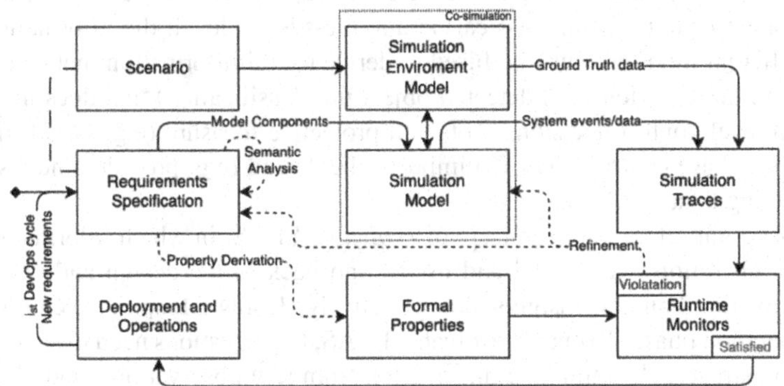

Fig. 4. FOCETA requirements specification/formalization approach

Simulation allows the designer to control the execution of scenarios and efficiently explore the systems operational design domain. Scenarios define the temporal evolution between several snapshots of the environments state in a sequence; they are specified as a set of actions and events, goals (e.g. staying between the lane markings) and values (e.g. prioritize safety of pedestrians).

To identify safety-critical scenarios, we adopt search-based testing (SBT), in which the testing is framed as an optimization problem that guides the search toward finding interesting/failure-revealing test cases. Such testing can be performed by applying the modular and extendable SBT framework OpenSBT [36] or a toolchain consisting of the Simcenter Prescan[3] and HEEDS[4] tools. In particular, Simcenter HEEDS provides solutions for optimization, test orchestration, and visualization and analysis, whereas Simcenter Prescan is a physics-based simulation platform for advanced driver assistance systems that has been integrated into the FOCETA Compositional Simulation Archi-

[3] https://www.plm.automation.siemens.com/global/en/products/simcenter/prescan.html.

[4] https://www.plm.automation.siemens.com/global/en/products/simcenter/simcenter-heeds.html.

tecture. In addition to classical SBT, we also explored black-box testing combined with light-weight learning [13] to accelerate generation of relevant tests.

3.3 Deployment, Operation and Analysis of LEAS at Runtime

The analysis of LECs and their integration into LEAS during design time, together with the protective mechanisms synthesized around LECs support the safety assurance of the overall system during real-time operation. These measures are complemented by runtime verification that plays a central role during the LEAS operation. Runtime monitors allow users to observe the system and its interaction with the environment and gather useful information regarding (1) violations of safety or other requirements, (2) new operational scenarios that were not captured by the training data and/or models, and (3) other unexpected situations and anomalies that are not characterized by the existing set of requirements. In order to be effective, monitors must be present both at the component level (LE and classical) and at the system level; the information gathered by different monitors must be fused to derive useful information that can be used to (1) ignore the situation (e.g. detected object misclassification) that does not impact the system-level control decision, (2) take a protective measure (e.g. switch from the advanced to a base controller) or (3) improve the design (e.g. provide a new scenario for the training data).

The last point refers to the concept of *evolvable* LEAS, in which information from the system operation is collected and used to go back to the design and enhance its functionality based on new insights, thus effectively closing a loop between the design and the operation phase. To enable evolvable LEAS, two questions need to be answered: (1) how to extract and summarize information from raw observations, and (2) how to use such information to increase the quality of the design.

In FOCETA, we advocate specification mining [2] as one approach to answer the first question. It is the process of learning system properties from observing its execution and the behavior of its environment. We use inferred specifications to understand the specificities of the system behavior, characterize its operational design domain (ODD) and identify system aspects that can be improved. However, specification mining has broader application potentials. Specifications mined from a system can be also used to complete the existing incomplete or outdated specifications, confirm expected behaviors, and generate new tests. Answering the second question is highly dependent on the specific component or sub-system that needs to be updated and improved over time. For example, we developed a proof-on-demand mechanism [28] to expand the region in which a data-driven controller can safely function without the need to activate the shield while the system is operating

3.4 Assurance Cases for LEAS

The continuous engineering of safety-critical LEAS requires constructing and maintaining an assurance case. In FOCETA, we adopted the off-the-shelf continuous integration framework Evidential Tool Bus (ETB) [10]. ETB allows: 1) the automated and decentralized execution of V&V tools to provide assurance evidence for an assurance case construction, and 2) incrementally maintain an assurance case. An incremental update is required when, for instance, the system under assurance changes, e.g., when the requirements of the system (e.g., its ODD) must be updated either after inference of corner case properties at runtime with specification mining or when the system must be deployed in another country with different regulations.

4 Case Studies Demonstrating the FOCETA Methodology

4.1 Traffic Speed Detection and Path Lane Following

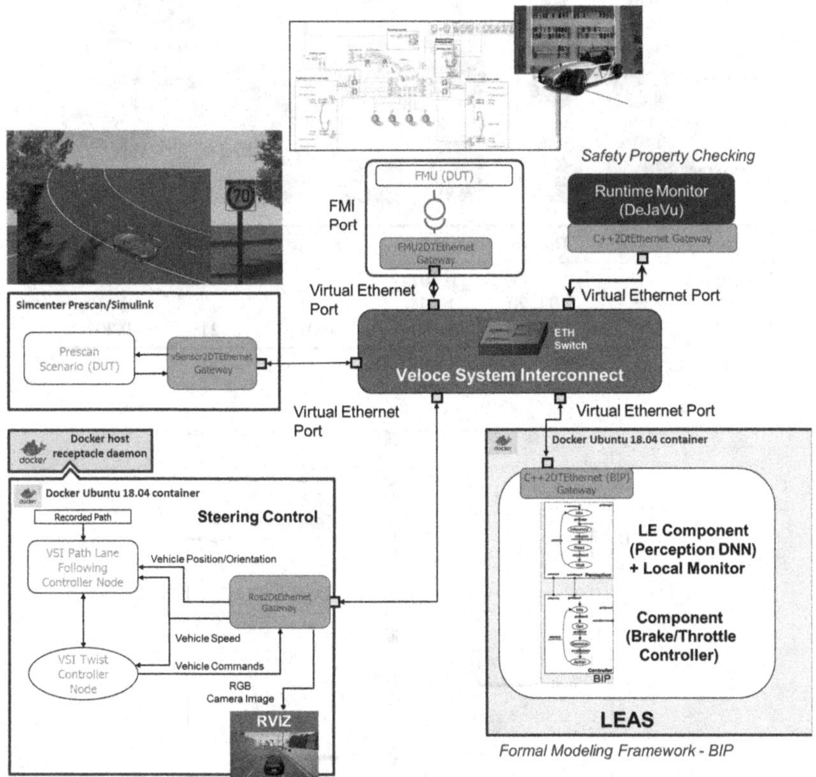

Fig. 5. ML-based traffic speed detection and Path Lane Following

Figure 5 depicts a SiL setup that shows how digital twin simulation is extended with formal analysis and runtime monitoring to verify the functionality of a traffic speed detection and path lane following system. In this case study, a formal model was developed for the perception and throttle/brake control modules of the LEAS using the BIP component framework. This executable model was then integrated with a Simcenter Prescan model for the environment, a Simcenter Amesim model for the EGO vehicle dynamics and a ROS-based implementation of the steering control for path lane following and twist control. The vehicle has an RGB camera sensor. The camera feed is sent to the BIP model for speed sign detection and classification, and the controller component takes the action of acceleration/deceleration based on the speed sign detected. Formal specifications derived from the system requirements using the FOCETA requirements formalisation tool (cf. Figure 4) are then used for synthesizing DeJaVu runtime monitors for safety property checking. DeJaVu monitors are then seamlessly integrated, together with the aforementioned components/models, into the compositional digital twin shown in Fig. 5 based on the VSI.

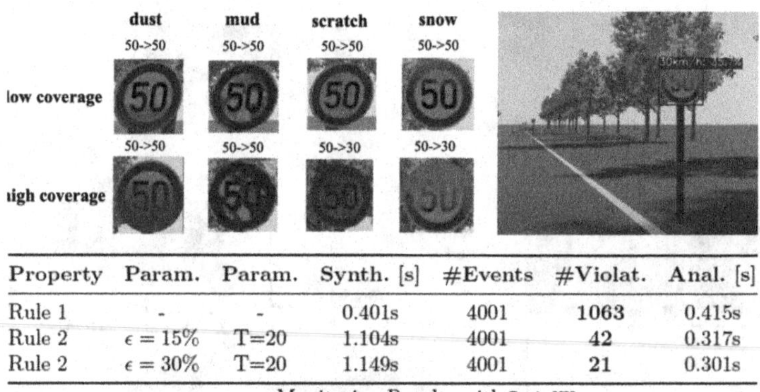

Property	Param.	Param.	Synth. [s]	#Events	#Violat.	Anal. [s]
Rule 1	-	-	0.401s	4001	**1063**	0.415s
Rule 2	$\epsilon = 15\%$	T=20	1.104s	4001	**42**	0.317s
Rule 2	$\epsilon = 30\%$	T=20	1.149s	4001	**21**	0.301s

Monitoring Results with `DejaVU`

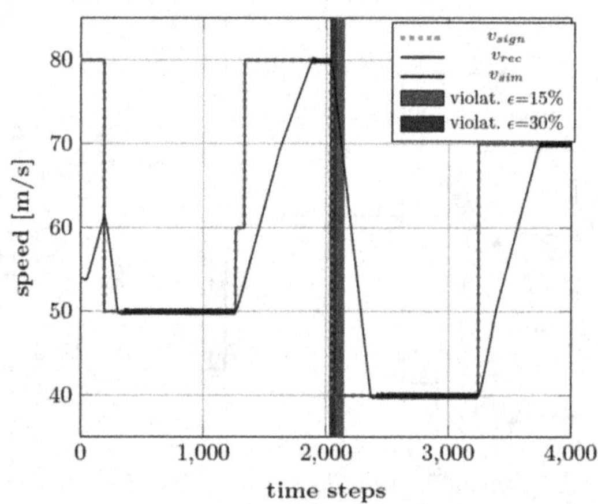

Fig. 6. A trace of the SiL example co-simulated for a horizon of 4001 time units, output: speed over time. The violating events of property/rule 2 are shown in red. Color figure online

The upper part of Fig. 6 shows how the classification of the YOLO model used for traffic sign detection is affected via imperfections of varying coverage due to various weather conditions. The tests took place by implementing different scenarios through

changing the types of imperfection in Prescan. Our YOLO model appears to be i) robust against low-coverage imperfections, and ii) sensitive against high-coverage scratch and snow. On the right, an incorrect prediction found is displayed, via a bounding box. In the table below, we provide the verification results over the simulation trace of a sample scenario with respect to the following properties:
P_1: "EGO should always identify the traffic sign value correctly and the vehicle's speed should be always smaller or equal to the current speed limit."
P_2:"If EGO detects a new speed limit, the speed should not exceed this speed limit by more than ϵ for T time units after detection, where ϵ is a given percentage.".

For simulation traces extended up to 4001 time units we found that property violations occur: (i) when a new traffic sign appears that changes the speed limit from a higher to a lower value, and (ii) due to oscillations of the vehicle speed, when reaching a new speed limit.

The results in Fig. 6 are for LEAS that do not account for potential failures of the YOLO model to correctly identify the speed limit. In this case, the combined interaction of the throttle/brake control and steering control modules will have to ensure that when an abrupt steering angle change is commanded, the vehicle's speed is less than a safe margin (constant ζ) relative to the speed limit. Figure 7 showcases the interactions between runtime monitors at two different levels. At a local level for monitoring the performance of the YOLO model, we employ a runtime monitoring technique from those discussed in Sect. 2.1. At the system level, we use a DeJaVu global monitor for verifying the following property:
P_3:"The traffic sign should be correctly detected (local monitor) and EGO's speed should be smaller than v_{det} (speed limit) if the difference δ_{st} between current and previous steering angle is less than ε_{deg_1} degrees, and v_{sim} should be smaller than v_{det} by at least ζ if δ_{st} is greater than ε_{deg_2}".

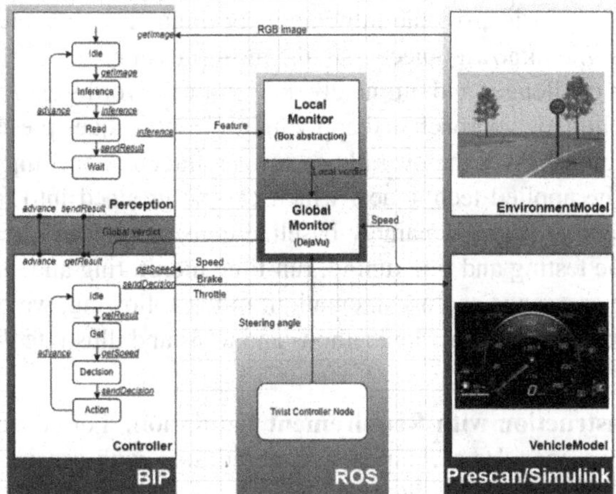

Fig. 7. Digital twin simulation with runtime monitoring the behaviour of a LEC

4.2 Safe and Secure Intelligent Automated Valet Parking

Fig. 8. *(Top)* An example pedestrian-avoiding scenario in the AVP use case. The left image shows a bird's eye view with the drop-off zone in yellow and the designated parking slot in red. The right image shows a driving view, highlighting a pair of pedestrians at risk. *(Bottom)* The effect of various environmental attributes including illumination and precipitation conditions.

This case study addresses an automated valet parking (AVP) system, a highly automated driving system in a relatively controlled environment, or technically termed operational design domain (ODD) [35]. Still, in this ODD, there may be mixed traffic that involves pedestrians as well as parked and moving vehicles. In addition, environmental attributes such as illumination, precipitation, and fog conditions may change. For example, Fig. 8 shows a functional scenario of pedestrian avoidance in a parking lot and the diversity of the ODD considered in this case study. As seen, even within a relatively controlled parking space, there can be many challenging factors, among them (i) the high variability of scenarios, (ii) the intricate actor dynamics, and (iii) the constantly changing world (e.g., unknown objects) are the most pressing.

To tackle such challenges and ultimately deliver a trustworthy AVP system, we follow the FOCETA holistic approach and apply multiple techniques presented in the previous sections. Figure 9 gives the overall use case architecture encompassing the baseline system and the applied techniques, which can be grouped into four phases in a continuous engineering process, namely baseline construction with requirement validation, design-time testing and fine-tuning, run-time monitoring and enforcement, and lastly incremental assurance and argumentation. In the following, we instantiate every phase of this workflow with concrete methods and tools and illustrate their application.

(A) Baseline Construction with Requirement Validation. For constructing an AVP baseline system, we consider a component-based design with sensing, planning, and acting components, as shown by the green area in Fig. 9. In particular, we implement two LECs, including an NN-based 3D object detector and an RL-based controller. We also focus on virtual testing in the Simcenter Prescan simulator[5]. Overall, this design

[5] The virtual simulation platform can be seamlessly changed for HiL or ViL testing.

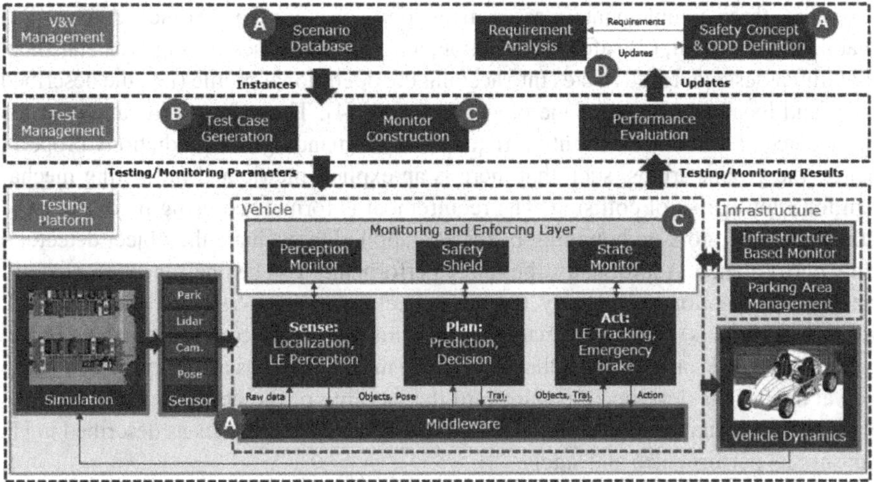

Fig. 9. The overall AVP use case architecture encompassing the testing platform and the V&V and testing techniques discussed in previous sections. The red tags mark the four phases in our continuous engineering process, including (A) baseline construction with requirement validation, (B) design-time testing and fine-tuning, (C) run-time monitoring and enforcement, and (D) incremental assurance and argumentation. color figure online

offers two benefits: (i) The assurance of the overall AVP system can now be attributed to more tractable and efficient verification efforts at the component level; (ii) Adopting the continuous engineering paradigm, we only need to refine and reverify components, typically the learning-enabled ones, that call for an incremental update at some point during testing or run-time.

To illustrate the benefits, we specify a high-level safety goal: The automated vehicle (AV) does not cause a collision unless it is hit by other actors in a static state. With the component-based design, the safety goal can be decomposed into low-level requirements. For instance, the learning-enabled controller is required to always follow a given path within a maximum deviation. Similarly, the (rule-based) emergency brake has to stop the AV whenever there is an obstacle situated within a safety distance (e.g., the pedestrians in Fig. 8). Intuitively, this safety distance can be derived from the maximum controller deviation and the maximum braking distance. Finally, the learning-enabled object detector must then always recognize an obstacle (e.g., the pedestrians) within the derived safety distance. We formally specify these requirements to facilitate rigorous V&V, testing, and monitoring of the AVP components/system. These requirements are managed and validated using semantic analysis based on the DSO modeled from the AVP system (see Sect. 3.1). More specifically, the analysis helps to identify potential weaknesses (e.g., incompleteness, inconsistency, and redundancy) in the requirements.

(B) Design-Time Testing and Fine-Tuning. During design time, testing is done at two levels. At the lower level, we focus on testing the two LECs. Due to the space limit, we provide here brief explanations and links to their results. As mentioned in Sect. 2, we propose three complementary assessment approaches for the 3D object detector: (1) reliability assessment, (2) safety verification, and (3) fault-based testing. The statistical reliability assessment study takes into account the operational profile (i.e., the described ODD) and local robustness of the object detector [44]. The safety verification for the object detector follows an intuitive requirement demanding the predictions properly enclose the ground truths, such that there is an explicit metric and mitigating mechanism for a lower risk of collision. The requirement is formalized using predicate logic with spatial operators on bounding boxes and applied to evaluate the object detector's safety performance. Additionally, the safety performance can be fine-tuned via a safety-oriented loss function [27]. Lastly, the fault injector simulates hardware faults (e.g. bit flips in NN weights) that allow analyzing their impact on the correctness of the object detector. Likewise, an additional fault mitigating mechanism based on neuron activation interval analysis is developed to safeguard the working of the object detector [15]. As for the learning-enabled controller, we apply RL guiding techniques as described in [1] to ensure its performance and safety.

With the components tested and integrated, system-level testing is then conducted (see Sect. 3.2). In particular, given the ODD, we employ search-based testing (SBT) with evolutionary algorithms for our AVP system [36]. Specifically, the following steps are taken: (1) Select a *scenario* within the ODD, e.g., the pedestrian-avoiding scenario in Fig. 8; (2) Define the variables and specify their ranges in which they will be varied to generate different instances of the scenario such as time of day (e.g., 9:00-17:00), precipitation (e.g., none, medium, or heavy rain), and different pedestrian types (e.g., child, adult, and elder); (3) Define fitness functions based on the introduced safety goal, e.g., the distance between the AV and the pedestrian and the velocity of the AV at its closest point to the pedestrian; (4) Apply a search algorithm and optimize the fitness functions to find failure-revealing test cases. Figure 10 shows two such critical cases qualitatively, and quantitatively we observe about 30% of generated test cases are critical to the AVP system using NSGA-II [11]. By doing such optimization-driven search-based testing, we are able to extensively test the AVP system and mitigate the challenge of high scenario variability.

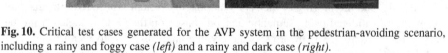

Fig. 10. Critical test cases generated for the AVP system in the pedestrian-avoiding scenario, including a rainy and foggy case *(left)* and a rainy and dark case *(right)*.

(C) Run-Time Monitoring and Enforcement. Considering the challenges of intricate actor dynamics and the ever-changing world, an AVP system can hardly be fully assured

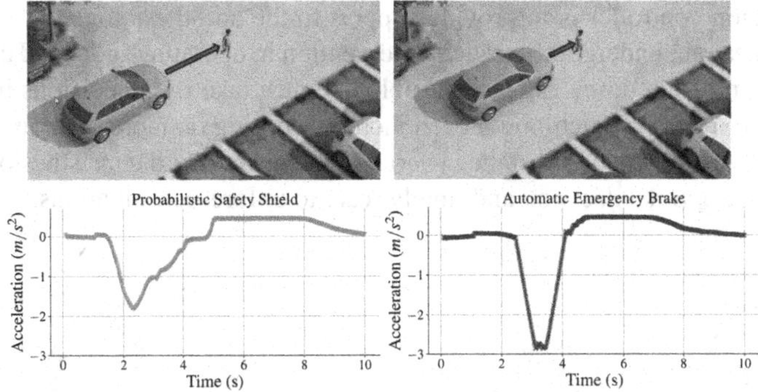

Fig. 11. In the pedestrian-avoiding scenario, the shield *(left)* mitigates the risk of colliding more smoothly and earlier than the baseline emergency brake *(right)*.

by design-time testing only. Therefore, monitors and enforcers are usually added to the system to safeguard it during run-time. We highlight two lines of work in this regard. Firstly, we create an out-of-distribution perception monitor (see Sect. 2.1) and link it to a system safety enforcer. Essentially, the perception monitor provides the confidence level of the object detector's prediction and triggers the system safety shield (see Sect. 2.2) to correct the underlying controller's action whenever needed [24]. Figure 11 demonstrates an interim result of applying the safety shield (with ground-truth perception). Secondly, a global state monitor modeled (see Sect. 3.2) with Signal Temporal Logic (STL) is implemented via RTAMT [32] to ensure the overall safety of the AVP system. For example, when the perception monitor sends a warning, the state monitor can check if the shield is actually activated. Additionally, it can also directly monitor different vehicle states such as tracking deviation, as decomposed from the high-level safety goal. Altogether, as depicted by the light blue area in Fig. 9, these techniques form another layer of safety measures at run-time for the AVP system.

(D) Incremental Assurance and Argumentation. Finally, to close the loop of the continuous engineering process, we underline the utilization of the specification mining technique (Sect. 3.3) [3] which helps characterize system behaviors or identify missing requirements with system operations. For instance, by repeating the simulation of the pedestrian-avoiding scenario in Fig. 8, we find that the AV (1) will never go within 0.5 m to the first pedestrian and (2) will only make a collision if the second pedestrian is a child (but not an adult or an elder). With these results, we can then refine or relax the original set of requirements (from phase A) and thereby repair or fine-tune our AVP system for incremental assurance (Sect. 3.4). Another iteration cycle of requirements validation will then have to take place (cf. Figure 4).

4.3 Anaesthetic Drug Target Control Infusion

This case study develops a concept design and a test platform, depicted in Fig. 12, for an intelligent infusion pump controller for Depth of Anaesthesia (DoA). The main aim for a smart infusion controller is to provide support to the anesthesiologist in monitoring the DoA of a patient undergoing surgical intervention in operating room and calculating the next drug infusion dose. The anesthesiologist must take right decisions in possibly stressful environments, which might even include working on more than one patient at the same time. This type of assistance is crucial to ensure that the anesthesiologist can always take the optimal decision and timely react to unforeseen situations.

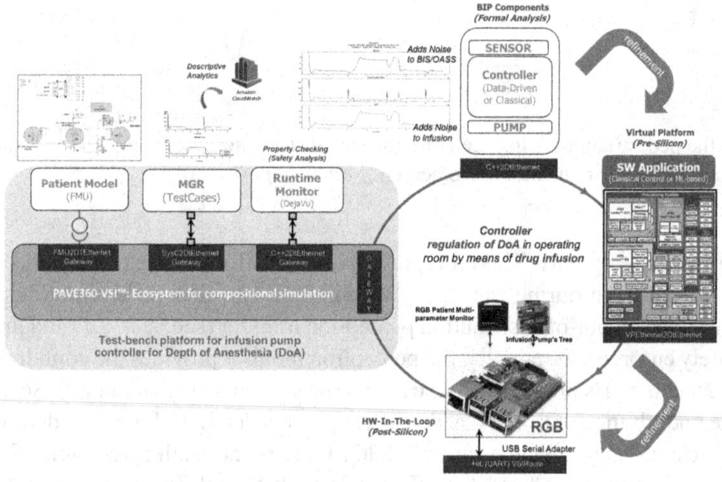

Fig. 12. HiL/SiL platform for the medical case study.

The main intelligence is embedded in the controller. We developed a data-driven controller based on a recurrent NN for the pump infusion from the collected data used for training. While the data-driven controller may provide near to optimal drug infusion doses, this process is not expected to be fully automated, both from the perspective of regulatory bodies and the user acceptance. Hence, we take the approach of having the *human shield* (anesthesiologist) that ensures the safety of the patient by taking the final decision regarding the next dose. Another LEC in design is the monitor that observes the vital signs of the patient and predicts her current DoA state.

To support the design of this intelligent drug pump controller, we need several other components and a virtual integration and testing platform. Given that no clinical studies can be done in FOCETA, there is a need for replacing the real patient in the platform. Hence, we developed a patient model in Simcenter Amesim. The model, based on the relevant research in the medical literature, is parameterizable in function of the patient's characteristics, such as the age, weight and gender. The patient is modelled using traditional compartmental analysis in which the interpersonal variability is considered. The patients model determines the DoA level achieved with a certain drug dose in bispectral index (BIS) values.

Another key component in this platform is the test case manager. It is used for the initial configuration of the other components according to the selected test case.

The main initial settings are the initial drug infusion dose and the target DoA level. The abstract test scenarios are (partially) constructed from interviewing doctors and recording their usual sequences of steps during operations.

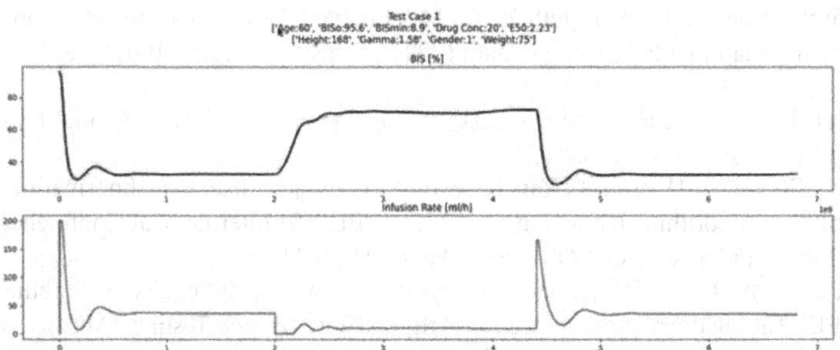

Fig. 13. Simulation results: BIS vs. infusion rate for a given patient Profile TestCase

We used the FOCETA Compositional Simulation Architecture (cf. Figure 3) to intergrate Simcenter Amesim, DejaVU (Runtime Monitoring), BIP (Component based Modeling), Virtual Platform Modeling, and HiL (external Hardware board), as shown in Figs. 12 and 13. Furthermore, we demonstrate the refinement of the DoA controller under test while keeping all other digital twin components intact within the loop (i.e. Testbench platform). The success criterion in this case was to obtain the same results, which affirms the effectiveness of the controller design refinement.

5 Conclusion

In this paper, we presented the FOCETA methodology that consists of two workflows: one for designing trustworthy LECs and one for building safe LEAS by integrating both classical and LE components. We summarized the main steps of the methodology and associated them to the most appropriate methods and tools developed in FOCETA. We finally showed how the case studies in FOCETA demonstrate the various facets of the methodology.

Acknowledgment. This project has received funding from the European Unions Horizon 2020 research and innovation programme under grant agreement No 956123.

References

1. Aguilar, E.A., Berducci, L., Brunnbauer, A., Grosu, R., Nickovic, D.: From STL rulebooks to rewards. CoRR, abs/ arXiv: 2110.02792 (2021)
2. Bartocci, E., Mateis, C., Nesterini, E., Nickovic, D.: Survey on mining signal temporal logic specifications. Inform. Comput., 104957 (2022)
3. Bartocci, E., Mateis, C., Nesterini, E., Ničković, D.: Mining hyperproperties using temporal logics. ACM Trans. Embed. Comput. Syst. (2023)

4. Basu, A., Bensalem, S., Bozga, M., Bourgos, P., Sifakis, J.: Rigorous system design: the BIP approach. In: Kotásek, Z., Bouda, J., Černá, I., Sekanina, L., Vojnar, T., Antoš, D. (eds.) MEMICS 2011. LNCS, vol. 7119, pp. 1–19. Springer, Heidelberg (2012). https://doi.org/10.1007/978-3-642-25929-6_1
5. Bensalem, S., et al.: Formal specification for learning-enabled autonomous systems. In: Software Verification and Formal Methods for ML-Enabled Autonomous Systems, pp. 131–143. Springer International Publishing, Cham (2022). https://doi.org/10.1007/978-3-031-21222-2_8
6. Berducci, L., Aguilar, E.A., Ničković, D., Grosu, R.: Hierarchical potential-based reward shaping from task specifications (2021)
7. Chen, Y., Cheng, C.-H., Yan, J., Yan, R.: Monitoring object detection abnormalities via data-label and post-algorithm abstractions. In: 2021 IEEE/RSJ International Conference on Intelligent Robots and Systems (IROS), pp. 6688–6693 (2021)
8. Cheng, C., Yan, R.: Testing autonomous systems with believed equivalence refinement. In: 2021 IEEE International Conference On Artificial Intelligence Testing (AITest), pp. 49–56. IEEE Computer Society (2021)
9. Cheng, C.-H.: Provably-robust runtime monitoring of neuron activation patterns. In: IEEE DATE (2021)
10. Cruanes, S., Hamon, G., Owre, S., Shankar, N.: Tool integration with the evidential tool bus. In: Verification, Model Checking, and Abstract Interpretation, 14th International Conference, VMCAI 2013, Rome, Italy, 20–22 January 2013. Proceedings, pp. 275–294 (2013)
11. Deb, K., Pratap, A., Agarwal, S., Meyarivan, T.: A fast and elitist multiobjective genetic algorithm: Nsga-ii. IEEE Trans. Evol. Comput. **6**(2), 182–197 (2002)
12. Eleftheriadis, C., Kekatos, N., Katsaros, P., Tripakis, S.: On neural network equivalence checking using smt solvers. In: Bogomolov, S., Parker, D. (eds.) Formal Modeling and Analysis of Timed Systems, pp. 237–257. Springer International Publishing, Cham (2022) https://doi.org/10.1007/978-3-031-15839-1_14
13. Fogler, R., Cohen, I., Peled, D.: Accelerating black box testing with light-weight learning. In: Model Checking Software - 29th International Symposium, SPIN 2023, Paris, France, 26–27 April 2023, Proceedings, pp. 103–120 (2023)
14. Geissler, F., Qutub, S., Paulitsch, M., Pattabiraman, K.: A low-cost strategic monitoring approach for scalable and interpretable error detection in deep neural networks. In: Computer Safety, Reliability, and Security - 42nd International Conference, SAFECOMP 2023, Toulouse, France, 19–22 September 2023, Proceedings (2023)
15. Geissler, F., et al.: Towards a safety case for hardware fault tolerance in convolutional neural networks using activation range supervision. CoRR, abs/ arXiv: 2108.07019 (2021)
16. Gräfe, R., Sha, Q.S., Geissler, F., Paulitsch, M.: Large-scale application of fault injection into pytorch models -an extension to pytorchfi for validation efficiency. In: 2023 53rd Annual IEEE/IFIP International Conference on Dependable Systems and Networks - Supplemental Volume (DSN-S), pp. 56–62 (2023)
17. Havelund, K., Peled, D., Ulus, D.: Dejavu: a monitoring tool for first-order temporal logic. In: 3rd Workshop on Monitoring and Testing of Cyber-Physical Systems, MT@CPSWeek 2018, Porto, Portugal, 10 April 2018, pp. 12–13 (2018)
18. Henzinger, T.A., Lukina, A., Schilling, C.: Outside the box: abstraction-based monitoring of neural networks. In: ECAI 2020, pp. 2433–2440. IOS Press (2020)
19. Huang, W., et al.: Coverage-guided testing for recurrent neural networks. IEEE Trans. Reliab. **71**(3), 1191–1206 (2022)
20. Huang, W., Zhao, X., Cox, V., Huang, X.: Hierarchical distribution-aware testing of deep learning, Alec Banks (2022)
21. Huang, W., Zhao, X., Jin, G., Huang, X.: Safari: versatile and efficient evaluations for robustness of interpretability. arXiv preprint arXiv:2208.09418 (2022)

22. Jin, G., Yi, X., Huang, W., Schewe, S., Huang, X.: Enhancing adversarial training with second-order statistics of weights. In: Proceedings of the IEEE/CVF Conference on Computer Vision and Pattern Recognition (CVPR), pp. 15273–15283 (June 2022)
23. Jin, G., Yi, X., Zhang, L., Zhang, L., Schewe, S., Huang, X.: How does weight correlation affect generalisation ability of deep neural networks? Adv. Neural Inf. Proc. Syst. **33**, 21346–21356 (2020)
24. Könighofer, B., Rudolf, J., Palmisano, A., Tappler, M., Bloem, R.: Online shielding for reinforcement learning. CoRR, abs/ arXiv: 2212.01861 (2022)
25. Kose, N., Krishnan, R., Dhamasia, A., Tickoo, O., Paulitsch, M.: Reliable multimodal trajectory prediction via error aligned uncertainty optimization. In Computer Vision - ECCV 2022 Workshops - Tel Aviv, Israel, 23–27 October 2022, Proceedings, Part V, pp. 443–458 (2022). https://doi.org/10.1007/978-3-031-25072-9_31
26. Liao, B.H.-C., Cheng, C.-H., Esen, H., Knoll, A.: Are transformers more robust? Towards exact robustness verification for transformers. In: SafeComp (2023)
27. Liao, B.H.-C., Cheng, C.-H., Esen, H., Knoll, A.: Improving the safety of 3D object detectors in autonomous driving using IoGT and distance measures. abs/ arXiv: 2209.10368 (2023)
28. Maderbacher, B., Schupp, S., Bartocci, E., Bloem,R., Nickovic, D., Könighofer, B.: Provable correct and adaptive simplex architecture for bounded-liveness properties. In: Model Checking Software - 29th International Symposium, SPIN 2023, Paris, France, 26–27April 2023, Proceedings, pp. 141–160 (2023)
29. Mahmoud, A., et al.: Pytorchfi: a runtime perturbation tool for dnns. In: 2020 50th Annual IEEE/IFIP International Conference on Dependable Systems and Networks Workshops (DSN-W), pp. 25–31 (2020)
30. Maler, O., Nickovic, D.: Monitoring temporal properties of continuous signals. In: Lakhnech, Y., Yovine, S. (eds.) FORMATS/FTRTFT -2004. LNCS, vol. 3253, pp. 152–166. Springer, Heidelberg (2004). https://doi.org/10.1007/978-3-540-30206-3_12
31. Mokos, K., Nestoridis, T., Katsaros, P., Bassiliades, N.: Semantic modeling and analysis of natural language system requirements. IEEE Access **10**, 84094–84119 (2022)
32. Nickovic, D., Yamaguchi, T.: RTAMT: online robustness monitors from STL. In: Automated Technology for Verification and Analysis - 18th International Symposium, ATVA 2020, Hanoi, Vietnam, 19–23 October 2020, Proceedings, pp. 564–571 (2020)
33. OpenAI. Gpt-4 technical report (2023)
34. Qutub, S., Geissler, F., Peng, Y., Gräfe, R., Paulitsch, M., Hinz, G., Knoll, A.: Hardware faults that matter: understanding and estimating the safety impact of hardware faults on object detection DNNs. LNCS, pp. 298–318. Springer International Publishing (2022). https://doi.org/10.1007/978-3-031-14835-4_20
35. SAE. J3016: Taxonomy and definitions for terms related to driving automation systems for on-road motor vehicles
36. Sorokin, L., Munaro, T., Safin, D., Liao, B.H.-C., Molin, A.: A modular framework for search-based testing of automated driving systems, Opensbt (2023)
37. Su, J., Vargas, D.V., Sakurai, K.: One pixel attack for fooling deep neural networks. IEEE Trans. Evolut. Comput. **23**(5), 828–841 (2019)
38. Temperekidis, A., Kekatos, N., Katsaros, P.: Runtime verification for fmi-based co-simulation. In: Dang, T., Stolz, V. (eds.) Runtime Verification, pp. 304–313. Springer International Publishing, Cham (2022). https://doi.org/10.1007/978-3-031-17196-3_19
39. Temperekidis, A., et al.: Towards a digital twin architecture with formal analysis capabilities for learning-enabled autonomous systems. In: Modelling and Simulation for Autonomous Systems, pp. 163–181. Springer International Publishing, Cham (2023). https://doi.org/10.1007/978-3-031-31268-7_10

40. Tripakis, S.: Bridging the semantic gap between heterogeneous modeling formalisms and FMI. In: 2015 International Conference on Embedded Computer Systems: Architectures, Modeling, and Simulation (SAMOS), pp. 60–69. IEEE (2015)
41. Wu, C., Falcone, Y., Bensalem, S.: Customizable reference runtime monitoring of neural networks using resolution boxes (2021)
42. Zuxuan, W., Lim, S.-N., Davis, L., Goldstein, T.: Real world adversarial attacks on object detectors, Making an invisibility cloak (2019)
43. Xu, P., Wang, F., Ruan, W., Zhang, C., Huang, X.: Sora: scalable black-box reachability analyser on neural networks. In: ICASSP 2023–2023 IEEE International Conference on Acoustics, Speech and Signal Processing (ICASSP), pp. 1–5. IEEE (2023)
44. Zhao, X., et al.: Assessing the reliability of deep learning classifiers through robustness evaluation and operational profiles. In: Proceedings of the Workshop on Artificial Intelligence Safety 2021 (co-located with IJCAI 2021), vol. 2916. CEUR Workshop Proceedings (2021)
45. Zhao, X.: Reliability assessment and safety arguments for machine learning components in assuring learning-enabled autonomous systems. ACM Trans. Embedded Comput. Syst. (2022)
46. Zhao, X., Huang, W., Huang, X., Robu, V., Flynn, D.: Baylime: bayesian local interpretable model-agnostic explanations. In: Proceedings of 37th Conference on Uncertainty in Artificial Intelligence, 27–30 Jul, vol. 161, pp. 887–896. PMLR (2021)

Benchmarks: Semantic Segmentation Neural Network Verification and Objection Detection Neural Network Verification in Perceptions Tasks of Autonomous Driving

Yonggang Luo(✉), Jinyan Ma, Sanchu Han, and Lecheng Xie

AI LAB, Chongqing Changan Automobile Ltd., Chongqing, China
{luoyg3,majy1,frankhan,xielc}@changan.com.cn

Abstract. The verification of the security of neural networks is cruicial, especially for the field of autonomous driving. Although there are currently benchmarks for the verification of the robustness of neural networks, there are hardly any benchmarks related to the field of autonomous driving, especially those related to object detection and semantic segmentation. Thus, a notable gap exists in formally verifying the robustness of semantic semantic segmentation and object detection tasks under complex, real-world conditions. To address this, we present an innovative approach to benchamark formal verification for autonomous driving perception tasks. Firstly, we propose robust verification benchmarks for semantic segmentation and object detection, supplementing existing methods. Secondly, and more significantly, we introduce a novel patch-level disturbance approach for object detection, providing a more realistic representation of real-world scenarios. By augmenting the current verification benchmarks with our novel proposals, our work contributes towards developing a more comprehensive, practical, and realistic benchmarking methodology for perception tasks in autonomous driving, thereby propelling the field towards improved safety and reliability. Our dataset and code used in this work are publicly available.

Keywords: Machine Learning · Formal Verification · Perception Tasks · Autonomous Driving

1 Introduction

The advent of autonomous driving technologies has ushered in a new paradigm for transportation, offering promise for improved safety and efficiency. Yet, they also pose significant challenges, particularly in perception tasks which are fundamental to their safe operation[1,2]. For example, by accurately segmenting the

[1] https://github.com/pomodoromjy/vnn-comp-2022-Carvana-unet.

[2] https://github.com/pomodoromjy/vnncomp-2023-CCTSDB-YOLO.

B. Steffen (Ed.): AISoLA 2023, LNCS 14380, pp. 279–290, 2024.
https://doi.org/10.1007/978-3-031-46002-9_16

drivable road surface from other areas, the vehicle can know where it can go. In the other case, the autonomous vehicle needs to detect pedestrians to ensure that it stops or slows down in time to avoid collisions. Reliable perception necessitates precise object detection and semantic segmentation under varied and often unpredictable real-world conditions [37], where semantic segmentation is the task of clustering parts of images together which belong to the same object class [40] and object detection is the task of identifying objects in the image along with their localizations and classifications [10].

Formal verification, grounded in rigorous mathematical and logical principles, has been identified as a potent mechanism for assuring the safety and performance of neural network. Many formal approaches are already able to verify variants of classification tasks [1,2,5,7,12,15,16,19–21,24,26,30,35,36,38,41,43,45–47,49–51]. The verification of safety and robustness specification of neural network controlled systems is explored by many works [22,23,42]. Furthermore, the performance of image-based controllers is discussed by concatenating the generator network with the control network [25]. However, only few work focuses on the formal approach for verifying semantic segmentation and object detection networks robustness using reachability analysis [44]. Moreover, existing formal verification methods often rely on assumptions of ideal operational environments, creating a potential divergance from the often unpredictable conditions encountered in real-world scenarios.

Given this context, although we have many benchmarks for formal verification methods [3,8,31], there is still a significant and unexplored need to benchmark formal verification methods for autonomous driving system in the wild. This approach allows for a more realistic assessment of perception neural networks' robustness under challenging real-world conditions, while also facilitating calibration of verification tools to better mirror reality. The motivation behind our work arises from the necessity to enhance the verification benchmarks for object detection and semantic segmentation tasks and to better align them with actual autonomous driving scenarios.

In this paper, we present a comprehensive approach to benchmark formal verification for autonomous driving perception tasks. Our primary contributions are two-fold: firstly, we propose robust verification benchmarks for object detection and semantic segmentation tasks. Secondly, and more importantly, we introduce a patch-level disturbance approach for object detection tasks, mirroring the complexities of real-world scenarios in a more realistic manner. Although pixel-level adversarial samples can effectively attack our perception models, in the real world, we seldom encounter disturbance patterns that exactly match adversarial samples. That is, it's nearly impossible to replicate pixel-level disturbances in the real world, so it's questionable whether we will encounter adversarial samples' interference patterns in the real world. On the contrary, patch-level disturbance patterns are a more common type of interference, and they are easier to replicate in the real world and are more likely to occur. For example, we only need to simply cut some black paper pieces to replicate the disturbance patterns we want to appear in the real world. By augmenting the existing verification benchmarks and proposing a novel patch-level disturbance approach, this work aims to provide a more comprehensive and practical benchmarking methodology for autonomous driving perception tasks, thereby advancing the field towards greater safety and reliability.

The paper is organized as follows: In Sect. 2, we provide a detailed relevent work. Section 3 introduces our semantic segmentation benchmark. In Sect. 4, we delve into our patch-level object detection benchmark. Finally, Sect. 5 presents the experiment of two benchmarks, and Sect. 6 concludes the paper with future work directions.

2 Related Work

Perception tasks in autonomous driving: Perception tasks hold a key role by playing a critical function in recognizing and understanding the various elements in the surrounding environments [48]. This understanding allows these perception tasks to extract vital semantic information necessary for safe and efficient driving. Such information includes the identification and detection of different road onjects. These could be pedestriants crossing the street, other vehicles in transit, or even potential obstacles that could hinder the smooth progress of the autonomous vehicle.

Moreover, object tracking is another crucial perception task, ensuring a continous understanding of the movement and position of surrounding entites. Another aspect of perception tasks involves semantic segmentation, a process that categorizes each pixel in an image to a particular class to help the vehicle better understand its environment. This not only includes road and off-road classification but also recognizes different lanes and traffic lights, aiding the vehicle's decision-making progress in different traffic scenarios.

These perception tasks rely heavily on the integration of multiple sensor inputs. These sensors typically include cameras, Light Detection and Ranging (LiDAR) systems and Radio Detection and Ranging (RADAR) sensors. The confluence of data from these diverse sensor systems feeds into the perception tasks, aiding the autonomous vehicle in understanding and navigating its surroundings efficiently and safely.

In this paper, we mainly focus on semantic segmentation and object detection tasks. Considering that the research in formal verification of neural networks is still unable to handle complex neural network models, we have simplified the model in our benchmarks, which is not intended for commercial mass production or practical use. At the same time, we are only considering the data of a single target in a single camera as the models' input. We will treat more complex perception models and multi-sensor inputs as future research directions.

Benchmarks: Well-known benchmarks for perception tasks are typically KITTI [17], nuScenes [9] and Waymo [39] in autonomous driving area, however they were designed for general purpose instead of performing robustness evaluation. In order to conduct evaluations of robustness, recent studies have been actively either developing new benchmarks based on the existing autonomous driving datasets [14], or constructing new datasets that consist of road anomalies, or those that represent extrem weather conditions [4,11,13,18,27,32,33].

In the field of robustness verification of neural networks, benchmarks are typically image classification tasks, though some recent studies have been actively proposing new benchmarks in many other tasks [3,8,31]. However, to the best of our knowledge, so far there is no paper focusing on benchmarks which evaluate formal verification tools for perception tasks of autonomous driving in the wild.

In this paper, we propose two benchmarks which are related to autonomous driving scenarios, and we present a detailed description of the background to highlight our benchmarks' relevance and the characteristics of the verification problems. The ONNX format and the VNN-LIB format were adpoted for our benchmarks.

3 Semantic Segmentation Benchmark–Carvana Unet

The motivation behind our proposed benchmarks is primarily the predominant focus of existing networks in the literature on image classification. We perceive the need for more emphasis on aspects such as object detection or semantic segmentation, particularly in real-world scenarios such as autonomous driving. In this section, we introduce a new suite of simplified Unet [34] benchmarks designed specifically for neural network verification on the Carvana dataset [6]. To respond to the practicality of current verification tools and the intricate nature of semantic segmentation, we construct this new series of simplified Unet benchmarks (model one consists of four Conv2d layers followed by BatchNorm (BN) and ReLu; model two builds upon model one, adding an AveragePool layer and a Transposed Conv Upsampling layer). We believe that it's vital for tools to address more pragmatic architectures and consider this simplified Unet as a step in that direction.

Furthermore, the Carvana dataset, composed of 5088 images representing 318 cars (16 images per car), has been divided into a test set of 318 images (one per car) and a training set of the remaining 4700 images. The input images should be normalized to a [0, 1] range. Ground truth masks, generated by running the model on original images, assign either a 0 or 1 to each pixel. Our proposal is to select 16 images randomly for verification from those whose over 98.8 percent and 99.0 percent of pixels are predicted correctly by model one and model two respectively. The input size is [1, 4, 31, 47], where '1' corresponds to the batch size, '4' to the number of channels, '31' and '47' to the height and width of samples respectively. The first three channels signify RGB values of images, and the last channel denotes the model-produced mask used for computing the quantity of accurately predicted pixels by the model. The model output is the count of pixels predicted correctly by the model, juxtaposed with the model-produced mask. We summarized the network details and implementation details in Appendix A and Appendix B.

4 Patch-Level Object Detection Benchmark–CCTSDB YOLO

While the Carvana Unet benchmark in Sect. 3 allows the application of neural network verification tools in autonomous driving scenarios, the pixel-level perturbation is still challenging to reflect the real-world situation. In this section, we are stepping up the challenge by introducing a new set of benchmarks for object detection within autonomous driving scenes. Given the practicality of current verification tools, we have modified Yolo-FastestV2 [29], based on a well-known end-to-end object detection framework Yolo. This architecture comprise backbone, neck, and head components.

To further alleviate computational burden, we have simplified the backbone and neck. For the head, we aim to facilitate single object detection while bypassing the need to conduct non-maximum suppression (NMS) operation within the model. To this end, we have replaced the box regression method with landmark regression for coordinate detection.

To the best of our knowledge, previous benchmarks were designed to test the model's digital world robustness. However, with an eye towards real-world practicality, we now suggest testing the model's robustness within the physical world. Specifically, we will supply an image with its corresponding label, as well as a fixed-size patch (either 1×1 or 3×3). Our goal is for the community to verify the model's robustness after applying the patch to any position within the image, all within the allocated time of specific time.

We utilized the training set from CCTSDB 2021 [52], which encompasses a total of 16356 images (26838 instances). Further division of all instances in a 9:1 ratio resulted in a training set comprising 23856 instances and a test set featuring 2982 instances. The input images and target coordinates need normalization within the range of 0–1. Targets are divided into three categories, signified by 0 (mandatory), 1 (prohibitory), and 2 (warning). We picked images with an intersection over union (IoU) greater than 0.5 and correct category classification from the test set. Eventually, 16 images will be selected at random for verification.

The model input consists of an array of 12296 elements, which include images (12288 elements), position (2 elements), and targets (6 elements). The model's single output is a combination of IoU between the predicted and actual bounding box, and the consistency of the predicted category with the actual category, as the Eq. 1.

$$output = IoU \times \begin{cases} 1, pred\_cls = gt\_cls \\ 0, pred\_cls \neq gt\_cls \end{cases} \tag{1}$$

If the final output for the input with the added patch is less than 0.5, the model is deemed non-robust for that patch. And vice versa. We summarized the network details and implementation details in Appendix A and Appendix B.

5 Experiments

For the Carvana Unet benchmark, three formal verification tools (α, β Crown [36, 45–47, 49–51], MN-BAB [16], and VeriNet [19–21]) have been successfully applied to our benchmark in VNN-COMP 2022 [31]. The number of instances that were solved by the different formal verification tools within a certain runtime for our benchmark is as illustrated in the Fig. 1. We expect more formal verification tools could be applied to the Carvana Unet benchmark in the future.

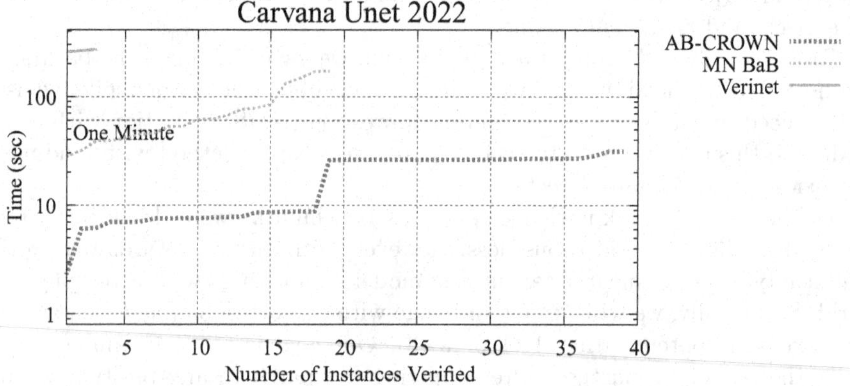

Fig. 1. The number of instances that were solved by the different formal verification tools within a certain runtime for Carvana Unet in VNN-COMP 2022 [31].

For the CCTSDB YOLO benchmark, we further conduct extensive experiments to prove the following properties; (1) The simplified object detection model can still accurately identify targets within the dataset. (2) By adding patches randomly, we can ensure an anomalous detection in some images while maintaining correct detection in others, thus preventing situations where all data are either hold or violated. The object detection model and the dataset are same as the description in Sect. 4. We summarize our experiment results in the Table 1.

Table 1. Object detection accuracy for the dataset with/without patches.

Model	without patch	with patch
Model1 (patch size 1×1)	0.968	0.805
Model2 (patch size 3×3)	0.978	0.253

As illustrated in the Table 1, the result shows that without the patch added, the model achieves successful detection rates of 0.968 and 0.978, indicating that its performance on our dataset has not significantly declined due to simplification. Moreover, after adding the patch, the detection rates drop to 0.805 and 0.253, ensuring that some data fails detection, thereby validating the effectiveness of our benchmark in evaluating the performance of formal verification tools (within a certain time limitation).

At the same time, we also show different types of detection errors in our benchmarks in Fig. 2. Except for the image in the upper left corner of the figure, the rest of the error are related to the incorrect positioning of the bounding box, even if the object classification within the bounding box is correct. But for the image in the upper left corner, the error lies in both the incorrect position of the bounding box and the incorrect classification of the object within the bounding box. We can further set the conditions for "hold" and "violated" based on the scenarios we use. For example, when we only care about the information of the traffic sign, and are less concerned about its position, we can rewrite Eq. 1, relying solely on whether the predicted and actual categories are consistent to determine its robustness.

Fig. 2. The different types of detection errors in benchmark CCTSDB YOLO. The yellow boxs represent the ground truth, while the blue boxes represent the predicted bounding boxes. The yellow and blue numbers respectively represent the actual and predicted categories. The image in the upper left corner contains two types of errors, while the rest of the images only have bounding box errors. (Color figure online)

6 Conclusion

In this paper, we show how perception tasks' performance can be further connected with robustness verification field by benchmarking formal verification for autonomous driving in the wild. Specifically, we propose two benchmarks consist of the pixel-level semantic segmentation benchmark (Carvana Unet) and the patch-level object detection benchmark (CCTSDB YOLO). Experiments results demonstrate the effectiveness of the proposed benchmark for evaluating formal verification tools in autonomous driving perception tasks. Future work will take into account more real-world autonomous driving tasks (e.g., 3D object detection, object tracking and LiDAR localization) and more variants of attached patches.

Acknowledgement. Yonggang Luo was supported by the Department of Human Resources and Social Security of Chongqing City, through the Chongqing Liuchuang Program. Sanchu Han was supported by the Department of Human Resources and Social Security of Chongqing City, through the Chongqing Talents Program.

A Network Details

In our benchmarks, we used a total of three networks, namely Unet_simp, Unet_upsample, and Yolo. Among them, Unet_simp and Unet_upsample correspond to benchmark Carvana Unet, while Yolo corresponds to benchmark CCTSDB YOLO. We have summarized the amount of parameters and the size of the models corresponding to these thress networks in the Table 2. The networks in benchmark Carvana Unet used operation such as Conv, BN, ReLu, AvgPool, ConvTranspose, etc., whereas the networks in benchmark CCTSDB YOLO used operations like Conv, BN, ReLu, MaxPool, interpolate, etc.

Table 2. Summary of the amount of parameters and model sizes of the three networks

Networks	The amount of parameters	Model sizes (M)	The number of layers
Unet_simp	149826	0.608	4
Unet_upsample	330370	1.333	6
Yolo	144583	0.668	Not defined due to existed branches

B Implementation Details

For the benchmark Carvana Unet, we used the RMSprop optimizer, where the weight decay was set to 1×10^{-8} and the momentum was set to 0.9. We initialized the learning rate to 1×10^{-5}, with a decay strategy of ReduceLROnPlateau, where the mode was chosen as max and patience was set to 2. We trained it for a total of 5 epochs.

For the benchmark CCTSDB YOLO, we used the SGD optimizer, where the weight decay was set to 0.0005 and the momentum was set to 0.949. We initialized the learning rate to 0.001, with a decay strategy of MultiStepLR, where the milestones was set to an array as [150, 250] and gamma was set to 0.1. We trained it for a total of 300 epochs.

References

1. Anderson, G., Pailoor, S., Dillig, I., Chaudhuri, S.: Optimization and abstraction: a synergistic approach for analyzing neural network robustness. In: Proceedings of the 40th ACM SIGPLAN Conference on Programming Language Design and Implementation, PLDI 2019, pp. 731–744. Association for Computing Machinery, New York (2019)
2. Bak, S.: nnenum: verification of ReLU neural networks with optimized abstraction refinement. In: Dutle, A., Moscato, M.M., Titolo, L., Muñoz, C.A., Perez, I. (eds.) NFM 2021. LNCS, vol. 12673, pp. 19–36. Springer, Cham (2021). https://doi.org/10.1007/978-3-030-76384-8_2
3. Bak, S., Liu, C., Johnson, T.T.: The second international verification of neural networks competition (vnn-comp 2021): Summary and results. arXiv: 2109.00498 (2021)
4. Bijelic, M., et al.: Seeing through fog without seeing fog: deep multimodal sensor fusion in unseen adverse weather. In: 2020 IEEE/CVF Conference on Computer Vision and Pattern Recognition (CVPR), pp. 11679–11689 (2020)
5. Botoeva, E., Kouvaros, P., Kronqvist, J., Lomuscio, A., Misener, R.: Efficient verification of relu-based neural networks via dependency analysis. In: AAAI Conference on Artificial Intelligence (2020)
6. Shaler, B.: DanGill, M.M.M.P.W.C.: Carvana image masking challenge (2017)
7. Brix, C., Noll, T.: Debona: decoupled boundary network analysis for tighter bounds and faster adversarial robustness proofs. arXiv: 2006.09040 (2020)
8. Brix, C., Muller, M.N., Bak, S., Johnson, T.T., Liu, C.: First three years of the international verification of neural networks competition (vnn-comp). ArXiv, abs/ arXiv: 2301.05815 (2023)
9. Caesar, H., et al.: nuscenes: A multimodal dataset for autonomous driving. In: 2020 IEEE/CVF Conference on Computer Vision and Pattern Recognition (CVPR), pp. 11618–11628 (2019)
10. Chahal, K.S., Dey, K.: A survey of modern object detection literature using deep learning. ArXiv, abs/ arXiv: 1808.07256 (2018)
11. Chan, R., et al.: Segmentmeifyoucan: A benchmark for anomaly segmentation. ArXiv, abs/ arXiv: 2104.14812 (2021)

12. Dathathri, S., et al.: Enabling certification of verification-agnostic networks via memory-efficient semidefinite programming. In: Larochelle, H., Ranzato, M., Hadsell, R., Balcan, M., Lin, H. (eds.) Advances in Neural Information Processing Systems, vol. 33, pp. 5318–5331. Curran Associates Inc. (2020)
13. Diaz-Ruiz, C.A., et al.: Ithaca365: dataset and driving perception under repeated and challenging weather conditions. In: 2022 IEEE/CVF Conference on Computer Vision and Pattern Recognition (CVPR), pp. 21351–21360 (2022)
14. Dong, Y., et al.: Benchmarking robustness of 3d object detection to common corruptions in autonomous driving. ArXiv, abs/ arXiv: 2303.11040 (2023)
15. Fazlyab, M., Morari, M., Pappas, G.J.: Safety verification and robustness analysis of neural networks via quadratic constraints and semidefinite programming. IEEE Trans. Autom. Control **67**(1), 1–15 (2022)
16. Ferrari, C., Mueller, M.N., Jovanović, N., Vechev, M.: Complete verification via multi-neuron relaxation guided branch-and-bound. In: International Conference on Learning Representations (2022)
17. Geiger, A., Lenz, P., Urtasun, R.: Are we ready for autonomous driving? the kitti vision benchmark suite. In: 2012 IEEE Conference on Computer Vision and Pattern Recognition, pp. 3354–3361 (2012)
18. Hendrycks, D., Basart, S., Mazeika, M., Mostajabi, M., Steinhardt, J., Song, D.X.: Scaling out-of-distribution detection for real-world settings. In: International Conference on Machine Learning (2022)
19. Henriksen, P., Lomuscio, A.: Efficient neural network verification via adaptive refinement and adversarial search (2020)
20. Henriksen, P., Lomuscio, A.: Deepsplit: an efficient splitting method for neural network verification via indirect effect analysis. In: Zhou, Z.-H. (ed.) Proceedings of the Thirtieth International Joint Conference on Artificial Intelligence, IJCAI 2021, pp. 2549–2555. International Joint Conferences on Artificial Intelligence Organization, Main Track (Aug 2021)
21. Henriksen, P., Hammernik, K., Rueckert, D., Lomuscio, A.: Bias field robustness verification of large neural image classifiers. In: British Machine Vision Conference (2021)
22. Huang, C., Fan, J., Li, W., Chen, X., Zhu, Q.: Reachnn: reachability analysis of neural-network controlled systems. ACM Trans. Embed. Comput. Syst. **18**(5s) (2019)
23. Ivanov, R., Weimer, J., Alur, R., Pappas, G. J., Lee, I.: Verisig: verifying safety properties of hybrid systems with neural network controllers. In: Proceedings of the 22nd ACM International Conference on Hybrid Systems: Computation and Control, HSCC 2019, pp. 169–178. Association for Computing Machinery, New York (2019)
24. Katz, G., et al.: The marabou framework for verification and analysis of deep neural networks. In: Dillig, I., Tasiran, S. (eds.) CAV 2019. LNCS, vol. 11561, pp. 443–452. Springer, Cham (2019). https://doi.org/10.1007/978-3-030-25540-4_26
25. Katz, S.M., Corso, A., Strong, C.A., Kochenderfer, M.J.: Verification of image-based neural network controllers using generative models. In: 2021 IEEE/AIAA 40th Digital Avionics Systems Conference (DASC), pp. 1–10 (2021)
26. Khedr, H., Ferlez, J., Shoukry, Y.: Effective formal verification of neural networks using the geometry of linear regions. ArXiv, abs/ arXiv: 2006.10864 (2020)
27. Li, K., et al.: A real-world road corner case dataset for object detection in autonomous driving. ArXiv, abs/ arXiv: 2203.07724 (2022)

28. Liu, X., Yang, H., Liu, Z., Song, L., Chen, Y., Li, H.H.: Dpatch: an adversarial patch attack on object detectors. In: Computer Vision and Pattern Recognition (2018)
29. Ma, X.: dog-qiuqiu/yolo-fastestv2: V0.2 (August 2021)
30. Mohapatra, J., Weng, T.-W., Chen, P.-Y., Liu, S., Daniel, L.: Towards verifying robustness of neural networks against a family of semantic perturbations. In: 2020 IEEE/CVF Conference on Computer Vision and Pattern Recognition (CVPR), pp. 241–249 (2020)
31. Muller, M. N., Brix, C., Bak, S., Liu, C., Johnson, T.T.: The third international verification of neural networks competition (vnn-comp 2022): Summary and results (2023)
32. Pinggera, P., Ramos, S., Gehrig, S., Franke, U., Rother, C., Mester, R.: Lost and found: detecting small road hazards for self-driving vehicles. In: 2016 IEEE/RSJ International Conference on Intelligent Robots and Systems (IROS), pp. 1099–1106 (2016)
33. Pitropov, M.A., et al.: Canadian adverse driving conditions dataset. Inter. J. Robo. Res. **40**, 681–690 (2020)
34. Ronneberger, O., Fischer, P., Brox, T.: U-net: convolutional networks for biomedical image segmentation. ArXiv, abs/ arXiv: 1505.04597 (2015)
35. Ruan, W., Wu, M., Sun, Y., Huang, X., Kroening, D., Kwiatkowska, M.: Global robustness evaluation of deep neural networks with provable guarantees for L0 norm. CoRR, abs/ arXiv: 1804.05805 (2018)
36. Salman, H., Yang, G., Zhang, H., Hsieh, C.-J., Zhang, P.: A convex relaxation barrier to tight robustness verification of neural networks. Adv. Neural. Inf. Process. Syst. **32**, 9835–9846 (2019)
37. Shen, J.,et al.: Sok: on the semantic ai security in autonomous driving. ArXiv, abs/ arXiv: 2203.05314 (2022)
38. Singh, G., Gehr, T., Püschel, M., Vechev, M.: An abstract domain for certifying neural networks. Proc. ACM Program. Lang. **3**(POPL) (2019)
39. Sun, P., Kretzschmar, H., et al.: Scalability in perception for autonomous driving: Waymo open dataset. In: 2020 IEEE/CVF Conference on Computer Vision and Pattern Recognition (CVPR), pp. 2443–2451 (2020)
40. Thoma, M.: A survey of semantic segmentation. ArXiv, abs/ arXiv: 1602.06541 (2016)
41. Tjeng, V., Xiao, K. Y., Tedrake, R.: Evaluating robustness of neural networks with mixed integer programming. In: International Conference on Learning Representations (2017)
42. Tran, H.-D., Cai, F., Diego, M. L., Musau, P., Johnson, T.T., Koutsoukos, X.: Safety verification of cyber-physical systems with reinforcement learning control. ACM Trans. Embed. Comput. Syst., **18**(5s) (2019)
43. Tran, H.-D., Bak, S., Xiang, W., Johnson, T.T.: Verification of deep convolutional neural networks using imagestars. In: Lahiri, S.K., Wang, C. (eds.) CAV 2020. LNCS, vol. 12224, pp. 18–42. Springer, Cham (2020). https://doi.org/10.1007/978-3-030-53288-8_2
44. Tran, H.-D., et al.: Robustness verification of semantic segmentation neural networks using relaxed reachability. In: Silva, A., Leino, K.R.M. (eds.) CAV 2021. LNCS, vol. 12759, pp. 263–286. Springer, Cham (2021). https://doi.org/10.1007/978-3-030-81685-8_12
45. Wang, S., et al.: Beta-CROWN: efficient bound propagation with per-neuron split constraints for complete and incomplete neural network verification. In: Advances in Neural Information Processing Systems 34 (2021)

46. Xu, K., et al.: Automatic perturbation analysis for scalable certified robustness and beyond. In: Advances in Neural Information Processing Systems 33 (2020)
47. Xu, K., et al.: Fast and complete: enabling complete neural network verification with rapid and massively parallel incomplete verifiers. In: International Conference on Learning Representations (2021)
48. Yurtsever, E., Lambert, J., Carballo, A., Takeda, K.: A survey of autonomous driving: common practices and emerging technologies. IEEE Access **8**, 58443–58469 (2019)
49. Zhang, H., Weng, T.-W., Chen, P.-Y., Hsieh, C.-J., Daniel, L.: Efficient neural network robustness certification with general activation functions. In: Proceedings of the 32nd International Conference on Neural Information Processing Systems, NIPS 2018, pp. 4944–4953. Curran Associates Inc., Red Hook (2018)
50. Zhang, H., et al.: General cutting planes for bound-propagation-based neural network verification. In: Advances in Neural Information Processing Systems (2022)
51. Zhang, H., et al.: A branch and bound framework for stronger adversarial attacks of ReLU networks. In: Proceedings of the 39th International Conference on Machine Learning, vol. 162, pp. 26591–26604 (2022)
52. Zhang, J., Zou, X., Kuang, L., Wang, J., Sherratt, R., Yu, X.: Cctsdb 2021: a more comprehensive traffic sign detection benchmark. Human-centric Comput. Inform. Sci. **12**, 23 (2022)

Benchmark: Neural Network Malware Classification

Preston K. Robinette(✉), Diego Manzanas Lopez, and Taylor T. Johnson

Vanderbilt University, Nashville, TN 37212, USA
{preston.k.robinette,diego.manzanas.lopez,taylor.johnson}@vanderbilt.edu

Abstract. As malware threats continue to increase in both complexity and sophistication, the adoption of advanced detection methods, such as deep neural networks (DNNs) for malware classification, has become increasingly vital to safeguard digital infrastructure and protect sensitive data. In order to measure progress in this safety-critical landscape, we propose two malware classification benchmarks: a feature-based benchmark and an image-based benchmark. Feature-based datasets provide a detailed understanding of malware characteristics, and image-based datasets transform raw malware binary data into grayscale images for swift processing. These datasets can be used for both binary classification (benign vs. malicious) as well as classifying known malware into a particular family. This paper, therefore, introduces two benchmark datasets for binary and family classification with varying difficulty levels to quantify improvements in malware classification strategies. Key contributions include the creation of feature and image dataset benchmarks, and the validation of a trained binary classification network using the feature dataset benchmark. Benchmarks as well as example training code are available.

Keywords: Malware · Verification · Benchmarks

1 Introduction

Malware is any software designed with malicious intent. Various types of harmful software include stealing sensitive data (data theft [4,6]), monitoring activity and passwords (espionage [15]), the creation of a 'botnet' (Distributed Denial of Service (DDoS) [1]), stealing data and holding it for ransom (ransomware attacks [7]), using someone else's system to mine cryptocurrency (cryptojacking [11]), and distributing spam [5]. To mitigate the harmful effects of malware, defense mechanisms rely upon the ability to distinguish between benign software and malicious software. If malware can be detected, it can be effectively isolated and neutralized before it has a chance to compromise the system. This early detection is not only pivotal for securing individual systems but also plays a crucial role in preventing the spread of malware across networks, thereby fortifying overall cybersecurity infrastructure. It also facilitates the process of reverse

B. Steffen (Ed.): AISoLA 2023, LNCS 14380, pp. 291–298, 2024.
https://doi.org/10.1007/978-3-031-46002-9_17

engineering the malware to understand its functionality and to devise robust countermeasures for similar threats in the future[1].

As the sophistication of these threats continues to increase, more advanced methods for detection and classification have become necessary. One such method is the application of deep neural networks (DNN) for malware classification [2,3,8,10,12,13]. Neural network malware classifiers are usually trained on either feature datasets or image datasets. Feature datasets consist of numerical or categorical attributes extracted from malware samples, such as opcode frequencies, system calls, file sizes, and other static or dynamic features. These feature sets are designed to capture the distinctive behaviors or properties of malicious software. On the other hand, image datasets involve a transformation of the raw binary data of malware files into grayscale images, which depict the visual patterns underlying the malware's binary structure.

Both approaches present their own advantages. Feature-based datasets can provide a detailed overview of the malware's characteristics, facilitating a deeper understanding of the malware's functionality and behavior. This approach, however, can be time-consuming and requires expert knowledge to identify and extract the most relevant features. In contrast, image-based datasets can be processed quickly and do not necessitate the tedious task of feature selection.

While feature datasets are most commonly used for binary classification of either benign or malicious, image datasets tend to also be used to classify malware families. This is particularly useful, as malware belonging to the same family often share a common code base and exhibit similar patterns of behavior. By identifying the malware family, cybersecurity experts can gain insights into the malware's likely origin, its potential behavior, and the most effective countermeasures. Additionally, this classification aids in tracking the evolution of different malware strains and anticipates emerging threats.

As threats continue to evolve and the methods we use to combat against them improve as well, it is imperative to provide benchmark datasets in this domain to quantify improvements in both classification strategies as well as verification tools. In addition to datasets utilized in this paper, which are representative of the state-of-the-art in this domain, the property verified is also an important factor as well. As this is the first benchmark for malware classification, the verification process needs to be thorough and comprehensive, ensuring that the system's robustness is not solely reliant on specific data but can generalize well across varied and potentially unseen malicious threats. Thus, this paper introduces two benchmark datasets (a feature dataset and an image dataset), which evaluate how robust a classifier is against adversarial attacks and dataset shifts. The contributions of this work, therefore, are the following:

1. Introduction of a feature dataset benchmark for binary classification, consisting of three different difficulty levels.
2. Introduction of an image dataset benchmark for family classification, consisting of three different difficulty levels.

[1] Code: https://github.com/pkrobinette/malware_benchmarks.

3. A trained binary classification network verified using the feature dataset benchmark.

2 Preliminaries

In this section, we introduce robustness and the malware datasets used for benchmarking: (1) a feature dataset, which represents malware samples as vectors of data such as byte entropy and string length, and (2) an image dataset, which represents malware samples as grayscale images.

2.1 Feature Datasets

Malware feature datasets are composed of 'features' extracted from collected samples, which can be either benign or malicious. Common features include file properties, binary content, API calls, network activities, registry key modifications, and embedded resources. These data points form a comprehensive profile of each software sample, providing vital clues about its behavior, origin, and potential harm. By analyzing these features, cybersecurity experts can accurately classify software as benign or malicious and identify novel malware variants. In addition to static features, feature datasets can include dynamic attributes, such as runtime behavior, system interactions, and state changes over time. Dynamic attributes provide insights into how the software behaves when executed, including changes made to files, registries, and the system memory. They can also capture network connections initiated, services used, and any suspicious activities like process injection, encryption of user files, or attempts to evade detection. These dynamic behaviors, combined with static features, help create a more holistic understanding of the malware's functionality and impact, enhancing the effectiveness of threat detection and prevention mechanisms.

BODMAS. While there are many publicly available feature datasets, we utilize the Blue Hexagon Open Dataset for Malware Analysis, or BODMAS [14]. BODMAS contains 77,142 benign samples (marked as label 0) and 57,293 malicious samples (marked as label 1). Each sample is represented by a vector of 2381 features extracted using both dynamic and static analysis methods with the aid of the LIEF project [9]. Table 1 shows the seven distinct datatype categories contained in the dataset. These data types are used to distinguish between benchmark difficulty levels.

2.2 Image Datasets

As extracting static and dynamic features requires expert knowledge and is time-intensive, researchers have also utilized image alternatives. A sample binary is segmented into bytes, and these bytes are then converted into grayscale pixel values. For instance, if the binary file contains the sequence 0100010010010111, this would be chunked into 8 bits (a byte): [01000100, 10010111], and converted

Table 1. The data types contained in the BODMAS dataset. Each feature data type has a distinct range, which demonstrates the need for a range-specific perturbation.

Feature Type	Count	Max Range Pre-Scale	Max Range Post-Scale	Example
Continuous	5	[5.0, 2.0e5]	[−0.1, 304.6]	Entropy of the file
Categorical	8	[0.0, 6.5e4]	[−0.0, 124.3]	Machine type
Hash Categorical	560	[−647.6, 15.4]	[0.0, 361.0]	Hash of original file
Discrete with Large Range	34	[0.0, 4.3e9]	[−0.0, 261.6]	Number of occurrences of each byte value within the file
Binary	5	[0.0, 1.0]	[−2.1, 0.5]	Presence of debug section
Hash Categorical Discrete	1531	[−8.0e6, 1.6e9]	[−327.9, 164.0]	Hash of target system type
Memory Related	16	[0.0, 4.0e9]	[−0.1, 307.5]	Size of the original file
Null	222	[−31.0, 60.0]	[−0.9, 160.4]	—

to decimal: [68, 151]. These would be two-pixel values in the corresponding grayscale image of the binary. Image-level representations provide a quick alternative to static and dynamic analysis, while still providing valuable insights into the structure and patterns inherent in the binary data. The graphical patterns formed by these binary sequences can be distinctive, enabling models to learn and identify specific behaviors and characteristics of the represented software. This approach significantly reduces the time and complexity of feature extraction while maintaining a high level of analysis precision.

Malimg. We utilize the Malimg Dataset in this work. The Malimg dataset is composed of 9339 malware images from 25 different malware families [8]. Table 2 shows the breakdown of samples per family as well as the family hierarchies. For instance, *Allaple.A* and *Allaple.L* are two different families that fall under the same type of attack: *Worm*. As there are large differences between the number of represented samples (*Allaple.A*: 2949 samples vs. *Skintrim.N*: 80 samples), this adds to the difficulty of verifying specific malware families.

2.3 Robustness

As malware attacks evolve, we want classification systems that are robust against changing adversarial attacks. To quantify this goal, these benchmarks focus on a robustness verification property – given changes in a sample (changing adversarial attacks), can the classification system correctly classify samples even in the presence of change? For instance, let a neural network classifier be denoted as f, an input $x \in \mathbb{R}^{n \times m}$, target $y \in \mathbb{R}^N$ where N is the number of classes, perturbation parameter $\epsilon \in \mathbb{R}$, and an input set R containing x_p such that $X_p = \{x : ||x - x_p||_\infty \leq \epsilon\}$ which represents the set of all possible perturbations

Table 2. Malimg dataset details.

No.	Family	Family Name	No. of Samples
01	Dialer	Adialer.C	122
02	Backdoor	Agent.FYI	116
03	Worm	Allaple.A	2949
04	Worm	Allaple.L	1591
05	Trojan	Alueron.gen!J	198
06	Worm:AutoIT	Autorun.K	106
07	Trojan	C2Lop.P	146
08	Trojan	C2Lop.gen!G	200
09	Dialer	Dialplatform.B	177
10	Trojan Downloader	Dontovo.A	162
11	Rogue	Fakerean	381
12	Dialer	Instantaccess	431
13	PWS	Lolyda.AA 1	213
14	PWS	Lolyda.AA 2	184
15	PWS	Lolyda.AA 3	123
16	PWS	Lolyda.AT	159
17	Trojan	Malex.gen !J	136
18	Trojan Downloader	Obfuscator.AD	142
19	Backdoor	Rbot!gen	158
20	Trojan	Skintrim.N	80
21	Trojan Downloader	Swizzor.gen!E	128
22	Trojan Downloader	Swizzor.gen!I	132
23	Worm	VB.AT	408
24	Trojan Downloader	Wintrim.BX	97
25	Worm	Yuner.A	800

of x where $||x - x_p||_\infty$ is the $\mathcal{L}_\infty$ norm. A model is robust at x if all the perturbed inputs x_p are classified to the same label as y, e.g., the system is **robust** if $f(x_p) = f(x) = y$ for all $x_p \in X_p$. In this way, we can verify that a classification system will be useful in future situations, not just against known malware patterns in the present.

3 Benchmarks

In this section, we introduce each of the malware benchmarks in more detail.

3.1 Malware Feature Benchmark

The malware feature benchmark consists of 200 samples taken from a stratified sampling of the entire BODMAS dataset, giving a split of 43% malicious samples. While the specific samples do not have varying levels of difficulty, the data type used during the perturbation as well as the size of the perturbation lends itself to levels of verification difficulty. The level, corresponding data type, and epsilon used for each benchmark are described in Table 3.

Table 3. Malware feature dataset details (BODMAS).

Benchmark Level	**Perturbation Data Type**	**Perturbation Size(ϵ^*)**
Level 1	Continuous	0.01
Level 2	Continuous and Discrete	0.025
Level 3	All	0.001

Table 4. Malware image dataset details (Malimg).

Benchmark Level	**Perturbation Size(ϵ)**
Level 1	5
Level 2	10
Level 3	15

The $\mathcal{L}_\infty$ perturbation of size ϵ^* is applied to the range of each feature of the corresponding datatype. For example, if feature 1 has a range $[3, 567]$, the $\mathcal{L}_\infty$ bound with $\epsilon^* = 0.1\%$ would be $\pm 0.56 = 0.1\% \times (567 - 3)$. ϵ^* here represents the modification to the range of each feature. For all samples s and for the designated features f (dependent on benchmark level) within that sample, the perturbation ϵ used for verification is defined as ϵ^* of the range of that feature, i.e., $\epsilon_{s,f} = \epsilon^* \text{range}_{s,f}$. This provides a more feature realistic perturbation to each sample. Even though the perturbed features will all be of the same datatype, the ranges for those features can be drastically different, making it important to consider the range for each particular feature of the corresponding datatype.

3.2 Malware Image Benchmark

Whereas the malware feature dataset verifies different data types and perturbation sizes, the malware image dataset only focuses on verifying different perturbation sizes in each level. The verification dataset consists of 5 randomly sampled images from each malware family, which makes a total of 125 images of pixel values in the range $[0, 255]$. Each level consists of an $\mathcal{L}_\infty$ perturbation on the pixel values of the verification image. A perturbation size of $\epsilon = 3$ indicates that the value of each pixel in the image is allowed to be changed by ± 3. The level and corresponding perturbation sizes ϵ are shown in Table 4.

4 Benchmark Demonstration

To demonstrate the use of these benchmarks, we demonstrate the verification of a binary neural network classifier trained on the BODMAS dataset. First, we train a neural network with an input layer of 2381, one hidden layer of size 32, and an output layer of size 2 (binary classification). This model is trained with an Adam optimizer and a learning rate of 0.001 for 20 epochs. The testing performance of this trained model is shown in Table 5.

Table 5. Binary neural network classifier model performance.

Metric	Value
Accuracy	1.0
Precision	0.99
Recall	1.0
F1	1.0

From these results, the model performs well on the test set, as indicated by the high value for each metric. We then verify this model using the level 2 feature benchmark, which results in the successful robustness verification of 103 out of 200 images[2]. This means that only about 50% of the tested samples were verified within the given perturbation; this does not bode well for the tested classifier as we would want a higher verification rate to ensure confidence in its robustness, especially in real-world scenarios where diverse adversarial attacks might be more prevalent. This result highlights the importance of using benchmarks to compare trained classifiers. Just based on the metrics, the trained model performs well. Considering the verification, however, our model may not be as robust as we would like.

5 Conclusion

In this work, we introduce two malware classifier benchmarks: a feature benchmark and an image benchmark. Each benchmark consists of 3 different difficulty levels. The feature benchmark is distinguished by the data types perturbed, whereas the image benchmark is distinguished by perturbation size. These novel benchmarks will be pivotal in quantifying improvements in the safety-critical domain of malware classification.

Acknowledgement. This paper was supported in part by a fellowship award under contract FA9550-21-F-0003 through the National Defense Science and Engineering Graduate (NDSEG) Fellowship Program, sponsored by the Air Force Research Laboratory (AFRL), the Office of Naval Research (ONR), and the Army Research Office (ARO). The material presented in this paper is based upon work supported by the National Science Foundation (NSF) through grant numbers 2220426 and 2220401,

[2] Code available here: https://github.com/pkrobinette/malware_benchmarks.

the Defense Advanced Research Projects Agency (DARPA) under contract number FA8750-23-C-0518, and the Air Force Office of Scientific Research (AFOSR) under contract number FA9550-22-1-0019 and FA9550-23-1-0135. Any opinions, findings, and conclusions or recommendations expressed in this paper are those of the authors and do not necessarily reflect the views of AFOSR, DARPA, or NSF.

References

1. Antonakakis, M., et al.: Understanding the MIRAI botnet. In: 26th {USENIX} security symposium ({USENIX} Security 17), pp. 1093–1110 (2017)
2. Awan, M.J., et al.: Image-based malware classification using VGG19 network and spatial convolutional attention. Electronics **10**(19), 2444 (2021)
3. Bhodia, N., Prajapati, P., Di Troia, F., Stamp, M.: Transfer learning for image-based malware classification. arXiv preprint arXiv:1903.11551 (2019)
4. Carvalho, M., DeMott, J., Ford, R., Wheeler, D.A.: Heartbleed 101. IEEE Secur. Privacy **12**(4), 63–67 (2014). https://doi.org/10.1109/MSP.2014.66
5. Khan, I., Kwon, Y.W.: Attention-based malware detection of android applications. In: 2022 IEEE International Conference on Big Data (Big Data), pp. 6693–6695 (2022). https://doi.org/10.1109/BigData55660.2022.10020684
6. Lipp, M., et al.: Meltdown: reading kernel memory from user space. In: 27th USENIX Security Symposium (USENIX Security 18) (2018)
7. McIntosh, T., Kayes, A.S.M., Chen, Y.P.P., Ng, A., Watters, P.: Ransomware mitigation in the modern era: a comprehensive review, research challenges, and future directions. ACM Comput. Surv. **54**(9) (2021). https://doi.org/10.1145/3479393
8. Nataraj, L., Karthikeyan, S., Jacob, G., Manjunath, B.S.: Malware images: visualization and automatic classification. In: Proceedings of the 8th International Symposium on Visualization for Cyber Security, pp. 1–7 (2011)
9. Oyama, Y., Miyashita, T., Kokubo, H.: Identifying useful features for malware detection in the ember dataset. In: 2019 Seventh International Symposium on Computing and Networking Workshops (CANDARW), pp. 360–366 (2019). https://doi.org/10.1109/CANDARW.2019.00069
10. Singh, A., Handa, A., Kumar, N., Shukla, S.K.: Malware classification using image representation. In: Dolev, S., Hendler, D., Lodha, S., Yung, M. (eds.) CSCML 2019. LNCS, vol. 11527, pp. 75–92. Springer, Cham (2019). https://doi.org/10.1007/978-3-030-20951-3_6
11. Tekiner, E., Acar, A., Uluagac, A.S., Kirda, E., Selcuk, A.A.: SOK: cryptojacking malware. In: 2021 IEEE European Symposium on Security and Privacy (EuroS&P), pp. 120–139. IEEE (2021)
12. Vasan, D., Alazab, M., Wassan, S., Naeem, H., Safaei, B., Zheng, Q.: IMCFN: image-based malware classification using fine-tuned convolutional neural network architecture. Comput. Netw. **171**, 107138 (2020)
13. Vasan, D., Alazab, M., Wassan, S., Safaei, B., Zheng, Q.: Image-based malware classification using ensemble of CNN architectures (IMCEC). Comput. Secur. **92**, 101748 (2020)
14. Yang, L., Ciptadi, A., Laziuk, I., Ahmadzadeh, A., Wang, G.: BODMAS: an open dataset for learning based temporal analysis of PE malware. In: 4th Deep Learning and Security Workshop (2021)
15. Zhang, F., Wang, H., Leach, K., Stavrou, A.: A framework to secure peripherals at runtime. In: Kutyłowski, M., Vaidya, J. (eds.) ESORICS 2014. LNCS, vol. 8712, pp. 219–238. Springer, Cham (2014). https://doi.org/10.1007/978-3-319-11203-9_13

Benchmark: Remaining Useful Life Predictor for Aircraft Equipment

Dmitrii Kirov[1(✉)] and Simone Fulvio Rollini[2]

[1] Collins Aerospace, Trento, Italy
dmitrii.kirov@collins.com
[2] Collins Aerospace, Rome, Italy

Abstract. We propose a predictive maintenance application as a benchmark problem for verification of neural networks (VNN). It is a deep learning based estimator of remaining useful life (RUL) of aircraft mechanical components, such as bearings. We implement the estimator as a convolutional neural network. We then provide mathematical formalizations of its non-functional requirements, such as stability and monotonicity, as properties. These properties can be used to assess the applicability and the scalability of existing VNN tools.

URL. Benchmark materials, such as trained models (.onnx), examples of properties (.vnnlib), test datasets, and property generation procedures, are available at https://github.com/loonwerks/vnncomp2022.

1 Introduction

Remaining Useful Life (RUL) is a widely used metric in Prognostics and Health Management (PHM) that manifests the remaining lifetime of a component (e.g., mechanical bearing, hydraulic pump, aircraft engine). RUL is used for *condition-based maintenance* to support aircraft maintenance and flight preparation. It contributes to such tasks as augmented manual inspection of components and scheduling of maintenance cycles for components, such as repair or replacement, thus moving from preventive maintenance to predictive maintenance (do maintenance only when needed, based on component's current condition and estimated future condition). This could allow to eliminate or to extend service operations and inspection periods, optimize component servicing (e.g., lubricant replacement), generate inspection and maintenance schedules, and obtain significant cost savings. RUL could also highlight areas for inspection during the next planned maintenance, i.e., it could be used to move up a maintenance/inspection action to prevent component failure. Finally, RUL function can also be used in airborne (in-flight) applications to dynamically inform pilots on the health state of aircraft components during flight.

Multivariate time series data is often used as RUL function input, for example, measurements from a set of sensors monitoring the component state, taken at several subsequent time steps (within a time window). Additional inputs may include information about current flight phase, mission and environment.

B. Steffen (Ed.): AISoLA 2023, LNCS 14380, pp. 299–304, 2024.
https://doi.org/10.1007/978-3-031-46002-9_18

Such highly multi-dimensional input space motivates the use of Machine Learning (ML), more precisely, Deep Learning (DL) solutions with their capabilities of performing automatic feature extraction from raw data. A number of solutions based on Deep Neural Networks (DNNs) has emerged over recent years (e.g., [4–6]).

An example of a DL-based RUL function is illustrated in Fig. 1. The DL model is a Convolutional Neural Network (CNN) that accepts as input a time window of length 40, i.e., snapshots reflecting the bearing state taken at 40 consecutive time steps. Each time step corresponds to 1 h. Each snapshot contains the following information:

- Seven Condition Indicators (CIs) that provide numerical information about the bearing degradation, obtained from signal processing of measurements of the vibration sensor attached to the bearing.
- Information about the current mission: current flight regime, such as ascent, cruise and descent, with corresponding nominal component load (bearing RUL heavily depends on how the component is loaded), mission type (a set of predefined mission patterns is available, e.g., long, short, mixed).
- Information about the current flight environment (e.g., desert or non-desert).

CI values are computed by the Health Usage Monitoring System (HUMS), while remaining inputs are provided by other avionics software. Snapshots are provided to the input generator, where they are stored in memory and periodically shifted to yield a new consecutive time window. Output of the CNN is a numerical non-negative value that represents the bearing RUL in hours. It is provided to the end users, such as pilots and MRO (Maintenance, Repair and Overhaul) via cockpit and ground station displays. Additional pre- and post-processing of the CNN (e.g., input normalization) is not described due to space limitations, details are available in [2].

2 Model Description

We propose a Convolutional Neural Network (CNN) model adapted from [1] as a benchmark for the competition. It corresponds to the use case described above. The CNN accepts as input a sequence (time window) of inputs. The inputs are snapshots of condition indicators at a given time step, as well as other metrics. Several convolutional layers are used to apply 1D convolutions to the inputs along the time sequence direction. Extracted features are then merged together via a fully connected layer. Dropout is used to mitigate overfitting. Activation functions at all layers are Rectified Linear Units (ReLUs). The CNN performs a regression task and outputs a numerical value, which is the RUL.

Several neural networks of different complexity are provided:

- **NN_rul_small_window20.onnx** (number of ReLUs - 5500)
- **NN_rul_full_window20.onnx** (number of ReLUs - 10300)
- **NN_rul_full_window40.onnx** (number of ReLUs - 28300)

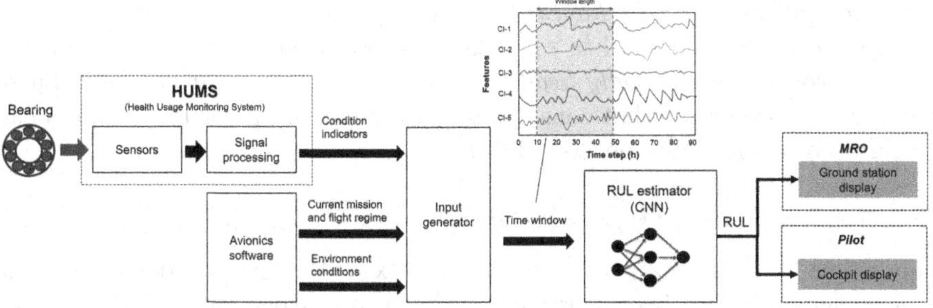

Fig. 1. Overview of the RUL estimator and its context.

All networks have been trained using the same dataset. The motivation for providing several networks is the scalability study. The number of ReLUs is different for each network. This seems to be one of the key complexity metrics for many VNN tools. Internally, networks have the same architecture/layers, but some different hyperparameters, such as the number of filters in convolutional layers ("small" networks have fewer filters, "full" networks have more). Also, two window sizes (20 and 40) have been used to generate the networks. While the number of input features remains constant for all networks, manipulating the window size allows to change the input space size (2× in the case of window sizes used). Change in window size has a more significant impact on the overall CNN complexity.

3 Properties Description

We propose several classes of properties for the NN-based RUL estimation function. First two classes (stability and monotonicity) are *local*, i.e., defined around a given point. To address the requirement for randomizing the inputs to VNN tools, we provide a script with adjustable random seed that can generate these properties around input points randomly picked from a test dataset. Properties of the last class ("if-then") are defined over input ranges. We have generated a list of such properties and provide means for randomly selecting properties from this list. Below, a short description of each property class is provided.

3.1 Stability Properties

ML model is *stable* if a small, bounded perturbation applied to its inputs in normal operating conditions, i.e., when the inputs are inside the ML model's operational design domain, does not cause a significant deviation in its output. Here, we focus on perturbations of condition indicator (CI) inputs. Corresponding model stability requirement could be formulated as follows: *"For a simultaneous perturbation of one or many CIs at a single time step (e.g., due to a resonance frequency) within any time window, the output deviation of the RUL* *estimator shall not exceed ϵ hours. The maximum admissible perturbation that can occur to a CI input shall be equal to δ% of the average initial value of that CI that corresponds to a fully healthy state of the bearing component".* Then, local stability properties that consider perturbations of one or more inputs can be expressed in the "delta-epsilon" form:

$$\forall \mathbf{x}' : \forall i \in S : |x_i'^t - x_i^t| < \delta_i |x_i^*| \implies |f(x') - f(x)| < \epsilon, \tag{1}$$

where prime (′) denotes a *perturbed* item (i.e., $\mathbf{x}'$ is the time window where one or more elements have been perturbed; $x_i'^t$ is a perturbed value of the CI i at time step t; $f(\mathbf{x}')$ is the ML model output computed from the perturbed input), x_i^* represents the average initial value of the CI i, computed over all data, S is a subset of the indexes corresponding to perturbed CIs, δ_i is the bound on the input perturbation for a chosen CI i *w.r.t.* x_i^* (expressed as a percentage), and ϵ is the maximum admissible output change.

The property requires that for any input perturbation applied to CIs from the set S, bounded by a corresponding δ_i, the output must not deviate by more than ϵ (L_∞ norm is used to define perturbations). Stability properties provided in this benchmark differ in the number of perturbed CIs and perturbation magnitudes.

3.2 Monotonicity Properties

Differently from stability requirements, the requirements on monotonicity of the RUL estimator concern all steps of the input window, i.e., within the entire window. This is a realistic situation that may occur, for example, due to damage or excessive load in the bearing that leads to an increased degradation rate. Therefore, such changes in the CIs over the entire time window shall not be identified by data quality indicators in the HUMS as abnormal (unlike random spikes/perturbations occurring at multiple time steps). Monotonicity requirements prescribe a non-increasing behavior of the estimator given a change in the growth rate (higher or smaller) of one or more condition indicators.

Condition indicators are correlated with component degradation and failures. Their values are expected to *monotonically increase* during the use of the bearing component, which reflects its degradation. Consequently, the bearing RUL is expected to *monotonically decrease.* Expected behavior of the RUL estimator output is monotonic with respect to the inputs (CIs), i.e., when CIs increase the RUL should decrease.

A growth rate increase of a CI by some percentage represents a different CI "trajectory" within the time window. Such new trajectory can be used as an upper bound, while the original CI growth trend represents a lower bound. The verification strategy is to analyze all possible CI trajectories within these bounds. Let $\mathbf{x_i}$ be the vector of values of some CI i in the time window, x_i^t being the CI value at time step t. Local monotonicity property for this CI can be formulated as

$$\forall \mathbf{x}' : \forall t : x_i^t \leq x_i'^t \leq x_i^t + \gamma|x_i^t - x_i^1| \implies f(\mathbf{x}') \leq f(\mathbf{x}) \tag{2}$$

where prime (′) denotes a modified item (i.e., $\mathbf{x}'$ is the time window, where one or more CIs have modified growth rates *w.r.t.* the original time window $\mathbf{x}$; $x_i'^t$ is a modified value of the CI i at time step t; $f(\mathbf{x}')$ is the ML model output computed from the modified input), and γ (gamma) is the parameter that regulates the CI slope change.

This property states that for any growing CI trajectory bounded by the original CI trajectory (lower bound) and the one changed by a percentage γ (upper bound), i.e., a steeper growth trend, the RUL shall be non-increasing *w.r.t.* the original CI trajectory. The difference $|x_i^t - x_i^1|$ represents an approximation of the CI slope in the interval $[1, t]$. Further discussion on formalization of monotonicity properties for the RUL is available in [2].

3.3 If-Then Properties

These properties are formulated as follows: IF the CNN inputs are in given ranges, THEN the output (RUL) must be in an expected range. To generate such properties, input ranges of some inputs have been broken down into several sub-ranges (e.g., Low, Medium, High) with corresponding lower and upper bounds. For each combination of these sub-ranges, an expected output range has been estimated. Given these numerical bounds on input/output ranges, if-then properties are straightforward to formulate.

NOTE. Given the number of combinations of input ranges, the number of if-then properties can be extremely large. Therefore, for this benchmark we have generated only a small subset of such properties with different complexity, based on size and the number of the ranges. The properties are randomly selected from this subset. If-Then properties are currently the hardest to verify.

4 Concluding Remarks

We have proposed a benchmark problem for neural network verification tools – a convolutional neural network that predicts remaining useful life of a mechanical component. Property verification an important capability in learning assurance. European Union Aviation Safety Agency (EASA) in their AI Concept Paper [3] emphasizes Formal Methods as anticipated means of compliance for the verification of ML models and their properties, such as robustness.

Acknowledgement. The authors wish to thank Eric DeWind and David F. Larsen for fruitful discussions and feedback about the RUL estimator and its properties, as well as for providing mechanical bearing degradation datasets to prepare this benchmark problem.

References

1. Remaining Useful Life Estimation using Convolutional Neural Network. https://www.mathworks.com/help/releases/R2021a/predmaint/ug/remaining-useful-life-estimation-using-convolutional-neural-network.html

2. EASA and Collins Aerospace: Formal Methods use for Learning Assurance (ForMuLA). Technical report (2023)
3. European Union Aviation Safety Agency (EASA): Concept Paper: Guidance for Level 1&2 Machine Learning Applications. Concept paper for consultation (2023)
4. Li, X., Ding, Q., Sun, J.Q.: Remaining useful life estimation in prognostics using deep convolution neural networks. In: Reliability Engineering & System Safety, pp. 1–11 (2018)
5. Ren, L., Cui, J., Sun, Y., Cheng, X.: Multi-bearing remaining useful life collaborative prediction: a deep learning approach. J. Manuf. Syst. **43**, 248–256 (2017)
6. Yuan, M., Wu, Y., Lin, L.: Fault diagnosis and remaining useful life estimation of aero engine using LSTM neural network. In: 2016 IEEE International Conference on Aircraft Utility Systems (AUS), pp. 135–140. IEEE (2016)

Benchmark: Object Detection for Maritime Search and Rescue

Dmitrii Kirov[1(✉)], Simone Fulvio Rollini[2], Rohit Chandrahas[3], Shashidhar Reddy Chandupatla[4], and Rajdeep Sawant[4]

[1] Collins Aerospace, Trento, Italy
dmitrii.kirov@collins.com
[2] Collins Aerospace, Rome, Italy
[3] Collins Aerospace, Bangalore, India
[4] Collins Aerospace, Hyderabad, India

Abstract. We propose an object detection system for maritime search and rescue as a benchmark problem for verification of neural networks (VNN). The model to be verified is a YOLO (You Only Look Once) deep neural network for object detection and classification and has a very high number of learnable parameters (millions). We describe the workflow for defining and generating robustness properties in the regions of interest of the images, i.e., in the neighborhood of the objects to be detected by the neural network. This benchmark can be used to assess the applicability and the scalability of existing VNN tools for perception systems based on deep learning.

URL. Benchmark materials, such as trained models (.onnx), examples of properties (.vnnlib), test images, and property generation procedures, are available at https://github.com/loonwerks/vnncomp2023.

1 Introduction

Generally, maritime surveillance has been conducted using means such as satellites and manned aircraft. These have been limited in their ability to provide high-resolution, real-time video processing for various reasons. For example, satellite bandwidth is not ideal to handle large amounts of real time data, while rotorcrafts and fixed wing platforms can be very expensive. Current developments with quadcopters and other small drones have enabled additional options that are much cheaper than larger aircraft. Such unmanned vehicles can be equipped with various sensors and signal processing algorithms to enable automated identification of regions where search and rescue efforts may be focused, thereby reducing the time to rescue that can be very limited [1].

One enabling technology for this application is computer vision that is powered by state-of-the-art Machine Learning (ML) algorithms and provides reliable object detection and classification functions. Trustworthiness of these ML-based functions is of paramount importance, because their degraded performances and failures may significantly reduce the chances of people in distress to be rescued timely, thus impacting the safety. Therefore, *learning assurance* process

B. Steffen (Ed.): AISoLA 2023, LNCS 14380, pp. 305–310, 2024.
https://doi.org/10.1007/978-3-031-46002-9_19

and methods [4] need to be applied to guarantee the expected performance and the robustness of the ML-based search and rescue system. In particular, *formal methods* can be effective means of assessing the robustness of perception-based models, for example, to noise and other adverse inputs [3].

This benchmark problem intends to challenge the VNN community in the direction of verifying properties of large-scale neural networks for computer vision, such as object detection networks. It has also been submitted to the 2023 VNNComp event[1], along with few other benchmarks on YOLO neural networks. To the best of our knowledge, this is the first time when such benchmarks have been proposed for VNN tools.

2 Model Description

The object detection model chosen as a basis of the benchmark is a YOLOv5-nano neural network (NN). The objective is to assess current capabilities of VNN tools for verifying properties of deep neural networks of high complexity, such as YOLOs. The "nano" version of a YOLO has been selected for the sake of an incremental approach to complexity. It contains much fewer learnable parameters compared to its original, full-scale YOLO version. Furthermore, to make the model supported by VNN tools, SiLU activation functions have been replaced with (piecewise linear) Leaky ReLU activations.

The model has been trained on the SeaDronesSee dataset[2] [2,5] consisting of maritime search and rescue scenarios captured using a drone, generated by the University of Tuebingen. Examples of images used in the benchmark are shown on Fig. 1. The dataset includes of 8930 training images and 1547 validation images, all of which are labelled with bounding boxes and corresponding classes. There are six classes in the dataset, such as "boat", "person", "jetski". The intended function of the YOLO model is to detect objects of these classes on the water surface, draw bounding boxes around them, and classify them. Model outputs can be communicated to the operator at the ground station who can use this information to dispatch rescue missions and vehicles.

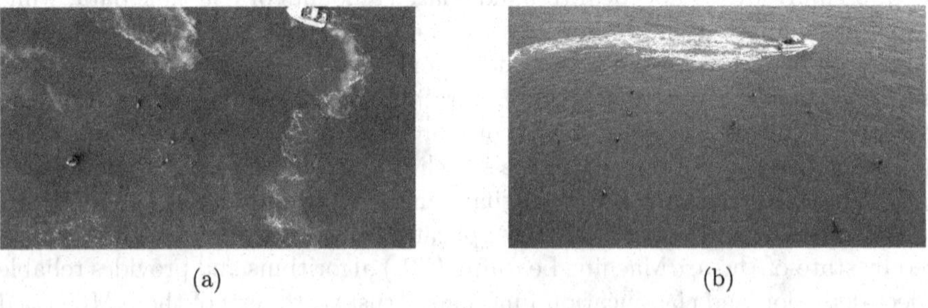

(a) (b)

Fig. 1. Examples of images used to formalize benchmark properties.

[1] https://sites.google.com/view/vnn2023.

[2] SeaDronesSee dataset is used on a license.

The YOLOv5-nano model has 157 layers and around 1.8×10^6 learnable parameters. The training has been done with an input image size of 640×640. The model has 3 output layers. The total input and output size of the model are, respectively, 1.2×10^6 and 277×10^3 (note that the numbers have been rounded).

3 Property Description

This benchmark focuses on robustness properties that are formalized using L_∞ norms, same as in many other existing benchmarks and applications. Such evaluation is an important starting point in assessing the applicability of VNN tools to object detection models, such as YOLO.

3.1 Robustness Properties Overview

Robustness properties are formulated by applying perturbations to selected inputs and requiring that the predicted class remains unchanged, while allowing for a bounded decrease of the confidence of object existence. The motivation is to keep the object detector robust, for example, to different lighting conditions and, possibly, to adversarial attacks. Robustness is particularly relevant to the detection of swimmers on the water surface, because misclassifications and false negatives can have a significant safety impact: for example, a person could not get noticed and, as a consequence, not rescued or rescued too late. The benchmark represents local robustness by applying L_∞ perturbations to the neighborhood of objects (e.g., persons, boats) in the image[3]. The neighborhood is determined from the bounding box, which corresponds to the model detection of the object on the original unperturbed image.

Mathematically, local robustness properties are defined in the "delta-epsilon" form, which makes use of the infinity norm:

$$||x' - x||_\infty < \delta \implies ||f(x') - f(x)||_\infty < \epsilon. \quad (1)$$

where $x \in X$ is the original input (image) belonging to the input space X of the ML model, $x' \in X$ is the perturbed input, $f(x)$ and $f(x')$ are ML model outputs for, respectively, x and x', δ and ϵ are as discussed above ($\delta, \epsilon \in \mathbb{R}_{>0}$), and $||\cdot||$ is a norm that measures the distance between original and perturbed inputs and outputs. Local robustness requires that for an input perturbation bounded by δ (precondition $||x' - x||_\infty < \delta$) the output must not deviate by more than ϵ (postcondition $||f(x') - f(x)||_\infty < \epsilon$).

[3] We note that in future work it may be possible to also identify more meaningful perturbations, such as changing the colors of certain objects in the image (e.g., life jackets from red to blue). Such modifications may require additional image processing to precisely identify the pixels to apply perturbation to, which brings additional challenges to be solved.

3.2 Robustness Properties for the YOLO Model

Current benchmark includes robustness properties for different pixel perturbation magnitudes δ, ranging from 0.1% to 10%. Pixel perturbations are applied in the neighborhood of objects on the water surface (e.g., swimmers, boats) in order to see whether their detection changes due to modification in (or near) the pixels belonging to the object. The following steps are executed to formalize a robustness property, for a given δ:

1. Randomly pick a dataset image x;
2. Downscale[4] the image (including padding, if necessary) to match the NN input size (640×640), obtaining image x_{in};
3. Perform NN inference on the downsized image to compute bounding boxes $b_i^{out} \in B^{out}$ and respective classes ($1 \leq i \leq |B^{out}|$, where B^{out} is the set of bounding boxes predicted for the image obtained after post-processing of the NN output);
4. Upscale bounding boxes to the original image size, getting the boxes $b_i \in B$ ($1 \leq i \leq |B|$, considering that $|B| = |B^{out}|$);
5. Randomly pick one bounding box b from B, corresponding to one of the objects detected on the image;
6. Define a space of possible perturbations on the original-size image x, by applying L_∞ to pixels inside the bounding box b, and downscale it to the NN input size (see next section for details). Impose input constraints that the input perturbation is within δ, i.e., pixel perturbations are bounded by $x - \delta$ and $x + \delta$ for the original size image and by $(x - \delta)_{in}$ and $(x + \delta)_{in}$ for the downscaled image;
7. Impose output constraints that (1) the bounding box class confidence on the perturbed image is still the highest among all classes and that (2) the object existence confidence does not deviate by more than $\epsilon = 10\%$.

In this procedure, input constraints correspond to the precondition of the local robustness property, while output constraints correspond to its postcondition.

Key Challenge. The main challenging aspect of the benchmark is the large number of inputs and outputs (on the order of, respectively, 10^6 and 10^5). The former is due to the need of using a high-resolution image in the search and rescue application, because some objects, such as swimmers, are often very small (e.g., due to high flight altitudes of the drone). Therefore, further decrease of the input size of the YOLO model significantly hampers its prediction performance.

4 Property Generation

The formulation of the properties required to address two technical issues. The first one is the mismatch between the size of original dataset images and the NN

[4] Resizing is performed via OpenCV `resize()` command (bilinear interpolation).

input size. To encode the input constraints, perturbation range for the pixels belonging to the selected area/bounding box is to be set to the range between $x-\delta$ and $x+\delta$. Since the selected bounding box b^{out} computed by the NN refers to the downscaled image x_{in}, b^{out} is first upsized to b on the original image x; then the perturbation is applied within b, leading to pixel perturbation range between $x-\delta$ and $x+\delta$, leaving the area of x outside of b unmodified. Finally, the images containing the two perturbed bounding boxes are downscaled to the NN input size as $(x-\delta)_{in}$ and $(x+\delta)_{in}$.

The second issue depends on the postprocessing applied to the NN output. The output bounding boxes and their respective classes are derived from the NN "raw" output of size ~25200 × 11, consisting of candidate boxes and probability estimates, by means of a non-trivial sequence of operations, including multiple phases of threshold-based filtering and the application of a Non-Maximum Suppression algorithm to resolve overlaps. To encode the output constraints, which are expressed in terms of the NN raw output, an algorithm has been implemented to trace the selected bounding box back to the corresponding raw data.

5 Concluding Remarks

Robustness assessment of vision-based systems, such as object detection, is one of their key certification objectives. European Union Aviation Safety Agency (EASA) in their Concept Paper for Level 1&2 Machine Learning Applications [4] emphasizes Formal Methods (FM) as anticipated means of compliance for the verification of robustness of ML models. FM tools can become a critical enabler of AI/ML trustworthiness [3], therefore, aviation industry is looking forward to maturation and improvement of relevant technologies. The proposed benchmark has the intent of being a motivating example of a realistic application in the aerospace domain.

Acknowledgement. The authors wish to thank Benjamin Kiefer et al. from the University of Tuebingen for the publication of the *SeaDronesSee* dataset, which has been used as a baseline in this research work.

References

1. Avalon - Aerial and vision-based assistance system for real time object detection in search and rescue missions. https://uni-tuebingen.de/fakultaeten/mathematisch-naturwissenschaftliche-fakultaet/fachbereiche/informatik/lehrstuehle/kognitive-systeme/projects/avalon/
2. SeaDronesSee dataset. https://seadronessee.cs.uni-tuebingen.de/dataset
3. EASA and Collins Aerospace: Formal Methods use for Learning Assurance (ForMuLA). Technical report (2023)

4. European Union Aviation Safety Agency (EASA): Concept Paper: Guidance for Level 1&2 Machine Learning Applications. Concept paper for consultation (2023)
5. Varga, L.A., Kiefer, B., Messmer, M., Zell, A.: Seadronessee: a maritime benchmark for detecting humans in open water. In: Proceedings of the IEEE/CVF Winter Conference on Applications of Computer Vision, pp. 2260–2270 (2022)

Benchmark: Formal Verification of Semantic Segmentation Neural Networks

Neelanjana Pal(✉), Seojin Lee, and Taylor T. Johnson

Institute for Software Integration and Systems, Vanderbilt University, Nashville, TN, USA
{neelanjana.pal,seojin.lee,taylor.johnson}@vanderbilt.edu

Abstract. Formal verification utilizes a rigorous approach to ensure the absence of critical errors and validate models against predefined properties. While significant progress has been made in verification methods for various deep neural networks (DNNs), such as feed-forward neural networks (FFNNs) and convolutional neural networks (CNNs), the application of these techniques to semantic segmentation remains largely unexplored. Semantic segmentation networks are vital in computer vision applications, where they assign semantic labels to individual pixels within an image. Given their deployment in safety-critical domains, ensuring the correctness of these networks becomes paramount. This paper presents a comprehensive benchmark study on applying formal verification techniques to semantic segmentation networks. We explore a diverse set of state-of-the-art semantic segmentation datasets and generate neural network models, including fully-convolutional networks and encoder-decoder architectures. Our investigation encompasses a wide range of verification properties, focusing on the robustness of these models against bounded adversarial vulnerabilities. To evaluate the networks' performance, we employ set-based reachability algorithms to calculate the output reachable set(s) and some state-of-the-art performance measures for a comparative study among the networks. This benchmark paper aims to provide the formal verification community with several semantic segmentation networks and their robustness specifications for future use cases in different neural network verification competitions.

Keywords: Semantic Segmentation · Adversarial Attack · Benchmarking · Reachability · Robustness · VNN-Comp

1 Introduction

The Significant Role of Semantic Segmentation. Over the past three decades, image segmentation [34] has been one of the most challenging problems in computer vision. In contrast to tasks like image classification or object recognition, image segmentation operates differently, as it does not rely on prior

B. Steffen (Ed.): AISoLA 2023, LNCS 14380, pp. 311–330, 2024.
https://doi.org/10.1007/978-3-031-46002-9_20

knowledge of visual concepts or objects within the image. Instead, it assigns a specific category label to every individual pixel in the image. This approach allows the model to accurately delineate distinct regions or objects present in the image, effectively dividing it into meaningful segments. The model creates a comprehensive and detailed representation of the image's content by associating each pixel with its corresponding category label. This capability to provide pixel-level category information has significant real-world applications [36], such as self-driving vehicles [23,45], pedestrian detection [5,12], defect detection [35], therapy planning [15,46], and computer-aided diagnosis [52,53]. The segmentation task empowers intelligent systems to grasp spatial positions and make critical judgments by offering detailed semantic information at the pixel level, setting it apart from other common computer vision tasks (Fig. 1).

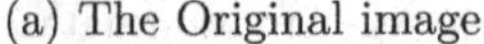

(a) The Original image

(b) Semantically Segmented Image

Fig. 1. An example of semantic segmentation vision tasks from CamVid dataset [7].

Deep Neural Networks (DNN) and Adversarial Attacks. Research has shown that even well-trained neural networks (NNs) are vulnerable to minor input modifications (i.e., adversarial attacks) that can cause significant changes in the output [27]. Similar to image classification neural networks, semantic segmentation networks (SSNs) are also known to be vulnerable to adversarial perturbations [50]. While deep neural network (DNN) verification is evolving as a well-established research area with numerous tools and techniques proposed to ensure the safety and robustness specifications of DNNs [24,48] and neural network-controlled systems [16,18,39,43] most state-of-the-art verification techniques for robustness validation in DNNs primarily focus on variations of classification tasks, often related to images [1,4,8,11,21,26,30,32,37,38,49,51]. In recent years, verification of segmentation networks has also gained immense focus from researchers all over [3,19,42].

Neural Network Verification Competitions. The proliferation of neural networks (NNs) in safety-critical applications has brought attention to their susceptibility to adversarial examples [33], where even minor input perturbations can significantly alter their outputs. Such perturbations, whether occurring randomly or due to malicious intent, emphasize the crucial need to rigorously analyze the robustness of deep learning systems before deploying them in safety-critical domains. Consequently, numerous methods and software tools [10,13,17,20] have been developed for this purpose. However, the increasing number and specialization of these tools have made it challenging for practitioners to choose the most suitable one for their needs.

In response to this dilemma, in 2020, a friendly International Competition on Verification of Neural Networks (VNN-Comp 2020) [2,6,28] was conducted to address the issue and allow researchers to compare their neural network verifiers across a wide range of benchmarks. Originally designed as a friendly competition with minimal standardization, the event evolved to introduce more standardization and automation. The goal was to ensure a fair comparison among verifiers on cost-equivalent hardware, utilizing standardized formats for properties and networks. This evolution aimed to facilitate informed decision-making by researchers and practitioners when selecting verification tools for their specific requirements. The VNN-Comp celebrates its 4th iteration this year and successfully presented the results at the Computer Aided Verification 2023 (CAV) conference.

Work Presented In This Paper. Despite the growing interest and competition in robustness verification, there remains a lack of appropriate benchmarks for evaluating different verifiers on semantic segmentation tasks. This research addresses this gap by introducing segmentation networks on two widely used datasets: MNIST [22], M2NIST (which is a multi-digit variant of MNIST suitable for segmentation evaluation) . Additionally, we define the specific properties that need to be verified for these networks.

An essential aspect of our work is its potential utility for the VNN-Comp's upcoming iterations. By providing these well-defined benchmarks for semantic segmentation, we hope to contribute to advancing and standardizing robustness verification techniques in this domain.

Contributions. In summary, this paper makes several key contributions:

1. We introduce NNs designed specifically for two different semantic segmentation datasets, providing a comprehensive benchmark dataset for evaluating their performance.
2. In this benchmark work, we not only showcase fully-convolutional NNs but also include encoder-decoder architectures, offering a diverse set of models to assess their effectiveness in different scenarios.
3. To assess the robustness of these networks against adversarial attacks, we define specific properties and constraints and represent them in vnnlib files, adhering to the guidelines set by VNN-Comp.
4. Furthermore, we present sample verification results, obtained using set-based reachability algorithms and performance measures. These results demonstrate

the networks' resilience and provide insights into their performance under different conditions, aiding researchers and practitioners in making informed decisions.

Outline. The paper is structured as follows: Sect. 2 introduces the benchmark design considerations for this proposal, while Sect. 3 presents an example verification task for the MNIST networks against an adversarial attack. Finally, Sect. 4 provides a summary of the main proposal, discusses its implications, and outlines potential avenues for future research.

2 Benchmark Design

In the following, we describe our benchmark: (i) the overall motivations and philosophy; (ii) the Datasets and their creation; (iii) the networks proposed; (iv) the unknown-bounded adversarial attack; (v) the metrics used for evaluation; and (vi) robustness property specification.

2.1 Philosophy

The motivation behind benchmarking formal verification techniques for semantic segmentation networks arises from the growing significance of deploying these networks in safety-critical applications. By establishing standardized benchmarks and datasets, researchers and practitioners can assess the strengths and limitations of various verification techniques. This enables them to make well-informed decisions when selecting the most appropriate verification methods, considering factors like accuracy, computational overhead, and scalability.

Benchmarking formal verification techniques drives innovation and encourages the development of more reliable and secure deep learning models. It paves the way for integrating formal methods into the training and deployment pipeline, instilling greater confidence in the safety and robustness of semantic segmentation networks for critical applications.

2.2 Datasets

The MNIST and M2NIST datasets provide a solid starting point for conducting image-segmentation benchmarking. In contrast to real-world images, especially those captured from autonomous vehicles, these datasets feature well-isolated digits positioned at the center of the images. Consequently, the task of segmentation is comparatively straightforward. The digits, which are the focal points of interest, exhibit distinct clarity and encounter minimal clutter or occlusion. A significant advantage of the MNIST and M2NIST datasets lies in their provision of well-defined ground-truth annotations. This feature greatly simplifies the accurate assessment of segmentation algorithms, enabling meticulous evaluation. Furthermore, these datasets often serve as valuable tools for conveying and elucidating image segmentation's core principles.

MNIST Dataset. The MNIST [22] dataset is a well-known dataset used for training and testing machine learning models, particularly for image classification tasks. It consists of handwritten digit images, where each image is a grayscale image of size 28×28 pixels and corresponding ground-truth-labeled masks representing random digit numbers ranging from 0 to 9. To facilitate our experiments, we divided the dataset into two sets: 50,000 images for training and 10,000 images for testing. Figure 2 displays sample images from the MNIST dataset.

Fig. 2. Sample images from MNIST dataset

M2NIST Dataset. The M2NIST dataset comprises images with dimensions of (64, 84, 1) and corresponding ground-truth-labeled masks depicting multiple (up to three) random digits ranging from 0 to 9. These digits are arranged in a manner that they do not overlap with each other within the images. For our experiments, we divided the original dataset into two sets: 50,000 samples for training and 10,000 for testing. Figure 3 displays sample images from the M2NIST dataset.

Fig. 3. Sample images from M2NIST dataset

2.3 Neural Network Models

MNIST Dataset. For the MNIST dataset, we utilize two pre-trained networks from [42], and we train a third network with 16 layers. The networks consist of an image input layer with the input size of (28, 28, 1) followed by two-dimensional convolution layers, ReLU layers and average-pooling layers.

M2NIST Dataset. For the M2NIST Dataset, we propose the three pre-trained networks used in [42] and two newly trained networks, as shown in Fig. 5. The input image size for these networks is changed to (64, 84, 1).

The performance measures of each of the proposed networks are shown in Table. 1.

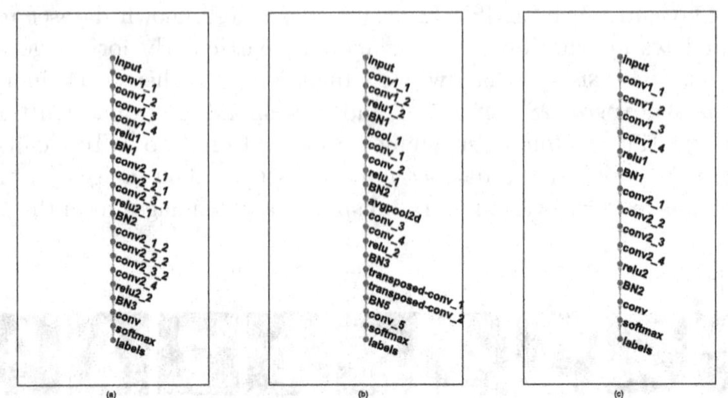

Fig. 4. Benchmark for MNIST Networks

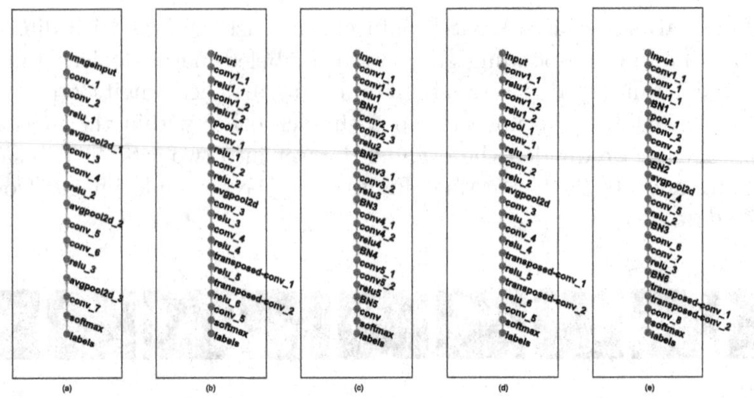

Fig. 5. Benchmark for M2NIST Networks

Table 1. Performances of different networks used for MNIST and M2NIST datasets

$Network_{MNIST}$	$Accuracy_{global}(\%)$	$Accuracy_{mean}(\%)$	IoU_{mean}	$IoU_{weighted}$
$mnist\_21\_iou83$	96.88	93.70	0.8335	0.9427
$mnist\_avg\_21$	97.28	96.20	0.8675	0.9490
$mnist\_16$	96.93	92.67	0.8376	0.9430
$Network_{M2NIST}$	$Accuracy_{global}(\%)$	$Accuracy_{mean}(\%)$	IoU_{mean}	$IoU_{weighted}$
$m2nist\_avg\_iou62$	96.61	88.30	0.6210	0.9464
$m2nist\_avg\_iou75$	98.03	97.60	0.7502	0.9660
$m2nist\_iou72\_24$	97.86	96.27	0.7271	0.9635
$m2nist\_avg\_22$	97.97	98.30	0.7495	0.9650
$m2nist\_avg\_24$	97.07	97.86	0.8321	0.9466

2.4 Segmentation in the Context of Proposed Datasets

The segmentation task in the MNIST and M2NIST datasets involves the process of precisely delineating and identifying individual digits within the given images. The goal is to assign a distinct label to each pixel or region that corresponds to a specific digit. This segmentation is vital for isolating and distinguishing the different digits present in the image, enabling accurate digit recognition and analysis.

MNIST Dataset. In the MNIST dataset, each image depicts a single handwritten digit (0–9). The segmentation task involves precisely outlining the boundaries of the digit, distinguishing it from the background. This process aims to identify the exact spatial extent of the digit, ensuring that every pixel belonging to the digit is correctly labeled while excluding pixels from the surrounding background.

M2NIST Dataset. The M2NIST dataset introduces a slightly more complex scenario. It consists of images containing two or three handwritten digits placed in non-overlapping arrangements. The segmentation task in M2NIST entails accurately segmenting each digit within the image, ensuring that the segmentation boundaries do not cross over into neighboring digits. This task becomes especially challenging when digits are in close proximity, as segmentation algorithms must correctly identify the boundaries between adjacent digits.

The segmentation task in both datasets essentially involves creating pixel-wise masks that outline the boundaries of individual digits. These masks indicate which pixels belong to each digit and which pixels constitute the background. The successful execution of the segmentation task is crucial for subsequent digit recognition, as the isolated digits can then be analyzed, classified, and identified accurately.

2.5 Adversarial Attacks

Inspired by the paper [42], we consider an unknown-bounded adversarial attack (UBAA) on input images in our study. The coefficient vector ϵ, representing the attack strength, is bounded by lower and upper bounds, denoted as $[\underline{\epsilon}, \overline{\epsilon}]$, with each ϵ_i satisfying $\underline{\epsilon_i} \leq \epsilon_i \leq \overline{\epsilon_i}$. We apply this attack concept to images, where pixel values range from 0 to 255, and consider the attack's impact on either a single pixel or multiple pixels within the image. By applying this attack, a set of images is generated, each having variations in pixel values within one or multiple locations, limited by the bounds $[\underline{\epsilon}, \overline{\epsilon}]$.

To illustrate this, we represent an adversarial image x^{adv} as follows:

$$x^{adv} = x^{org} + \Sigma_{i=1}^{n} \epsilon_i \cdot x_i^{attack} \tag{1}$$

where x^{org} and x^{adv} are the original and adversarial images, respectively. The variable n denotes the total number of pixels in the image, and ϵ_i represents the attack coefficient for the pixel at position i.

Within this benchmark study, we subject each image, x, to an UBAA across the test datasets. Here we darken a pixel $x(i,j)$ by 1 unit if its value exceeds a specified threshold, denoted as d. In mathematical terms, the adversarial darkening attack on an image x can be described as follows:

$$x^{adv} = x + \epsilon \cdot x^{noise},\ 1 - \Delta_\epsilon \le \epsilon \le 1,$$
$$x^{noise}(i,j) = -1,\ \text{if } x(i,j) > d,\ \text{otherwise } x^{noise}(i,j) = 0.$$

For $\epsilon = 1$, we darken all pixels by 1 unit whose values exceed the threshold d (set to 150 for this work and $\epsilon = 1$), resulting in $x^{adv}(i,j) = x(i,j) - 1$. The size of the input set affected by the attack is determined by Δ_ϵ. A larger value of Δ_ϵ corresponds to a larger input set after applying the attack.

By varying the values of ϵ and d, we generate different robustness properties to verify.

2.6 Evaluation Metrics

For evaluation purposes, we used the traditional concept of Intersection-over-Union (IoU) for both segmentation model performances and model robustness checking. Following [42], we also used the concept of robustness value (RV) and robustness sensitivity (RS).

Robustness Value (RV). An SSN's Robustness Value (RV) characterizes its resilience against an adversarial attack. Specifically, for an unknown bounded adversarial attack applied to an input image, the RV is defined as follows:

$$RV = \frac{N_{robust}}{N_{pixels}} \times 100\%, \tag{2}$$

where N_{robust} is the total number of robust pixels[1] under the attack, and $N_{pixels} = h \cdot w$ is the total number of input image pixels.

Robustness Sensitivity (RS). The Robustness Sensitivity (RS) quantifies the network's susceptibility under the adversarial attack, revealing the average number of pixels in the segmentation output image that are influenced (either becoming non-robust or unknown) when a single pixel in the input image is attacked. The robustness sensitivity of an SSN corresponding to an unknown bounded adversarial attack applied to an input image is defined as

$$RS = \frac{N_{nonrobust} + N_{unknown}}{N_{attackedpixels}}, \tag{3}$$

where $N_{nonrobust}$ is the total number of non-robust pixels under the attack, $N_{unknown}$ is the total number of pixels whose robustness is unknown (i.e., the verifier can not guarantee on the robustness; it may or may not be robust), and $N_{attackedpixels}$ is the total number of attacked pixels of the input image.

[1] In this context, "Robust pixels" refer to those pixels that maintain their correct classification even in the presence of an adversarial attack..

Robust Intersection-over-Union (IoU). The robust IoU (R_{IoU}) concept shares similarities with the traditional IoU, a fundamental metric used to evaluate accuracy during the training of semantic segmentation networks (SSNs). The robust IoU of a semantic segmentation network (SSN) when subjected to an unknown-bounded adversarial attack on an input image is calculated as the average IoU of all labels that remain robust under the attack.

Consider a segmentation ground-truth image denoted as x and the verified segmentation image under the adversarial attack as y. Then the IoU (IoU_p) for the pth label in the label images x and y is computed as the intersection of the label images divided by their union for the ith label. , then the R_{IoU} of the SSN is computed by:

$$R_{IoU} = \frac{\Sigma_{p=1}^{L} IoU_p}{L}. \tag{4}$$

In our context, we leverage the robust IoU concept in conjunction with the robustness value and robustness sensitivity as core metrics to assess the robustness of an SSN when subjected to adversarial attacks within the verification framework. Instead of solely measuring accuracy, these metrics comprehensively evaluate the network's resilience against such attacks.

2.7 Robustness Property Specification

In semantic segmentation examples, while each pixel is assigned a class label, individual pixels do not determine the object classification. Instead, a cluster of pixels with the same class collectively contributes to the final object decision. As a result, the robustness property defined for classification models is not directly applicable to segmentation models. Therefore, we focus on evaluating the Intersection over Union (IoU) measures of the segmentation output image w.r.t its original counterpart.

To characterize the robustness properties of a specific SSN for a given input image, we define its corresponding Robustness Value (RV) and Robustness Sensitivity (RS) within a specified range. This range represents the maximum allowable deviation the SSN is allowed to exhibit to be within a safe region. Consequently, for an adversarial input image set denoted as X^{adv} and its output segmentation image set as Y^{adv}, the robustness property for RV is defined as follows:

$$RV_{min} \leq RV_{org} \leq RV_{max} \tag{5}$$

where $[RV_{min}, RV_{max}]$ is the permissible bounds for the RV and RV_{org} is the actual RV for the unperturbed image.

Similarly, we can get the robustness property for the RS of the same example as:

$$RS_{min} \leq RS_{org} \leq RS_{max} \tag{6}$$

where $[RS_{min}, RS_{max}]$ is the permissible bounds for the RS and RS_{org} is the actual RS for the unperturbed image.

The IoU robustness property can be given by the equation:

$$R_{IoU_{min}} \leq R_{IoU_{org}} \leq R_{IoU_{max}} \tag{7}$$

where $[R_{IoU_{min}}, R_{IoU_{max}}]$ is the permissible bounds for the IoU and $R_{IoU_{org}}$ is the actual IoU for the unperturbed image.

2.8 Verification Property Specifications in Vnnlib Files: Illustrated with an Example

Vnnlib File Format. Following the competition protocol, we propose the robustness specification in a vnnlib file [9]. A vnnlib file is a standard format for representing neural network verification problems. It provides details about the neural network, input constraints, and properties to be verified. The vnnlib file format is widely adopted in formal verification for neural networks [2,14,28,31]. The verification specification in a vnnlib file involves defining properties using a specific syntax. The structure of a vnnlib file typically includes the following components:

1. **Input Constraints:** This section defines the input bounds or constraints for the neural network.
2. **Output Behavior Specification:** This section contains the expected output or behavior of the neural network for the specified input constraints.
3. **Property Specification:** This section specifies the neural network properties to be verified. These properties include safety and robustness verification properties.

Example. To illustrate this format, we consider the example in Fig. 6.

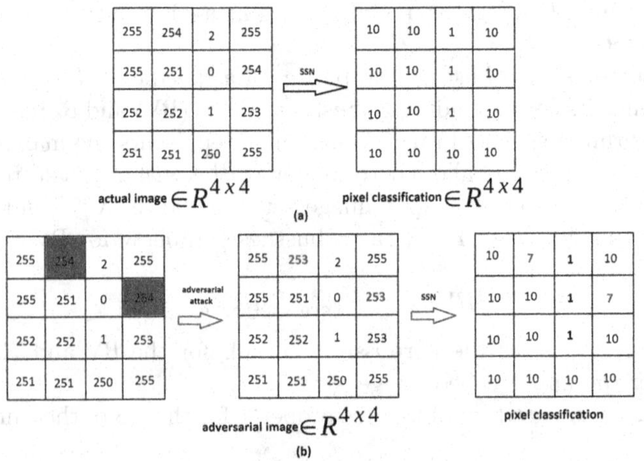

Fig. 6. The robustness verification specification for a Semantic Segmentation Network (SSN) is illustrated as follows: (a) Example image and its corresponding pixel classification. (b) Location of the adversarial attack (red), the pixel darkened by 1 (original value 254), and the resulting pixel classification after the adversarial attack. (Color figure online)

List 1. Input Constraints

```
; Verification Property Specification
(declare-const X_0 Real)
(declare-const X_1 Real)
(declare-const X_2 Real)
(declare-const X_3 Real)
(declare-const X_4 Real)
(declare-const X_5 Real)
(declare-const X_6 Real)
(declare-const X_7 Real)
(declare-const X_8 Real)
(declare-const X_9 Real)
(declare-const X_10 Real)
(declare-const X_11 Real)
(declare-const X_12 Real)
(declare-const X_13 Real)
(declare-const X_14 Real)
(declare-const X_15 Real)
; Unscaled Input 0: (255, 255)
(assert (<= X_0 255))
(assert (>= X_0 255))

; Unscaled Input 1: (255, 255)
(assert (<= X_1 255))
(assert (>= X_1 255))

; Unscaled Input 2: (252, 252)
(assert (<= X_2 252))
(assert (>= X_2 252))

; Unscaled Input 3: (251, 251)
(assert (<= X_3 251))
(assert (>= X_3 251))

; Unscaled Input 4: (253, 254)
(assert (<= X_4 254))
(assert (>= X_4 253))

; Unscaled Input 5: (251, 251)
(assert (<= X_5 251))
(assert (>= X_5 251))

; Unscaled Input 6: (252, 252)
(assert (<= X_6 252))
(assert (>= X_6 252))

; Unscaled Input 7: (251, 251)
(assert (<= X_7 251))
(assert (>= X_7 251))

; Unscaled Input 8: (2, 2)
(assert (<= X_8 2))
(assert (>= X_8 2))

; Unscaled Input 9: (0, 0)
(assert (<= X_9 0))
(assert (>= X_9 0))

; Unscaled Input 10: (1, 1)
(assert (<= X_10 1))
(assert (>= X_10 1))

; Unscaled Input 11: (250, 250)
(assert (<= X_11 250))
(assert (>= X_11 250))

; Unscaled Input 12: (255, 255)
(assert (<= X_12 255))
(assert (>= X_12 255))

; Unscaled Input 13: (253, 254)
(assert (<= X_13 254))
(assert (>= X_13 253))

; Unscaled Input 14: (253, 253)
(assert (<= X_14 253))
(assert (>= X_14 253))

; Unscaled Input 15: (255, 255)
(assert (<= X_15 255))
(assert (>= X_15 255))
```

In this example, we focus on an input image represented as a 4×4 2-dimensional array with pixel values from 0 to 255. The output of the Semantic Segmentation Network (SSN) pixel classification layer is also a 4×4 2-dimensional array, assigning classes to each pixel. For this image, we highlight the digit '1', with the first three rows in column 3 of the output classified as '1' and the remaining rows labeled as background (represented by '10').

Next, we explore an Unbounded Adversarial Attack (UBAA) on the image, targeting pixels with a value of 254, reducing them to 253. To ensure a bounded attack, we set the upper bound of the attacked image as the original image itself [Fig. 6 (b) left], and the lower bound as the image with darkened pixels [Fig. 6 (b) middle].

To specify the input properties in a vnnlib file, we first flatten the input image column-wise and then define the upper and lower bounds for each pixel representing the attack. In the case of the provided image example, the input properties in a vnnlib file should be structured as depicted in List. 1. This allows for a comprehensive representation of the image and its bounds, facilitating the verification process.

Similar to the input specification, for generating the output specification, we also need to flatten the output column-wise as in List. 2.

List 2. Output Behavior Specification

```
(declare-const Y_0 Real)
(declare-const Y_1 Real)
(declare-const Y_2 Real)
(declare-const Y_3 Real)
(declare-const Y_4 Real)
(declare-const Y_5 Real)
(declare-const Y_6 Real)
(declare-const Y_7 Real)
(declare-const Y_8 Real)
(declare-const Y_9 Real)
(declare-const Y_10 Real)
(declare-const Y_11 Real)
(declare-const Y_12 Real)
(declare-const Y_13 Real)
(declare-const Y_14 Real)
(declare-const Y_15 Real)

; pixel classification constraints
(assert(== Y_0 10))
(assert(== Y_1 10))
(assert(== Y_2 10))
(assert(== Y_3 10))
(assert(== Y_4 10))
(assert(== Y_5 10))
(assert(== Y_6 10))
(assert(== Y_7 10))
(assert(== Y_8 1))
(assert(== Y_9 1))
(assert(== Y_10 1))
(assert(== Y_11 10))
(assert(== Y_12 10))
(assert(== Y_13 10))
(assert(== Y_14 10))
(assert(== Y_15 10))
```

In the example, we also make an assumption, as depicted in [Fig. 6 (b) right] that the SSN misclassifies two pixels due to the darkening effect, classifying them as '7' instead of '10'. Consequently, following the definition of robustness measures, we obtain the values for both the unperturbed image and the one corresponding to the UBAA attack as shown below in Table. 2. Here we need to emphasize that following Sect. 2.6 the concept of robustness sensitivity is only valid for an adversarial input.

Table 2. Robustness measures for both the unperturbed image and the one corresponding to the UBAA attack

RobustnessMeasures	*Unperturbed*	*Under UBAA*
RV	1	0.8750
RS	-	1
RIOU	1	0.6154

Drawing on the concept of robustness measures for SSN verification against adversarial attacks, we introduce additional output verification properties. These properties are derived from the output pixel classification constraints, as provided in List. 3. For the example shown in Fig. 6 we restrict the considerable RV in $[0.9, 1]$, RIoU in $[0.8, 1]$ and RS to be always ≤ 100, for the output reachable set to be in the safe region. The proposed properties are as follows:

List 3. Verification Property Specification: Robustness Measures

```
; robustness measures specification
(assert(<= RV 1))          (assert(<= RIOU 1))
(assert(>= RV 0.9))        (assert(>= RIOU 0.8))
(assert(<= RS 0.8))
```

3 Evaluation

3.1 Reachability Analysis

To assess the impact of the adversarial attack on each dataset, we employ reachability analysis, a widely used concept [16,25,29,40–42,47]. The perturbed input is represented as a bounded set, and we compute the output reachable set layer-by-layer for the SSN. For the final layer of an SSN, i.e., pixel-classification layer, the pixel-class reachable set at a specific pixel is denoted as $pc(i, j) = \{l_1, ..., l_m\}$. This set is obtained by determining all cross-channel max-point candidates for each pixel in the input set. Consequently, we can obtain the pixel-class reachable set of the layer, which is equivalent to the reachable set of the SSN, denoted as $R_f = [pc(i, j)]_{h \times w}$, i.e., the collection of pixel classes at every index (i; j) [42].

Subsequently, we calculate the Robustness Values (RVs), Robustness Sensitivities (RSs), and Robust Intersection-over-Union (IoU) scores for all the images in the adversarial set based on the output reachable set.

We employ the "approx-star" method for reachability analysis in this paper. This method is preferred due to its computational efficiency, requiring less time and memory than "exact-star" methods. We direct our readers to refer to [40–42] for a more comprehensive understanding of the Star-based reachability analysis.

3.2 Neural Network Verification (NNV) Tool

For calculating the output reachable set using "approx-star," we make use of a readily available tool called "Neural Network Verification (NNV) Tool" [44]. It is a comprehensive set-based framework for verifying neural networks (NNs). It supports multiple reachability algorithms, enabling safety verification and robustness analysis of various deep neural network (DNN) types.

In the context of reachability analysis, the NNV tool computes output reachable sets layer-by-layer, starting from a given input. This input is defined by upper and lower bounds, representing perturbations around the actual input. As the analysis progresses through the layers, the reachable sets at the final layer represent the collection of all possible states of the DNN.

The primary objective of the NNV tool is to determine whether the DNN is deemed "safe." A DNN is considered safe when the specified safety properties determine no intersection between the output sets and the predefined unsafe region. By verifying safety conditions and analyzing robustness, the NNV tool aids in ensuring the reliability and trustworthiness of neural networks in various applications.

3.3 Results

In this section, we present a sample plot [Fig. 7] illustrating the average robustness measures of three MNIST networks, as described in Sect. 2.3. We conduct the analysis by subjecting 100 random digit images to the UBA attack and calculating the networks' average robustness against this attack with the following details: (1) max number of pixels attacked under UBAA: [1 2 3 4 5] and (2) $\epsilon = 1$ [Sect. 2.5].

When analyzing the outcomes of our experiment, we made several notable observations that shed light on the behavior of different robustness measures under varying degrees of adversarial attacks. These observations provide valuable insights into how these measures respond and behave in the face of adversarial perturbations.

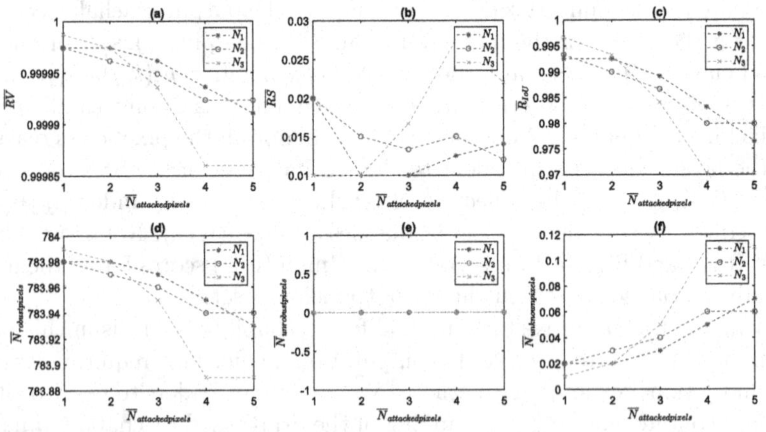

Fig. 7. The average robustness value, sensitivity, and IoU of MNIST SSNs.

Specifically, as we increased the number of adversarial attacks, we noticed a consistent downward trend in both the robustness value and the robust IoU (Intersection-over-Union). The robustness value quantifies the extent to which the SSN's predictions remain accurate after exposure to adversarial perturbations. In our analysis, this value consistently decreased with a greater number of attacks. Similarly, the robust IoU, which measures the overlap between predicted and ground-truth segments, also demonstrated a decreasing pattern with increased attacks. This reduction suggests that the adversarial perturbations adversely affect the network's ability to segment objects within images accurately.

Interestingly, we encountered a nuanced behavior when examining the robustness sensitivity. Unlike the robustness value and robust IoU, the trend in robustness sensitivity was not strictly uniform as the number of attacks increase. Robustness sensitivity gauges how sensitive the SSN's output segmentation is to changes in input pixels due to an attack. Our observations found that this sensitivity did not consistently follow a rigid trend with escalating adversarial attacks. This variability aligns with the inherent nature of robustness sensitivity, which can be influenced by the distribution and complexity of perturbations introduced by different attacks.

Overall, these observations reaffirm the theoretical definitions and expectations of these robustness measures in the context of various adversarial attacks. The decreasing trends in robustness value and robust IoU highlight the vulnerability of the SSN's segmentation performance to increasing adversarial perturbations. The non-uniform trend in robustness sensitivity emphasizes the intricate interplay between attack characteristics and the network's responsiveness to perturbations, leading to varying degrees of sensitivity under different attack scenarios. Such insights are crucial for understanding the strengths and limitations of these robustness measures and guiding the development of more resilient semantic segmentation networks in the future.

4 Conclusion and Future Ideas

In this paper, we proposed a benchmark framework for the formal verification of semantic segmentation neural networks. Our study aimed to address the challenges in ensuring the safety and reliability of these networks, which are increasingly being utilized in critical applications such as autonomous vehicles, medical imaging, and surveillance systems. By establishing a standardized benchmark, we aimed to facilitate the first step towards a fair comparison of different verification methods and tools, promoting advancements in the field of formal verification for semantic segmentation neural networks. The benchmark framework we presented encompasses a diverse set of neural network architectures, datasets, and verification properties, representing two commonly used datasets: MNIST and M2NIST. We also provided a detailed specification format in vnnlib files to describe the verification properties, enabling the seamless integration of different tools and approaches. This standardization allows researchers and developers to easily evaluate and compare the effectiveness of their verification techniques.

While our proposed benchmark framework represents a significant step towards formal verification in semantic segmentation neural networks, there are several avenues for future research and enhancement. Firstly, we plan to continuously update and expand the benchmark by incorporating new neural network architectures, datasets, and verification properties that emerge in the field. This will ensure that the benchmark remains up-to-date and reflective of the latest advancements in semantic segmentation tasks. Moreover, we aim to collaborate with the research community to gather feedback and incorporate suggestions for improving the benchmark. This will allow us to refine the benchmark based on the practical experiences and insights of researchers working on formal verification for semantic segmentation networks. Furthermore, we intend to conduct comprehensive evaluations and comparisons of existing formal verification methods and tools using the benchmark. By doing so, we can identify the strengths and limitations of different approaches, helping to guide researchers in selecting the most suitable verification techniques for their specific use cases. Lastly, we will explore the integration of novel techniques and advances in formal verification to enhance the benchmark's capabilities and coverage. This may include leveraging machine learning-based methods, formal synthesis, and abstraction techniques to address the challenges posed by the complexity and scalability of large-scale semantic segmentation networks.

In conclusion, our proposed benchmark framework for the formal verification of semantic segmentation neural networks lays the foundation for advancing the safety and reliability of these networks in critical applications. We look forward to collaborating with the research community to further refine and expand the benchmark, fostering progress in the field of formal verification for semantic segmentation neural networks.

Acknowledgements. The material presented in this paper is based upon work supported by the National Science Foundation (NSF) through grant numbers 1910017, 2028001, 2220426, and 2220401, and the Defense Advanced Research Projects Agency (DARPA) under contract number FA8750-23-C-0518, and the Air Force Office of Scientific Research (AFOSR) under contract number FA9550-22-1-0019 and FA9550-23-1-0135. Any opinions, findings, conclusions, or recommendations expressed in this paper are those of the authors and do not necessarily reflect the views of AFOSR, DARPA, or NSF. We also want to thank our colleagues, Tianshu and Serena for their valuable feedback.

References

1. Anderson, G., Pailoor, S., Dillig, I., Chaudhuri, S.: Optimization and abstraction: A synergistic approach for analyzing neural network robustness. In: Proceedings of the 40th ACM SIGPLAN Conference on Programming Language Design and Implementation, pp. 731–744. PLDI 2019, Association for Computing Machinery, New York, NY, USA (2019). https://doi.org/10.1145/3314221.3314614
2. Bak, S., Liu, C., Johnson, T.: The second international verification of neural networks competition (vnn-comp 2021): Summary and results. arXiv preprint arXiv:2109.00498 (2021)

3. Blum, H., Sarlin, P.E., Nieto, J., Siegwart, R., Cadena, C.: Fishyscapes: A benchmark for safe semantic segmentation in autonomous driving. In: Proceedings of the IEEE/CVF International Conference on Computer Vision Workshops (2019)
4. Botoeva, E., Kouvaros, P., Kronqvist, J., Lomuscio, A., Misener, R.: Efficient verification of relu-based neural networks via dependency analysis. Proc. AAAI Conf. Artif. Intell. **34**(04), 3291–3299 (2020). https://doi.org/10.1609/aaai.v34i04.5729
5. Brazil, G., Yin, X., Liu, X.: Illuminating pedestrians via simultaneous detection & segmentation. In: Proceedings of the IEEE International Conference on Computer Vision, pp. 4950–4959 (2017)
6. Brix, C., Müller, M.N., Bak, S., Johnson, T.T., Liu, C.: First three years of the international verification of neural networks competition (VNN-Comp). Int. J. Softw. Tools Technol. Transfer **25**, 329–339 (2023)
7. Brostow, G.J., Fauqueur, J., Cipolla, R.: Semantic object classes in video: A high-definition ground truth database. Pattern Recogn. Lett. **30**(2), 88–97 (2009)
8. Dathathri, S., et al.: Enabling certification of verification-agnostic networks via memory-efficient semidefinite programming (2020)
9. Demarchi, S.: VNN-LIB – vnnlib.org. https://www.vnnlib.org/ Accessed 31 Aug 2023
10. Ehlers, R.: Formal verification of piece-wise linear feed-forward neural networks. In: D'Souza, D., Narayan Kumar, K. (eds.) Automated Technology for Verification and Analysis, pp. 269–286. Springer, Cham (2017). https://doi.org/10.1007/978-3-319-68167-2_19
11. Fazlyab, M., Morari, M., Pappas, G.J.: Safety verification and robustness analysis of neural networks via quadratic constraints and semidefinite programming. IEEE Trans. Auto. Control **67**(1), 1–15 (2022). https://doi.org/10.1109/TAC.2020.3046193
12. Flohr, F., Gavrila, D., et al.: Pedcut: an iterative framework for pedestrian segmentation combining shape models and multiple data cues. In: BMVC (2013)
13. Gehr, T., Mirman, M., Drachsler-Cohen, D., Tsankov, P., Chaudhuri, S., Vechev, M.: Ai2: Safety and robustness certification of neural networks with abstract interpretation. In: 2018 IEEE Symposium on Security and Privacy (SP), pp. 3–18. IEEE (2018)
14. Girard-Satabin, J., Alberti, M., Bobot, F., Chihani, Z., Lemesle, A.: Caisar: A platform for characterizing artificial intelligence safety and robustness. arXiv preprint arXiv:2206.03044 (2022)
15. Guo, Y., Gao, Y., Shen, D.: Deformable MR prostate segmentation via deep feature learning and sparse patch matching. IEEE Trans. Med. Imaging **35**(4), 1077–1089 (2015)
16. Huang, C., Fan, J., Li, W., Chen, X., Zhu, Q.: Reachnn: Reachability analysis of neural-network controlled systems. ACM Trans. Embedded Comput. Syst. (TECS) **18**(5s), 1–22 (2019)
17. Huang, X., Kwiatkowska, M., Wang, S., Wu, M.: Safety verification of deep neural networks. In: Majumdar, R., Kunčak, V. (eds.) Computer Aided Verification: 29th International Conference, CAV 2017, Heidelberg, Germany, July 24-28, 2017, Proceedings, Part I, pp. 3–29. Springer, Cham (2017). https://doi.org/10.1007/978-3-319-63387-9_1
18. Ivanov, R., Weimer, J., Alur, R., Pappas, G.J., Lee, I.: Verisig: verifying safety properties of hybrid systems with neural network controllers. In: Proceedings of the 22nd ACM International Conference on Hybrid Systems: Computation and Control, pp. 169–178 (2019)

19. Kamann, C., Rother, C.: Benchmarking the robustness of semantic segmentation models. In: Proceedings of the IEEE/CVF Conference on Computer Vision and Pattern Recognition, pp. 8828–8838 (2020)
20. Katz, G., Barrett, C., Dill, D.L., Julian, K., Kochenderfer, M.J.: Reluplex: an efficient SMT solver for verifying deep neural networks. In: Majumdar, R., Kunčak, V. (eds.) Computer Aided Verification: 29th International Conference, CAV 2017, Heidelberg, Germany, July 24-28, 2017, Proceedings, Part I, pp. 97–117. Springer, Cham (2017). https://doi.org/10.1007/978-3-319-63387-9_5
21. Katz, G., et al.: The Marabou framework for verification and analysis of deep neural networks. In: Dillig, I., Tasiran, S. (eds.) Computer Aided Verification: 31st International Conference, CAV 2019, New York City, NY, USA, July 15-18, 2019, Proceedings, Part I, pp. 443–452. Springer, Cham (2019). https://doi.org/10.1007/978-3-030-25540-4_26
22. LeCun, Y.: The mnist database of handwritten digits. http://yann.lecun.com/exdb/mnist/ (1998)
23. Li, B., Liu, S., Xu, W., Qiu, W.: Real-time object detection and semantic segmentation for autonomous driving. In: MIPPR 2017: Automatic Target Recognition and Navigation. vol. 10608, pp. 167–174. SPIE (2018)
24. Liu, C., Arnon, T., Lazarus, C., Strong, C., Barrett, C., Kochenderfer, M.J., et al.: Algorithms for verifying deep neural networks. Found. Trends® in Optimization **4**(3–4), 244–404 (2021)
25. Lomuscio, A., Maganti, L.: An approach to reachability analysis for feed-forward relu neural networks. arXiv preprint arXiv:1706.07351 (2017)
26. Mohapatra, J., Weng, T.W., Chen, P.Y., Liu, S., Daniel, L.: Towards verifying robustness of neural networks against a family of semantic perturbations. In: Proceedings of the IEEE/CVF Conference on Computer Vision and Pattern Recognition (CVPR) (2020)
27. Moosavi-Dezfooli, S.M., Fawzi, A., Frossard, P.: Deepfool: a simple and accurate method to fool deep neural networks. In: Proceedings of the IEEE Conference on Computer Vision and Pattern Recognition, pp. 2574–2582 (2016)
28. Müller, M.N., Brix, C., Bak, S., Liu, C., Johnson, T.T.: The third international verification of neural networks competition (vnn-comp 2022): summary and results. arXiv preprint arXiv:2212.10376 (2022)
29. Ruan, W., Huang, X., Kwiatkowska, M.: Reachability analysis of deep neural networks with provable guarantees. arXiv preprint arXiv:1805.02242 (2018)
30. Ruan, W., Wu, M., Sun, Y., Huang, X., Kroening, D., Kwiatkowska, M.: Global robustness evaluation of deep neural networks with provable guarantees for the l_0 norm. arXiv preprint arXiv:1804.05805 (2018)
31. Shriver, D., Elbaum, S., Dwyer, M.B.: DNNV: a framework for deep neural network verification. In: Silva, A., Leino, K.R.M. (eds.) Computer Aided Verification: 33rd International Conference, CAV 2021, Virtual Event, July 20–23, 2021, Proceedings, Part I, pp. 137–150. Springer, Cham (2021). https://doi.org/10.1007/978-3-030-81685-8_6
32. Singh, G., Gehr, T., Püschel, M., Vechev, M.: An abstract domain for certifying neural networks. Proc. ACM Programm. Lang. **3**(POPL), 41 (2019)
33. Szegedy, C., et al.: Intriguing properties of neural networks. arXiv preprint arXiv:1312.6199 (2013)
34. Szeliski, R.: Computer vision: algorithms and applications 2nd edition (2021)
35. Tao, X., Zhang, D., Ma, W., Liu, X., Xu, D.: Automatic metallic surface defect detection and recognition with convolutional neural networks. Appl. Sci. **8**(9), 1575 (2018)

36. Thoma, M.: A survey of semantic segmentation. arXiv preprint arXiv:1602.06541 (2016)
37. Tjeng, V., Xiao, K.Y., Tedrake, R.: Evaluating robustness of neural networks with mixed integer programming. In: International Conference on Learning Representations (2019)
38. Tran, H.-D., Bak, S., Xiang, W., Johnson, T.T.: Verification of Deep Convolutional Neural Networks Using ImageStars. In: Lahiri, S.K., Wang, C. (eds.) Computer Aided Verification: 32nd International Conference, CAV 2020, Los Angeles, CA, USA, July 21–24, 2020, Proceedings, Part I, pp. 18–42. Springer, Cham (2020). https://doi.org/10.1007/978-3-030-53288-8_2
39. Tran, H.D., Cei, F., Lopez, D.M., Johnson, T.T., Koutsoukos, X.: Safety verification of cyber-physical systems with reinforcement learning control. In: ACM SIGBED International Conference on Embedded Software (EMSOFT'19). ACM (2019)
40. Tran, H.D., et al.: Star-based reachability analysis of deep neural networks. In: Formal Methods-The Next 30 Years: Third World Congress, FM 2019, Porto, Portugal, October 7–11, 2019, Proceedings 3, pp. 670–686. Springer (2019)
41. Tran, H.-D., et al.: Star-based reachability analysis of deep neural networks. In: ter Beek, M.H., McIver, A., Oliveira, J.N. (eds.) Formal Methods – The Next 30 Years: Third World Congress, FM 2019, Porto, Portugal, October 7–11, 2019, Proceedings, pp. 670–686. Springer International Publishing, Cham (2019). https://doi.org/10.1007/978-3-030-30942-8_39
42. Tran, H.-D., et al.: Robustness verification of semantic segmentation neural networks using relaxed reachability. In: Silva, A., Leino, K.R.M. (eds.) Computer Aided Verification: 33rd International Conference, CAV 2021, Virtual Event, July 20–23, 2021, Proceedings, Part I, pp. 263–286. Springer, Cham (2021). https://doi.org/10.1007/978-3-030-81685-8_12
43. Tran, H.D., Xiang, W., Johnson, T.T.: Verification approaches for learning-enabled autonomous cyber-physical systems. IEEE Design & Test (2020)
44. Tran, H.-D., et al.: NNV: the neural network verification tool for deep neural networks and learning-enabled cyber-physical systems. In: Lahiri, S.K., Wang, C. (eds.) Computer Aided Verification: 32nd International Conference, CAV 2020, Los Angeles, CA, USA, July 21–24, 2020, Proceedings, Part I, pp. 3–17. Springer, Cham (2020). https://doi.org/10.1007/978-3-030-53288-8_1
45. Tseng, Y.H., Jan, S.S.: Combination of computer vision detection and segmentation for autonomous driving. In: 2018 IEEE/ION Position, Location and Navigation Symposium (PLANS), pp. 1047–1052. IEEE (2018)
46. Wang, Z., Wei, L., Wang, L., Gao, Y., Chen, W., Shen, D.: Hierarchical vertex regression-based segmentation of head and neck CT images for radiotherapy planning. IEEE Trans. Image Process. **27**(2), 923–937 (2017)
47. Xiang, W., Johnson, T.T.: Reachability analysis and safety verification for neural network control systems. arXiv preprint arXiv:1805.09944 (2018)
48. Xiang, W., et al.: Verification for machine learning, autonomy, and neural networks survey. arXiv preprint arXiv:1810.01989 (2018)
49. Xie, X., Kersting, K., Neider, D.: Neuro-symbolic verification of deep neural networks. arXiv preprint arXiv:2203.00938 (2022)
50. Yuan, X., He, P., Zhu, Q., Li, X.: Adversarial examples: attacks and defenses for deep learning. IEEE Transac. Neural Netw. Learn. Syst. **30**(9), 2805–2824 (2019)
51. Zhang, H., Weng, T.W., Chen, P.Y., Hsieh, C.J., Daniel, L.: Efficient neural network robustness certification with general activation functions. In: Bengio, S.,

Wallach, H., Larochelle, H., Grauman, K., Cesa-Bianchi, N., Garnett, R. (eds.) Advances in Neural Information Processing Systems. vol. 31, pp. 4939–4948. Curran Associates, Inc. (2018)
52. Zhu, X., Suk, H.I., Lee, S.W., Shen, D.: Subspace regularized sparse multitask learning for multiclass neurodegenerative disease identification. IEEE Trans. Biomed. Eng. **63**(3), 607–618 (2015)
53. Zhu, X., Suk, H.I., Shen, D.: A novel matrix-similarity based loss function for joint regression and classification in ad diagnosis. Neuroimage **100**, 91–105 (2014)

Empirical Analysis of Benchmark Generation for the Verification of Neural Network Image Classifiers

Diego Manzanas Lopez(✉) and Taylor T. Johnson

Vanderbilt University, Nashville, TN, USA
{diego.manzanas.lopez,taylor.johnson}@vanderbilt.edu

Abstract. Deep Learning success in a wide range of applications, such as image recognition and natural language processing, has led to the increasing usage of this technology in many domains, including safety-critical applications such as autonomous cars and medicine. The usage of the models, e.g., neural networks, in safety critical applications demands a thorough evaluation from a component and system level perspective. In these domains, formal methods have the ability to guarantee the correct operation of these components. Despite great efforts in the formal verification of neural networks in the past decade, several challenges remain. One of these challenges is the development of neural networks for easier verification. In this work, we present an empirical analysis, presented as a Latin Hypercube experiment design, in which we evaluate how regularization and initialization methods across different random seeds on two datasets affect the verification analysis of a reachability analysis technique for the verification of neural networks. We show that there are certain training routines that simplify the formal verification task. Lastly, a discussion on how these training approaches impact the robustness verification and reachability computation of the method utilized is included.

Keywords: Formal Verification · Medical Imaging · Deep Learning · Reachability Analysis

1 Introduction

Neural Networks (NN) are a type of machine learning models that are able to learn complex patterns from data, and have been used to achieve state-of-the-art results in a wide variety of tasks such as image recognition [6,14,23] and natural language processing [7,29,32]. However, their usage in safety-critical domains requires an extensive and rigorous analysis of these models from both a component and system level perspective. Formal methods are techniques that are able to provide guarantees on the functionality of these models to ensure the correct behavior in these domains. In the past several years, there have been

B. Steffen (Ed.): AISoLA 2023, LNCS 14380, pp. 331–347, 2024.
https://doi.org/10.1007/978-3-031-46002-9_21

numerous formal verification methods and tools developed to address this challenge [2,22,27,28,30,31,35,41,48,49]. Despite recent efforts, several challenges in existing state-of-the-art methods and tools remain due to the complexity of these models and constant and rapid development of new NN architectures and models. One of the main challenges is the scalability of verification methods to large models, such as those use in Semantic Segmentation [31,45] or LLMs [32]. Another challenge is the disconnect between NN development and verification. Typically, first goes the development and training of the neural network, followed by the verification approach on the learned network (fixed parameters). If the networks do not meet the formal requirements or the methods are not able to prove them due to the complexity of the models, either new methods are needed to be developed or a new model is needed to be trained.

In this manuscript, we focus on the latter challenge, with the goal of providing some guidance and understanding on how training procedures affect formal verification methods. This idea of this project began when we discovered a large difference in the reachability computation times (order of 10 to 100 times faster) when analyzing the robustness of a neural network classifier on a medical image dataset. These findings were present not only in individual instances of a class, but were general to the whole set of images analyzed from the same class. After these observations, we decided to dig a little deeper to understand the reason behind these differences. Is it specific to the images evaluated? Is it just for a specific model? What if we change the training method, will a similar verification patter hold for the new method as well?

In this manuscript, we present a set of experiments that provide some insights to these questions using the verification tool NNV [30,46]. The contributions of this work are:

- Introduction of a new benchmark for neural network verification in the area of medical imaging (MedNIST [1]).
- Compute the formal verification of two benchmarks, both trained on grayscale image datasets, consisting of a total of 45 models and 300 instances analyzed per benchmark.
- Analysis of NNV [30,41] methods on these two benchmarks, including a discussion of the training effects on the reachability method used.

2 Related Work

Neural Network Verification. The area of neural network verification has grown immensely in recent years, having the community establish and develop standard input formats[1]. These have been especially useful for friendly competitions [28,31] as well as for method and tool comparison that enable a faster and (hopefully) fairer comparison across tools [2,21,22,30,31,46,48,49]. Despite recent efforts, the majority of these methods focus on verifying feedforward and convolutional NN architectures. These approaches can generally be classified

[1] vnnlib: https://www.vnnlib.org.

into sound or unsound, and complete or incomplete. Unsound approaches are less common for NN verification than sound approaches, as they cannot provide formal guarantees on the computer results. They usually refer to probabilistic analysis such as [42] or under approximations of the actual verification result, which are typically faster to compute than sound approximations [17]. Complete and sound methods refer to algorithms that can precisely analyze whether a given property holds on a model, also referred to as exact methods. A disadvantage from these methods is how computationally expensive these are, often becoming prohibitive to compute, thus suffering from scalability issues for large models or inputs sets [31,45]. These methods are often limited in the type of layers and architectures they can be used for. These can be Satisfiability Modulo Theories (SMT) based methods [21,22], Mixed Integer Linear Program (MILP) based methods [40], reachability analysis methods [45], and others such as branch and bound methods [5]. To overcome some of these challenges, sound and incomplete methods have been developed. These methods often introduced a tradeoff between precision, scalability and computational power needed. These methods are capable of computing the verification results faster than sound and complete methods, however, due to the overapproximation computations, unknown results may arise (cannot guarantee specification is violated nor satisfied). Several of these methods are based on abstract interpretation, some of which have demonstrated to outperform complete methods by orders of magnitude (time wise) [31]. Recent work in [11] has enhanced the abstraction-based verification of neural networks via residual reasoning.

Training and Verification and Repair. There have also been some works focusing on repairing or retraining neural networks when a specification is violated [8,13,39]. Many of these efforts focus on fine-tuning or retraining the network when inputs violating the output constraints are found [10,33,36,51], directly modifying the parameters of the network to correct violating inputs [9,16,47], or on modifying the architecture of the neural network to facilitate the repair of the model such as in [37]. Another area that has seen some efforts is to directly train neural networks for enhancing the verification approaches. Some works focus on replacing the ReLU layers by Parametric ReLUs to enhance both robustness and verification scalability [26], others have focused on using stability training methods for ReLUs to pre-estimate the bounds for all ReLU neurons [50], providing local Lipschitz bounds to the networks to simplify its verification [20], using interval bound propagation during training to improve the verified robustness of the models [34], or developing regularization methods for improving robustness and reducing the verification time for autoencoders [4].

3 Evaluation

We use two datasets in our evaluation: MNIST [25], and a medical image dataset, MedNIST [1]. The MedNIST dataset was assembled by B.J. Erickson (Department of Radiology, Mayo Clinic).[2] The dataset contains 58954 medical images

[2] Available at https://github.com/Project-MONAI/MONAI/.

belonging to 6 classes: AbdomenCT, BreastMRI, ChestCT, CSR, Hand, and HeadCT, which are depicted in Fig. 1. Each of the classes contains 10,000 images except for BreastMRI, which contains 8,954 images.

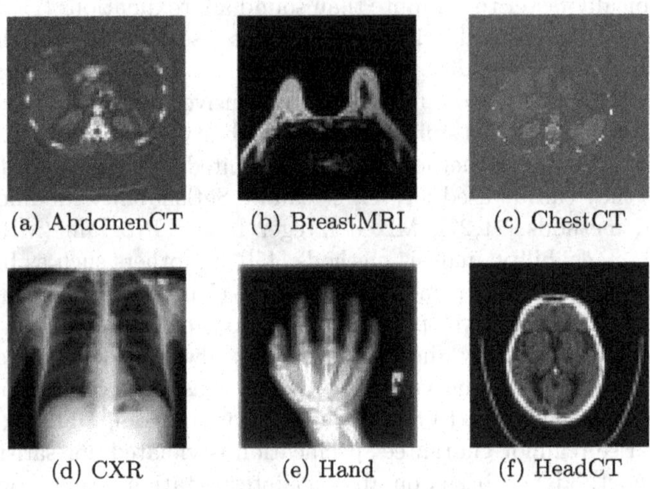

(a) AbdomenCT (b) BreastMRI (c) ChestCT

(d) CXR (e) Hand (f) HeadCT

Fig. 1. MedNIST dataset visualization.

We present our study as a Latin Hypercube experiment design. A Latin hypercube typically consists of N variables divided into M equally sized intervals or discrete values, where each sample is unique: each sample is the only one in each axis-aligned hyperplane containing it [12]. Our experimental design consists of 3 variables (*init_method*, *reg_method*, *random_seed*), the first two containing 3 different values and the latter one with 5 possible values. The experiments consist of training 45 different models, 5 models per combination of hyperparameters: initialization *init_method* $\in$ {He [18], Glorot [15], narrow_normal[3]}, and regularization scheme *reg_method* $\in$ {Dropout [38], Jacobian [19], L_2 [24] }. Each of these models are initialized with a different random seed, *random_seed* $\in \{0, 1, 2, 3, 4\}$, to evaluate the training combination of *init_method* $\times$ *reg_method*.

Once all models are trained, we perform a verification analysis, for which we select 300 images from the test dataset, and apply an L_∞ attack with an $\epsilon = \{3/255\}$, for a total of 300 images evaluated for each of the 45 neural networks[4]. To verify the robustness of these networks against adversarial attacks, we only chose images that are correctly classified by all networks, and select the same number of images per class in each dataset: 50 images per class in MedNIST, and 30 for MNIST. Formally, we evaluate the robustness of a neural network

[3] Weights are independently sampled from a normal distribution with 0 mean and standard deviation of 0.01.

[4] The model architecture is depicted in Fig. 9 in the Appendix.

$\mathcal{F}(z)$, with input image $z \in \mathbb{R}^{i \times j}$, perturbation parameter $\epsilon \in \mathbb{R}$ and an input set Z_p containing z_p such that $Z_p = \{z : ||z - z_p|| \leq \epsilon\}$ that represents the set of all possible perturbations of z. The neural network is locally **robust** at z if it correctly classifies all the perturbed inputs z_p to the same label as z, i.e., the system is **robust** if $\mathcal{F}(z_p) = \mathcal{F}(z)$ for all $z_p \in Z_p$.

Our goal is to gain some insights to the following questions:

- Is there a training procedure that facilitates the verification of these models?
- Can the training and verification trends hold across datasets?
- How much of an effect has the initial random seed on our evaluation?
- Are there specific classes that are harder or easier to verify than others?

4 Results

We analyze the verification results based on 1) initialization, 2) regularization, and 3) random seed, with respect to every class in the dataset. It is important to remember that the robustness percentage may be greater than the accuracy, as we only evaluated the models in images correctly classified by all of them. On Figs. 2 to 7, on the left (subfig. *a*) we present the average percentage of instances verified to be robust with respect to each image class, and on the right (subfig. *b*), we present the average computation time to verify each instance with respect to each image class[5]. In addition, we present a summary of the verification results in the Appendix in Tables 1 and 2 for MedNIST and MNIST respectively.

4.1 Initialization

In Fig. 2 we present the average robustness percentage and computation time across all 15 models trained using each initialization method on the MedNIST dataset. We observe that we are able to verify the largest number of instances of the models trained using the *narrow-normal* initialization method, and much faster than the other ones.

In Fig. 3 we present the average robustness percentage and computation time across all 15 models trained using each initialization method on the MNIST dataset. Similar to the MedNIST results but less pronounced, we observe that we are able to verify the largest number of instances of the models trained using the *narrow-normal* initialization method, and faster than the other ones, but very close to the *he* initializer.

4.2 Regularization

In Fig. 4 we present the average robustness percentage and computation time across all 15 models trained using each regularization method on the MedNIST dataset. We observe that we are able to verify the largest number of instances of

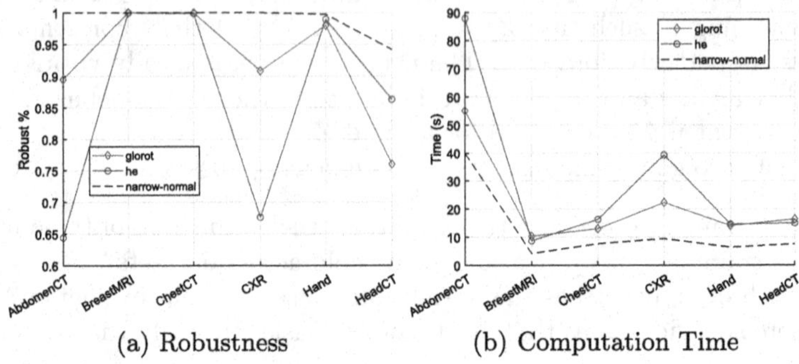

(a) Robustness (b) Computation Time

Fig. 2. *MedNIST Results.* Comparison across initialization schemes with respect to each image class.

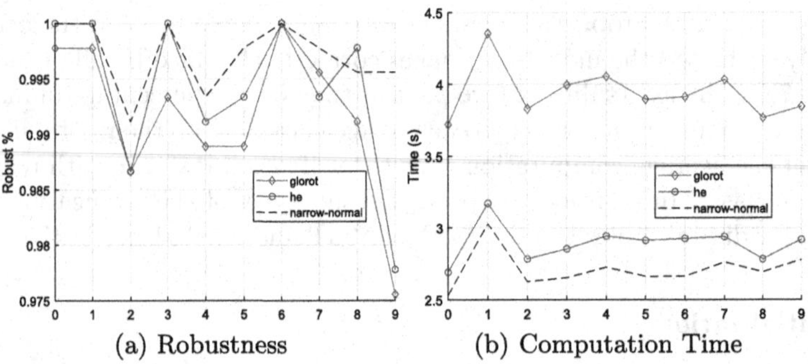

(a) Robustness (b) Computation Time

Fig. 3. *MNIST Results.* Comparison across initialization schemes with respect to each image class.

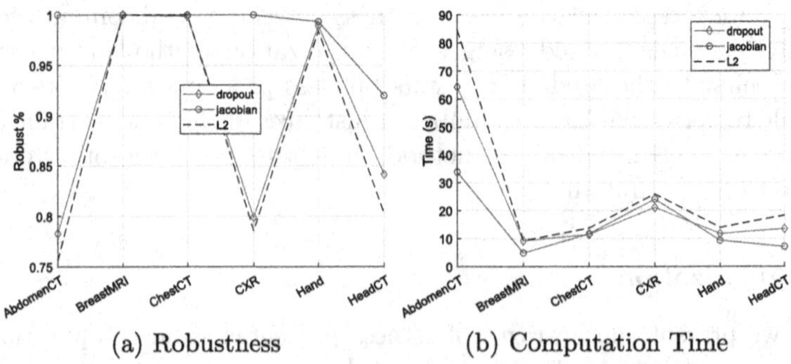

(a) Robustness (b) Computation Time

Fig. 4. *MedNIST Results.* Comparison across regularization techniques with respect to each image class.

the models trained using the *Jacobian* regularization method, and slightly faster than the other ones.

In Fig. 5 we present the average robustness percentage and computation time across all 15 models trained using each regularization method on the MNIST dataset. We observe that we are able to compute the verification result of the models using the dropout regularization method the fastest, about 2× faster than *Jacobian* (fastest on MedNIST), but the number of instances across them is very similar.

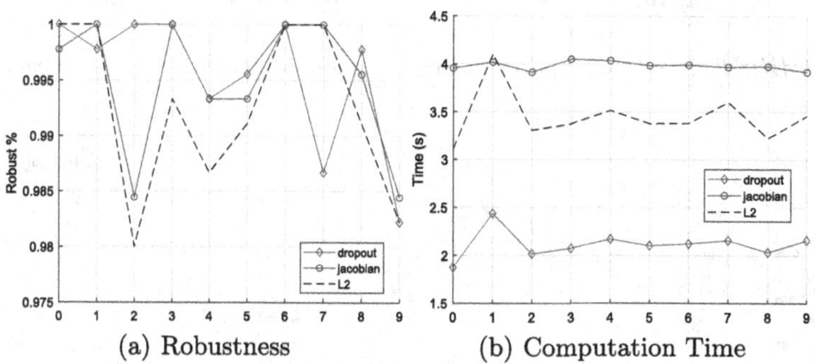

Fig. 5. *MNIST Results.* Comparison across regularization techniques with respect to each image class.

4.3 Random Seed

In Fig. 6 we present the average robustness percentage and computation time across all 9 models initialized using each random seed on the MedNIST dataset. Models with random seed *1* are slightly faster to verify, with a larger number of instances verified.

In Fig. 7 we present the average robustness percentage and computation time across all 9 models initialized using each random seed on the MNIST dataset. In this case, there is not a clear "winner" in terms of number of instances verified, but interestingly, there is a very defined pattern in the verification computation across the random seeds, being *2* the fastest and *3* the slowest.

Regularization and Initialization Combinations. Looking into these results, we would expect to have several models with 100 % verified instances on the MNIST dataset (total of 10, as observed in Table 2, and having the fastest models to verify to be a model trained using the narrow-normal initialization with the dropout regularizer, depicted in Fig. 8(b). For the MedNIST dataset,

[5] Code is available at: https://github.com/verivital/nnv/tree/master/code/nnv/examples/Submission/AISOLA2023.

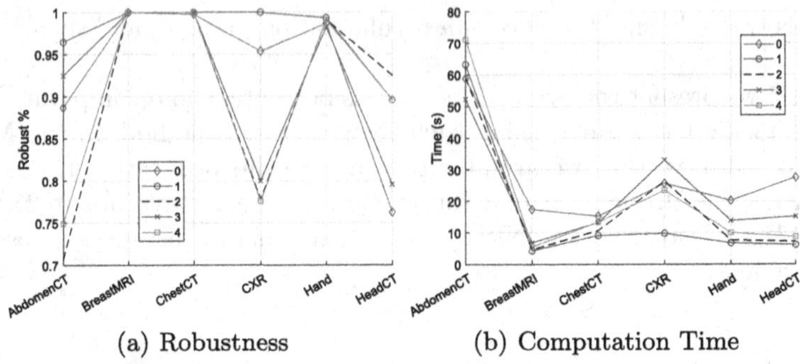

(a) Robustness (b) Computation Time

Fig. 6. *MedNIST Results.* Comparison across random seeds with respect to each image class.

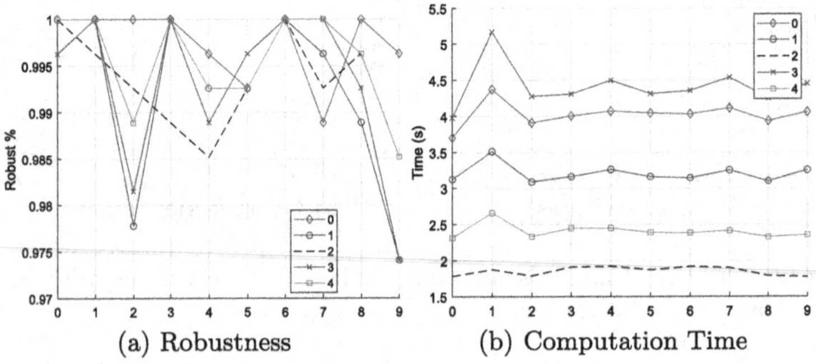

(a) Robustness (b) Computation Time

Fig. 7. *MNIST Results.* Comparison across random seeds with respect to each image class.

the fastest combination is expected to be a narrow-normal initialized model with either dropout or Jacobian regularization, as observed in Fig. 8(a). A surprising result is that there are 6 models with 100 % verified instances on the MedNIST benchmark, 4 of which are models trained using Jacobian regularization and narrow-normal initialization method, as observed in Table 2.

5 Discussion

Based on the results from Figs. 2 to 7, one can observe that there are trends that hold across the datasets, while some other results are very different from each other. We begin with the similarities between the two datasets in terms of verification results. Looking into the initialization schemes (Figs. 2 and 3), we observe similar results, being *narrow-normal* initializer the fastest to verify across both datasets, and the one with the highest number of instances verified. Another common result from both datasets is L_2 regularizer having the least number of instances verified, and the slowest for MedNIST and second slowest for MNIST, closer to the slowest (Jacobian) than the fastest (dropout).

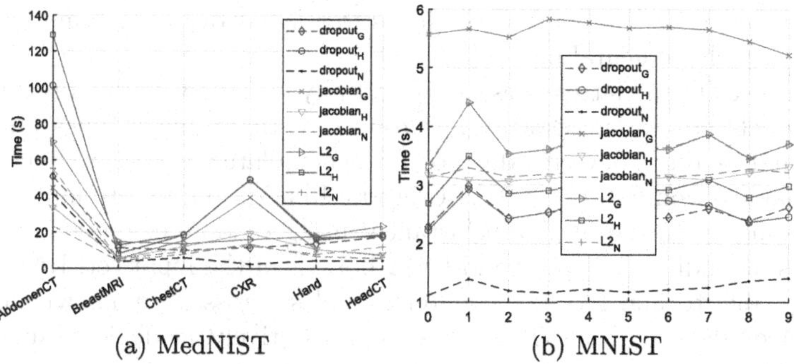

(a) MedNIST (b) MNIST

Fig. 8. *Combination Results.* Comparison across regularization & initialization combinations in terms of verification computation time in seconds for MedNIST and MNIST benchmarks.

There are also some clear differences across the datasets. For the MNIST models, the computation time trends are held across all the classes, indicating that the verification computation depends more on the model than the image class evaluated, except for class *1* which is slightly slower. On the other hand, for the MedNIST models, the verification times are very dependent on the image type, as we can observe in Figs. 2, 4, and 6, where the verification of *AbdomenCT* images is the slowest, up to 10× slower than other classes, and *CXR* the second slowest with 4× to 5× slower than other classes. *AbdomenCT* is also the class with the least number of instances verified, followed by *HeadCT* and *CXR*.

These last results prompt two questions:

1. Why is there such a big difference in the computation time of the same model when looking at two different images from the same dataset?
2. Do the lower robustness percentages mean the models are less robust, or are these models harder to verify?

To answer these, we need to understand the verification method used. In this paper, we use a sound and incomplete reachability method described in [41,44]. This method represents the sets using ImageStars [41], and computes the output set using a layer-by-layer approach. We run several examples and timed every operation within the reachability computation to understand where the timing difference lies, and discovered (as expected) that the largest percentage of the computation time is in the reachability computation of the ReLU layers. More specifically, in the computation of the solution of the Linear Programming (LP) problems. When using the approach in [44], if the estimated range contains the zero point, we solve two LP problems to get the range of this specific input. The solution to each of these LP problems is an overapproximation of the exact range (sound and incomplete). Thus, it is not a coincidence that the class with the slowest verification computation (AbdomenCT) is also the class with the least number of instances verified. These two variables are correlated, as the larger number of LP problems solved leads to a larger overapproximation of the reachable set of the neural network.

The answer to the latter question is partially covered with the previous one. These models are not necessarily less robust to these image types under L_∞ attacks, but harder to verify due to the accumulated overapproximations in the reachability computation of ReLU layers. In addition, we attempted to find counterexamples to the unknown instances using random examples within the input sets, including the upper and lower bounds of the input set. However, we were only able to find 2 and 1 counterexamples across all unknown instances for the MedNIST and MNIST benchmarks respectively, as depicted in Tables 1 and 2.

Limitations.

Dataset Coverage. For the robustness analysis, we randomly select 20 images per class, which is less than 1% of the images in the dataset.

Model Architecture. The analysis is limited to a single architecture with a convolutional, a batch normalization, a ReLU, an average pooling and a fully-connected layer. When looking closely at the results, we observe that the *harder* examples (in terms of computation time) tend to *activate* both sides of the ReLU neurons (input interval is less than 0 and greater than 0), requiring to solve a larger amount of Linear Programming (LP) problems, e.g., taking up to 80% to 90% of the total reachability computation time for some instances. Using other activation function or architectures may reduce the complexity of these *harder* instances.

Methods Evaluated. We were able to discover some trends on finding harder verification examples for NNV, which is a reachability based tool using Star sets [3,41,44,46]. Although we expect similar results in terms of computation time trends, more evaluations are needed to determine if these trends also hold when using other methods such as SMT or MILP based (e.g., Marabou [22]).

Complete vs Incomplete Verification. We evaluate the robustness of the networks using a sound but incomplete method, so we can only guarantee the number of instances verified to be robust, but no guarantees on the others. To prove the network is not robust, we would have to find counterexamples, or we would need to run a complete verifier (*exact* reachability methods in NNV) to determine the certified robustness score of each network. However, the goal of this paper is to understand the complexity of the verification analysis on different training routines, and we would expect to observe a similar trend for the exact analysis on the computation time aspect (the larger computation times come from having to compute the reachability of ReLU neurons when the input interval value is less than 0 and greater than 0, which has a similar effect on the complete methods [43]).

6 Conclusion

In this study, we have presented two neural network verification benchmarks, one from the MedNIST dataset [1] and one from MNIST [25] consisting of 45 neural networks and 300 verification instances per network, for each of the benchmarks. On these, we have analyzed how different training procedures affect a sound and incomplete reachability analysis technique implemented in NNV [41,44]. We can observe that there are training combinations that lead to models that are easier to verify using these methods. For the more challenging verification instances, we discuss the reasons behind it: input ranges to the neurons in the ReLU layers are "activating" both sides of the function ($max(0, input)$), requiring to solve a larger number of LP problems, which in turn leads to a larger overapproximation of the output reachable set, making the computation slower and more complex.

Acknowledgements. The material presented in this paper is based upon work supported by the National Science Foundation (NSF) through grant numbers 2028001, 2220426 and 2220401, the Defense Advanced Research Projects Agency (DARPA) under contract number FA8750-23-C-0518, and the Air Force Office of Scientific Research (AFOSR) under contract number FA9550-22-1-0019 and FA9550-23-1-0135. Any opinions, findings, and conclusions or recommendations expressed in this paper are those of the authors and do not necessarily reflect the views of AFOSR, DARPA, or NSF.

A Appendix

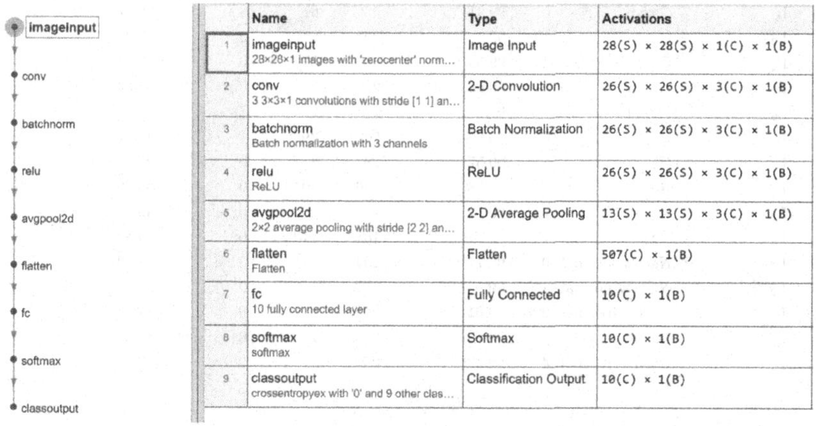

imageinput → conv → batchnorm → relu → avgpool2d → flatten → fc → softmax → classoutput

	Name	Type	Activations
1	imageinput 28×28×1 images with 'zerocenter' norm...	Image Input	28(S) × 28(S) × 1(C) × 1(B)
2	conv 3 3×3×1 convolutions with stride [1 1] an...	2-D Convolution	26(S) × 26(S) × 3(C) × 1(B)
3	batchnorm Batch normalization with 3 channels	Batch Normalization	26(S) × 26(S) × 3(C) × 1(B)
4	relu ReLU	ReLU	26(S) × 26(S) × 3(C) × 1(B)
5	avgpool2d 2×2 average pooling with stride [2 2] an...	2-D Average Pooling	13(S) × 13(S) × 3(C) × 1(B)
6	flatten Flatten	Flatten	507(C) × 1(B)
7	fc 10 fully connected layer	Fully Connected	10(C) × 1(B)
8	softmax softmax	Softmax	10(C) × 1(B)
9	classoutput crossentropyex with '0' and 9 other clas...	Classification Output	10(C) × 1(B)

Fig. 9. Neural network architecture of the models trained on MNIST. The architecture for the MedNIST models is created with the same parameters as the MNIST ones, but the difference is the size of the input. MNIST input is 28 × 28, while MedNIST images are 64 × 64, thus leading to small differences such as in the number of weights across some of the layers.

Table 1. MedNIST summary results

Model			**Accuracy (%)**	**Verification Results**			
Regularization	*Initialization*	*Seed*		*Robust*	*Unkown*	*Not Robust*	*Avg. Time (s)*
Dropout	Glorot	0	99.27	276	24	0	28.87
Dropout	Glorot	1	99.51	294	6	0	13.33
Dropout	Glorot	2	99.52	285	15	0	11.93
Dropout	Glorot	3	99.57	257	43	0	24.53
Dropout	Glorot	4	99.63	286	14	0	17.36
Dropout	He	0	99.65	257	43	0	43.81
Dropout	He	1	99.60	286	14	0	22.23
Dropout	He	2	99.57	203	96	0	28.40
Dropout	He	3	99.73	235	65	0	42.11
Dropout	He	4	99.70	196	104	0	43.95
Dropout	Narrow-normal	0	99.55	300	0	0	10.49
Dropout	Narrow-normal	1	99.50	294	6	0	11.72
Dropout	Narrow-normal	2	99.61	293	7	0	14.85
Dropout	Narrow-normal	3	99.55	296	4	0	5.17
Dropout	Narrow-normal	4	99.66	300	0	0	9.35
Jacobian	Glorot	0	99.79	288	12	0	19.55
Jacobian	Glorot	1	99.79	291	9	0	20.80
Jacobian	Glorot	2	99.80	289	11	0	19.97
Jacobian	Glorot	3	99.80	289	11	0	19.98
Jacobian	Glorot	4	99.78	292	8	0	21.76
Jacobian	He	0	99.67	300	0	0	14.46
Jacobian	He	1	99.75	298	2	0	14.72
Jacobian	He	2	99.74	298	2	0	14.85
Jacobian	He	3	99.74	298	2	0	14.81
Jacobian	He	4	99.77	297	3	0	15.00
Jacobian	Narrow-normal	0	99.69	300	0	0	10.32
Jacobian	Narrow-normal	1	99.76	295	5	0	9.51
Jacobian	Narrow-normal	2	99.77	300	0	0	10.33
Jacobian	Narrow-normal	3	99.78	300	0	0	10.32
Jacobian	Narrow-normal	4	99.78	300	0	0	10.31
L_2	Glorot	0	99.31	239	61	0	38.67
L_2	Glorot	1	99.51	292	8	0	18.25
L_2	Glorot	2	99.55	273	27	0	16.24
L_2	Glorot	3	99.60	229	71	0	32.63
L_2	Glorot	4	99.65	277	22	1	23.67
L_2	He	0	99.69	260	39	1	45.94
L_2	He	1	99.57	292	8	0	27.76
L_2	He	2	99.58	196	104	0	39.09
L_2	He	3	99.72	274	26	0	42.45
L_2	He	4	99.72	188	112	0	44.44
L_2	Narrow-normal	0	99.71	294	6	0	35.24
L_2	Narrow-normal	1	99.53	292	8	0	10.52
L_2	Narrow-normal	2	99.61	293	7	0	17.80
L_2	Narrow-normal	3	99.55	298	2	0	9.21
L_2	Narrow-normal	4	99.68	299	1	0	12.43

Table 2. MNIST summary results

Model			**Accuracy (%)**	**Verification Results**			
Regularization	*Initialization*	*Seed*		*Robust*	*Unkown*	*Not Robust*	*Avg. Time (s)*
Dropout	Glorot	0	95.61	300	0	0	4.15
Dropout	Glorot	1	95.54	299	1	0	3.87
Dropout	Glorot	2	93.43	293	7	0	0.32
Dropout	Glorot	3	96.56	298	2	0	3.90
Dropout	Glorot	4	94.10	298	2	0	0.41
Dropout	He	0	92.79	297	3	0	4.04
Dropout	He	1	93.62	299	1	0	0.32
Dropout	He	2	93.82	299	1	0	0.26
Dropout	He	3	95.97	299	1	0	4.19
Dropout	He	4	95.81	299	0	1	4.05
Dropout	Narrow-normal	0	95.92	300	0	0	0.52
Dropout	Narrow-normal	1	93.31	299	1	0	0.32
Dropout	Narrow-normal	2	94.67	299	1	0	0.38
Dropout	Narrow-normal	3	96.03	300	0	0	4.53
Dropout	Narrow-normal	4	95.84	300	0	0	0.48
Jacobian	Glorot	0	96.37	299	1	0	4.65
Jacobian	Glorot	1	96.86	298	2	0	6.11
Jacobian	Glorot	2	97.03	299	1	0	6.32
Jacobian	Glorot	3	97.16	296	4	0	5.58
Jacobian	Glorot	4	97.08	299	1	0	5.36
Jacobian	He	0	94.81	298	2	0	5.89
Jacobian	He	1	96.04	297	3	0	3.93
Jacobian	He	2	96.56	299	1	0	2.57
Jacobian	He	3	96.97	299	1	0	1.75
Jacobian	He	4	96.83	296	4	0	1.57
Jacobian	Narrow-normal	0	96.50	300	0	0	6.08
Jacobian	Narrow-normal	1	97.12	299	1	0	3.46
Jacobian	Narrow-normal	2	96.97	300	0	0	2.53
Jacobian	Narrow-normal	3	97.23	299	1	0	1.96
Jacobian	Narrow-normal	4	97.20	299	1	0	1.98
L_2	Glorot	0	96.11	300	0	0	3.64
L_2	Glorot	1	95.63	296	4	0	7.00
L_2	Glorot	2	94.49	293	7	0	0.30
L_2	Glorot	3	96.29	295	5	0	7.08
L_2	Glorot	4	94.49	299	1	0	0.42
L_2	He	0	92.88	300	0	0	3.54
L_2	He	1	93.73	295	5	0	3.60
L_2	He	2	93.47	300	0	0	0.27
L_2	He	3	96.03	296	4	0	3.72
L_2	He	4	96.18	300	0	0	3.67
L_2	Narrow-normal	0	96.20	299	1	0	3.72
L_2	Narrow-normal	1	93.27	297	3	0	0.29
L_2	Narrow-normal	2	94.97	299	1	0	3.72
L_2	Narrow-normal	3	96.68	299	1	0	7.02
L_2	Narrow-normal	4	95.72	298	2	0	3.70

References

1. apolanco3225: Medical mnist classification. https://github.com/apolanco3225/Medical-MNIST-Classification (2017)

2. Bak, S.: nnenum: verification of ReLU neural networks with optimized abstraction refinement. In: Dutle, A., Moscato, M.M., Titolo, L., Muñoz, C.A., Perez, I. (eds.) NASA Formal Methods: 13th International Symposium, NFM 2021, Virtual Event, May 24–28, 2021, Proceedings, pp. 19–36. Springer, Cham (2021). https://doi.org/10.1007/978-3-030-76384-8_2
3. Bak, S., Duggirala, P.S.: Simulation-equivalent reachability of large linear systems with inputs. In: Majumdar, R., Kunčak, V. (eds.) Computer Aided Verification, pp. 401–420. Springer International Publishing, Cham (2017)
4. Böing, B., Müller, E.: On training and verifying robust autoencoders. In: 2022 IEEE 9th International Conference on Data Science and Advanced Analytics (DSAA), pp. 1–10 (2022). https://doi.org/10.1109/DSAA54385.2022.10032334
5. Bunel, R., et al.: Branch and bound for piecewise linear neural network verification. J. Mach. Learn. Res. **21**(1) (2020)
6. Cireşan, D., Meier, U., Schmidhuber, J.: Multi-column deep neural networks for image classification. arXiv preprint arXiv:1202.2745 (2012)
7. Collobert, R., Weston, J.: A unified architecture for natural language processing: Deep neural networks with multitask learning. In: Proceedings of the 25th international conference on Machine learning, pp. 160–167. ACM (2008)
8. Cruz, U.S., Ferlez, J., Shoukry, Y.: Safe-by-repair: A convex optimization approach for repairing unsafe two-level lattice neural network controllers. In: 2022 IEEE 61st Conference on Decision and Control (CDC), pp. 3383–3388 (2022). https://doi.org/10.1109/CDC51059.2022.9993239
9. Dong, G., Sun, J., Wang, J., Wang, X., Dai, T.: Towards repairing neural networks correctly (2021)
10. Dreossi, T., Ghosh, S., Yue, X., Keutzer, K., Sangiovanni-Vincentelli, A., Seshia, S.A.: Counterexample-guided data augmentation. In: Proceedings of the 27th International Joint Conference on Artificial Intelligence, pp. 2071–2078. IJCAI'18, AAAI Press (2018)
11. Elboher, Y.Y., Cohen, E., Katz, G.: Neural network verification using residual reasoning. In: Schlingloff, B.-H., Chai, M. (eds.) Software Engineering and Formal Methods: 20th International Conference, SEFM 2022, Berlin, Germany, September 26–30, 2022, Proceedings, pp. 173–189. Springer, Cham (2022). https://doi.org/10.1007/978-3-031-17108-6_11
12. Fisher, R.A.: Statistical methods for research workers. In: Kotz, S., Johnson, N.L. (eds.) Breakthroughs in Statistics, pp. 66–70. Springer, New York, NY (1992). https://doi.org/10.1007/978-1-4612-4380-9_6
13. Fu, F., Li, W.: Sound and complete neural network repair with minimality and locality guarantees. In: International Conference on Learning Representations (2022). https://openreview.net/forum?id=xS8AMYiEav3
14. Gatys, L.A., Ecker, A.S., Bethge, M.: Image style transfer using convolutional neural networks. In: Proceedings of the IEEE Conference on Computer Vision and Pattern Recognition, pp. 2414–2423 (2016)
15. Glorot, X., Bengio, Y.: Understanding the difficulty of training deep feedforward neural networks. In: Teh, Y.W., Titterington, M. (eds.) Proceedings of the Thirteenth International Conference on Artificial Intelligence and Statistics. Proceedings of Machine Learning Research, vol. 9, pp. 249–256. PMLR, Chia Laguna Resort, Sardinia, Italy (2010)
16. Goldberger, B., Katz, G., Adi, Y., Keshet, J.: Minimal modifications of deep neural networks using verification. In: Albert, E., Kovacs, L. (eds.) LPAR23. LPAR-23: 23rd International Conference on Logic for Programming, Artificial Intelligence

and Reasoning. EPiC Series in Computing, vol. 73, pp. 260–278. EasyChair (2020). https://doi.org/10.29007/699q, https://easychair.org/publications/paper/CWhF
17. Goubault, E., Putot, S.: Rino: robust inner and outer approximated reachability of neural networks controlled systems. In: Shoham, S., Vizel, Y. (eds.) Computer Aided Verification, pp. 511–523. Springer, Cham (2022)
18. He, K., Zhang, X., Ren, S., Sun, J.: Delving deep into rectifiers: Surpassing human-level performance on imagenet classification. In: 2015 IEEE International Conference on Computer Vision (ICCV), pp. 1026–1034 (2015). https://doi.org/10.1109/ICCV.2015.123
19. Hoffman, J., Roberts, D.A., Yaida, S.: Robust learning with Jacobian regularization (2019)
20. Huang, Y., Zhang, H., Shi, Y., Kolter, J.Z., Anandkumar, A.: Training certifiably robust neural networks with efficient local lipschitz bounds. In: Ranzato, M., Beygelzimer, A., Dauphin, Y., Liang, P., Vaughan, J.W. (eds.) Advances in Neural Information Processing Systems. vol. 34, pp. 22745–22757. Curran Associates, Inc. (2021)
21. Katz, G., Barrett, C., Dill, D.L., Julian, K., Kochenderfer, M.J.: Reluplex: an efficient SMT solver for verifying deep neural networks. In: Majumdar, R., Kunčak, V. (eds.) Computer Aided Verification: 29th International Conference, CAV 2017, Heidelberg, Germany, July 24-28, 2017, Proceedings, Part I, pp. 97–117. Springer, Cham (2017). https://doi.org/10.1007/978-3-319-63387-9_5
22. Katz, G., et al.: The marabou framework for verification and analysis of deep neural networks. In: Dillig, I., Tasiran, S. (eds.) Computer Aided Verification: 31st International Conference, CAV 2019, New York City, NY, USA, July 15-18, 2019, Proceedings, Part I, pp. 443–452. Springer, Cham (2019). https://doi.org/10.1007/978-3-030-25540-4_26
23. Krizhevsky, A., Sutskever, I., Hinton, G.E.: Imagenet classification with deep convolutional neural networks. In: Advances in neural information processing systems, pp. 1097–1105 (2012)
24. Krogh, A., Hertz, J.A.: A simple weight decay can improve generalization. In: Proceedings of the 4th International Conference on Neural Information Processing Systems, pp. 950–957. NIPS'91, Morgan Kaufmann Publishers Inc., San Francisco, CA, USA (1991)
25. LeCun, Y., Cortes, C., Burges, C.: Mnist handwritten digit database. ATT Labs http://yann.lecun.com/exdb/mnist 2 (2010)
26. Leofante, F., Henriksen, P., Lomuscio, A.: Verification-friendly networks: the case for parametric relus. In: Workshop on Formal Verification of Machine Learning, Colocated with ICML 2022. IEEE (2022)
27. Liu, C., Arnon, T., Lazarus, C., Strong, C., Barrett, C., Kochenderfer, M.J.: Algorithms for verifying deep neural networks. Found. Trends Optimization **4**(3–4), 244–404 (2021). https://doi.org/10.1561/2400000035
28. Lopez, D.M., et al.: Arch-comp22 category report: Artificial intelligence and neural network control systems (ainncs) for continuous and hybrid systems plants. In: Frehse, G., Althoff, M., Schoitsch, E., Guiochet, J. (eds.) Proceedings of 9th International Workshop on Applied Verification of Continuous and Hybrid Systems (ARCH22). EPiC Series in Computing, vol. 90, pp. 142–184. EasyChair (2022)
29. Luong, M.T., Pham, H., Manning, C.D.: Effective approaches to attention-based neural machine translation. arXiv preprint arXiv:1508.04025 (2015)
30. Lopez, D.M., Choi, S.W., Tran, H.-D., Johnson, T.T.: NNV 2.0: the neural network verification tool. In: Enea, C., Lal, A. (eds.) Computer Aided Verification: 35th

International Conference, CAV 2023, Paris, France, July 17–22, 2023, Proceedings, Part II, pp. 397–412. Springer, Cham (2023). https://doi.org/10.1007/978-3-031-37703-7_19
31. Müller, M.N., Brix, C., Bak, S., Liu, C., Johnson, T.T.: The third international verification of neural networks competition (vnn-comp 2022): Summary and results (2022)
32. OpenAI: Gpt-4 technical report (2023)
33. Ren, X., et al.: Few-shot guided mix for dnn repairing. In: Proceedings - 2020 IEEE International Conference on Software Maintenance and Evolution, ICSME 2020, pp. 717–721. Proceedings - 2020 IEEE International Conference on Software Maintenance and Evolution, ICSME 2020, Institute of Electrical and Electronics Engineers Inc., United States (2020). https://doi.org/10.1109/ICSME46990.2020.00079
34. Shi, Z., Wang, Y., Zhang, H., Yi, J., Hsieh, C.J.: Fast certified robust training with short warmup. In: Ranzato, M., Beygelzimer, A., Dauphin, Y., Liang, P., Vaughan, J.W. (eds.) Advances in Neural Information Processing Systems. vol. 34, pp. 18335–18349. Curran Associates, Inc. (2021). https://proceedings.neurips.cc/paper_files/paper/2021/file/988f9153ac4fd966ea302dd9ab9bae15-Paper.pdf
35. Singh, G., Gehr, T., Mirman, M., Püschel, M., Vechev, M.: Fast and effective robustness certification. In: Bengio, S., Wallach, H., Larochelle, H., Grauman, K., Cesa-Bianchi, N., Garnett, R. (eds.) In: Advances in Neural Information Processing Systems, vol. 31. Curran Associates, Inc. (2018)
36. Sinitsin, A., Plokhotnyuk, V., Pyrkin, D., Popov, S., Babenko, A.: Editable neural networks. In: International Conference on Learning Representations (2020)
37. Sotoudeh, M., Thakur, A.V.: Provable repair of deep neural networks. In: Proceedings of the 42nd ACM SIGPLAN International Conference on Programming Language Design and Implementation, pp. 588–603. PLDI 2021, Association for Computing Machinery, New York, NY, USA (2021). https://doi.org/10.1145/3453483.3454064
38. Srivastava, N., Hinton, G., Krizhevsky, A., Sutskever, I., Salakhutdinov, R.: Dropout: a simple way to prevent neural networks from overfitting. J. Mach. Learn. Res. **15**(56), 1929–1958 (2014). http://jmlr.org/papers/v15/srivastava14a.html
39. Tao, Z., Nawas, S., Mitchell, J., Thakur, A.V.: Architecture-preserving provable repair of deep neural networks. Proc. ACM Program. Lang. 7(PLDI), 443–467 (2023). https://doi.org/10.1145/3591238
40. Tjeng, V., Xiao, K., Tedrake, R.: Evaluating robustness of neural networks with mixed integer programming. arXiv preprint arXiv:1711.07356 (2017)
41. Tran, H.-D., Bak, S., Xiang, W., Johnson, T.T.: Verification of deep convolutional neural networks using imagestars. In: Lahiri, S.K., Wang, C. (eds.) Computer Aided Verification: 32nd International Conference, CAV 2020, Los Angeles, CA, USA, July 21–24, 2020, Proceedings, Part I, pp. 18–42. Springer, Cham (2020). https://doi.org/10.1007/978-3-030-53288-8_2
42. Tran, H.D., Choi, S., Okamoto, H., Hoxha, B., Fainekos, G., Prokhorov, D.: Quantitative verification for neural networks using probstars. In: Proceedings of the 26th ACM International Conference on Hybrid Systems: Computation and Control. HSCC '23, Association for Computing Machinery, New York, NY, USA (2023). https://doi.org/10.1145/3575870.3587112
43. Tran, H.-D., et al.: Star-based reachability analysis of deep neural networks. In: ter Beek, M.H., McIver, A., Oliveira, J.N. (eds.) Formal Methods – The Next 30 Years: Third World Congress, FM 2019, Porto, Portugal, October 7–11, 2019,

Proceedings, pp. 670–686. Springer, Cham (2019). https://doi.org/10.1007/978-3-030-30942-8_39
44. Tran, H.D., et al.: Verification of piecewise deep neural networks: A star set approach with zonotope pre-filter. Form. Asp. Comput. **33**(4–5), 519–545 (2021)
45. Tran, H.-D., et al.: Robustness verification of semantic segmentation neural networks using relaxed reachability. In: Silva, A., Leino, K.R.M. (eds.) Computer Aided Verification: 33rd International Conference, CAV 2021, Virtual Event, July 20–23, 2021, Proceedings, Part I, pp. 263–286. Springer, Cham (2021). https://doi.org/10.1007/978-3-030-81685-8_12
46. Tran, H.D., et al.: NNV: The neural network verification tool for deep neural networks and learning-enabled cyber-physical systems. In: 32nd International Conference on Computer-Aided Verification (CAV) (2020)
47. Usman, M., Gopinath, D., Sun, Y., Noller, Y., Păsăreanu, C.S.: Nnrepair: constraint-based repair of neural network classifiers. In: Silva, A., Leino, K.R.M. (eds.) Computer Aided Verification, pp. 3–25. Springer, Cham (2021)
48. Wang, S., Pei, K., Whitehouse, J., Yang, J., Jana, S.: Formal security analysis of neural networks using symbolic intervals. In: 27th {USENIX} Security Symposium ({USENIX} Security 18), pp. 1599–1614 (2018)
49. Wang, S., et al.: Beta-CROWN: Efficient bound propagation with per-neuron split constraints for complete and incomplete neural network verification. In: Advances in Neural Information Processing Systems 34 (2021)
50. Xiao, K.Y., Tjeng, V., Shafiullah, N.M.M., Madry, A.: Training for faster adversarial robustness verification via inducing reLU stability. In: International Conference on Learning Representations (2019). https://openreview.net/forum?id=BJfIVjAcKm
51. Yang, X., Yamaguchi, T., Tran, H.D., Hoxha, B., Johnson, T.T., Prokhorov, D.: Neural network repair with reachability analysis. In: Bogomolov, S., Parker, D. (eds.) Formal Modeling and Analysis of Timed Systems, pp. 221–236. Springer, Cham (2022)

AI Assisted Programming

AI Assisted Programming
(AISoLA 2023 Track Introduction)

Wolfgang Ahrendt[1(✉)] and Klaus Havelund[2(✉)]

[1] Chalmers University of Technology, Gothenburg, Sweden
ahrendt@chalmers.se
[2] Jet Propulsion Laboratory, California Institute of Technology, Pasadena, USA
klaus.havelund@jpl.nasa.gov

Abstract. The paper is an introduction to the track 'AI Assisted Programming', organized at the AISoLA conference during the period October 23–28, 2023. The theme of AISoLA 2023 is: 'Bridging the Gap Between AI and Reality'. The motivation behind the track is the emerging use of Large Language Models for construction and analysis of software artifacts. An overview of the track presentations is provided.

1 Introduction

Neural program synthesis, using Large Language Models (LLMs) which are trained on open source code, are quickly becoming a popular addition to the software developer's toolbox. Services like, for instance, OpenAI's ChatGPT [8], Google's Bard [6], and GitHub's Copilot [5] can generate code in many different programming languages from natural language requirements. This opens up for fascinating new perspectives, such as increased productivity and accessibility of programming also for non-experts. However, neural systems do not come with guarantees of producing correct, safe, or secure code. They produce the most probable output, based on the training data, and there are countless examples of coherent but erroneous results. Even alert users fall victim to automation bias: the well studied tendency of humans to be over-reliant on computer generated suggestions. The area of software development is no exception to this automation bias.

The track *AI Assisted Programming* at AISoLA 2023 is devoted to discussions and exchange of ideas on questions like: What are the capabilities of this technology when it comes to software development? What are the limitations? What are the challenges and research areas that need to be addressed? How can we facilitate the rising power of code co-piloting while achieving a high level of correctness, safety, and security? What does the future look like? How should

K. Havelund—The research performed by this author was carried out at Jet Propulsion Laboratory, California Institute of Technology, under a contract with the National Aeronautics and Space Administration.

B. Steffen (Ed.): AISoLA 2023, LNCS 14380, pp. 351–354, 2024.
https://doi.org/10.1007/978-3-031-46002-9_22

these developments impact future approaches and technologies in software development and quality assurance? What is the role of models, tests, specification, verification, and documentation in conjunction with code co-piloting? Can quality assurance methods and technologies themselves profit from the new power of LLMs?

2 Contributions

These questions are taken up by the participants of the track in 10 talks. Three talks [2–4] were associated with regular papers, one talk [7] was associated with an extended abstract, and one talk [1] with a one page abstract. The remaining five talks do not have associated papers in the proceedings. Presenters have been offered to publish regular papers in a subsequent post-conference proceedings.

2.1 Talks with Papers in the Proceedings

Lenz Belzner, Thomas Gabor, and Martin Wirsing [2] (*Large language model assisted software engineering: prospects, challenges, and a case study*) discuss the potential benefits and challenges associated with the adoption of LLMs in software engineering. They explore the opportunities for requirements engineering, system design, code generation, test generation, code reviews, and software processes. The paper includes a comprehensive review of the state-of-the-art of the use of LLMs for software development. A case study is presented, illustrating the prompt-based development of a simple "search and rescue" application.

Daniel Busch, Gerrit Nolte, Alexander Bainczyk, and Bernhard Steffen [3] (*ChatGPT in the loop: a natural language extension for domain-specific modeling languages*) present an approach that combines the use of Domain-Specific Languages (DSLs) and natural language prompting using LLMs. The user provides first a context in the form of a DSL model, creating a frame in which ChatGPT can generate code that fits the code skeleton generated from the model. The resulting code is verified using automata learning and subsequent model checking. The ideas are demonstrated with the development of a classical river crossing game.

Itay Cohen and Doron Peled [4] (*Integrating distributed component-based systems through deep reinforcement learning*) present the idea of using deep reinforcement learning to learn how concurrently executing components can communicate in a more optimal way, in order to avoid failed communication attempts, where one components attempts to communicate with another component, which, however, is not willing to communicate at that moment. The components are considered "black boxes", where their internal structure is not known, and the learning is performed in a distributed manner.

Moa Johansson [7] (*What can large language models do for theorem proving and formal methods?* - extended abstract) investigates how to best combine the capabilities of LLMs with symbolic verification systems such as theorem provers. LLMs are noted to be unreliable and prone to hallucinate, also in mathematical reasoning. It is suggested that a more reliable way is to let the LLM provide inputs, specifically invent lemmas and conjectures, to a theorem prover, which can then do the formal reasoning. In a case study it is explored how GPT-4 performs on lemma discovery for the Isabelle/HOL proof assistant.

Bernhard K. Aichernig and Klaus Havelund [1] (*AI-assisted programming with test-based refinement* - abstract) explore the idea of program development in Scala by refinement using ChatGPT. The authors refine a classic bridge controller, originally used as an example illustrating Event-B, through several steps, each generated by ChatGPT from natural language prompts. The refinements are tested using refinement mappings and property-oriented testing with ScalaCheck. This in contrast to the Event-B effort, which proves the refinements correct.

2.2 Talks Without Papers in the Proceedings

Wolfgang Ahrendt, Dilian Gurov, Moa Johansson, and Philipp Rümmer (*TriCo - LLM supported Development of Robust Software*) suggest an agile software development workflow which addresses the commonly seen lack of trust in code generated by LLMs. The proposed approach, named TriCo (Triple Co-piloting), integrates in an IDE a LLM with formal methods, automated testing, and machine learning. A change in one of these three artifacts, will cause the IDE to suggest changes to the other two artifacts, keeping them consistent.

Saddek Bensalem, Kaiwen Cai, Yi Dong, Andre Freitas, Wei Huang, Xiaowei Huang, Gaojie Jin, Ronghui Mu, Mustafa A. Mustafa Yi Qi, Wenjie Ruan, Changshun WU, Dengyu Wu, Sihao Wu, Peipei Xu, Yanghao Zhang, and Xingyu Zhao (*A Survey of Safety and Trustworthiness of Large Language Models through the Lens of Verification and Validation*) present a survey exploring the safety and trustworthiness of LLMs. The authors review and categorize known vulnerabilities of LLMs. They then investigate if and how verification and validation techniques developed for traditional software and deep learning models can be integrated during the life-cycle of LLMs to make them safer and more trustworthy.

Dirk Beyer (*Software Verification in the Presence of Generated Programs*) discusses the problem of formally verifying that a program generated by a LLM satisfies a formal specification. In order to prove this, it is commonly necessary to formulate and prove program invariants. The talk focuses on automatic construction of such invariants as first-class interchangeable objects, not just code annotations, and their automatic verification. It is also discussed how to produce comprehensible error reports when a specification is violated.

Dan Boneh, Deepak Kumar, Neil Perry, and Megha Srivastava (*Do Users Write More Insecure Code with AI Assistants?*) conduct a study examining how users interact with an AI Code assistant to solve a variety of security related tasks across different programming languages. The authors observe that the uncritical use of an AI code assistant generally results in less secure code. Additionally, users with access to an AI assistant seem more likely to believe they write secure code. The authors perform an analysis of the users' language and interaction behaviours, and release an interface to conduct similar studies in the future.

Martin Leucker and Gerardo Schneider (*Some Experiments in Chatbot-Assisted Program Development*) report on experiments with ChatGPT. In particular, the authors explore the use of ChatGPT to generate simple programs, point out deficiencies in programs, generate test cases, generate temporal logic formulae, and deal with automata specifications. Furthermore it is shown how to build a simple chatbot that can run dedicated analysis tools, such as a model checker, locally, as a step towards full-scale chatbot-assisted program development.

3 Conclusion

The presentations in this track cover the use of LLMs in the context of all phases of software development, including requirements, designs, coding, testing and verification. This includes their use in combination with specification languages and domain-specific languages. It is explored how LLMs can be used to support formal methods and testing, and in the other direction it is explored how these techniques can support the use of LLMs, both wrt. safety, security, and correctness of software. Other machine learning topics are covered as well. Some case studies are furthermore presented. This covers an already interesting spectrum of AI assisted programming at this very early stage of LLMs. We hope that this track, with its talks, discussions, and papers, contributes to a future of AI assisted programming which exploits the strengths of arising AI technologies while mitigating the corresponding risks. We are convinced that many communities within computing have a lot to contribute to such a development, and look forward to future initiatives and contributions towards this aim.

References

1. Aichernig, B.K., Havelund, K.: AI-assisted programming with test-based refinement. In: Steffen, B. (ed.) AISoLA 2023. LNCS, vol. 14380, p. 453. Springer, Cham (2023)
2. Belzner, L., Gabor, T., Wirsing, M.: Large language model assisted software engineering: prospects, challenges, and a case study. In: Steffen, B. (ed.) AISoLA 2023. LNCS, vol. 14380, pp. 355–374. Springer, Cham (2023)
3. Busch, D., Nolte, G., Bainczyk, A., Steffen, B.: ChatGPT in the loop: a natural language extension for domain-specific modeling languages. In: Steffen, B. (ed.) AISoLA 2023. LNCS, vol. 14380, pp. 375–390. Springer, Cham (2023)
4. Cohen, I., Peled, D.: Integrating distributed component-based systems through deep reinforcement learning. In: Steffen, B. (ed.) AISoLA 2023. LNCS, vol. 14380, pp. 395–417. Springer, Cham (2023)
5. GitHub. Copilot (2023). https://copilot.github.com. Accessed 27 Aug 2023
6. Google. Bard (2023). https://bard.google.com. Accessed 27 Aug 2023
7. Johansson, M.: What can large language models do for theorem proving and formal methods? In: Steffen, B. (ed.) AISoLA 2023. LNCS, vol. 14380, pp. 391–394. Springer, Cham (2023)
8. OpenAI. ChatGPT (2023). https://chat.openai.com. Accessed 27 Aug 2023

Large Language Model Assisted Software Engineering: Prospects, Challenges, and a Case Study

Lenz Belzner[1], Thomas Gabor[2], and Martin Wirsing[2](✉)

[1] TH Ingolstadt, Ingolstadt, Germany
lenz.belzner@thi.de
[2] Ludwig-Maximilians-Universität München, München, Germany
{gabor,wirsing}@ifi.lmu.de

Abstract. Large language models such as OpenAI's GPT and Google's Bard offer new opportunities for supporting software engineering processes. Large language model assisted software engineering promises to support developers in a conversational way with expert knowledge over the whole software lifecycle. Current applications range from requirements extraction, ambiguity resolution, code and test case generation, code review and translation to verification and repair of software vulnerabilities. In this paper we present our position on the potential benefits and challenges associated with the adoption of language models in software engineering. In particular, we focus on the possible applications of large language models for requirements engineering, system design, code and test generation, code quality reviews, and software process management. We also give a short review of the state-of-the-art of large language model support for software construction and illustrate our position by a case study on the object-oriented development of a simple "search and rescue" scenario.

Keywords: large language model · GPT · Bard · LLM-assisted · software engineering · state-of-the-art · challenges · requirements · design · validation · verification

1 Introduction

Software engineering (SE) has traditionally been a highly manual, human-driven process that involves a range of activities from requirements gathering and analysis, to system design, implementation, and testing. Recent advances in artificial intelligence (AI) have led to the development of powerful natural language processing models such as OpenAI's GPT [6,34,36] or Google's Bard [42], known as large language models (LLMs). For an overview on current LLMs see [32,49].

LLMs have opened a wide array of applications in various domains, including applications in software engineering processes. In contrast to classical software development support, textual interaction with an LLM-based development

B. Steffen (Ed.): AISoLA 2023, LNCS 14380, pp. 355–374, 2024.
https://doi.org/10.1007/978-3-031-46002-9_23

environment is not command-based but intent-based [33] and conversational: a developer engages in a dialogue with the system in which she asks questions or describes the desired outcome, but does not state how that outcome is constructed or calculated.

Vision. Our vision is that the use of LLMs will lead to a paradigm shift in software development. In "LLM-assisted software engineering" the LLM acts together with other supporting bots and tools to help the human developers in all phases of the software lifecycle. The LLM plays the role of development expert whereas developers act as domain experts. Humans specify and clarify to the LLM the intended requirements, judge and correct the software design proposals and the code produced by the LLM-bot and other bots the LLM cooperates with. In the validation and verification phase the LLM serves as testing and verification expert. It autonomously generates tests, invokes appropriate testing and verification goals and tools, and converses with the human for uncovering unexpected issues with requirements and design specifications. Moreover, an LLM may also play the role of a software process expert and plan the forthcoming development activities in agile development process.

However, to realize this vision many challenges still need to be overcome ranging from integrating LLMs into the larger domain and technical context as well as evaluating and testing the quality of the output generated by LLMs to many further issues in practical use. If all these challenges can be resolved, we see (at least) three scenarios of how our vision for integrating LLMs into software engineering might play out: (1) integration of today's LLMs into the standard tooling for routine software development, (2) integration into the standard software engineering processes so that LLMs take over some expert roles and thus replace some human experts, and (3) integration into each stage of software development so that the role of human software developers changes entirely to a manager of AI-induced software development processes.

Contribution. This paper presents our position on the potential benefits and challenges of LLM-assisted software engineering, with a particular focus on requirements engineering, system design, code and test generation, and code quality reviews. We give a short overview of the current (July 2023) state-of-the-art of large language model support for software construction and illustrate our position by exemplary dialogues with ChatGPT and Bard on object-oriented development of a simple "search and rescue" scenario.

Our work provides an initial exploration into the application of LLMs throughout the full software development lifecycle, encompassing requirements engineering, system design, development, and quality assurance. We also provide a case study with illustrative examples of LLM application in selected phases of the software development lifecycle. By setting the scope that comprises the early development phases, code and artifact generation, and the integration into software engineering processes, we aim to stimulate a broader discussion and uncover potential avenues for the application of LLMs in software engineering. We hope this exploration can serve as a starting point for more comprehensive investigations in the future.

Outline. The paper is organized as follows: Sect. 2 describes our view of the prospects of software engineering applications of LLMs and the current state-of-the-art. Section 3 reports on our case study dialogues with ChatGPT and Bard for developing requirements, design and test cases of a "search and rescue" scenario. Section 4 discusses the challenges in adopting LLMs for software engineering, Sect. 5 depicts scenarios that could evolve if some or all of the challenges can be surpassed, and Sect. 6 concludes the paper.

2 LLMs in Software Engineering: Prospects and State-of-the-Art

The idea of embodying human expertise in a software system goes back to the roots of AI, to knowledge-based systems [20] and in particular expert systems [7]. Expert systems had applications in various domains, ranging from mathematics to healthcare and also software engineering [5]. A further step is conversational software engineering, i.e. engineering with the help of software-based systems which are capable of processing natural language data to simulate a smart conversational process with humans [31]. The first ideas for conversational software engineering go back to [38], which proposes an architecture for enabling assistant agents to reply to questions asked by naive users about the structure and functioning of graphical interfaces. [31] gives an overview on the field of conversational agents and their impact in the field of software engineering, but LLMs are not among the surveyed techniques nor are software development activities among the surveyed applications.

LLM-assisted software engineering goes a step further and promises to support developers in a conversational way with expert knowledge along the whole software lifecycle. Today, there are first experiments with LLMs helping software developers with common software engineering tasks such as ambiguity resolution in software requirements, method name suggestion, test case prioritization, code review, and log summarization [41]. In [43], a catalogue of prompt patterns is proposed that guide software developers in performing common software engineering activities using LLMs, such as disambiguating specification, creating APIs, proposing software architectures, or simulating web application APIs.

The paper [37] presents an LLM-assisted prototype system, called the Programmer's Assistant, that supports conversational interactions of developer and system. The Programmer's Assistant is based on a code-fluent large language model and helps the developer by answering general programming questions, by generating context-relevant code, by enabling the model to exhibit emergent behaviors, and by enabling users to ask follow-up questions that depend upon their conversational and code contexts. The AutoScrum system [40] supports a highly iterative Scrum process between LLM and humans where the LLM generates small chunks of text or code at a time, which are reviewed by the user and then committed into the database. The GPT2SP system [17] helps in estimating story points for implementing agile product backlogs.

In the following we will discuss how LLM-assisted software engineering can support the classical phases of a software development life cycle (for AI-based systems see, e.g., [18,19,44]), i.e., requirements engineering, design, validation and verification. A case study with illustrative examples for some of the approaches outlined here is given in Sect. 3.

2.1 Requirements Engineering

Requirements Engineering (RE) is a critical process in the development of software systems, involving the definition, documentation, and maintenance of software requirements. This is a multidimensional task that requires robust information retrieval, effective communication with diverse stakeholders, and the production of detailed textual descriptions. It is an endeavor that can prove challenging due to the complexity and breadth of the tasks involved. LLMs can significantly facilitate this process, providing support in several areas of RE such as requirements elicitation, specification extraction and refinement, and generating solution concepts and system architectures.

Extraction and Elicitation. First experiments report that LLMs can be very helpful in specification extraction from documents. According to a recent study [46], LLMs that are coached by few-shot learning achieve better extraction results than state-of-the-art techniques such as Jdoctor [4] and DocTer [45].

In addition to specification extraction, LLMs can also be used to support the refinement of system specifications and other artifacts such as epics, stories, and tasks in agile development. For instance, an LLM can be prompted to ask questions to identify and fill gaps in system specifications. This can be particularly beneficial during the refinement processes in agile environments. Leveraging the domain expertise exhibited by LLMs, the refinement process can be tailored to different perspectives and roles such as development, testing, and security. For instance, our case study (see Sect. 3) is a simple example for elaborating and refining requirements to obtain a system design and test cases.

Moreover, the translation and summarization capabilities of LLMs can be used to generate a system concept. By appropriately prompting the LLM, it can organize the generated summary or system concept along certain axes, such as system goals, stakeholders, functional and non-functional requirements, and so on. Interestingly, LLMs can also be prompted to explicitly express any missing information for certain aspects, thereby providing a comprehensive picture of the system's requirements.

In terms of user interaction, LLMs can generate and elaborate on user flows in an application. This can be especially beneficial in the absence of an interactive system during the RE process. LLMs have demonstrated their capacity to derive plausible user stories from system descriptions, thereby providing a tangible rendering of the user experience.

Use Case Design. In use case design LLMs exhibit considerable utility. For example, given a comprehensive system specification, LLMs can ascertain the various use cases present. This involves extraction and description of the specified interactions between the users and the system, as well as the system's response to these interactions.

LLMs can construct illustrative use case and sequence diagrams from the identified use cases. Use case diagrams provide a graphical representation of the system's intended interactions with its environment and users, making the system's functionality more understandable. Sequence diagrams detail the sequential order of interactions between different system components corresponding to a specific use case, adding another layer of clarity to the system's operations.

The use of LLMs in requirements engineering not only speeds up the process but also reduces costs, making them an efficient alternative to manual labor. This, coupled with the ability of LLMs to gather information regarding a particular target artifact, offers an intriguing and promising avenue for future exploration.

2.2 System Design

In the realm of system design, Large Language Models (LLMs) are emerging as beneficial tools. Their capabilities range from proposing design alternatives to identifying trade-offs. Given a description of a system's functionalities, LLMs can suggest varied design solutions, and generate diagrams for visual communication. This enables designers to survey design alternatives more efficiently, thereby expediting decision-making.

Architecture. Large Language Models (LLMs) could play a crucial role in the formulation of architectural views, which are vital in providing a comprehensive overview of a system's structure. These views take into consideration both functional and non-functional requirements of a system, aiding in visualizing the system's organization and functionality. LLMs can also help in data modeling and API design.

In creating architectural views, LLMs can explore and present a multitude of possible architectural configurations. Each option is accompanied by an analysis of its strengths and weaknesses, providing a balanced evaluation of each potential architectural design. This ability to critically evaluate each option makes the decision-making process more efficient and data-driven. In [47], it is shown how this can be used for hardware-software Co-Design of Accelerators for deep neural networks. The experimental results indicate a substantial speedup compared to a state-of-the-art method. [43] provide a prompt pattern that helps developers in requesting different architectural possibilities from the LLM.

Beyond suggesting and evaluating design options, LLMs can also proactively identify potential risks associated with each architectural option. Recognizing these risks early in the design phase can prevent costly errors down the line. Also, LLMs can potentially offer possible mitigation strategies to minimize these risks, thereby adding another layer of robustness to the system design process.

A possible advantage of utilizing LLMs in this way is the alignment it creates between system design choices and the system's requirements. This harmonization ensures that the chosen architectural design adequately meets the system's functional and non-functional requirements, leading to a more effective and optimized system. If there are trade-offs involved, LLMs can help to document these and support decision making in the architectural design process.

The capability of LLMs to align requirements and design is also particularly valuable in architectural reviews. It may enable a streamlined and efficient review process, with LLMs effectively serving as tools for cross-verifying the alignment between system requirements and design choices.

Data Modeling. LLMs can identify and define core entities within a system. Core entities in a system refer to the main components or elements that make up that system, and understanding these entities and their interactions is crucial for effective system design and development.

When using LLMs for identifying and defining core entities, we are essentially harnessing their capability to understand and interpret natural language descriptions of a system. Given a detailed description of the system's features, functions, and behaviors, an LLM could potentially highlight what the central entities are, based on frequency of mentions, context, and importance in achieving system functionalities.

LLMs can generate relational data models from context descriptions. These models can be expressed in domain-specific languages like mermaid.js[1] for visual representation. LLMs can also accommodate different levels of abstraction in data models, such as those seen in ELT or ETL pipelines.

API Design Based on use cases that are identified and described in requirements engineering, LLMs can further assist in the design process by defining endpoints for a corresponding REST API. In a web application, endpoints are the URIs (Uniform Resource Identifiers) where specific resources reside and can be manipulated via HTTP methods such as GET, POST, PUT, and DELETE. An LLM can derive these endpoints from the use cases, ensuring that the functionality encapsulated in each endpoint aligns with a specific user-system interaction.

By extracting use cases and generating REST endpoints from system specifications, LLMs streamline the design process, reducing time and effort required and minimizing the potential for human error. LLMs can also help the designers to create ansd simulate APIs (see, e.g., the corresponding patterns in [43]). This allows designers to devote more attention to other critical aspects of the system design, such as performance optimization and user experience.

2.3 Code Generation

Code generation and testing are key components of the implementation phase in software engineering. LLMs show remarkable capabilities in code generation, given a distinctive task specification for a small enough coding task [12]. We think that the combination of these coding capabilities with systematic problem

[1] https://github.com/mermaid-js/mermaid.

decomposition assisted by LLMs could greatly expand the application domain from only coding singular tasks to providing code artifacts for large, complex, coordinated software systems.

LLMs have shown promising results in generating code snippets and test cases, tailored to specific requirements and design specifications. E.g., by combining code snippet generation of ChatGPT with tools for Language-Driven Engineering and modelchecking, [8] achieve a no-code development of a point-and-click adventure web game. Other interesting LLM-applications are generating code guided by test-driven user-intent formalization [24], or translating code with the help of LLM-based transpilers [21]. By automating such tasks, software engineers can focus more on solving complex problems while trusting the LLMs for routine and repetitive tasks.

These approaches can be combined with artifacts from the previous phases. For example, it is possible to create unit tests for REST endpoints and their respective description and sequence diagrams. Following for example a test-driven development approach, this test can the be passed to a subsequent call to the LLM asking for an implementation based on the specification that aims to pass the unit test.

2.4 Quality Assurance, Testing and Verification

As software projects grow in size and complexity, code reviews become crucial to maintaining the quality and integrity of the codebase. LLMs can be employed to conduct automatic code quality assessments, identifying potential problems, suggesting improvements, and providing recommendations based on best practices. There are several approaches for enhancing code review using LLMs, e.g. for providing useful suggestions on human-written code [30] or for supporting code review of pull requests of GitHub workflows [16]. This can lead to a more efficient code review process and improve overall code quality. However, currently ChatGPT can recognize some security code flaws but – not being trained for such applications – it recognizes many false positives so that its output has to be examined with great care [1].

The paper [14] provides an overview of conversational and potentially autonomous testing agents and proposes a framework for conversational testing agents that are potentially autonomous and supported by existing automated testing techniques. Such an LLM-system could not only become an intelligent testing partner to a human software engineer, but also be able to handle typical testing related tasks autonomously. Similarly, in [39] an adaptive test generation technique is presented that uses an off-the-shelf LLM for automatically generating unit tests. Still, tests generated by ChatGPT often suffer from correctness issues [48]. As a remedy, in [48] an iterative test refiner is proposed for reducing compilation errors and incorrect assertions of ChatGPT-generated tests.

Furthermore, as current programming benchmarks are limited in both quantity and quality, Liu et al. [27] present a ChatGPT-based evaluation framework, called EvalPlus, for automatically generating and diversifying test inputs. The authors show that EvalPlus can considerably improve the popular HUMANEVAL benchmark [12].

Combining LLMs with automated verification tools is a promising avenue. In [11], a symbolic bounded model checker cooperates with an LLM for debugging and verifying code. If the model checker detects a violation of a memory safety property, the code is fed to the LLM for repair. The corrected code is passed again to the model checker for a verification check. As mentioned above, in [8] model checking ensures the correctness of an LLM-generated web application.

3 Case Study

For illustrating the software development abilities of LLMs we considered a simple search-and-rescue scenario (see [3]) and focus on the early phases, i.e., requirements engineering and design as well as testing.

In the scenario, a robot agent searches for victims in a probabilistic environment over a discrete graph of locations. Locations can be in fires that can ignite and cease. The goal of the agent is to rescue the victims and to bring them to safe locations. Note that a version of our example is accessible via the web (e.g. [3]), and therefore potentially part of ChatGPT's training data.

By interacting with ChatGPT and also with Bard we conducted two systematic developments consisting of a (textual) requirements specification and an object-oriented design specification in form of a class diagram and of pseudocode of the agent behavior. With Bard, we also developed the basic unit tests and system tests of the scenario. In the following we present excerpts of these developments and comment the results.

The conversation with ChatGPT-3.5, July 20, 2023 version was held on July 25, 2023 and the one with Bard on July 16, 2023. See the footnotes for links to the conversation with ChatGPT[2] and the one with Bard[3].

3.1 Requirements

First, we ask ChatGPT and Bard whether they can model a search and rescue scenario as a simulation for autonomous planning agents. Both give appropriate answers: Bard proposes an abstract earthquake scenario and some of the challenges for a simulation such as the complexity of the environment; ChatGPT provides a more operational description of the key elements of the simulation (see Fig. 1).

Then we ask both LLMs to instantiate the abstract model to just one agent with global observability and an environment consisting of a graph-like structure of locations where locations may be on fire. Again both LLMs answer with appropriate textual requirements descriptions, the one of ChatGPT being more concrete and proposing also two possible graph search algorithms (see Fig. 2).

[2] ChatGPT https://chat.openai.com/share/a93d844d-e542-4997-a7d5-0d254e007c08.

[3] Bard https://g.co/bard/share/c51838296a3c.

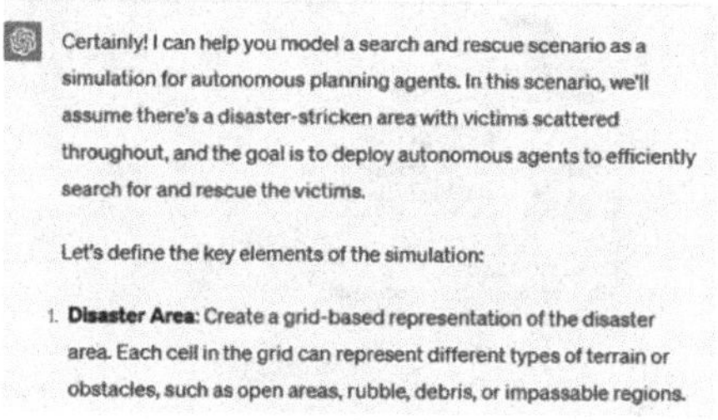

Certainly! I can help you model a search and rescue scenario as a simulation for autonomous planning agents. In this scenario, we'll assume there's a disaster-stricken area with victims scattered throughout, and the goal is to deploy autonomous agents to efficiently search for and rescue the victims.

Let's define the key elements of the simulation:

1. **Disaster Area:** Create a grid-based representation of the disaster area. Each cell in the grid can represent different types of terrain or obstacles, such as open areas, rubble, debris, or impassable regions.

Chat GPT.

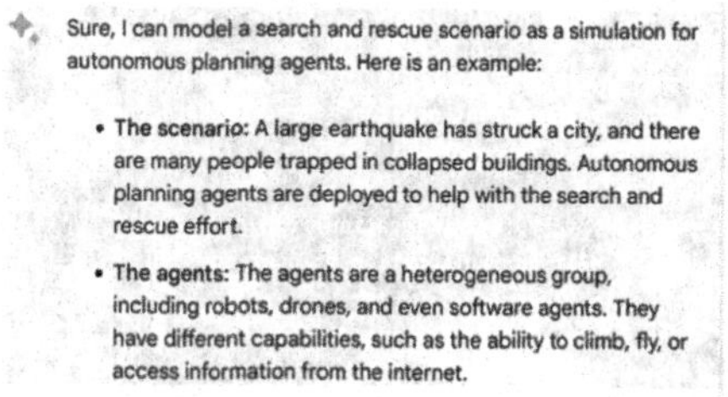

Sure, I can model a search and rescue scenario as a simulation for autonomous planning agents. Here is an example:

- **The scenario:** A large earthquake has struck a city, and there are many people trapped in collapsed buildings. Autonomous planning agents are deployed to help with the search and rescue effort.
- **The agents:** The agents are a heterogeneous group, including robots, drones, and even software agents. They have different capabilities, such as the ability to climb, fly, or access information from the internet.

Bard.

Fig. 1. Search-and-Rescue Requirements (excerpts).

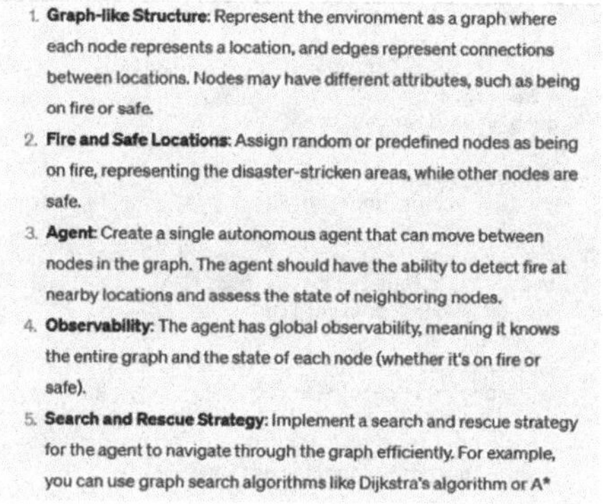

1. **Graph-like Structure:** Represent the environment as a graph where each node represents a location, and edges represent connections between locations. Nodes may have different attributes, such as being on fire or safe.
2. **Fire and Safe Locations:** Assign random or predefined nodes as being on fire, representing the disaster-stricken areas, while other nodes are safe.
3. **Agent:** Create a single autonomous agent that can move between nodes in the graph. The agent should have the ability to detect fire at nearby locations and assess the state of neighboring nodes.
4. **Observability:** The agent has global observability, meaning it knows the entire graph and the state of each node (whether it's on fire or safe).
5. **Search and Rescue Strategy:** Implement a search and rescue strategy for the agent to navigate through the graph efficiently. For example, you can use graph search algorithms like Dijkstra's algorithm or A*

Chat GPT.

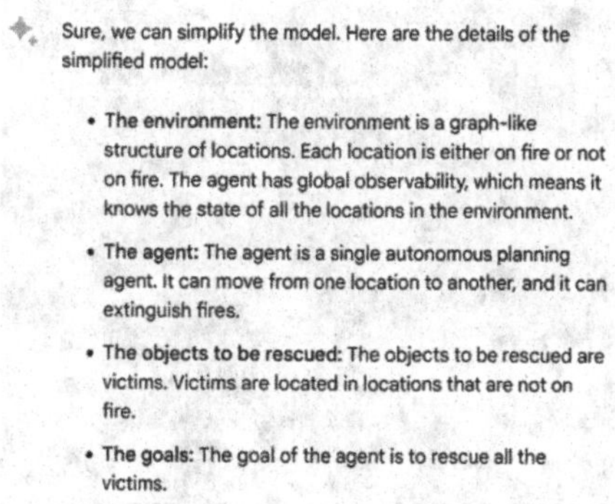

Sure, we can simplify the model. Here are the details of the simplified model:

- **The environment:** The environment is a graph-like structure of locations. Each location is either on fire or not on fire. The agent has global observability, which means it knows the state of all the locations in the environment.
- **The agent:** The agent is a single autonomous planning agent. It can move from one location to another, and it can extinguish fires.
- **The objects to be rescued:** The objects to be rescued are victims. Victims are located in locations that are not on fire.
- **The goals:** The goal of the agent is to rescue all the victims.

Bard.

Fig. 2. Simplified Search-and-Rescue Requirements (excerpts).

3.2 Design

For developing a design specification, first we ask the LLMs to provide a UML diagram of the scenario domain. Both LLMs present plausible class diagrams and corresponding pseudocode of the important classes and their relationships. Asked about operations, they also add appropriate methods. Concerning the additional constraint that the agent should extinguish the fire when it moves to a location in fire, ChatGPT adds a corresponding clause to the body of the "move" operation (see Fig. 3 left) whereas Bard remains abstract (see Fig. 3 right) and mentions the constraint only in the documentation.

Then we want to construct an online planning algorithm for the agent to perform effective rescuing. Both LLMs give informed discussions about possible algorithms. ChatGPT proposes A* search and mentions also "planning algorithms like D* Lite, Incremental A*, or variants of Monte Carlo Tree Search (MCTS)." Bard proposes A* search and Dijkstra's shortest path algorithm as well as probabilistic and Bayesian planning; it also mentions MCTS for probabilistic scenarios. Concerning MCTS, both LLMs provide appropriate pseudocode for MCTS and also for the behavior of the agent using MCTS for online

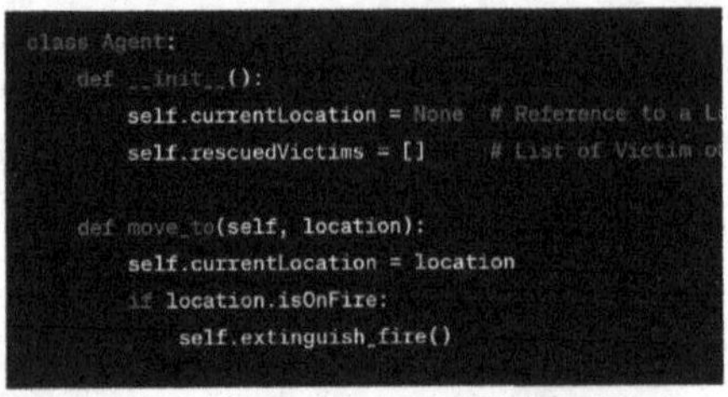

```
class Agent:
    def __init__():
        self.currentLocation = None  # Reference to a Lo
        self.rescuedVictims = []     # List of Victim o

    def move_to(self, location):
        self.currentLocation = location
        if location.isOnFire:
            self.extinguish_fire()
```

Chat GPT Move operation.

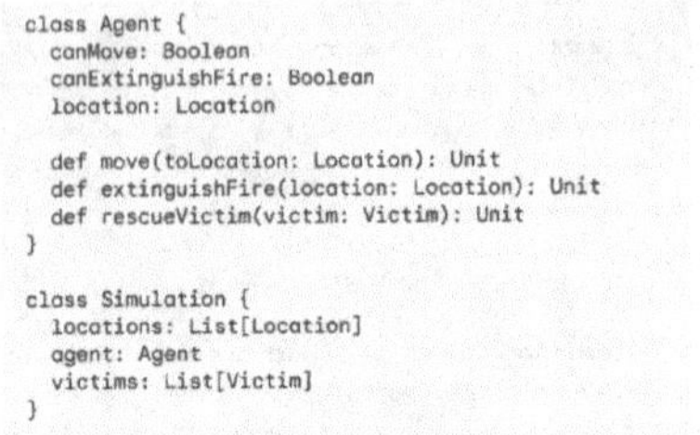

```
class Agent {
  canMove: Boolean
  canExtinguishFire: Boolean
  location: Location

  def move(toLocation: Location): Unit
  def extinguishFire(location: Location): Unit
  def rescueVictim(victim: Victim): Unit
}

class Simulation {
  locations: List[Location]
  agent: Agent
  victims: List[Victim]
}
```

Bard Move operation.

Fig. 3. Search-and-Rescue Class Diagram (excerpts).

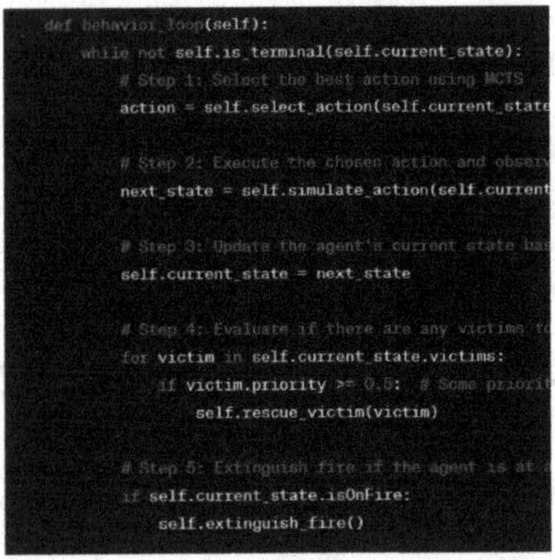

```
def behavior_loop(self):
    while not self.is_terminal(self.current_state):
        # Step 1: Select the best action using MCTS
        action = self.select_action(self.current_state

        # Step 2: Execute the chosen action and observ
        next_state = self.simulate_action(self.current

        # Step 3: Update the agent's current state bas
        self.current_state = next_state

        # Step 4: Evaluate if there are any victims to
        for victim in self.current_state.victims:
            if victim.priority >= 0.5:  # Some priorit
                self.rescue_victim(victim)

        # Step 5: Extinguish fire if the agent is at a
        if self.current_state.isOnFire:
            self.extinguish_fire()
```

Chat GPT.

```
def agent_behavior(agent, environment):
  # Monitoring
  data = environment.monitor()

  # Analysis
  goals = agent.analyze(data)

  # Planning
  tree = MCTS(agent, data, goals)
  action = best_action(tree)

  # Execution
  environment.execute(action)

  # Logging
  agent.log(data, goals, action)

  return action
```

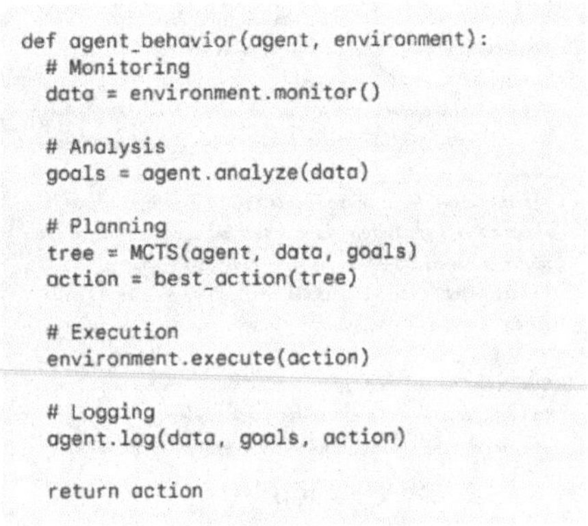

Bard.

Fig. 4. Search-and-Rescue Agent Behavior (excerpts).

planning. ChatGPT is again more concrete and considers the constraint concerning the fires (see the last two lines of Fig. 4 left) whereas Bard remains abstract (see Fig. 4 right).

3.3 Testing

Asked about unit and system tests, both LLMs proposed relevant tests for both test categories. Again Bard is more abstract and proposes unit tests corresponding to the abstract operations of the MAPE loop whereas ChatGPT defines more concrete tests using the unittest testing framework. Concerning the system tests, ChatGPT offers a simple concrete scenario (consisting of three locations and two victims) whereas Bard defines abstract tests for a simulated and a real-world environment (see Fig. 5).

3.4 Discussion

We observed interesting and stimulating generated outputs for the software engineering tasks in our case study. The example is quite simplistic, so the scalabil-

```
class TestSearchAndRescueSystem(unittest.TestCase):
    def setUp(self):
        # Create the graph and locations for testing
        self.graph = Graph()
        self.location1 = Location()
        self.location2 = Location()
        self.location3 = Location()
        self.graph.add_location(self.location1)
        self.graph.add_location(self.location2)
        self.graph.add_location(self.location3)
```

Chat GPT Test Scenario.

```
def test_agent_in_simulated_environment(agent):
  environment = Environment()
  agent.simulate(environment)
  assert agent.has_achieved_goals()

def test_agent_in_real_world_environment(agent):
  environment = Environment()
  agent.run(environment)
  assert agent.has_achieved_goals()
```

Bard System Tests.

Fig. 5. Search-and-Rescue Tests (excerpts).

ity of our "naive" prompting approach remains to be evaluated. At times, we observed a difference between the generated artifacts (e.g. the relation multiplicities in a class diagram) and our expectations. We attribute this to ambiguities in our description of the requirements. We think that systematic and potentially automated evaluation of such qualitative divergences is a highly interesting and valuable direction for future research (see also Sect. 4.2 for challenges of evaluating generated output).

4 Challenges in Adopting LLMs for Software Engineering

In the following we outline several challenges that need to be addressed when adopting LLMs in software engineering.

4.1 Integration with Large Context

Integrating LLMs into a larger domain and its context, such as existing processes, background knowledge, technical environments, and tools, is challenging. LLMs need to understand and capture the context-specific information to provide meaningful and actionable insights to software engineers, requiring new methods and processes for contextualization [35].

Divide and Conquer Utilizing a large language model necessitates an organized, progressive approach, particularly for tackling intricate tasks such as the design of a software architecture. The first step entails employing the model to construct a high-level plan. This involves identifying the key components of the architecture, comprehending how these parts interrelate, and outlining the basic procedures necessary to create the structure. It is crucial at this stage to recognize that the output will be a broad overview, serving as a roadmap for subsequent, more detailed design stages.

After crafting a high-level plan the model is directed to focus on each component individually. This involves generating detailed information for each part, treating them as separate tasks. This methodology enables a deeper exploration of the unique characteristics of each component.

Several open-source projects explore LLM-based automated decomposition for software engineering, e.g., AutoGPT[4], MetaGPT[5], GPT-Synthesizer[6], and gpt-engineer[7]. However, finding the "right" level of abstraction remains challenging. For further evaluation or even automating and improving abstraction level decisions, introducing quantifiable or ranking (comparative) quality measurements would be highly valuable. These metrics could assess the relevance, coherence, and depth of the generated content w.r.t. a given task, offering potential avenues for future research. See also the following Sect. 4.2 on evaluation and testing of generative output for further elaboration on this matter.

Scaling to Large Context. Managing large domain contexts within the constraint of LLM's limited prompt sizes poses a significant challenge. Prompt engineering, leveraging known relations and abstractions in software engineering, can help circumvent this issue. By distilling complex concepts into concise, structured prompts, we can guide the model's responses more effectively. Additionally, vector database approaches that utilize embeddings of code and documentation artifacts can help manage these large contexts. These embeddings capture semantic information in a compact form, aiding in maintaining contextual continuity across prompts.

Combining LLMs with knowledge graphs is another promising avenue to scale to larger contexts [35]. Knowledge graphs provide structured and interconnected representations of domain knowledge, which can be leveraged to provide context to LLMs beyond their prompt limits. The graph's nodes and edges can be transformed into prompts or fed into the model as needed to support context-rich generation tasks. Creating heuristics of how to organize prompt information from knowledge graphs, or how to use LLM's agentic capabilities to derive these heuristics contextually on the fly seems a large area for future research. Also, incorporating knowledge graphs already when training or finetuning LLMs is an interesting but challenging direction.

Semantic Interfaces for Natural Language Artifacts. When managing numerous components in a larger artifact, the task of keeping track of their interfaces and relations can become highly complex. The context window of a large language model (LLM) is limited, making it unfeasible to hold all the component details simultaneously. However, if each component is well-defined, it is not necessary to retain all details; maintaining a record of their interfaces in the LLM context would suffice. In addition to generating the complete component, it is thus pivotal to create a succinct interface for the LLM context.

This concept is well-established for formal artifacts such as code, where interfaces denote a defined point of interaction between two components. However, the notion of an interface becomes nebulous when dealing with natural language artifacts, which are inherently ambiguous and lack the structured nature

[4] https://github.com/Significant-Gravitas/Auto-GPT.
[5] https://github.com/geekan/MetaGPT.
[6] https://github.com/RoboCoachTechnologies/GPT-Synthesizer.
[7] https://github.com/AntonOsika/gpt-engineer.

of formal code. The challenge lies in defining these interfaces for natural language artifacts. LLMs, with their robust language understanding capabilities, could be a valuable tool for creating interfaces for these ambiguous, natural-language-based artifacts. However, the method of achieving this remains unclear and requires further exploration. This could be a promising avenue of research for more efficient utilization of LLMs in complex, multi-component tasks.

4.2 Evaluating and Testing Generative Outputs

Evaluating the output generated by LLMs is a crucial aspect of their deployment. Primarily, this involves measuring the factuality, relevance, coherence, and depth of the generated content. LLMs are known to suffer from so called hallucinations that create seemingly plausible but factually or logically wrong outputs [2,22]. Therefore, accurately evaluating facual correctness of generated outputs is highly important. However, it is unclear how to perform such an evaluation without human labor in the abscence of an already labeled ground truth dataset. Relevance assesses whether the output corresponds well with the input prompt, coherence measures the logical consistency and fluidity of the response, and depth gauges the level of detail and complexity. These evaluations can be conducted both qualitatively, through human reviewers, and quantitatively, using metrics such as BLEU, ROUGE (for references see [9]), and METEOR [25]. Furthermore, evaluation might also consider the model's ability to avoid generating harmful or biased content. However, these metrics should be used in combination with human judgment, as they may not capture all nuances of language and context. For a recent survey on LLM evaluation, see [10].

A novel challenge arises when the output from the LLM is "better" than the ground truth, which refers to the model generating a response that is more accurate, insightful, or comprehensive than the expected answer. In this case, traditional metrics that penalize divergence from the ground truth could unfairly penalize the model. Therefore, flexible evaluation methods that can appreciate and reward such enhancements are necessary. One approach could be to utilize expert human reviewers who can appreciate such improvements in the context of the task at hand. Additionally, considering the use of "range-based" or "bucket" scores, which allow for a certain degree of deviation from the ground truth without penalty, could be another viable approach. These evaluations should be designed in a way that they encourage innovative and high-quality responses, rather than just adherence to a predefined answer. However, this area remains largely unexplored and warrants further research.

4.3 Challenges in Practical Use

Evaluating Value Creation and Utility. In some instances, the time invested in scrutinizing, understanding, and modifying the output generated by an LLM could potentially outweigh the advantages of automation. It is therefore essential to identify the scenarios where LLMs can add true value and efficiency in terms of time and resources. In these scenarios, LLMs can augment human productivity by automating tasks such as code generation, bug detection, and documentation, among others.

Accountability for Generated Content. Maintaining human accountability for the outputs generated by LLMs is of utmost importance, particularly when automatic evaluation of generated output remains an open research issue (as discussed in Sect. 4.2). These models, while powerful, are tools that aid in various tasks, and the ultimate responsibility for their application rests with the humans employing them. This accountability is pivotal in ensuring ethical, lawful, and appropriate use of LLMs. Particularly in fields like software engineering, where potential consequences of errors can be significant, human oversight of model outputs is crucial. This situation accentuates the importance of robust review capabilities within systems deploying LLMs. As long as the automatic evaluation of generated outputs is not entirely reliable or comprehensive, the human review and revision of these outputs not only ensure quality but also embed a layer of human judgement and responsibility, adding a vital layer of safety and accountability.

Legal Uncertainty and Copyright Issues. Legal issues regarding the copyright of content generated by large language models (LLMs) represent a complex and as yet unresolved area of discussion. Traditional copyright laws are designed around human authorship, and how these apply to machine-generated content remains a matter of debate. Questions about who owns the rights to the content generated by these models – the developers of the model, the users who prompt the generation, or perhaps no one at all – are currently under examination. Furthermore, there is the question of whether LLM outputs, if they inadvertently reproduce or mimic copyrighted content, constitute a violation of existing copyright laws.

Privacy Concerns. Privacy and personally identifiable information (PII) considerations are paramount when using large language models (LLMs) in a professional context, such as in requirements engineering, system design, code generation, and quality assurance in software engineering. Since these models learn from the data they are trained on, there is a risk they may inadvertently memorize and reproduce sensitive information. In a professional setting, this could lead to the disclosure of confidential business information, proprietary algorithms, or personal data of stakeholders, potentially violating privacy laws and ethical guidelines. As LLMs increasingly find use in diverse fields, it becomes crucial to implement robust mechanisms to prevent the leakage of sensitive information. These might include data anonymization techniques, strict access controls, and regular audits. Also, clear guidelines about what types of data should and should not be input into the model are essential. Given the seriousness of these concerns, the ongoing development and refinement of privacy-preserving techniques in AI models represent an area of significant importance in the field of AI ethics and governance [23,26].

Hosting open-source LLMs in private environments can help alleviate these concerns. This allows organizations to keep their data in a secure network, reducing the risk of data breaches. Strict access controls and security protocols can further enhance data security.

Model Efficiency. Increasing the resource efficiency of large language models (LLMs) is a vital consideration, especially as the scale and complexity of these models continue to grow. One way to achieve this is through model compression techniques, which aim to reduce the size of the model without significantly impacting its performance. Methods such as quantization, pruning, and knowledge distillation are commonly employed. Quantization reduces the precision of the numbers used in the model's computations, effectively shrinking its size [13]. Pruning involves removing less important connections in the model's neural network, leading to a sparser but still effective model [15]. Knowledge distillation, on the other hand, is a process where a smaller model (student) is trained to mimic the behavior of a larger model (teacher), thereby achieving similar performance with less computational resources. These techniques can hopefully lead to more efficient LLMs that maintain high performance while reducing both the computational power required and the currently associated resource requirements and carbon footprint [29].

5 What Could Happen if the Challenges Are Resolved?

So far we have been concerned with the software engineering applications of LLMs *at hand.* As the discipline is shifting, we see major opportunities as well as severe challenges. Naturally, no one can predict future developments that this new technology might bring about, but we can imagine various scenarios of how the integration of LLMs into software engineering might play out; we might mostly sort these scenarios by the (necessary) involvement of LLMs in all standard tasks of software engineering and likewise by the impact they might have on the discipline.

The simplest assumption we might make is just based on the capabilities we have seen LLMs exert today. Through integration of today's LLMs into the standard tooling for routine software development, we achieve Scenario 1.

Scenario 1 (A Better Bat). *LLMs become integrated into standard tools for software engineering. As such, they augment software IDEs with features like integrated code suggestion, adaptation of code samples from the web, or the generation of documentation from code (or vice versa). As sketched throughout this paper, they might also augment tools concerned with requirement analysis (by allowing to automatically generate summaries or check for inconsistencies in given descriptions) and thus aid and accelerate the whole software engineering life cycle. However, the standard processes involved in software engineering remain intact (albeit somewhat shifted w.r.t. the distribution of human effort) and well-known models for software engineering still apply. The long-term impact of LLMs is somewhat comparable to that of more powerful debuggers or better IDEs in the past.*

As long as LLMs are not entirely disregarded as a technology, the achievement of Scenario 1 appears almost inevitable.

Scenario 2 (A Game Changer). *LLMs become integrated into the standard model for software engineering processes and profoundly alter the way software is developed. Standard techniques (and standard implementations of them) are established that can reform or entirely replace parts of the software engineering process. As such, variants of LLMs might take over some roles (providing an AI scrum master, e.g.) or tasks (writing and updating documentation, e.g.). Education for software developers now has to include correctly dealing with LLMs and shift focus towards the remaining "human tasks" in software development. However, the produced artifacts (the compiled software, documentation, etc.) still closely resemble those generated before and compatibility with earlier products and also with earlier processes is maintained: Human developers are easily able to alter (and, if necessary, emulate) any machine output and scale LLM integration according to their preference. Through more powerful development processes, new software products may emerge whose complexity was previously not feasible for development teams not using LLM-enhanced processes (quickly coding against a wide range of semantically similar but syntactically diverse APIs, e.g.). The long-term impact of LLMs is somewhat comparable to that of (increasingly) higher programming languages or development paradigms in the past.*

For this range of APIs we might imagine a smart home device that can be enabled to talk to refrigerators without the need for a standardized API for refrigerators, but by describing the desired interaction as well as a long list of vendor-specific API calls and thereby generating modules for hundreds or thousand different devices within a reasonable time frame. However, what we end up with is still just a large code base that *could* have been written by a (albeit larger) human team.

Scenario 3 (An Entirely New Game). *LLMs fundamentally change the way we think about software and software development. LLMs become integrated in any stage of software development (and might even be the glue that keeps the process together or drives the process in the first place) and/or integrated into many artifacts that are produced. The pervasive accessibility of LLMs blurs the border between the artifact and the process that generates it, as capable LLMs can further develop (parts of) the software at any stage without human interaction. As such, LLMs become an inalienable part of any software product as even shipped software might self-adapt according to a specific user's preference via an LLM that can re-program (parts of) the original product or utilize LLMs for any means of inter-application communication (instead of protocols and APIs in today's sense). Software in today's sense is either reduced to work as a foundation of an LLM-based software ecosystem (similar to how Unix commands support today's software products) and/or its functionality is quickly re-implemented within that ecosystem. Akin to the vision of software gardening replacing software engineering [18], the role of human software developers changes entirely to a manager of AI-induced software development processes. These big changes* *in the software ecosystem are either justified by vastly increased productivity or entirely new capabilities only reached by this new kind of software.*

Naturally, what new capabilities software might reach in the future remains yet to be seen. However, we feel positive that more powerful development paradigms enable more powerful software products in the long run.[8]

As a possible endpoint to that line of thought, Liventsev et al. [28] already invoke the vision of "fully autonomous programming" (for now) by running an LLM-based loop for improving a sought-for program aided by prompt generation provided by a genetic algorithm.

6 Concluding Remarks

LLM-assisted software engineering holds a significant potential for revolutionizing software processes. However, there are challenges that need to be addressed, such as evaluating generative output, integration with business and technical contexts, and understanding the practical implications of automation. As research continues to advance in this area, we can expect considerable improvements in the right direction, providing new opportunities for the software engineering domain to embrace the power of large language models.

Addressing the challenges discussed, future work in LLM-assisted software engineering should delve deeper into using LLMs across various facets of the software process lifecycle that have not yet been thoroughly explored. Beyond the application examples we outlined in this work, additional application areas include implementation of generated system designs, operations and monitoring, where LLMs could potentially contribute to automated incident detection, root cause analysis, and decision support for resolution strategies. Combining verification tools with LLMs and applying LLMs to system security are other promising directions. Additionally, there is the domain of data engineering where LLMs could assist in tasks like data cleaning, transformation, and metadata management. Furthermore, leveraging LLMs in analytics to generate insights from complex and diverse data sets, automating data interpretation, or enhancing decision-making processes also presents compelling research opportunities.

Acknowledgements. We thank the anonymous reviewer for constructive criticisms and helpful suggestions.

References

1. Anley, C.: Security code review with ChatGPT. NCC Group (2023). https://research.nccgroup.com/2023/02/09/security-code-review-with-chatgpt/. Accessed 20 June 2023

[8] Despite the validity of the Church–Turing thesis, more powerful tools enable more products in practice.

2. Bang, Y., et al.: A multitask, multilingual, multimodal evaluation of ChatGPT on reasoning, hallucination, and interactivity. arXiv preprint arXiv:2302.04023 (2023)
3. Belzner, L., Hennicker, R., Wirsing, M.: OnPlan: a framework for simulation-based online planning. In: Braga, C., Ölveczky, P.C. (eds.) FACS 2015. LNCS, vol. 9539, pp. 1–30. Springer, Cham (2016). https://doi.org/10.1007/978-3-319-28934-2_1
4. Blasi, A., et al.: Translating code comments to procedure specifications. In: Tip, F., Bodden, E. (eds.) Proceedings of the 27th ACM SIGSOFT International Symposium on Software Testing and Analysis, ISSTA 2018, Amsterdam, The Netherlands, 16–21 July 2018, pp. 242–253. ACM (2018)
5. Blum, B.I., Wachter, R.F.: Expert system applications in software engineering. Telematics Inform. **3**(4), 237–262 (1986)
6. Brown, T., et al.: Language models are few-shot learners. Adv. Neural. Inf. Process. Syst. **33**, 1877–1901 (2020)
7. Buchanan, B.G., Davis, R., Smith, R.G., Feigenbaum, E.A.: Expert systems: a perspective from computer science. Cambridge Handbooks in Psychology, 2nd edn, pp. 84–104. Cambridge University Press (2018)
8. Busch, D., Nolte, G., Bainczyk, A., Steffen, B.: ChatGPT in the loop. In: Steffen, B. (ed.) AISoLA 2023. LNCS, vol. 14380, pp. 375–390. Springer, Cham (2023)
9. Chang, E.Y.: Examining GPT-4: capabilities, implications, and future directions (2023)
10. Chang, Y., et al.: A survey on evaluation of large language models. CoRR, abs/2307.03109 (2023)
11. Charalambous, Y., Tihanyi, N., Jain, R., Sun, Y., Ferrag, M.A., Cordeiro, L.C.: A new era in software security: towards self-healing software via large language models and formal verification. CoRR, abs/2305.14752 (2023)
12. Chen, M., et al.: Evaluating large language models trained on code. arXiv preprint arXiv:2107.03374 (2021)
13. Dettmers, T., Lewis, M., Belkada, Y., Zettlemoyer, L.: Llm.int8(): 8-bit matrix multiplication for transformers at scale. CoRR, abs/2208.07339 (2022)
14. Feldt, R., Kang, S., Yoon, J., Yoo, S.: Towards autonomous testing agents via conversational large language models. CoRR, abs/2306.05152 (2023). Accessed 29 June 2023
15. Frantar, E., Alistarh, D.: SparseGPT: massive language models can be accurately pruned in one-shot. CoRR, abs/2301.00774 (2023)
16. Fu, M.: A ChatGPT-powered code reviewer bot for open-source projects. Cloud Native Computing Foundation (2023). https://www.cncf.io/blog/2023/06/06/a-chatgpt-powered-code-reviewer-bot-for-open-source-projects/. Accessed 20 July 2023
17. Fu, M., Tantithamthavorn, C.: GPT2SP: a transformer-based agile story point estimation approach. IEEE Trans. Software Eng. **49**(2), 611–625 (2023)
18. Gabor, T.: Self-adaptive fitness in evolutionary processes. Ph.D. thesis, LMU (2021)
19. Gabor, T., et al.: The scenario coevolution paradigm: adaptive quality assurance for adaptive systems. Int. J. Softw. Tools Technol. Transf. **22**(4), 457–476 (2020)
20. Goldstein, I., Papert, S.: Artificial intelligence, language, and the study of knowledge. Cogn. Sci. **1**(1), 84–123 (1977)
21. Jana, P., Jha, P., Ju, H., Kishore, G., Mahajan, A., Ganesh, V.: Attention, compilation, and solver-based symbolic analysis are all you need. CoRR, abs/2306.06755 (2023)

22. Kabir, S., Udo-Imeh, D.N., Kou, B., Zhang, T.: Who answers it better? An in-depth analysis of ChatGPT and Stack Overflow answers to software engineering questions. CoRR, abs/2308.02312 (2023)
23. Kim, S., Yun, S., Lee, H., Gubri, M., Yoon, S., Oh, S.J.: Propile: probing privacy leakage in large language models (2023)
24. Lahiri, S.K., et al.: Interactive code generation via test-driven user-intent formalization. CoRR, abs/2208.05950 (2022)
25. Lavie, A., Agarwal, A.: METEOR: an automatic metric for MT evaluation with high levels of correlation with human judgments. In: Callison-Burch, C., Koehn, P., Fordyce, C.S., Monz, C. (eds.) Proceedings of the Second Workshop on Statistical Machine Translation, WMT@ACL 2007, Prague, Czech Republic, 23 June 2007, pp. 228–231. Association for Computational Linguistics (2007)
26. Li, Y., Tan, Z., Liu, Y.: Privacy-preserving prompt tuning for large language model services (2023)
27. Liu, J., Xia, C.S., Wang, Y., Zhang, L.: Is your code generated by ChatGPT really correct? Rigorous evaluation of large language models for code generation. CoRR, abs/2305.01210 (2023)
28. Liventsev, V., Grishina, A., Härmä, A., Moonen, L.: Fully autonomous programming with large language models. In: Proceedings of the Genetic and Evolutionary Computation Conference (GECCO 2023) (2023)
29. Luccioni, A.S., Viguier, S., Ligozat, A.-L.: Estimating the carbon footprint of bloom, a 176b parameter language model. CoRR, abs/2211.02001 (2022)
30. McColl, R.: On-demand code review with ChatGPT. NearForm blog (2023). https://www.nearform.com/blog/on-demand-code-review-with-chatgpt/. Accessed 20 June 2023
31. Motger, Q., Franch, X., Marco, J.: Software-based dialogue systems: survey, taxonomy, and challenges. ACM Comput. Surv. **55**(5), 91:1–91:42 (2023)
32. Naveed, H., et al.: A comprehensive overview of large language models. CoRR, abs/2307.06435 (2023)
33. Nielsen, J.: AI is first new UI paradigm in 60 years. Jakob Nielsen on UX (2023). https://jakobnielsenphd.substack.com/p/ai-is-first-new-ui-paradigm-in-60. Accessed 03 July 2023
34. Ouyang, L., et al.: Training language models to follow instructions with human feedback. In: NeurIPS (2022)
35. Pan, S., Luo, L., Wang, Y., Chen, C., Wang, J., Wu, X.: Unifying large language models and knowledge graphs: a roadmap (2023)
36. Radford, A., Wu, J., Child, R., Luan, D., Amodei, D., Sutskever, I.: Language models are unsupervised multitask learners. OpenAI, San Francisco, California, United States (2019). https://cdn.openai.com/better-language-models/language_models_are_unsupervised_multitask_learners.pdf. Accessed 05 July 2023
37. Ross, S.I., Martinez, F., Houde, S., Muller, M., Weisz, J.D.: The programmer's assistant: conversational interaction with a large language model for software development. In: Proceedings of the 28th International Conference on Intelligent User Interfaces, IUI 2023, Sydney, NSW, Australia, 27–31 March 2023, pp. 491–514. ACM (2023)
38. Sansonnet, J.-P., Martin, J.-C., Leguern, K.: A software engineering approach combining rational and conversational agents for the design of assistance applications. In: Panayiotopoulos, T., Gratch, J., Aylett, R., Ballin, D., Olivier, P., Rist, T. (eds.) IVA 2005. LNCS (LNAI), vol. 3661, pp. 111–119. Springer, Heidelberg (2005). https://doi.org/10.1007/11550617_10

39. Schäfer, M., Nadi, S., Eghbali, A., Tip, F.: Adaptive test generation using a large language model. CoRR, abs/2302.06527 (2023)
40. Schröder, M.: Autoscrum: automating project planning using large language models. CoRR, abs/2306.03197 (2023)
41. Sridhara, G., Mazumdar, S.: ChatGPT: a study on its utility for ubiquitous software engineering tasks. CoRR, abs/2305.16837 (2023)
42. Thoppilan, R., et al.: Lamda: language models for dialog applications. arXiv preprint arXiv:2201.08239 (2022)
43. White, J., Hays, S., Fu, Q., Spencer-Smith, J., Schmidt, D.C.: ChatGPT prompt patterns for improving code quality, refactoring, requirements elicitation, and software design. CoRR, abs/2303.07839 (2023)
44. Wirsing, M., Belzner, L.: Towards systematically engineering autonomous systems using reinforcement learning and planning. In: López-García, P., Gallagher, J.P., Giacobazzi, R. (eds.) Analysis, Verification and Transformation for Declarative Programming and Intelligent Systems. LNCS, vol. 13160, pp. 281–306. Springer, Cham (2023). https://doi.org/10.1007/978-3-031-31476-6_16
45. Xie, D., et al.: Docter: documentation-guided fuzzing for testing deep learning API functions. In: Ryu, S., Smaragdakis, Y. (eds.) ISSTA 2022: 31st ACM SIGSOFT International Symposium on Software Testing and Analysis, Virtual Event, South Korea, 18–22 July 2022, pp. 176–188. ACM (2022)
46. Xie, D., et al.: Impact of large language models on generating software specifications. CoRR, abs/2306.03324 (2023)
47. Yan, Z., Qin, Y., Hu, X.S., Shi, Y.: On the viability of using LLMS for SW/HW co-design: an example in designing cim DNN accelerators. CoRR, abs/2306.06923 (2023)
48. Yuan, Z., et al.: No more manual tests? Evaluating and improving ChatGPT for unit test generation. CoRR, abs/2305.04207 (2023). Accessed 29 June 2023
49. Zhao, W.X., et al.: A survey of large language models. CoRR, abs/2303.18223 (2023)

ChatGPT in the Loop: A Natural Language Extension for Domain-Specific Modeling Languages

Daniel Busch(✉), Gerrit Nolte, Alexander Bainczyk, and Bernhard Steffen

Department of Computer Science, Chair for Programming Systems,
TU Dortmund University, 44227 Dortmund, Germany
{daniel2.busch,gerrit.nolte,alexander.bainczyk,
bernhard.steffen}@tu-dortmund.de

Abstract. This paper presents an approach to no-code development based on the interplay of *formally defined* (graphical) Domain-Specific Languages and *informal, intuitive* Natural Language which is enriched with contextual information to enable referencing of formally defined entities. The paper focuses on the use and automated integration of these enriched intuitive languages via ChatGPT-based code generation to exploit the best of both language paradigms for domain-specific application development. To compensate for the lack of control over the intuitive languages we apply automated system-level validation via automata learning and subsequent model checking. All this is illustrated using the development of point-and-click adventures as a minimal viable example.

Keywords: Software Engineering · Low-Code/No-Code · Language-driven Engineering · Large Language Models · Automata Learning · Verification · Prompt Engineering · Web Application

1 Motivation and Introduction

GitHub Copilot [16] and ChatGPT [28] have opened a totally new programming experience: Code for diverse programming languages can be generated from just a few lines of natural language descriptions, and even simple programs can be generated fully automatically in a similar fashion. In particular, Large Language Model (LLM)-based programming exceeds what would have been expected in the past by far. On the other side, generated code of machine learning models may have surprisingly severe mistakes. Thus, LLM-based programming is bound to be supervised.

In this paper, we present an approach to software development based on the interplay of Domain-Specific Languages (DSLs) and Natural Language (NL) descriptions. Conceptually, our approach is an extension of Language-Driven Engineering (LDE) [15] to allow natural language specifications for process requirements. We call a natural language which is contextualized with additional

B. Steffen (Ed.): AISoLA 2023, LNCS 14380, pp. 375–390, 2024.
https://doi.org/10.1007/978-3-031-46002-9_24

information about the domain models a Domain-Specific Natural Language (DSNL). This special kind of DSLs ensures that users do not need to specify implementation details, but all necessary information for LLM-based code generation is contained in the additional context. The role of these languages is sketched in Fig. 1 which we explain along the description of our concept in Sect. 3. We illustrate this concept in Sect. 4 using the example of the river crossing puzzle [3]. In this puzzle a farmer is confronted with the problem to cross the river with a wolf, a goat, and a cabbage in a boat that is so small that it can only take one of the three items at a time. In order to avoid damage, the farmer must make sure that neither the wolf and the goat, nor the goat and the cabbage are on the same side of the river whilst the farmer is on the other side.

Our accompanying example concerns the automatic generation of a point-and-click adventure which is won exactly when all the items are safely transferred from one side of the river to the other. The landscape of the point-and-click adventure can easily be specified graphically. For our puzzle we only have to draw the two sides of the river and mutual connections for modeling the potential boat transfer as shown in Fig. 2. This is enough to generate

- a Prompt Frame that provides contextual information to the NL description, so that it can be used as a DSNL, and
- the code that is meant to be extended by the LLM via code generation and code merging.

The example used in this paper focuses on the specification of the puzzle's constraints in natural language, enriched to talk about the objects of the graphical model. These specifications are fed into the Prompt Frame to generate code that extends the code generated from the graphical model. The resulting (merged) code can then be deployed to a fully running web application.

Our approach relies heavily on natural language descriptions with all its ambiguities. This reduces the number of properties which can be validated by the inherent properties of DSLs alone. As a result, we verify them via black box checking [6] of the overall system. Concretely, we combine active automata learning [2,4,5] to infer behavioral models of generated applications via testing and model checking to verify runtime properties formulated in temporal logic. To achieve a full no-code solution, our generators are implemented to generate instrumented web applications that are *learnable by design* [21]. Only the model checker requires manual input in terms of the property to be verified. In our example, we consider the property that the farmer can succeed to cross the river with all three 'items' while assuring that no damage occurs.

It should be noted that our solution is fully no-code and only requires domain experts to:

1. graphically model the architectural information,
2. to specify the process logic in natural language, and
3. to observe the feedback of automated model verification.

All of this can be done via an accessible web application which we will make publicly available for experimentation.

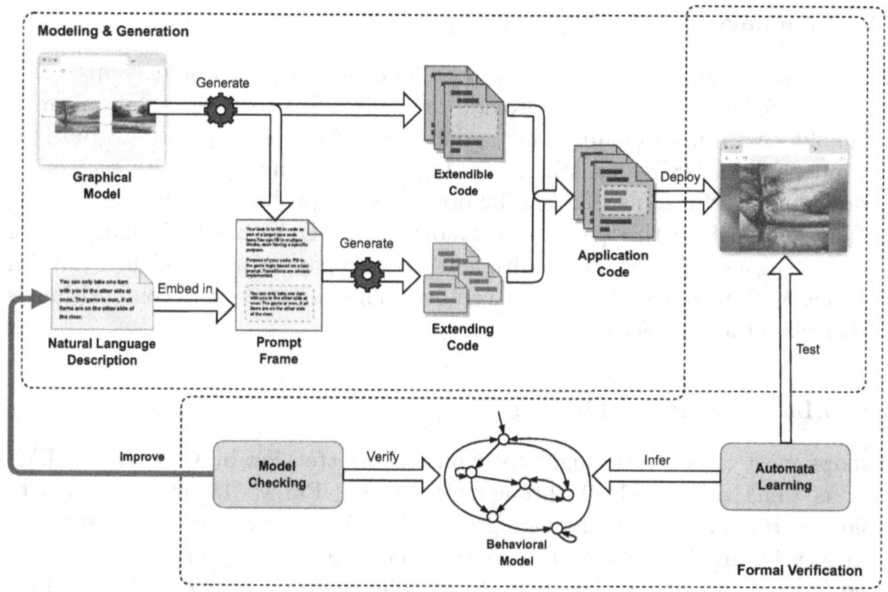

Fig. 1. Concept overview.

Outline. In Sect. 2, we introduce the three fundamental topics of this paper, LDE, LLMs in the context of programming, and learning-based testing. From there, we introduce the concept of utilizing natural language in a domain-specific environment in Sect. 3, and present implementation details in the context of an exemplary implementation in Sect. 4. Section 5 discusses the potential and drawbacks of the presented approach and also compares our contribution to related work. Finally, Sect. 6 concludes the paper, giving an overview, reflecting on the presented approach, and providing ideas for future work.

2 Preliminaries

DSLs and Natural Language Processing (NLP) are two very different approaches to interacting with machines. Each of these approaches has advantages and disadvantages. However, both their advantages and their disadvantages seem to be complementary. This is one of the main reasons why our approach attempts to merge the two paradigms to create one that benefits from the advantages of both while trying to overcome their disadvantages.

This section provides a brief overview of DSLs and NLP and describes their advantages and disadvantages. In addition, learning-based testing is presented as a means to enable a validation feedback loop for users using DSNLs in a no-code environment.

2.1 Language-Driven Engineering

LDE is a paradigm that brings DSLs into focus for solving problems in specific domains [15,17,24]. It aims to provide multiple DSLs for each subproblem or stakeholder within a domain. This is done by decomposing potential solutions into independent DSLs that still have a high degree of interplay with each other to provide powerful tools that can be used to solve problems with ease.

The approach in this paper also follows an LDE approach. But instead of decomposing a single DSL into multiple DSLs, this paper's approach uses natural language within a domain-infused context. This concept of decomposition is further elaborated in Sect. 3.2

2.2 LLMs and Programming

Perhaps most famously brought to mainstream attention by ChatGPT, LLMs such as LLaMa [32], GPT1 through GPT4 [25], PaLM [18] etc. have led to rapid progress in natural language processing. Most commonly, LLMs are used as generative models, taking in a natural language description and returning some form of output, such as text (ChatGPT), images (Stable Diffusion [19]), audio (MusicLM [20]) or, most importantly for this work, code.

Modern LLMs have shown increasingly promising performances with regards to code generation, with model performance steadily increasing. As an example, GPT-4 [28] reached a score of 67% on the Human-Eval dataset [16] where GPT-3.5 only reached 48.1%.

2.3 Learning-Based Testing

Learning-based testing [7] is an approach to fully automated testing of black-box systems using *Active Automata Learning* [2]. In this context, *active learning* refers to a process in which a so-called *learner* interacts directly with a System Under Learning (SUL) via its public interfaces. By posing automatically constructed test queries over some input alphabet and recording the reactions of the SUL, automata models representing the system behavior can be inferred. Often, learning is combined with model checking to automatically verify system properties on inferred models. The practice of testing web applications via learning-based testing also has a long history in research [8,9,11,12,17], where Mealy machines proved to be an adequate representation for verifying user-level specific system properties.

Learning web applications[1] typically requires users to specify an input alphabet and implement system-specific *mappers* [10] that provide an interface for learning algorithms to interact with the target SUL. To address this problem, [21] introduces the *learnability-by-design* framework, which includes the instrumentation DSL iHTML. The language enables developers to instrument HTML

[1] In this work, the term *learning* refers to the use of active automata learning and is not related to the field of deep learning or other AI-based approaches.

code in a way that allows learning algorithms to incrementally mine behavioral models simply by analyzing the Document Object Model (DOM) of the website, without explicitly specifying an input alphabet.

3 Concept

In this section, we introduce a method for code generation that produces code from combined DSL and natural language descriptions. The core concept of this approach is twofold:

1. providing additional domain information to the LLM to generate code that satisfies specific requirements so that it can be used contextually, and
2. extending code that has been generated by traditional code generation.

With reference to Fig. 1, the user creates the graphical model and automatically generates the extensible code and the prompt frame from it. Next, they can use NL to describe additional program logic that is embedded in the prompt frame so that the LLM can generate code from it. This code is then automatically merged into the previously generated extensible code of the graphical model, which together form the resulting application code. Automatic validation is performed on the running instance of the application, which outputs an automaton of accessible system states and can be used to provide feedback to the user using model checking on this automaton.

3.1 Goals

Code generation from formally defined DSLs is well-understood and scalable, in contrast to code generation with LLMs which, at least today, lacks

Control. In general it is hard to predict whether the generated code will be syntactically correct, let alone that it solves the intended task.
Scalability. Feasible problem descriptions are strongly limited in size and conceptual complexity.

To deal with these weaknesses, our approach is designed to only require the generation of small, clearly defined code blocks from natural language that are as independent as possible from the rest of the code-base (which is generated in a structured, rigorous fashion from a DSL model). Of course, we cannot guarantee semantic correctness even for these small code blocks, but we can assure that their aspect-oriented integration maintains executability. This allows us to validate runtime properties of the resulting applications using black-box checking.

3.2 Language Integration

Our approach is characterized by decomposing the overall specification into a formal and an intuitive part, both supported by dedicated DSLs. Such a decomposition is typical for LDE, but the required language integration is new. It requires special care to let ChatGPT generate code that is ready for aspect-oriented merging with code generated from the graphical model. It is the role of the *Prompt Frame* to guarantee that the code generated by the LLM fits the code generated by the graphical DSLs. In particular, it must use the same programming language and utilize the desired functions and global variables.

3.3 Contextualization

To actually use the formal properties of DSLs in an LLM environment, the LLM needs further information about the context for which it should generate code. Thus, the actual prompt must be primed with information about its expected behavior, constraints and details about the graphically modeled instances, and about the expected output code. We call this priming information, into which the user prompt will later be embedded, the Prompt Frame.

Since the LLM's output code is expected to extend the code generated by the DSLs, the LLM is also provided with code stubs and descriptive comments. As a consequence, the Prompt Frame also contains this information about the expected output structure. We call this sub-frame, into which the LLM fills its code, the Generation Frame. The example in Sect. 4 takes advantage of aspect-oriented extensions by using this ensured LLM output structure.

The following paragraphs describe the Prompt Frame and its Generation Frame part in more detail, including their goals and overall purpose.

Prompt Frame. The Prompt Frame should serve two purposes: (1) to provide the LLM with information about the concrete model instances of the DSLs, and (2) to communicate requirements for the generated code that go beyond the general structure provided by the Generation Frame.

The information provided to the LLM should include, for example, information about available states and global variables, as exemplified in Listing 1.1. Any entity that has been modeled in an accompanying DSL and that should be able to interact with the logic prompts fed into the LLM should be mentioned in the prompt frame. Other information may include the desired programming language, or that the LLM should output only code and no supporting text.

Generation Frame. The Generation Frame is a part of the Prompt Frame and consists of code parts that the LLM should fill-in, as seen in Listing 1.2. It is used to ensure that the LLM outputs exactly the functions with the correct signatures that are needed by the DSLs' generated code, which enables the code generated by the DSLs to safely call the functions implemented by the LLM. This allows for easy extensions of the underlying program in an aspect-orientated fashion.

Information about which code is expected in each function is provided through comments or as additional descriptions in the outer Prompt Frame. Besides, LLMs are also able to extract semantic information from the names and signatures of functions and fill in code accordingly.

3.4 Validation and Feedback

In the context of this work, we leverage iHTML in our approach by embedding learnability-by-design practices into our manually implemented code generator, which generates the code frame for the LLM-based generator from our DSL. As a result, arbitrarily generated applications are automatically learnable, allowing us to infer behavioral models that represent user-level interaction processes. For verification purposes, desired system properties can be formulated in temporal logic, Computation Tree Logic (CTL) [1] in our case, to automatically verify learned models with a model checker. Feedback from the model checker is used to refine the natural language prompt, as discussed in Sect. 4.5.

4 Example Implementation

This section shows a sample implementation of the concept presented in this paper. For this, the point-and-click adventure mentioned before is implemented. In our scenario it consists of a puzzle with two locations: the left and the right side of a river. At the beginning there are three objects on the left side of the river: a wolf, a goat and a cabbage. The game is *won* when all three items have been moved to the right side in a fashion satisfying the following constraints: The player can only take one item at a time and at no time the wolf and the goat or the goat and the cabbage are on the same side of the river while the player is on the other side. To implement this puzzle, we chose the graphical DSL Webstory [13], created with the IME workbench Cinco [14].

As the title of this paper suggests, the LLM used for this example is ChatGPT in its API version "gpt-3.5-turbo". Conceptually, this choice is not important, but the use of other LLMs may well lead to different results.

Fig. 2. Examplary WebstoryGM model on Cinco product level.

4.1 Model Decomposition

When creating a point-and-click adventure, two aspects are most important: (1) the design of each game screen and its reachability, and (2) the game logic about when the game is won or lost, as well as the existence and behavior of game objects. Following our approach, we decompose our example into *WebstoryGM*, a graphical DSL to model game screens and transitions between them and *WebstoryNL*, the domain-specific natural language to express the game logic:

- WebstoryGM is suitable to visually specify a high level overview of the game with game screens as images that are actually used in the game, and arrows to model their connections.
- WebstoryNL allows to describe the win and lose conditions using natural language without requiring any form of formalization.

4.2 Graphical Modelling

In its original version, Webstory includes three basic elements for modeling point-and-click adventures: screens, click areas, and transitions. Using these three types of elements, users can define images for game screens and where to click to trigger transitions to different screens. In addition, the original version of Webstory allows users to graphically model game logic. This can be done using graphical representations for variables and adding guards to transitions to change the behavior of screen transitions depending on the overall state of the game. However, implementing game logic using the graphical method is rather tedious, and its semantics cannot be immediately deduced by just looking at the model.

As described in Sect. 4.1, WebstoryGM should only be used to create a sitemap-like overview of all available game screens and their general reachability for this example. Thus, the original Webstory has been modified to contain only screens and transitions, resulting in the desired WebstoryGM. These two elements allow the user to create such a sitemap from which all the information needed to generate the base code, the Prompt Frame and the Generation Frame can be derived. In addition, game screens for a losing and a winning state have been added. These screens don't need to be modeled by the user, as they are implicitly accessible when the player reaches a winning or losing state, as specified by the natural language description of the game logic.

Figure 2 shows an example model for the river crossing puzzle. It consists only of the left and right sides of the river, starting on the left side.

4.3 Prompt Frame and Generation Frame

The game's logic should be described and generated using natural language and ChatGPT as an LLM. To be able to extend the underlying game modelled using the WebstoryNL as described earlier in Sect. 3 the Prompt Frame, as seen in Listing 1.1, contains the following information:

- names of the available game screens
- the desired programming language; in this case JavaScript
- a general directive that should be concise and produce nothing more than the desired code, so it can be easily merged with the code of the graphical models
- expected general properties like the already implemented transitions that are derived from the game objects the LLM should provide, or the general scenario of a point-and-click adventure

```
Your task is to fill in code as part of a larger JavaScript code base.

You can fill in multiple blocks, each having a specific purpose.

Larger context for code: a point-and-click adventure with state
     transitions. All code that you write is part of a game with
     attributes states=["leftRiver", "rightRiver"] and currentState
     which holds the currently visited river side and is therefore one
     of either values of states. These attributes are already written
     and you can safely assume that the rest of the code works as
     intended.

Purpose of your code: Fill in the game logic based on a text prompt.
     Game objects beside states and currentState should be objects
     having a name, and potentially multiple transition objects that
     contain a screen property which is the name the transition can be
     triggered on, and a function property which is the transition
     function for this screen. Game objects are considered present in a
     state if they possess the currentScreen property of the state.

The code blocks for you to implement:

// [...], see Listing 2

Prompt: // [...], see Listing 3

Answer as follows: Write down ONLY the filled in code blocks with the
     code that you seem fit. Add comments if you want but do NOT explain
     anything about the code, your answer should ONLY contain javascript
     code.
```

Listing 1.1. Excerpt of the generated Prompt Frame.

As another part of the Prompt Frame, the LLM is provided with code stubs, as illustrated in Listing 1.2, it has to fill-in as part of the Generator Frame. This Generator Frame comprises

- the function `initVariables()` for game objects, `checkWin()` and `checkLoss()` for implementations of the winning and losing conditions
- Comments with further information about the expected game objects or to mark the positions where the LLM-generated code has to be inserted.

The Prompt Frame (including the Generation Frame) is sufficient to prime ChatGPT in a way that it generates code that is ready to be merged into the code generated from the WebstoryGM model.

```
function initVariables() {
  // state objects should be of the following form
  // this.gameObjects = [
  //   {
  //     name: 'someName',
  //     currentScreen:'someState',
  //     transitions: [
  //       {
  //         screen: 'someState',
  //         function: () => ()
  //       }
  //     ],
  //   }
  // ]
  // they can possess multiple transitions and are only
  // rendered on screens they have transitions for

  this.gameObjects = []; // fill in
}

function checkWin() { // fill in }

function checkLoss() { // fill in }
```

Listing 1.2. The example Generation Frame.

```
On the left side of the river there are a wolf, a goat, and a cabbage.
The game is won if every object has been brought to the right side of
    the river.
The game is lost if the wolf and the goat are on the same side of the
    river, while the player is on the other side, or if the cabbage and
    the goat are on the same side of the river while the player is on
    the other side.
```

Listing 1.3. Example for a natural language description.

4.4 Resulting Web Application

Once the user has modeled the WebstoryGM model as in Fig. 2 and generated the extensible code and prompt frame from it, the DSNL prompt can be added to state the desired game logic.

An example prompt to let ChatGPT implement the game logic of the river crossing example can be seen in Listing 1.3. Once the prompt has been inserted into the prompt frame, it can be sent to ChatGPT either through its API or through the web interface. ChatGPT will only respond with the desired JavaScript code which is then merged into the base code generated from the graphical model. Two screens of the resulting example game can be seen in Fig. 3.

After automatic deployment, the desired point-and-click adventure is ready to use. Initially, the player sees the screen of the left side of the river where the wolf, the goat, and the cabbage are represented as buttons which, when clicked, transfer the corresponding object and the player to the other side of the river.

Fig. 3. The initial game screen (left) after full code generation and the screen after taking the goat to the right riverside (right).

In addition to the buttons, ChatGPT has also implemented the `checkWin()` and `checkLoss()` functions that check after each step whether the game is won or lost. If one of these conditions holds, the corresponding win or loss screen is displayed.

4.5 Model Learning and Verification

After deploying the generated web application, we can learn the instance using Malwa, the tool introduced in [21] to learn instrumented web applications just by providing the URL to the server where the application is deployed to the tool. Note that, because of the instrumentation, we do not need to specify an input alphabet for the learning algorithm, as it is build incrementally just by analyzing and observing the DOM of the website. The learning process results in the eleven-state automaton displayed in Fig. 4. It represents the user-level interaction graph that results from the interactions with the user interface of the Webstory product by clicking on the generated buttons. We represent models using Moore automata[2] to simplify model checking and visual analysis, since each state is linked to exactly one screenshot, thus accurately reflecting user-level interactions with the website.

Upon visual inspection, one can see that the generation resulted in an application that adheres to the constraints formulated in our natural language prompt and that the game can be played as intended. The property that it is possible to win the game can also easily be seen as the *won* screen is reachable in the learned

[2] Moore automata are semantically equivalent to Mealy automata which are the standard target automaton type for active learning of web applications.

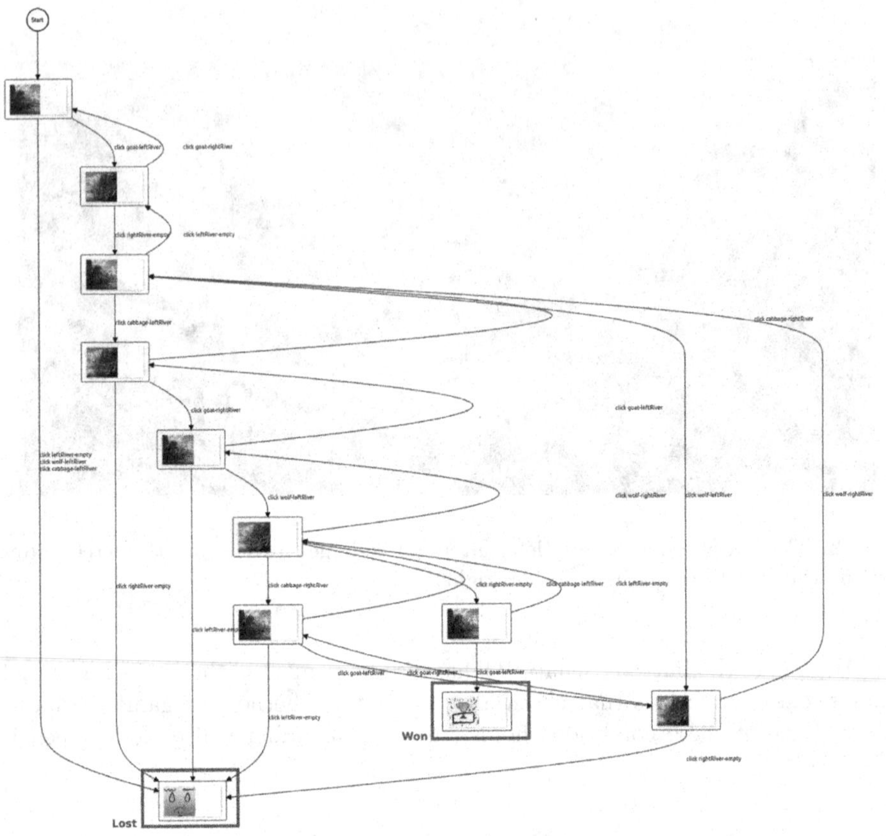

Fig. 4. Learned model of the generated Webstory.

model. For larger models, model checking is an ideal means to verify such properties. Our solution supports CTL model checking using our model checker GEAR for this purpose. Currently, this requires the manual specification of the intended formula which, in particular, may still require to identify dynamically generated atomic propositions, a task that we are aiming to automatically support in the future.

5 Discussion and Related Work

Unsurprisingly, the novel ability to both understand and generate code from natural language descriptions (although still limited) has attracted attention from the software engineering community.

At present, applications of LLMs in software engineering are in very early stages and most work on LLMs and their role in software development focuses on supportive applications in traditional software engineering contexts [22]. In most of these works, LLMs are not tasked with full code generation but predominantly with tasks such as: Explaining code to a human, providing feedback to a human, finding potential bugs in human-written code or generating small-scale helper functions. Moreover, most of these works focus on applications of ChatGPT as it is one of the strongest and most widely used LLMs at present.

The authors of [31] apply ChatGPT to a range of code generation benchmark tasks as well as supporting tasks such as code summarization, bug fixing and program repair. They note that, while ChatGPT is neither able to repair, explain or generate programs reliably on its own, it can often provide a range of possible solutions from which an expert programmer can choose an adequate one and propose ChatGPT as "programming support" in software engineering. In this context, [26] propose a continuous improvement cycle where code generated by the LLM is model checked and counterexamples are fed back to the LLM to incrementally improve the generated code until all properties are satisfied.

Quite similarly, the authors of [30] evaluate ChatGPT's performance on bug fixing and program repair and, again, find empirically that performance is only adequate if a human programmer works in tandem with ChatGPT.

This point of view is also reflected in current industrial applications. Commercial tools such as GitHub Copilot [27] show that this is currently the predominant application of LLMs in software engineering.

An approach to using LLMs for the entirety of software development has been investigated by [23]. They investigate the potential of using LLMs for design, code generation, and testing processes. From their findings and their case study, they derive challenges to be addressed and possible future scenarios for LLM-based software engineering.

Larger-scale code generation has been attempted by AutoGPT [29]. Using specific prompts, AutoGPT forces ChatGPT to divide a larger task into multiple subtasks and iterate upon its earlier results to solve more complex problems in a divide and conquer fashion.

The idea to decompose a complex programming task into small pieces is similar to our approach, but the means are different: Whereas AutoGPT uses ChatGPT for handling the decomposition also, we use a formally defined DSL which provides us with better control and scalability. In particular, we can guarantee the executability of the overall generated application, a precondition to apply black-box checking.

We are not aware of any approach that aims at a similarly holistic integration of natural language-based specifications into a (no/low code) development framework.

6 Conclusion

We have presented an approach to no-code development based on the interplay of formally defined (graphical) Domain-Specific Languages and informal, intuitive Natural Language which is enriched with contextual information to enable referencing of formally defined entities. Our implementation within the LDE ecosystem which is designed to support application development using multiple DSLs has illustrated how one can exploit the best of the two language paradigms:

- the control provided by the graphical DSL to ensure executability of the developed application, a precondition to apply black-box checking for validation, and
- the ease of prompting ChatGPT with natural language which enables people without any computational knowledge to specify process requirements.

Technically, our approach depends on enhancing the code generator for the graphical modeling language to also generate an appropriate prompt frame that guarantees that the code generated from the natural language specification can be merged into the code generated from the graphical model while guaranteeing that the resulting application is executable.

Our approach has been illustrated in detail using the development of point-and-click adventures as minimal viable application scenario. More concretely, we stepwise developed a point-and-click adventure that is inspired by the river crossing puzzle.

Guaranteed executability is essential to provide non-technical users also with no-code validation, but it is not sufficient as the required automata learning typically requires to provide a dedicated learning alphabet. In our application scenario, the code generator guarantees that the generated applications are learnable by design: the required learning alphabet can be incrementally deduced from the Document Object Models (DOM) as part of the learning process. In contrast, the subsequent model checking requires the manual specification of the intended formula which, in particular, may still require to identify dynamically generated atomic propositions. We are currently investigating how far this identification can be automated.

The enormous potential of intuitive specifications became evident with the recent development of LLMs, and we are only at the beginning of understanding what their combined power with formal specifications might be. In this paper we have shown how to gain some control over LLM-generated code by embedding it into 'traditionally' generated code. This has allowed us to guarantee the executability of the generated overall applications, a precondition for applying validation techniques like black box checking. We are convinced that this kind of embedding LLM-based code generation into formal methods-based application development is a promising way to exploit the power of natural language specification while taming its shortcomings.

References

1. Clarke, E.M., Emerson, E.A., Sistla, A.P.: Automatic verification of finite-state concurrent systems using temporal logic specifications. In: ACM Transactions on Programming Languages and Systems, vol. 8, no. 2, pp. 244–263 (1986). https://doi.org/10.1145/5397.5399
2. Angluin, D.: Learning regular sets from queries and counterexamples. Inf. Comput. **75**(2), 87–106 (1987). https://doi.org/10.1016/0890-5401(87)90052-6

3. Burkholder, P.: Alcuin of York's propositiones ad acuendos juvenes: introduction, commentary & translation. Hist. Sci. Technol. Bull. **1**(2) (1993)
4. Kearns, M.J., Vazirani, U.V.: An Introduction to Computational Learning Theory. Cambridge, MA, USA (1994). ISBN: 0-262-11193-4
5. Balcázar, J.L., Dýéaz, J., Gavaldá, R.: Algorithms for learning finite automata from queries: a unified view. In: Advances in Algorithms, Languages, and Complexity, pp. 53–72 (1997)
6. Peled, D., Vardi, M.Y., Yannakakis, M.: Black box checking. In: Wu, J., Chanson, S.T., Gao, Q. (eds.) Formal Methods for Protocol Engineering and Distributed Systems. IAICT, vol. 28, pp. 225–240. Springer, Boston, MA (1999). https://doi.org/10.1007/978-0-387-35578-8_13
7. Hungar, H., Margaria, T., Steffen, B.: Test-based model generation for legacy systems. In: Test Conference, 2003. Proceedings. ITC 2003. International, vol. 1, pp. 971–980 (2003). https://doi.org/10.1109/TEST.2003.1271205
8. Raffelt, H., Steffen, B., Margaria, T.: Dynamic testing via automata learning. In: Yorav, K. (ed.) HVC 2007. LNCS, vol. 4899, pp. 136–152. Springer, Heidelberg (2008). https://doi.org/10.1007/978-3-540-77966-7_13
9. Raffelt, H., et al.: Dynamic testing via automata learning. In: International Journal on Software Tools for Technology Transfer (STTT), vol. 11, issue 4, pp. 307–324 (2009). ISSN: 1433–2779. https://doi.org/10.1007/s10009-009-0120-7
10. Jonsson, B.: Learning of automata models extended with data. In: Formal Methods for Eternal Networked Software Systems: 11th International School on Formal Methods for the Design of Computer, Communication and Software Systems, SFM 2011, Bertinoro, Italy, June 13–18, 2011. Advanced Lectures. Ed. by Marco Bernardo and Val-erie Issarny. Berlin, Heidelberg: Springer, Berlin Heidelberg, pp. 327–349 (2011). ISBN: 978-3-642-21455-4. https://doi.org/10.1007/978-3-642-21455-4_10
11. Neubauer, J., Windmüller, S., Steffen, B.: Risk-based testing via active continuous quality control. Int. J. Softw. Tools Technol. Transfer **16**(5), 569–591 (2014). https://doi.org/10.1007/s10009-014-0321-6
12. Bainczyk, A., Schieweck, A., Steffen, B., Howar, F.: Model-based testing without models: the TodoMVC case study. In: Katoen, J.-P., Langerak, R., Rensink, A. (eds.) ModelEd, TestEd, TrustEd. LNCS, vol. 10500, pp. 125–144. Springer, Cham (2017). https://doi.org/10.1007/978-3-319-68270-9_7
13. Lybecait, M., Kopetzki, D., Zweihoff, P., Fuhge, A., Naujokat, S., Steffen, B.: A tutorial introduction to graphical modeling and metamodeling with CINCO. In: Margaria, T., Steffen, B. (eds.) ISoLA 2018. LNCS, vol. 11244, pp. 519–538. Springer, Cham (2018). https://doi.org/10.1007/978-3-030-03418-4_31
14. Naujokat, S., et al.: CINCO: a simplicity-driven approach to full generation of domain-specific graphical modeling tools. Int. J. Softw. Tools Technol. Transfer **20**, 327–354 (2018)
15. Steffen, B., et al.: Language-driven engineering: from general-purpose to purpose-specific languages. In: Computing and Software Science: State of the Art and Perspectives, pp. 311–344 (2019)
16. Chen, M., et al.: Evaluating large language models trained on code. In: arXiv preprint arXiv:2107.03374 (2021)
17. Bainczyk, A., et al.: Towards continuous quality control in the context of language-driven engineering. In: Leveraging Applications of Formal Methods, Verification and Validation. Software Engineering. Ed. by Tiziana Margaria and Bernhard Steffen, pp. 389–406. Springer Nature Switzerland, Cham (2022). ISBN: 978-3-031-19756-7. https://doi.org/10.1007/978-3-031-19756-7_22

18. Chowdhery, A., et al.: PaLM: scaling language modeling with pathways. In: arXiv preprint arXiv:2204.02311 (2022)
19. Rombach, R., et al.: High-resolution image synthesis with latent diffusion models. In: Proceedings of the IEEE/CVF Conference on Computer Vision and Pattern Recognition, pp. 10684–10695 (2022)
20. Agostinelli, A., et al.: MusicLM: generating music from text. In: arXiv preprint arXiv:2301.11325 (2023)
21. Bainczyk, A.: Simplicity-oriented lifelong learning of web applications. [work in progress]. PhD thesis. Dortmund, Germany: TU Dortmund University (2023)
22. Beganovic, A., Abu Jaber, M., Abd Almisreb, A.: Methods and applications of ChatGPT in software development: a literature review. SE Eur. J. Soft Comput. **12**(1), 08–12 (2023)
23. Belzner, L., Gabor, T., Wirsing, M.: Large language model assisted software engineering: prospects, challenges, and a case study. In: Steffen, B. (ed.) Bridging the Gap between AI and Reality, AISoLA 2023, LNCS 14380, pp. 355–374. Springer, Heidelberg (2023)
24. Boßelmann, S.: Evolution of ecosystems for language-driven engineering. PhD thesis. Dortmund, Germany: TU Dortmund University (2023). https://doi.org/10.17877/DE290R-23218
25. Bubeck, S., et al.: Sparks of artificial general intelligence: early experiments with GPT-4. arXiv preprint arXiv:2303.12712 (2023)
26. Charalambous, Y., et al.: A new era in software security: towards self-healing software via large language models and formal verification (2023). https://doi.org/10.48550/arXiv.2305.14752
27. GitHub. GitHub Copilot (2023). https://copilot.github.com/. Accessed 21 July 2023
28. OpenAI. GPT-4 Technical Report. ArXiv abs/2303.08774 (2023)
29. Richards, T.B.: Auto-GPT: an autonomous GPT-4 experiment (2023). https://github.com/Significant-Gravitas/Auto-GPT. Accessed 21 July 2023
30. Sobania, D., et al.: An analysis of the automatic bug fixing performance of ChatGPT. arXiv preprint arXiv:2301.08653 (2023)
31. Tian, H., et al.: Is ChatGPT the ultimate programming assistant-how far is it? In: arXiv preprint arXiv:2304.11938 (2023)
32. Touvron, H., et al.: LLaMA: open and efficient foundation language models. arXiv preprint arXiv:2302.13971 (2023)

What Can Large Language Models Do for Theorem Proving and Formal Methods?

Moa Johansson(✉)

Chalmers University of Technology, Gothenburg, Sweden
moa.johansson@chalmers.se

Abstract. With the introduction of large language models, AI for natural language have taken a leap. These systems are now also being used for tasks that has previously been dominated by symbolic methods, such as program synthesis and even to support formalising mathematics and assist theorem provers. We survey some recent applications in theorem proving, focusing on how they combine neural networks with symbolic systems, and report on a case-study of using GPT-4 for the task of automated conjecturing a.k.a. theory exploration.

1 Introduction

With recent developments of very capable Large Language Models (LLMs) such as GPT-4 [14], many of us now investigate how to best combine the generative capabilities of LLMs with symbolic systems like theorem provers. LLMs are sometimes unreliable and prone to hallucinate, simply "invent" stuff, and occasionally fail on seemingly trivial problems. While there is work on using LLMs to directly reason in mathematics, via chain-of-thought prompting and similar techniques e.g., [12], we believe a more reliable way forward is to induce the LLM to provide inputs to symbolic systems, like theorem provers to do the actual reasoning. Work on *autoformalisation* [17], concerns the task of translating problems expressed in natural or informal language into the input languages of interactive theorem provers such as Mizar [10] and recently also, by using LLMs, Isabelle/HOL [19] or Coq [2]. There is also work on getting LLMs to generate proof-scripts, or parts thereof [5,6,20]. These proof scripts may of course contain errors, but these will be flagged when run through the corresponding proof-assistant and can be patched by a human user or (symbolic) automated proof repair tools. Finally, we also mention that GPT-4 has recently been fitted with the capability to interact with external tools like Wolfram Alpha, via its Code Interpreter interface. This way, certain problems can be outsourced to external systems, for which suitable symbolic inputs are generated. Early results on problems from maths and science were mixed [3].

B. Steffen (Ed.): AISoLA 2023, LNCS 14380, pp. 391–394, 2024.
https://doi.org/10.1007/978-3-031-46002-9_25

2 Automated Conjecturing

We are interested in the task of inventing suitable lemmas or conjectures, which can help theorem provers by enriching their background theories, in particular for automating proofs by induction [8,9,16]. Given a set of datatypes and function definitions, what interesting properties can be discovered? The problem of automated conjecturing is certainly not new to research in (symbolic) AI: there are several early systems based on specialised heuristics such as AM and Graffiti [4,11], followed later by HR (integer sequences) and MATHsAiD (algebra) [1,13]. The above-mentioned systems all use search, but there is also work on neural network driven methods [15,18] which has managed to generate some lemmas, however also producing many repetitions of known lemmas and non-theorems.

2.1 Case Study: Theory Exploration in GPT-4

In a recent case-study (described in more detail in [7]), we wanted to investigate how the GPT-4 system would perform on a lemma discovery task, zero-shot. We prompted GPT-4 with theories written in the syntax of the Isabelle/HOL proof assistant and asked it to provide lemmas also in this syntax. This approach requires some care: as GPT-4 is trained on code from GitHub, we were aware that our benchmarks used from our Hipster theory exploration system [9], very likely were in the training data (which also was confirmed by GPT-4 occasionally producing close copies to Hipster's output), together with existing libraries for Isabelle/HOL. We thus instead chose to port a Haskell library about drawings and geometry to Isabelle. Some interesting observations can be made: Generally, GPT-4 was very consistently producing outputs in correct Isabelle syntax, which could be pasted into the proof-assistant with little or no further editing. Each run will differ slightly, as the system is probabilistic, but it consistently produces "generic" lemmas, such as associativity, commutativity and distributivity for binary functions and unary functions being their own inverses. As these properties are quite common, it is probably sensible suggestions, but does not take anything else from the function definitions into account, and hence lead to many non-theorems (false statements). Occasionally though, GPT-4 came up with other useful lemmas, for instance relationships between rotating drawings varying degrees.

Compared to a symbolic theory exploration system, GPT-4 can use the semantics of function names to occasionally "hallucinate" some additional function which could be of interest, but the user had not thought of including. It also does not have any restrictions of the size and shape of the lemmas generated, so no special treatment is needed for implications compared to equalities, unlike symbolic systems. On the downside, GPT-4 is less predictable than a symbolic system and will need to be run several times to achieve decent coverage. It is also difficult to fairly evaluate, as we don't know exactly what is in its training data.

3 Conclusions and Further Work

Using LLMs for lemma discovery has some complementary features to fully symbolic systems. How to customise and use such systems for making analogies between theories, use them to make analogies between theories and potentially combine them with symbolic lemma discovery systems is interesting further work. Lemma discovery systems have so far been limited to simple toy theories and simple functional programs, of little use to formal methods and more advanced mathematics, where proofs typically require highly contextualised lemmas of larger size than symbolic systems deal with well. Whether LLMs can help narrowing this gap is still an open question.

References

1. Colton, S.: The HR program for theorem generation. In: Voronkov, A. (ed.) CADE 2002. LNCS (LNAI), vol. 2392, pp. 285–289. Springer, Heidelberg (2002). https://doi.org/10.1007/3-540-45620-1_24
2. Cunningham, G., Bunescu, R.C., Juedes, D.: Towards autoformalization of mathematics and code correctness: experiments with elementary proofs (2023)
3. Davis, E., Aaronson, S.: Testing GPT-4 with Wolfram Alpha and Code Interpreter plug-ins on math and science problems (2023)
4. Fajtlowicz, S.: On conjectures of Graffiti. Ann. Discrete Math. **38**, 113–118 (1988)
5. First, E., Rabe, M.N., Ringer, T., Brun, Y.: Baldur: Whole-proof generation and repair with large language models (2023). https://arxiv.org/abs/2303.04910
6. Jiang, A.Q., et al.: Thor: Wielding hammers to integrate language models and automated theorem provers. In: Oh, A.H., Agarwal, A., Belgrave, D., Cho, K., editors, Advances in Neural Information Processing Systems (2022). https://openreview.net/forum?id=fUeOyt-2EOp
7. Johansson, M., Smallbone, N.: Exploring mathematical conjecturing with large language models. In: Proceedings of NeSy 2023, 17th International Workshop on Neural-Symbolic Learning and Reasoning (2023)
8. Johansson, M., Dixon, L., Bundy, A.: Conjecture synthesis for inductive theories. J. Autom. Reason. **47**(3), 251–289, Oct (2011). ISSN 1573–0670. https://doi.org/10.1007/s10817-010-9193-y
9. Johansson, M., Rosén, D., Smallbone, N., Claessen, K.: Hipster: integrating theory exploration in a proof assistant. In: Watt, S.M., Davenport, J.H., Sexton, A.P., Sojka, P., Urban, J. (eds.) CICM 2014. LNCS (LNAI), vol. 8543, pp. 108–122. Springer, Cham (2014). https://doi.org/10.1007/978-3-319-08434-3_9
10. Kaliszyk, C., Urban, J., Vyskocil, J.: System description: statistical parsing of informalized Mizar formulas. In: 2017 19th International Symposium on Symbolic and Numeric Algorithms for Scientific Computing (SYNASC), pp. 169–172 (2017). https://doi.org/10.1109/SYNASC.2017.00036
11. Lenat, D.B.: AM, an artificial intelligence approach to discovery in mathematics as heuristic search (1976)
12. Lewkowycz, A., et al.: Solving quantitative reasoning problems with language models. In: Oh, A.H., Agarwal, A., Belgrave, D., Cho, K., editors, Advances in Neural Information Processing Systems (2022). https://openreview.net/forum?id=IFXTZERXdM7

13. McCasland, R.L., Bundy, A., Smith, P.F.: MATHsAiD: automated mathematical theory exploration. Appl. Intell. **47**(3), 585–606 (2017). https://doi.org/10.1007/s10489-017-0954-8
14. OpenAI. GPT-4 technical report. Technical report (2023). https://cdn.openai.com/papers/gpt-4.pdf
15. Rabe, M.N., Lee, D., Bansal, K., Szegedy, C.: Mathematical reasoning via self-supervised skip-tree training. In: International Conference on Learning Representations (2021). https://openreview.net/forum?id=YmqAnY0CMEy
16. Smallbone, N., Johansson, M., Claessen, K., Algehed, M.: Quick specifications for the busy programmer. J. Functional Program., 27 (2017). https://doi.org/10.1017/S0956796817000090
17. Szegedy, C.: A promising path towards autoformalization and general artificial intelligence. In: Benzmüller, C., Miller, B. (eds.) CICM 2020. LNCS (LNAI), vol. 12236, pp. 3–20. Springer, Cham (2020). https://doi.org/10.1007/978-3-030-53518-6_1
18. Szegedy, C.: A promising path towards autoformalization and general artificial intelligence. In: Benzmüller, C., Miller, B. (eds.) CICM 2020. LNCS (LNAI), vol. 12236, pp. 3–20. Springer, Cham (2020). https://doi.org/10.1007/978-3-030-53518-6_1
19. Wu, Y., et al.: Autoformalization with large language models. In: Oh, A.H., Agarwal, A., Belgrave, D., Cho, K., editors, Advances in Neural Information Processing Systems (2022). https://openreview.net/forum?id=IUikebJ1Bf0
20. Yang, K., et al.: LeanDojo: theorem proving with retrieval-augmented language models. arXiv preprint arXiv:2306.15626 (2023)

Integrating Distributed Component-Based Systems Through Deep Reinforcement Learning

Itay Cohen and Doron Peled(✉)

Bar Ilan University, 52900 Ramat Gan, Israel
doron.peled@gmail.com

Abstract. Modern system design and development often consists of combining different components developed by separate vendors under some known constraints that allow them to operate together. Such a system may further benefit from further refinement when the components are integrated together. We suggest a learning-open architecture that employs deep reinforcement learning performed under weak assumptions. The components are "black boxes", where their internal structure is not known, and the learning is performed in a distributed way, where each process is aware only on its local execution information and the global utility value of the system, calculated after complete executions. We employ the proximal policy optimization (PPO) as our learning architecture adapted to our case of training control for black box components. We start by applying the PPO architecture to a simplified case, where we need to train a single component that is connected to a black box environment; we show a stark improvement when compared to a previous attempt. Then we move to study the case of multiple components.

1 Introduction

The process of system development often involves partitioning the system's task into different components that work in tandem. These components can be developed in-house by different groups and can also include parts outsourced to other software houses or off-the-shelf elements. Recently, we see a growing research effort on the automatic construction of system components directly from the specification. We are also starting to witness the automatic synthesis of code based on natural language requirements, e.g., as part of the capabilities of the chatbot ChatGPT [1] that is based on large-scale deep learning. Constructing a system from concurrently performing components that are developed by different groups and using different methodologies may require some means of control for optimizing the combined behavior. In particular, the goal of such control can be the following: as components can interact with one another, one would

This project has received funding from the European Union's Horizon 2020 research and innovation programme under grant agreement No 956123 - FOCETA.

B. Steffen (Ed.): AISoLA 2023, LNCS 14380, pp. 395–417, 2024.
https://doi.org/10.1007/978-3-031-46002-9_26

like to avoid situation where a large number of attempts to interact would be unsuccessful due to the lack of knowledge of components about the current state of one another.

In this work, we address the problem of providing distributed control to a system that is developed from multiple components that interact with each other, i.e., a *multi-agent system*. The internal structure of these components is unknown (due to their development process), i.e., each component is considered to be a *black box* with respect to each other; only the types of interactions with the other processes is known to each process. We suggest that the components are designed with local provisions for establishing control based on deep learning. We do not want to rely on shared information for achieving control during their joint execution. Thus, the learning process can use only the locally observed information of a component.[1] Our goal is then to choose an effective learning-open architecture for distributed control for optimizing the joint execution of a multi-agent system. As a specific goal that we can demonstrate and experiment with, we chose to minimize the overall number of failed interactions between the processes (components) of a multi-agent system, i.e., the number of times that a process offers an interaction to another process while the other process is not ready for it. While this optimization criterion is natural and attainable, our control synthesis method does not have to be confined to it. A more general goal we considered is to maximize the cumulative rewards assigned for each type of action in a process (component).

Since each component sees the rest of the system as a black box with which it can interact, we adopt a reinforcement learning approach where the control is synthesized based on observations performed on the integrated system. However, due to using components developed independently, during training each component has access only to its local information. Our suggested approach can be considered as a version of *multiagent reinforcement learning (MARL)* [2]. In particular, we employ *deep* multiagent reinforcement learning [9], where trained neural networks undertake the task of controlling the components. While there is a large number of models and architectures designed for MARL, we seek an architecture and a training methodology that best suite our targeted systems, consisting of concurrent black box components that interact with one another. We refrain from allowing interactions between the learning components, e.g., the sharing of information at training time (as of a shared critique) [15]. We also concentrate on using state-of-the art techniques, including the *proximal policy optimization* (PPO) algorithm [13], a reinforcement learning algorithm that is employed also in chatGPT.

We developed our approach in two steps. In the first step we considered a simplified model that has concurrent synchronous components, which was first introduced in [7]. This allowed us to concentrate first on the selection of the deep

[1] This can also be easily generalized to employ a utility function that is calculated from the local utility functions of each component; for example, each component can calculate some measure of success (e.g., in form of a discounting sum) on performing interactions, and the global utility can be the sum of this measure over the participating processes.

learning architecture and parameters, and to compare to experiments that were done with respect to this limited model. This model includes a finite state component that we call the *system*, which interacts with a black-box *environment*. The control is only imposed on the system component and the environment component is uncontrollable. In each step, the system and the environment stay synchronized, where the communication between them is in the form of an handshake. The system makes a choice for the next action, and the environment must follow that choice if the action is enabled. Otherwise, a failed interaction occurs and the system does not move while the environment makes some independent progress. The control enforces the choice of the system's next action based on the available partial information, which involves its sequence of local states and actions that occurred so far and the indication of success/failure to interact with the environment at each point. The control goal is to minimize the number of times that the system will offer an action that will result in a failed interaction.

As part of the first step of our approach, we devise an alternative deep reinforcement learning approach for the simplified setting, based on the Proximal Policy Optimization algorithm. We integrate a Recurrent Neural Network (RNN) with the network architecture of PPO, to capture the long term history of the executions. We show that this approach improves the experimental results of [7].

After experimenting with the restricted model, the second step included a full and more realistic model that encapsulates multiple concurrent components executing asynchronously. Although the model is asynchronous, it preserves the handshake-like form of communication; a pair of components should offer each other the same type of action to establish a successful interaction. We introduce a generalized approach that derives control for *multiple* components that can interact with one another, where a separate control, based on a trained RNN, is imposed on each component. Controlling the different components is obtained in a distributed fashion, where each component considers the others as its environment. The only signal that is shared between the components in whether an interaction succeeded, failed or missed.

To motivate our deep learning framework, consider the dinning philosophers problem, which is a classical problem involving scheduling and interaction between concurrent processes. It involves a number of philosophers (often five) sitting around a table, with a fork between each two of them. Each philosopher needs to capture two forks to eat. After eating, he can release the forks. In order to let all the philosophers eat, a strategy involving capturing the forks is needed. A bad strategy can, e.g., let each philosopher capture the left fork first; then they discover that no one can eat, then trying the right fork, etc. In [10], it was proven that there is no deterministic (i.e., non probabilistic) and symmetric solution to the dining philosophers problem. In our framework, there is also the additional factor that the philosophers do not known the structure of each other (they are black boxes), hence the sought strategy needs to be discovered by experiments. Our deep reinforcement learning approach learns such strategies, represented within the used neural networks.

We implemented our proposed methodology using the PyTorch library [12]. To test our implementation, we devised small but somewhat challenging examples. These examples allowed us to evaluate the results of our experiments. The different parameters of our approach were also fine-tuned as a result of experimenting with these examples. Our experiments consist of a comparison between the performance of our implementation and the optimal strategy for each example.

2 Preliminaries

We study systems that are constructed from finite state components and interact with each other. At any state a component can choose between a set of actions. A controller supervising a component can observe the current state of the system and can impose restrictions to the set of actions allowed at the current state. Such a mechanism is standard in control theory, and a formalization can be found e.g., in [3]. In particular, we look at a system constructed from multiple components running concurrently. The actions that are mutual to a pair of components can be considered as *interactions* and both components need to select the same action in order to successfully interact. In models like CSP [6] the interaction can be asymmetric, where one side is a sender and the other one is a receiver. In other models the interactions are defined in a more general context, not necessarily associated with message passing [4].

A Simplified Model. Initially, we look at a simplified case, where one component (process) is a given state machine that we term "the system", and the other one is a black box machine we term "the environment". The set of actions is joined by both components. We further assume that the system and the environment are executing synchronously. The system has priority in selecting the next action (it is the "master") and if the action it offers the environment is currently available by the environment (which is the "slave"), they will both interact and move to their respective state. Note that the state of the environment and the set of actions enabled from it are unknown, as the environment is a black box. If the environment cannot participate in the action offered to it by the system (it is not enabled), then it chooses one of its other enabled actions and progresses according to it. Note that here, for simplicity of the model, the environment progresses on one of the interactions without the system taking part in it; this modeling assumption will be removed in the more advanced model. In the simplified model case, the control is enforced only on the system, where the environment is to be left as is.

The details of this model were selected in order to simplify both the implementation and the presentation. This is also the model used in [7] and adopting the model allows us to compare the training architecture that we use here with the results of that work.

Example. Consider the system in Fig. 1 (left) and its environment (right). This system can always make a choice between the actions a, b and c, and the environment has to agree with that choice if it is enabled from its current state.

Remember that the system is unaware of the environment's internal state. If the system selects actions according to $(abc)^*$ then the environment can follow that selection with no failures. On the other hand, if the system selects actions according to $(baa)^*$ it will fail constantly, while the environment keeps changing states. Our goal is to construct a control that restricts the system's actions at each step such that the number of failed interactions will be minimal.

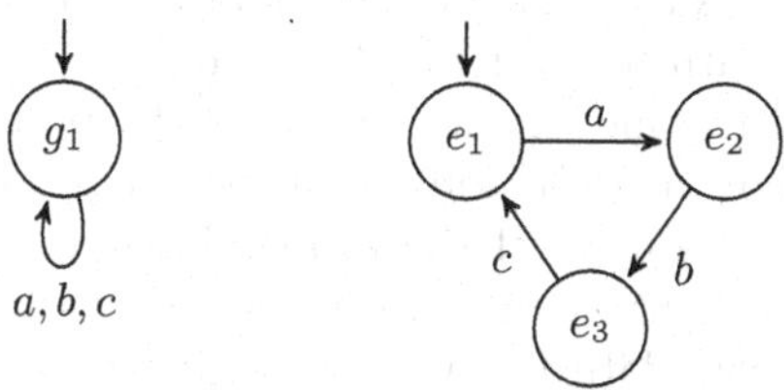

Fig. 1. *permitted*: System (left) and Environment (right).

A More Advanced Model. In the advanced model, components (processes) can interact with one another. All the interactions involve pairs of components. Each component may also have local actions (which may model interactions with yet another component, when we want to abstract away some of the components). All the components are black boxes. There is no explicit notion of *environment* is this model; in a sense, each process can consider the rest of the processes combined as its environment. Control is applied, separately, to each component. If an agreed upon interaction is not selected, a component can select to perform a local action, but unlike the simpler case, cannot decide to participate unilaterally in an interaction. The execution is now asynchronous, with components performing according to their own speeds. The choice of an asynchronous execution model further justifies the use of deep reinforcement learning as a method for learning to control the components; the relative speed of the different concurrent components contributes to the nondeterminism in the execution. Changing only the timing parameters of a single system would potentially change the optimal control strategies for the rest of the components. Hence it is the actual experience that is used in the training that allows us to effectively control the system; thus, a preliminary learning of finite state models of the components would take into account the timing parameters.

Reinforcement Learning. Reinforcement learning (RL) includes methods for controlling the interaction with an environment [14]. The goal is to maximize the expected utility value that sums up the future rewards/penalties; these can be discounted by γ^n with respect to its future distance n from the current point, with $0 < \gamma \leq 1$, or be summed up with respect to a finite distance (horizon). Typically, the model for RL is a Markov Decision Process (MDP), where there is a probability distribution on the states that are reached by taking an action from a given state. When the current state of the environment is not directly known to the controller during the execution, the model is a Partially Observable MDP (POMDP).

A *value-based* control policy (strategy) can be calculated by maximizing either a state-value function $V(s)$ or a state-action value $Q(s,a)$. Assuming acting according to a certain strategy, the value function $V(s)$ is equal to the expected discounted sum of rewards of a controller starting from state s. The state-value function means the expected discounted sum of rewards received by the controller starting with an action a from state s. When the environment is fully observable, and the model that indicates the probability to move from one state to another (given an action) is known, a procedure based on Bellman's equation [14] can be used. If the probabilities are unknown but we can still observe the environment, a randomized-based (*Monte Carlo*) exploration method can be used to update the value function and converge towards the optimal policy.

Policy based RL methods avoid calculating the optimal utility value directly at each state, hence are more effective when the number of possible states is huge. The policy is parametric and its parameters are optimized based on gradient descent. Such parameters can be, in particular, the weights of a neural network. The class of reinforcement learning algorithms that utilize neural networks to represent a parametric policy, or to estimate state-action values is called *deep reinforcement learning.*

Deep Learning. Deep learning is a collection of methods for training *neural networks*, which can be used to perform various tasks such as image and speech recognition or playing games at an expert level. A neural network consists of a collection of nodes, the *neurons*, arranged in several layers, where each neuron is connected to all the neurons in the previous and the next layer. The first layer is the *input layer* and the last layer is the *output layer*. The other layers are *hidden*.

The value x_i of the ith neuron at layer $j+1$ is computed from the column vector $\mathbf{y} = (y_1, \ldots, y_m)$ of all the neurons at layer j. To compute x_i, we first apply a transformation $t_i = \mathbf{w}_i \mathbf{y} + b_i$ where $\mathbf{w}_i$ is a line vector of *weights*, and b_i a number called the *bias*. Then we apply to the vector $\mathbf{t} = (t_1, \ldots, t_n)$ an *activation function*, making the value of each neuron a non-linear function of the values of neurons at the preceding layer. Typical activation functions include the *sigmoid* and *tanh* functions, as well as *ReLU* and *softmax*.

The ReLU (rectified linear unit) activation function is defined as the positive part of its argument. When applied on a vector, it is defined as a vector of the positive part of each of its coordinates.

$$ReLU(x) = \begin{cases} x & \text{if } x > 0 \\ 0 & \text{otherwise.} \end{cases}$$

The *softmax* activation function takes a vector of values and normalizes it into a corresponding vector of probability distributions, i.e., with values between 0 and 1, summing up to 1.

$$softmax(t_1, \dots, t_n) = \left(\frac{e^{t_1}}{\Sigma_i e^{t_i}}, \dots, \dots, \frac{e^{t_n}}{\Sigma_i e^{t_i}} \right)$$

Given values for all neurons in the input layer, we can compute the values for all neurons in the network. Overall, a neural network represents a function $\mathbb{R}^n \rightarrow \mathbb{R}^m$ where n is the size of the input layer, and m the size of the output layer.

The values of the weights w_i and the biases b_i are modified through *training*. A *loss function* provides a measurement of the distance between the actual output of the neural network and the desired output. The goal of training is to minimize the loss function. Optimizing the parameters is performed from the output layer backwards based on gradient descent.

For applications where sequences of inputs are analyzed, as e.g., in language recognition, one often uses a form of network called *Recurrent Neural Network* (RNN). An RNN maintains a feedback loop, where values of some neurons are fed back to the network as additional inputs in the next step. In this way an RNN has the capability of maintaining some long term memory that summarizes the input sequence so far. A more specific type of RNN that intends to solve this problem is a *Long Short-Term Memory*, LSTM. It includes components that control what (and how much) is erased from the memory layer of the network and what is added.

Proximal Policy Optimization. Proximal Policy Optimization (PPO) [13] is a deep reinforcement learning algorithm that is based on a policy gradient method; it searches the space of policies rather than assigning values to state-action pairs. The policy π is represented by a neural network, and its set of parameters is denoted by θ. A detailed description of the network architecture will follow. This algorithm uses the notion of the *advantage* of an action with respect to a certain state. An advantage $A(s, a)$ measures how much an action is a good or a bad decision given a certain state. Formally, is it defined as $A(s, a) = Q(s, a) - V(s)$. To trace the impact of the different actions, the algorithm calculates the probability of the action under the current policy $\pi(a \mid s)$, and divides it by the probability of the action under the previous policy $\pi_{old}(a \mid s)$. For timestep t, this ratio is denoted by $r_t(\theta)$, where

$$r_t(\theta) = \frac{\pi_\theta(a_t \mid s_t)}{\pi_{\theta_{old}}(a_t \mid s_t)}$$

When $r_t(\theta)$ is greater than one, the relevant action is more probable in the current policy than in the old one. $r_t(\theta)$ that is between zero and one indicates that the action is less probable in the current policy than in the old one.

The algorithm uses the *clipped surrogate objective* function L^{CLIP} to optimize the policy's set of parameters θ. This function is maximized using stochastic gradient ascent. It is defined as follows:

$$L^{CLIP}(\theta) = \hat{E}_t[min(r_t(\theta)\hat{A}_t, clip(r_t(\theta), 1-\varepsilon, 1+\varepsilon)\hat{A}_t)]$$

where

- $\hat{E}_t$ denotes the empirical expectation over timesteps.
- $\hat{A}_t$ is the estimated advantage of the selected action at time t.
- *clip* is a function that clips the values of $r_t(\theta)$ between $(1-\epsilon, 1+\epsilon)$. Formally, it is defined as follows:

$$clip(r_t(\theta), 1-\varepsilon, 1+\varepsilon) = \begin{cases} 1+\varepsilon & \text{if } r_t(\theta) \geq 1+\varepsilon \\ 1-\varepsilon & \text{if } r_t(\theta) \leq 1-\varepsilon \\ r_t(\theta) & \text{otherwise.} \end{cases}$$

Note that when $r_t(\theta)$ is not in the interval $(1-\epsilon, 1+\epsilon)$, the gradient of $clip(r_t(\theta), 1-\varepsilon, 1+\varepsilon)$ is zero.

The main idea of this objective function is to incentivize actions that led to higher rewards. However, we would like to restrict the amount that the policy can change in every optimization, to help guarantee that it is monotonically improving. This restriction is reflected by the clipping mechanism of the objective function. Consider a case where a certain action became significantly more probable under the current policy rather than the old one, and its advantage is positive, meaning that it had an estimated positive effect on the outcome. If there were no restrictions, we might perform a relatively big optimization step, that might destruct our policy in the future. With the clipping mechanism of $r_t(\theta)$, its gradient would be considered as zero if it exceeded the threshold of $1+\epsilon$, and we would ignore the potential optimization step as a result.

According to the algorithm, we use the current policy π_θ to sample a constant number of episodes, and calculate the *reward-to-go* for every action in each episode. The reward-to-go of a state-action pair is the discounted sum of rewards from this point and up until the end of the episode. It is denoted by $\hat{R}(s_t, a_t)$. This value is often used as a local approximation of the state-action value $Q(s, a)$. The estimated advantage of a chosen action is then calculated by $\hat{A}_t = \hat{R}(s_t, a_t) - V_\varphi(s_t)$, where V_φ is a state-value function that is also optimized throughout the same learning process. Then, the policy parameters are optimized according to the clipped surrogate objective function. Later, the parameters of the state-value function are optimized according to the mean-squared loss with respect to the reward-to-go:

$$MSE(\varphi) = \hat{E}_t[(V_\varphi(s_t) - \hat{R}(s_t, a_t))^2]$$

3 The Proposed Approach

3.1 Overview

Initially, we suggest a PPO based approach that constructs a controller for the single system component in the simplified model. It strives to minimize the number of failures of interactions offered by the system component to the black box environment component. Controlling the selection of the system component's actions at each step assumes that it is unaware of the environment's internal state. In fact, the only information that is available from the environment at each execution step is whether the interaction succeeded or not.

Later, in the case of the more advanced model which includes multiple components and local actions, we suggest an architecture where each component is learning-enabled, equipped with its own neural network. The neural network is trained to control the process within the context of the entire system, based on a given utility measurement. The training of the different components is performed simultaneously, based on executions of the entire system; however, each component is trained within that context locally, based on the local information of the components.

To get an informed decision regarding the next action to be selected by the system component, our proposed controller, utilizes both long term and short term histories of the current execution. The short term history consists of the latest execution step from the component's perspective: the latest action selected by the component, whether this interaction was successful, and the current component state as a result of the interaction. The long term history is a finite representation of the past selected actions of the component, including their status (successful or not), and the past states. This finite representation is a summary of the execution so far from the component point of view. It is necessary to represent the long term history in a finite way, since we design our controller to operate under unbounded execution lengths.

At each execution step the controller receives both the short term and the long term histories, selects the next interaction to be offered, and updates the long term history representation accordingly.

3.2 Suggested Deep Learning Architecture

The Controller's State Space Representation. As mentioned above, the controller receives two inputs - the short and the long term histories. A short term history is represented by a matrix M of size $|S^s| \times |T^s|$, where S^s is the system's state space and T^s is the system's set of actions. We assume a fixed order on the elements in S^s and T^s. The only non-zero cell of the matrix is M_{ij}, if the last offered action was $t_j \in T^s$, and the current system state as a result is $s_i \in S^s$. The value of M_{ij} is 1 if the interaction was successful and -1 otherwise. The controller's state space is the set of all valid short term histories, denoted by S'. Note that the state space does not provide any information about the long term history. This is due to the fact that short term history usually have greater impact on the selection of future actions than long term history. Hence, we wanted to emphasize these elements in terms of the actor network's course of action.

Actor-Critic Based Implementation. To construct the controller, we implemented a variant of the PPO algorithm with a few modifications. Our variant relied on the *Actor-Critic* architecture [5].

Actor-Critic learning is a deep reinforcement learning technique that utilizes both an actor neural network and a critic neural network. The actor network is responsible for generating *actions* based on the current state, while the critic network evaluates the quality of the different *states* of the network. The two networks are trained in a cooperative manner, where the idea is that the critic provides feedback to the actor. To capture the long term history in a finite representation, we incorporated an RNN layer in the architecture of both the actor and the critic networks.

The actor network represents the policy $\pi_\theta(a \mid s')$, where $s' \in S'$, and θ is a the set of the network's parameters. The input layer is a vector that represents the short term history matrix, of size $|S^s| \times |T^s|$. This vector is passed through an LSTM layer, which is followed by a few linear layers separated by a ReLU activation function. The output of the last layer is a vector of size $|T^s|$. It is passed through a softmax function to give the actual output of the network in a form of a probability distribution over the possible interactions T^s. The parameters of this network are optimized to maximize the objective function L^{CLIP}.

The critic network serves as the estimated state-value function of the current policy π_θ induced by the actor. Its structure is almost identical to the actor network. It differs only in the last layer, which has only one neuron. This single neuron's value is the approximated value of the input state vector $V(s')$. The estimated advantages are calculated based on the controller state values received from this network, and the reward-to-go values derived from the sampled episodes. The critic parameters are optimized to minimize the *MSE* loss function.

The Training Phase. Our goal is to find a set of parameters θ that maximizes the successful number of interactions with the environment. We start by training the actor and the critic networks. At the beginning of every optimization phase of the two networks, we use our current actor network π_θ to sample a constant number of episodes of the same length. At each timestep, the actor network returns a probability distribution over all the possible interactions.

On the one hand, we can exploit the current knowledge of the actor network and always choose the interaction with the highest probability to maximize the number of successful interactions. On the other hand, exploring new interactions with lower probabilities may be necessary to gather information about the environment and discover new and potentially better interactions.

We observed that a decaying level of exploration over time helps in finding optimal policies in our setting. Hence, we chose our next action in the training phase according to the *Boltzmann Exploration* technique. Instead of deriving the distribution over the possible interactions based on the regular softmax function, we used a softmax function with a temperature parameter T.

$$softmax(t_1, \dots, t_n; T) = \left(\frac{e^{\frac{t_1}{T}}}{\Sigma_i e^{\frac{t_i}{T}}}, \dots, \dots, \frac{e^{\frac{t_n}{T}}}{\Sigma_i e^{\frac{t_i}{T}}} \right)$$

We sample the next interaction according to this distribution. The temperature parameter is used to control the degree of exploration, with higher temperatures leading to more exploration and lower temperatures leading to more exploitation. We start the training phase with an initial temperature value of T_0 and gradually decay it in a geometric fashion. We stop decaying it when $T = 1$.

In [7], exploration is performed during training by selecting a random action in generating the current execution of the system; exploitation is done by selecting the action with the highest probability among the probability distribution provided by the network. A constant ϵ represented the probability for exploring the environment. Note that this exploration technique ignores any information the controller network might hold regarding the actions. Even if one action is less probable to select than another action according to the network's action distribution, the two would be selected with an equal probability as part of an exploration step. On the contrary, our approach uses the actor network to both explore and exploit. By sampling the next action directly from the action distribution, less probable actions according to the actor network would be selected less frequently than the more probable ones.

We assigned two reward values for the offered interactions in the collected episodes. A reward of 1 was given to a successful interaction and a reward of -1 was given otherwise. After optimizing both networks according to their objective functions L^{CLIP} and *MSE*, a new optimization step begins. Note that we do not directly use the critic network to select an interaction. The critic network is used as a mean to estimate the value of a controller state, as a part of the estimated advantage calculation of every observed state-action pair. The training phase ends upon completing a predefined number of optimization steps.

Another difference between our approach and the previously mentioned approach is the frequency and the timing of the optimization steps. In the previous approach, more local optimization steps are performed. This started with a loss function that was calculated after every interaction with the environment, and optimized the parameters according to its gradient. The loss function definition differed depending on whether the last interaction succeeded or not. However, local optimization steps may not always yield optimal policies. In some cases we need to look beyond the immediate outcome of an interaction to make an informed decision. Consequently, an addition of a *lookahead* parameter allowed them to optimize the network after observing the outcome of a sequence of interactions. Longer lookahead assisted in learning optimal policies for a relatively more complex scenarios. The controller's network was optimized in the previous work according to this loss function. This optimization approach may be unstable for two reasons. First, a fraction of an execution may be insufficient for optimizing the networks parameters. In some cases, we would know if a certain action paid off only at the end of an execution. Another reason is that information from a single execution may not adequately represent the effectiveness of a given policy; i.e., an excellent policy on average can, by chance, show weak performance.

PPO performs an optimization step only after at least a few full executions are evaluated. This is reflected in the L^{CLIP} objective function, where an empirical expectation over all batch timesteps is taken. The fact that outcome of full executions is considered essentially eliminates the need for lookahead.

The Evaluation Phase. After training, we only exploit the actor network to evaluate its performance. At this point, the critic network in not used at all. In our experiments we assumed that the optimal policies are deterministic rather than stochastic. Hence, exploitation in our context would be selecting the action with the highest probability at each timestep. Stochastic policies might be achieved by sampling interactions from the actor network's distribution.

3.3 An Extension of the Proposed Approach to the Advanced Model

We now generalize our approach to synthesize a control for the more advanced model where components may interact with each other asynchronously, with local actions in addition to their regular way to interact.

Our system consists now of multiple components with extended functionalities that interact with one another; interactions are allowed only between pairs of components. All the components consider each other as a black box. This time, each action may be associated with one of two types:

- *Interactions* - these actions behave as a standard action in the simplified model, and indicate an attempt of two components (agents, processes) to interact.
- *Local actions* - these actions are performed independently with respect to their component. A necessary and sufficient condition for a local action to be triggered, is to be enabled and selected by the respective component.

As mentioned above, the execution is *asynchronous*, with components performing according to their own speeds; each component operates according to its own internal clock, where a fixed time interval represents the duration of every timestep in the execution. Note that different components may have different time intervals. Despite the asynchronous nature of the joint execution, the interaction between components is still established in an handshake form.

At each timestep, a component may offer an interaction to another component, or perform a local action. If an interaction was offered, it would wait the entire timestep for a response. We first examine the case where two components chose to interact with each other. Here, both components would be informed whether or not their interaction was successful. The interaction is considered successful when the same action was proposed by both components. In this case, the two components change their respective states according to the proposed action. If two different actions were offered, the interaction *fails*. Then, both sides uniformly sample at random some enabled local action and move accordingly.

A component that chose to interact but received no feedback until the end of the timestep may either wait for a response in the next timestep or give up. If it gives up, its action would be considered as a *missed* interaction from its perspective, and it would remain at its current state. Obviously, a component that selected a local action does not need a feedback for a its action, since it is always successful regardless of the other components. In this case the component immediately changes its state according to the selected local action.

Note that it is not clear what is the goal of each component in this scenario. Maximizing the individual sum of rewards in this case does not always maximize social welfare. However, when the reward given to a local action is lower than a reward of a successful interaction, then an individual maximization of the accumulated sum of reward should also lead to the optimal result, with respect to the social welfare. We therefore assumed that local actions are always less rewarding than interactions in the more advanced model.

In light of this insight, we modified our approach to adapt our advanced model. We assigned each component's controller a pair of actor and critic networks, and used the same training routine in parallel with respect to each controller. This setup is often called *decentralized training* [16]. In each one of their optimization steps, the components obtain their collection of episodes by interacting with each other.

When the different controllers are trained in a decentralized fashion, each one of them considers the others as the environment. However, while a standard environment in reinforcement learning has Markovian behavior, our controllers constantly change their strategies throughout the training phase, completely invalidating the Markovian assumption on their strategy.

As a result of the constantly changing behavior of the components in the training phase, we tested different parallel exploration techniques in our experiments. Specifically, we tested the efficiency of different techniques on scenarios with two components. We started by alternately applying the same exploration or exploitation policy for both components. i.e. in each optimization step the two controllers selected their actions according to Boltzmann exploration, or they both exploited their neural network, selecting the most probable action.

We examined an additional exploration technique. According to this technique, in every optimization step, only one of the components performs Boltzmann exploration, while the other always exploits its network. In the next optimization step, the components change their roles with respect to their exploration/exploitation strategies. The idea behind this technique is that the exploring component would be able to learn a more stabilized version of his peer, which in constantly exploiting, thus acting in a more predictable way.

Finally, the most stable results were achieved where both components were exploring according to Boltzmann exploration throughout the entire training phase. It seems that the optimization steps of PPO are small and cautious enough, so both agents can explore simultaneously and still converge to strategies that maximize their individual cumulative rewards with a relatively high probability. We observed than this exploration technique is efficient also for scenarios with more than two components. The results are further described in the experiments section.

4 Experiments

We present here the experimental results for our proposed approach. The experiments consist of two parts. In the first part we tested our approach with respect to six existing examples of the simplified model. The second part examines our extended approach in the more advanced setting. All the experiments were conducted on the same machine with an Intel® Core™ i5 CPU at 2.4 GHz and 8GB of RAM, running on a Windows 11 operating system. Our approach was implemented in Python, using the PyTorch library.

4.1 Experiments with the Simplified Model

In [7], six different examples of system and environment pairs to experiment with were studied. The first four are relatively simple. The latter two are more complex, combining the behaviors of two simple examples. The first simple example - *permitted*, was described in Sect. 2. We present here two additional simple examples.

In example *schedule* in Fig. 2, the controller must make sure that the system will never choose an a. Otherwise, after interacting on a, the environment will progress to e_3, and no successful interaction with b will be available further. A controller with two states that alternates between b and c, i.e., allows exactly the sequence of interactions $(bc)^*$ is sufficient to guarantee that no failure ever occurs.

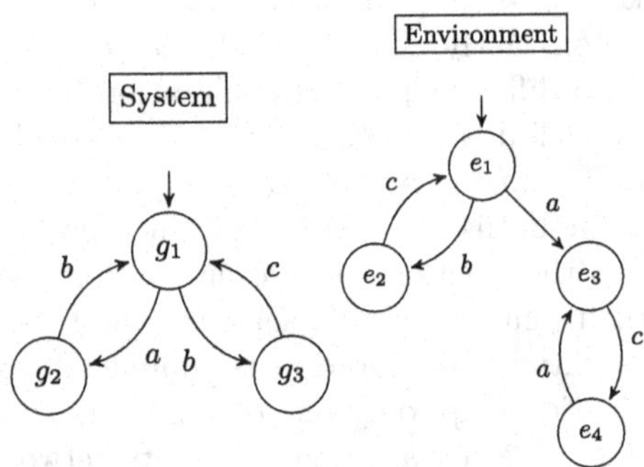

Fig. 2. *schedule*: The control needs to avoid the action a as its initial choice.

In the example *cases* in Fig. 3, the system is obliged to offer an a from its initial state. The environment allows initially only b or c. Hence, the interaction will fail, the system will stay at the same state and the environment will progress to e_2 or to e_3, according to its choice, which is not visible to the system. After the first a, the system does not change state, hence a is again the only action that it offers.

An optimal controller for this example has to consider the execution history to make an informed decision. After the system offers the first a, which is due to fail, it checks whether offering a fails again. If it does, then the next interaction to be offered is c. Otherwise, it selects the action b.

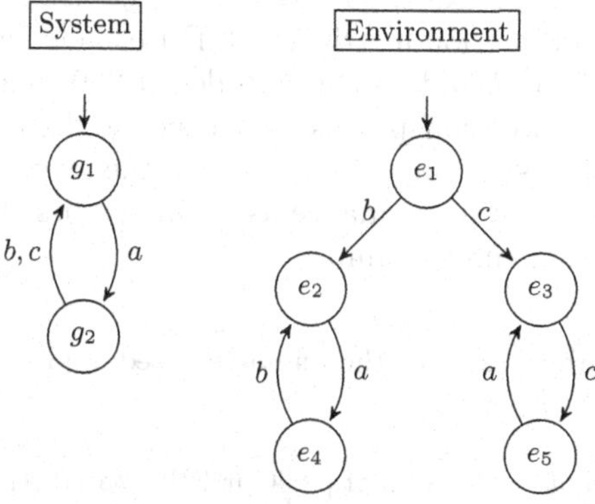

Fig. 3. *cases*: Needs to check if a succeeded.

In their experiments, the hyperparameter values that achieved the optimal results were different for each example. In addition, their training routine for the complex examples was different comparing to their simpler examples. We tested our approach against all six examples. The last complex example (*cycle scc*) assumed to be the most difficult one, since it had the highest average failure rate. Table 1 exhibits the properties of the tested experiments.

Table 1. Experiments list. Failure percentages are per episodes with 200 timesteps.

Experiment	Environment States	Best Failure Rate (%)
Permitted	3	0
Schedule	4	0
Cases	5	1.5
Choice-scc	25	1.5
Schedule-cycle	4	0
Cycle-scc	25	1.5

In our experiments, we used the same training routine for all examples. Moreover, the values of the different hyperparameters in our approach did not vary between different examples. We trained our actor and critic network as presented in the previous section, with 160 sampled episodes of length of 25 in each optimization phase, for a maximum of 150 optimization phases. In most of the cases, the optimal policy was found in less than 100 optimization steps.

We used *Adam* [8] to optimize the weights of both the actor and the critic networks, with a learning rate of 0.01. Adam is an adaptive learning rate optimization algorithm that has been designed specifically for training deep neural networks. The PPO clipping parameter ϵ was set to 0.2, and the initial exploration temperature was $T_0 = 2$ with a geometric decay rate of 1.008. The discount factor for the calculated reward-to-go was set to $\gamma = 0.99$.

We used the same evaluation metric as [7]. For each example, we trained the model and evaluated it on 100 different episodes of 200 timesteps. We repeated the training and the evaluation process ten times and calculated the average failure rate. Table 2 shows a comparison between the average failure rates. Our approach achieves the same performance as [7] in the first three examples, and outperforms it in the last three examples.

Table 2. Average failure rates (%) - the reinforce-based approach vs. our PPO-based approach.

Experiment	Results of [7]	Our PPO based Approach
Permitted	0	0
Schedule	0	0
Cases	0	0
Choice-scc	4.5	1.5
Schedule-cycle	5	0
Cycle-scc	33.5	3

4.2 Experiments with the Advanced Model

We tested the extension of our approach on examples with multiple components, with both interactions and local actions. The rewards that were given to failed and successful interactions were identical to previous experiments. The reward for local actions was lower than the one given for interactions, and varied between examples. Each example was tested with respect to two different execution profiles. The first profile is the case when the two components perform according to the same speed, while in the second one the execution speed of one components is two times faster than the other throughout the whole execution. Here we did not consider the failure rate, but the average cumulative rewards (CR) throughout the execution.

We started to test our approach on an example called *hold back*. It is described in Fig. 4; the action l is a local action in both components, while all the others are interactions. The reward for local actions was set to 0.5, and the reward for a successful interactions was set to 1. A reward of 0 was given for a missed interaction, while a failed interaction had a reward of -1.

In this example, both components are faced with three consecutive decisions, where they have to choose between two options with different payoffs. The optimal result for them may be achieved only if they both choose the least rewarding course of action at every decision point. In an execution profile where there are different execution speeds, the faster process may have to wait after the three first local actions before successfully triggering the action a.

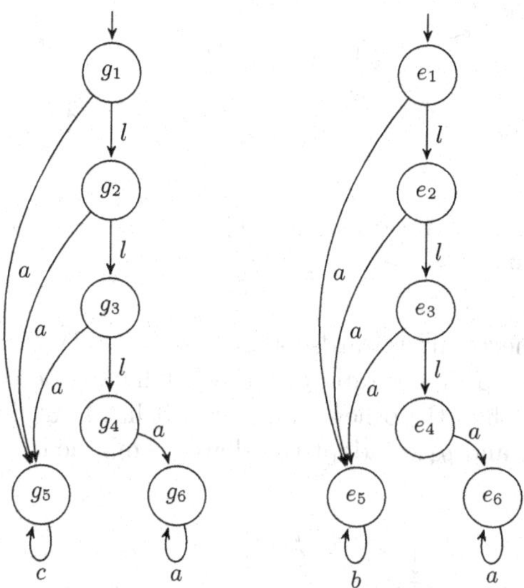

Fig. 4. *hold back*: Three consecutive decisions with different payoffs. The action l is a local action in both components, while all the others are interactions.

The second example we designed is called *abcde coordination*. It is depicted in Fig. 5. In this example, the maximal cumulative reward of each process is achieved if both components learn to repeat the following sequence of interactions: $a\ b\ c\ d\ e$, where l is a local action. It is not a simple task to coordinate this pattern of interactions; both components have some self-loop actions that should be triggered at the right time. Moreover, this task is even more difficult in an execution profile where the two components have different execution speeds. For instance, if the component on the right is faster than the other one, an optimal strategy for it would be utilizing the local actions on its self loops in between interactions, so it can be correlated with the slower component. Here, the rewards for interactions are identical to the hold back example, and the reward for local actions was set to 0.1.

The third example we introduce in Fig. 6 is called *wait to succeed*. The actions l, l_1 and l_2 are local actions in this example. All the reward values are identical to the values in abcde coordination, except of the local action reward that was set to 0.02. As part of the optimal strategy in this example, both components would aim to end the execution with a sequence of consecutive successful interactions of type d. To achieve that in the equal-speeds execution profile, they would have to coordinate on the sequence $a\ b\ c$, and then trigger two local actions before initiate an interaction of type d. Both the preliminary sequence and the two local

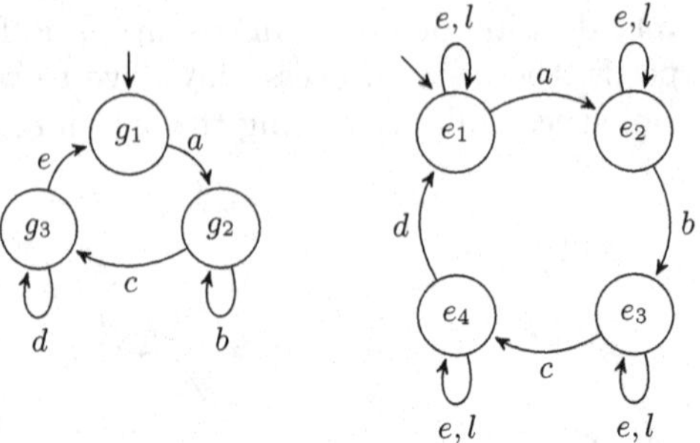

Fig. 5. *abcde coordination*: A certain repeating sequence leads to a non-failure execution. l is a local action.

actions waiting are necessary towards having a successful sequence of interactions of type d. Now, the optimal strategy of the left hand side component changes assuming it is faster than the other component. It has to utilize the local actions of from states g_2, g_3 and g_4 to adapt the slower component.

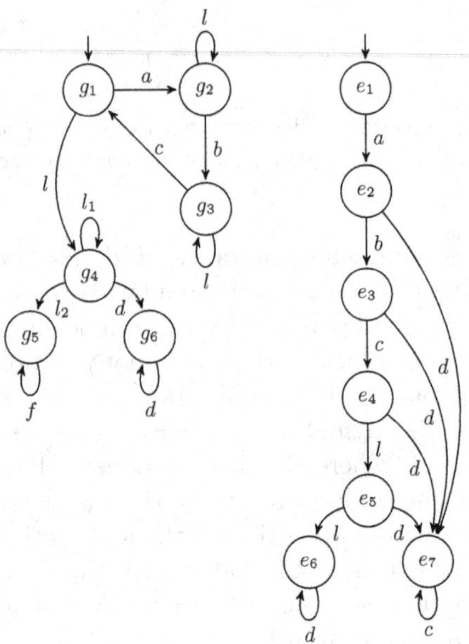

Fig. 6. *wait to succeed*: The two components will have to coordinate with respect to a specific sequence, then trigger a few local actions before they may continue with a long sequence of consecutive successful interactions of type d. The actions l, l_1 and l_2 are local actions.

The fourth example, which is called *triple coordination*, consists of three asynchronous components. It is described in Fig. 7. The actions l, l_1, l_2 are local actions, while all the others are interactions. The reward for local actions was set to 0.1, and the reward for a successful interaction was set to 1. A reward of 0 was given for a missed interaction, while a failed interaction had a reward of -1. In this example, component (a) is able to interact with both components (b) and (c). However, components (b) and (c) cannot interact with each other. In order to achieve an optimal performance, component (a) would aim to end its execution with a sequence of alternating interactions from s_1, where f is offered to component (b), and e is offered to component (c). This execution suffix would have been possible only if component (a) and (b) had coordinated on the sequence a b c at the beginning of the execution. We denote the first execution profile by p_1. In this profile, the components have equal speeds. In the second execution profile, denoted by p_2, components (a) and (c) have equal speeds, while component (b) is two times slower.

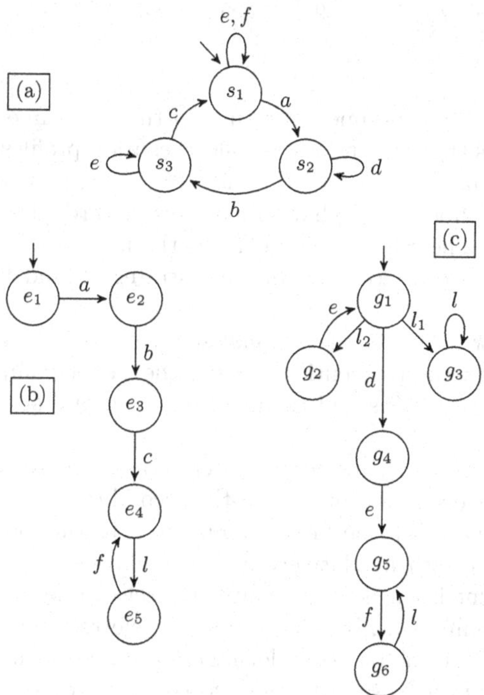

Fig. 7. *triple coordination*: The actions l, l_1, l_2 are local actions, while all the others are interactions. Component (a) is able to interact with both (b) and (c). However, components (b) and (c) cannot interact with each other.

Most of the hyperparameter values were identical to previous experiments. We slightly changed the initial exploration temperature to 2.5, and the geometric decay rate to 1.01. As mentioned before, both components were exploring according to Boltzmann exploration throughout the entire training phase. Again, we trained the controllers and evaluated them on 100 different episodes of 200 timesteps. We repeated the training and the evaluation process ten times.

Table 3. Average and median cumulative rewards - a model with two asynchronous components with local actions.

Experiment	Optimal CR		Our Avg. CR		Our Med. CR	
	Cp.a	*Cp.b*	*Cp.a*	*Cp.b*	*Cp.a*	*Cp.b*
hold-back-p_1	198.80	198.80	155.20	155.20	198.80	198.80
hold-back-p_2	98.80	98.80	98.80	98.80	98.80	98.80
abcde-p_1	200	200	163.20	163.40	200	200
abcde-p_2	100	101	67	67.74	95.60	96.01
w.t succeed-p_1	198.04	198.04	158.80	158.02	197.02	197.02
w.t succeed-p_2	98.14	98.04	96.85	96.83	97.02	97.02

Table 3 exhibits the experimental results of the first three examples. p_1 and p_2 are referred to as the first and the second execution profiles. The table shows that the average cumulative rewards in most of the experiments are lower than the optimal ones, while the median cumulative rewards are close or equal to the optimal values. The reason behind this is the fact that in some repetitions, the interfaces could not learn their optimal strategies, and had a sub-optimal performance.

In the *hold back* example, the optimal strategy was learned in most of the repetitions. In the second execution profile, the faster component learned to trigger its three local actions and then to wait for a first successful interaction of type a.

In *abcde coordination*, the optimal strategy was achieved in most of the repetitions for the first execution profile. In the second execution profile, the right component was selected as the faster component. In this profile, the majority of executions ended with a relatively high cumulative reward. In some cases, the faster component learned to intermittently select a local action in order to adapt the slower component. In other cases, it preferred to wait for a successful interaction rather than intersperse a local action in between.

In the example *wait to succeed*, the two components managed to learn the behavior that leads to the optimal results in most of the cases. In the second execution profile, we selected the left component to be the faster one. In this profile, a common behaviour for the left component was to select local actions before trying interactions from states g_2 and g_3. However, when being in state g_4, the typical behaviour was to wait for a successful interaction of type d.

The performance of our extended approach on the triple coordination example is described in Table 4. It shows a comparison between the optimal strategy's cumulative rewards and the average cumulative rewards according to our extended approach. It is observed that in the first execution profile, the three components manage to learn the behavior that leads to the optimal result. In the second execution profile, component (a) learns a strategy that is slightly less beneficial than its optimal strategy. Despite having different speeds, component (a) learns how to alternately interact with components (b) and (c) in the suffix of the execution.

Table 4. Average cumulative rewards - a model with three asynchronous components with local actions.

Experiment	Optimal CR			Our Avg. CR		
	$Cp.a$	$Cp.b$	$Cp.c$	$Cp.a$	$Cp.b$	$Cp.c$
triple coord.-p_1	200	191.9	189.9	200	191.9	189.9
triple coord.-p_2	152	55.8	109.8	151	55.8	109.8

5 Conclusion

We presented a deep reinforcement learning approach that constructs control for concurrent components of a system that are capable of interacting with one another, with a limited knowledge of one another's structure and execution history. We started by designing an approach that improved on the REINFORCE-based method used in [7] for the simplified model.

Our approach is an Actor-Critic implementation of the PPO algorithm with some modifications. We have distinguished between two types of execution histories: short and long term histories, and handled them in different ways. The short term history was encoded as part of the control's state space representation, while the long term history was captured by the recurrent layers we have integrated in both the actor and the critic networks. In addition, we found an exploration strategy that suited all the tested examples in our experiments. In the tested experiments, not only did our approach outperform the method presented in [7], but it was capable of using a single set of hyperparameter values and training routine for all tested examples.

We have suggested an architecture for optimizing the integration of systems that consist of multiple processes. According to this learning-open architecture, each component is equipped with a local neural network that can be trained to control its behavior. As the different components can be constructed separately, the training of the system does not involve the sharing of information between the deep learning components; each process (and its controller) is aware only of its own states, and the outcome of the interactions. Hence, deep reinforcement learning methods such as DQN [11], which focus on estimating the utility value of each state in the state space are less suitable for our task. We conclude that policy gradient methods such as PPO are more adequate in case of a state space with limited observability.

Our approach appears to be stable with optimization steps that are relatively small and rely on full sampled episodes. As opposed to the previously mentioned approach that relies on a single episode each time, in our approach each optimization step may be more significant. Moreover, the nature of PPO inherently eliminates the use of a lookahead. We do not need to consider a limited horizon and optimize the parameters after every timestep, it can be done once after generating a batch of full episodes. On the other hand, in most of the cases, our approach would need to sample relatively more executions to construct an effective strategy. Apparently, in this case, the effectiveness and the robustness of our approach in different scenarios come at a cost.

We realized that our approach requires only a few minor modifications to adapt to the more advanced setting, even though the Markovian assumption no longer holds for each component. In the examples we tested, the components manage to converge towards an optimal outcome with high probability, despite the scarce signals that are transmitted between the different components. Future directions of this research include applying this approach to more complex components with more states and extended functionality. In addition, our approach should also be evaluated in settings where maximizing the individual objective may not lead to the optimal global outcome, e.g., when two or more components have conflicting objectives.

References

1. Brown, T.B., et al.: Language models are few-shot learners. In: Advances in Neural Information Processing Systems 33: Annual Conference on Neural Information Processing Systems 2020, NeurIPS 2020, December 6–12, 2020, virtual (2020)
2. Busoniu, L., Babuska, R., Schutter, B.D.: A comprehensive survey of multiagent reinforcement learning. IEEE Trans. Syst. Man Cybern. Part C **38**(2), 156–172 (2008)
3. Cassandras, C.G., Lafortune, S.: Introduction to Discrete Event Systems, 2nd edn. Springer, Cham (2008). https://doi.org/10.1007/978-0-387-68612-7
4. Gößler, G., Sifakis, J.: Composition for component-based modeling. Sci. Comput. Program. **55**(1–3), 161–183 (2005)
5. Haarnoja, T., Zhou, A., Abbeel, P., Levine, S.: Soft actor-critic: Off-policy maximum entropy deep reinforcement learning with a stochastic actor. In: International Conference on Machine Learning, pp. 1861–1870. PMLR (2018)
6. Hoare, C.A.R.: Communicating sequential processes. Commun. ACM **21**(8), 666–677 (1978)
7. Iosti, S., Peled, D., Aharon, K., Bensalem, S., Goldberg, Y.: Synthesizing control for a system with black box environment, based on deep learning. In: Margaria, T., Steffen, B. (eds.) ISoLA 2020. LNCS, vol. 12477, pp. 457–472. Springer, Cham (2020). https://doi.org/10.1007/978-3-030-61470-6_27
8. Kingma, D.P., Ba, J.: Adam: a method for stochastic optimization. arXiv preprint arXiv:1412.6980 (2014)
9. Kravaris, T., Vouros, G.A.: Deep multiagent reinforcement learning methods addressing the scalability challenge. Appl. Intell. (2023)
10. Lehmann, D., Rabin, M.O.: On the advantages of free choice: a symmetric and fully distributed solution to the dining philosophers problem. In: Proceedings of the 8th ACM SIGPLAN-SIGACT Symposium on Principles of Programming Languages, pp. 133–138 (1981)

11. Mnih, V., et al.: Playing Atari with deep reinforcement learning. arXiv preprint arXiv:1312.5602 (2013)
12. Paszke, A., et al.: Pytorch: an imperative style, high-performance deep learning library. In: Advances in Neural Information Processing Systems 32, pp. 8024–8035. Curran Associates, Inc. (2019). http://papers.neurips.cc/paper/9015-pytorch-an-imperative-style-high-performance-deep-learning-library.pdf
13. Schulman, J., Wolski, F., Dhariwal, P., Radford, A., Klimov, O.: Proximal policy optimization algorithms. arXiv preprint arXiv:1707.06347 (2017)
14. Sutton, R.S., Barto, A.G.: Reinforcement Learning - An Introduction. Adaptive Computation and Machine Learning, 2nd edn. MIT Press, London (2018)
15. Tan, M.: Multi-agent reinforcement learning: Independent versus cooperative agents. In: Utgoff, P.E. (ed.) Machine Learning, Proceedings of the Tenth International Conference, University of Massachusetts, Amherst, MA, USA, June 27–29, 1993, pp. 330–337. Morgan Kaufmann (1993)
16. Zhang, K., Yang, Z., Liu, H., Zhang, T., Basar, T.: Fully decentralized multi-agent reinforcement learning with networked agents. In: International Conference on Machine Learning, pp. 5872–5881. PMLR (2018)

Automotive Driving

Safe AI in Autonomous Vehicles
Track at AISoLA 2023

Falk Howar[1(✉)] and Hardi Hungar[2]

[1] Dortmund University of Technology and Fraunhofer ISST, Dortmund, Germany
falk.howar@tu-dortmund.de
[2] German Aerospace Center, Braunschweig, Germany
hardi.hungar@dlr.de

Abstract. Today, the most prominent application of AI technology in the automotive domain is in the realm of environment perception. The diversity of the traffic environment and the complexity of sensor readings make it impossible to specify and implement perception functionality manually. Deep learning technology, on the other hand, has proven itself capable of solving the task very well. However, it is important to note that effectiveness alone does not guarantee a comprehensive solution, and the issue of validation currently remains unsatisfactorily resolved. The track provided different perspectives on the challenges pertaining to the use of AI/ML technology in highly automated driving functions, including considerations on safety verification and validation techniques for AI-based autonomous vehicles, formal methods and their application in assuring the safety of AI-based autonomous systems robustness and resilience of AI algorithms in uncertain and open environments, system architectures for AI-based autonomous vehicles, data-driven approaches for safety assurance and risk analysis in autonomous driving, safety standards, regulations, and certification processes for AI-based autonomous vehicles, as well as testing, simulation, and validation methodologies for autonomous vehicle systems.

Track Description

Autonomous vehicles and highly automated driving functions have been a focus of research and development for roughly two decades since the 2004 DARPA grand challenge [5]. Most major carmakers and tech companies as well as a bunch of startups have engaged in a fierce competition for the first truly driverless vehicle.

Today (2023), fleets of driverless taxis are being tested in San Francisco (California), Phoenix (Arizona), and in several other cities across the world [8]. The company Cruise, e.g., operates driverless taxis that do not have a safety driver in the vehicle in San Francisco. Tesla delivered the biggest fleet of vehicles with a advanced driver assistance systems: Autopilot/FSD is a SAE Level 2 assistance systems that controls lateral and longitudinal movement of a vehicle under constant supervision of its driver. As of early 2023, more than 360,000 vehicles outfitted with this system are being driven on public roads by their owners [9].

B. Steffen (Ed.): AISoLA 2023, LNCS 14380, pp. 421–425, 2024.
https://doi.org/10.1007/978-3-031-46002-9_27

Mercedes Benz is the first company to announce the release of a SAE Level 3 automated driving function. The so-called "drive pilot" will take over driving completely on highways in certain conditions. The human driver/operator does not have to constantly supervise the systems but must be able to take over driving when requested by the system within a reasonable amount of time. The system has been certified in the U.S. state of Nevada in January of 2023 and is announced to be released in the U.S. in 2024 [3].

From this description of the current state of development, one could incorrectly infer that autonomous driving is a solved problem. This, however, is not true. Several major challenges remain unsolved, e.g., pertaining to system design and development, safety assurance, as well as legal and economic aspects (which we will not further discuss here):

System Design and Development

One of the greatest challenges for automated driving lies in the complexity and heterogeneity of the environment in which the vehicle must operate. Above all, the automation has to form a sufficiently comprehensive and accurate picture of the environment. All relevant elements must be seen, recognized, and assessed as far as possible. And where uncertainties remain, these must be taken into consideration. AI/ML technology today provides the essential building blocks for practical solutions (e.g., semantic classification for analyzing camera images).

Models for these tasks, however, are trained, which relies on training data, and when the training data does not include certain situations, the vehicle will not recognize these situations. Reported examples of misclassified or missed objects include child-like objects [6]. Then, these models do not encode common sense: they e.g., have been reported to recognize traffic lights transported in the back of a truck as floating on the freeway. Mechanisms for dealing with features of the environment that were not present in the training data and for validating the perceived environment remain to be developed.

Safety Assurance

To this day, it is not clear if and how we can document the safety of automated driving systems. The used AI/ML components are black-boxes. Verification techniques for such components are still in their infancy and mostly focus on robustness. It remains an open question, if and how their intended behavior can be specified beyond the set labelled training data. At the system level, it is not clear how safety can be assured in complex open environments. One current strategy is breaking down automated driving into many specific operational design domains (ODD)s and then specifying, developing, testing, and releasing functions for domains of increasing complexity and increasingly associated with risk over time - starting with highway driving, to urban driving, to mixed environments.

A number of industry standards is being developed that e.g., mandate ODD specification (ISO 34503 [7]), scenario-based testing of the intended functionality (ISO 21448 [1]), and safety of automotive AI components (ISO 8800 [2]). However, finding a balance between pace of deployment and safety is not trivial: Autonomous taxis have caused disruptions and outright dangerous situations in their urban environments. Reported incidents include blocking lanes when autonomous driving fails, not following police instructions, blocking ambulances, interfering with fire fighters, and creating a multiple vehicle roadblock close to a bigger event (triggered by overload in the mobile network) [4].

Contributions

The track on Safe AI in the Automotive Domain at AISoLA 2023 aimed at bringing together researchers, practitioners, and experts from formal methods, AI/ML communities, and the automotive domain to discuss the sketched challenges in the broader context of "bridging the gap between AI and reality". The contributions to this track study different aspects of the role of AI technology in autonomous systems. They span the spectrum from requirements to implementation to verification of AI in perception, and the approaches partly employ AI themselves.

1. Starting with the requirements for the systems, today there is no established approach how to formalize them. First of all, a language is needed that precisely grasps the phenomena of the traffic world. The presentation on *"Situation Recognition in Complex Operational Domains using Temporal and Description Logics - A Motivation from the Automotive Domain"* by Westhofen, Neurohr, Neider and Jung proposes to use Description Logics (ontologies) for this purpose. These provide a basis for expressing the traffic objects, their states and static relationships to each other. On top of that, they use temporal logic operators, with which durations and sequences of conditions can be described. This results in a description language that is powerful enough to express the relevant sequences, such as the way in which a particular critical situation arises. On the other hand, the constructors of the language are chosen such that it remains computable when a description applies to an observed sequence of events. The authors announce that they will develop an evaluation routine for their language: *"Mission-Time Linear Temporal Logic over Conjunctive Queries"*.
2. When considering the need to prove the safety of the system for homologation, the standards ISO 26262 (functional safety) and ISO 21448 (safety of the intended functionality, SOTIF) must be observed. A SOTIF analysis entails the study of triggering conditions leading to unintended functionality. How to identify, analyze and test such condition are questions only sparsely covered by research so far. *"Identifying and Testing SOTIF Triggering Condition for the Safety Verification and Validation of Automated Driving Systems"* by Zhu and Howar addresses this topic systematically. The contribution provides a formalization of three main types of triggering conditions. Then, it introduces

a knowledge-driven method for systematically identifying such conditions. With a data-driven method, scenarios relevant to a condition can be extracted from real-life test data. And based on that, a strategy is developed by which triggering conditions can be incorporated into a testing process complying to the requirements of the ISO 21448.
3. Concerning the functionalities of perception, their AI based implementation makes verification and validation very difficult. In his presentation on *"A Note on Confidence Awareness in Automotive Perception"*, Hungar makes a point of making confidence in perception a first-order citizen in the argumentation. Results of verification and validation would be much better if the quality information of the perception output was computed compositionally over the system architecture, starting with adequately captured current quality of sensor readings. The AI components interpreting the sensor readings would be one stage of the system particularly important to be characterized in their contribution to potential inaccuracies or mistakes. Also, the sensor models used in simulating an automated driving system would have to produce the additional quality information.
4. Another aspect of compositionality concerns not the verification, but the construction of the perception itself. The current focus of applying AI technology is on single AI models, i.e., it is model-centric, disregarding the challenges of engineering systems with multiple components that need to interact to realize complex functionality. Applications of machine learning (ML) should be able to support architectures that can integrate and chain ML components. This requires systems-centric methods and tools. This is discussed in *"Towards ML-Integration and Training Patterns for AI-Enabled Systems"* by Peldszus, Knopp, Sens, and Berger. They analyze the limitations of currently applied training processes when engineering multi-ML systems, and discuss possible patterns for training and integration to facilitate the effective and efficient development, maintenance, and evolution of such complex systems.
5. Even if today's AI technology, both in multi-level systems as well as in the form of single models, does not yet provide perception results of the desired level of confidence, in the way one makes use of the results one may attain the desired level of safety. This is shown by Fränzle in *"Maximizing Confidence in Safety-Critical Decisions of Automated Vehicles that are Grounded in ML-based Environmental Perception - Rendering AVs 'Safer than Perception'"*. The approach starts from the observation that critical maneuvers are generally safeguarded by complex spatio-temporal conditions that combine multiple percepts. Evaluation of these conditions, and thereby drawing safety-relevant decisions, exposes all kinds of masking effects between individual misperceptions. The masking can be influenced by rewriting the conditions. This implies that these conditions can be analyzed and modified for their error propagation, optimizing them to limit the negative safety-related effect of ML-induced misperceptions to a societally acceptable level.
6. Finally, AI techniques can be used not only in the construction of automated driving systems, but also in their verification, as Hungar presents in the contribution *"Using AI in the Verification and Validation of Automated Driving*

Systems". This includes the analysis of data from the real world and from simulation, recognition of maneuvers in real-world data, detection and evaluation of criticality, construction of scenarios, compilation of scenario catalogs, different kinds of simulations, in particular the exploration of scenario spaces, and assignment of real-world data to scenarios.

Moreover, the track included the demonstration of the DevOps-inspired process implemented by TU Dortmund university's formula student team in the development of their autonomous driving system.

References

1. ISO 21448:2022. Road vehicles - Safety of the intended functionality. Standard, International Organization for Standardization, Geneva, CH (2022)
2. ISO/CD PAS 8800. Road Vehicles - Safety and artificial intelligence. Standard, International Organization for Standardization, Geneva, CH (under development)
3. Hawkins, A.J.: Mercedes-Benz is the first to bring Level 3 automated driving to the US 2023. https://www.theverge.com/2023/1/27/23572942/mercedes-drive-pilot-level-3-approved-nevada. Accessed Sept 2023
4. Public Utilities Commission of the State of California. Resolution approving authorization for cruise llc's expanded service in autonomous vehicle passenger service phase i driverless deployment program (2023). https://docs.cpuc.ca.gov/PublishedDocs/Published/G000/M516/K812/516812218.PDF. Accessed Sept 2023
5. Defense Advanced Research Projects Agency. Grand Challenge 2004: Final Report (2004). https://www.esd.whs.mil/Portals/54/Documents/FOID/Reading%20Room/DARPA/15-F-0059_GC_2004_FINAL_RPT_7-30-2004.pdf. Accessed Sept 2023
6. Helmore, E.: Tesla's self-driving technology fails to detect children in the road, group claims (2023). https://www.theguardian.com/technology/2022/aug/09/tesla-self-driving-technology-safety-children. Accessed Sept 2023
7. Road Vehicles - Test scenarios for automated driving systems - Specification for operational design domain. Standard, International Organization for Standardization, Geneva, CH (2023)
8. Muller, J.: Robotaxis hit the accelerator in growing list of cities nationwide (2023). https://www.axios.com/2023/08/29/cities-testing-self-driving-driverless-taxis-robotaxi-waymo. Accessed Sept 2023
9. National Highway Traffic Safety Administration. Full Self-Driving Software May Cause Crash (2023). https://static.nhtsa.gov/odi/rcl/2023/RCAK-23V085-2525.pdf. Accessed Sept 2023

Responsible and Trustworthy AI

Normative Perspectives on and Societal Implications of AI Systems

Kevin Baum[1], Thorsten Helfer[2], Markus Langer[3], Eva Schmidt[4], Andreas Sesing-Wagenpfeil[5], and Timo Speith[6](✉)

[1] German Research Center for Artificial Intelligence, 66123 Saarbrücken, Germany
[2] Department of Philosophy, Saarland University, 66123 Saarbrücken, Germany
[3] Philipps-University of Marburg, 35037 Marburg, Germany
[4] TU Dortmund and Lamarr Institute for Machine Learning and Artificial Intelligence, 44227 Dortmund, Germany
[5] Institute of Legal Informatics, Saarland University, 66123 Saarbrücken, Germany
[6] University of Bayreuth, 95447 Bayreuth, Germany

Abstract. As AI technology becomes increasingly integrated into diverse sectors of society, the importance of guaranteeing its reliable and ethical development and utilization increases as well. This conference track seeks to unite interdisciplinary research spanning fields such as philosophy, law, psychology, computer science, economics, and other pertinent areas. Its overarching goal is to investigate the ethical perspectives and societal implications associated with the creation and deployment of AI systems.

1 Motivation

While artificial intelligence (AI) systems are becoming increasingly integrated into every facet of our lives, it is imperative to ensure their ethical and trustworthy development and application. The track "Normative Perspectives on and Societal Implications of AI Systems" serves as a platform for interdisciplinary research. Experts from fields including philosophy, law, psychology, computer science, economics, and related domains will explore the ethical dimensions and societal ramifications of AI system creation and deployment.

The central objective of this conference track is to address the critical challenges of setting minimum requirements tailored to specific domains for the verification, explanation, and assessment of machine learning systems. By doing so, the track aims to foster responsible and dependable utilization of AI technologies in real-world applications. Attendees can expect a deep dive into the ethical considerations surrounding AI, as well as discussions on normative viewpoints on and societal consequences of current developments in AI.

This special track received funding from the Volkswagen Foundation grants AZ 98509, AZ 98510, AZ 98511, AZ 98512, AZ 98513, and AZ 98514 "Explainable Intelligent Systems" (EIS) and from the DFG grant 389792660 as part of TRR 248. We also thank the Lamarr Institute for Machine Learning and Artificial Intelligence for providing scholarships for some of our speakers.

B. Steffen (Ed.): AISoLA 2023, LNCS 14380, pp. 429–430, 2024.
https://doi.org/10.1007/978-3-031-46002-9

2 Program

The track received 33 submissions, of which 22 were accepted. These 22 submissions have been divided into 6 different thematic blocks, each of which has one day of the track dedicated to it.

Day 1: Risks and Privacy The first day of the conference track is focused on exploring the inherent risks and privacy concerns associated with the proliferation of AI systems. Experts in the field will delve into the intricate issues of data privacy, fears regarding AI systems, and the potential consequences of unchecked AI applications for individual liberties and societal norms.

Day 2: Trustworthiness and Explainability On the second day, the track turns its attention to the fundamental principles of trustworthiness and explainability in AI. Speakers will address the critical question of how to assess the trustworthiness of an AI model. The sessions will also provide insights into innovative approaches and tools for explaining AI decisions, thereby fostering calibrated user trust and confidence in these systems.

Day 3: Regulating AI The third day is dedicated to AI regulation. Various legal and policy experts will discuss the challenges and opportunities in regulating AI technologies to ensure their responsible deployment. Topics will include the role of stakes, the new AI act, and experimental sandboxes for AI regulation.

Day 4: Explainability, Responsibility, and Liability Addressing issues that were already implicit in the first three days, the fourth day of the track is devoted to the interplay between explainability, responsibility, and liability in AI systems. Attendees will gain insights into the legal and ethical dimensions of AI decision-making, including who should be held accountable when AI systems make consequential choices. This session aims to shed light on the evolving legal and ethical landscape surrounding AI technologies and their impact.

Day 5: The Impact of (Creative) AI on Democracy The track's fifth day examines the impact of AI, particularly creative AI, on democratic processes. Speakers will discuss the potential influence of AI in shaping public opinion, disseminating information, and impacting the democratic decision-making process.

Day 6: Fairness of AI Systems The track concludes with an analysis of fairness in AI systems. Topics include the interplay between fairness, explainability, and appropriate reliance in AI systems, as well as frameworks for fairness in AI.

Nature of AI-Based Systems

The Nature of AI-Based Systems Track Introduction

Bernhard Steffen(✉)

TU Dortmund University, Dortmund, Germany
Steffen@cs.tu-dortmund.de

We are only at the very beginning of understanding the power and impact of Ecorithms as presented by Leslie Valiant in his book Probably Approximately Correct. They provide a new computational paradigm which is based on learning from observation/examples (rather than on conceptual design) and which Valiant therefore characterizes as theoryless. The power of ecorithms, which largely escape human control, becomes particular apparent with today's large language models. Valiant recognized the importance of ecorithms very early. In fact, he conjectured already a decade ago that they may even serve as a new paradigm for explaining the process of evolution and, in particular, its short timeframe.

The track *The Nature of AI-Based Systems* aims at shedding light on what makes AI-based system so special, to reveal their current impact and limitations, and to speculate where all this will lead to.

Main part of the track are the three keynotes:

- **Deep Neural Networks, Explanations, and Rationality** by Edward Lee,
- **Human or Machine: Reflections on Turing-Inspired Testing** for the Everyday by David Harel, and the more technical keynote
- **Graph Neural Networks: Everything is Connected** by Matthias Fey

which are complemented by podium discussions.

B. Steffen (Ed.): AISoLA 2023, LNCS 14380, p. 433, 2024.
https://doi.org/10.1007/978-3-031-46002-9

Digital Humanities

Digital Humanities and Cultural Heritage in AI and IT-Enabled Environments

Ciara Breathnach and Tiziana Margaria(✉)

HRI, Lero and CRT-AI, University of Limerick, Limerick, Ireland
{Ciara.Breathnach,Tiziana.Margaria}@ul.ie

Summary

We are in the middle of an AI and IT revolution and at a point of digital cultural heritage data saturation, but humanities' scholarship is struggling to keep pace.

In this Track we discuss the challenges faced by both computing and historical sciences to outline a roadmap to address some of the most pressing issues of data access, preservation, conservation, harmonisation across national datasets, and governance on one side, and the opportunities and threats brought by AI and machine learning to the advancement of rigorous data analytics.

We concentrate primarily on written/printed documents rather than on pictures and images.

We stress the importance of collaboration across the discipline boundaries and their cultures to ensure that mutual respect and equal partnerships are fostered from the outset so that in turn better practices can ensue.

In this track we welcome contributions that address these and other related topics:

- Advances brought by modern software development, AI, ML and data analytics to the transcription of documents and sources
- Tools and platforms that address the digital divide between physical, analog or digital sources and the level of curation of datasets needed for modern analytics
- Design for accessibility an interoperability of data sets, including corpora and thesauri
- Tools and techniques for machine-understanding form-based documents, recognition of digits and codes, handwriting, and other semantically structured data
- Knowledge representation for better analysis of semi-structured data from relevant domains (diaries, registers, reports, etc.)
- Specific needs arising from the study of minority languages and populations, disadvantaged groups and any other rare or less documented phenomena and groups
- Challenges relative to the conservation, publication, curation, and governance of data as open access artefacts

B. Steffen (Ed.): AISoLA 2023, LNCS 14380, pp. 437–438, 2024.
https://doi.org/10.1007/978-3-031-46002-9

- Challenges relative to initial and continuing education and curricular or extracurricular professional formation in the digital humanities professions
- Spatial digital humanities
- Digital humanities aspects concerning occupation, medicine and health.

In this Track, we welcome contributions that elucidate the role of AI and Machine Learning to support digital transcription of archival documents, the use of evolving AI techniques to support the detection of loneliness, the application of knowledge graphs to cultural heritage, the use of GIS to follow the transformation of built space and land property and usage over the centuries, the linking of data from different registers and provenance to reconstruct family and community lives and lifestyles, and also the use of digital rhetoric to study the change of communication and oratory across time.

RAISE

Research in Advanced Low-Code/No-Code Application Development: Aspects Around the R@ISE Approach

Tiziana Margaria(✉) and Mike Hinchey

Lero and CRT-AI, University of Limerick, Limerick, Ireland
{Tiziana.Margaria,Mike.Hinchey}@ul.ie

Summary

The R@ISE project serves as a catalyst for the development of a strong Low-Code/No-Code (LCNC) research and adoption capability for Ireland. Supported by eminent scholars, international domain experts and corporate and public sector partners, this multi-dimensional and visionary project will lead research and dissemination programmes in both core (Low Code/No Code development platforms) and applied Software Engineering (Digital Thread). The project was launched on April 4th in the University of Limerick.

Software increasingly pervades every aspect of our society and economy. Software development has never been more important, and yet organizations are struggling to find enough skilled developers. Businesses have an unmet need for code that works. Low-code is a new way for developers of all skill levels to design applications quickly and with minimum hand-coding. No-code is a way to help those who may not know how to program but want to develop an application for their specific use case.

Low-code and no-code (LC/NC) development tools enable the rapid deployment of powerful computerized functionalities without the need for a developer to have deep knowledge of the underlying platform or of computer science. LC/NC development tools speed up the delivery of applications. LC/NC tools have been used by governments around the world to handle the spread of COVID-19.

LC/NC can meet the unmet needs of government and business. Digital businesses' demand for ever-more software ever-more-quickly is the big driver of LC/NC adoption. In an influential report, Gartner predicted in 2019 that by 2023, over 50% of medium to large enterprises will have adopted low-code or no-code as one of their strategic application platforms. In 2021, Gartner forecasted that by 2025, the value of these technologies will reach $29 billion, with a compound annual growth rate of over 20%. Gartner also predict that by 2025, 70% of new applications developed within enterprises will use no-code or low-code technologies.

Given these trends and the national importance of software, the goal of the R@ISE programme is to act as a catalyst for the development of a strong research

B. Steffen (Ed.): AISoLA 2023, LNCS 14380, pp. 441–442, 2024.
https://doi.org/10.1007/978-3-031-46002-9

and application LC/NC capability for Ireland. R@ISE is uniquely placed to accelerate this development into the future of LC/NC with industry partners like Tines, ADI, Stripe and J&J. We also partner with Limerick City and County Council to embed LC/NC approach within a public policy context.

R@ISE is expected to become the research catalyst platform of a unique industry partnership supporting the development and adoption of technologies, methodologies and test beds of national strategic importance that harnesses national and international academic knowledge with industrial know-how and experience in LC/NC. R@ISE's impact will be through

1. A comprehensive platform for LC/NC development.
2. A shared cohesive vision and strategy for the growth of LC/NC research, education and tool development
3. An unprecedented level of participation and partnership of academic and industry partners committed to the LC/NC vision.
4. The extended dissemination of high-calibre and research-led insights relating to the evolving LC/NC field.

The exponential growth of high-class LC/NC deployment by small and large actors, furthering increased corporate automation and revenue generation on a national scale and beyond.

In this Track, we welcome contributions that elucidate the role of formal methods, modern development techniques like DSLs, microservices, test first, and other approaches that increase encapsulation and reuse, and anticipate the validation, verification and checks to design time instead of runtime, as well as new techniques for better, more automated integration and deployment, and generative approaches, be this from specifications, models or even natural language, perhaps integrated via technologies like ChatGPT.

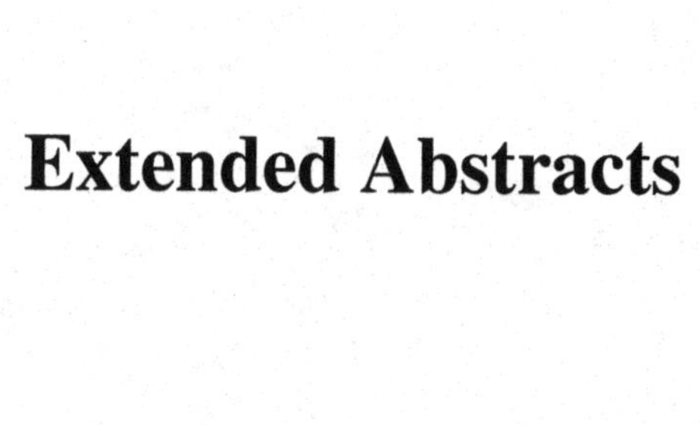

Extended Abstracts

Distribution-Aware Neuro-Symbolic Verification

Faried Abu Zaid [1(✉)], Dennis Diekmann [2], and Daniel Neider [3]

[1] Transferlab, appliedAI Institute, Munich, Germany
[2] Carl von Ossietzky University, Oldenburg, Germany
[3] Verification and Formal Guarantees of Machine Learning, TU Dortmund University, Dortmund, Germany

Abstract. We propose distribution aware neuro-symbolic verification as a way to restrict verification processes to the data distribution (or other distributions). We propose the NICE Laplacianizing flow as suitable density model because of two major properties. First, we show that the log-density function associated to a NICE Laplacianizing flow is piece-wise affine and hence applicable for SMT based approaches using linear arithmetic. Second, each NICE flow maps the upper log-density level sets of the data distribution to the upper log-density level sets of the latent Laplacian, which gives rise to potential applications within interval bound propagation methods.

1 Introduction

Neuro-symbolic verification has recently emerged as a new technique to verify semantic properties of neural networks [6, 8, 10]. In a nutshell, reference networks are used to express high-level properties which can be addressed as predicates in an otherwise logical specification. Popular ways of performing the verification are the reduction to SMT solving or the use of interval-bound propagation methods. Low-level properties such as adversarial robustness are expressible in the neuro-symbolic framework in the same way as high-level properties such as "a self-driving car will always hold in front of a stop sign". In case of a violation of the property, many verification methods are able to provide concrete counter examples. However, searching for counter examples in the entire feature space might return instances which are not in the support of the data distribution. Xie et al. [10] propose an auto-encoder based method to ensure that counterexamples are contained in the data distribution. We build upon this idea and refine it to yield probabilistically interpretable results. We achieve this by replacing the auto-encoder with a density estimator and adjust the verification task to verify properties only for the upper density level set of a specified probability mass. Since computing upper-level density sets for a given estimator is computationally infeasible in general, we employ a special flow architecture based the non-linear independent component estimator (NICE) by Dinh et al. [2] and show that upper-level density sets of the target distribution have very simple latent representations in these flows, which makes them accessible for SMT based on linear arithmetic and interval propagation based techniques.

B. Steffen (Ed.): AISoLA 2023, LNCS 14380, pp. 445–447, 2024.
https://doi.org/10.1007/978-3-031-46002-9

We believe that restricting verification tasks to the support of a meaningful input distribution is very important for the verification of real world systems since in practice areas outside of the support of the input distribution might be meaningless and we might therefore not be interested in the behavior of the model in this area. Additionally, the far tail of a distribution is by nature poorly represented in data, which leads to high epistemic uncertainty about the tail even after seeing the data. We would expect that a model which takes uncertainty because of the lack of data into account produces much less confident predictions in the tail of the distribution, which is an behavior that we might want to verify separately.

While auto-encoder implicitly capture the data distribution through the reconstruction error, they are not trained to align the reconstruction error with the underlying density function. Hence, upper- and lower reconstruction error level sets are not probabilistically interpretable. The natural replacement to solve this issue are upper density level sets $L_D^{\uparrow}(t) = \{x \in \mathbb{R}^d \mid p_D(x) > t\}$, where p_D is the density of the input distribution. In this case we can even bound the failure probability relative to the reference distribution: A successful verification of the property on $L_D^{\uparrow}(t)$ implies a failure probability of at most $1 - p_D(L_D^{\uparrow}(t))$.

2 Applications

2.1 Verification within the Data Distribution

This is our motivating example from the introduction. In a practical scenario, we would like to specify acceptable failure probability p rather than an acceptable log-density threshold. Hence, we propose the following abstract procedure for verification of machine learning models within the center of the data distribution:

1. For a given $p \in [0, 1]$, determine the log-density $\log t_p$ with $p_D(L_D^{\uparrow}(t_p)) = p$.
2. Verify that $\forall x : \log p_D(x) > \log t_p \rightarrow \varphi(x)$

Where φ is the neuro-symbolic property that we want to verify. Note that since we are able to sample from our flow model, estimating $\log t_p$ can easily be done empirically with high accuracy [1, 9].

2.2 Verification of Correct Epistemic Uncertainty Quantification

As we argued earlier, for the far tail of the data distribution there are usually no samples available. Hence, any model trained purely from data has never gotten information about these areas. Without any inductive bias, the uncertainty estimates given e.g. by a classifier should converge towards a uniform distribution as we move further outwards in the tail [4, 5]. However, it is known that many deep neural network training methods produce badly calibrated networks with overconfident predictions, especially in areas of high epistemic uncertainty [3, 7]. Our approach can be used to verify that the network takes epistemic uncertainty into account. E.g. for a binary classifier C:

1. For a given (very small) $p \in [0, 1]$, determine the log-density $\log t_p$ with $p_D(L_D^{\downarrow}(t_p)) = p$.
2. Verify that $\forall x : \log p_D(x) \leq \log t_p \rightarrow C(x) \in \left[\frac{1}{2} - \epsilon, \frac{1}{2} + \epsilon\right]$ for a given tolerance ϵ.

References

1. Cadre, B., Pelletier, B., Pudlo, P.: Estimation of density level sets with a given probability content **25**(1), 261–272
2. Dinh, L., Krueger, D., Bengio, Y.: NICE: non-linear independent components estimation. In: Bengio, Y., LeCun, Y. (eds.) 3rd International Conference on Learning Representations, ICLR 2015, San Diego, CA, USA, 7–9 May 2015, Workshop Track Proceedings
3. Guo, C., Pleiss, G., Sun, Y., Weinberger, K.Q.: On calibration of modern neural networks. In: Proceedings of the 34th International Conference on Machine Learning, pp. 1321–1330
4. Hüllermeier, E., Waegeman, W.: Aleatoric and epistemic uncertainty in machine learning: an introduction to concepts and methods **110**(3), 457–506
5. Kendall, A., Gal, Y.: What uncertainties do we need in Bayesian deep learning for computer vision? In: Proceedings of the 31st International Conference on Neural Information Processing Systems, NIPS 2017, pp. 5580–5590. Curran Associates Inc.
6. Liu, C., et al.: Algorithms for verifying deep neural networks **4**(3–4), 244–404
7. Minderer, M., et al.: Revisiting the Calibration of Modern Neural Networks
8. Müller, M.N., Brix, C., Bak, S., Liu, C., Johnson. T.T.: The Third International Verification of Neural Networks Competition (VNN-COMP 2022): Summary and Results. CoRR abs/2212.10376
9. Tsybakov, B.: On nonparametric estimation of density level sets **25**(3), 948–969
10. Xie, X., Kersting, K., Neider, D.: Neuro-symbolic verification of deep neural networks. In: Proceedings of the Thirty-First International Joint Conferences on Artificial Intelligence

Towards Verification of Changes in Dynamic Machine Learning Models Using Deep Ensemble Anomaly Detection

Tim Katzke(✉), Bin Li, Simon Klüttermann, and Emmanuel Müller

TU Dortmund, Dortmund, Germany
{tim.katzke,bin.li,simon.kluettermann,
emmanuel.mueller}@cs.tu-dortmund.de

Abstract. Formal verification of machine learning models is of major importance for safety critical systems. However, in case of dynamically changing data distributions, such verification has to consider the temporal representation of state changes as the context of a dynamic machine learning model. For instance, one has to verify a time-dependent machine learning model w.r.t. distinct states of an evolving time series. As an illustration, environmental time series encompassing variables such as temperature, humidity, illumination are used to train such models w.r.t. seasonal states like spring, summer, autumn and winter.

In general, such machine learning models are trained under so-called concept drift and have been developed to capture changing data distributions with internal representation learning. For formal verification, however, this implicit representation lacks explicit delineation of states, descriptions of transitions, and their human-understandable interpretability. Hence, we aim to extend powerful neural network verification to dynamic machine learning models trained under dynamic data changes. We consider the formal representation of a minimal state transition model as the first open challenge for an interpretable as well as efficient verification of such time-dependent machine learning models.

This presentation presents work in progress on defining a novel co-training procedure that uses our deep ensemble anomaly detection (DEAN-TS) algorithm to detect state changes in an unsupervised fashion and learn a finite-state automaton in parallel to the training of any state-of-the-art machine learning model under concept drift. In a naïve setup, one could simply create one new state for each newly detected concept in the data. However, as we aim at an interpretable as well as efficient verification, we optimize for a minimal automaton by incrementally merging similar concepts/states. In particular, our novel DEAN-TS algorithm provides us with an un-likelihood of erroneous states by exploiting the unique characteristics of different anomaly types vs. normal data. Using feature bagging, each ensemble submodel considers a subset of time series components to identify characteristic feature importance distributions. This unique approach allows us to describe each state in our automaton with the most important features and consequently provide human users with the ability to add corresponding semantics.

Keywords: Learning · Finite-state automaton · Verification · Time series · Change detection · Deep ensemble · Anomaly detection

B. Steffen (Ed.): AISoLA 2023, LNCS 14380, p. 448, 2024.
https://doi.org/10.1007/978-3-031-46002-9

Benchmark: Neural Networks for Anomaly Detection in Batch Distillation

Simon Lutz[1,2(✉)] and Daniel Neider[1,2]

[1] TU Dortmund University, Dortmund, Germany
simon.lutz@tu-dortmund.de
[2] Center for Trustworthy Data Science and Security, UA Ruhr, Germany

Abstract. In recent years, deep learning has achieved considerable success in the field of anomaly detection. These models have to work safely and reliably when deployed in safety-critical applications, such as chemical plants: Failure to report anomalies may result in imminent hazards to the environment and harm to human life. Contrary, false alarms may lead to substantial financial or scientific loss due to unnecessary downtime of a plant. In this paper, we present a benchmark suite for verifying neural networks used in anomaly detection for the batch distillation chemical process.

This work presents the abstract for a talk at AISoLA 2023.

Anomaly detection is the task of detecting behavior which diverges from the norm. Motivated by its the success in other applications, there has been a rise of interest in developing deep learning approaches for anomaly detection in recent years. Before deploying these models in safety-critical applications, such as chemical plants, we need to ensure they work safely and reliably: Failure to report anomalies may result in imminent hazards to the environment and harm to human life. Contrary, false alarms may lead to substantial financial or scientific loss due to unnecessary downtime. In this talk, we present a benchmark suite for verifying neural networks used in anomaly detection for batch distillation, a chemical process. This benchmark suit arises from an interdisciplinary project on deep learning on chemical process data.

Batch distillation is a chemical process that uses a so-called distillation column (see Fig. 1) to separate a liquid mixture into multiple, possible unknown chemical components. To this end, the mixture is filled into the distillation still, a vessel connected to a heat source, and heated up until it boils. The resulting vapor rises up through the rectifying column, containing a sequence of packings or plates, until it is condensed in the condenser at the top of the column. The condensate is cooled and split into two separate streams. One part of the condensate is withdrawn as distillate while the other, often larger fraction of the condensate called reflux is returned to the column top. There, the countercurrent

B. Steffen (Ed.): AISoLA 2023, LNCS 14380, pp. 449–452, 2024.
https://doi.org/10.1007/978-3-031-46002-9

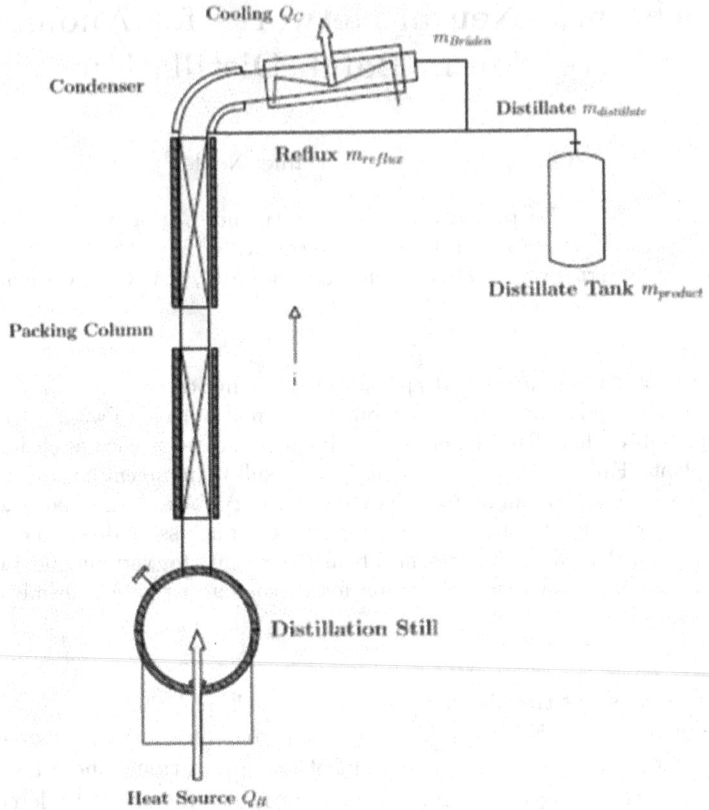

Fig. 1. The simplified schematics of a distillation column

of downflowing liquid and uprising vapor is constantly in contact, enabling a material flow improving the separation of the components in the mixture.

By measuring, for instance, the temperature, pressure, and concentration of the individual components throughout multiple experiments we collect a data set of multi-modal sequential data on which we train a variety of (deep) anomaly detectors. These models take multi-modal sequences of a fixed length k as input (typically the values of the last k points of time) and predict whether the current time point is an anomaly or not.

To verify the safety and reliability of these anomaly detectors, we composed a list of specifications over multi-modal sequences which need to be fulfilled when the batch distillation works properly. Conversely, whenever one of the properties is violated the anomaly detector should report an anomaly.

In order for an automated verifier to process theses specifications, we formalize them in a specification logic. Working on multi-modal sequences of measurements over time, this specification logic must be able to express two main properties: On the one hand, we need to express relations between real-valued variables, e.g., the values of a temperature sensor. One the other hand, we need to model temporal relations and properties, for instance, that a condition will always hold. To this end, our specification logic combines the theory of Linear Real Arithmetic (LRA), to express relations between real-valued variables, and Linear Temporal Logic [1], to express the temporal properties. Note that we consider only sequences of equal and finite length which would allow us to just use LRA by introducing a variable for each point in the sequence. To not clutter this section to much we omit a formal definition of our specification language at this point. Whenever we refer to "measurements", we mean a specific input to the neural network at a fixed position in its input.

We categorize our formal specifications into three groups: The first group consists of properties that define bounds on the measurements. This includes properties like 'The pressure must always be greater than zero'. Recall that the inputs to our network are multi-modal sequences of, for instance, temperature, pressure, or concentrations of a component s measured over time at different positions in the distillation column. We denote each such sequence by t_i, p_i, and c_i^s, respectively, where the index indicates the position within the column (from distillations still to the top of the column). Using the temporal operator G (globally) to indicate that a property has to hold at any point of the sequence, we formalize the above property as follows:

$$\mathrm{G}(\bigwedge_{i=0}^{n_p} p_i > 0)$$

The second group of specifications defines relations between two measurements, either of different sensors or at different points in time. These include properties like 'The temperature has to decrease from distillation still to the top of the packing column' or 'The temperature in the distillation still increases over time'. For instance, we formalize the former specification as:

$$\mathrm{G}(\bigwedge_{i=0}^{n_t-1} t_i > t_{i+1})$$

Due to the nature of the ongoing chemical processes, the conditions within the distillation column can not change too rapidly but must exhibit a certain degree of continuity. Preserving this continuity, for instance, over time, is expressed by the specifications of the third group. One example for such a specification is 'Continuity over time for pressure (i.e., the value may only change by at most ε_p)' which we formalize as:

$$\mathrm{G}(\bigwedge_{i=0}^{n_p} p_i - \varepsilon_p \leq \ominus p_i \wedge \ominus p_i \leq p_i + \varepsilon_p)$$

In conclusion, this talk will present a benchmarks set arising from chemical process engineering. More precisely, the neural networks trained are deep anomaly detectors, and the specifications express sanity checks on these networks. Until the conference in October, we plan to train a variety of (deep) anomaly detectors. Afterwards, we will evaluate our benchmark suite and make the results as well as the benchmark suite publicly available.

Reference

1. Pnueli, A.: The temporal logic of programs. In: 18th Annual Symposium on Foundations of Computer Science (sfcs 1977), pp. 46–57 (1977). https://doi.org/10.1109/SFCS.1977.32

AI-Assisted Programming with Test-Based Refinement

Bernhard K. Aichernig[1] and Klaus Havelund[2(✉)]

[1] Institute of Software Technology, Graz University of Technology, Graz, Austria
[2] Jet Propulsion Laboratory, California Institute of Technology, Pasadena, USA
havelund@gmail.com

Abstract. Neural program synthesis, based on Large Language Models (LLMs) which are trained on open source code, are quickly becoming a popular addition to the software developer's toolbox. Services like, for instance, Open AI's GPT4, Google's Bard, and GitHub's Copilot, can generate code in many different programming languages from natural language requirements entered as "prompts". However, prompt-based programming seems to work best for development of smaller programs. It currently appears infeasible to generate large and complex programs from natural language prompts. We refer to this as the *complexity problem.* Furthermore, neural systems do not come with guarantees of producing correct, safe, or secure code, what we shall refer to as the *verification problem.* We propose test-based refinement to address these two problems. Specifically, to approach the *complexity* problem, we propose a method based on program *refinement*, where a program is developed in a stepwise manner, starting with a very high level abstract program, and then refining it iteratively, towards a final implementation. At each refinement step, the LLM can provide assistance by generating code suggestions and refining existing code snippets. To approach the program *verification* problem, we suggest to apply automated *testing* to test that each refinement implements the previous step. Literature on program refinement usually approaches the verification problem as a deductive proof problem. Proofs are, however, hard to carry out for humans, even with automated proof tools. The experiments are carried out by developing a classical bridge controller in the Scala programming language using the ScalaCheck property-based testing library.

The research performed by the second author was carried out at Jet Propulsion Laboratory, California Institute of Technology, under a contract with the National Aeronautics and Space Administration.

B. Steffen (Ed.): AISoLA 2023, LNCS 14380, p. 453, 2024.
https://doi.org/10.1007/978-3-031-46002-9

Author Index

B. Steffen (Ed.): AISoLA 2023, LNCS 14380, pp. 455–456, 2024.
https://doi.org/10.1007/978-3-031-46002-9

Printed in the United States
by Baker & Taylor Publisher Services